FINANCIAL ENGINEERING

The Robert W. Kolb Series in Finance provides a comprehensive view of the field of finance in all of its variety and complexity. The series is projected to include approximately 65 volumes covering all major topics and specializations in finance, ranging from investments to corporate finance and financial institutions. Each volume in the Kolb Series in Finance consists of new articles written especially for the volume.

Each Kolb Series volume is edited by a specialist in a particular area of finance, who develops the volume outline and commissions articles by the world's experts in that particular field of finance. Each volume includes an editor's introduction and approximately 30 articles to fully describe the current state of financial research and practice in a particular area of finance.

The essays in each volume are intended for practicing finance professionals, graduate students, and advanced undergraduate students. The goal of each volume is to encapsulate the current state of knowledge in a particular area of finance so that the reader can quickly achieve a mastery of that special area.

FINANCIAL ENGINEERING

The Evolution of a Profession

Tanya Beder
Cara M. Marshall

The Robert W. Kolb Series in Finance

John Wiley & Sons, Inc.

Published by John Wiley & Sons, Inc., Hoboken, New Jersey.
Published simultaneously in Canada.

For general information on our other products and services or for technical support, please contact our Customer Care Department within the United States at (800) 762-2974, outside the United States at (317) 572-3993 or fax (317) 572-4002.

Wiley also publishes its books in a variety of electronic formats. Some content that appears in print may not be available in electronic formats. For more information about Wiley products, visit our Web site at www.wiley.com.

Library of Congress Cataloging-in-Publication Data:

Financial engineering : the evolution of a profession / Tanya S. Beder and Cara M. Marshall, editors.
     p. cm. – (Robert W. Kolb series ; 2)
  Includes index.
  ISBN 978-0-470-45581-4 (hardback); ISBN 978-0-470-88981-7 (ebk);
  ISBN 978-0-470-88982-4 (ebk); ISBN 978-0-470-88983-1 (ebk)
 1. Financial engineering.   I. Beder, Tanya S.   II. Marshall, Cara M.
  HG176.7.F558 2011
  332–dc22

                      2010049290

Printed in the United States of America

10 9 8 7 6 5 4 3 2 1

To my mother, Margaret, and in memory of my father, Clarence, with gratitude for your inspiration, love, and support.

—Tanya Beder

To my father and mother, Jack and Joanne, and to my in-laws Jim and Marie. Thank you for all that you do.

—Cara M. Marshall

Contents

Introduction

TANYA BEDER
Chairman, SBCC and SBCC Group Inc.

CARA M. MARSHALL
Queens College of the City University of New York

T he past three decades have been a remarkable period for innovation. This is no less true, and probably truer, for financial innovation. No prior period of equal length has ever witnessed anything that even comes close. This innovation has included amazing advances in financial theory, computational capability, new product design, new trading processes, new markets, and new applications. In fact, each of these innovations has supported and reinforced the others. In the early 1990s, practitioners and academics alike began to recognize that this spate of innovation was not just a passing fad. Rather, something fundamental had changed. Indeed, something had, and the new profession known as financial engineering emerged. These think-out-of-the box, often technologically and/or quantitatively sophisticated, individuals are the drivers behind the new finance.

All periods of innovation are traumatic. The old, only grudgingly, makes way for the new. Adapting to a new environment takes effort, and not all will survive. For example, many floor traders on stock, futures, and options exchanges fought tooth and nail to prevent the introduction of electronic trading platforms. But, in the end, the new platforms won out. Why? Because they are better—they are faster, less error prone, and they lead to tighter bid-ask spreads, which means lower transaction costs for investors.

Innovation is not without its problems. Good ideas often have unintended consequences. Cell phones, for example, have made it possible for anyone to reach almost anyone else at any time in real time. How can that be bad? But cell phones and their associated capabilities, such as text messaging, have increased road hazards, become an annoyance to anyone dining out, attending a theater, or just trying to read in peace on the commute home. Similarly, financial innovation has often had unintended consequences. The financial crisis that began in 2007 and, some would say, continues as of this writing, has been blamed in part on the securitization of subprime mortgages and other financial innovations. Securitization dramatically changed the way mortgage lending worked. It brought huge amounts of capital to the mortgage market, making it faster and easier for would-be home-buyers to secure the necessary financing for their purchase. How could making it easier to achieve the American Dream possibly be bad? But securitization has had unintended consequences. Many mortgage originators changed their focus from managing their credit risk to originating as much volume as possible with little regard to credit quality. Securitization had made credit risk "someone else's problem."

The years ahead will be a period of great change for financial engineering. Investors, borrowers, regulators, supervisors, boards of directors, legislators, and individuals alike will need to determine what to keep—and what to throw out. This book is designed to help readers do precisely that. Whether experienced or new to financial engineering, this book will help you focus on not only established activities but also the areas of greatest opportunity and need.

For those who are new to financial engineering, Part I of this book (Chapters 1 through 3), provides a history of financial innovation and the commensurate growth of financial engineering as a profession. In this same section, various types of financial engineering occupations are discussed, but not to the point of being exhaustive. Also in this section, financial engineering curricula and programs are discussed. Many of these programs carry a label other than financial engineering (e.g., quantitative finance, risk management, mathematical finance, and so forth), but they are nevertheless subsets within the broader field of financial engineering. A website, www.wiley.com/go/bedermarshall/ (password: kolb) has been provided to allow the prospective student to get a good sense of which universities offer financial engineering-related programs and what these programs contain. The data is not exhaustive because our survey did not reach all universities with financial engineering-related programs, some of the schools we sent our survey to did not respond in a timely fashion, and new programs are being introduced regularly. We apologize to any university that feels they have a program that should have been included. We invite them to contact Survey@sbccgroup.com to have their institution's programs added to our data base.

The chapters included in this book are organized around several key themes.

THEME 1: DERIVATIVES WILL CONTINUE TO PLAY A CRITICAL, VALUABLE, AND PERMANENT ROLE IN THE GLOBAL CAPITAL MARKETS

According to the Bank for International Settlements, notional principal for derivatives outstanding peaked in 2007 at US$ 1,444 trillion (all types combined). This number declined significantly during the global financial crisis, but by the latter part of 2009 it was again rising rapidly. Because this figure is notionals outstanding, it can be misleading. Many prefer to measure the size of the market in terms of gross market value, which is the cost of replacing existing contracts. Gross market value is typically a small fraction of the notionals outstanding. Nevertheless, by any measure, the derivatives markets are massive in size and, by all accounts, are once again growing rapidly.

Although some derivatives, most notably futures, have a very long history, as chronicled in the financial engineering history chapter, many of the more important derivatives have been around for less than 35 years. These include swaps, most types of options, caps, floors, collars, and the more complex combinations thereof. After the introduction of these latter derivatives, innovation took off and continues at breakneck speed. Today financial derivatives are a core part of the global capital markets. They continue to assist borrowers to achieve lower-cost funding, investors to achieve greater rates of return and/or more desirable risk/reward tradeoffs, and financial and nonfinancial firms to better manage risks linked to interest rates, currencies, commodities, equities, credit, weather, and greenhouse gases, among others. With such rapid growth it is not surprising that the drivers of some derivatives strategies and financially-engineered products had some problems. Despite these, and the fact that some pioneers of financial engineering feel they unwittingly helped to make an atom bomb in the financial markets with the advent of certain types of securitized products, we believe that derivatives will continue to play a critical, valuable, and permanent role in the global capital markets.

Part II (Chapters 4 through 9) examines each of the major markets, one per chapter. Not surprisingly, derivatives play an important role in each of these markets. Specifically Part II addresses, sequentially, financial innovation and engineering associated with the fixed-income markets, the mortgage market more narrowly, the equity markets, the foreign exchange markets, the commodity markets, and the credit markets.

THEME 2: RISK MEASUREMENT AND MANAGEMENT WILL CHANGE SUBSTANTIALLY FOLLOWING LESSONS LEARNED FROM THE MELTDOWN THAT MANIFESTED IN 2007

Since the onset of the financial meltdown, losses have been realized by almost every type of firm on every continent. Trillions in taxpayers' funds have been deployed by countries around the world to try to stabilize firms and markets. Disclosed losses involved not only exotic or highly leveraged securities, but simple products as well. As we continue to work our way through these losses, it is clear that risk measurement and risk management failed to identify some exposures. Further, many supervisors, boards of directors, senior managers, and other overseers were seduced by a dangerous sense of calm, placing too much faith in data derived during a relatively benign period in the history of the capital markets.

Revising risk measurement methodologies and risk management techniques will be an important focus of the financial engineering community over the next decade. So-called once-in-100-year events have occurred all too frequently, thereby exposing serious flaws in current techniques for identifying and managing risks. Further, the risk that a model's value may be different from that ultimately obtained in the market reared its head globally and without prejudice as to continent or type of firm, costing trillions. Those who assumed that engaging in multiple activities in multiple geographic markets would provide so-called natural diversification lost breathtaking sums; and different financial markets and different types of financial services were found to be much more interconnected during times of stress than their risk measurement systems predicted.

Part III (Chapters 10 through 16) examines a number of recent important innovative applications of financial engineering that have made news over the past decade and that will continue, in our opinion, to do so in the years ahead. Important among these are the advent of securitized products—both those that contributed to the financial crisis and those that did not; structured products, which have become an important new bank funding tool; the importance of obtaining independent valuation of financially-engineered products; and new, highly-quantitative trading strategies for both equities and fixed income. Also included in Part III are some thoughts on how risk management might be retooled to reflect what has been learned as a result of the financial crisis and how new financial products may make it possible to manage the risks associated with macroeconomic uncertainties.

THEME 3: FINANCIALLY-ENGINEERED SECURITIES AND STRATEGIES WILL EVOLVE TO INCLUDE MORE TRANSPARENCY AND BETTER WARNING LABELS

The successful financial engineer is always re-evaluating what has gone before and how it might be done better in the future. To fully appreciate what can go wrong, one has to be willing to examine failure. Indeed, one can often learn more from failure than from success.

Part IV (Chapters 17 through 22) deals with case studies in which some sort of operational failure led to a financial calamity. In all cases these were large failures, some of which led to the demise of the companies with which they were associated. In other cases, the companies were able to survive—often thanks to an acquisition or government bailout. We are grateful to Algorithmics for allowing us to draw on their extensive and proprietary data base of operational risk case studies. We are particularly grateful to Penny Cagan, formerly of Algorithmics, for assembling these case studies for incorporation in this book.

The cases that are included discuss risk themes that have led to losses across multiple market environments, including what we have experienced recently. These include the stories of Countrywide, Northern Rock, Société Général, Barings, Allied Irish/Allfirst, Allstate, Long-Term Capital Management, the state of Florida's Local Government Investment Fund, Orange County (California), American International Group (AIG), and Merrill Lynch.

THEME 4: THE DEGREE TO WHICH INCREASED REGULATION WILL STYMIE FINANCIAL ENGINEERING AND INNOVATION IS UNCERTAIN

Not all financially-engineered securities pose the same risks. Some are inherently riskier than others. Some anxiety-ridden legislators, regulators, academics, and supervisors have taken the extreme step of suggesting that *all* engineered securities should be purged from some firms' activities. Other stakeholders have made the mistake of assuming that without engineered securities, risk going forward will be under control. Sadly, not only would many firms with purged activities have greater residual risk, but they are likely to be noncompetitive in the global arena.

We do not think it is advisable to put the securitization genie back into the bottle, and we agree with the stakeholders and overseers who have taken a more constructive approach. Greater transparency and disclosure regarding financially-engineered securities are at the center of how these firms plan to continue to use these products while learning from past losses.

In Part V (Chapters 23 through 29), we address special topics of interest to various segments of the financial engineering community and those who would employ the services of financial engineers. This is a rather eclectic mix. We begin by taking a look at compensation and performance fees. There is little doubt that risk-sensitive compensation frameworks will evolve as a direct result of the crisis as supervisors, government officials, company executives, and directors work to overcome the consequences of what many now view as too many short-term and one-sided incentives. We then continue with thoughts on hedging and the implications of hedge accounting for the volatility of corporate earnings; issues in operational risk and legal risk; the porting of alpha in the current market environment; and the essence of the no-arbitrage condition in valuation and its role in financial engineering.

Although the technological and transaction bridges across markets are well established, the social and political structures supporting cross-border and cross-institution transactions will take years to catch up. Through the meltdown, linkages in the global economy revealed that a shock in a key sector or country can reverberate rapidly through the world. The untoward results were increasingly accompanied by the question of whether government intervention became too lax, and whether supervisors did adequate jobs (including regulators, senior managers, boards of directors, and other overseers). Further, the question of whether protectionism and/or regionalism will overtake ongoing globalization has started to appear with increasing frequency in the debate. We close this book (Chapter 29) with some thoughts on the role of the public sector in the management of systemic risk.

At this writing, the world continues its de-risking and de-leveraging. In April of 2010 the IMF revised downward to US$2.3 trillion its earlier estimate of global write-downs by banks. This number exceeds considerably the new capital raised by banks during the same period. The substantial losses by investors in certain types of financially engineered credit instruments and the incineration of trillions of dollars of value have resulted in the nationalization of numerous financial firms and global companies plus breathtaking bailouts by governments around the world. While some instruments are well into their write-down cycles (for example, residential mortgage-backed securities), other instruments are just beginning a likely write-down cycle (for example, commercial mortgage-backed securities and prime residential mortgage-backed securities). Given the huge injections of funds, we encourage you to think about whether governments and stakeholders (i.e., taxpayers) will demand higher levels of regulation and oversight in exchange for those bailout monies. There certainly seems a palpable probability that a reduction in the freedom of global banks is possible as countries and/or regions focus on limiting damage from future crises.

We have included several appendices at the end of this book (Part VI) that we believe can be useful to the beginning student looking forward to a career in financial engineering. These appendices include a brief look at some of the computational and information technology tools available to the financial engineer (Appendix A); and, as already noted, an overview of the survey of financial engineering programs and programs with a financial engineering component (Appendix B).

The authors wish to specially thank John F. Marshall for his insights, advice, and experience drawn from the publication of numerous past books and articles on many of these topics. His input was invaluable to the completion of this book. The authors also wish to thank the staff at SBCC Group Inc. for research and fact checking throughout numerous drafts. We also thank the entire team at John Wiley & Sons for their efforts and support. Finally, and perhaps foremost, we thank the innumerable executives, directors, regulators, risk managers, traders, investors, borrowers, academics and students who have shared their experiences and their challenges over the past three decades.

FINANCIAL ENGINEERING

PART I

Overview

1

CHAPTER 1

The History of Financial Engineering from Inception to Today*

TANYA BEDER
SBCC Group Inc.

WHAT IS FINANCIAL ENGINEERING?

Financial engineering may be broadly defined as the development and creative application of innovative financial technology. Financial technology includes financial theory, quantitative techniques, financial products, and financial processes. At a microeconomic level, the motivation behind financial engineering is to produce profits for the innovators by finding better ways to address society's needs. At a macroeconomic level financial engineering helps improve the allocation of scarce resources. Allocation of resources is the fundamental objective of any economic system. Indeed, financial engineering epitomizes Joseph Schumpeter's view of capitalism as "creative destruction." New products replace old products, new theory improves on old theory, and new processes supplant old processes.

Financial engineering borrows heavily and liberally from other disciplines, which helps explain why the field has attracted people from across the scientific spectrum. The key to understanding financial engineering is understanding innovation in all of its dimensions and turning this innovation into practical solutions. While, in some sense, financial engineering has been with us since the innovation of money, financial engineering has not, until quite recently, been recognized as a profession. What has changed, more than anything else, is the pace of innovation.

The history of financial engineering is presented in the segments illustrated in Exhibit 1.1.

---

*© Copyright 2010 by Tanya Beder, chairman, SBCC Group Inc. The author wishes to thank Helen Lu for her valuable assistance for portions of the research regarding this chapter.

Exhibit 1.1   Financial Engineering Time Line

Inception and Early Stages (1970–1997)	**Rationalization** (from 2007, ongoing)
• Deregulation of interest rates, currencies, and commodity prices creates need to manage risks.	• Global financial markets melt down and continue in various states of disarray, starting with residential
• Tools created to do so (derivatives, theoretical pricing models, risk measures).	mortgages and progressing to commercial real estate, financial firms, corporate, municipal and sovereign risks.
• Technology provides platform and drives globalization (telecom advances, hardware, software, first PCs).	• Troubled assets and liquidity crises lead to trillions in bailouts and drive global de-leveraging and de-risking.
• Financial firms build businesses to intermediate risk in addition to capital.	• A dramatic "re-think" of the role of governments/greater regulation/need to manage systemic risk underway.

Massive Growth (1998–2006)
- The world of "monoline" financial firms ends as banks, insurers, traditional, and alternative asset managers combine and enter each others' businesses globally.
- Asian currency crisis, Russian crisis, and LTCM launch global growth of the business of enterprise risk management.
- Ongoing deregulation and freer markets spur growth.
- Credit derivatives and securitization grow from zero into the hundreds of trillions, massively changing how risk and return are originated, held, and transferred.
- BRICs, sovereign wealth funds emerge as major players in the world capital market, vastly fueling globalization.
- Huge liquidity, low risk premiums, and low interest rates drive massive growth in the size of firms (from banks to hedge funds), capital markets (from emerging to established), and the use of leverage.

Source: SBCC Group Inc.

WHY DIDN'T FINANCIAL ENGINEERING START SOONER?

Markets and some financial functions have been around for thousands of years. There is evidence, for example, that the Romans may have invented checking as early as 352 B.C. By the year 1750 the basic financial firms were established to take deposits; make loans; write insurance; provide investments (savings and pension products); intermediate (checking, crossing trades, brokering); underwrite; distribute; and facilitate trade. From the 1700s until about 1970 (more than 200 years), the development of financial firms was continuous and done at a manageable pace. But the period was also one of frequent violent upheaval, as wars repeatedly ravaged nations and populations. New firms were born and others went out of business, but the basic functions of banks, insurance companies, asset managers, company pension funds, central banks, brokers, and dealers did not change radically. Most firms had monoline business models, and the primary business was the intermediation of capital.

As summarized in Exhibit 1.1, the pace of innovation was slow, but there were notable developments in the four decades leading up to the inception of financial engineering. Harry Markowitz published his seminal work on portfolio theory in the 1950s; the first Eurobonds were issued in the early 1960s, and certificates of deposit were introduced in the late 1960s. There were advancements in technology, but most were not broad-based consumer products: Chester Carlson invented xerography (photocopying) in 1938; the first computer (the ENIAC) was unveiled in the 1940s; Bell Systems revealed the transistor that would revolutionize telecommunications in 1947; the first modem enabling communication between machines was developed in the late 1950s; and the National Aeronautics and Space Administration (NASA) launched the first communications satellite in 1962. As the 1960s ended, Texas Instruments developed the first handheld calculator, which retailed for $2,000.

The decades after World War I right through to the early 1970s were a period of ever-increasing financial market regulation. This period included episodes of currency instability, devastating inflation in some countries, the Great Depression, World War II, and the rebuilding of Europe and Japan in the wake of that global calamity. Substantial regulation was put in place to promote the safety and soundness of individual countries' financial systems. Most regulations adopted were rule-based by category/type of firm versus by function. In addition, there were important agreements made between countries; for example, fixed exchange rates were established between major countries at the Bretton Woods Conference of 1944. The interest rates paid by savings banks were capped. Commodity prices were kept artificially low by many governments. Hence, there was little price volatility to manage. Also of note is that fewer than 350 companies worldwide had assets in excess of US$500 million, so most financial activities were local (within home countries) rather than global. Losses by financial firms during this era were either credit-based (for example, the failure of the Austrian bank Credit Anstalt that led to substantial overnight foreign exchange losses for counterparties) or operational-based (for example, the United States' paper crunch during which trading volume outstripped settlement capabilities, leading to the failure of 160 members of the New York Stock Exchange).

Toward the end of the period, glimmers of deregulation and technology advances laid the groundwork for the beginning of financial engineering.

INCEPTION AND THE EARLY STAGES (1970 TO 1997)

During the latter part of the twentieth century, four forces worked together to drive the separation between the past and the present businesses of financial firms:

1. Technology
2. Globalization
3. Deregulation
4. Risk intermediation

By 1970 the business of financial firms had begun to change radically and irrevocably. Banks, insurance companies, funds, central banks, brokers, dealers, government entities, and others faced difficult new risks and challenges to their profitability. As summarized in Exhibit 1.2, interest rates and currencies were deregulated, and the Organization of Petroleum Exporting Countries (OPEC) was established—all leading to substantial new volatilities to manage. Increasingly, global corporations struggled as well to manage their income statements, balance sheets, and raw material costs.

Technology was the first force. Until the advent of personal computers and parallel processing in the 1980s, most technology was too slow to be utilized in the

Exhibit 1.2 Early Stages (1970–1997)

Date	New Products/ Risk Innovations	Technology	Deregulation/ Regulatory Change	Key Milestones for Different Types of Financial Firms
1970–1975	EEC common exchange rates (snake).	The invention of the floppy disk provides the first source of portable storage of data (1970).	U.S. President Nixon ends Bretton Woods system and takes away gold standard, while still keeping fixed exchange rates (1971); by 1973, floating exchange system adopted globally.	State and federal deregulation of financial institutions initiated S&L institutions to engage in riskier investments in sectors such as real estate, construction, and services.
	Early GAP analysis for banks & thrifts.	Intel introduces the world's first single chip microprocessor (1971).	Oil shocks of 1970s: OPEC increased price of oil due to the devaluation of U.S. dollar—received less real income, and political conflicts in the Middle East at the time also spurred unpredictable changes in oil prices.	Multinational corporations were on the rise—7,000 parent companies by 1970; 333 had assets of at least $500 million, and one-third of those corporations had assets of at least $1 billion.
	Capital Asset Pricing Theory	NASDAQ began its operations as "the world's first electronic stock market" (1971).	U.S. removed capital controls.	Government National Mortgage Association, or Ginnie Mae, introduces first mortgage pass-through securities (1970).
	The Black-Scholes model	The advent of the Monroe 1272, the first electronic bond yield calculator (1971).	Australia begins process of financial deregulation—continues on through to mid-1980s.	William Fouse and John McQuown created first index fund; today known as The Vanguard Group (1971).
	Prudent-person theory	First email program created by Ray Tomlinson of BBN Technologies (1972).	Commodity Futures Trading Commission Act (1974).	

	Extension of portfolio theory to hedging with futures. Mortgage-backed bonds Chicago Board Options Exchange (CBOE) was opened for trading options on common stocks (1973). Floating rate notes (Euromarkets 1970, U.S. market 1974). Exchange-traded futures on interest rates and currencies (1972–1977).		Employee Retirement Income Security Act (ERISA) provided pension fund rights for employees (1974).	
1976–1980	Puttable bonds (1976) European currency unit (1979)	First supercomputer crafted by Seymour Cray (1976).	International Banking Act (1978) Great Britain removes capital controls (1979).	
1981–1985	Application of Macauley's duration (published in 1938).	IBM designs the modern computer ("PC" or "personal computer") (1981).	The Depository Institutions Deregulation and Monetary Control Act (DIDMCA) of 1980 and Garn–St. Germain Depository Institutions Act of 1982 began process of bank deregulation by removing restrictions on real-estate loans and raising deposit insurance limits.	The decade of hostile takeovers and leveraged buyouts; easier to finance because of rise of Michael Milken's junk bond market.

(Continued)

Exhibit 1.2 (*Continued*)

Date	New Products/ Risk Innovations	Technology	Deregulation/ Regulatory Change	Key Milestones for Different Types of Financial Firms
	Equivalents	Hewlett-Packard introduces its HP 12c financial calculator, which eventually became a standard tool for financial professionals (1981).		Currency swaps first introduced when World Bank swapped dollars with IBM for IBM's excess Swiss francs and German marks (1981).
	Convexity	Microsoft Corporation launches the Windows© program—still predominant software used in finance (1985).		
	Sharpe ratio The Greeks for options (delta, gamma, "vega," theta, rho). Stress testing Scenario analysis Option-adjusted spread Portfolio Insurance Bonds with warrants Municipal bonds with 7-day puts. Silver-indexed bonds Zero coupon bonds (1981) Dual currency bonds (1981) Swaps, caps (1981) Stock index futures (1982) Options on futures (1982) Adjustable rate and money market preferred stock (1982–1984). Collateralized mortgage obligations (1983).			

| 1986–1990 | Risk-adjusted return on capital (1983).

Asset-backed securities (1985)

Inverse floaters (1986)

Limits on exposure by duration bucket (1986).

Credit card receivable-backed securities (1987). | Lotus Notes is the first commercially released product that features document sharing and remote location communication, and becomes one of the most powerful web conferencing tools (1989). | Undertakings for Collective Investments in Transferable Securities (UCITS) (1985).

"Big Bang" reforms in U.K.: eliminating fixed commission system, allowed more foreign investment, and improved screen technology for trading.

Basel 1—provided minimum capital requirements for banks and introduced to members of the G-10 (1988).

Financial Institutions Reform, Recovery and Enforcement Act (FIRREA) makes major regulation changes to savings and loan industry. (1989) | Tax Reform Act of 1986 prevented commercial banks from purchasing municipal securities.

Junk-bond market increased from $10 billion in 1978 to $189 billion 1989 (about 34% increase each year).

Double-digit performance of Julian Robertson's Tiger Fund astounds the public and initiates great interest in hedge fund industry.

Insurance companies began offering catastrophe bonds that are linked to major catastrophic, often natural-caused, events. Insurance companies transfer some of their risk obligations to investors.

End of 1980s and beginning of 1990s, all European countries established derivatives exchanges—amount of derivatives outstanding increased from $2.7 billion (1986) to $2.4 trillion (2001) |

(Continued)

Exhibit 1.2 (*Continued*)

Date	New Products/ Risk Innovations	Technology	Deregulation/ Regulatory Change	Key Milestones for Different Types of Financial Firms
	CBO/CLOs (1987)			Over $80 billion of foreign investment in developing nations by multinational corporations.
	Principal exchange-rate-linked securities (1987).			Long-Term Capital Management formed in 1994; strategy concentrated on "convergence-arbitrage" trades, trying to profit from small price differences among similar securities; used very high leverage, ratio of 25:1.
	Swaptions (1988)			After Bill Clinton passed a law in 1995 that allowed easy access to bank credit, commercial banks began issuing large numbers of sub-prime mortgage loans.
1991–1996	Bonds with earthquake puts.	CNBC expands its broadcasting at an international scale with the launch of CNBC Asia. CNBC Europe begins its programming a year later (1995).	Japan begins process of financial deregulation.	

Credit default swaps—total-return swaps—credit-linked notes.

Palm, Inc. introduces the first successful handheld computer (also known as PDAs, or personal digital assistants), the Palm Pilot (1996).

CMT derivatives
Power structures
Energy derivatives

Commodity indexed notes (1991)
Structured notes (1991)
Path-dependent derivatives (1991–94)
Equity linked notes (1993)
Market risk, operational risk and other non-credit based reserves.
Value at Risk
M-squared
Multi-period and Monte Carlo methods for options models.
Sensitivity to model risk.
Portfolio allocation according to expenditure of risk.
Risk Metrics (1994)

Equity with litigation-output option.
Derivatives based on the Euro.
Inflation-linked US Treasuries (1996).
Act of God bonds (1996)
Balance sheet CLOs (1996)

context of the capital markets. Prior to the advances in technology, mathematical techniques long used in the sciences could only be used *theoretically* in finance due to the inability to wait hours or days for answers. As this period progressed, many techniques whose power was only dreamed about in the early 1900s became employable *practically* by dealers, end users, regulators, and others. This created not only greater opportunities to see both risk and reward, but also a shortened cycle of innovation.

Dramatic comparisons are evident—a list of *all* innovations in the early 1970s began to be matched by those in a single quarter. With the exceptions of commodity futures and currency and commodity forwards, derivatives markets that were nonexistent in 1970—for example, interest rate swaps and currency swaps—topped $50 trillion outstanding by the end of 1998.[1] Structured notes, collateralized mortgage obligations (CMOs), and asset-backed securities (ABS) were all introduced. Advances in technology changed how firms and individuals participated in the capital markets. Transactions became ever less "hard copy and local" and ever more "electronic and global." The contrasts make the beginning of this period sound like the Dark Ages: At the beginning of this period, we did not have the personal computer; instead, handwritten spreadsheets and calculators were used to perform calculations, and pools of typists painstakingly produced single documents on wide-carriage typewriters. We did not have desktop publishing; instead, typesetters placed lead type in individual rows, and many an all-nighter was spent proofreading the lines as they were changed. We did not have mortgage calculators to perform interest and principal calculations; instead, bankers looked up monthly payment amounts in books that contained tables of principal and interest for different rates.

Globalization was the second force. With technology arrived e-mail and satellite communications. Information flow became cheap and virtually instantaneous, and cross-border transactions were executed in seconds versus days at the beginning of the period. A related result was that capital market events began to transcend borders, sometimes causing sympathy crashes or other market moves as traders tried to anticipate one market's reaction to another's event. Yet another change was that financial firms began to shop the world's markets for the best deal, not only for themselves but also for their customers. At the beginning of the period, a U.S. corporation looked to its lead bank or to the domestic debt and equity markets to raise capital, and it was rare to issue a Eurobond, a Samurai bond, or a Yankee bond. During this period, the list of capital-raising alternatives grew much longer, and it became standard to include the public and private European and Asian capital markets, as well as new financial lenders such as mutual funds. Often, new markets were used in combination with derivatives so that borrowers or investors could swap back or transform the currency or interest rate basis to a preferred structure. In addition, borrowers and investors alike began to use futures and over-the-counter derivatives, notably caps, collars, and floors, to alter the risk/return structures of assets and liabilities.

Deregulation was the third force. In 1971, the Bretton Woods system, which, through government intervention, had worked remarkably well in maintaining stable exchange rates since the end of World War II, collapsed. This was followed by a dramatic increase in the volatility of exchange rates. As this period began, Canada and Germany had begun interest rate deregulation. In 1979, Paul Volcker, succumbing to the powerful forces of disintermediation brought on by inflation, freed short-term U.S. interest rates. Banks would now pay market-determined rates rather than government-mandated rates. In 1980, the United States began a process of deregulating its savings, commercial, and investment banks. France deregulated many financial institutions in 1981, and Great Britain deregulated securities firms with the so-called Big Bang in 1986. The oil shocks of the 1970s, and again later during the Gulf War, rather than being managed by governments, were left to market forces. As a result of deregulation and the other forces, the currency, interest rate, commodity, and stock markets experienced unprecedented volatility.

The fourth force was the expansion of financial institutions' businesses to include the intermediation of *risk* in addition to the intermediation of capital. No longer would monoline financial intermediaries handle all aspects of the borrowing and lending transaction. During this period, not just banks but mutual funds, insurance companies, brokers, government agencies, and credit unions became ever more likely to stand in between, not only to move capital, but also to move risk from suppliers to users. Large world events further drove the need to manage risk: For example, the historical volatility of oil had a high of about 30 percent but increased to 300 percent during the Gulf War. In other words, the likelihood that oil prices would change over a given period of time increased tenfold. Globalization and technology had enabled the proliferation of products to manage such risks: Analysis and computations previously untenable in a volatile environment had grown feasible. Financial firms stepped in to design and execute risk management products, not only to manage their own risks but also to service their customers.

The collapse of Bretton Woods (1971); the oil shocks (1973, 1979, and 1990); a major stock market crash (1987); and dramatic currency moves (notably the Japanese yen, Italian lira, and Mexican peso in the 1990s) made it clear to corporations and financial institutions that active risk management was essential to their financial health and competitiveness. Whereas it had been acceptable to most shareholders in 1970 for corporations to announce increased sales but decreased profits due to currency exchange losses or volatile raw materials costs, this was no longer the case by the end of the period. Shareholders demanded that corporations employ risk/reward management tools to keep risk within acceptable bounds.

The now-infamous savings and loan (S&L) crisis provides an excellent example of how the new products offered by financial firms could be used to better control risk. In the late 1960s the business of S&Ls was, essentially, as it had been since the emergence of these institutions in the United States after World War II. Simply stated, S&Ls invested short-term depositors' funds in long-term mortgage loans to homeowners. This asset-liability mismatch caused few problems while interest rates were low and stable. However, when interest rates rose, disintermediation became inevitable. A deregulation of interest rates in 1979 became a necessity for the United States to remain competitive in the new global playing field. As interest rates tripled to over 20 percent in 1979–1980, S&Ls had to raise rates paid on their deposits beyond those received on their existing mortgage loan portfolios, creating huge losses that the industry could not sustain. A government bailout resulted, and the need for greater risk management was clear. By the end of this period, simple interest rate swaps, one of the most common risk management products today, and engineered securities in the form of CMOs and structured deposits, assisted S&Ls in managing their risks profitably.

The interaction of these forces was at many times painful but also helpful to financial firms and corporations. On the painful side, at the same time that many financial firms struggled with default crises in less-developed country debt, high-yield debt, and commercial real estate, deregulation reduced profits or produced negative profit margins. On the helpful side, many new innovative products, markets, and delivery channels opened to financial institutions through technology and others' deregulation. In addition, the need to manage increased volatility, combined with the ability to deploy technology within the time frame of traded markets, provided the means to create new multitrillion-dollar markets such as risk advisory services, derivatives, and financially engineered securities, which bolstered profits and risk management capabilities at a critical time.

In summary, during this phase, financial firms were very much in the business of responding to their own needs to manage risk and clients' needs to manage risk. They created new products, notably derivatives (at first called "synthetics") and financially-engineered securities. They added risk intermediation to the business of capital intermediation. During this period, the financial engineer was born and financial engineering became its own profession. Organizations such as the International Association of Financial Engineers[2] were founded; finance curriculum expanded to include derivatives, risk management, new products, and hedging techniques. There was such a need for trained quants that dozens of graduate programs were launched at major universities to produce financial engineers. Over the three decades leading up to 1998, firms like J.P. Morgan, Swiss Bank Corporation (SBC) (later to become part of UBS, AG), Deutsche Bank, Equitable Companies, Fidelity Funds, Citibank, Goldman Sachs, and some new boutiques emerged in powerful positions.

But others were not as lucky or as quick to acknowledge the sea change in their businesses and markets or to manage the changing risk profiles of the capital markets and their firms. Spectacular downfalls ensued for Kidder Peabody, Barings Bank, Granite Funds, Daiwa's U.S. Bank, Toyo Shinkin Bank, Nissan Mutual Life Insurance, Confederation Life, the Maxwell Companies' pension funds, Drexel Burnham Lambert, Continental Illinois, and Bank of Credit and Commerce International (BCCI), plus many regional savings and loans and credit unions in Japan, Great Britain, Switzerland, and the United States. A lucky few were forgiven by the capital markets long before their woes were over (notably Orange County, California). A few survived with the assistance of governments or via takeovers by stronger partners, but many did not.

During this period, it was no longer possible to distinguish financial institutions merely by their names. For example, insurance companies and mutual funds both made loans and offered check writing (traditional banking functions), while banks began to write insurance and offer families of mutual funds (traditional insurance and investment management functions). The overlap and expansion of businesses changed how top firms were measured. For example, 10 to 20 years earlier the top banks had been measured by total assets, total loans, and total capital.

In the new era, rankings were expanded to include a host of additional measures such as "best foreign exchange house," "best risk management adviser," "best equity dealer," "best commodity house," and so forth. Another contributor to the transformation of finance was the emergence of off-balance-sheet businesses for many financial institutions. According to the Bank for International Settlements, by March 1995 the notional amount of derivatives outstanding exceeded $40 trillion and translated into over $3 trillion in market exposure. By the mid-1990s, some financial institutions had more off-balance-sheet business than on-balance-sheet business. A good example was Bankers Trust, which, as the eighth-largest U.S. bank in 1994, had about $70 billion in total assets and over $1 trillion notional amount in off-balance-sheet items. Less than 20 years earlier, the reverse had existed: Off-balance-sheet businesses were at that time dominated by on-balance-sheet businesses for all financial firms.

During this period, central banks and national governments faced increasing difficulty in monitoring off-balance-sheet exposures and in resolving large-scale, cross-border financial problems such as the freezing of Iranian assets, BCCI, Barings, Olympia & York, and Lloyd's due to the lack of a uniform commercial code across nations. Trading blocks in North America, Europe, and Asia emerged, driven by the need for regions with similar economic interests to cooperate and address such issues. A notable turning point in the history of financial engineering came with three financial calamities: the Asian financial crisis of 1997–1998, followed by the Russian financial crisis, followed by the downfall of Long-Term Capital Management (LTCM) in 1998. All of these events raised fears of a global economic meltdown. Also notable at the end of 1998 was the creation of the financial behemoth, Citigroup, that challenged the separation of banking and insurance under the then-in-effect Glass-Steagall Act.

THE MASSIVE GROWTH PERIOD (1998 TO 2006)

The Asian financial crisis began with the financial collapse of Thailand's currency, the Thai baht. Currencies across Asia slumped at the same time that equity and other asset markets devalued. These events, in turn, caused a precipitous increase in borrowing. Widespread civil unrest and rioting forced President Suharto to resign after being at the helm in Indonesia for 30 years. A slump in world commodity prices triggered a Russian financial crisis. At the time, oil and gas, timber, and metals accounted for 80 percent of Russia's exports. A collapse of Russia's currency, bond, and equity markets followed. On the heels of the Russian financial crisis, Long-Term Capital Management lost almost $5 billion in less than four months. Fearing potential interlinkages, the Federal Reserve supervised a forced bailout of the hedge fund by major banks and broker-dealers.

These crises led to a new focus on enterprise risk management and the creation of the so-called "enterprise risk manager." As summarized in Exhibit 1.3, there also was rapid innovation in credit-linked derivatives, plus financially-engineered instruments. During this period, interest rate swaps and currency swaps grew sixfold to almost $350 trillion,[3] and credit default swaps grew from about $350 billion in 2001 to over $45 trillion. The economic environment during this period was one of remarkable stability and included flush liquidity, relatively low volatility, low

Exhibit 1.3 Massive Growth (1997–2006)

Date	New Products/ Risk Innovations	Technology	Deregulation/ Regulatory Change	Key Milestones for Different Types of Financial Firms
1996–2000	Synthetic CLOs (1997)	The Blackberry goes mainstream when Research In Motion (RIM) introduces the Blackberry Email Solution (1999).	Objectives and Principles of Securities Regulation (IOSCO Principles) (1998).	Collapse of Long-Term Capital Management (1998).
	Volatility swaps (1998)	CNBC's release of Worldwide Exchange, the first live news broadcast that is globally integrated, combining the financial markets of the United States, Europe, and Asia (2005).	Repeal of Glass-Steagall Act, thus allowing the merging of commercial and investment banks (1999).	
	Correlation options (1999)	Apple launches the iPhone (2007).	First Asian CDO deals were balance sheet transactions issued by Japanese banks.	
	Integration of credit and market risk (1998).	Amazon releases the Kindle, setting competitors into finding ways to enter the newly emerging market of e-book readers (2007).	Guidelines set by Insurance and Superannuation Commission allows use of derivative instruments, but very strict guidelines (1997).	
2001–2007	Principal Protected Note (PPN)		Commodity Futures Modernization Act (2000)	National Credit Union Administration (NCUA) allowed Western Corporate Federal Credit Union (WesCorp) to organize a program providing federal credit unions with easy access to financial derivatives market (2000.)

16

Repackaged assets	Sarbanes-Oxley Act (2002)	DBS Bank securitized $1.5 billion of CDS on corporate loans in the first Asian synthetic balance sheet CDO deal (2001).
Merrill Lynch introduces first rated collateralized foreign exchange obligation (CFXO) (2007).	Basel II Accord (2004)	By 2004, over-the-counter (OTC) derivatives market reaches $248 trillion worldwide (market value about $9 trillion). 40% of volume is traded in U.S., 40% in Europe (mostly London and Frankfurt), and 20% in Asian (mostly Tokyo).
Binary options (2007)	Requirement for hedge fund investors to register under the Investment Advisor's Act of 1940 (2004).	Total volume of non-life insurance-linked securities (ILS) was estimated to be more than $8 billion, while hedge funds contributed another $10 billion to other ILS investments in industry-loss warranties (ILW), sidecars, and cat bonds (2006).
Macroprudential indicators/analysis (2000) Enterprise-wide risk management (2000) Expected Shortfall (ES) Financial Soundness Indicators (FSI) Methodology (established by IMF) (2004).		

interest rates, rising equity and real estate prices, and easy-to-obtain leverage. The capital markets absorbed several large market corrections, including substantial accounting scandals (e.g., Enron and Parmalat) and the bursting of the tech bubble. During this period, the landscape of financial firms changed substantially:

- Citigroup's Sanford Weill became known as the "shatterer of Glass-Steagall" in the United States.
- Around the world, massive deregulation of financial firms commenced as the business models of investment banks, commercial banks, and broker-dealers converged with private equity, alternative asset management, and insurance.
- Several financial firms rode the wave of the massive derivatives and structured products growth, and so joined the ranks of top derivatives and structured products behemoths, including UBS, ING, HBC, Barclays, Lehman Brothers, Merrill Lynch, Bear Stearns, and American International Group (AIG), among others.
- Whereas hedge funds were almost exclusively based in the United States at the beginning of the period, hedge funds in Asia grew to $110 billion, and in Europe to $400 billion, by the end of 2006.
- Central banks and sovereign wealth funds in Asia and the Middle East accumulated an estimated $7 trillion to $10 trillion in assets, becoming increasing purchasers of U.S. debt and net suppliers of global capital.
- Asset managers such as Fidelity, which had taken over five decades to grow to a few hundred billion in assets under management (AUM), more than tripled their assets during the period to AUMs measured in the trillions.
- Freddie Mac, Fannie Mae, Bank of America, Washington Mutual, Ameriquest, and others became the leaders in sectors of the U.S. subprime mortgage market.
- Quantitative trading grew substantially, due to the success of Renaissance Technologies LLC and many commodity-trading advisors (CTAs).
- G-7 investors massively increased their global presence, focusing particularly heavily on Brazil, Russia, India, and China (BRIC) and other emerging markets.
- Multibillion-dollar so-called club deals (multiple private equity firms pooling their assets to take over huge firms) became common.
- Whereas the International Monetary Fund (IMF) had played a substantial role in the Asian and Russian financial crises, it was fighting for relevancy as the strong economic environment continued into 2006.

During this period, enterprise risk reporting added many new dimensions, especially to capture correlation risk (the risk that multiple asset classes or exposures will deteriorate in concert). Further, value at risk (VaR—a widely used measure of the risk of loss), stress tests, and Monte Carlo simulations continued as day-to-day features of a best-practice risk management program. A notable turning point came in 2007 with the subprime mortgage crisis that exposed pervasive weaknesses in the measurement of risk, particularly with respect to how interconnected many institutions had become. Consequently, the debate about national and global financial re-regulation focused the spotlight on systemic risk.

THE RATIONALIZATION PERIOD (2007 TO DATE, ONGOING)

Expansionary monetary and fiscal policies, combined with substantial deregulation of capital markets and financial firms, had facilitated explosive growth in financial engineering. While there were some signs of a weakening residential mortgage market in the United States in 2005, as well as weakening loan markets that had earlier fueled hugely appreciated assets in other countries (for example, Ireland, England, and Spain), the beginning of the current financial crisis commonly is linked to the United States' subprime mortgage defaults that began in earnest in 2007. Early in the crisis, a huge focus was placed on credit derivatives, securitization, high leverage, off-balance-sheet financing, and failures in specific and enterprise risk management. As the crisis continues to unfold, additional focus has been placed on pro-cyclical regulatory, accounting, and risk management practices; also, compensation practices have been placed under the spotlight as strong contributors to the global crisis (for financial and nonfinancial firms alike). The question of whether government regulation had become too lax and whether supervisors did adequate jobs (including regulators, senior managers, boards of directors, and other overseers) is at the heart of current discussion. And the question of whether protectionism and/or regionalism will overtake ongoing globalization appears with increasing frequency in the debate.

At the same time, the practical result has been de-risking and de-leveraging, with global write-downs by banks at $1.5 trillion at the end of 2009 and with IMF estimating in April 2010 that the global bank write-downs will reach $2.3 trillion by the time the crisis is completely resolved. This is considerably more than banks raised in new capital during the same period. The substantial losses by investors in certain types of financially engineered credit instruments, and the incineration of trillions of dollars of value, have resulted in the nationalization of numerous financial firms and global companies plus staggering bailouts by governments around the world. While some instruments are well into their write-down cycle (for example, residential mortgage-backed securities), other instruments are just beginning a likely write-down cycle (for example, commercial mortgage-backed securities and prime residential mortgage-backed securities). Given the breathtaking injections of funds, we pose the question: Will governments and stakeholders (i.e., taxpayers) demand higher levels of regulation and oversight in exchange for those bailout monies? There certainly seems a palpable probability that a reduction in the freedom of global banks is possible as countries and/or regions focus on limiting damage from future crises. Another key factor to consider will be how governments, consumers, and firms respond, determining whether the BRICs/Middle East/sovereign wealth funds emerge with more than 50 percent of the global gross domestic product (GDP) pie after global growth recovers. This will be the first era during which these countries/regions may dominate the global capital markets.

Financial engineering has been forced to enter a rationalization phase. Most firms are in the process of reviewing, rethinking, and/or retooling the procedures, policies, assumptions, and techniques underneath both their specific and enterprise risk management. Regulators, supervisors, and legislators are in the process of conducting substantial reviews and hearings regarding systemic risk and existing regulatory frameworks. They are conducting investigations into firms that failed or were nationalized. There is little doubt that as Exhibit 1.4 is updated, there will be substantial additions to the "Regulatory Change" and "Risk Innovation" columns.

Some of the questions that will shape this new phase in the evolution of financial engineering are:

- Will increased regulation stifle financial engineering innovation and the over-the-counter derivatives markets?
- How will transparency be increased?
- How will the accountability of overseers (regulators, boards of directors, senior management, and others) be increased?
- What (permanent) changes will be made to compensation models at firms (both financial and nonfinancial)?
- How can data and information sharing, plus cooperation, be improved across central banks, regulators, and policy makers?
- Will the financial utility functions (for example, monetary flows) be separated from financial risk-taking functions (for example, riskier proprietary trading)?
- How will additional regulation or other changes impact the cost structure of financial firms?
- Will stakeholders during this era focus more on revenue and earnings growth (as in prior eras) or more on stable and well-funded balance sheets?
- How will the mix of short-term and long-term funding change, and what will be the impact on the activities of firms?
- How will consumers change savings patterns, and if savings rise substantially, how severely will this rise impact growth?
- Will ratings agency debt ratings be viewed as accurate measures of credit risk?
- How will the aging populations in the established economies impact the next generation of financially engineered products, especially those linked to insurance and pension products?
- What are the new risk measurement models that will be added to value at risk, stress testing, and simulation to improve risk management?
- How can multiple models be used to conduct more thorough analysis of worst cases or expected losses?
- How did common regulatory, accounting, and risk management approaches contribute to pro-cyclicality and the systemic issues?
- Are there new measures of liquidity risk that reveal exposures better?
- How should stress tests be revised, given their weaknesses as set tests that look at past moves and/or have fixed parameters designed for specific positions or strategies?
- How will "too large to fail" or "too linked to fail" change the global landscape of firms?
- What will replace agency ratings as a tool for assessing risk?
- How will firms better align compensation and excessive risk taking?
- Which firms will successfully focus on new business models and business strategies and adapt to the substantial changes in the next phase of the

Exhibit 1.4 Rationalization Period (2007–Present)

Date	New Products/ Risk Innovations	Technology	Deregulation/ Regulatory Change	Key Milestones for Different Types of Financial Firms
2007				Rating agencies have been questioned regarding the accuracy of their ratings of certain financial instruments, especially residential mortgage-backed securities (2007).
2008–2009	IBRD and IDA offer high-risk countries weather derivatives to help with loss of food supply. Pay-option adjustable-rate mortgages for the worst residential mortgage credits.	The Cray XT5 supercomputer, also known as the "Jaguar," is bestowed the title of world's fastest computer, with the ability to process 1.75 petaflops (quadrillions of floating point operations per second) (2009).	Financial Services Authority (FSA) introduces remuneration code of practice, which requires banks, building societies, and broker dealers in the U.K. to implement policies that promote effective risk management (2009).	Insurance giant AIG became government-controlled after the Federal Reserve saved the firm through an $85 billion bailout; government feared the possible collapse of AIG because it had provided numerous insurance contracts to investors who bought complex securitized products. Two of the largest investment banks, Morgan Stanley and Goldman Sachs, create commercial bank branches (2008). Barclays Capital purchases Lehman Brothers' broker-dealer unit, which potentially pushes the U.K. bank into top 10 positions across many parts of investment banking, such as global M&A, and global equity and debt capital markets (2008).

(Continued)

Exhibit 1.4 (*Continued*)

Date	New Products/ Risk Innovations	Technology	Deregulation/ Regulatory Change	Key Milestones for Different Types of Financial Firms
2010			U.S. announces intention to collect "TARP" tax from financial firms (2010). Hearings continue regarding systemic risk and the role played by various financial firms around the world (2010). European Commission continues to review restructuring plans submitted by nationalized banks of member countries (2009, 2010). Obama, following a suggestion by Volcker, announces he will pursue the separation of the utility functions of banks from the risk-taking function of banks. Britain announces windfall tax on bonuses given by financial firms (2010).	PIMCO Total Return Fund, the world's largest bond fund, contains nearly $193 billion in total assets, much of which has been accumulated through derivative exposures—the fund buys futures contracts or other derivatives in order to obtain exposure to bonds. NCUA took over U.S. Central Federal Credit Union (with $34 billion assets) and WesCorp (with $23 billion assets). After a stress-test of the asset-backed securities held by the two credit unions NCUA concluded that the risk of the securities were too high. Hundreds of additional smaller bank failures are expected in the United States and around the world (2010).

capital markets and financial engineering, and which will lose their way by focusing too narrowly on their response to the financial crisis?

HISTORICAL READINGS

Here is a comprehensive list of relevant readings that you can locate if you are interested:

Abbott, Charles C. 1947. "The Commercial Banks and the Public Debt." *American Economic Review* 37:2, 265–276.

Aldcroft, Derek Howard. 1993. *The European Economy, 1914–1990.* 3rd ed. London: Routledge.

Andrews, Edmund L., Michael J. de la Merced, and Mary Williams Walsh. 2008. "Fed's $85 Billion Loan Rescues Insurer." *New York Times,* September 16, A1.

Australia, Parliament, House of Representatives, Standing Committee on Economics, Finance, and Public Administration. 2000. "Inquiry into the International Financial Market Effects on Government Policy," March 22.

Bank for International Settlements. 2008. "Financial Market Developments and Their Implications for Monetary Policy." BIS Papers 39.

Barr, Paul G. 1996. "Institutions Cut Derivative Use." *Pensions & Investments* 24:15, 3–5.

Beder, Tanya S. 1999. "The Great Risk Hunt." *Journal of Portfolio Management,* 25th Anniversary Special 25:5, 28–34.

Beder, Tanya S. 1995. "VAR: Seductive but Dangerous." *Financial Analysts Journal* 51:5, 12–24.

Beder, Tanya S. 1997. "What We've Learned about Derivatives Risk in the 1990s." *Journal of Economic Notes.* Banca Monte dei Paschi di Siena SpA (January 1997).

Beder, Tanya S., with Michael Minnich, Hubert Shen, and Jodi Stanton. 1998. "Vignettes on VaR." *Journal of Financial Engineering* 7:3/4, 289–309.

Bellis, Mary. "Timelines and Inventions of the 20th Century." *About.com.* http://inventors.about.com/od/timelines/a/twentieth.htm.

Bing, Liang. 2001. "Hedge Fund Performance: 1990–1999." *Financial Analysts Journal* 57:1, 11–18.

Braham, Lewis, with Tara Kalwarski. 2009. "What's Inside PIMCO?" *BusinessWeek,* November 19, 72–73.

Brouwer, Gordon. 1999. "Deregulation and Open Capital Markets: The Australian Experience before Wallis." *Agenda* 61:51–68.

Choudhry, Moorad. 2004. "Securitization: Global Financial Market Development for the 21st Century." *Euromoney* 35:2–5.

Comissão de Valores Mobiliários: 30th Anniversary Conference. 2006. September 4–5, Rio de Janiero, Brazil.

Csiszar, Ernest N. 2007. "An Update on the Use of Modern Financial Instruments in the Insurance Sector." *Geneva Papers* 32:319–331.

Cummins, J. David, Richard D. Phillips, and Stephen D. Smith. 1996. "Corporate Hedging in the Insurance Industry: The Use of Financial Derivatives by US Insurers." Wharton Financial Institutions Center, September 19.

Curry, Timothy, and Lynn Shibut. 2000. "The Cost of the Savings and Loan Crisis: Truth and Consequences." *FDIC Banking Review* 13:2, n.pg.

Davis, Charles H. 2003. "The History of Computers." www.city-net.com/~ched/help/general/tech_history.html.

Davis, Os. 2006. "How Exchange-Traded Funds Came to Be." *Associated Content*, June 27. www.associatedcontent.com/article/40099/how_exchangetraded_funds_came_to_be.html.

Dodd, Randall. 2000. "The Role of Derivatives in the East Asian Financial Crisis." CEPA Working Paper Series III, no. 20.

Eichengreen, Barry, and Donald Mathieson. 1999. "Hedge Funds: What Do We Really Know?" *Economic Issues* 19 (September): n.pg.

Ely, Bert, "Savings and Loan Crisis." 2008. In *The Concise Encyclopedia of Economics*, 2nd edition.

Embrechts, Paul. "Statistics and Quantitative Risk Management." Department of Mathematics, ETH Zurich, n.d.

Farley, Tom. "Mobile Telephone History." 2005. *Telektronikk* (March 4): n.pg.

Federal Communications Commission. 2005. "Historical Periods in Television Technology." *Communications History* 21 (November).

Federal Deposit Insurance Corporation. 2000. "An Examination of the Banking Crises of the 1980s and Early 1990s" (June 5).

Financial Advisor. 2008. "Barclays Buys Lehman's Broker-Dealer Unit." September 17.

Finnerty, John D., and Douglas R. Emery. 2002. "Corporate Securities Innovation: An Update." *Journal of Applied Finance* 12:1, 21.

Fortson, Danny. 2006. "The Day Big Bang Blasted the Old Boys into Oblivion." *The Independent*, October 29.

Fratzscher, Oliver. 2006. "Emerging Derivative Markets in Asia." *Asian Financial Market Development*, World Bank, (March). http://siteresources.worldbank.org/INTEAPREGTOPFINFINSECDEV/Resources/589748-1144293317827/EAFinance_bkgrnd_Derivative_Markets.pdf (accessed December 1, 2009).

Gordon, Marcy. 2009. "WesCorp, U.S. Central: U.S. Regulators Seize Control of Two Credit Unions." *Huffington Post*, March. www.huffingtonpost.com/2009/03/20/wescorp-us-central-regula_n_177584.html.

Greer, Jed, and Kavaljit Singh. 2000. "A Brief History of Transnational Corporations." *Global Policy Forum*.

Harmon, Florence E. 2007. "Self-Regulatory Organizations: The Options Clearing Corporation; Notice of Filing of a Proposed Rule Change Relating to Binary Options." United States Securities and Exchange Commission, September 19.

"Hedge Fund History." *Hedge Fund History*, n.p., n.d.

Hoadley, John, and Al Javed. 2005. "Overview: Technological Innovation for Wireless Broadband Access." *Nortel Technical Journal* 2 (July):1–5.

Hodgson, Raphael. 2009. "The Birth of the Swap." *Financial Analysts Journal* 65:3, 1–4.

Howell, Paul L. 1958. "A Re-Examination of Pension Fund Investment Policies." *Journal of Finance* 13:2, 261–274.

Hundman, Katie. 1999. "An Analysis of the Determinants of Financial Derivative Use by Commercial Banks." *Park Place Economist* 7. www.iwu.edu/economics/PPE07/katie.pdf.

Investment U Research Team. "The History of Private Equity." *The Oxford Club: Investment U*. The Oxford Club, LLC, n.d.

Investopedia, 2009. *Investopedia ULC*. www.investopedia.com/.

Israkson, Daylin. 2008 "Pension Funds—A Historical Overview." *Associated Content*, October. www.associatedcontent.com/article/1118718/pension_funds_a_historical_overview.html?cat=55.

Jameson, Rob. 2002. "Case Study: US Savings and Loan Crisis." *Ambit ERisk*, (August).

Jorion, Philippe. 2000. "Risk Management Lessons from Long-Term Capital Management." *European Financial Management* 6:3, 277–301.

Karchmer, Jennifer. 2000. "Tiger Management Closes." *CNNMoney*, Cable News Network, A Time Warner Company, March 30.

Kemp, Robert S., Sharon Graham, and S. Brooks Marshall Jr. 1986. "An Analysis of the Investment Decision of Defined Benefit Pension Funds from the Corporate Perspective." *Benefits Quarterly* 2:1, 18–25.

Kindleberger, Charles P. 1993. *"A Financial History of Western Europe.* "New York: Oxford University Press.

Kindleberger, Charles P. 2000. *"Manias, Panics and Crashes: A History of Financial Crises."* New York: John Wiley & Sons.

Kiviat, Barbara. 2009. "A Brief History of Ratings Agencies." *Time* 173:12, 18.

Koski, Jennifer Lynch, and Jeffrey Pontiff. 1999. "How Are Derivatives Used? Evidence from the Mutual Fund Industry." *Journal of Finance* 54:2, 791–816.

Lanchester, John. 2009. "Outsmarted: High Finance vs. Human Nature." Review of *Fool's Gold*, by Gillian Tett, *A Failure of Capitalism*, by Richard A. Posner, and *Animal Spirits: How Human Psychology Drives the Economy, and Why It Matters for Global Capitalism*, by Robert J. Schiller and George A. Akerlof. *New Yorker*, June 1.

Ledrut, Elizabeth, and Christian Upper. 2007. "Changing Post-Trading Arrangements for OTC Derivatives." *BIS Quarterly Review* (December).

Maremont, Mark. 2009. "U.S. Moves to Bail Out Credit Union Network." *Wall Street Journal*, January 29, A1.

New York Times (1857–Current File). 1960. "Big Mutual Fund Sets Assets Mark: '59 Report of Massachusetts Investors Also Shows Share Value at Peak." January 27, 48.

New York Times (1857–Current File). 1950. "Investors Trust Increases Assets: Massachusetts Organization Reports $27,490,665 Dec. 31, Against $207,322,061." January 31, 39.

New York Times (1857–Current File). 1935. "SEC Acts to Rule 'Outside' Trading: All Brokers and Dealers in Over-the-Counter Securities Are Ordered to Register; Must Give Reports July 1; New Regulations Aim to Protect Customers Who Invest Outside Regular Exchanges." May 6.

New York Times (1857–Current File). 1940. "Trust Increases Its Asset Value: Massachusetts Investors Trust Reports $18.18 a Share on Sept. 30." October 21.

O'Kelly, Grellan. 2009. "UCITS Funds Gain Popularity, Increasingly Employ Hedge Fund Strategies." *FINalternatives* (September 1).

Park, Yung Chul, and Kee-Hong Bae. 2002. "Financial Liberalization and Economic Integration in East Asia." *PECC Finance Forum Conference*, August 11–13, Hilton Hawaiian Village, Honolulu, Hawaii.

Pogue, Thomas F., and Robert M. Soldofsky. 1969. "What's in a Bond Rating." *Journal of Financial and Quantitative Analysis* 4:2, 201–228.

Qudrat, Abir. "Financial Derivatives and the Global Financial Crisis." *Financial Express*, n.d.

Reckard, E. Scott. 2009. "Federal Regulator Is Blamed in Bank Failures." *Los Angeles Times*, June 18.

Remolona, Eli M., and Ilhyock Shim. 2008. "Credit Derivatives and Structured Credit: The Nascent Markets of Asia and the Pacific." *BIS Quarterly Review*, (June). www.bis.org/repofficepubl/arpresearch_dev_200806.01.pdf?noframes=1 (accessed December 1, 2009).

Rubin, Howard. 2009. "Dynamics of Technology Economy Are Key to Mastering Balance of Expense and Value." *Wall Street & Technology*, November 16.

Sangha, Balvinder S. 1995. "Financial Derivatives: Applications and Policy Issues." *Business Economics* 30:1, 46–53.

Schapiro, Mary. 2009. "Testimony Concerning the Over-the-Counter Derivatives Markets Act of 2009, before the House Committee on Agriculture." U.S. Securities and Exchange Commission, September 22.

Setton, Dolly, et al. 1999. "A Century of Deals." *Forbes* 163:8, 265–272.

South Australia, Legal Services Commission. 2007. "Superannuation." *Law Handbook*, June 27.

United States Securities and Exchange Commission. 2008. "The Laws That Govern the Securities Industry." SEC, September 26.

Wall Street & Technology Daily. 2009. "*WS&T*'s 2009 Gold Book: Wall Street's Top Technology Leaders Drive Innovation in Tough Times." October 19.

Wargo, Brian. 2009. "Credit Union Chief: Cash Infusion Would Fund More Loans." *Las Vegas Sun*, December 29.

Wells, Brenda P., et al. 2009. "Risky Asset Substitution in the Insurance Industry: An Historical Example." *Journal of Insurance Regulation* 27:3, 67–90.

World Council of Credit Unions. "The Birth of World Council of Credit Unions." http://www.woccu.org/about/heritage.

Yamazaki, Tomoko. 2009. "Hedge Funds Post Best Performance Since February 2000 (Update 1)." http://www.canadianhedgewatch.com/content/news/general/?id=4820.

NOTES

1. Source: International Swaps and Derivatives Association, Inc. (www.ISDA.org)

2. www.iafe.org.

3. Source: International Swaps and Derivatives Association, Inc. (www.ISDA.org)

ABOUT THE AUTHOR

Tanya Beder is currently chairman of SBCC in New York and SBCC Group Inc. in Connecticut. SBCC, founded in 1987, has a broad base of hedge fund, global bank, private equity, asset management, financial services, and corporate clients. From 2004 to 2006, Tanya was CEO of Tribeca Global Management LLC, Citigroup's USD 3 billion multi-strategy hedge fund, and from 1999 to 2004 was managing director of Caxton Associates LLC, a USD 10 billion investment management firm. Tanya sits on several boards of directors, including a major mutual fund complex and the National Board of Mathematics and their Applications. She has taught courses at Yale University's School of Management and Columbia University's Graduate School of Business and Financial Engineering. She speaks and guest lectures globally. Tanya has published in the *Journal of Portfolio Management*, *Financial Analysts Journal*, *Harvard Business Review*, and the *Journal of Financial Engineering*. She holds an MBA in finance from Harvard University and a BA in mathematics and philosophy from Yale University.

CHAPTER 2

Careers in Financial Engineering

SPENCER JONES
SBCC Group, Inc.

INTRODUCTION

The evolution and growth of financial engineering as a profession has been accompanied by an ever-increasing demand for qualified job candidates. The field is interdisciplinary and had existed under a number of different, sometimes inappropriate, labels for some time before industry and academia finally settled on the more accurate descriptor of "financial engineer." The roots of financial engineering trace back to major theoretical contributions made by financial economists during the 1950s, 1960s, and 1970s. They include names like Harry Markowitz, Merton Miller, Franco Modigliani, Eugene Fama, William Sharpe, Myron Scholes, Fischer Black, Robert Merton, Mark Rubinstein, John Cox, Stephen Ross, and many others that walked with them or followed the trail they pioneered. These men brought a new set of tools and a more scientific approach to finance to our understanding of financial markets, financial products, and financial relationships. However, as important as these contributions were in planting the seeds for a new profession, the blossoming of that profession did not occur until the financial markets began to experience an influx of highly skilled professionals from other, traditionally more quantitative, disciplines. These new entrants to the financial markets included ever more physicists, mathematicians, statisticians, astrophysicists, various types of engineers, and others who shared a love for quantitative rigor. Some of these people came to finance because they reached a point in their lives when they simply wanted to do something different. Others came because they were displaced by a changing world.

As the years passed, the initially fragmented discipline began to coalesce into an increasingly recognized and respected profession with its own professional organizations and recognized leaders. As the field evolved, it attracted some of the most respected minds from academia, both in traditional finance programs at respected business schools but also at leading engineering schools. Many of these people were drawn to financial engineering by the nascent markets for derivatives and later by the advent of securitization. While the opportunities and the variety of employment roles that are available to prospective financial engineers have increased dramatically over the years, the popular press all too often names the people engaged in the profession as "quants" (short for quantitative analyst). Nevertheless, not all financial engineering careers require an advanced study of mathematics. While many do, and some quantitative training certainly does help, there are many niches to be filled in which mathematics plays a less important role.

There are, today, a wealth of career opportunities available to competent financial engineers. As the field, first defined and given a name only about twenty years ago, has grown, over 150 universities and colleges have introduced courses and/or degree and certificate programs devoted to dimensions of financial engineering.[1] In this chapter, we present a framework to examine the range of career opportunities available.

In the most recent survey of financial engineering graduates, performed by the International Association of Financial Engineers (IAFE), career objectives showed a remarkable homogeneity. Of all the students surveyed, 56 percent of graduates wanted to work in a field related to derivatives pricing or trading, with a further 21 percent pursuing opportunities within risk management. This survey was performed in advance of the credit crisis. What is most surprising is that—with the extensive variety of opportunities available—over three-quarters of graduates were interested in such a concentrated group of fields. With over 5,000 financial engineering students now graduating annually,[2] it is important to more fully appreciate the wide set of opportunities outside of derivatives.

At first glance, it is understandable why students are drawn towards derivatives. Derivatives have become the archetype of financially engineered securities. They can be found in almost every market sector. But derivatives are far from the only area in which financial engineers are needed. The growth of automated trading strategies, for example, is but one of the many new opportunities in the markets where financial engineers are much in demand, as was securitization before that. With the massive spread of complex securities, opportunities and challenges abound in managing the risks faced by firms. With an estimated 750,000[3] risk practitioners across all industries, risk management remains one of the largest areas in which financial engineers can build a career.

The purpose of this chapter is to give the reader a sense of the breadth of financial engineering careers and to make it a bit easier to understand what skill sets are sought when the student reads job-posting notices. For example, within the realm of job postings titled "Quantitative Analyst," there is great variety in the types of analysis to be performed and in the nature of the employers. Quantitative analysts, and therefore financial engineers, are not simply in demand for roles on the CDO structuring desk within global banks. Rather, they are in demand across a broad spectrum of firms and in a large number of roles. The requirement and demand for quantitative analytical skills bridges across from banks, financial services firms and insurance companies to corporations, service companies, governments, and non-governmental organizations (NGOs). The skills developed during a financial engineering program are understood to apply far beyond the technical scope of financial instruments. Employers seek the strong analytical skills instilled during the student's program of study. These characteristics are also why the profession continues to draw people from other analytical backgrounds, applying their skills to financial problems.

The job functions of individual financial engineers can vary dramatically despite similar job titles, firms, and even business divisions. This will become noticeable if the reader reviews the details in a number of similar-sounding job postings. The similarities will generally be immediately apparent, but there will also be many subtle differences. A prospective candidate should be able to quickly identify the variety of businesses that employ financial engineers. Yet, beneath this, there are numerous roles that include programming, financial modeling, and data analysis. For some new entrants to the industry this can be challenging. To assist you, we have attempted to present the roles available by highlighting key components. Our hope is that, by doing this, you will be able to use this chapter in conjunction with job descriptions to better understand the nature of the role advertised.

At the conclusion of this chapter the reader will find tables that present a summary of the types of roles and opportunities available to a financial engineering graduate. When we first sat down to write this chapter, we were tempted to simply populate the tables with the role "Quantitative Analyst." This would have served to make the point of how widespread quantitative analytical roles have become—originally, of course, in the securities and derivatives markets, but later spreading to such things as analyzing data trends for superstore purchases, marketing analysis, and even journalism. While we have tried to illustrate the range of employment opportunities that require financial engineering skills, the areas we have identified below should not be considered exhaustive by any means. The range of employment opportunities will continue to evolve—along with financial engineering as a profession.

A WORLD OF OPPORTUNITIES

It is a challenge to illustrate the opportunities available to job candidates who have qualified themselves in financial engineering, whether through a formal course of study or through sufficient applicable experience. To assist the reader in understanding the variety of career paths available, we have developed the diagram in Exhibit 2.1. We envision a series of concentric circles, each of which depicts a functional area within a business or governmental entity. Think of these functional areas as the ingredients necessary to bake a pie. The "pie" is then sliced up into nine industry sectors that employ financial engineers and/or where quantitative analysts are sought. Some areas, such as "Services," are defined very broadly and encompass a great many roles and business types. The objective of the image is to highlight the range of fields available to financial engineers and quants, digesting the multitude of possible career paths into an approachable framework.

The concentric circles, which can also be thought of as representing levels of core competencies, illustrate the variety of functions within each of the sectors. In certain sectors, the differences in the job roles across the levels will be significant; in others, the differences will be minimal. Differentiating between the two is important if the job candidate is to identify the opportunities for which he or she is best suited.

The range of opportunities can be identified in part by reviewing the scale of offerings available within each sector. Risk Management, as highlighted earlier, is a sector in which over 750,000 professionals are estimated to be employed. Within academia, there are already 150 programs that are called, or offer substantial coursework in, financial engineering. Each employs a number of professors.

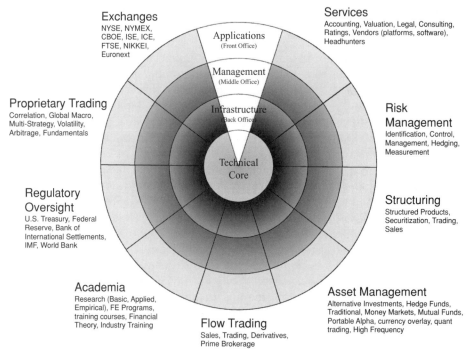

Exchanges
NYSE, NYMEX, CBOE, ISE, ICE, FTSE, NIKKEI, Euronext

Services
Accounting, Valuation, Legal, Consulting, Ratings, Vendors (platforms, software), Headhunters

Applications
(Front Office)

Management
(Middle Office)

Infrastructure
(Back Office)

Technical
Core

Proprietary Trading
Correlation, Global Macro, Multi-Strategy, Volatility, Arbitrage, Fundamentals

Risk Management
Identification, Control, Management, Hedging, Measurement

Regulatory Oversight
U.S. Treasury, Federal Reserve, Bank of International Settlements, IMF, World Bank

Structuring
Structured Products, Securitization, Trading, Sales

Academia
Research (Basic, Applied, Empirical), FE Programs, training courses, Financial Theory, Industry Training

Asset Management
Alternative Investments, Hedge Funds, Traditional, Money Markets, Mutual Funds, Portable Alpha, currency overlay, quant trading, High Frequency

Flow Trading
Sales, Trading, Derivatives, Prime Brokerage

NB–Examples below pie slices are illustrative and not complete

Exhibit 2.1 Career Wheel for Financial Engineers

Additionally, an even greater number of academics are employed within university finance departments at business schools that do not have a formal financial engineering program. For Asset Management, on top of all the pure asset management firms, a search identified 244 insurance companies in the United States alone that each employed more than 1,000 people and had annual revenues of USD 100 million.[4] In surveys of the Hedge Fund industry, over 18,000 hedge funds and 7,050 fund-of-funds were identified, collectively managing approximately USD 1.4 trillion.[5] In Regulatory Oversight, the Bank for International Settlements (BIS) recognizes 166 central banks on its website, from Afghanistan to Zimbabwe. Within each central bank there are likely to range from tens to hundreds of employment opportunities for financial engineers.

FUNCTIONAL AREAS

Technical Core

The technical core section for any career path encompasses the theories and principles that are the foundation for the field. The technical core underpins the field, providing idea growth and advancement in the field, both in academia and industry. It is unusual in that it need not be embedded within the business itself, often operating in areas that provide advisory solutions or thought leadership. This occurs within firms, but also within academia and specialized research firms.

The technical core will often center around research and development; developing and testing new theories and product possibilities that can, in time, be developed into an active business line. Most cutting edge firms require a continuous flow of fresh ideas. This often means that there will be a direct link to both established and emerging leaders in the academic community and a regular need to review work published in research outlets. Within risk management and asset management, for example, the role will involve extensive work in identifying new methods of creating and managing risk exposures for the business or for its clients. These roles require that the financial engineer keep himself or herself at the forefront of developments as they pertain to the business, either through incorporating academic research or actively engaging in research on their own.

Roles within the technical core may be captured under titles such as *theoretical model review, product design, new applications, business strategy* or *business development*. Roles also include lecturers and professors. The titles should not conceal the potential for extensive quantitative and theoretical analysis within these roles. Technical core roles will necessitate a more empirical analysis, analyzing the fundamentals and the principles that exist within each market space. Application of developments made in the technical core ultimately lead to new products and markets. The technical core is the area where financial engineers are most likely to need to apply computer programming skills (or work with those who do so).

Infrastructure

Underlying every successful business is a strong business architecture or infrastructure upon which all other areas can confidently rely. The business infrastructure is often referred to in a trading environment as the back office, a reflection of best-practice business segmentation. Today, the back office increasingly sits at the table with, and is compensated equally to, the front office for critical positions. The business infrastructure is the backbone that provides assurance within a successful operation. The infrastructure area within most financial institutions is responsible for the processing and verification of all activity with external parties—be this through brokers, exchanges, dark pools, Treasury auctions, over-the-counter transactions, or any other vehicle of exchange. The challenge for those working in business infrastructure is to provide assurance that all risk positions held by the firm are those into which it intended to enter, and all those that were not intended are resolved as quickly as possible.

The infrastructure role provides an important checkpoint within the business. It acts as an area of day-to-day operations and quality control, ensuring that all data and information are accurate within databases or models or transactions. With the increase in compliance-related reporting necessitated by Sarbanes-Oxley, the demand for financial engineers has increased dramatically within infrastructure departments. The function requires specialized skills in the stratification of data, so that information can be processed accurately without demanding excessive resources or time. Infrastructure departments also employ advanced data mining techniques to identify data mismatches and any inconsistencies that can reflect fraudulent activity within the business conducted.

Management

Acting as the interface between applications and infrastructure, the management area within the middle office holds responsibility for the oversight of activity, aggregation, and verification of business practices. The management function is most commonly identified as the center of risk management and control within the enterprise. With the evolution of more complex business strategies and financial products, the management function faces an ever-increasing challenge in the comprehension of risks within the business, and also the communication of these risks to both the front office and executive offices. The complexity and challenge within the area provides two main avenues of opportunity for financial engineers.

First, financial engineers have numerous opportunities available in the area of reporting. Moving from raw business data to a risk report creates a requirement for extensive data synthesis, computer programming, and mathematical manipulation. As executives seek reporting with greater immediacy and increasing accuracy, financial engineers must deliver on these requirements.

Second, management areas need to consistently work to identify or create new metrics to highlight the risks embedded within products and the risks held within the business. Researching and identifying new metrics and approaches within the management function can often lead to a role in the applications area; new risk perspectives and approaches can redefine the business approach, developing new products or strategies by identifying risk categories. By working to better understand and communicate the risks the business has, management can better position the firm to decide which risks it should keep and which risks it should not take (at least in the present).

Applications

The applications area, alternatively known as the front office, is the area where products often are designed, priced, and ownership is transferred. Acting as the interface between the firm and its customers, this area depends heavily on its technology and requires a solid infrastructure that can expeditiously and accurately price products and provide information on positions.

The front office will be, in part, serviced by software and reporting that is compatible with that provided by risk management and the technical core. The primary function for financial engineers within applications is in the development of tools to best assist the firm in assuming new risks. These models will combine elements from inventory, risk mitigation prospects, and market information to best comprehend the price that the market can bear, and also the price at which it is economically acceptable for the firm to assume the risk. Front-line applications are critical for ensuring that new transactions are entered into without the firm either losing money or assuming risk without adequate compensation.

The nature of the applications area differs across different types of businesses. It can involve working as the lead author in drafting articles on financial markets and events, leading relationship teams for regulators, or implementing software solutions for clients. All of these roles require the ability to configure products to best suit customer needs, to quickly adapt to a changing environment, and to complete tasks to a high standard.

SPECIFIC CAREER PATHS

From the illustration in the previous section, it should be apparent that there are many more career paths for financial engineers than one might initial think. Further, within the functional areas of applications, management, and infrastructure, multiple roles exist in each of the different sectors mentioned in the preceding section.

The reader will notice that we have altered the specific careers discussion below a bit from the diagram that we laid out above. This was done to highlight the variety of roles included within the Regulatory Oversight and Services sectors of the diagram. These are expanded a bit below to better identify different opportunities with software firms, service companies, consultants, and ratings agencies, covering a diverse grouping of roles within the Services sector.

Sell Side

The term "sell side" refers, primarily, to the global bank and broker-dealer community where the principal business is "selling" financial instruments and research. The term "selling" actually includes both the buying and the selling of financial instruments in the capacity of dealers, which, of course, requires that they provide both a bid and an offer. Nevertheless, "sell side" is well understood to refer to the global bank and broker-dealer community. Sell side firms make both the primary and the secondary markets for securities. The former involves the initial sale of a security by an issuer. This could take the form of stock being sold in an initial public offering (IPO) or an established public company selling additional stock in a seasoned public offering (commonly called a follow-on offering). Primary market offerings of debt securities include the underwriting of bonds, the private placement of structured securities, and the syndication of loans. The secondary market involves all transactions in a security following the initial sale of the security—that is from investor-to-investor rather than issuer-to-investor. Sell-side firms participate in the secondary markets in two distinct but related ways: They broker transactions in exchange for fees called commissions, and they make markets by acting as dealers. For many, market making is the essence of their business and rewards them through the bid-ask spread associated with the financial instruments they trade.

Sell-side firms seek to handle as large a volume of transactions as possible while holding the minimum inventory sufficient to function efficiently. They leverage their distribution networks to buy side firms, and through institutional and retail brokerage units. Historically, these services were rendered by the firm's trading floor personnel. Increasingly, however, much of this activity has moved over to specialized prime brokerage units that have grown extensively over the past few decades.

With the revocation of Glass-Steagall in the United States, a number of traditional sell-side firms began to add components traditionally associated with the buy side (e.g., insurance, and asset management). The recent Dodd-Frank legislation is expected to reduce the scale of this overlap going forward. Here we consider firms whose principal activity is to provide sell-side functionality to clients, irrespective of their proprietary trading activities.

Examples of sell-side firms include investment banks, commercial banks, broker-dealers, and global banks.

Buy Side

The buy side is typified by firms that are entering the financial markets to implement an investment strategy. In some ways, it is the inverse of the sell side, where the objective is to minimize inventory and facilitate transfer; a buy-side firm seeks to accumulate a specific inventory through market transfer.

Whereas the sell side format is relatively homogenous, buy-side firms are highly varied in their objectives, strategies, and scale. Buy-side firms include the traditional types, such as insurance companies, pension funds, endowment funds, mutual funds, and unit trusts, but they also include some non-traditional types, such as hedge funds and private equity funds. The non-traditional types are often called alternative investments, and they differ from more traditional buy-side firms in several important ways. These include manpower, infrastructure, regulation, and the investment approaches they employ (we treat alternative investments separately later). The holding period of an investment position by buy-side firms can vary from several years (e.g., pension funds) to much shorter terms. The number of invested positions held can vary from just a handful to hundreds. Also the risk appetite and investment instruments available to the firm can vary greatly, with differing levels of proprietary trading decision making permissible.

Examples of buy-side firms include fund managers, exchange-traded funds, pension funds, insurance companies, mutual funds, and investment manager.

Alternative Investments

In the context in which it is applied here, "alternative investments" captures the firms within the buy-side space that require their investors to satisfy, at a minimum, the accredited investor condition under the Securities and Exchange Commission's Regulation D. Alternative investment firms will typically aim to outperform a benchmark index, similar to the objective of other buy-side firms. The difference is that these firms are prepared to take on more risk and employ higher degrees of leverage in their strategies to achieve their return objectives.

Many alternative investment firms employ strategies that carry a reduced level of diversification and, in some cases, deliberately take on concentrated exposures. These vary from high-speed, low-latency trading strategies that employ artificial intelligence programming and that hold positions for, at most, months, to global macroeconomic strategies and private equity where positions are often held for years or even decades.

A key difference to job applicants between alternative investment buy-side firms and traditional buy-side firms is most often one of scale. While these firms may have significant amounts of funds under management, they will typically operate in a very lean manner with considerable overlap among job roles. Also, they occupy a space that, at present, operates in a much different regulatory environment to that of pension funds, insurance firms, and mutual funds.

Examples of alternative investment firms include hedge funds, fund of funds, private equity, and alternative asset managers.

Central Banks

Central banks operate as important governmental participants within the markets. They are principally involved in managing the money stock, liquidity, the cost of credit and foreign exchange. They actively participate through open market operations in the purchase and sale of sovereign debt, and they intervene when they feel it necessary in the foreign exchange markets. Though less common, they may also participate in the commodities markets and the non-governmental debt markets when necessary (for example, the Troubled Asset Relief Program). Consequently, the central banks require the same expertise and knowledge required of all active private sector market participants.

Regulators

Most countries separate the regulatory oversight function of the markets and market participants from the functions of their central banks. Often this involves multiple regulators, each dedicated to oversight by product, sector, or function. For example, securities markets may be overseen by one regulator while commodities markets are overseen by a different regulator. Banks may be overseen by several different regulators depending on the purpose of the regulation. Insurance companies, too, often have their own specialized regulators. In order for a regulator to properly analyze the activity within the market where they have oversight responsibility, regulators require experienced participants and strong analytical departments.

Rating Agencies

The rating agencies perform the valuable service of opining on the credit worthiness of various institutions, sovereign states, and individual securities. The assessment of credit worthiness involves a detailed analysis of legal structures, credit hierarchy, accounting, and supporting assets. The ratings of rating agencies are an important component of many institutions' investing rules, which, oftentimes, only allow investment in assets of a certain credit grade. The credit assessment also plays a major role in the pricing of debt facilities (i.e., bonds, loans, revolving lines of credit, etc.).

Three firms—Standard & Poor's, Moody's, and Fitch—have dominated the market. There are, however, numerous other ratings agencies, some limiting themselves to specific asset classes. These include Kroll, Dun & Bradstreet, Egan-Jones, Dominion, and Baycorp Advantage.

Service Providers

Service providers capture the array of auxiliary businesses that have developed around financial firms, typically operating to provide information services or prepackaged solutions and tools. The most ubiquitous and generalized firm within this space is Bloomberg LLP. Bloomberg not only provides real-time or delayed market data to licensed users, but has expanded to provide extensive analytical tools, including pricing tools, and other trading services. Many of the simple-to-use functions available to subscribers actually embody extensive financial modeling—but this is transparent to the user. For example, the system allows users to select from a variety of pre-engineered yield curves. And users can interact with the system to create their own curves using customized splines and other techniques. Behind the user-friendly front end lies sophisticated programming, financial engineering, and product development that has to adapt to ever-changing market dynamics.

There are multiple businesses that operate within niche spaces, providing custom data solutions for credit derivatives (e.g., MarkIt), financial statement analysis (e.g., Capital IQ), or some that compete across multiple fields (e.g., Reuters Thompson). In addition to acting as conduits for data flowing from the markets, these firms play significant roles in data synthesis, analysis, and modeling prior to delivering the data to clients. These activities require large numbers of highly competent technical specialists.

Custom Solutions

Custom solutions captures the over-the-counter market, where customized exposures are created for clients. The most publicly-visible structured products in recent years have been collateralized debt obligations (CDOs), a product involving extensive tailoring and orchestration to bring to market. Custom solutions can work with clients to create a bespoke exposure to meet their requirements—ranging from equity derivatives and commodities hedging tools to tax and funding solutions. The process for customizing solutions can be time consuming and is not comparable to the frenetic pace often seen on trading floors where standardized products trade. A customized solution often goes through numerous iterations and adjustments before it precisely meets the requirements of the client, obtains ratings agency acceptance, and achieves appropriate risk management comfort levels. Only after these things have been accomplished can custom solutions move forward and initiate the structure.

USING THE TABLES

Exhibits 2.2 through 2.7, contain a series of tables that illustrate the many roles for financial engineers and quantitative analysts. To illustrate to the reader how to read the tables, we will run through a few examples of the roles depicted in the table. We will explain why the same role appears in different boxes, and also how that role or job title may differ from one box to another.

Exhibit 2.2 Roles in Financial Companies: Applications/Front Office

	Sales	Trading	Custom Solutions	Risk	Regulations	Reporting	Research
Sell Side	• Salesman • Structurer • Quant Pricing • Modeler • Risk Manager	• Flow Trader • Proprietary Trader • Quant Trader • Structurer • Desk Quant • Modeler • Risk Manager	• Structurer • Trader • Quant Pricing • Modeler • Risk Manager	• Live risk management • Hedging • Risk modeling • Structuring	• Full Position Monitoring • Hedging • Risk • Modeling	• End of Day P&L • Position reporting • Pricing • Exposure modeling	• Strategist • Technical research • Quant development • Structuring
Buy Side	• Client Marketing • Model backtest/ strategy testing • Performance records	• Portfolio Manager • Quant Trader • Structurer • Desk Quant • Modeler • Risk Manager	• Structurer • Quant Trader • Desk Quant • Modeler • Risk Manager	• Live risk management • Hedging • Modeling • Scenario testing • Structuring	• Large Exposures • Regulatory ordinance	• End of Day P&L • Position reporting • Pricing • Exposure modeling	• Strategist • Technical research • Quant development • Macro modeling
Alternative Investments	• Client Marketing • Model backtest/ strategy testing • Performance records • Prime Broker	• Proprietary Trader • Quant Trader • Desk Quant • Modeler • Quant • Research • Risk Manager	• Structurer (custom exposure) • Quant Trader • Desk Quant • Modeler • Risk Manager	• Live risk management • Modeling • Scenario testing • Quant Programming • Structurer	Dodd-Frank Act	• End of Day P&L • Position reporting • Pricing • Exposure modeling	• Portfolio Manager • Strategist • Quant Researcher • Research Analyst
Other	• Product Specialists • Hedging Specialists • Exotics	• Back Book • Corporate Treasury • Programmer • Risk Trader • Hedging • Risk Manager • Asset Manager	• Corporate Treasury • Asset-Backed Securities • Leasing • Exposure management • Commodities hedging	• Corporate Treasury • Liquidity and Funding Risk Management		• Corporate Treasury • End of Day P&L • Position reporting • Pricing • Exposure modeling	• Corporates • Quantitative marketing and strategy • Pricing strategies • Market Analyst

Exhibit 2.3 Roles in Non-Financial Companies: Applications/Front Office

Non-Financial Companies Applications/Front Office*

	Sales	Trading	Custom Solutions	Risk	Regulatory	Reporting	Research
Central Banks		• Quant Trader • Structurer • Open-market intervention	• Quant Analyst • Structurer • Modeler	• Quant Risk • Risk Modeler • Systemic analysis		• Market Analyst	• Market analysis and dynamics
Regulators	• Rules analysis & litigation	• Strategy analysis • Liquidity Analyst		• Regulation observation Intervention	• Trading Regulation design		• Market trend and distortion analytics
Rating Agencies	• Quant Analyst • Structurer • Modeler		• Quant Analyst • Structurer • Modeler	• Risk Modeler • Ratings Analyst • Quant Analyst		• Rating Disclosures	• Macro trend analysis • Industry Analyst
Consultants	• Performance Analyst • Pricing Tool Modeler	• Strategy analysis • Performance Benchmarks	• Structure • Due diligence • Strategy Analysis	• Risk Consultancy • Quant Consultant			• Best practice analysis
Service Providers	• Date provision • User interfaces	• Data provision • User interfaces	• Data provision • User interfaces	• Data provision • User interfaces	• Compliance support		
Software Vendors		• Trading Software, pricing, programming	• Collateral management • Software pricing tools	• Risk and pricing • Systems mitigation tools	• Regulatory reporting • Software	• Front-office accounting • Portfolio software	
Academia		• Strategy Analyst • Empirical studies	• ABS, CDO research, analysis, teaching	• Empirical and theoretical risk research • Training	• Market efficiency studies • Proposals	• Accounting standards	
Other		• Exchange trader • Exchange oversight	• Journalist • Market Analyst	• Journalist • Market Analyst			

* Incomplete listing

Exhibit 2.4 Roles in Financial Companies: Management/Middle Office*

Financial Companies Management/Middle Office*

	Sales	Trading	Custom Solutions	Risk	Regulatory	Reporting	Research
Sell Side	• Policy compliance • Risk control	• Hedging instructions • Hedging strategies	• Risk mitigation strategies • Performance management	• Intra-day risk reporting • Mark to model • Model validation • Risk appetite	• Stress testing • Modeler • Data analysis • Compliance	• Risk reporting • Analyst • Compliance • Structuring reporting	• Regulatory Framework research • Risk innovation
Buy Side		• Hedging instructions • Hedging strategies	• Risk analysis • Risk appetite assessment • Performance management • Quant analysts	• Asset liability management • Mark to model • Portfolio analysis	• Stress Test modeling • Data analysis • Compliance	• Positions, mismatches & exceptions reports • Daily P&L verification • Structure monitoring	• Capital management • Analyst liquidity • Management researcher
Alternative Investments		• Hedging instructions • Hedging strategies	• Risk analysis • Risk appetite assessment • Performance management • Quant Analysts	• Asset liability management • Risk limits • Intra-day reporting	• Regulatory negotiations	• Internal financial reporting • Positions, mismatches & exceptions reports	• Peer group analysis
Other		• Outsources • Reporting solutions		• Corporate • Asset liability management • Risk limits • Intra-day reporting			

* Incomplete listing

Exhibit 2.5 Roles in Non-Financial Companies: Management/Middle Office

Non-Financial Companies Management/Middle Office*

	Sales	Trading	Custom Solutions	Risk	Regulatory	Reporting	Research
Central Banks		• Data processing and trend analysis • Systemic analysis	• Systemic risk analysis	• Macro market systemic analysis and oversight	• Macro market systemic analysis and oversight		
Regulators	• Sales practice analysis, investigation				• Market Analyst		
Rating Agencies	• Ratings control and management		• Structure analysis • Stress testing	• Model validation • Ratings analyst (reviews)			
Consultants	• Strategy analysis benchmarks	• Strategy analysis benchmarks	• Modeling and pricing Analytics	• Best practices benchmarks			
Service Providers		• Outsourced solutions		• Shareholder analytics		• Data filings and reports databases	
Software Vendors		• Risk reporting software • Data management		• Risk management software & models	• Regulatory reporting software	• Standardized reporting tools	
Academia				• International standards			

* Incomplete listing

42

Exhibit 2.6 Roles in Financial Companies: Infrastructure/Back Office

Financial Companies Infrastructure/Back Office

	Sales	Trading	Custom Solutions	Risk	Regulations	Reporting	Research
Sell Side	• Trade processing • Data capture • Data verification • Data synthesis	• Trade processing • Data capture • Data verification • Data synthesis	• Trade processing • Data capture • Data verification • Data synthesis	• Data stratification • Exceptions reporting • Trade verification • Mark-to-market	• Regulatory filings • Data programming	• Statutory accounting • Structuring skills	• Data processing • Database management • Data quality
Buy Side	• Portfolio data subsets & analysis	• Portfolio reconcilation, verification, assurance • Tri-Party Repo & Custodian management	• Portfolio update capture • Covenant testing	• Exceptions Capture trade verification (fraud check) • Portfolio assembly	• Regulatory filings • Data programming	• Statutory accounting • Management/Fund accounting	• Data processing • Database management • Data quality
Alternative Investments	• Prime brokerage • Relationship management	• Portfolio reconcilation, verification, assurance • Tri-Party Repo & Custodian management	• Portfolio update capture • Covenant testing	• Exceptions capture trade verification (fraud check) • Portfolio assembly		• Investor reporting • Management accounting	• Data processing • Database management • Data quality
Other		• Outsourced confirmations and reconciliations	• Outsourced portfolio management	• Outsourced risk control			

* Incomplete listing

Exhibit 2.7 Roles in Non-Financial Companies: Infrastructure/Back Office

Non-Financial Companies Infrastructure/Back Office*

	Sales	Trading	Custom Solutions	Risk	Regulatory	Reporting	Research
Central Banks		• Settlement analysis • Liquidity analysis	• Asset control	• Data management inventory		• Market metrics	
Regulators		• Market manipulation analysis		• Data management	• Filings Analysis rule enforcement		
Rating Agencies			• Portfolio updates • Rating capture			• Credit-worthiness standards	
Consultants		• Processing optimization • Latency analysis	• Pricing practices • Portfolio practices	• Operations Process anaylsis		• Accounting advisory	
Service Providers		• Mark-to-market reconciliation • Data summarizing	• Back-office data services • Outsourcing	• Encryption • Data security	• Data analysis • Forensic data research		
Software Vendors		• Data process optimization • Data mining tools	• Data management tools	• Data process optimization • Database systems	• Regulatory filing programs	• Accounting software	
Academia		• Operations analysis	• Legal structure analysis				
Other		• Exchange position management					

* Incomplete listing

"Structurer"

Roles within structuring have been among the most coveted positions for financial engineering graduates over the last decade. The area has experienced extensive innovation and growth during this time period, leading to considerable diversity in the forms of structuring positions available.

The most common interpretation of a structurer would be the role played by an individual specializing in customized solutions in the front office of a sell-side firm. This is the area that is involved in creating the financial structure for the client and the active management of the resultant security. The structurer is involved in the selection of assets, working in conjunction with the client, rating agencies, and lawyers in building a structure that meets the objectives of the transaction.

There are several different structurer positions within sell-side firms, however. Both sales and trading require specialists within structuring to provide expertise to the market. Sales structurers operate within both the primary market, selling various tranches of structures created by custom solutions, and also within the secondary market to facilitate effective trading of existing holdings. Trading structurers need to be able to assess securities available in the market, provide valuation services, and be able to assess how the structure can be hedged. Trading roles will depend upon candidates being able to create bespoke models to aid price discovery within the marketplace. Within sales and trading roles, the emphasis of the structurer is on the analysis of a large assortment of structures; whereas the customs solutions structurer will work with a lower volume of securities, tailoring the product through numerous iterations.

Risk management also requires expertise in structuring, such that they can accurately manage and report the risks associated with structured securities, both prior to distribution and while the securities are held on the bank's balance sheet. Risk management and modeling will interact with the trading desk, potentially sharing components that feed into the tools for pricing securities. Research and strategy similarly require structuring expertise to produce market commentary and to make recommendations to clients and (or) to traders. Researchers will take an active role in analyzing securities, with strategists working on more macro-economic analysis of the marketplace.

Similar structuring roles exist on the buy side. Buy-side firms interact with structured securities to create exposure to markets they would not be able to access and also, rather famously, by providing insurance wrappers to senior tranches on structured securities. Subsequently, the buy-side firms need structurers to identify opportunities where they can create beneficial structures. Buy-side structurers need equally strong, if not stronger, skills in structured securities because the buy-side firm has the objective of keeping the exposure created, rather than selling it. Buy-side firms require structurers who can work with the sell side's trading and customized solutions personnel, but also with their own risk management departments, who must opine on the risks associated with the final product.

Alternative investment firms also employ structurers in a buying capacity. A notable example of this that attracted considerable regulatory scrutiny and press coverage was the involvement of Paulson & Co. Inc. (representing the buy side) in the design of the Abacus structure with Goldman Sachs (the sell side). As is common within alternative investments firms, there will be significant overlap between roles as the firm has a much smaller headcount. The role of a structurer will overlap with research and, potentially, risk management as the firm seeks to tailor an investment that reflects its market views. Risk management will be involved in the active mitigation of exposures that the firm does not wish to bear. Alternative investments firms are often active in very specific markets, with growth seen in the distressed structured credit market in recent years.

Structuring specialists are also required in the industrial sector, as some large firms use structured securities to manage their risks. Beyond the use of interest rate swaps and foreign exchange hedging tools, corporations have been active in the hedging of commodities within their product lines and cost structures. Structuring specialists within firms are able to work with their sell-side counterparts in creating the securities to mitigate risks, much as structurers on the buy side work to create risk.

The final group of market participants to require structuring specialists is the central banks. With the actions taken during the credit crisis, central banks now find themselves with large structured asset portfolios. They have moved to supplement their structurers engaged in systemic analysis of the products with structurers focused on trading, portfolio management, and risk management. Going forward, central banks will undoubtedly perform extensive monitoring of the marketplace, working alongside regulators to ensure systemic risks are minimized.

Opportunities outside of financial firms (applying the Dodd-Frank interpretation) for structuring specialists do not necessarily imply the role has less market involvement. Ratings agencies, while not actively participating within the market, require extensive structuring skill to model, assess, and evaluate individual structures before they are brought to market. The work performed at the ratings agencies mirrors the pricing, risk, and research functions within a sell-side bank, though they are employed to render an objective credit evaluation of the products.

Service providers and software developers also require structured products modeling specialists. Here the demand is for the technical expertise and understanding of the intricacies within structured products, in order to develop resources that will benefit market participants. These companies focus on providing tools that assist in analyzing, pricing, and quantifying the risks associated with these securities, so their role is not dissimilar to that of the structurers who support trading on the sell side or buy side. Consultants specializing in structured products will also provide modeling expertise and risk management alongside asset management strategies and—in some cases—the outsourcing of the management of a portfolio of structured securities. The consultant's ability to interact across all aspects of structured products is relatively unique in the spectrum of roles.

Structuring specialists are also found in other business lines that require a deep understanding of structured products. Within accounting and reporting, specialists with an understanding of structured products are needed due to the specific treatment required by each structure. Risk management needs to monitor the structures, identifying risk indicators and methodologies for portfolios of securities. Lawyers employ structured product specialists due to the non-standard legal documentation required by each new issuance. People familiar with the structures need to work to price the securities daily prior to their sale (as opposed to pricing for trading), either working from market prices of traded products or by building appropriate, often complex, valuation models.

What should be apparent here is that there are many job functions at different types of firms that have a need for a similar set of skills. Indeed, the need is far greater than one might expect. Further, due to the complexity of structured products, all of the roles require extensive knowledge of the product and typically have demands for financial modeling and programming to work with the scale of the assets.

"Quantitative Trader"

Our review of the possible employment opportunities for those financial engineers interested in structuring illustrated the varied nature of the types of firms that require this talent. While the type of work was similar in all cases, the types of firms hiring people with structuring expertise and their reasons for requiring the skill set are quite different. An examination of opportunities for quant traders, on the other hand, illustrates just how varied the type of work can be despite the similarity of job descriptions. With the Dodd-Frank reform, the quant trader may well find previously available opportunities on the sell side restricted. But quant trading jobs will not go away; they will simply move to another venue. In addition to earning their keep for the firms that employ them, they provide valuable liquidity to the markets. Quantitative traders are, in large part, the drivers behind electronic trading which continues to grow and develop. But, even on the sell side, quantitative roles will continue, but they will evolve. Developing dark pool and grey pool environments and improved price optimization techniques for transactions are examples of the forms this evolution will take. Quant trading may also involve building instantaneous hedging systems and the automation of the hedging processes. Quant traders can also work on structured products, using programming to identify prospective assets to substitute into and out of the original structure.

Aside from the sell side, quant trading can involve any strategy that the trader can develop. Here the focus is on creating profitable trading opportunities. Trading strategies can vary from high frequency approaches that profit by providing liquidity, to those that operate on a signals basis to generate buy and sell orders to capture trends and exploit pricing inefficiencies. The methods and processes that drive these models are only limited by the creativity of the trader programming the strategy.

The existence of quantitative trading strategies, which now drive an extraordinary percentage of stock market volume, creates a demand for expertise among risk management departments, central bankers, and regulators. These people will be involved in either reverse-engineering the processes used or in developing metrics that assess the performance of the strategies. Given that the quant trading strategy will typically run automatically, pressure is placed on risk management and reporting to fully comprehend the trading methods that are employed and in determining what is critical to maintaining confidence in the system.

COMPUTER PROGRAMMING SKILLS

While it is only a prerequisite for specific roles within the discipline, it is important to address computer programming for financial engineers interested in the development and the maintenance of models. In the most quantitative of roles utilizing financial engineering skills, C++ remains the mainstay of programming and is the most frequently observed programming requirement within job postings. Given the complexity of working within C++ it is not uncommon for financial engineers to write code using Visual Basic for Applications (VBA) for quicker results. The relative importance of each will depend on the nature of the programmer's position. If the quant is expected to create quick, prototype models that can be used within a short time frame, programming in VBA will be more likely. The importance of the ability to create financial engineering tools within the Excel VBA environment should not be underestimated.[6] It immediately dovetails with a universal piece of software.

For more complex and stable models, coding will most commonly be in C++, or, alternatively, C# (pronounced "C sharp"), or Java. Fortunately, there are significant overlaps between the three languages. Understanding C++ will better prepare a financial engineer for working with legacy models, as the language has been in use for longer than most Masters of Financial Engineering (MSFE or MFE) candidates have been alive, and it typically embeds better with other systems capabilities. Given that many roles will involve inheriting models that need to be migrated to a more stable environment, the ability to program in C++ is valuable.

For work between full development and Excel-based functionality, there are a number of programming skills that are in demand at financial firms. SAS and SQL are commonly applied for accessing the array of databases within the institutions. MatLab is sometimes applied for intermediate coding work, but it is less common and will not be available at all firms.

CONCLUSION

The job of any two financial engineers is very unlikely to be the same, and can often vary significantly, even within the same firm. We hope that the tables included in this chapter (2.2–2.7, following) help financial engineering students and graduates of financial engineering programs to navigate through the wealth of opportunities available to them, and assist them in identifying the subtle differences between job postings.

What is most important, however, is the asterisk on each of the tables (i.e., "* Incomplete Listing"). The listings provided in this text are incomplete, with many more potential paths available to candidates. Much as physicists never saw "quantitative analyst" among their potential career paths just a few decades ago, the opportunities that will be available to those entering financial engineering today will be unrecognizable when compared to those opportunities available in the field's infancy, and considerably beyond those captured in this chapter. What is apparent is that the roles that utilize the skill sets that financial engineering students acquire will continue to increase.

NOTES

1. For example, mathematical finance programs are a subset of financial engineering programs. Similarly, risk management programs are a subset of financial engineering programs.

2. Based on 150 programs, the median number of candidates in current class sizes from the Financial Engineering Program Survey was 36 students.

3. There are over 250,000 members of PRMIA and GARP, the leading risk management professional associations. Allowing for overlap, with consideration that many professionals do not join these Associations, makes 750,000 a somewhat conservative estimate, especially when risk can be a small component of a role, and considering that both Associations have a Financial Services bias.

4. Search performed using Manta.com. Also identified were 190 banks within the United States that met these metrics.

5. PerTrac Hedge Fund Database Study, 2009. Morningstar tracks 8,000 Active Hedge Funds.

6. Excel is a trademark of Microsoft Corporation.

ABOUT THE AUTHOR

Spencer Jones is currently an associate at SBCC Group, where he has worked on projects including bank restructuring, structured credit portfolio analysis, and municipal risk management. From 2005 to 2007 he was a risk manager in Barclays Treasury, responsible for risk management across two divisions of the bank, including two M&A projects. From 2000 to 2004 he was an Analyst with HBOS, working in Asset & Liability Management developing risk models. He received an MBA, with distinction, from New York University and an MA in Economics with First Class Honours from the University of Edinburgh.

CHAPTER 3

A Profile of Programs and Curricula with a Financial Engineering Component

JOHN CORNISH
SBCC Group, Inc.

INTRODUCTION

As should have been made clear from the preceding chapter on career paths, financial engineers pursue employment in a number of different functional areas that may be thought of as subspecialties within the discipline. As the demand for quantitatively trained finance professionals has grown across many industries, so too have the programs offered by colleges and universities. Today, worldwide, an estimated 5,000 students graduate each year with some substantive training in financial engineering.[1] As also noted in the preceding chapter, different jobs within the broader field of quantitative finance require somewhat different skill sets. Employers' job postings may seek individuals with expertise in derivatives, risk management, mathematical modeling, computer programming, structured finance, and/or other specialized areas. Not surprisingly, many of the programs now offered do not explicitly incorporate the term "financial engineering" in their degree title. Nevertheless, they do provide the requisite training that distinguishes quantitative finance and financial engineering graduates from other degree majors. Even though the program titles and contents vary, for ease of discussion we refer to them all, in this chapter, as financial engineering programs.[2]

An understanding of the similarities and differences among financial engineering programs is important both to prospective students who are considering enrolling in a quantitative finance program and to employers who are seeking to hire properly trained financial engineers. The differences are also important to practitioners who are required to keep current on emerging trends in the field and to academics who are seeking input to their own programs. Despite the interest that employers, academics, and practitioners should have in program content, this chapter is written, for the most part, for the benefit of the prospective student.

The chapter on financial engineering careers should have helped to broaden the prospective student's appreciation for the diversity of jobs available to graduates trained in financial engineering. It should also have helped to explain why a similar level of diversity has evolved within the programs that offer some type of training in financial engineering. This is important to consider when choosing a program. While this chapter will not rank the various programs and has no opinion on which is "best," it should be clear that not all programs are created equal in relation to a particular student's academic and professional goals. Likewise, not all programs are created equal with respect to the knowledge base and skill set sought by an employer.

Also important for the student to consider is that, while the aggregate demand for trained financial engineers has increased steadily over the years, the demand for financial engineers in specific niche roles has varied. This variability in demand is a reflection of a business environment that continues to evolve and adapt to changing conditions. For example, in response to the credit crisis that began in 2007, the role of risk management has been in the spotlight throughout the global financial community. Increased demand for competent risk managers and for specialty risk management consulting firms will undoubtedly grow in response. Educational programs will adapt as well, by increasing their focus on risk measurement and risk management. Conversely, the decade prior to the burst of the housing bubble saw a steady increase in demand for financial engineers in structured finance departments, particularly those who could structure collateralized debt obligations backed by home mortgages, commercial mortgages, credit cards, automobile loans, and virtually any other asset with predictable cash flows. As the credit crisis spread in 2007–2008, liquidity for these sorts of assets dried up, and the demand for new structured products virtually disappeared. As a result, the demand for financial engineers to structure these products declined as well. This is not to say that demand for structuring specialists will not return. Indeed, some of the same people hired to structure the products are now working to restructure the products. The upshot of these examples is that the current business climate and expectations about the future business climate should be important to the prospective student when choosing a program.

It is important for the prospective student to consider the recent and expected future evolution of each of the markets and each of the subject areas that relate to financial engineering. Consider, for example, the subject area known as legal risk, which is covered later in this book. Pending regulations around the world threaten to restrict proprietary trading at large banks. For the individual hoping to get a job as a quantitative trader on a proprietary trading desk at a large financial institution, it is important to understand how pending or current legislation may affect each jurisdiction and to plan his/her enrollment and curriculum accordingly.

It is not the goal of this chapter to endorse a particular program. Rather, the purpose of this chapter is to introduce the prospective student to variations among the programs offered worldwide. It is up to the prospective student to identify his or her academic and professional goals and to consider the list of available programs through that lens. This chapter first presents some background information on programs offering training in financial engineering. As noted earlier, these programs carry different labels and are sponsored by different departments at different academic institutions. For example, some programs are offered by engineering schools, others by mathematics departments, and still others by business schools. Next, we discuss the curricula offered across the range of programs including a discussion of required and elective courses, course tracks, internships, research, and faculty. Finally we wrap up with a discussion of the advantages offered by various programs with respect to job placement.

Most of the information offered in this chapter comes directly from the academic institutions offering the programs. We distributed a survey to 150 programs offered by academic institutions worldwide and compiled the responses. A list of programs contacted appears in the Appendix at the end of the chapter. The survey asked for the following information:

- Program contact
- Program website
- Describe awards/recognition of the program
- What aspects of the program distinguish it from similar ones offered at other universities?
- Degrees offered (up to six)
- What are the fundamental and advanced core classes (up to six)?
- What are the available electives (up to six)?
- What course tracks are available (up to six)?
- What type of research is required (up to six)?
- Dean/Department Chair
- Program e-mail address
- Students per faculty member
- Professor/Instructor (up to six)
  - Name
  - Title
  - Department
  - Full/part-time
  - Areas of interest
  - Degrees received
- Number of applications
- Acceptance rate
- Average test scores of accepted students
- Undergraduate students
- Graduate students
- Full-time students
- Part-time students
- Primary nationality of students (up to five)
- Total number of countries represented
- Work experience (up to six jobs)
- Minimum time to complete program
- Job placement

Not every program to which the survey was distributed responded in time to meet our publishing deadline, and the sample lists that appear throughout the chapter as exhibits are not intended to be exhaustive. Further, the information provided in this chapter for each and every program cited is necessarily incomplete. For these reasons, prospective students should thoroughly research any programs they are interested in before making any enrollment decisions. Another useful resource for information on financial engineering programs is the International Association of Financial Engineers (IAFE), which posts information about programs on its website, www.iafe.org.

BACKGROUND INFORMATION ON FINANCIAL ENGINEERING PROGRAMS

While more established programs of study in other disciplines are relatively uniform in nature across academic institutions that offer them, financial engineering is an evolving field of study and distinctly unique, in that degree programs are offered under a variety of names and are sponsored by many different university departments. Program names and sponsoring departments are worth a little elaboration.

Program Name

The first programs offering training in financial engineering were developed as master's programs. Today, most degrees are still offered at the master's level; however, some universities offer training in financial engineering at the bachelor's and doctoral levels. Some universities also offer certificate programs, which are typically geared towards students holding a graduate degree who wish to expand their areas of proficiency.

Within each of the bachelor's, master's and doctoral levels, there are a variety of financial engineering-related degrees under names other than "financial engineering." Often the name of the degree depends on the department or departments sponsoring the degree. The next section will discuss the variety of departments that offer financial engineering–related degrees. Examples of program names that do not include the term "financial engineering" are provided in Exhibit 3.1. Note that this is not a complete list. It is for illustration purposes only.

Exhibit 3.1 Examples of Program Names

School	Degree
Georgia State University (U.S.)	MS in Mathematical Risk Management (MS MRM)
North Carolina State University (U.S.)	Masters of Financial Mathematics
University of Westminster (UK)	MSc in Investment and Quantitative Finance
Lehigh University (U.S.)	Master of Science in Analytical Finance
Dublin City University (IE)	MSc in Financial and Industrial Mathematics
Columbia University (U.S.)	MA in Mathematics of Finance
Case Western Reserve University (U.S.)	MSM Finance
Oxford University (UK)	MSc in Mathematical and Computational Finance
University of Twente (NL)	Master in Applied Mathematics
University of the Witwatersrand–Johannesburg (ZA)	BSc Honours in Advanced Mathematics of Finance
Boston University School of Management (U.S.)	Ph in Mathematical Finance
University of Minnesota (U.S.)	Post Bacaulareate Certifications—Fundamentals of Quantitative Finance (FQF)

Exhibit 3.2   Examples of Departments Offering FE-like Programs

School	Degree	Department
Columbia University (U.S.)	Master of Science in Financial Engineering	Industrial Engineering and Operations Research Department
University of Waterloo (CA)	Master of Quantitative Finance	Centre for Advanced Studies in Finance
The Hong Kong University of Science and Technology (CN)	Master of Science in Mathematics (Financial Mathematics and Statistics)	Department of Mathematics
Nanyang Technological University (SG)	Master of Science (Financial Engineering)	Nanyang Business School
Rensselaer Polytechnic University (U.S.)	MS in Financial Engineering and Risk Analytics	Lally School of Management and Technology

Department

Financial engineering draws on many disciplines. These include mathematics, statistics, finance, computer science, and engineering. It makes sense, therefore, that financial engineering programs have originated independently within various departments across the spectrum of academic institutions. Examples of departments offering financial engineering-like programs are provided in Exhibit 3.2.

Financial engineering programs are sometimes jointly sponsored by multiple departments within a university. Exhibit 3.3 provides some examples.

The department or departments that offer a financial engineering degree are significant factors in determining the program's content. Nevertheless, the content of each program will vary even when programs have similar titles and are offered by offered by similar departments.

Exhibit 3.3   Examples of Multiple Departments Sponsoring Programs

School	Degree	Departments
University of Illinois (U.S.)	Master of Science in Financial Engineering	College of Engineering and College of Business
University of Dayton (U.S.)	Master's of Financial Mathematics	MBA program and Department of Mathematics
Bogazici University (TR)	MS in Financial Engineering	Engineering, Management, and Mathematics departments
University of Birmingham (UK)	MSc in Mathematical Finance	School of Mathematics and Business School's Department of Economics
Claremont Graduate University (U.S.)	MS Financial Engineering (MSFE)	The Peter F. Drucker Graduate School of Management and The School of Mathematical Sciences

CURRICULA

The variety of firms and institutions seeking financial engineers and the resulting variety of programs offered means that prospective students must carefully consider how prepared they can reasonably expect to be for their desired professional field given the strengths and weaknesses of each program. The term "strengths and weaknesses" does not mean "good or bad." Rather, it is an acknowledgement that some programs focus more on math and less on finance, or more on finance and less on math, have a more theoretical or a more practical focus, offer greater or lesser flexibility with electives, and so on.

Consider the difference between the following two prospective students: Student A has a BS in computer programming and has two years of work experience at a well-respected software development firm. Student B has a BS in Finance and has two years of work experience at an investment banking firm. Both students plan to compete for jobs as quantitative traders. In order to be effective in their desired careers, each student will need to supplement their existing qualifications with a different knowledge base and skill set.

In this section we discuss the similarities and differences in pre-enrollment requirements (prerequisites), required courses and electives, course tracks, and faculty assigned to various programs that offer financial engineering programs.

Pre-Enrollment Requirements

Most programs do not require prior work experience. The nature of required course work completed prior to enrollment varies. Generally, programs look for students who have completed a significant number of courses in either math or finance. Oklahoma State University's (U.S.) Master of Science in Quantitative Financial Economics (MSQFE) program is representative of most programs in this regard:

> *The MSQFE Program offers a flexible curriculum suitable for two streams of students. Students entering the program from engineering, physics, mathematics and statistics have highly-developed analytical abilities and seek to gain insight into the financial applications of these skills. Students with a background in business and economics tend to have a better understanding of the context of financial applications, yet seek additional refinement of their analytical abilities.*

Required Courses and Electives

The range of required and elective courses in each program's curriculum varies greatly. Some common themes across curricula for master's programs include required courses on stochastic processes or time series analysis, computational finance, derivatives, fixed-income securities, financial modeling, investment, and asset pricing. Generally, these will not all be required courses within the same program.

Some programs require students to take courses in basic finance or economics, such as the University of Alabama's (U.S.) Master of Finance program, which requires courses in Financial Management, Microeconomics, and Macroeconomics. Some do not. Interestingly, programs requiring a course in pure computer programming, such as The Hong Kong University of Science and Technology's (CN) Master of Science program, which requires a course in C++ programming, are in the minority. However, what you do not take as a required course you can often take as an elective course.

Elective courses range from those centered on the fundamentals of finance or math to those focused on specific subject matter. Elective courses with a more general focus can offer students an opportunity to catch up on relatively basic subject matter, which perhaps was not the focus of their prior coursework. For example, the student seeking to supplement their training in basic finance can find elective courses such as Financial Statement Analysis at Claremont Graduate University (U.S.), Bond Markets or Macro Economic Analysis at North Carolina State University (U.S.), Corporate Finance or Financial Accounting at the University of Illinois (U.S.), International Finance at Case Western Reserve University (U.S.), and Valuation of Equity Securities or Financial Statement Analysis at New York University's Polytechnic Institute (U.S.). The prospective student seeking to supplement their training in math can find courses such as Intro to Financial Mathematics at Rensselaer Polytechnic Institute (U.S.), Data Mining and Analysis at Stanford University (U.S.), Mathematical Statistics at the University of Southern California (U.S.), and Regression Analysis at the University of Dayton (U.S.).

Typically, it is electives that afford the student some flexibility to tailor the curriculum to their preferred career path and to gain the knowledge base and skill set they need in order to pursue it. There are many different electives offered across the range of programs. Consider the sample depicted in Exhibit 3.4.

Some programs will offer electives focused on particular applications. These will be useful for prospective students who are relatively certain of a career path, and who know the specific skills they need to competitively pursue it. Exhibit 3.5 provides examples of these.

Course Tracks

Some programs offer course tracks that will provide the student with a more structured curriculum. Some examples include American University (U.S.), which offers five different tracks, including Investments, Corporate Finance, Risk Management, International Finance, and Real Estate; Rensselaer Polytechnic Institute (U.S.), which offers a Financial Technology track and a Financial Analysis track; the University of Twente (NL), which offers a Management track and a Mathematics track; and Florida State University (U.S.) which offers a Concentration in Actuarial Science track and a Concentration in Regression and Financial Time Series track.

Conversely, some programs, such as the University of Florida's (U.S.) Master of Science in Finance program, have very few required courses and are extremely flexible in their curricula. Both tracked programs and flexible programs have their pros and cons, but only the prospective students can determine which is best for them and should do so in the context of their career goals.

Exhibit 3.4　Sample Electives

School	Degree	Elective
University of Waterloo (CA)	Master of Quantitative Finance	Portfolio Optimization
Baruch College, City University of New York (U.S.)	MS in Financial Engineering	Time Series Analysis and Algorithmic Trading
Bogazici University (TR)	MS in Financial Engineering	FE 538 Valuation with Real Options
Nanyang Technological University (SG)	MSc (Financial Engineering)	Exotic Options & Structured Products
NYU–Polytechnic Institute (U.S.)	Master of Science in Financial Engineering	Behavioral Finance, Trading and Investment Strategy
Georgia State University (U.S.)	MS in Mathematical Risk Management (MS MRM)	Stochastic Term Structure and Credit Risk Models
Baruch College, City University of New York (U.S.)	MS in Financial Engineering	Commodities and Futures Trading
University of the Witwatersrand–Johannesburg (ZA)	MSc in Advanced Mathematics of Finance	Swaps & Exotic Options
Ecole Polytechnique Fédérale de Lausanne (CH)	Master of Sciences in Financial Engineering	Private equity
Nanyang Technological University (SG)	MSc (Financial Engineering)	Energy Derivatives
Rensselaer Polytechnic Institute (U.S.)	Master of Science in Financial Engineering and Risk Analytics	Risk Management
North Carolina State University (U.S.)	Masters of Financial Mathematics	Dynamic Programming
Olin Business School, Washington University in St. Louis (U.S.)	Master of Science in Finance	Fixed Income Derivatives
University of Limerick (IE)	MSc in Computational Finance	Portfolio Risk Analysis
Carnegie Mellon University (U.S.)	Masters of Science in Computational Finance	Credit Derivatives
Olin Business School, Washington University in St. Louis (U.S.)	Master of Science in Finance	Finance Consulting Seminar (applied learning course)
University of Alabama (U.S.)	Master of Science in Finance	Mergers and Acquisitions
University of California–Los Angeles (U.S.)	Master of Financial Engineering	MBS & ABS Markets
Columbia University (U.S.)	MA in Mathematics of Finance	Emerging Markets

Exhibit 3.5 Examples of More Focused Electives

School	Degree	Elective
Dublin City University (IE)	MSc in Financial and Industrial Mathematics	Coding and Cryptography
University of Birmingham (UK)	MSc in Mathematical Finance	Semidefinite Programming
University of Birmingham (UK)	MSc in Mathematical Finance	Combinatorial Optimisation
University of Twente (NL)	Master in Applied Mathematics	Stochastic Filtering and Control Theory
Oklahoma State University (U.S.)	Masters of Science in Quantitative Financial Economics	Power Systems and Regulation

Internships/Research

Some programs require an internship or research experience as part of their curriculum. Kent State University's (U.S.) Master of Science in Financial Engineering program, for example, requires relevant internship experience as part of its program. The University of Twente's (NL) Master in Applied Mathematics program requires full-time research in a financial institution during the second semester of the second year of study.

Faculty

Faculties across the range of programs offering training in financial engineering typically include some faculty who can offer a solid theoretical foundation and other faculty who can offer experience in real-world financial engineering–related problem solving. Faculty members offering real-world experience are often practitioners who contribute to the program as adjunct faculty. Many full-time faculty also have real-world experience in financial engineering, however, and a review of faculty across programs will reveal a broad range of experience upon which students can draw.

Some programs are more balanced than others in terms of offering both a theoretical foundation and real-world problem solving experience. The importance of each depends on the knowledge base and skill set sought by the prospective student.

Hands-on experience can be important to employers who are seeking graduates with specific and immediately applicable skills. Two professors teaching a course by the same name will impart to their students different levels of practical experience and different depths of theoretical foundation. An employer will want to gauge the level of each when hiring a graduate. Some employers will prefer to hire a graduate who has a solid theoretical foundation and who can be taught a number of skills on the job. Others are looking for specific skills and problem solving abilities, which may or may not have been taught depending on the faculty. Either way, a review of the faculty teaching in a degree program will be important in determining the suitability of the graduating student to a particular position within a firm.

JOB PLACEMENT

The goal of the prospective student is employment. Some students will know generally which field they wish to enter. Others will know the geographical area. Others will know exactly the firm for which they wish to work. However specific the employment goals are of the prospective student, there are also considerations to be made outside of the classroom regarding each program's ability to help the student meet them. For example, most programs provide an internship and job placement rate, which the prospective student can review in advance of enrolling. This section will discuss some additional considerations: institutional relationships, alumni networks, and geography.

Institutional Relationships

Most programs have developed institutional relationships, which their students are able to leverage when seeking employment. The strength and nature of these relationships differ among programs. Some programs have relationships with employers across a broad range of industries, and others have very strong ties to a particular industry. Some programs have developed strong ties to local industries, which may offer an advantage to the prospective student who knows they want to work in a particular location. For example, consider Case Western Reserve University's MSM Finance and MSM Finance/MBA Dual Degree programs, which offer the following unique advantage:

> *Cleveland offers visibility to a wealth of banking firms, a Federal Reserve, financial institutions, hedge funds and medium/large international firms. The faculty work closely with many of these firms and our alumni are a terrific resource for seminars, internship opportunities, etc.*

Or the University of Witwatersand's BSc Honours, MSc, and PhD in Advanced Mathematics of Finance programs, which boast the "largest faculty in South Africa" and have "long-standing connections to the SA financial sector."

Some programs offer a unique opportunity to gain exposure in foreign markets. The China Center at the University of Minnesota, for example, offers students exposure to China's emerging markets.

All schools have some form of Alumni network which the student can leverage.

Geographic Location

Today there are financial engineering programs in all of the developed markets and in many of the less developed ones as well. For the prospective student who knows in which geographic market they wish to work, and even for the prospective student who is not yet sure, the location of the program should play a role in the decision making process. But it should not be the deciding factor. For example, employers in Singapore hire graduates from programs in New York, and employers in New York hire graduates from programs in Singapore. Prospective students should consider the markets in which, and the firms for which, they wish to work and should research which programs are most likely to gain them access to those markets or firms. Employers should understand the range of programs outside the firm's immediate geographical market, from which qualified graduates may be recruited.

Some programs have developed across borders, offering students exposure to multiple geographic markets. The Nanyang Business School's MSc (Financial Engineering) program in Singapore, for example, is offered in collaboration with Carnegie Mellon University in the United States. Students spend seven weeks taking courses at Carnegie Mellon University and earn a Certificate in Computational Finance from Carnegie Mellon, in addition to the MFE degree awarded by Nanyang Technological University.

CONCLUSION

The common theme in any discussion of financial engineering programs is variety. There are a number of different departments at academic institutions around the world offering different degrees with varying curricula. This presents prospective students of financial engineering with an excellent opportunity to tailor their decision regarding program enrollment to their career goals. It should be stressed that the variety among financial engineering programs means that nothing should be taken for granted with respect to a particular program. Each program should be researched fully before the prospective student makes a judgment about the suitability of a program to his/her goals.

APPENDIX: PROGRAMS CONTACTED

For inclusion in the survey please contact info@sbccgroup.com.

School	Program	Location
Birkbeck College, University of London	MSc Financial Engineering	London, UK
Birkbeck College, University of London	MSc Finance	London, UK
Birkbeck College, University of London	MSc Finance & Commodities	London, UK
Brunel University	MSc Modelling and Management of Risk	Middlesex, UK
Cambridge University, Judge School	Master of Finance	Cambridge, UK
Cambridge University, Judge School	MPhil Finance (Financial Engineering Specialisation)	Cambridge, UK
City University, Cass School	MSc Financial Mathematics	London, UK
City University, Cass School	MSc Quantitative Finance (Formerly FEE)	London, UK
City University, Cass School	MSc Mathematical Finance & Trading	London, UK
Dublin City University	MSc Financial & Industrial Mathematics	Dublin, Ireland

(continued)

School	Program	Location
Herriot Watt University	MSc Financial Mathematics	Edinburgh, UK
Imperial College Business School	MSc Mathematics & Finance	London, UK
Imperial College Business School	MSc Risk Management and Financial Engineering	London, UK
King's College, London	MSc Financial Mathematics	London, UK
Queen's University, Belfast	MSc Finance	Belfast, Ireland
Leeds University	MSc Financial Mathematics	Leeds, UK
Leicester University	MSc Financial Mathematics & Computation	Leicester, UK
Liverpool John Moores University	MSc International Banking & Finance	Liverpool, UK
London Business School	MSc Finance	London, UK
Manchester Business School, Manchester University	MSc Finance	Manchester, UK
Manchester Business School, Manchester University	MSc Finance & Economics	Manchester, UK
Manchester Business School, Manchester University	MSc Quantitative Finance (Financial Engineering or Risk Management Track)	Manchester, UK
Manchester Business School, Manchester University	MSc Mathematical Finance	Manchester, UK
Oxford University, Saïd Business School	MSc Financial Economics	Oxford, UK
Oxford University	MSc Mathematical & Computational Finance	Oxford, UK
University of Birmingham	MSc Mathematical Finance	Birmingham, UK
University College Dublin, Smurfit School	MSc Finance	Dublin, Ireland
University College Dublin, Smurfit School	MSc Quantitative Finance	Dublin, Ireland
University College Dublin, Smurfit School	MSc Risk Management	Dublin, Ireland
ICMA Centre, University of Reading	MSc Financial Engineering	Reading, UK
ICMA Centre, University of Reading	MSc International Securities, Investment and Banking	Reading, UK
ICMA Centre, University of Reading	MSc Financial Risk Management	Reading, UK
University of Dublin, Trinity College	MSc Finance	Dublin, Ireland
University of Essex	MSc Computational Finance	Essex, UK
University of Exeter	MSc Financial Mathematics	Exeter, UK
University of Limerick, Kemmy School	MSc Computational Finance	Limerick, Ireland
University of Westminster	MSc Investment & Risk Finance	London, UK
University of York	MSc Mathematical Finance	York, UK
Warwick University	MSc Financial Mathematics	Warwick, UK

School	Program	Location
American University, Kogod School of Business	MS Finance	Washington, DC
Asbury College	BA Financial Mathematics	Wilmore, KY
Baruch College (City University of New York)	MS Financial Engineering	New York, NY
Ball State University	BS Financial Mathematics	Muncie, IN
Bentley College	MS Finance	Waltham, MA
Boston College, Carroll School	MS Finance	Boston, MA
Boston University	MS Mathematical Finance	Boston, MA
Brandeis University	MS Finance	Waltham, MA
Carnegie Mellon University, Tepper School	MS Computational Finance	Pittsburgh, PA
Carnegie Mellon University, Tepper School	MBA Financial Engineering	Pittsburgh, PA
Case Western University, Weatherhead School	Master of Science in Management in Finance	Cleveland, OH
Claremont Graduate University, Drucker School	MS Financial Engineering	Claremont, CA
Clark University	MS Finance	Worcester, MA
Columbia University	MA Mathematics of Finance	New York, NY
Cornell University	MSc Engineering (Concentration in Financial Engineering)	Ithaca, NY
DePaul University	MS Computational Finance	Chicago, IL
DePaul University, Kellstadt School	MS Finance	Chicago, IL
Drexel University	MS Finance	Philadelphia, PA
Fairfield University, Dolan School	MS Finance	Fairfield, CT
Florida State University	MS Financial Mathematics	Tallahassee, FL
Fordham University	MS in Quantitative Finance	New York, NY
Fordham University	Advanced Certificate in Financial Computing	New York, NY
George Washington University	MS Finance	Washington, DC
Georgia Institute of Technology	MS Quantitative and Computational Finance	Atlanta, GA
Georgia State University	MSc Mathematical Risk Management	Atlanta, GA
Golden Gate University	MS Finance	San Francisco, CA
Hofstra University	MS Quantitative Finance	Hempstead, NY
James Madison University	BS Quantitative Finance	Harrisonburg, VA
Johns Hopkins University—Carey School	MS Finance (Part-Time)	Baltimore, MD
Illinois Institute of Technology, Stuart School	MS Finance	Chicago, IL
Kent State University	MS Financial Engineering	Kent, OH
Lehigh University	MS Analytical Finance	Bethlehem, PA

(continued)

School	Program	Location
Louisiana State University, EJ Ourso School	MS Finance with Minor in Mathematics	Baton Rouge, LA
Loyola College, Sellinger School	MS Finance	Baltimore, MD
Massachusetts Institute of Technology	MF in Finance	Cambridge, MA
New Mexico State University	Professional MS in Financial Mathematics	Las Cruces, NM
New York University, Courant Institute	MS Mathematical Finance	New York, NY
North Carolina State University	MS Financial Mathematics	Raleigh, NC
Northwestern University, Kellogg School	Ph in Finance	Evanston, IL
Oklahoma State University, Spears School	MS Quantitative Financial Economics	Stillwater, OK
Polytechnic Institute of New York University	MS Financial Engineering	New York, NY
Princeton University	MF in Finance	Princeton, NJ
Purdue University, Krannert School	MS Finance	West Lafayette, IN
Purdue University	MS Mathematics with specialisation in Computational Finance	West Lafayette, IN
Purdue University	MS Statistics with specialisation in Computational Finance	West Lafayette, IN
Queens College (City University of New York)	MS in Risk Management	New York, NY
Rensselaer Polytechnic Institute, Lally School	MS in Management (Concentration in Financial Engineering & Risk Analytics)	Troy, NY
Rutgers University (New Brunswick–Piscataway)	MS Mathematical Finance	Piscataway, NJ
Rutgers University	MS Quantitative Finance	Newark, NJ
Saint Mary's College of California	MS Financial Analysis and Investment Management (FAIM)	Morago, CA
San Diego State University	BS in Applied Mathematics (Emphasis in Mathematical Finance)	San Diego, CA
Seattle University, Albers School	MS Finance	Seattle, WA
Stanford University	MSc Financial Mathematics	Stanford, CA
State University of New York–Buffalo	MS Finance	Buffalo, NY
Stevens Institute of Technology	MS Financial Engineering (Technology Track)— Distance Learning	Hoboken, NJ

School	Program	Location
Stony Brook University	MS Financial Mathematics	Stony Brook, NY
Temple University, Fox School of Business	MS Financial Engineering	Philadelphia, PA
Texas A&M University	MS Financial Mathematics	College Station, TX
Tulane University, Freeman School	MF in Finance	New Orleans, LA and Houston, TX
UC Berkeley, Haas School	MS Financial Engineering	Berkeley, CA
University of Alabama–Culverhouse	MS Finance	Tuscaloosa, AL
University of Arizona–Eller	MS Finance	Tucson, AZ
University of California–Los Angeles	MS Financial Engineering	Los Angeles, CA
University of California–Santa Barbara	BS Financial Mathematics and Statistics	Santa Barbara, CA
University of Chicago	MS Financial Mathematics	Chicago, IL
University of Connecticut	Professional MS Applied Financial Mathematics	Storrs, CT
University of Dayton	Master in Financial Mathematics	Dayton, OH
University of Denver, Daniels College of Business	MS Finance	Denver, CO
University of Florida, Hough Graduate School	MS Finance	Gainesville, FL
University of Hawaii, Shidler College of Business	MS Financial Engineering	Honolulu, HI
University of Houston, Bauer College of Business	MS Finance	Houston, TX
University of Illinois at Urbana-Champaign	MS Finance	Urbana-Champaign, IL
University of Illinois at Urbana-Champaign	MS Financial Engineering	Urbana-Champaign, IL
University of Michigan	MS Financial Engineering	Ann Arbor, MI
University of Minnesota	Master in Financial Mathematics	Minneapolis, MN
University of North Carolina at Charlotte	MS Mathematical Finance	Charlotte, NC
University of Pittsburgh	Professional Science MS Mathematical Finance	Pittsburgh, PA
University of Rochester, Simon School	MS Finance	Rochester, NY
University of Southern California	MS Mathematical Finance	Los Angeles, CA
University of Tulsa	MS Finance	Tulsa, OK
University of Wisconsin–Madison	Quantitative Masters in Finance	Madison, WI
Vanderbilt University, Owen School	MS Finance (Quantitative Track)	Nashville, TN

(continued)

School	Program	Location
Washington University in St. Louis, Olin School	MS Finance	St. Louis, MO
Worchester Polytechnic Institute	MSc Financial Mathematics	Worchester, MA
HEC Montreal	MSc Financial Engineering	Montreal, QB
McMaster University	MSc in Financial Mathematics	Hamilton, ON
Université de Montreal	MSc Financial Mathematics & Computational Finance	Montreal, QB
Université Laval	MSc Financial Engineering	Quebec, QB
University of Toronto	MS Mathematical Finance	Toronto, ON
University of Waterloo	MSc Quantitative Finance	Waterloo, ON
University of Western Ontario	MS Applied Mathematics (Research in Financial Mathematics)	London, ON
Université du Québec à Montréal (UQAM)	MSc Applied Finance	Montreal, QB
York University	MS Financial Engineering	Toronto, ON
City University–Hong Kong	MSc Finance	Hong Kong, Hong Kong
City University–Hong Kong	MSc Financial Engineering	Hong Kong, Hong Kong
Hong Kong University (HKU)	MF in Financial Engineering	Hong Kong, Hong Kong
Hong Kong University of Science of Technology (HKUST)	MSc Investment Management	Hong Kong, Hong Kong
Hong Kong University of Science of Technology (HKUST)	MSc Financial Analysis	Hong Kong, Hong Kong
Hong Kong University of Science of Technology (HKUST)	MSc Mathematics (Financial Mathematics & Statistics)	Hong Kong, Hong Kong
Macquarie University	Masters of Applied Finance	Sydney, Australia
Nanyang Technological University (NTU)	MSc Financial Engineering	Singapore, Singapore
National Tsing Hua University	MSc Quantitative Finance	Taipei, Taiwan
National University of Singapore (NUS)	MSc Financial Engineering	Singapore, Singapore
National University of Singapore (NUS)	MSc Quantitative Finance	Singapore, Singapore
Singapore Management University (SMU)	MSc Applied Finance	Singapore, Singapore
University of Melbourne	MSc Applied Finance	Melbourne, Australia
University of New South Wales	MSc Finance	Sydney, Australia
University of Technology Sydney	MSc Quantitative Finance	Sydney, Australia

School	Program	Location
Bar Ilan University	MSc Financial Mathematics	Ramat Gan, Israel
Bogaziçi University	MSc Financial Engineering	Istanbul, Turkey
Duisenberg School of Finance	MSc Risk Management	Amsterdam, Netherlands
Duisenberg School of Finance	MSc Corporate Finance and Banking	Amsterdam, Netherlands
Ecole Polytechnique Fédérale de Lausanne	MSc Financial Engineering	Lausanne, Switzerland
EDHEC	MSc Finance	Lille, France
ETH/UZH–Zurich	Master of Science in Quantitative Finance	Zurich, Switzerland
European School of Management (ESCP-EAP)	Specialized Master in Finance	Paris, London, Madrid
Frankfurt School of Finance & Management	MSc Quantitative Finance	Frankfurt, Germany
Frankfurt School of Finance & Management	MSc Finance	Frankfurt, Germany
HEC	MSc International Finance	Paris, France
International University of Monaco	Masters in Finance	Monaco, Monaco
ISCTE Business School	MSc Finance	Lisbon, Portugal
Middle East Technical University	MSc Financial Mathematics	Ankara, Turkey
Tilburg University	MSc Quantitative Finance and Actuarial Science	Tilburg, The Netherlands
Tilburg University	MSc Finance	Tilburg, The Netherlands
Universidad Carlos III de Madrid	MSc Financial Analysis	Madrid, Spain
Università Bocconi	MA Quantitative Finance & Risk Management	Milan, Italy
Universität Konstanz	Masters in Mathematical Finance	Constance, Germany
Université de Genève (HEC)	MSc Finance	Geneva, Switzerland
Université de Lausanne (HEC)	MSc Finance	Lausanne, Switzerland
Université de Neuchâtel	MSc Finance	Neuchâtel, Switzerland
Université Panthéon–Assas	MS Finance	Paris, France
University of St. Gallen	MSc Quantitative Economics and Finance	St. Gallen, Switzerland
University of Twente	MSc Applied Mathematics and MSc Industrial Engineering & Management (Specialisation in Financial Engineering)	Twente, The Netherlands

(continued)

School	Program	Location
Universiteit van Amsterdam, Amsterdam Business School	Master in International Finance (Quantitative Finance Track)	Amsterdam, The Netherlands
Universiteit van Amsterdam, Korteweg-de Vries Institute with Vrije Universteit & Universiteit Utrecht	MSc Stochastics and Financial Mathematics	Amsterdam, The Netherlands
Università di Torino	MSc Quantitative Finance	Torino, Italy
University of Piraeus	MSc in Banking and Financial Management	Piraeus, Greece
Vienna Institute of Technology	Masters in Finance	Vienna, Austria
Warsaw University	Masters in Quantitative Finance	Warsaw, Poland
North-West University	MSc Financial Mathematics	Potchestroom, South Africa
North-West University	MSc Quantitative Risk Management	Potchestroom, South Africa
University of Capetown	MSc Mathematics of Finance	Capetown, South Africa
University of Pretoria	MSc Financial Engineering	Pretoria, South Africa
University of Pretoria	MSc Mathematics of Finance	Pretoria, South Africa
University of São Paulo (Portuguese)	Professional Masters—Mathematical Modeling in Finance	São Paulo, Brazil
University of Stellenbosch	MComm in Financial Risk Management	Stellenbosch, South Africa
University of the Free State	MSc Mathematical Statistics	Bloemfontein, South Africa
University of the Witwatersrand	MSc Mathematics of Finance	Johannesburg, South Africa

NOTES

1. Median number of students (36) enrolled in programs who responded to the survey multiplied by number of programs having substantial components of financial engineering in their curricula worldwide (approximately 150).

2. Note that some universities interpret the term "financial engineering" more narrowly than we do, often limiting their interpretation to structuring roles. Some of these institutions prefer to think of financial engineering as a subset of quantitative finance. We employ a broader interpretation here that is consistent with that used by the International Association of Financial Engineers (IAFE).

ABOUT THE AUTHOR

John Cornish is an analyst at SBCC Group Inc. Since joining SBCC in January of 2009, John's independent advisory projects have spanned a diverse range of clients including hedge funds, multibillion-dollar asset management complexes, large global banks, endowments, municipalities, insurance companies and corporations. John's experience includes equities, fixed income, derivatives (both exchange traded and OTC) and structured products, the valuation of complex financially engineered securities, merger arbitrage, quantitative trading, transition trading and the liquidation of both equity and fixed income portfolios. John received his BSM in finance from the A.B. Freeman School of Business at Tulane University in 2008 and is a Level II candidate in the CFA program.

PART II

Financial Engineering and the Evolution of Major Markets

CHAPTER 4

The Fixed Income Market

PERUVEMBA SATISH
Allstate Investments, LLC

Fixed Income Market Snapshot

History: The interest rate derivatives markets began to develop in the late 1970s. Early on, the instruments that were traded were mainly used for risk management purposes by corporations exposed to interest rate fluctuations. However, the instruments were soon applied by other types of users for their hedging and investment needs. Eventually, the early derivatives led to the development of more complex, structured financial products. For these reasons, interest rate derivatives eventually became the largest segment, by far, of the global derivatives markets.

Size: The interest rate market is the largest component of both over-the-counter (OTC) and exchange-traded derivatives. The size of the OTC interest rate derivatives market has grown from $50 trillion at the end of 1998 to about $449 trillion at the end of 2009, while the exchange-traded derivatives side has evolved from $12.6 trillion in 1998 to $67 trillion in 2009.

Products: Over-the-counter products include interest rate swaps (either fixed-for-fixed or fixed-or-floating swaps), caps, floors, collars, corridors, swaptions, warrants, forward rate agreements (FRAs), and bond options. Exchange-traded instruments consist of a variety of interest rate futures on Treasury bonds and bills, Federal Funds, Eurodollars, and EuroYen.

First Usage: In 1975, the Chicago Board of Trade created the first interest rate futures contract based on Ginnie Mae mortgage pass-throughs. Though it met with initial success, the contract eventually died. The first successful interest rate futures contract, a 90-day U.S. Treasury bill futures contract, was produced by the Chicago Mercantile Exchange in the same year. One of the first interest rate swaps was transacted in 1982 by the Student Loan Marketing Association (Sallie Mae) in a successful effort to convert fixed-rate payments for its intermediate-term debt to floating rate payments indexed to the three-month Treasury bill rate.

Selection of Famous Events:

1989: The British local government of Hammersmith and Fulham Borough Council defaulted on about $10 billion worth of interest rate swaps and options contracts when rising interest rates reversed their income flow. Eventually, British courts ruled that Hammersmith and Fulham, as well as other local government councils that also participated in derivatives trading, had exceeded their legal powers by entering into the interest rate derivative contracts

1994: Procter & Gamble and Bankers Trust Company entered into two highly leveraged interest rate swaps, which made them more susceptible to market swings. The products were structured to pay off handsomely for P&G if interest rates continued to fall. They did not. A sudden increase in interest rates resulted in P&G incurring a $157 million loss.

1994: Air Products & Chemicals also entered into a derivative transaction with Bankers Trust. It wanted to lower its interest costs on $1.8 billion of loans and bonds and use the swaps to convert its fixed, high-interest rate obligations to lower variable rates. To achieve this, the company purchased five leveraged interest-rate swap contracts. When rates rose, the company suffered a pre-tax loss of $96.4 million.

Best Providers (as of 2009): The Best Interest Rate Derivative Provider, as ranked by Global Finance magazine, is JP Morgan in North America, Standard Chartered in Europe, and Royal Bank of Scotland (RBS) in Asia.

Applications: Some of the ways in which interest rate derivatives can be used include hedging against exposure to fluctuations in interest rates, mitigating cash flow volatility, lowering funding costs, and arbitraging debt price differences in the capital markets.

Users: Investors in interest rate derivatives include corporations (both financial and non-financial), government agencies, and various types of international institutions.

INTRODUCTION

Global fixed income markets cover a broad array of securities and vary considerably in their structure and complexity. Such fixed-income securities represent a significant portion of the asset allocation mix of institutional investors. They offer proprietary traders and hedge fund managers large and liquid markets to implement relative value, arbitrage and directional strategies. They provide investors, directly and indirectly, a wealth of information on the health of financial markets and macroeconomic conditions.

Over the past 10 years, investments in fixed income have outperformed investments in equities. From September 2000 to September 2010 the annual return on S&P 500 index was −1.4 percent and 1.6 percent for the MSCI Developed World (except the United States). In contrast, the Barclays US Corporate bond index was up 6.9 percent, the Barclays U.S. High Yield bond index returned 9.4 percent and the return on Barclays Euro Corporate bond index was 9.4 percent. In emerging markets, sovereign debt and equities performed equally well. The MSCI Emerging Market stock index was up 11.2 percent, while the Barclays Sovereign Debt index was up 11 percent. Today, as global economies recover from the 2008 credit crisis, the fixed income markets are entering a period of uncertainty and are poised for remarkable change.

On the demand side, after the collapse of the financial markets in 2008, investors have shown an insatiable appetite for fixed income securities. According

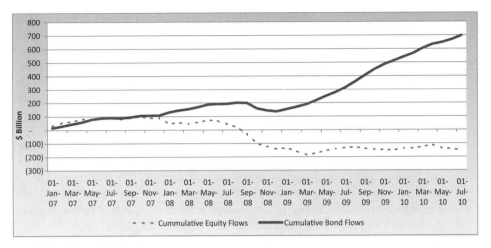

Exhibit 4.1 Cumulative Long-Term U.S. Mutual Fund Flows, January 2007–July 2010
Source: Investment Company Institute (http://www.ici.org).

to the Investment Company Institute, between January 2007 and July 2010 a total of $698 billion flowed into U.S. bond mutual funds while $153 billion flowed out of equity funds during the same period. Around 70 percent of the bond inflow took place since September 2008. These flows are depicted in Exhibit 4.1.

The desire for income in a low global interest rate environment, disappointment with performance of equity markets over the last several years, concerns about high risk with equity investment due to the slowdown in economic growth, and a growing fear of deflation have all contributed to this flood of money into fixed income markets. Moreover, with an aging population in the developed world, it is likely that the flows will persist, as the retiring population directs more of its investment to fixed income markets. Toward this goal, pension funds will further increase their allocation to these markets as they pursue liability-driven investments.

On the supply side, an entirely different dynamic is playing out. The massive deleveraging of the financial system and corporate balance sheets is resulting in a decline in the supply of fixed income securities. Several financial products that were manufactured during the credit bubble will not survive. Partially offsetting this is a flood of new government debt securities issued to fund massive budget deficits brought on by efforts to stimulate the economy. The challenges of reinvesting debt that is rolling over, the gap between the supply and demand for securities, and concerns about emerging sovereign debt crises in the developed economies are fundamentally altering the landscape of fixed income markets. In the near term, it is likely that the money flows into some of the corners of the fixed income markets (such as emerging markets) will reach levels beyond the size of these markets, thus potentially causing another bubble and elevating liquidity risks. Market price and yield relationships within the fixed income markets that have been relatively stable for decades, and never been in doubt, are beginning to unravel. The 30-year U.S. dollar interest rate swap spread has turned negative, something not observed in the past. It is likely that the rationale for several market relationships will be revisited, and a new investment paradigm may emerge. Some of the emerging market economies are in a strong fiscal position while the developed markets struggle with deficit and debt. The credit spreads between the sovereign debt of emerging and developed markets will need to recalibrated. Regulatory reforms, reduced risk-taking by dealers, and the exit of many participants, have all affected market liquidity and trading volume. In the past, the behavior of the fixed income markets has been defined by interest rate levels and interest rate volatilities. This will continue, but, as we go forward, it will be just as important to understand and closely watch investor perceptions of demand and supply to fully evaluate the risks and returns in the fixed income markets.

The fixed income markets can be divided into cash and derivative markets. The cash side of the U.S. fixed income market is by far the largest debt market globally. U.S. Treasury debt and mortgage-backed securities (MBS) combined constitute approximately 50 percent of the cash market. Corporate debt comprises about 20 percent. Exhibit 4.2 depicts the composition of the cash market at the end of the first quarter of 2010.

New U.S. debt issuance for the full year 2009, shown in Exhibit 4.3, follows a similar break-down with U.S. Treasuries and MBS dominating the market.

The derivatives side of the fixed income market includes both instruments that trade on exchanges and instruments that trade in over-the-counter (OTC) dealer markets. Fixed income derivatives represent the largest part of the total derivative market, with much of the trading activity taking place in the OTC markets. At the end of 2009, the total notional value of all outstanding OTC derivative contracts stood at $614 trillion. Interest rate derivatives made up 73 percent of this. This is depicted in Exhibit 4.4.

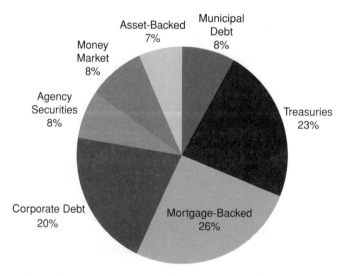

Exhibit 4.2   U.S. Bond Market, Q1 2010 Total Debt: $35 Trillion
Source: SIFMA (http://www.sifma.org).

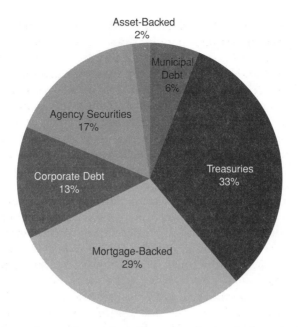

Exhibit 4.3   U.S. Bond Issuance, 2009 Total Issuance: $6.7 Trillion
Source: SIFMA (http://www.sifma.org).

This chapter is an introduction to the fixed income markets. Section 2 reviews the cash component of the fixed-income securities markets. Agency and mortgage-backed securities are excluded as they are a topic of discussion elsewhere in this book. Fixed income derivative products are covered in section 3. Sections 4, 5, and 6 presents some key topics related to analysis of fixed income securities. In section 7 a few trading strategies are outlined.

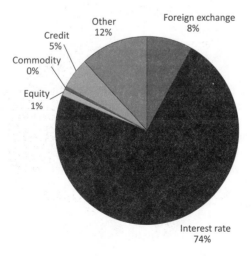

Exhibit 4.4   Over-the-Counter Derivatives Market, 2009 Total Outstanding: $614 Trillion
Source: BIS (http://www.bis.org).

THE CASH MARKETS

Treasury Debt

The roughly $13 trillion U.S. Treasury debt market is the largest fixed income market in the world. This market represents debt issued by the U.S. government, and the payment is guaranteed by the taxing authority of the United States. It is the principal means of financing the U.S. federal deficit and refinancing maturing debt.

Ownership and Make-Up: Historically, due to the reserve currency status of the U.S. dollar (hereinafter referred to as USD), U.S. Treasuries have established a unique status as a storehouse of value. The USD is considered a safe haven, with investors ranging from central banks to pension funds to individual investors. Approximately 60 percent of the debt is public-marketable, with the rest accounted for by public non-marketable and intra-governmental holding that includes the U.S. Federal Reserve and the Social Security Trust Fund.

As of December 2009, approximately 30 percent of total outstanding U.S. Treasuries were held by foreign and international entities. Another 15 percent were held by Pension Funds, Insurance Companies, Mutual Funds, and State and Local Governments.

Among foreign and international entities, China and Hong Kong are the largest owners, with 25 percent of ownership. They are followed by Japan at 20 percent and the United Kingdom at nine percent. BRIC nations (Brazil, Russia, India, and China), along with Hong Kong, Japan, and the United Kingdom, make up 62 percent of the foreign U.S. Treasury ownership.

The eight trillion dollars of public marketable Treasury securities can also be categorized by maturity as T-bills, T-notes, and T-bonds, plus an inflation-indexed product called Treasury Inflation-Protected Securities (TIPS). When looked at this way, the market consists of:

T-Bills—22 percent
T-notes—61 percent
T-bonds—10 percent
TIPS—7 percent

T-bills are short-term securities sold at a discount, whereas notes and bonds are interest-bearing obligations that pay a coupon semi-annually. TIPS also pay interest semi-annually, but the principal is indexed to the CPI-U. The CPI-U is the non-seasonally adjusted *U.S. City Average All Items Consumer Price Index for All Urban Consumers*, published monthly by the Bureau of Labor Statistics of the U.S. Department of Labor. In case of deflation, the principal is adjusted downwards resulting in a lower interest payment, but at maturity the Treasury guarantees repayment of the original principal if the adjusted principal falls below the original principal.

New Issuance: Treasuries are regularly issued via a cycle of announcements followed by auctions. The 4-week, 13-week, and 26-week Treasury bills are auctioned each week while the 52-week bills are offered every four weeks. The 2-year, 5-year, and 7-year notes are normally announced in the second half of the month and auctioned a few business days later. The 3-year and 10-year auctions are announced during the first half of the month. More specifically, the 10-year is usually announced during the months of February, May, August, and November. The 5-year TIPS are auctioned in April (reopened in October), 10-year TIPS are auctioned in January and July (reopened in March, May, September, and November), and 30-year TIPS are auctioned in February (reopened in August). A reopened Treasury has the same coupon rate, payment date, and maturity date but a different price.

The Treasury auction process begins with the announcement of the auction for a specified amount. The auction process determines the coupon rate and the issue price of the debt. Immediately following the auction announcement, dealers begin to trade the security on a when-issued basis. Securities purchased and sold on a when-issued basis settle on the issue date of the security, unlike normal secondary market transactions in Treasuries that settle in one business day. When-issued trading reduces uncertainty, enhances transparency, and facilitates price discovery. Potential bidders use the information to bid at the auction. Prior to 1992, Treasury auctions followed a multiple-price format, wherein each competitive bidder paid prices computed from their bid yield. However, in 1992, the U.S. Treasury adopted a single-price format for the auction.

Market participants submit either one or more competitive bids specifying the yield and quantity, or a noncompetitive bid specifying the quantity they are willing to purchase at the price established by the competitive bidders. The Treasury Department limits each bidder to 35 percent of the offering, less the bidder's "reportable net long position."

The Treasury, after subtracting noncompetitive bids, accepts competitive bids in the order of increasing yield until all securities being offered are exhausted. The highest accepted yield, called the "stop," establishes the single clearing price. Bids below the stop are filled in full, at the stop are filled prorated, and above the stop are rejected. The coupon rate is set to the highest level, in 1/8th percent increments, so as to not exceed a price of 100 percent.

Auctions for T-bills are similar except that competitive bids are in terms of discount rates. The auction market underwent several changes in 1992 after the discovery of a significant violation of bidding rules by Solomon Brothers. The firm bid inappropriately, such that it gained as much as 86 percent of a new issue.

Exhibit 4.5 reports the result from a recent 10-year auction held on August 11, 2010. FIMA stands for Foreign and International Monetary Authority and SOMA is the Federal Reserve System's Open Market Account. The bid/cover ratio, which is the ratio of total bids (excluding SOMA) to the total amount sold, was 3.04. The bid/cover ratio for the 10-year U.S. Treasury over the last 10 years has ranged between 3.7 and 1.2, with an average of around 2.4. The bid/cover ratio is a gauge of market demand for the debt and has taken on an added importance since 2008.

While, traditionally, the U.S. Treasuries have held significant weight in the asset allocation of investors globally, the future is more uncertain. The U.S. Treasury's debt has increased exponentially in the last few years; more than 50 percent since December 2006. This has been the result of U.S. central bankers' and policy makers' aggressive monetary and fiscal policies to counter the economic fallout from

Exhibit 4.5   Results of 10-Year U.S. Treasury Auction

Treasury Auction Results: August 11, 2010

Issue Date	16-Aug-10	
Maturity Date	15-Aug-20	
Original Issue Date	16-Aug-10	
Coupon Rate	2.625%	
High Yield	2.73%	
Allotted at High	10.57%	
Price	99.087	
Median Yield	2.67%	
Low Yield	2.66%	
	Tendered	**Accepted**
Competitive	$72,820,240,000	$23,824,219,500
Noncompetitive	$125,810,700	$125,810,700
FIMA (Noncompetitive)	$50,000,000	$50,000,000
Subtotal	*$72,996,050,700*	*$24,000,030,200*
SOMA	$1,437,197,100	$1,437,197,100
Total	*$74,433,247,800*	*$25,437,227,300*
	Tendered	**Accepted**
Primary Dealer	$49,067,000,000	$10,375,725,500
Direct Bidder	$9,936,000,000	$2,532,513,000
Indirect Bidder	$15,817,240,000	$10,915,981,000
Total Competitive	*$72,820,240,000*	*$23,824,219,500*

the 2008 credit crisis. The U.S. Treasury debt to GDP (see Exhibit 4.6) is 100 percent. This alarming rise in debt has led many leading investment professionals to question the status of U.S. Treasuries as a safe haven and to question its AAA credit rating. Any change in demand for U.S. Treasuries or investor perception will have enormous implications for fixed income markets, given the dominance of the U.S. Treasuries in the market. Also, the purchase and sales decisions of a few foreign and international entities will have significant impact on the Treasury market given the concentration of international ownership.

International Debt

The international debt market can be classified into domestic bonds, foreign bonds, and Eurobonds. Domestic bonds are issued by domestic borrowers in their local currency and sold locally. The foreign bond market is debt issued by foreign borrowers in domestic currency and sold domestically. An example of the latter would be a Japanese issuer selling a bond in the United States that is denominated in USD.

The foreign bonds traded in the foreign bond markets constituted a significant portion of the international bond market until a few decades ago. Foreign bond issuers typically include national governments and supranationals. For example,

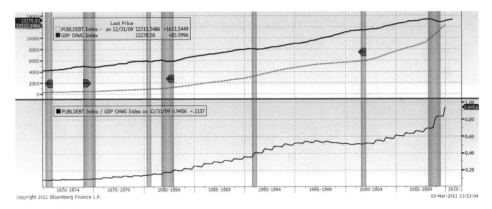

Exhibit 4.6 Total U.S. Treasury Debt Q1 1970–Q2 2010
Used with permission of Bloomberg Finance L.P.

in September 2010, BNP Paribas went to the Japanese capital market with a 5-year 1.04 percent JPY 59.3 billion bond issue (referred to as a Samurai bond). Yankee bonds are foreign bonds issued in USD in the U.S. market.

Eurobonds differ from the others in that they are not sold in any particular domestic bond market. Eurobonds are denominated in a currency not native to the country where they are issued. So if a Eurobond is denominated in the U.S. dollar, it would not be sold in the United States. The 5-year USD 2 billion 3.625 percent Russian debt issuance in April 2010 is an example of a Eurobond.

Historically, the pound Sterling used to play a key role in international trade. This predominance ended following the Bretton Woods conference in 1944 and the subsequent Sterling crisis. Today the USD is the largest reserve currency, followed by the Euro, the pound Sterling, and the Japanese yen. These currencies dominate the global foreign exchange markets and also make up much of the international debt market. Exhibit 4.7 shows marketable government debt for the top 25 OECD countries.

U.S. Treasuries and Japanese Government Bonds (JGB) dominate the government debt market, followed by Italy, France, UK, and Germany.

The Italian BOTs are short-term bonds with maturity up to one year. CTZs are zero coupon Italian bonds with two-year maturities. The Italian Treasury bonds with maturities of 3, 5, 10, 15, and 30 years are called BTPs. The Italian Treasury also issues bonds indexed to the Euro-zone inflation rate and are called BTP Euro i notes. These bonds are issued with 5-, 10-, 15-, and 30-year maturities.

OATs, BTANs, and BTFs are the French long-term, medium-term (two to five years) and short-term bonds. Maturity and coupon dates of fixed rate OATs are either 25th April or 25th October. In addition, there are inflation-linked OATs indexed to a French consumer price index (excluding tobacco) or to the Euro-zone inflation index.

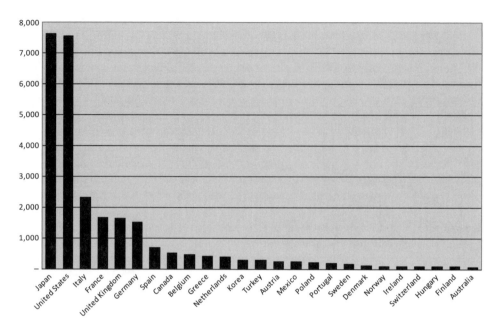

Exhibit 4.7 Sovereign Debt Outstanding Q4 2009
Source: OECD (http://stats.oecd.org).

The largest share of the UK government's debt are conventional gilts described by a coupon rate, a maturity date, and paid semi-annually. Index-linked gilts are the largest part of the gilt market after conventional gilts. They also pay a coupon semi-annually, but the principal is adjusted according to the UK Retail Price Index.

The German bond market consists of Bunds, Bobls, and Schatz. Bund maturities range from 10 to 30 years. Bobls are five-year notes and Schatz refers to the two-year notes. Another significant German debt market is the Pfandbrief. The total Pfandbrief outstanding, as of 2009, was EUR 719 billion. These are medium- to long-term covered bonds issued by German credit institutions (Pfandbriefbanken). The bonds are secured or "covered" by a pool of eligible cover assets, such as mortgages or public sector loans. Pfandbrief debt issues are governed by the German Pfandbrief Act which imposes strict legal requirements on the quality and over-collateralization of assets.

The Eurozone, with a common currency and the European Central Bank administering the monetary policy, is the largest liquid government debt market outside the United States. However, the government debt of Eurozone countries is far from uniform. There is substantial economic disparity among these countries, resulting in considerable differences in yield and trading activity of the debt of these countries. The market's perception of an issuer's credit quality is best illustrated by the price (called a spread) of purchasing credit protection on that debt by way of a credit default swap (CDS). Exhibit 4.8 illustrates comparative spreads for the debts of different countries.

Exhibit 4.8 Major Developed Market Government Bond Yield and CDS Spreads

Country	5-yr. Bond Yield (%)	10-yr. Bond Yield (%)	5-yr. CDS Spread (bps)
Australia	4.61	4.91	48.7
Austria	1.70	2.72	82.6
Belgium	1.95	2.98	117.2
Canada	2.20	2.94	
Denmark	1.06	2.42	35.5
Finland	1.52	2.53	27.2
France	1.62	2.63	74.5
Germany	1.34	2.36	36.2
Greece	11.49	11.04	890.0
Ireland	4.52	5.59	334.5
Italy	2.60	3.80	188.0
Japan	0.30	1.14	67.6
Netherlands	1.43	2.51	43.6
New Zealand	4.55	5.25	60.3
Norway	2.65	3.39	23.2
Portugal	4.10	5.50	296.7
Spain	2.96	4.01	222.5
Sweden	1.97	2.49	35.5
Switzerland	0.67	1.25	41.0
United Kingdom	1.73	3.00	63.6
United States	1.49	2.70	44.7

Source: Bloomberg Finance L.P.

Municipal Debt

The $2.8 trillion U.S. municipal bond market consists of taxable and tax-exempt bonds. U.S. individuals and mutual funds (money market funds, bond funds, and closed-end funds) constitute the largest owners. This is depicted in Exhibit 4.9. Further, the municipal bonds can be classified as General Obligation (GO) bonds and revenue bonds. GO bonds are secured by the unlimited taxing power of the state and local governments. This means that if the municipality encounters financial problems it will need to raise taxes to repay the bondholders. In many states, such as California, the constitution demands that the bondholders of state-backed debt be paid back first before using money for any other purposes. Local governments back their GO debt with taxes from property. GO bonds are generally considered the safest form of municipal debt. The interest and principal repayments on the revenue bonds are backed by the revenues from the project being financed.

Examples of revenue bonds are Airport, Hospital, University, Industrial Development, Water and Sewer, and Toll Road. Unlike GO bonds, the revenue bonds are more risky as they are only supported by the revenues from the project. Revenue bonds issued for essential services such as water, sewer, and power are generally considered safer than non-essential service bonds. In 2009, $221 billion of municipal bonds were issued, 40 percent GO and 60 percent revenue bonds. The U.S. municipal bond market is entirely a domestic market. The primary motivation to hold this

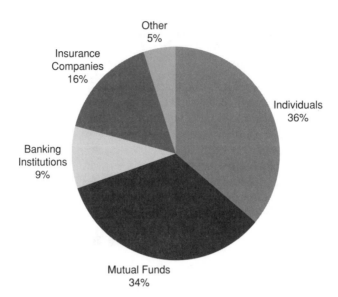

Exhibit 4.9 Municipal Debt Ownership Total Debt Outstanding: $2.8 Trillion
Source: SIFMA (http://www.sifma.org), with data from the Federal Reserve System.

debt is the exemption of U.S. federal taxes on the interest payment. The state taxes may also be exempt if the investor is a resident of the state issuing the bonds. Due to the tax-exempt status of municipal bonds they generally pay a lower interest rate compared to corporate bonds. The attractiveness of the debt is therefore a function of the marginal tax rate of an investor and other U.S. tax regulations.

Taxable municipal bonds had made up a very small fraction of total municipal bond issuance. However, this has changed since 2009 with the introduction of Build America Bonds (BABs). BABs are taxable municipal bonds that were authorized under the America Recovery and Reinvestment Act of 2009 and signed into law in February 2009. BABs can be direct pay or tax-credit BABs. They offer states and local governments an alternative to issuing tax-exempt municipal bonds. They cannot be used for refunding, working capital, private activities, or 501(c)(3) tax-exempt organizations. Since the interest on BABs is taxable, the interest rates are higher than tax-exempt municipal bonds. The federal government makes up for the lack of benefits associated with tax-exemption. In the case of direct pay BABs, the federal government provides a cash subsidy payment equal to 35 percent of their interest costs to issuers of BABs. The investors of tax-credit BABs receive a federal income tax credit equal to 35 percent of their BABs interest income. Since 2009, $130 billion of BABs have been issued. Most issuances have been direct pay BABs. California, Illinois, New York, and Texas have been the largest BABs issuers. This is depicted in Exhibit 4.10.

While U.S. Treasury securities have generally been considered a proxy for a risk-free asset, municipal bonds are not. Historically, municipal bond defaults have been low, and their ultimate recovery high. No state has defaulted on state GO municipal bonds since the Civil War. For instance, in the most notable default in 1994 by Orange County, California, the investors were paid back 100 percent with interest within 18 months. Most defaults were linked to poor debt management and

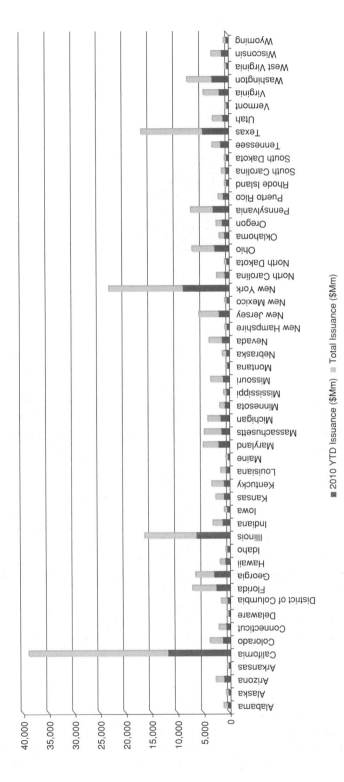

Exhibit 4.10 BABs Issuance by States

Source: Bloomberg Finance L.P.

Exhibit 4.11   Municipal Bond Default

	2008		2007		2006	
	# of Issue	Notional ($M)	# of Issue	Notional ($M)	# of Issue	Notional ($M)
Q1	21	862	11	113	20	542
Q2	52	1120	4	86	15	315
Q3	27	1225	4	33	9	62
Q4	36	4306	10	97	16	226
Total	136	7513	29	329	60	1145

Source: "Muni Bond Default Parade Plays On," January 15, 2009, Forbes.com.

financing arrangements. The default of municipal bonds was less of a consideration for the investor in the past, since many issuers insured their bonds against default with private insurance companies, such as MBIA, Ambac, or FIGIC. However, the municipal bond market is undergoing a regime shift following the 2008 credit crisis. With the demise of many bond insurers and the difficult fiscal position of many states, it is no longer a pure play on taxes and interest rates. The likelihood of a further increase in municipal bond defaults is making this a testing market for inexperienced investors. The current $3-billion-a-year collective default rate is three times the historic collective default rate of $1 billion or less a year going back to 1983. *Bloomberg Businessweek* reported that thirty-five municipal bond issues, totaling $1.5 billion, defaulted in 2010. It was 194 issues, totaling $6.9 billion, in 2009. (Default totals for some earlier years are depicted in Exhibit 4.11.) Macroeconomic conditions, credit analysis, and legal structure will all be equally important to evaluate the risk and rewards in this market.

Repurchase Agreements

A repurchase agreement or repo is a sale of a security combined with an agreement to repurchase the same security at a later date. A reverse repo is the other side of the transaction. Normally the repurchase price is higher than the sale price, and the difference represents the interest rate, known as the repo rate. A repo is thus similar to a collateralized lending, with the caveat that the title passes at the opening and the closing of the transaction. The passing of the title reduces counterparty risk for the lender of the cash against default events. While statistics on the total repo market are difficult to find, some estimate the U.S. repo market to be around $12 trillion. The Federal Reserve Bank of New York (FRBNY) reports the repo and reverse repo financing by primary dealers (see Exhibit 4.12).

Repos can be overnight, term (with a specified end date), or open (with no end date). They can also be classified as General Collateral (GC) or Specified Collateral (sometimes called specific collateral). In a GC, the lender of cash is willing to accept any of a variety of Treasury and other related securities as collateral. A specified collateral repo requires the borrower of cash to post a specific security as collateral. The repo rate for a specified collateral repo is always lower than the GC repo, and can even be negative if the security posted as collateral is in short supply.

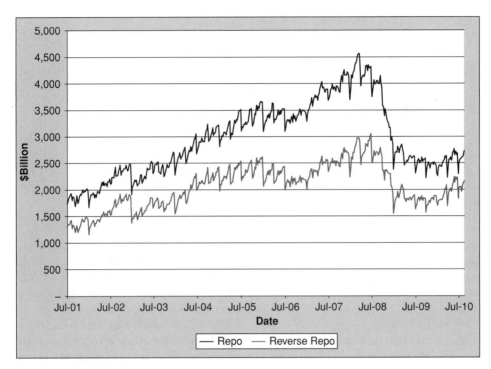

Exhibit 4.12 Primary Dealer Financing: Repo and Reverse Repo
Source: Federal Reserve Bank of New York.

A repo transaction can be executed as a bilateral repo or tri-party repo. In a bilateral repo, the counterparty borrows cash directly against a security, which is posted as collateral or via an executing broker. In a tri-party repo, a tri-party agent—normally a custodian bank—acts on behalf of the transacting parties to carry out the transaction requirements, such as settlement, margin maintenance, and collateral substitution. A tri-party repo reduces execution risk for lenders of cash and provides borrowers of cash greater flexibility with collateral substitution. Today, tri-party repos are the most prevalent form of repo contract in the United States. According to the Payments Risk Committee, FRBNY, as of Q1 2010, the U.S. tri-party repo market was estimated to be around $1.7 trillion, down from $2.8 trillion in early 2008. It is also a highly concentrated market with the top 10 cash borrowers accounting for 85 percent of the tri-party repo. The top 10 cash lenders provided 65 percent of the funds. Bilateral repos and tri-party repos are contrasted in Exhibits 4.13 and 4.14, respectively.

The repo is a money market instrument that plays a critical role in the efficient functioning of the bond market. It is the lifeline of modern financial markets, as it allows dealers and other market participants to access liquidity to finance their trading and risk-management activities. Underwriters of a new issue in government or corporate debt can hedge by taking an offsetting short position in an existing issue with similar risk. A liquid repo market allows the underwriter to borrow the security in the repo market and deliver against the short position. It also enables short sales by market participants. Central Banks use the repo market to add to

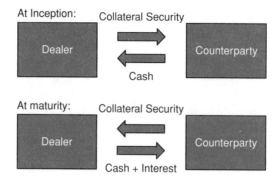

Exhibit 4.13   Bi-Lateral Repo

and withdraw reserves from the banking system to manage their monetary policy. During market turbulence, central banks have used repo markets to quickly pump liquidity into the financial system and control systemic risk. Recently, policy makers at the FRBNY have been testing the reverse repo as a potential tool to unwind the bank's massive liquidity infusion program following the 2008 credit crisis.

Due to the wider selection of collaterals that can be posted against a GC repo, these repos are uniform across financial institutions for each maturity and are closely correlated to unsecured money market rates. The specified repo rate on a specific security, on the other hand, can be lower than the GC repo rate. If so, the difference represents the implicit borrowing fee for the security, and the security is said to have been "on special." If the GC repo rate is low, then a security that has gone special can even have a negative repo rate. This allows holders of the security to earn excess return on their holdings. Negative repo rates for some securities are common during short squeezes. During a short squeeze there is heavy demand from short sellers to borrow the specified security for delivery against their short position. Negative repo rates can occur often in "on the run" government securities or "cheapest to deliver" bonds in the bond futures market.

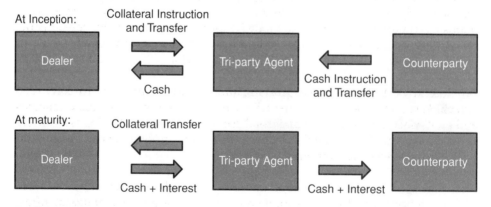

Exhibit 4.14   Tri-Party Repo

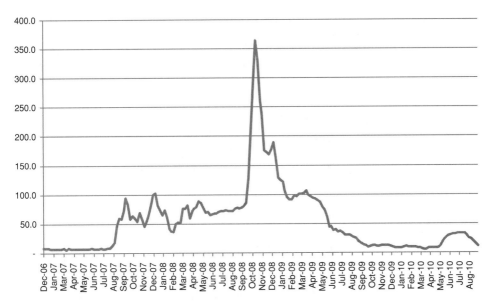

Exhibit 4.15   USD 3-Month Libor-OIS Spread
Source: Bloomberg Finance L.P.

Even though a repo is similar to secured lending it does not eliminate all credit risk. If the seller fails to fulfill his obligation at the repo's maturity to repurchase the security previously sold, the buyer may keep the security, and liquidate it to recover the cash. However, the buyer may incur a loss if, during this period, the security has lost value. To mitigate this risk repos are over collateralized (haircut), as well as subject to daily mark-to-market margining.

Since the repo market is a key provider of liquidity, its failure can cause a liquidity crisis. Gorton (2009) argued that the 2007 panic was caused by the repo market. He argues that until August 2007 the haircut on structured debt was close to zero. This went up to 45 percent by the end of 2007. The increase in haircut forced a massive deleveraging causing a panic in the market. A good barometer for the health of the repo market and its liquidity is the statistics on repo "fails" published by the FRBNY and the Libor-OIS spread. The Libor-OIS spread is the rate differential between the London Interbank Offered Rate (hereinafter LIBOR) and the overnight swap index. This unusual behavior of this spread is evident in Exhibit 4.15.

Recently, the FRBNY looked into the infrastructure supporting tri-party repo agreements. Subsequently they issued a white paper to discuss policy concerns and established a task force to address these concerns. The following issues were believed to have the potential to amplify instability in the financial system and cause severe market disruption:

- The markets' reliance on large amounts of intra-day credit made available to cash borrowers by the clearing banks that provided the operational infrastructure for the transactions.

- The risk management practices of cash lenders and clearing banks that were inadequate and vulnerable to pro-cyclical pressure.
- Lack of effective plans by market participants for managing the tri-party collaterals of a large securities dealer in default, without creating potentially destabilizing effects on the broader financial system.

The repo market is smaller today as the financial system de-leverages and market participants adjust their investment management practices.

DERIVATIVES MARKETS

Derivatives play a key role in fixed-income portfolio management. A derivative is a financial instrument (or contract between two parties) whose value is dependent upon, or derived from, the price of one or more "underlying" financial instruments. Institutional portfolio managers use derivatives to manage the overall risk and positioning of their portfolios. Dealers of derivative products offer investors customized solutions for their hedging needs. Some derivatives are structured to be tax efficient. Issuers use derivatives to manage their funding structure or hedge their issue risk.

Together, the cash and derivative markets offer traders seeking alpha opportunities a sizable investment universe. Most derivatives trade over-the-counter, but financial reforms, being put in place following the credit crisis in 2008, are beginning to transform this market with the expectation of a significant expansion of exchange involvement. Dealers in derivatives markets provide products with both simple and complex cash flows that are used by both portfolio managers and risk managers. According to the Bank for International Settlements (BIS), the total notional amount of interest rate contracts outstanding has grown from $50 trillion in 1998 to $449 trillion in 2009. This is a validation of the tremendous success and importance of these products in the global capital markets. The recent growth of the fixed income derivatives markets is depicted in Exhibit 4.16.

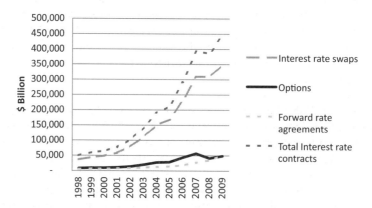

Exhibit 4.16   OTC Interest Rate Derivative Notional Outstanding
Source: BIS Quarterly Review, June 2010.

While the landscape of derivatives can be overwhelmingly complex for many investment professionals, the plain-vanilla products can accomplish most portfolio objectives. The liquidity and transparency of such products usually more than offset the additional structural benefits of the more complex instruments. The plain vanilla products include futures, swaps, swaptions, caps, and floors.

Interest Rate and Government Bond Futures

Interest Rate and Government bond futures provide market participants with liquid, standardized exchange-traded instruments to manage their interest rate risk.

Interest Rate Futures: These are obligations that commit market participants to lend or borrow a specified notional amount at a specified interest rate on a specified future date for a specified term. Buying an interest rate futures contract is equivalent to lending the notional amount, while selling an interest rate futures contract is equivalent to borrowing the notional amount. Eurodollar futures contracts, which trade on the Chicago Mercantile Exchange (CME), Euribor futures, which trade on the Euronext, Short Sterling futures, which trade on the London International Financial Futures, and Options Exchange (LIFFE), and Euroyen futures, which trade at the Tokyo Financial Exchange (TFX) are some of the major interest rate futures contracts traded globally.

Interest rate futures are quoted as 100, less the futures interest rate expressed on an annual basis. That is, the futures price rises when the rate goes down and declines when the rate goes up. For example, the 3-month Eurodollar futures traded on the CME indicate the 3-month rate on U.S. dollars deposited in commercial banks outside the United States (Eurodollar time deposit or LIBOR rate) at the final settlement date for the contract and quoted 100 less this rate. If the price today for December 2011 Eurodollar futures contract is 99.15 then it implies that the futures LIBOR rate for 3-months beginning December 2011 is 0.85 percent. The daily price fluctuations of a futures contract reflect the market expectations for the designated interest rate on the final settlement date. During the life of the futures contract, the futures rate will be less closely related to the current cash market interest rate and more closely related to the forward rate for the final settlement date. However, as the contract approaches the final settlement date, the futures rate begins to converge to the cash market interest rate. On the final settlement date, the futures rate will be exactly the same as the cash market interest rate. This convergence is guaranteed by the fact that the final settlement price of the Eurodollar futures contract is determined by the 3-month LIBOR cash market rate on the last day of the trading.

Government Bond Futures: A government bond futures contract is an obligation to take or to deliver—depending on whether one is long or short—a specified security at a future settlement date. Settlement can be with cash or delivery of the specific security, depending on the terms of the contract. Most traders will close their position by an offsetting transaction prior to the last trading date in the contract's life. However, if a deliverable contract remains open at the expiration of a contract, then it requires physical transfer of the security. Some of the leading government bonds futures contracts are: the U.S. Treasury note and bond futures (CBOT), U.K. Gilt futures (LIFFE), Japanese JGB futures (TSE), and the German Bobl, Schatz, and Bund futures (Eurex). The contract specifications for the various interest rate and bond futures that trade on the CBOT is given in Exhibit 4.17.

It is important to note that, due to the bond and note futures contract specifications, the buyer of a futures contract is simultaneously short several delivery options. In the case of U.S. Treasury futures, the seller of the futures contract can choose which bond to deliver (quality option), delay the delivery between the futures close and notification deadline (wildcard option), and switch the bond to be delivered between the futures close and the notice date (switch option).

Forward Rate Agreements and Interest Rate Swaps

Forward Rate Agreements (FRAs): These are contracts that pay or receive a fixed rate of interest on notional principal in exchange for receiving or paying the going Libor rate at a future point in time. The payment is made at the reset, but discounted from final maturity because the underlying cash instrument would be paid then. The market convention is to reference the purchaser of a FRA as the one paying the fixed rate. Note that, because of its structure, buying an interest rate future is equivalent to selling an FRA with the same International Monetary Market (IMM) dates.

Interest Rate Swaps: Interest rate swaps are agreements between two counterparties to exchange one stream of interest payments for another stream of interest payments. The interest payments are calculated based on a specified notional principal with typically no exchange of this notional principal. The most common interest rate swap involves the exchange of a fixed interest payment for a floating interest rate payment based on a reference rate (such as LIBOR). An interest rate swap agreement wherein the counterparty receives a fixed interest rate and pays a floating interest rate has a position equivalent to the economic risk of purchasing a bond.

There are many varieties of interest rate swaps that are considered exotic instruments. A callable swap allows one of the counterparties to cancel the swap. Effectively it is a swap with an embedded swaption. Another variant is the switchable swap. It is like the callable swap except the terms of the swap are changed rather than cancelled. For example, a counterparty can switch a floating leg to a fixed leg. The change of terms in callable swaps and switchable swaps is discretionary, whereas in the case of trigger swaps it is specified. For instance, the swap changes if the LIBOR on any roll day exceeds a specified level.

The standard LIBOR fixed-for-float interest rate swap is priced such that the present value of the fixed payment is equal to the present value of the floating rate payment. The discount rate for discounting the cash flows and the floating rate (or forward rate) is obtained from the swap yield curve. Since interest rate swaps are OTC instruments,[1] it exposes the involved parties to counterparty credit risk. The absence of any exchange of principal lowers this risk. Additionally, the terms of the contract specify margining requirements that further mitigate this counterparty credit risk. Historically, USD interest rate swap rates have been quoted at a spread over Treasury yields of the same maturity. This is called a swap spread. The spread has been viewed as a reflection of the credit risk premium on the banking system. However, swap spreads are not the same across currencies. Therefore the idea that swap spreads reflect the banking credit risk has been a less than satisfactory

Exhibit 4.17 CBOT Interest Rate and Treasury Futures Contract Specifications

Product	Underlying Instrument	Contract Size	Last Trading Day	Contract Months
Short Term Interest Rates				
Eurodollar	Eurodollar Time Deposit, 3-month maturity	$1,000,000	2nd London bank business day prior to 3rd Wednesday of contract month (11:00 A.M. GMT)	40 Quarters (10 years)
30-day Federal Funds	Avg. overnight Fed. Funds Rate for the contract month	$5,000,000	Last business day of delivery month (4:00 P.M. EST)	24 months
3-month OIS	Compounded daily effective Fed. Funds rate 3-month reference quarter	$1,000,000	Last day of reference quarter (4:00 P.M.) EST	Eight quarterly months
1-month Eurodollar	Eurodollar Time Deposit, 1-month maturity	$3,000,000	2nd London bank business day prior to 3rd Wednesday of contract month (11:00 A.M. GMT)	First 12 calendar months
Treasuries				
2-year U.S. Treasury Note	ORIGINAL MATURITY: ≤ 5 years, 3 months. REMAINING MATURITY: ≥ 1 year, 9 months from first day and ≤ 2 years from last day.	$200,000	Last business day of the contract month (12:01 P.M.)	Five quarterly months
3-year U.S. Treasury Note	ORIGINAL MATURITY: ≤ 5 years, 3 months. REMAINING MATURITY: ≥ 2 years, 9 months from first day and ≤ 3 years from last day.	$200,000	Last business day of the contract month (12:01 P.M.)	Five quarterly months
5-year U.S. Treasury Note	ORIGINAL MATURITY: ≤ 5 years, 3 months. REMAINING MATURITY: ≥ 4 years, 2 months from first day	$100,000	Last business day of the contract month (12:01 P.M.)	Five quarterly months
10-year U.S. Treasury Note	ORIGINAL MATURITY: ≤ 10 years. REMAINING MATURITY: ≥ 6 years, 6 months from first day.	$100,000	7th business day prior to last business day of contract month (12:01 P.M.)	Five quarterly months
U.S. Treasury Bond	REMAINING MATURITY: ≥ 15 years from first day.*	$100,000	7th business day prior to last business day of contract month (12:01 P.M.)	Three quarterly months
Long-Term "Ultra" U.S. Treasury Bond	REMAINING MATURITY: ≥ 25 years from first day.	$100,000	7th business day prior to last business day of contract month (12:01 P.M.)	Three quarterly months

*Effective with the March 2011 expiry, the underlying instruments for Treasury Bond futures will include bonds with remaining terms to maturity of at least 15 years, but less than 25 years.
Source: CME.

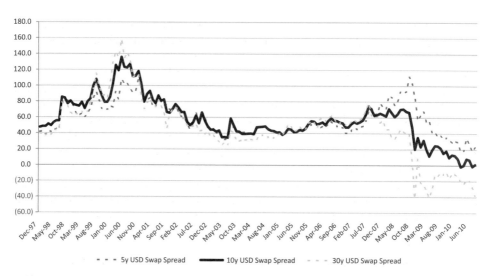

Exhibit 4.18 USD Swap Spreads, December 1997–August 2010
Source: Bloomberg Finance L.P.

explanation. Much has been debated and written about the rationale for USD swap spreads to be wider than EUR swap spreads when the same financial institutions dominate both these markets. The difference has been explained based on technical factors and differences in the financing activities of the corporate sector in the US and Europe. If there is one fact that has been accepted uniformly, it is that the swap spread would be positive. The collapse of Long-Term Capital Management in 1998 was a painful lesson for some on the dangers of hedging interest rate risk by shorting Treasuries. The hedging strategy failed in 1998 as a flight to quality resulted in Treasuries rallying while the swap spread widened. As a result, there has been a migration from Treasuries to interest rate swaps for hedging interest rate risk.

However, after the September 2008 bankruptcy of Lehman, the market behavior of the swap spread changed significantly. The USD 5-year, 10-year, and 30-year swap spreads reacted very differently in the months after the bankruptcy of Lehman, and they now trade at very different levels. The five-year swap spread widened and subsequently declined. The 10-year and 30-year swap spreads, instead of widening, declined, and have traded down. In August 2008 the 5-year, 10-year, and 30-year swap spreads were around 93bps, 68bps, and 40bps, respectively. At the end of August 2010 these were at 23bps, 1bps, and -38bps. These low, even unthinkable, negative swap spreads for the 30-year, were initially viewed as a short-term phenomenon driven by technical factors, such as the unwinding of relative value trades, and other duration hedging activities by institutional investors. But, as of the time of this writing, this condition has not changed and it is unclear if it will continue. The August 2010 swap spreads are depicted in Exhibit 4.18.

Options

Interest Rates Futures Options: These are exchange-traded options on interest rate futures contracts (e.g., Eurodollar futures). A call option gives its holder the right, but not the obligation, to buy the underlying futures contract while the put option gives its holder the right, but not the obligation, to sell the underlying futures contract. An American-style contract allows the exercise of the option at any time on or before the expiration date, whereas a European-style contract can only be exercised on the expiration date. The buyer of a call option in effect has the right to establish a long position in the underlying futures contract, while the buyer of a put option has the right to establish a short position in the underlying futures contract. The price at which the option holder can exercise his option to buy or sell is referred to as the strike price. Since the futures price moves inversely with the interest rate, the purchaser of a call option will profit when the interest rate declines further than the rate implied by the strike price. Similarly, a holder of a put option will gain when the interest rate rises more than the rate implied by the strike price. Options can be traded on the Eurodollar, the Euribor, the Euroyen, and short Sterling futures contracts. Generally these options are American-style.

Bond Futures Options: Similar to interest rate futures options, the bond futures options are exchange-traded options on government bond futures contracts. The option can be a call or a put option and are generally American-style.

Caps and Floors: A caplet is a call option on an FRA, that is the right to pay fixed at the expiration date. A floorlet is a put option on an FRA. Caps and floors are collections of consecutive caplets/floorlets with each caplet/floorlet being independently exercisable. A long cap position pays out when the rate is above the cap rate. This is similar to a put option on a bond. Similarly, a long position in a floor pays out when the rate is below the floor rate, which is similar to a call option on a bond.

Swaptions: The European swaption is the right to enter into an interest rate swap at an agreed-upon fixed interest rate on the expiration date of the contract. The right to pay a fixed interest rate is called a payer swaption, and the right to receive a fixed interest rate is called a receiver swaption. It is important to distinguish caps and floors from swaptions. Caps and floors are portfolios of options on FRAs, while swaptions are options on portfolios of FRAs.

The derivatives markets are undergoing dramatic changes as market participants and regulators globally respond with reforms. The traditionally over-the-counter derivative market is moving to exchanges. Under the Dodd-Frank Wall Street Reform and Consumer Protection Act passed by U.S. lawmakers, plain-vanilla swaps must be cleared through a registered clearinghouse and executed on a registered trading platform, that is, exchanges. Only non-financial entities will be exempt from clearing requirements, provided that they are not "major swap participants," use the swaps to hedge commercial risks, and are able to meet their financial obligations. The swaps include commodity, credit, currency, equity, interest rate, and foreign exchange swaps. The margin and capital requirements for major swap participants will be set higher by the regulators. Additionally, there will be more extensive reporting requirements on swap activities. This is a significant change for the derivative market that has caused considerable anxiety as the market awaits more clarity. The silver lining in all this is that it will bring much-needed transparency and stability to the derivatives markets. The benefits of derivative products include the ability to effectively hedge portfolio risks, manage asset-liability risks, and reposition portfolios efficiently. The derivatives markets are, and undoubtedly will continue to be, an integral part of investing, hedging, and debt issuance for financial and non-financial entities alike.

PRICE–YIELD RELATIONSHIP

The relationship between a bond's price and its yield is nonlinear and can further vary depending on the terms of the security. For a bond with no embedded option this can be expressed as follows:

$$Price = \sum_{i=1}^{N} \frac{C}{(1 + \alpha(t_{i-1}, t_i) \times y)^{t_i}} + \frac{Par}{(1 + y)^{t_N}}$$

where C is the coupon, $\alpha(t_{i-1}, t_i)$ is the accrual factor between time t_i and t_{i-1}, y is the bond's yield, Par is the principal, and t_N is the maturity in years. Macaulay (1938) proposed duration as a measure for the price volatility of a bond investment. (Note that the price equation above and the Macaulay duration equation below are both assuming that there is only one coupon payment per year.)

$$D_{Macaulay} = \frac{\sum_{i=1}^{N} \frac{t_i C}{(1 + \alpha(t_{i-1}, t_i) \times y)^{t_i}} + \frac{t_N Par}{(1 + y)^{t_N}}}{Price}$$

Macaulay's Duration measures the average life of a bond investment where the weight is the present value of each cash flow divided by the price of the bond. The concept of duration has since been modified and interpreted as price sensitivity of a bond to a change in its yield. Below is the relationship between Modified Duration and Macaulay's Duration. (Note: frequency refers to the number of coupon payments per year. If the bond paid semiannually, for example, the frequency would be 2.)

$$D_{Modified} = \frac{1}{\left(1 + \frac{y}{frequency}\right)} D_{Macaulay}$$

Market convention uses the term "duration" to refer to modified duration. Mathematically, duration is the linear approximation or the first-order effects of the price yield curve. Higher coupon bonds have a lower duration compared to lower coupon bonds for the same maturity. Longer maturity bonds have a higher duration than shorter maturity bonds. Another important bond attribute is "Convexity." It is the change in duration as the yield changes. Convexity is the quadratic term or the second-order effects of the price-yield relationship. Convexity captures the curvature of the price-yield curve. The relationship between the change in the price of a bond, P, and a change in its yield, y, can be approximated by the first and second terms of a Taylor series expansion.

$$\frac{\Delta P}{P} = \frac{1}{P} \frac{dP}{dy} \Delta y + \frac{1}{2} \frac{1}{P} \frac{d^2 P}{dy^2} (\Delta y)^2 + error$$

For a small change in yield we can ignore the error term and rewrite the above expression as follows:

$$\frac{\Delta P}{P} = -duration \; \Delta y + \frac{1}{2} convexity \; (\Delta y)^2$$

For a bond with no embedded options, the bond's price is negatively related to its yield and has positive convexity. Positive convexity means that for a given change in yield, a bond's price increases more when the yield declines than when the yield rises. Coupon, maturity, call, put, and sinking fund features can change the degree of convexity, and change it from positive to negative. Bonds that are callable will display negative convexity in some regions, since the call option limits price appreciation when yields decline. The duration and dispersion of cash flow determines the level of convexity. The convexity of a non-callable bond is proportional to the square of its duration, and it is higher when the dispersion of cash flow is higher. Therefore, long-term bonds are more convex than short-term bonds. Among a portfolio of bonds with the same duration, the zero-coupon bond will have the least convexity since it has no cash flow dispersion. Positive convexity is a desirable property since it can enhance returns. This bias is reflected in market prices, and its value depends on yield volatility. Understanding both duration and convexity is important in bond portfolio management. For example, a barbell portfolio of short-term and long-term zero-coupon bonds with more dispersed cash flow has more convexity than a similar duration, intermediate term, zero-coupon bond.

The price-yield curves for several U.S. Treasury bonds with different coupon rates and maturity are depicted in Exhibit 4.19. As the yield declines, the UST 3.5% 2/15/2039, the lowest coupon bond, begins to increase more rapidly than the others. On the other hand, as yield increases, the lowest coupon-paying bond's price declines more than the price of the higher coupon-paying bond.

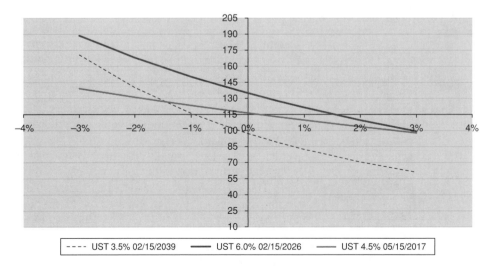

Exhibit 4.19 Bond Price versus Yield

Not all bonds have fixed interest cash flows with a bullet maturity. The terms of a bond can include floating rate payments, step-up or step-down coupon payments, sinking fund and amortization schedules, call provisions (callable), or put provisions (putable). Duration and convexity can be difficult to calculate analytically, given the possibility of a variety of bond payment terms and embedded options. Moreover, the analytical calculation is accurate only for a small change in yield and not practical for a large portfolio of bonds. Therefore, in practice, duration and convexity are estimated numerically by changing the yields and repricing the bonds. This process then allows for inclusion of the effects of non–plain vanilla features, such as optionality. The resultant measures are called effective duration and effective convexity.

$$D_{Effective} = \frac{1}{P(y^0)} \left(\frac{P(y^-) - P(y^*)}{y^+ - y^-} \right)$$

$$C_{Effective} = \left(\frac{P(y^+) + P(y^-) - 2P(y^0)}{P(y^0)(y^+ - y^-)^2} \right)$$

where $P(y^0)$ is the current price at yield y^0, $P(y^+)$ is the bond price when yield increases to y^+ and $P(y^-)$ is the bond price when yield decreases to y^-. This is simply a numerical method to estimate first- and second-order derivatives (in the mathematical sense of a derivative). Exhibit 4.20 below shows the effective duration, the effective convexity, and the change in price for various changes in yield for a portfolio of U.S. Treasury bonds. The duration of the UST 3.5% 2/15/2039 bond is 17.17, meaning that for a 100bps change in yield the price will change by 17.17 percent. Its convexity is 4.03, which implies that for a 100bps change in yield the convexity will add another 2.01 percent price change.

The duration and convexity of a portfolio can be estimated by using the change in value of the entire portfolio. For a small change, in yield the estimated price

Exhibit 4.20   Duration and Convexity for a Sample of U.S. Treasuries

CUSIP	Coupon Rate	Current Price	Maturity Date	Yield	Effective Duration	Effective Convexity
UST 3.5% 2/15/2039	3.50	97.25	2/15/2039	3.69	17.17	4.06
UST 6.0% 2/15/2026	6.00	6.00	2/15/2026	3.16	10.70	1.46
UST 4.5% 5/15/2017	4.50	116.34	5/15/2017	1.91	5.83	0.40

CUSIP	Down 300bps	Down 200bps	Down 100bps	Down 50bps	Current Price	Up 50bps	Up 100bps	Up 200bps	Up 300bps
UST 3.5% 2/15/2039	170.73	140.05	116.09	106.11	97.25	89.37	82.35	70.49	60.99
UST 6.0% 2/15/2026	188.62	168.16	150.38	142.38	134.91	127.93	121.41	109.61	99.27
UST 4.5% 5/15/2017	139.17	131.02	123.43	119.82	116.34	112.97	109.71	103.53	97.75

change, using duration and convexity as the basis for the estimate, will be close to the actual change. However, as the change in yield gets larger, the estimation error can increase considerably.

Duration and convexity are useful tools for government bond futures trading. Government bond futures generally permit the delivery of bonds within a range of maturities. This is known as the deliverable basket. For example, the 10-year U.S. Treasury bond futures permit delivery of coupon-bearing U.S. Treasuries with remaining term to maturity of at least 6.5 to 10 years from the first day of the delivery month. Since many bonds are available for delivery, the exchange homogenizes it with the use of a fixed conversion factor. The conversion factor for the 10-year U.S. Treasury bond is determined so that if every bond eligible for delivery yielded 6 percent, then there would be no preference for delivering any particular bond. The invoice price for the futures contract at the last settlement date is the futures settlement price, times a conversion factor, plus accrued interest. Since it is unlikely that all bonds in the market yield 6 percent, the further the market is away from 6 percent the less effective the homogenization becomes. The bond that is cheapest to deliver, known as the CTD bond, has the lowest basis. Basis is the price of a deliverable bond less the futures invoice price. Net basis is basis less carry, where carry is the bond coupon plus accrued interest, less the funding cost. The funding cost is determined by the repo rate. The duration and convexity of each bond in the basket is important in determining which deliverable bond could become the cheapest to deliver under different rate scenarios. This is the key to understanding a complex and highly sophisticated form of fixed income trading known as basis trading.

Exhibit 4.21 shows the price changes for two deliverable bonds normalized by their respective conversion factors. When the yield declines, the low-duration bond becomes more attractive to deliver. High-duration bonds are attractive to

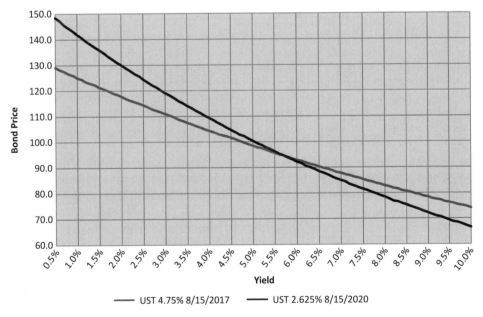

Exhibit 4.21   U.S. Treasury Bond Price Yield Normalized by Conversion Factor

deliver when yields rise. The shape of the yield curve (to be discussed later) will also affect the relative cheapness. If the yield curve steepens as yield falls, then, this will offset some of the incentive to deliver the low-duration bond. Similarly, if the yield curve flattens as yield rises, the incentive to deliver high-duration bonds will be somewhat offset. If the yield curve is inverted, then shorter-maturity bonds will be cheaper to deliver.

THE YIELD CURVE

Term Structure

The term structure of interest rates, commonly referred to as the "yield curve," describes the relationship between the market yield and maturity for securities with a similar credit risk. Typically, the yield curve is upward-sloping. That is, long-term rates are higher than short-term rates. The upward-sloping yield curve has been rationalized based on several plausible explanations including (1) a liquidity risk premium for investing longer term, (2) a term risk premium for higher volatility assets, and (3) inflationary expectations. An inverted yield curve has generally been viewed as a precursor of recession.

The yield curve plays a central role in the valuation, trading, and risk management of fixed income portfolios. The yield curve has embedded in it the consensus market views on the economy, inflation expectation, risk premia, and demand/supply imbalances. Several trading strategies and portfolio actions are driven by views on the current and future shape of the yield curve. The yield curve is essential to the valuation and hedging of fixed income assets. Since a fixed income portfolio pays out a stream of cash flows, a more appropriate gauge of its interest rate sensitivity is the "Key Rate Duration." The key rate duration for a bond is the price sensitivity of the bond to different points on the yield curve. This is done by changing the rates at different points along the yield curve and repricing the bond. Embedded in the yield curve is the market's implied forward rate curve, which is the short-term rate at various forward dates. Trading in futures and interest rate swaps is motivated by a trader's views on the implied forward curve.

Exhibit 4.22 depicts the yield curves for the United States, the European Union, the United Kingdom, and Japan based on benchmark government bonds. The money market deposit and LIBOR swap rates for USD, EUR, JPY, and GBP are shown in Exhibit 4.23. These quoted market rates are only indicative of the interest rate term structure and not applicable for many trading decisions and valuations. More precise and accurate information on the yield curve is needed. This is done by building the discount curve, par curve, zero-coupon curve, and forward rate curve from the quoted market rates. The discount curve indicates the discount rate for discounting cash flow at future dates, while the par curve represents the yields on bonds issued at par at different maturity dates. The zero-coupon curve, also known as the spot rate curve, represents the yields on zero coupon bonds for different maturity dates. The forward rate curve shows the implied forward rates for specific terms at different dates in the future. These curves are related to one another and can be viewed as just alternate representation of the same information. It is also important to note that the expected interest rates implied by these curves (particularly the forward curve) are unique in that they are the prevailing rate

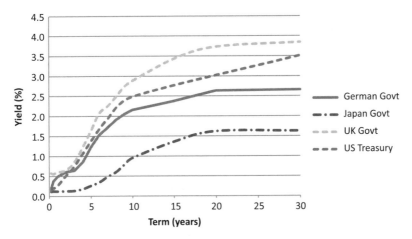

Exhibit 4.22   Benchmark Government Bond Yield Curve, August 16, 2010

currently offered by the market and can be locked-in. This can be done with a FRA or with an interest rate futures contract. In the LIBOR swap market, the method used to construct the yield curve is called bootstrapping the yield curve, and in the government bond market it is called the fitted yield curve.

Bootstrapping the Yield Curve

Bootstrapping the yield curve (also called zero coupon stripping) refers to a process whereby each data point along the yield curve is generated progressively, so that it is consistent with the market interest rates used as inputs. The LIBOR swap curve is built by splicing together rates from multiple markets and instruments.

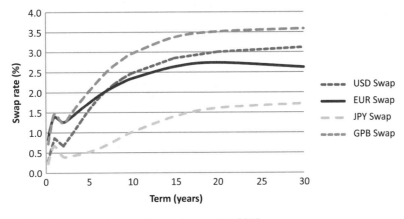

Exhibit 4.23   Deposit and Swap Rates, August 16, 2010

The selection of markets and instruments depends on the purpose and currency, but it is generally built using a combination of money market deposit rates, interest rate futures prices, and swap rates. Since the objective of building the yield curve is to derive the term structure of interest rates for trading, hedging, and valuation purposes, a prudent rule to follow is to use the rates and prices that are the most liquid and actively traded in the market as input quotes. It is common to use money market deposit rates from overnight to the first few weeks or months, followed by interest rate futures for several quarters, depending on market liquidity, and, finally, the swap rate.

The extraction of the discount factor from the deposit rate is the most straightforward, due to the simplicity of the money market instrument.

$$Z(t_0, t_1) = \frac{1}{(1 + r(t_1) \alpha(t_0, t_1))}$$

where t_0 is the current date, $Z(t_0, t_1)$ is the discount factor for time t_1, $r(t_1)$ is the deposit rate for time t_1, and $\alpha(t_0, t_1)$ is the interest-accrual factor based on the day count convention for the interest rate.

The relationship between discount rate and forward rate can be summarized as follows:

$$Z(t_0, t_2) = Z(t_0, t_1) \frac{1}{(1 + f(t_1, t_2) \alpha(t_1, t_2))}$$

where $f(t_1, t_2)$ is the forward rate between time t_1 and t_2. If the discount factor to time t_1 is known, and the forward rate between time t_1 and t_2 is known, then the discount factor for time t_2 can be calculated. The forward rate can be calculated from the futures prices. If, as a quick approximation, the forward rate can be assumed to be equal to the futures rate, then it is simply 100 less the futures price. However, if one would like to be more precise, then the futures rate needs to be adjusted for convexity bias to derive the forward rate. Convexity bias arises since the futures contract is settled daily and is linear with respect to the interest rate whereas a FRA is non-linear with respect to the interest rate (due to the discounting mechanism) and settled at maturity. Due to this difference in the settlement procedure, there is an advantage to consistently short the FRA and hedge it with a short futures contract. This is recognized by the market and reflected in the market prices of the futures contract. The convexity bias is small for near-dated futures contracts but can be larger for far-dated contracts. The convexity bias will result in the futures rate being adjusted downwards, and depends on the volatility of the forward rate, and the correlation between the forward rate and the zero-coupon bond price at the maturity of the forward rate. Each discount factor can be progressively calculated with the help of the above expression until all futures prices have been used.

The par swap rate, $S(t_0, t_n)$, for time t_n, can be linked to the discount factors as below:

$$S(t_0, t_n) = \frac{1 - Z(t_0, t_n)}{\sum_1^n \alpha(t_{i-1}, t_i) Z(t_{i-1}, t_i)}$$

Alternatively,

$$Z(t_0, t_n) = \frac{1 - S(t_0, t_n) \sum_1^{n-1} Z(t_{i-1}, t_i)}{1 + \alpha(t_{i-n}, t_i) S(t_0, t_n)}$$

If all the discount factors up to time t_{n-1} are known then, using the swap rate for time t_n, we can determine the discount factor for $Z(t_0, t_n)$ for time t_n.

Since the market may not trade all points on the yield curve, any deposit rate or swap rate that is needed for building the curve, but not quoted, must be interpolated from the other quoted market rates. The interpolation techniques used to stitch the curve between deposit rates and futures rates and determining any unknown swap rates is important, so as to obtain a smooth yield curve or smooth forward curve.

With the discount curve, it is now possible to calculate the zero-coupon curve, forward curve, and par curve. The discount curve can be directly used in discounted cash flow models to value other financial instruments. Examples are depicted in Exhibit 4.24.

Perhaps the most important perspective on the market can be obtained by looking at the forward curve. The forward curve shows the evolution of the yield curve as implied by the current market yield curve. Exhibit 4.25 depicts the current versus implied forward curve for USD for December 2010 and March 2011. This indicates that the market is expecting short-term rates to rise by around 60bps and the yield curve to flatten slightly. If a trader believes that the rates will increase significantly more, or if he expects the curve to flatten more significantly, then he can execute transactions in the cash and/or derivative market to monetize the view.

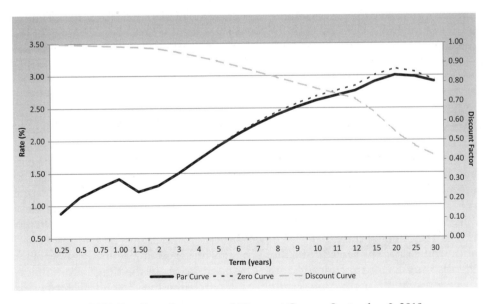

Exhibit 4.24 USD Par, Zero-Coupon, and Discount Curves, September 3, 2010

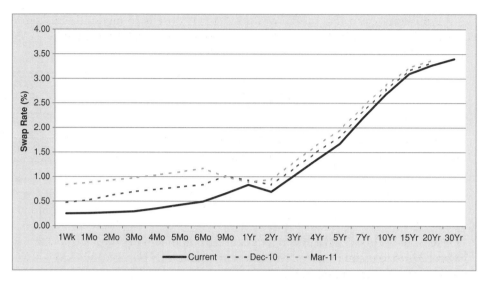

Exhibit 4.25   USD Forward Curve, September 3, 2010

Fitted Yield Curve

The bond market trades a wide range of bonds that differ in their coupons, payment dates, and maturities. Unlike the swap market, which quotes uniform rates for any specific term, the prices of bonds for any maturity can differ widely due to differences in liquidity, coupon, and other factors. Therefore, in the bond market, a fitting algorithm is needed to construct a yield curve. The motivation for bootstrapping the yield curve in the swap market was driven by the need to gain an insight into the market's implied expectations and for the valuation of many OTC products. The objective of the fitted yield curve in the bond market is for time series analysis of the yield curve and rich/cheap analysis of the bonds for relative-value trading strategies. The fitting algorithm is useful in identifying bonds that are significant outliers compared to historical norms. A bootstrapping algorithm guaranteeing that the constructed yield will recover the bond prices is not desirable if there is recognition that technical factors in the market can distort some bond prices. The objective is to apply a consistent methodology to identify the outliers for trading purposes.

    The fitting algorithm for bond yield curves can be distinguished by those that fit the bond yields and those that fit the market prices. The models that fit the yield specify a functional form for the yield curve and use a least squares method to estimate the coefficient of the function that can best fit the bond yield used in the sample. The methodology, with a suitable function, can produce a smooth yield curve but can still be theoretically unsound. The biggest objection to this approach is that it does not require that cash flows occurring at the same date be discounted at the same rate. The price-fitting model begins by specifying a functional form for the discount factor function, and uses the bond prices in the sample to estimate the coefficient of the function. Further, constraints that the discount factor be one at time zero, and be downward sloping with respect to time, can be explicitly incorporated.

A simple function that works well for this purpose is to model the discount curve as a linear combination of m basis functions where each basis function is an exponential function. In this approach, the discount factor at time t_n is

$$Z(t_0, t_n) = \sum_{k=1}^{m} a_k \left(e^{-bt_n}\right)^k$$

where a_k and b are the unknown coefficients to be estimated. Since the discount factor is one at time zero the following constraint can be derived:

$$Z(t_0, t_0) = 1 = \sum_{k=1}^{m} a_k$$

A reasonably good fitting yield curve can be obtained with five basis functions. The procedure to estimate the coefficients for a sample of bonds can be done with ordinary least-squares regression.

INTEREST RATE MODELS

Interest rate models are important for managing interest rate risk and for the valuation of securities. Interest rate modeling can be viewed from two different perspectives depending on the market. Fixed income cash bond portfolio managers have an interest in the statistical modeling of the time series properties of interest rates for predictive purposes. Volatility and correlation are estimated using observed market data. Often, techniques such as principal component analysis are used to explain the movements in the yield curve. In the interest rate derivatives market, on the other hand, the preferred approach to modeling interest rates is to derive it from market prices. Volatility and correlation are implied from the prices of liquid plain-vanilla derivative products.

Black-Scholes (1973) pioneered the approach to pricing derivative securities. If the terminal payoffs of a derivative security can be perfectly replicated then, under no-arbitrage conditions, the value of the derivative security should be the same as the value of the replicating strategy. This was the main principle behind their pricing equation for an equity call option. Their model assumed that the underlying stock price follows a lognormal distribution. The Black-Scholes intuition of perfect replication continues to be the fundamental principle behind the design and valuation of derivative securities in the market. Another perspective on the Black-Scholes approach is the principle of "risk-neutral" valuation. Since a derivative instrument's payoff can be perfectly replicated, it is valid to assume a market that is risk-neutral, that is, indifferent to individual risk preferences. The value of a derivative instrument, therefore, is the present value of the expected payoffs where the expected payoffs are determined according to the risk-neutral distribution and discounted by the risk-free rate. A few years after the Black-Scholes seminal paper was published, Black (1976) presented a modified approach to price options on futures. This model assumes that futures prices are lognormally distributed. This model has been used by the market to value options on interest rate futures, options on bond futures, caps, floors, and swaptions. From a strictly theoretical perspective, the use of the Black (1976) model to price all these instruments is inconsistent. A lognormal forward rate is not consistent with a lognormal swap rate. Likewise, a lognormal bond price is not consistent with a lognormal swap rate. The market is fully aware of these inconsistencies and reflects them in the volatilities used to price these instruments using the Black model. Therefore, in the plain vanilla interest rate derivative markets, the model simply acts as a way to translate price into implied volatilities.

Options embedded in bonds or in derivative securities with a more complex payoff cannot always be priced with the Black model. A more explicit model for the evolution of interest rates is needed to price these securities. These interest rate models follow the basic principle of the Black-Scholes model, namely, a no-arbitrage principle. However, they also bring other elements unique to interest rates, such as mean reversion. The early models for interest rate derivatives were called the short-rate models. These models began with an assumption of a stochastic process for instantaneous short rates. The models are designed to be consistent with today's term structure of interest rates. Hence they are also called no-arbitrage models. Ho and Lee (1986), Hull, and White (1990), Black, Derman and Toy (1990), and Black and Karasinski (1991) are some examples of short-rate models. The consistency of these models to the options market is achieved by calibrating the model. The models are used to price calibrating instruments (generally plain-vanilla swaptions or caps and floors) and parameters estimated so it can best fit the price of the calibrating instruments.

The next-generation models moved away from modeling the short rate and switched to modeling the entire term structure of interest rates. An early pioneer of this approach was the model by Heath, Jarrow, and Morton (1992) (HJM). They proposed a model for the evolution of a continuum of forward rates. The volatilities of the forward rates and correlations between them are left as exogenous inputs. The covariance function and the initial yield curve are the only inputs. The problem with HJM is that a continuum of instantaneous forward rates does not exist. The market is liquid only in certain instruments and at certain maturities. HJM does not have a satisfactory analytical solution and the numerical simulation can be computationally demanding. The Brace, Gatarek, and Musiela (1997) (BGM) model is a practical, discrete-time implementation of an HJM-type model. The BGM model considers a set of consecutive forward LIBOR rates and assumes that they follow a log-normal distribution. Since the assumption of log-normal forward rates is in keeping with the market convention of using the Black model to price vanilla options, market volatility can be employed directly as an input into the model.

Interest rate derivative models are complex, therefore their calibration is an essential part of model development. It is critical to understand the objective of calibration. Since the model is used not only for valuation but also for hedging, it is necessary that the model not only recover the market price, but that it is also able to track the evolution of volatility and correlation in the market.

Trading Strategies

The breadth and depth of fixed income markets offers investors opportunities to implement a variety of strategies to exploit their views and observations on the market. Two common strategies are government bond basis trading and curve trading.

Government Bond Basis Trading: Basis trading is the buying (selling) of government bonds and the simultaneous selling (buying) of government bond futures. A trade that involves buying the government bond in the cash market and selling the bond futures contract is referred to as "going long the basis." The opposite strategy is referred to as "going short the basis." When the basis is tight, long basis trades can be profitable. When the basis is wide, short basis trades can be profitable. It is unusual to have a negative basis. If the basis were to become negative, a trader could realize arbitrage profits by buying the cash bond and delivering it against the futures contract. The risk and return of such a trade is generally very low and requires a lot of capital.

A trader would normally employ a lot of leverage to improve the return on capital from such trades. Changes in repo rate, yield curve, and supply factors are important determinants of basis. Another key determinant for changes in basis is the conversion factor used by exchanges to adjust the futures invoice price for each bond in the deliverable basket. The futures invoice price of any two deliverable bonds always moves at a fixed ratio based on the conversion factor; it does not change as the bond prices changes. As the market moves away from par, the conversion factor begins to disproportionately affect the basis of each bond. When the price rises, the price of the high coupon (low duration) bond will change less than the low coupon (high duration) bond with the same maturity. The reverse is true when the bond price declines. Since the conversion factor does not change, this cheapens the high coupon/low duration bonds in a rally. During a sell-off, the low coupon/high duration bonds become cheaper. Basis trading is not without risks. Due to the high leverage employed by the strategy, it is subject to significant risk if the repo counterparty fails to deliver.

Curve Trading: The U.S. bond markets offer many kinds of inter- and intra-market spread-trading opportunities. The on-the-run versus off-the-run spreads involve trading the benchmark bond against an older bond with similar maturity. In the case of a swap spread trade, a bond is traded against a swap. In contrast, curve trading involves trading the slope and the shape of the yield curve.

The classic trade is the curve steepener or curve flattener. Exhibit 4.26 depicts the 10-year and 2-year U.S. Treasury bond spread along with a recession indicator. Historically, the slope of the curve has been a function of the strength of the economy and Fed actions. Policy rate cuts by the Fed have been accompanied by a steepening of the yield curve while rate hikes have been accompanied by a flattening of the yield curve. A curve steepener involves shorting a longer-dated bond against a shorter-dated bond. (That is, you go short on the long-maturity bond and long the short-maturity bond.) The weights of the long position and short position are selected so as to be duration-neutral, but the position may have convexity risk. Another type of curve trade is based on views about the curvature of the yield curve. This involves going long on both a short-maturity bond and a long-maturity bond, while simultaneously going short on an intermediate-maturity bond. This is called a butterfly strategy. The weight on the bonds can be adjusted to be duration-neutral or dollar-neutral.

Consider, for example, the spread between the yields on the 5-year and 30-year U.S. Treasuries. (These are depicted in Exhibit 4.27.) The spread that was close to flat in December 2006 is at 230bps in September 2009. If a trader believes that the curve will flatten, he can sell the 5-year bond and buy the 30-year bond. The trade

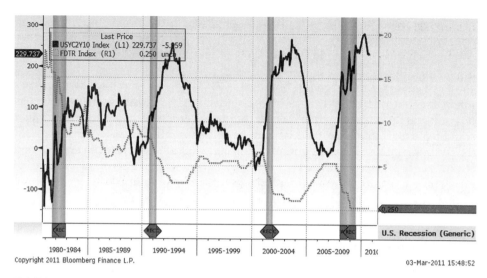

Exhibit 4.26   The 10-year and 2-year U.S. Treasury spreads: September 1980–July 2010
Used with permission of Bloomberg Finance L.P.

can be done so the dollar value of the bond sold is equal to the dollar value of the bond purchased. However, this is not a risk-neutral trade. The trader is exposed to the risk of a parallel shift in the yield curve while he is waiting for the curve to flatten. To avoid this risk, the relative sizes of the positions should be adjusted in such a fashion that the net position is duration-neutral. In Exhibit 4.28, a duration-neutral transaction is depicted together with the expected profit or loss if the yield curve steepens or flattens.

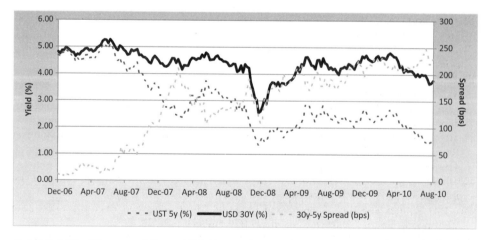

Exhibit 4.27   30-year and 5-year U.S. Treasury Yield and Spreads: December 2006–August 2010
Source: Bloomberg Finance L.P.

Exhibit 4.28   30-year, 5-year U.S. Treasury spread trade

Trade	Security	Quantity	Yield	Price	Duration	DV01
Sell	UST 1.25% 8/31/15	1000	1.568	98.48	4.72	472
Buy	UST 3.875% 8/15/40	265	3.839	100.64	17.17	471

		Market Value	Flattener 100bps	Flattener 50bps	Steepener 50bps	Steepener 100bps
			Profit/Loss			
Sell	UST 1.25% 8/31/15	−985	−30.77	−17.44	8.76	22
	UST 3.875% 8/15/40	266.7	53.35	25.23	−22.38	−43
	Net		22.58	7.79	−13.62	−21

NOTE

1. This is beginning to change with a push by regulators to move more derivatives trading to exchanges.

REFERENCES

Black, F. 1976. "The Pricing of Commodity Contracts," *Journal of Financial Economics* 3 (March): 167–79.

Black, F., E. Derman, and W. Toy. 1990. "A One-Factor Model of Interest Rates and Its Application to Treasury Bond Options." *Financial Analysts Journal* (January/February): 33–39.

Black, F., and P. Karasinski. 1991. "Bond and Option Pricing When Short Rates Are Lognormal," *Financial Analysts Journal* (July/August): 52–59.

Black, F., and M. Scholes. 1973. "The Pricing of Options and Corporate Liabilities." *Journal of Political Economy* 81 (May/June): 637–59.

Brace, A., D. Gatarek, and M. Musiela. 1997. "The Market Model of Interest Rate Dynamics." *Mathematical Finance* 7:2, 127–55.

Gorton, G. 2009. "Information, Liquidity, and the (Ongoing) Panic of 2007." American Economic Review Papers and Proceedings.

Heath, D., R. Jarrow, and A. Morton. 1990. "Bond Pricing and the Term Structure of Interest Rates: A Discrete Time Approximation." *Journal of Financial and Quantitative Analysis* 25:4, 419–40.

Heath, D., R. Jarrow, and A. Morton. 1992. "Bond Pricing and the Term Structure of the Interest Rates: A New Methodology." *Econometrica* 60:1, 77–105.

Ho, T. S. Y., and S.-B. Lee. 1986. "Term Structure Movements and Pricing Interest Rate Contingent Claims." *Journal of Finance* 41 (December): 1011–29.

Hull, J., and A. White. 1990. "Pricing interest-rate derivative securities." *The Review of Financial Studies* 3:4, 573–592.

Hull, J., and A. White. 1993. "Bond Option Pricing Based on a Model for the Evolution of Bond Prices." *Advances in Futures and Options Research* 6: 1–13.

Hull, J., and A. White. 1993. "One-Factor Interest Rate Models and the Valuation of Interest Rate Derivative Securities." *Journal of Financial and Quantitative Analysis* 28 (June): 235–54.

Hull, J., and A. White. 1994. "Numerical Procedures for Implementing Term Structure Models I: Single-Factor Models." *Journal of Derivatives* 2:1, 7–16.

Hull, J., and A. White. 2000. "Forward Rate Volatilities, Swap Rate Volatilities, and the Implementation of the LIBOR Market Model." *Journal of Fixed Income* 10:2, 46–62.

Jamshidian, F. 1977. "LIBOR and Swap Market Models and Measures." *Finance and Stochastics* 1:4, 293–330.

Jamshidian, F. 1989. "An Exact Bond Option Pricing Formula." *Journal of Finance* 44 (March): 205–9.

Macaulay, F. 1938. "Some Theoretical Problems Suggested by the Movements of Interest Rates, Bond Yields, and Stock Prices in the US since 1856." National Bureau of Economic Research.

Rebonato, R. 1996. *Interest Rate Option Models.* Chichester, UK: John Wiley & Sons.

Rebonato, R. 2004. *Volatility and Correlations: The Perfect Hedger and the Fox.* Chichester, UK: John Wiley & Sons.

ABOUT THE AUTHOR

Peruvemba Satish is managing director and chief risk officer (CRO) of Allstate Investments, LLC. He has held senior leadership responsibilities in the areas of risk management, portfolio management, and quantitative research for the past 15 years. Prior to joining Allstate, Satish was the CRO of Jamison Capital Partners. Earlier, he was a partner and the CRO of DKR Capital Partners LP. From 2001 to 2004 Satish was director of risk management at Soros Fund Management. Satish received his MA (Honors) in Economics from SUNY Binghamton in 1990 and a PhD in Finance from the University of Texas at Austin in 1994. He holds degrees in Mechanical Engineering and Economics from BITS, Pilani, India. Satish is also a CFA charter holder.

CHAPTER 5

The U.S. Mortgage Market

BRUCE McNEVIN
The Midway Group

Mortgage Market Snapshot

History: After the Great Depression, the United States federal government created several government and government-sponsored agencies in order to
provide government-guaranteed mortgage insurance and create a liquid
secondary market so that more loans could be issued. The secondary mortgage market in the United States became active in the 1970s, and extended
to the private sector when Bank of America National Trust & Savings
Association became the first truly private issuer of mortgage-backed securities in 1977. The secondary mortgage market reached great heights by
the mid-2000s; however, with the recent subprime mortgage crisis, people have been rethinking the ways in which mortgage-related instruments
have been packaged and issued.

Size: Total outstanding mortgage-related debt in the United States is about
$14.1 trillion as of the first quarter of 2010, according to the Federal Reserve.

Products: Today's market offers investors an array of investment options,
ranging from simple generic pass-through bonds to a diverse set of
structured mortgage-backed securities (MBSs) with very complicated
cash flow patterns.

First Usage: In 1970, the Government National Mortgage Association, or
Ginnie Mae, issued the first mortgage pass-through security that passed
the principal and interest payments on mortgages to investors by pooling
together qualified mortgage loans.

Selection of Famous Events:

1994: Harris Trust and Savings Bank, a subsidiary of the Bank of Montreal,
suffered losses of $51.3 million from investments in risky mortgage
derivatives that were supposedly kept in low-risk institutional customer accounts.

2007: In August 2007, rising defaults in subprime loans rattled not only
the secondary mortgage market, but also financial markets in general.
Many feared that Countrywide Financial, the largest mortgage lender
in the United States, would teeter toward bankruptcy. Indeed, first, it
accepted a credit line of $11.5 billion from banks, then later a financing
of $2 billion from Bank of America, which eventually acquired the
mortgage lender in 2008 for about $4 billion in stock. Countrywide

announced a $1.2 billion third-quarter loss in October 2007, its first
reported loss in 25 years. In addition to tremendous losses on subprime loans, the mortgage lender was also under FBI investigation for
mortgage fraud, including misleading investors about the extent of
the credit risk involved in maintaining its market operations.

2007–2008: Lehman Brothers Holdings Inc. was a global financial services
firm that was also hit hard by the subprime mortgage crisis. By 2007,
the firm closed down its subprime lender, BNC Mortgage, took an
after-tax charge of $25 million, and a goodwill write down of $27 million due to poor market conditions in the mortgage realm. However,
Lehman continued to suffer from the continuing subprime mortgage
crisis. With falling stock share prices and rising losses in low-rated
mortgage securities, it eventually succumbed to bankruptcy in 2008,
while posting a third-quarter loss of $3.9 billion. Lehman's bankruptcy
filing sparked worries around the world about the health of the global
financial system.

Applications: Mortgage-backed securities can be used to satisfy specific risk
preferences on a number of dimensions, including prepayment, duration,
and credit risk.

Users: Investors in the secondary mortgage market include investment banks
as well as corporations and individual investors.

INTRODUCTION

In 1970, when the Government National Mortgage Association (Ginnie Mae) issued its first mortgage pass-through security, the secondary mortgage market was
little more than an inchoate assemblage of government housing initiatives. Today,
total outstanding mortgage-related debt is over $10 trillion, making mortgages
the largest segment of the U.S. bond market (see Exhibit 5.1). The structure of the
market has also undergone a significant change.

The growth in market size was accompanied by a broad-based expansion in
the variety of mortgage-derivative products available to investors. Today's market
offers investors an array of investment options ranging from simple generic

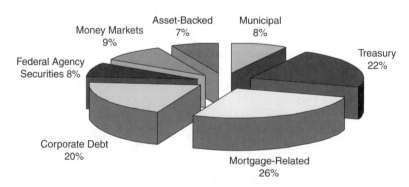

Exhibit 5.1 Outstanding U.S. Bond Market Debt, Q4 2009
Source: Securities Industry Financial Markets Association (SIFMA).

pass-through bonds, like those first issued by Ginnie Mae in 1970, to a diverse set of structured products with very complicated cash-flow patterns, designed to satisfy specific risk preferences on a number of dimensions including prepayment, duration, and credit risk. Many of the changes in the market for mortgage-backed securities since the early 1970s can be attributed to the theoretical, methodological, and computational achievements of financial engineering during the same time period. The story of the evolution of the market for mortgage-backed securities is entwined with the evolution of financial engineering as a discipline.

The one factor that distinguishes MBSs from most other fixed-income products is the uncertainty of the cash flows and the consequential complexity of the valuation process. The primary reason for the uncertainty is that borrowers hold an option to prepay their mortgages. If, and when, a borrower exercises this option depends on general economic conditions (e.g., interest rates, home price appreciation) and circumstances specific to each borrower (e.g., relocation, divorce, job loss). An estimate of the cash flow at a future point in time requires an estimate of the probability that a loan will prepay at that point. The expected future probability that a borrower will exercise the prepayment option may be characterized as being dynamic, path dependent, and uncertain. It is dynamic in the sense that it changes over time; path dependent in the sense that at any point in time it depends on current and previous states of the world; and uncertain in the sense that at the time of valuation it requires knowledge of future states of the world.

Thirty-five years ago, the tools, methods, and computing power required to properly value mortgage-backed securities were not generally available to investors. The prevailing method of valuation was cash flow yield (also known as mortgage yield). This is a static method that does not properly capture the value of the prepayment option. Out of necessity, the decision to invest in an MBS was made with very little information about the underlying collateral, and very little understanding of how the characteristics of the borrowers might impact cash flows.

Today's investors, in contrast, have access to tools that allow them to routinely process and analyze massive amounts of loan-level information in short periods of time and use this information to value very complex mortgage derivatives. This capability is largely due to advances in financial engineering, which has championed the development of high-speed, theoretically sound valuation methods that employ simulation techniques to value the prepayment option. The development of sophisticated valuation tools has, in turn, led to the development of a more diverse set of mortgage-derivative products that better meet the preferences of investors.

This chapter is a discussion of the evolution of the market for mortgage-backed securities (or the secondary mortgage market), its institutions, participants, products, and analytic methods, and the role of financial engineering. We begin with a discussion of government housing policy and its role in the establishment of the market. This is a brief but important discussion, insofar as understanding the current state of the MBS market and its future direction is concerned. Indeed, the housing policy established by Congress 50 or even 80 years ago lies at the heart of our current economic situation, and will for the foreseeable future. Having established the institutional framework of today's mortgage market, we proceed to discuss the historical development of the suite of mortgage derivatives currently available to investors. As we will see, the evolution of the different types of mortgage-backed securities available to investors reflects the development of

financial engineering methods. We then discuss the current state of mortgage valuation with an emphasis on the role of prepayments and defaults. The information
available to value a MBS, and the computational ability to process that information,
have changed significantly over the history of the secondary mortgage market. In
fact, this is an area that has seen major advances in the past 8 to 10 years. In the
final section, we discuss current market conditions, the future of key institutions,
and the role of financial engineering in the mortgage market of the future.

A BRIEF HISTORY OF THE ORIGIN OF THE MARKET FOR MORTGAGE-BACKED SECURITIES

The secondary market for mortgages, and the history of mortgage-backed securities
in general, has its roots in the Great Depression. In 1934, Congress passed the
National Housing Act, which established the Federal Housing Authority (FHA).
The legislation was enacted in response to the very high rate of mortgage defaults
between 1929 and 1934. By some estimates, homeowner default rates were as
high as 25 to 30 percent nationally. The defaults were driven by a combination of
high unemployment, a steep decline in housing prices, and the practice of issuing
balloon mortgages.[1]

The FHA was established to provide insurance on mortgages issued by FHA-
approved lenders. The intent of the program was to encourage lending by reducing
the risk of loss associated with a mortgage default. The mortgage insurance premium was paid by the borrower through an increase in monthly payments. The
FHA insurance program is still in existence, and has played a very important role in
the recent housing crisis. In addition to providing insurance to lenders, the underwriting standards on FHA-approved loans are less stringent than those of standard
mortgages. Borrowers can secure an FHA loan with a very small cash investment,
and income requirements are less rigorous than standard mortgages. The FHA is
currently part of the Department of Housing and Urban Development (HUD).

In 1938, using authority granted under the National Housing Act of 1934,
the FHA chartered the Federal National Mortgage Association (Fannie Mae). The
purpose of establishing Fannie Mae was to provide liquidity to the mortgage
market by creating a secondary market for mortgages. Fannie Mae bought FHA-
insured mortgages from lenders and either held them in its own portfolio or sold
them to investors. Lenders were motivated to underwrite FHA-insured loans,
since they were confident that they could sell them. Selling the loans provided
lenders with new capital to write additional loans. Creating a secondary market
for mortgages also facilitated the flow of capital across geographic regions, which is
critical for a market such as housing that is inherently local. In the late 1940s Fannie
Mae expanded its buying program to include loans guaranteed by the Veterans
Administration (VA).

In 1968, the Federal National Mortgage Association was split into two entities,
one public and one privately owned. The privately owned entity kept the name
Fannie Mae, and the publicly owned entity was named the Government National
Mortgage Association (Ginnie Mae). The establishment of these two entities was
an important step by the federal government toward expanding the secondary
market for mortgages, and advancing its policy of providing housing assistance

to Americans. Ginnie Mae was specifically created to expand affordable housing. In 1970, the government established a third entity, the Federal Home Loan Mortgage Corporation (Freddie Mac), which, like Fannie Mae, was privately owned. One of the primary reasons for establishing Freddie Mac was so that Fannie Mae would not be a monopoly. These two institutions, Fannie and Freddie, are, technically, government-sponsored enterprises (GSEs), which means they are federally chartered, but privately owned. These two GSEs, plus Ginnie Mae, are collectively referred to as agencies. As a group, the agencies have been crucial to the development and robust growth of the secondary market for mortgages.

AGENCY MORTGAGE PASS-THROUGH SECURITIES

In 1970, Ginnie Mae introduced the first mortgage pass-through security, which effectively marked the beginning of the modern-day market for mortgage-backed securities. A mortgage pass-through is a bundle or pool of mortgages that have similar characteristics such as maturity, origination date, interest rate, mortgage type (fixed rate versus adjustable rate), and property type (single-family home or multifamily home). An investor who purchases a mortgage pass-through security is entitled to the principal and interest payments[2] from the mortgages in the pool. Under the Ginnie Mae mortgage pass-through program, loans are pooled by approved issuers and resold in the secondary mortgage market. Ginnie Mae does not actually issue the securities, but it does guarantee the principal and interest payments of pools issued by its approved issuers.

Ginnie Mae took the lead in introducing mortgage pass-throughs, and the two GSEs eventually followed (Freddie Mac in 1972 and Fannie in 1981). It is important to note that unlike Ginnie Mae, the GSEs actually purchase mortgages, and then either retain them in their own portfolios or securitize and sell them in the secondary market. Also, in keeping with its mission of assisting low- and moderate-income home buyers, the Ginnie Mae pass-through program issues pools of mortgages that are primarily FHA insured or VA guaranteed. These loans are commonly referred to as government loans.

The vast majority of mortgage pass-through securities are traded in the to-be-announced (TBA) market. A TBA is a contract to buy or sell a set of pools or mortgages at some future date. The TBA market gets its name from the fact that the buyer does not know the specific pools that will be delivered until two days before delivery. The TBA market trades on the assumption that the pools are homogeneous and therefore fungible. As an example, an investor can enter into a contract to buy pass-throughs backed by Fannie Mae 5 percent, 30-year fixed-rate loans, but the investor will not know the average age of the loans in the pools, the average loan size, or even the average mortgage rate on the pools until 48 hours before delivery. TBAs settle according to a monthly schedule set by the Securities Industry Financial Markets Association (SIFMA). Mortgage originators use the TBA market to fund originations by negotiating contracts several months in advanced of the settlement date, effectively allowing them to lock in a price for mortgages that they are still in the process of originating. SIFMA also provides guidelines for "good delivery" of TBAs, which generally address settlement issues, such as the maximum number of pools that can be delivered per $1 million of TBAs, and the variance of the delivery amount of the trade and the agreed-upon amount.

Mortgage pass-throughs also trade as specified pools, meaning that investors can purchase pools for their specific characteristics, such as loan balance (low, medium, or high); geography (location of the homes underlying the pools); credit-worthiness of the borrower; occupancy type (primary residence, investor owned); and property type (single-family residence, multifamily, condo, co-op). The specified pool market places special value on certain loan characteristics, and in that sense it is antithetical to the TBA market, which operates under the assumption of pool homogeneity. The specified pool market has become very active in the past five to six years, as the agencies have provided more information about the characteristics of the loans within the pools. For instance, in 2003 the agencies began reporting weighted averages and quartiles for FICO scores, loan-to-value (LTV) ratios, occupancy type, mortgage purpose (home purchase, cash-out refinance, rate refinance), and average loan size for all pools originating from 1996 onward. In early 2006, Freddie Mac began reporting loan-level information for the loans backing their pools, but, interestingly, it did not provide an indicator of which pool the loan belongs to, so the information is of limited use. However, the availability of this information, along with information on the geographic concentration of the loans within a pool, has spurred growth of the specified pool market. It has also provided investors with a wealth of information that they have used to improve MBS valuation models.

Agency Market Structure

MBS market segmentation is largely collateral-based in the sense that the segments reflect fundamental differences in borrower characteristics.[3] Borrower characteristics are a key determinant of the expected probabilities of prepayment. Consequently, the market segmentation scheme reflects fundamental differences in security valuation. In effect, for a given state of the economy, each segment of borrowers has a different propensity to prepay. Market segments are important differences that must be accounted for in the valuation process. Advances in financial engineering since the creation of the MBS market have enabled investors to incorporate these differences into the valuation process.

Ginnie Mae pools are comprised of government-guaranteed loans primarily from the VA and FHA loan programs. GSE pools, unlike Ginnie Mae, do not limit securitization to pools backed by government-guaranteed loans. Most of the loans in GSE pools are nongovernment loans. These loans are referred to as conventional loans. Pools backed by conventional loans tend to have different prepayment speeds from pools backed by government loans. Part of the reason for this is that the government loan programs have higher loan-to-value (LTV) limits and the loans tend to be smaller.

Agency loan standards generally require that borrowers provide written proof (documentation) of employment and income. In addition, conventional loan standards typically require that borrowers have a loan-to-value ratio of less than 80 percent, satisfy a minimum level of creditworthiness, and meet certain minimum levels of debt-to-income ratios. Government loans often have LTVs higher than 80 percent. Nongovernment loans that do not meet GSE standards are typically securitized by private-label issuers and sold in the non-agency market.

All three agencies limit eligibility based on loan size, known as the conforming balance limit. In 2009 the conforming balance limit was $729,500 for temporary high-cost areas, $625,500 for permanent high-cost areas, and $417,000 in all other areas. The limit is reset annually based on the level of home price appreciation. Conventional loans that exceed the conforming balance limit are not eligible for securitization in an agency pool, and are referred to as jumbo loans. Securities backed by jumbo loans trade in the non-agency market.

One important feature of MBS market segmentation that is not based on borrower characteristics relates to credit risk. Setting aside differences in loan characteristics, from an investor's point of view Ginnie Mae pass-throughs and GSE pass-throughs are not perfect substitutes because of an important difference in the guarantee of principal and interest payments. All of the agencies guarantee investors the timely payment of principal and interest, but only the Ginnie Mae guarantee carries the full faith and credit of the U.S. government. The GSEs have traditionally been viewed as having the implicit guarantee of the U.S. government because of their GSE designation. In principle, because of the difference in the credit risk, GSE pass-throughs should trade at a discount to Ginnie Mae pass-throughs. In fact, the government intervention and conservatorship of Fannie and Freddie in 2008 made the implicit guarantee quite explicit. Private issuers of MBSs do not provide any guarantee.

The introduction of pass-throughs was a major step toward establishing a liquid secondary mortgage market. Pass-throughs facilitated investors' ability to trade lots of relatively homogenous mortgages. Pooling mortgages with similar characteristics meant that pool-level, average characteristics were generally representative of the underlying loans. This moderate level of homogeneity facilitated the security valuation process. By setting conforming loan standards, the GSEs have helped to establish national underwriting standards for mortgages. Today the mortgage pass-through security market is the most popular type of mortgage-backed security, and GSE issuance's share of agency pass-throughs far exceeds that of Ginnie Mae.

PRICING MORTGAGE-BACKED SECURITIES

On the surface, a mortgage pass-through is not a particularly complex instrument. The owner of a mortgage pass-through receives monthly payments of principal and interest from the loans backing the pool(s). Valuing a pass-through, however, is not a trivial exercise since it requires valuing a borrower's option to prepay the mortgage. Financial engineers have made significant contributions in this area, providing investors with fast, practical, and easily implementable MBS valuation tools.

As is the case with any asset, the value of a mortgage-backed security is determined by the present value of its cash flow. What makes a MBS different from, say, a Treasury bond, is that the cash flow is uncertain. The basic price equation for a pass-through is:

$$Price = \sum_{t=1}^{T} \frac{CF_t}{(1+y)^t}$$

where CF_t = scheduled principal + scheduled interest + prepaid principal, and y = mortgage yield. CF_t cannot be determined with certainty, because the amount of prepaid principal each month is unknown. Borrowers have the option to prepay some of the principal balance on a mortgage (known as a curtailment), prepay all of the principal balance (known as a prepayment), pay the scheduled portion of the principal balance, or pay none of the principal balance (known as a default). A homeowner has the right to call the loan at any time, so from an investor's perspective, owning a mortgage pass-through is equivalent to the following:

$$MBS = Treasury + Short\ Call$$

In addition to the uncertainty in the cash flows, there is also uncertainty associated with the interest rate used to discount the cash flows. We will discuss each of these issues, and the current financial engineering methods for valuing mortgage-backed securities.

We begin by discussing voluntary prepayments, since they can have a very large impact on MBS valuation. There are two primary reasons why a borrower voluntarily prepays a loan: The borrower either moves or gets a lower mortgage rate. Every month (on the close of the fourth business day for fixed-rate mortgages), the agencies report pool factors that indicate the remaining balance in a pool per dollar of original balance. Given the scheduled balance of principal for a pool, one can calculate the fraction of the pool balance that was prepaid—that is, the unscheduled fraction of the balance that was paid off by borrowers. Prepayments are measured as the fraction of the pool at the beginning of the month that was prepaid during the month. This measure is called the single monthly mortality (SMM) rate. The annualized SMM is called the constant prepayment rate (CPR). The history of monthly SMMs for the entire set of pools for an agency is typically used to estimate an econometric model with the goal of explaining the determinants of SMM. Ultimately, the model is used to forecast SMM. Usually the same prepayment model can be used for Fannie Mae and Freddie Mac pools, but a separate model needs to be estimated for Ginnie Mae pools because of the high concentration of loans for low-income borrowers.

The typical prepayment model has two parts: a turnover equation that estimates the determinants of homeowner mobility on prepayments, and a refinance model that estimates the effect of interest rates on prepayments. Each model has a number of determinants, which typically impact SMM nonlinearly. For the turnover model, the key determinants[4] of SMM include:

- *Loan age.* Mortgages exhibit a very strong seasoning effect, meaning that the SMM ramps up as a loan ages. A pool of 20-month-old loans will have a higher rate of prepayment than a pool of two-month-old loans. Seasoning usually takes about 30 months.
- *Relative mortgage rate.* The lower the average mortgage rate for a pool of loans—referred to as the weighted average coupon (WAC)—relative to the market rate for mortgages, the greater the disincentive of a borrower to move.
- *Seasonality.* Home sales exhibit very strong seasonal patterns, being highest in the summer months and lowest during January and February.

The turnover model has a difficult task in that it uses aggregate information on loan characteristics to estimate the likelihood that a group of individuals will move to a new house.

For the refinance model, one of the key determinants is relative mortgage rate. As the market mortgage rate drops relative to the rate on an existing mortgage, the probability that a loan will refinance increases nonlinearly, initially at an increasing rate and then at a decreasing rate until it eventually reaches an asymptote. This is illustrated in Exhibit 5.2, where the ratio of WAC to the market rate measures the degree to which a pool is at a premium. A ratio of 1.0 indicates that the average mortgage rate for a pool of loans is equal to the market rate and borrowers in the pool do not, on average, have a rate incentive to refinance.

Exhibit 5.2 illustrates the actual refinance curve for Fannie Mae pools based on 10 years of historical data (1999–2009). We see that as the incentive to refinance reaches a ratio of 1.25 the SMM stops increasing. Also, notice that SMM drops off slowly as the refinance ratio falls below 1.0. This illustrates the rate disincentive that movers face. Finally, note that the curve does not approach zero as the incentive falls below 1.0 since there will always be movers.

Other important variables that impact the probability of refinancing include the following:

- *Credit score.* The lower the credit score of a borrower, the more difficult it is to get a loan, and therefore the lower the probability of prepaying.
- *Loan-to-value ratio.* A borrower with a high LTV has lower probability of refinancing. One of the biggest drivers of LTV in today's market is housing prices.
- *House price appreciation.* As home prices increase, the probability that a borrower will refinance to get cash from the house increases. This is called cash-out refinancing, and it was a very common phenomenon from 2005 through the middle of 2007. Similarly, as home prices drop, LTV increases and borrowers are unable to refinance unless they put additional capital into the house.

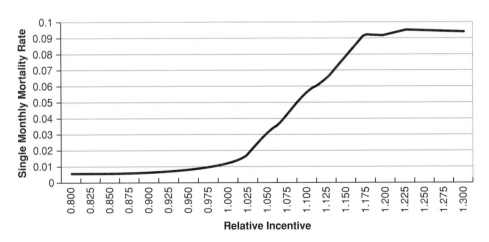

Exhibit 5.2 Refinance Curve

- *Loan size.* For a given rate incentive, the higher the loan balance, the greater the probability a borrower will refinance. To the extent that the mortgage payment on a large loan constitutes a greater portion of a borrower's income, a borrower will be relatively more sensitive to mortgage rates.
- *Geography.* Home price appreciation aside, the condition of the local economy can have a very important differentiating effect on prepayments. Some states, such as those in the Rust Belt,[5] have chronic high unemployment, which may suppress prepayments (but increase defaults). State tax policy can also have a significant impact on prepayments. For instance, New York State taxes mortgage refinancing, and as a result, after adjusting for differences in all other factors, prepayments in New York can be as much as 30 percent lower than prepayments in some other states.

In addition to the loan characteristics, there are two other market factors that have been found to significantly impact the probability of prepayment.

1. *Media effect.* When mortgage rates reach historically low levels, media coverage tends to raise borrower awareness of rate levels, and prepayment activity tends to surge. This was certainly the case in the summer of 2003 when 30-year fixed mortgage rates reached a historical low of 5.21 percent and prepayments on many premium pools surged to 80 CPR. However, it was not the case in 2009 when rates fell as low as 4.7 percent for 30-year fixed mortgage rates, and prepayment activity averaged only 20 to 25 CPR. The 2009 experience reflects lender constraints, since even though a borrower holds an option to prepay her mortgage, she must still meet underwriting standards of the lender to exercise the option.
2. *Burnout.* When the market mortgage rates fall below the average mortgage rate—weighted average coupon (WAC)—of a pool, the pool will experience an increase in prepayments. However, not all of the loans in the pool will prepay, even if there is a strong incentive to do so. If we assume that the borrowers in the pool are rational, one explanation for this behavior is the existence of one or more unobserved heterogeneities, such as transaction costs. Burnout is the observed effect of these unobserved heterogeneities. When there is a rate incentive to prepay, a self-selection process takes place—pools with low transaction costs prepay. As a result, the average propensity to refinance for the pool declines. The pool is said to have experienced burnout since in the future, if there is a similar incentive to refinance, the prepayment rate for the pool will be lower than it was the first time.

Forecasting prepayments is critical to valuing an MBS when the degree of uncertainty is high. The information that exists is largely inadequate for the task. The agencies primarily report aggregate pool-level data, and while private issuers usually report loan-level information, none of the available data contains demographic information, such as age, gender, employment status, income, occupation, number of children, and wealth of the borrower. These unobserved variables all contribute to forecast bias and error.

In addition to prepayments, the other key determinant of cash flow is defaults. Historically, this has not been a major concern for the loans in agency pools, or even for grade A private-issuer collateral. However, this has all changed in the recent economic downturn, and default modeling has taken on much greater importance. Most of the factors that impact the probability of a loan prepaying also impact the probability of a default. In addition, defaults are also very sensitive to local economic conditions, so the unemployment rate is usually included in a default model.

Prepayment and defaults are the two biggest factors to consider when forecasting cash flow. They are often modeled separately, which is interesting, since the probability of a default is not independent of the probability of a prepayment. Recent modeling initiatives have recognized this dependence, and now the two are often modeled using *competing risk* models, which calculate the probability of both default and prepayment, recognizing that they are not independent.

Interest Rate Models

The other source of uncertainty in MBS valuation is the interest rate. This is an area where financial engineering has made a major contribution. There are a number of models that can be used to forecast interest rates. We will focus on the Cox-Ingersoll-Ross (CIR)[6] model for illustrative purposes and provide a brief summary. A basic knowledge of the interest rate process is crucial to understanding MBS valuation. CIR models the change in the short-term interest rate using the following stochastic differential equation:

$$dr_t = a\,(b - r_t)\,dt + \sigma\,\sqrt{r_t}\,dw_t$$

where b is the equilibrium or mean of the short-term rate, a is the rate of reversion to the mean, σ is the standard deviation of the short-term rate, and w_t is a Weiner process intended to represent random market risk. This is a mean-reversion model, meaning that if this period's short-term rate is above the mean it will move down over time, and it will move up if it is below the mean rate. This first part of the equation says that the change in the short-term interest rate from t to $t + 1$ is a function of the distance of the actual short-term rate at time t from its mean, the rate of reversion to the mean, and the change in time. The second part of the equation says that change in the short-term rate is determined by volatility of the rate, the level (square root) of the rate, and a market risk factor. This model is used to forecast the short-term rate from which arbitrage-free bond prices can be derived and the term structure can be calculated.

The interest rate model process has been an area of intense focus for financial engineers. As we will see in the next section, mortgage-backed securities are valued using a simulation process that requires the calculation of hundreds of interest rate forecasts for the term of the bond. It is a process that is feasible only with high-speed, efficient programs.

MBS Valuation

The current state of practice for MBS valuation is the option-adjusted spread (OAS) approach. This is a method that has been in practice since the mid-1980s. In the OAS method, the security price is given, and an interest rate model such as CIR is used to forecast interest rates on many paths over the life of the collateral. A prepayment model is used to forecast cash flows given the interest rate, and OAS is the single spread that makes the average of the discounted cash flows along all interest rate paths equal to the market price of the security. The OAS, which is measured in basis points, is interpreted as the cost of the prepayment option.

The two key inputs into the valuation of an MBS are the prepayment forecast and the term structure of interest rates. The basic valuation equation is:

$$\text{Price} = \frac{1}{N} \sum_{i=1}^{N} \sum_{t=1}^{T} \frac{CF_{t,i}}{\prod_{s=1}^{t} (1 + r_{i,s} + OAS)}$$

$N =$ number of simulation paths,
$T =$ number of cash flow periods,
$r =$ short term rate

The typical OAS valuation involves the following three steps:

1. Simulate 500 interest rate paths.
2. Calculate prepayments on each path.
3. Calculate the yield spread of the MBS to London Interbank Offered Rate (LIBOR) (Treasury) curve so the average price across all paths just equals the price of the MBS. This is the expected yield pickup to LIBOR (Treasury) curve, after adjusting for prepayment risk.

The simulation process is computationally intensive. As an example, consider a 30-year fixed-rate pass-through security based on collateral that was just issued. For a 500-path analysis, the OAS method requires the term structure forecast for 359 months along each path and a prepayment forecast for 359 months on each of the 500 paths. For the calculation of duration, this would be done three times, first using the current yield curve to start the simulation process of 500 paths, then shifting the curve up and down 50 basis points, and repeating the process two more times. The magnitude of the computation is also affected by the collateral used to value the security. An agency security might be valued at the pool level or using a more aggregate grouping; in either case, a prepayment forecast and cash flow calculation is required, so if there are 300 pools, the cash flow calculation is done for each pool. In the non-agency world, the collateral is often available at the loan level, and a bond may have 3,000 or 4,000 loans. It is not uncommon to forecast the probability of prepayment and default for each loan at each point in time on each interest rate path (times 3 to calculate duration). This is an area where financial engineering has made an enormous contribution in terms of the development of the analytic methodology, reducing the number of calculations, and generally making sophisticated valuation tools more accessible to a wide group of investors. Today it may take only a minute or two to calculate the duration of a very complex cash flow structure at the loan level.

BEYOND PASS-THROUGHS: COLLATERALIZED MORTGAGE OBLIGATIONS (CMOs)

One of the most important outcomes arising from the development of the OAS valuation tool has been the development of more complex mortgage securities. OAS valuation facilitated the evolution of mortgage-backed securities from simple pass-throughs to a variety of much more complex cash-flow structures called collateralized mortgage obligations (CMOs). A collateralized mortgage obligation is a claim to specific cash flows from a set of underlying mortgages, as opposed to a mortgage pass-through, which is a claim to a pro rata share of all principal and interest payments (less a servicing fee) from the underlying mortgages. The CMO market evolved because there was often a mismatch between the cash flow characteristics of pass-throughs being traded in the secondary mortgage market and the needs of investors. For instance, in the early days of the MBS market, investors with a need to hedge a liability with a two-year duration might have difficulty finding an out-of-the-money pass-through with a matching duration. The first CMO, which was issued by Freddie Mac in 1983, was specifically designed to address investors' need for greater variability in duration. Additional types of CMOs, designed to offer investors varying levels of exposure to an assortment of risks, soon followed. Today CMO issuance is over $1 trillion per year.

In the most general sense, CMOs use predetermined rules to allocate the principal and interest payments of an underlying set of mortgages to different tranches. The result is a set of bonds with cash flow patterns and risk exposures that can be very different from pass-throughs, and much more suitable to the heterogeneous preferences of investors. Financial engineering has played a very important role in the development of the CMO market, as the techniques for applying the rules, and valuing the tranches, are a computationally intensive application of fixed-income valuation principles.

The earliest CMOs, called sequential bonds, were designed to address the duration mismatch problem. Sequential bonds divide the principal payments from the underlying mortgage collateral into classes that amortized sequentially. For instance, the Class A tranche may pay principal for the first five years while the other three tranches do not make any principal payments. At the end of five years, Class A is fully amortized and the Class B tranche begins to pay principal, which may also amortize over five years. This sequential process continues until the remaining classes are paid off. Thus, the different tranches provide investors with an array of mortgage-backed securities to choose from, each with a different duration. It is important to note that the actual principal payments depend on both the amortization schedule and the actual level of prepayment and default activity. For instance, if prepayments decrease, the duration of all classes in the sequential bond will increase. Sequential bonds satisfy a need for variation in duration, but still expose investors to prepayment risk. The prepayment risk of a sequential bond varies across tranches, and requires an OAS methodology to size and value.

In the mid-1980s, several other types of CMOs were developed that not only provided investors with an array of durations to choose from, but also provided varying levels of exposure to prepayment risk. We will briefly discuss several of these bonds to get a sense of the design and complexity. The planned amortization class (PAC) structure was designed to provide investors with prepayment protection. The PAC structure is composed of two basic types of bonds: the PAC bond and the support bond. The principal payment schedule of the PAC bond is defined as the minimum cash flow associated within a band of prepayment rates. The PAC bond maintains its scheduled principal payments through the use of a support bond. When prepayments are fast, the support bond pays off at a faster rate, allowing the PAC bond to maintain its principal schedule. When prepayments are slow, principal payments to the support bond are delayed so that the PAC schedule can be met. PAC and support bonds are also amortized sequentially to create tranches with different maturities. While the PAC bond does not guarantee principal payments, even if the prepayment rates stay within the predetermined bounds, it does provide limited exposure to prepayment risk, and consequently provides some stability to principal payments. There are a number of different types of PACs that offer different degrees of prepayment protection.

Unlike the sequential and PAC structured bonds, which alter duration and exposure to prepayment risk by restructuring principal payments, floater and inverse floater CMOs are used to create tranches with varying risk exposures by changing the coupon rate. The floater/inverse floater is created by splitting a fixed-rate CMO into two pieces (floater and inverse floater) that amortize simultaneously and have variable rates. The floater has a coupon rate that resets periodically and is calculated using an index (often the one-month LIBOR) plus a margin or spread. The floater rate typically has a lifetime cap and floor, and often has an intermediate cap and floor. The inverse floater has a coupon rate that resets in the opposite direction of the floater and also has caps and floors. A floater/inverse floater structure can be produced from another CMO structure, including a PAC and a sequential bond.

Another important set of CMOs developed in the mid-1980s are the interest-only (IO)/principal-only (PO) bonds (or strips, as they are commonly called). As the name suggests, the IO receives 100 percent of the interest payments from the underlying collateral and the PO receives 100 percent of the principal payments. IOs have negative duration, meaning that when interest rates fall their prices decrease. IO prices are very sensitive to interest rate changes, since a drop in the interest rate will trigger prepayments, resulting in a permanent loss of cash flow. IOs and POs derived from agency collateral trade in a very large, liquid market.

THE NON-AGENCY MARKET

The non-agency (private issue) market originated as a market for loans that were not eligible for securitization by the agencies. Non-agency share of issuance was negligible in the 1980s but grew steadily, reaching 10 percent in 1996 and peaking at 43 percent in 2006. Share of issuance has dropped off considerably since 2006 as the housing market declined. Developments in financial engineering played an important role in the growth of the non-agency market. Non-agency collateral is much more heterogeneous than agency collateral, making the valuation process more information-intensive. Valuation and analysis are typically done at the loan level, as opposed to agency deals, which do not provide loan-level information. In addition, non-agency bond structures tend to be more complex because they incorporate credit enhancements not present in agency CMOs.

There are several fundamental differences between agency and non-agency collateral, bonds, and market structures. First, unlike agency bonds, which are guaranteed by the U.S. government either explicitly (Ginnie Mae) or implicitly (Fannie Mac, Freddie Mac), non-agency bonds do not have a guarantee of timely payment of principal and interest. Non-agency CMO issuers have attempted to compensate for this additional level of credit risk by incorporating a credit tranche structure into their CMOs.[7]

There are also important differences in the quality of agency and non-agency collateral. While many of the loans that are bundled into non-agency CMOs meet agency underwriting standards, there are also loans that do not. For instance, a borrower's credit score may be too low to qualify for an agency loan, or the borrower may not provide the necessary documentation to qualify for an agency loan. A large portion of the non-agency loans do not have full documentation, meaning that the borrower does not provide written proof of employment, income level, and/or net wealth. For these partial-documentation loans, the lender accepts a written, unverified statement of employment and/or income from the borrower in lieu of verification. These loans have become known as *liar loans*. Another important difference in loan quality is that non-agency loans can have an LTV that exceeds 80 percent, whereas agency collateral cannot. At the height of the recent housing boom, some non-agency loans originated with 100 percent financing. Finally, agency and non-agency loans can differ by loan size. The non-agency issuance is not restricted by the *conforming balance* limit. As a result there is an entire market segment (called jumbos) of conventional loans that are ineligible for agency securitization.

Up until the early 1990s, a non-agency deal could contain any type of loan, regardless of whether it was a jumbo loan with a high credit score and a low LTV, or a conforming balance loan with a low credit score and no documentation. The heterogeneous nature of the underlying collateral of non-agency bonds restricted its appeal to investors. Low- and high-quality collateral generally appeal to investors with very different risk preferences. Heterogeneity also made the bonds difficult to value. Factors such as loan size, credit score, LTV, and documentation type are each important determinants of prepayment and default risk. The ability to produce a reasonable forecast of expected cash flow requires loan-level data processing, models, and analysis, which is an effective barrier to entry. Segmenting the market was a logical step toward increasing the appeal of non-agency bonds to investors.

In 1993, private banks began issuing CMOs with credit grades based on the characteristics of the underlying collateral. The three main categories that were created and are still in use today include *jumbo prime*, which is comprised of loans that exceed the conforming balance limit but are otherwise equivalent in quality to agency loans; *Alt-A*, which are grade A bonds backed by loans that have balances below the conforming limit but do not meet agency underwriting standards because the credit score is too low, the LTV is too high, or the borrower failed to provide full documentation; and *subprime*, which are grade B and grade C bonds backed by poor credit-quality loans, such as a loan with a low credit score, high LTV, and no documentation. The definitions are not hard-and-fast, but the segmentation provided a degree of homogeneity that facilitated valuation and generally increased investor appeal.

Even with credit segmentation, the characteristics and creditworthiness of non-agency collateral tend to be much more heterogeneous than agency collateral, so the models used to forecast prepayments and defaults tend to be much more complex. Analysis and valuation of non-agency bonds typically use loan-level information, whereas agency bonds are valued at the pool level or a more aggregate level since virtually no useful loan information is available from the agencies. As a result, the valuation process for non-agency bonds tends to be computationally more demanding than agency valuation. Many investors in the non-agency market recognize the need to analyze deals at the loan level, and have the capability to do so.

The rapid growth in non-agency issuance share, from 10 percent in 1996 to 43 percent in 2006, can be attributed in part to the segmentation of the market in the early 1990s. It can also be attributed to a significant increase in the origination of so-called *affordability* products such as adjustable-rate mortgages (ARMs), hybrid ARMs, nonamortizing (interest-only loans) loans, and option ARMs, all of which were designed to provide borrowers with lower monthly loan payments, but typically just do so temporarily. In 2001, approximately 75 percent of all Alt-A originations were fixed-rate mortgages. By 2005 only about 20 percent were fixed-rate mortgages.[8]

In the five-year period leading up to its peak in 2006, the increase in non-agency issuance was accompanied by a decline in the quality of borrower characteristics. For instance, the percentage of Alt-A loans with full documentation declined from 35 percent in 2001 to 16 percent in 2006. The percentage of Alt-A loans with silent second mortgages increased from 1 percent in 2001 to 39 percent in 2006. (A silent second mortgage is a second mortgage that was not disclosed to the first mortgage lender at origination.) The average LTV on a subprime loan was 86 percent in 2006 compared with 80 percent in 2001.[9] Banks were lending money to riskier borrowers, and many of the loans found their way into non-agency CMOs, which, unlike agency CMOs, do not have an implicit or explicit guarantee of timely payment of principal and interest.

Non-Agency CMOs

Because non-agency bonds do not have a credit guarantee, issuers use a senior/ subordinate structure to create credit tranches and redistribute credit risk. A common non-agency CMO structure[10] is illustrated in Exhibit 5.3. Principal and interest payments flow from the top down, giving the senior tranche, which is typically rated AAA, priority to the principal and interest payments from the collateral. The subordinate tranches have lower credit ratings and may or may not be investment grade. The bottom tranche, often called the junior tranche, may not be rated at all.

In addition to the top-down flow of principal and interest, the senior tranche is protected by making it the last to incur losses. Losses are allocated from the bottom up, meaning that the lowest-rated tranche is the first to receive principal losses. The subordinate bonds protect the senior bond until their principal is depleted. In Exhibit 5.3 the subordinates will absorb the first $23.1 million in losses before the senior tranche suffers any loss. The relative size of the subordinate tranches

Bond	Rating	Amount	% of Deal
Senior	AAA	382.9	95.00%
Subordinate 1	AA	12.1	3.00%
Subordinate 2	A	4.0	1.00%
Subordinate 3	BBB	3.0	0.75%
Subordinate 4	BB	2.0	0.50%
Subordinate 5	B	1.0	0.25%
Subordinate 6	Not Rated	1.0	0.25%

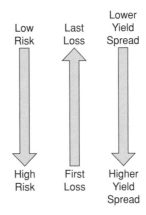

Exhibit 5.3 Generic Non-Agency CMO Structure

dictates the level of protection. The protection afforded by this credit-enhancing structure allows the senior tranche to hold its triple-A rating.

Non-agency CMOs often provide additional credit protection to the senior tranche by allocating the subordinate bond's share of any prepayments to the senior for a fixed time period, often referred to as the lockout period. The lockout period can vary from five to 10 years depending on the type of collateral. For instance, in the case of a CMO backed by 30-year fixed-rate Alt-A mortgages, all prepaid principal may be allocated to the senior tranche for the first five years of the bond's life. This is called a shifting interest structure. It has the effect of increasing subordination over time by making the subordinate bonds larger. Finally, the individual credit tranches in a deal may also be split into sequential bonds, PAC bonds, interest-only/principal-only bonds, floaters/inverse floaters, and other types of structures, which, as we previously discussed, have the effect of shifting prepayment and/or interest rates.

The level of credit protection provided to the senior bonds by the senior-subordinate structure depends on the size or thickness of the subordinate piece. Establishing an appropriate level of subordination for a deal requires an estimate of losses, or mortgage defaults. Statistical models for forecasting the probability of default depend on historical experience. Most models use data from the past 15 years to forecast defaults. The national level of defaults for the period 2007–2009 has been greater than for any other period except the Great Depression. As a result, default models have grossly underforecasted default rates, and subordination levels have in many instances been inadequate to protect the triple-A rating of senior tranches.

FINANCIAL ENGINEERING AND THE FUTURE OF THE SECONDARY MORTGAGE MARKET

The economic downturn has taken its toll on the market for mortgage-backed securities. In 2008, total MBS issuance declined by 35 percent to $1.3 trillion. This is roughly half the level of total issuance in the peak year 2003. There are signs of a recovery for the MBS market as a whole, with total issuance up 40 percent in 2009. But aggregate statistics often tell a misleading story. Agency issuance declined only 5 percent in 2008, and it increased 43 percent in 2009. Non-agency issuance, however, plummeted, declining 95 percent in 2008 and an additional 47 percent in 2009. As a result, the non-agency share of issuance declined in 2009 to a mere 1.3 percent.

Although Fannie Mae and Freddie Mac are in financial straits, the agency market will eventually rebound. The federal government is still committed to a housing policy that helps provide affordable housing. The 2009 federal tax credit for first-time home buyers has stimulated the origination of FHA-insured loans, which are typically securitized by Ginnie Mae. The explicit federal guarantee of the timely payment of principal and interest has increased the demand for Ginnie Mae bonds. Agency CMOs as a whole comprise the highest-quality mortgages. The logic of carving up the cash flows from high-quality loans to create bonds that meet the needs of investors is still sound, and as a result, agency CMOs will always be in demand.

The future of the non-agency market will depend on its ability to adapt to the new economic reality. Credit risk has proven to be much greater than ever anticipated, and the rejuvenation of the non-agency CMO market will depend on the ability of issuers to structure CMOs that provide greater protection. For instance, the level of subordination in a deal will probably have to be much higher than it has been in the past. In the future, a 5 percent cushion of subordination will probably be deemed too low to protect a senior tranche. In addition, the valuation process will have to make greater use of loan-level data. Investment decisions

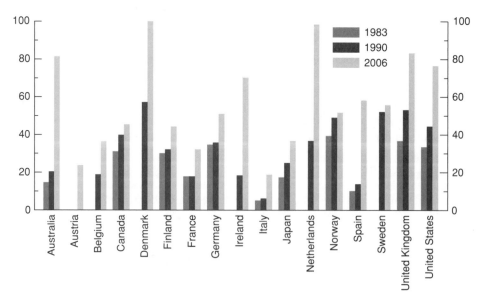

Exhibit 5.4 Mortgage Debt Outstanding (percent of GDP)
Source: IMF. This chart was published in 2008 and can be accessed at: www.imf.org/external/pubs/ft/weo/2008/01/c3/Fig3_1.pdf.

will require improved methods for evaluating the multiple dimensions of risk in a non-agency CMO, and financial engineering will necessarily play a key role.

A NOTE ON THE GLOBAL GROWTH OF THE MORTGAGE MARKET

The enormous growth of mortgage lending experienced in the United States over the past few decades is not unique. Similar patterns have been experienced throughout the world. Exhibit 5.4 depicts the size of the mortgage markets for a number of countries for select years.

NOTES

1. The prevalent fixed-rate 30-year mortgage of today was rare in the 1930s. Many mortgages were balloon loans where the entire principal payment was due at one time, usually three to five years after origination.
2. The investor receives principal plus interest, less a fee paid to the mortgage servicer for collecting payments from the borrower.
3. One major exception to this characterization, as we will see, relates to differences in credit risk.
4. Some additional determinants often included in a turnover model are credit score, loan-to-value ratio at origination, slope of the yield curve at origination, and spread between the borrower's mortgage rate and the average mortgage rate at origination.
5. The Rust Belt includes parts of the northeastern United States, the mid-Atlantic states, and portions of the eastern midwest.
6. The CIR model was one of the first internally consistent term structure models. See Rebonato (2004) for a survey of interest rate models.
7. Credit enhancement and non-agency CMO structure are discussed in the next section.
8. See Kramer and Sinha (2006).
9. Loan performance in Ashcraft and Schuermann (2008).
10. This structure is common for CMOs backed by non-agency Alt-A and jumbo prime collateral. CMOs backed by subprime mortgages often provide additional credit enhancement through excess spread and overcollateralization.

REFERENCES

Ashcraft, Adam A., and Til Schuermann. 2008. "Understanding the Securitization of Subprime Mortgage Credit." Federal Bank of New York Staff Report No. 318.

Fabozzi, Frank J. 2005. *The Handbook of Mortgage-Backed Securities.* 6th ed. New York: McGraw-Hill.

Gorton, Gary. 2008. "The Panic of 2007." Unpublished paper prepared for the Federal Reserve Bank of Kansas City, Jackson Hole Conference, August.

Kramer, Bruce, and Gyan Sinha. 2006. *Bear Stearns Quick Guide to Non-Agency Mortgage Backed Securities.* Bear Stearns, September.

McDonald, Daniel J., and Daniel L. Thornton. 2008. "A Primer on the Mortgage Market and Mortgage Finance." *Federal Reserve Bank of St. Louis Review* (January/February 2008): 31–46.

Rebonato, Riccardo. 2004. "Interest Rate Term-Structure Pricing Models: A Review." *Proceedings: Mathematical, Physical and Engineering Sciences* 460:2043, 667–728.

ABOUT THE AUTHOR

Bruce McNevin is the managing director of Mortgage Research at The MidWay Group, a hedge fund specializing in mortgage-backed securities. His primary responsibilities include directing development of mortgage prepayment models and conducting relative value research on MBSs. Dr. McNevin holds a PhD in economics from the City University of New York.

CHAPTER 6

The Equity Market

GARY L. GASTINEAU
ETF Consultants LLC

JOHN F. MARSHALL
Marshall Management Services

Equity Market Snapshot

History: Although some forms of equity derivatives have been around for many years, the growth of the equity derivatives markets has accelerated dramatically within the past fifteen years, with increasing volumes of equity derivatives traded due to improving technology and changing market infrastructure. One of the most successful equity products developed by financial engineers within the past two decades is the exchange-traded fund (ETF).

Size: In comparison to other markets, the over-the-counter and exchange-traded portions of the equity derivatives market have grown at roughly the same pace, and are close in size. The OTC equity derivatives market has expanded from $1.5 trillion in 1998 to $6.6 trillion in 2009, while the exchange-traded derivatives market has grown from $1.2 trillion in 1998 to $5.8 trillion in 2009.

Products: Exchange-traded equity products include equity options, index options, index futures, single-stock futures, and exchange-traded funds (ETFs). OTC equity products include, primarily, equity options and swaps, basket options and swaps, index and share-linked swaps, warrants, forward contracts, and contracts-for-difference (CFDs).

First Usage: The first standardized stock call options began trading in 1973 on the Chicago Board Options Exchange (CBOE). Previously, equity options were bought and sold only in the OTC market as individually negotiated contracts.

Selection of Famous Events

1996: Bing Sung, a trader at Rhumbline Advisers, a firm that mostly managed funds that mirrored the performance of stock indices, made large unauthorized bets on the direction of technology stocks. Rhumbline had agreed to manage AT&T's options portfolios in a conservative manner, but beginning in 1995, Sung had begun to exceed the limits imposed by AT&T and was eventually discovered when those option positions went awry due to market conditions. Rhumbline had

131

amassed losses of $150 million for AT&T's pension fund, as well as $12 million for a pension fund of Massachusetts teachers and state employees.

1998: The Union Bank of Switzerland had racked up large losses on its equity derivatives in Singapore, amounting to about $700 million. At the same time, the bank also incurred losses from problems at the hedge fund Long-Term Capital Management (LTCM), accumulating total losses of $1.2 billion for the year. The bank's problems served as one of the reasons for its merger with Swiss Bank Corporation (SBS) to form UBS during the same year.

2008: A team from the large French mutual bank, Groupe Caisse d'Épargne, made bad bets on equity derivatives linked to the CAC-40, the French equivalent of the Dow Jones Industrial Average. Because the stock markets had plunged during a week in October, the proprietary trading positions that the team held quickly soured. In addition, the trades made were unauthorized, with volume and amount of derivative positions exceeding the risk limits of the bank. The total losses incurred from these derivatives totaled about €600 million ($807 million).

Best Providers (as of 2009): Bank of America Merrill Lynch was named Best Provider of Equity Derivatives in North America by Global Finance magazine, while Société Générale received the award for both Europe and Asia.

Applications: Equity derivatives can be used for investing, hedging, enhancing tax efficiency, and cost savings.

Users: Investors in equity derivatives range from professionals, such as investment banks, fund managers, and securities houses, to private individual investors.

INTRODUCTION

This chapter examines some of the ways financial engineering has contributed, and will continue to contribute, to the growth of trading and the development of new products in the equity markets. The authors' familiarity with U.S. markets is greater than their familiarity with other markets. Consequently, most of the examples are U.S. examples. This parochialism is not a significant disadvantage, because a similar story with similar examples is applicable to most of the world's equity markets.

CASH MARKET—ORIGINS

The cash equity markets exist to facilitate (1) the raising of equity capital by corporate issuers, and (2) the transfer of ownership interests in corporate entities among investors. The equity markets provide the essential mechanics and the necessary liquidity to accomplish these key objectives. Historically, the markets consisted of both centralized, highly organized, self-policing exchanges, and a less formal, over-the-counter component with markets made by dealers. In recent years a number of novel platforms have been introduced, including such things as "dark pools," in which investors can trade anonymously. The roots of the modern equity markets in the United States trace back over 200 years, to the founding of what are now called the Philadelphia Stock Exchange and the New York Stock Exchange, respectively—both of which have undergone many transformations and mergers over the years.

The organization of equity markets varies from country to country, and, even within a country, there can be multiple market structures. Increasingly, mergers between exchanges, particularly cross-border mergers, have made the operation of equity markets a global enterprise. These mergers themselves can be seen as a form of financial engineering, as technologies developed and applied in one market are then transferred to another market. We will have more to say about the recent history of the cash equity markets later. But first we will consider some of the equity derivative products that have been developed and introduced over the past thirty or so years. These products represent milestones in the history of financial innovation. The more important of these are equity options, index options, stock index futures, equity swaps, and ETFs. Much of this chapter will be devoted to the latter.

EQUITY DERIVATIVES

There are a number of different types of equity derivatives, including equity options, exchange-traded index options, stock-index and single-stock futures, and equity swaps.

Equity Options

An equity option is routinely defined as the "right but not the obligation to buy or sell a specific number of shares of a specific stock at a specific price for a specific period of time." The specific stock is called the "underlying asset" or simply the "underlying" (some people say "underlier"). The seller of the option is called the "writer," the buyer of the option is called the "holder" or the "purchaser." The seller is *short* the option, and the holder is *long* the option. For the "right" that the option conveys, the buyer of the option pays the seller of the option a "fee" up front, known as the "option premium." The premium is the price paid for the option. It should not be confused with the strike price, which is a separate price paid if and only if the option is exercised. If the option gives its holder the right to *buy* the stock, it is known as a "call option," or simply a "call." If the option gives its holder the right to *sell* the stock, it is known as a "put option," or simply a "put." The specific price at which the option can be "exercised" is called the option's "strike price" (also sometimes known as the "exercise price"), and the life of the option is called its "time to expiration" or "time to expiry." The actual date of expiration is called "expiration date" or "expiry."

Options come in a variety of "types," sometimes called "styles." These include American-type, European-type, and Bermudan-type. American-type options can be exercised by the holder at any time from the moment they are written until the moment they expire. European-type, on the other hand, can only be exercised at the very end of their lives. Bermudan-type are in between American and European, in that they can be exercised at several distinct points in their lives, but are not continuously exercisable the way American-type options are.

Equity options have traded informally in an over-the-counter environment for a very long time, but it wasn't until the formation of the equity options exchanges that standardization and clearinghouses were introduced. The first of these to trade equity options in the United States was the Chicago Board Options Exchange (CBOE), which began trading calls in 1973 and soon after introduced puts. Other exchanges followed, and eventually there were a handful of exchanges trading, essentially, the same products but written on different underlyings. That is, each exchange had a monopoly on the "names" it traded, which made it possible for market makers to maintain rather wide bid-ask spreads. Eventually, under pressure from regulators and potential competitors, these monopolies gave way to competition and, not surprisingly, bid-ask spreads soon narrowed.

In the same year that exchange-traded equity options were introduced, two academics, Fischer Black and Myron Scholes (later to be considered two of the most important contributors to the field that eventually became known as financial engineering), published the first complete option pricing model. It is not that others had not tried to develop option pricing models, but none had completely succeeded. Black and Scholes demonstrated that, under a specific set of assumptions, the value of an equity option is a function of five variables. These are sometimes referred to as the option's "value drivers." They are (1) the current spot price of the underlying stock, (2) the strike price of the option, (3) the time to option expiration, (4) the interest rate, and the (5) the volatility of the price of the underlying stock. In their model, Black and Scholes assumed away dividends.

The Black-Scholes model was soon improved upon by Robert Merton. Their collective work is now often referred to as the Black-Scholes-Merton option pricing model. These models were revolutionary theoretical and technological breakthroughs that were derived using principles of stochastic calculus. At the time, few people working in finance had the necessary quantitative skills to fully appreciate these models. Nevertheless, it was possible to develop "tables" to tell a trader what an option was worth under a given set of value drivers.

In time, a number of alternative approaches were developed to value equity options. These included finite difference methods, numerical models, and simulation models, among others. Each approach has its own strengths and its own weaknesses. For example, some models are easily adapted to fit a slightly different set of assumptions (such as if the stock pays dividends); others are not easily adapted. At the same time, the less flexible model might be computationally faster than more flexible models.

Over time, options were introduced on a variety of underlyings, in addition to equities. These included options on interest rates, options on commodities, options on futures, and so on. With each new type of underlying and each new set of contract specifications, new models needed to be developed. Because models employ assumptions and reality does not necessarily accord with the assumptions, new models are continuing to be introduced and old models refined. The goal is always to more accurately estimate the true value of the option. Indeed, option valuation modeling is one of the critical components of financial engineering expertise, and it is where you see the importance of a good quantitative skill set. It is also, in part, the reason that people associate financial engineering with quantitative finance—even though there are areas of financial engineering that do not require strong quantitative skills. Because this is not a chapter on derivatives valuation, we will only highlight the more elementary issues. We assume that the reader has access to more detailed literature on the mathematics of derivatives valuation.[1]

Today, equity options exchanges can trade options that are either physically deliverable or cash settled. Physically deliverable options require that, if the option is exercised, the physical underlying be transferred from one party to the other with payment simultaneously made at the contract's strike price. If the recipient of the underlying does not want the underlying, he or she can sell it in the cash market. Cash-settled options dispense with the physical transfer of the underlying and settle up at expiry for the cash equivalent of transferring the underlying and making a corresponding cash market transaction. For some purposes traders prefer physically deliverable options, but for other purposes cash settlement is more efficient.

Exchange-traded equity options employ a clearinghouse to remove the counterparty credit risk between the long and the short.[2] That is, no matter with whom the actual trade is made when buying or selling the option, the trader's counterparty becomes the clearinghouse. The clearinghouse requires the option writer to post margin to protect the clearinghouse from credit risk. The buyer of the option pays the premium to the seller but does not post margin with the clearinghouse.

Even though not all options are cash-settled, and exchange-traded equity options are usually physically deliverable, we can talk about them as though they are all cash-settled since we can always synthesize cash settlement by a cash market transaction. We adopt this convention here.

Exchange-traded equity options in the United States usually expire on the third Friday of the month. So, for example, a June call option on Microsoft (ticker MSFT) would expire on the third Friday of June. It is not necessary to point this out since all traders are familiar with this expiration convention. Now suppose that it is presently March 15 and the June option expires on June 19. That is 96 days to expiry. Suppose that MSFT is currently trading at $25.30 (the spot price), the relevant interest rate is 2 percent, and the annualized volatility of MSFT is 30 percent. Suppose further that MSFT will not pay any dividends between March 15 and June 19. We are interested in a call option having a strike price of $25. In this scenario, using a Black/Scholes' set of assumptions, the value of this call is $1.76. Thus, ignoring a small bid-ask spread, the market maker would charge a $1.76 premium for this slightly "in-the-money" call option. The "per-share-covered" payoff to the option holder at expiry on June 19th would be given by the following equation:

$$\text{Terminal Payoff} = max[S - X, \ 0]$$

where *max* denotes the "maximum" function defined as the larger of the two values in brackets at expiration, S denotes the spot price of the stock (i.e., stock price) at expiration, and X denotes the strike price. A call is described as "in-the-money" when $S > X$; "at-the-money" when $S = X$, and "out-of-the-money" when $S < X$. Since the strike price of $25 was set at the time the option was written and does not change, we can fill this in and get:

$$\text{Terminal Payoff} = max[S - \$25, \ 0]$$

It should be plainly obvious that, at expiry, the option has zero value at any stock price at or below $25. The call will have a positive value (payoff) equal to the difference between S and X whenever $S > X$. Suppose, for example, that MSFT is trading at $32.10 at the time of the option's expiration. Then the payoff is given by:

$$\text{Terminal Payoff} = max[\$32.10 - \$25.00,\ 0] = \$7.10$$

Importantly, this terminal payoff should not be confused with "profit." After all, the option holder paid the option writer $1.76 for the option when he or she bought it. Therefore, profit at expiration is given by:

$$\text{Profit/Loss} = max[S - X,\ 0] - \text{Premium Paid}$$

In our specific example, the profit would be $5.34 (i.e., $7.10 – $1.76). Of course, this calculation is for each share covered by the option. On U.S. and most other countries' exchanges, options typically cover 100 shares, so the actual premium paid and the actual profit earned on this contract would be $176 and $534, respectively.

Graphically, the profit diagram that corresponds to the profit/loss function above is depicted in Exhibit 6.1. Notice the characteristic "hockey stick" shape of the profit diagram. Whenever "hockey stick" shaped profit diagrams are encountered, one should always expect to find some sort of option.

Analogous arguments can be made for put options. In these cases, the terminal payoff is given by:

$$\text{Terminal Payoff} = max[X - S,\ 0]$$

And the profit function at expiration is given by:

$$\text{Profit/Loss} = max[X - S,\ 0] - \text{Premium Paid}$$

Not surprisingly, a put option is in-the-money when $S < X$, at-the-money when $S = X$, and out-of-the-money when $S > X$.

Suppose now that the put has a strike price of $25, the stock price is again $25.30 at the time the option is written, the annual volatility is 30 percent, the interest rate is 2 percent, and the option has 96 days to expiry. The fair value of this

Exhibit 6.1   Profit Diagram: Call

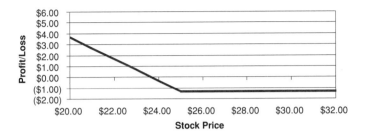

Exhibit 6.2 Profit Diagram: Put

slightly out-of-the-money put is $1.33, and we will assume that this is the price the buyer of the put pays. The profit function at expiry would then be given by:

$$\text{Profit/Loss} = max[\$25.00 - S, \ 0] - \$1.33$$

And the profit diagram is given in Exhibit 6.2.

Exchange-Traded Index Options

Exchange-traded index options are options written on stock indexes, such as the S&P 500 or the NASDAQ 100. That is, the index is the underlying. They are typically cash settled at expiration rather than physically delivered. The key difference between equity options and index options is that the former are written on individual equities, while the latter are written on stock indexes. Pricing models for index options are similar to option pricing models for equity options. The terminal payoff function, the profit/loss function, and the profit diagrams for index calls and puts are identical to those for single-stock calls and puts.

Index options were introduced by the CBOE in 1983 under long-term licensing agreements from the publishers of the indexes (i.e., the trademark holders). This has given the CBOE a monopoly position in these contracts and has made it difficult for other exchanges to compete in these product areas. Similar index option products were introduced on European and Asian exchanges.

Stock-Index and Single-Stock Futures

In the United States, stock index futures contracts were introduced in 1982 by the Chicago Mercantile Exchange (CME). The CME, like the Chicago Board of Trade (CBOT),[3] started out as a commodities exchange (also known as a commodity futures exchange). It wasn't until the 1980s that the CME began to introduce futures on underlyings that were not "commodities" in the traditional sense. The introduction of non-commodity futures, such as stock index futures and certain types of interest rate futures, required a "re-think" of the delivery rules for futures trading. The key innovation in the introduction of these two products, now some of the most heavily traded futures in the world, was the recognition that physical delivery could be replaced by cash settlement, provided that transparent cash settlement rules could be adopted.

It is important to note that index futures, like all futures, are guaranteed by a clearinghouse designated by the exchange. This effectively eliminates counterparty risk for the trading public. This is the same mechanism used to guarantee performance on exchange-traded equity options. However, in the case of futures, both parties to a futures contract post margin, which, in turn protects the clearinghouse from counterparty risk. Futures contracts are discussed much more thoroughly in the Commodity Market chapter of this book, so we will not spend precious space here describing the market mechanics of futures. Suffice it to say that stock index futures provided portfolio managers with a very useful hedging tool for their equity portfolios. They also provided investors with a highly-leveraged product that could be used to quickly and easily take either long or short positions on the broad market. Arbitrageurs, too, found uses for stock index futures, including various forms of basket trading that collectively became known as program trading.

As a side note, in 2002 a number of exchanges began trading single-stock futures (SSFs). These are similar in concept to commodity futures, in that each futures contract is written on one specific underlying stock, just as a commodity futures contract is written on one specific underlying commodity. The mechanics of SSFs, with respect to clearing and trading, are the same as the mechanics for index futures, and we won't elaborate on them here. The SSF market is small, but it has considerable future potential.

Equity Swaps

In 1989, Banker's Trust (later acquired by Deutsche Bank) introduced equity swaps. Equity swaps work on the same principle as interest rate swaps. These are over-the-counter derivatives and lack the standardization of most exchange-traded products. Indeed, that is one of their key strengths—they can be tailored to suit the specific needs of the client. In an equity swap, one counterparty pays the other counterparty a fixed or floating rate in exchange for receiving a floating rate determined by the behavior of a stock index (or a specific equity). The latter is paid on what is called the "equity leg." The swap can make use of the "price return" of the stock or index, or it can make use of the "total return" of the stock, or index on the equity leg. Total return includes dividends, price return does not. A typical equity swap with a fixed or floating rate on the non-equity leg is depicted in Exhibit 6.3.

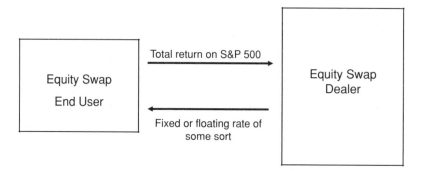

Exhibit 6.3   Structure of an Equity Swap

Equity swaps have many innovative uses, and the market for them grew rapidly after their introduction. The creation of this product was, of course, another exercise in financial engineering. So, too, was the introduction of each new variant of this product. Today there are dozens of such variants. The innovative applications of equity swaps are not to be neglected. These are best viewed as examples of applied financial engineering. We will consider one such example.

Suppose we have a hedge fund that seeks to earn the return on a bond portfolio. The hedge fund wants to "enhance" the return on the bond portfolio with some "alpha" earned from its expertise in the stock market. That is to say, the hedge fund manager believes he or she has the ability to outperform some equity benchmark (let's make it the S&P 500) on a risk-adjusted basis. So, the hedge fund purchases a carefully selected portfolio of equities. It then enters into an equity swap with an equity swap dealer. This equity swap is tailored a bit so that the hedge fund pays the dealer the total return on the S&P 500 quarterly for two years. In return, the equity swap dealer pays the hedge fund the total return on a particular bond index. Notice that this is the total return on an equity index for the total return on a bond index.

The logic here is that the hedge fund earns for its investors the total return on the bond index, just as if it had invested in the bonds that make up the index. But, it also keeps the difference between what it earned on its cash equity portfolio and what it pays on the equity leg of the swap. Assuming that the systematic risk of the equity portfolio and the systematic risk of the index used for the equity leg of the swap are the same, any difference could be a manifestation of "alpha." This alpha can then be paid out with the bond index return to the investors in the fund. This is an example of using equity swaps to "port" alpha from one asset class (equities) to another asset class (bonds). Portable alpha is discussed later in this book in more detail. The structure is depicted in Exhibit 6.4.

Equity swaps have become particularly popular in Europe as a vehicle to avoid taxes on equity transactions. For example, the U.K. government levies a 0.5 percent "stamp duty" (the term comes from the old practice of requiring stamped paper for legal documents) on the purchase side of an equity transaction. By structuring an equity swap to synthesize a long or short position in equities, the investor does not have to pay this tax. Equity swaps of this sort are commonly called "contracts for difference" (CFD). CFDs are typically contracts between investors and dealer banks. At the end of the contract, the parties exchange the difference between the starting and ending prices of the underlying financial instrument. As a side point, investors in these sorts of equity swaps can also benefit by avoiding custody fees, withholding taxes on dividends, and restrictions on shorting stock. Recent estimates place CFD-backed trades at the equivalent of 25 percent to 30 percent of equity transactions on the London Stock Exchange.

The same OTC derivatives dealers that make markets in equity swaps also, often, make markets in equity options. These differ from exchange-traded equity options in that all terms are negotiable. Additionally, it is possible to create extraordinarily "exotic" equity swaps and equity options, which have many uses. These exotic products tend to be introduced when a client has a problem that none of the existing products neatly addresses. Once a novel product is introduced, it is often added to the dealer's toolkit and recycled to other clients. Through this process, the tailored exotic gradually becomes another off-the-shelf tool.

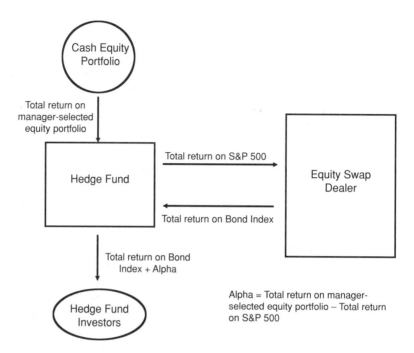

Exhibit 6.4   A Typical Structure for Porting Alpha

DECLINING TRADING COSTS INCREASE FINANCIAL ENGINEERING OPPORTUNITIES, AND FINANCIAL ENGINEERING OFTEN REDUCES TRADING COSTS

In 1968, the average daily volume of stock trading on the New York Stock Exchange (NYSE) was about 13 million shares. Just 40 years later, in 2008, the average daily trading volume in NYSE-listed stocks was about six billion shares per day. This is roughly a 450 times increase in volume, yet it still *understates* the significance of the increase in equity trading volume. In 1968, the trading volume on other exchanges and the over-the-counter market (not yet NASDAQ) was a small fraction of the trading volume on the New York Stock Exchange, and ETFs did not exist. In 2009, total equity trading volume was nearly 10 billion shares a day and about 20 percent of that volume was in ETFs.

New York Stock Exchange trading volumes in 1968 were at record levels—up from just three million shares a day in 1960. In fact, one reason for selecting 1968 as a starting point for this commentary is that this high volume (by the standards of the day) created massive operating problems for U.S. securities markets. The NYSE closed early on many days in the first half of 1968 and closed every Wednesday during the second half of the year to deal with a "paperwork crisis."

The dramatic growth in trading over the next 40 years—without a repeat of the operational chaos of 1968—is the result of two kinds of changes that are at the heart of many examples of financial engineering: improvements in technology and corresponding changes in the economics of trading and in the instruments available to trade. The computerization of both trading and back office operations has sharply reduced commissions and trading spreads for small trades and for trading baskets of securities since 1968. The costs of large trades in a single issue have not, on the other hand, declined much, if at all, because their largest cost element is the price of the liquidity they demand.

Long before 1968 and for a few years thereafter, New York Stock Exchange commissions were fixed at a high level. The average commission on a stock purchase or sale in 1968 was significantly more than 1 percent of the value of the transaction. Bid-ask spreads were generally measured in quarters ($0.25) rather than the penny ($0.01) spreads common for small trades in many actively traded shares today. The market impact of a large trade was significant in 1968, as it is today. The growth of institutional investing was just getting under way in 1968, so large trades were much less common than they became in the 1970s and 1980s.

Punch-card accounting was still common in 1968, but the early computer systems available then were dramatic innovations relative to the handwritten ledgers and clerks with iconic eyeshades that were the state of the art 40 years earlier in the late 1920s. The technology introduced since the paperwork crisis of 1968 has made much higher volumes possible with far less hands-on human involvement in every step of the trading and trade settlement process.

The workday population on the New York Stock Exchange floor grew for a number of years after 1968, but floor trading activity is not meaningful today. Most recent live videos from the NYSE floor show more quotation monitors than people to watch them. The visitors gallery has been closed since September 11, 2001 and the floor is often most crowded during the cocktail parties that begin shortly after the formal close of trading. Automated trading and trade processing have changed the visualization, as well as the economics, of trading.

The total cost to buy or sell stock in 1968 approached 2 percent of the value of the stock. With some fairly rough rounding, total trading costs probably represented a little more than 0.2 percent of the value of the trade for the average transaction by a retail investor in 2008. The average cost of a typical retail transaction fell by a factor of nearly 10 while *total* transaction costs in the stock market increased by a multiple of as much as 50. The reduction in the cost of each trade brought in more traders—and facilitated a number of feats of financial engineering. While the increases in trading volume and in total trading costs are dramatic, they are an almost inevitable consequence of changes in technology and market infrastructure that stimulated a broad range of financial market innovations.

In some respects, the most dramatic equity trading stories are the stories of new equity derivatives markets and new derivative products that have been introduced on equity markets over the past 40 years. Many of these markets and products were briefly discussed in the first part of this chapter. These new equity derivatives markets have their own eye-popping figures for transaction volumes and the notional values of both trading and open interest in equity derivatives contracts. While new equity derivatives have stimulated stock volume, the notional volume in some of these equity derivatives markets exceeds the dollar value of the underlying equity market volumes.

As noted earlier, exchange-traded equity derivatives, such as index futures, single-stock futures, and equity options, all employ a clearinghouse to guarantee performance and ameliorate counterparty credit risk. OTC products, such as equity swaps, equity forwards, and OTC equity options have not, generally, employed a clearinghouse to guarantee performance. Instead, each participant in these bilateral transactions needed to consider the creditworthiness of its counterparty. This, of course, tended to push the end users of these contracts toward more highly rated dealers. Banks often responded by setting up "best credit" subsidiaries to serve as the dealer function. These would typically be very well-funded and have an excellent credit rating. However, in the wake of the credit issues that surfaced in 2007 and 2008, many of these OTC instruments will be cleared through clearinghouses in the future.

ARBITRAGE COMPLEXES

The relationships between trading in equities and trading in various equity derivatives markets are best understood by considering how an arbitrage complex works. The arbitrage complex provides a useful way to think about the range of choices open to users of index (or portfolio basket) financial instruments. The arbitrage complex consists of a number of related financial instruments, or groups of financial instruments, based on a common group of underlying assets. The principal underlying assets behind each of the instruments in an arbitrage complex may consist of an index, an arbitrary stock basket, an exchange-traded fund (ETF), or even an individual security or commodity. The arbitrage complex can cover domestic and/or foreign markets. An arbitrage complex can include components that are nominally debt instruments (structured notes), and it can include options and other components that have a nonsymmetric response to changing prices.

Exhibit 6.5 lists some typical equity index arbitrage complex instruments. Among the traditional securities positions, the members of the equity index arbitrage complex are program or portfolio trading of baskets of equity securities and exchange-traded funds. These are simply combinations and extensions of the traditional underlying securities that compose equity portfolios. Trading securi-

Exhibit 6.5   Equity Index Arbitrage Complex Instruments

ties in a basket or as an index derivative is a natural extension of both trading technology improvements and modern portfolio theory.

The second category in the arbitrage complex is symmetric derivatives. By symmetric, we mean that they move up and down very much like the underlying index portfolio or position that determines their market risk characteristics. The most important symmetric equity index instruments are stock index futures, ETF single-stock futures contracts, and equity index swaps.

To round out the instruments that make up an equity index arbitrage complex, there are index options and structured notes based on indexes. In contrast to the instruments we have discussed so far, instruments with embedded options have convexity; that is, they have payoffs that are not straight-line functions of an underlying price variable.

We plan to spend most of the balance of this chapter illustrating and analyzing some of the things financial engineers have done and continue to do to transform key segments of the market in equity securities. The development of these markets illustrates some of the ways in which trading in the components of an arbitrage complex interact and contribute to pricing efficiency and trading cost reduction.

EQUITY STRUCTURED PRODUCTS AND EXCHANGE-TRADED FUNDS (ETFs)

The equity structured products that financial engineers have developed over the years are extraordinarily diverse. These structured products have ranged from structured notes (debt instruments with embedded equity elements) and covered warrants to Americus Trust primes and scores, which were similar to a number of products now available on the listed options markets. The most successful of the equity instruments developed by financial engineers go under the broad label of exchange-traded funds (ETFs). Not all the products called ETFs are funds, but most of them share a common genesis in basket or portfolio trading and index arbitrage. A few of them are simply different ways to package something—gold, for example—to make it easier for investors to hold and trade as a security. They are all exchange-traded. The fact that investors can trade most of the products called ETFs at market-determined prices that are close to the intraday value of an underlying portfolio or index is one common feature of most of these securities. At various times, the ETF label has been attached to:

- Closed-end funds (e.g., Nuveen).
- Grantor trust products based on fixed portfolios (e.g., HOLDRs).
- Grantor trust products based on holdings of a single commodity (e.g., Gold and Silver Trusts).
- Currency money market trusts (e.g., Euro Currency Trust).
- Commodity indexed trusts (e.g., iShares Goldman Sachs Commodity Index Trust).
- Open-end structured notes (e.g., iPath GSCI Total Return Index Notes).
- Mutual fund exchange-traded share classes (e.g., Vanguard ETFs).
- Standard & Poor's depositary receipt (SPDR)-style indexed portfolios (e.g., SPDRs, QQQs, World Equity Benchmark Shares [WEBS], iShares, etc.).

Each of these products has an interesting history, and most can serve as models for further financial engineering. For reasons of space, our focus will be on the last group. It includes the largest number of products and competes head-to-head with conventional mutual funds, a product family in serious need of some structural innovation. As we look at ETF evolution we will take quick looks at where a few of the other products fit into the history of equity market innovation.

When we examine these products, it is important to bear in mind that many of the early ETFs were not created to provide a superior investment vehicle. Some of the most successful of these products were developed primarily to provide something to trade, not to create the ideal product for investors. Most of the products that are called ETFs rely heavily on a low-cost equity trading environment. Because of diverse motives and structural choices, it is often difficult to pin down the economic incentives to various parties behind a particular product or structure. Nonetheless, an important part of the financial engineer's job is to understand the economic incentives that will make a new product or market succeed. Cost reduction is usually a large part of the explanation for the success of a new product or market. Keep an eye out for examples of cost reduction as we trace the history of the ETFs' antecedents—the proto-products that led to the current generation of ETFs—and set the stage for products yet to come.

PORTFOLIO TRADING AND STOCK INDEX FUTURES CONTRACTS

The basic idea of trading an entire portfolio in a single transaction did not originate with the Canadian Toronto Index Participation Securities (TIPs) or the U.S. SPDRs, the earliest examples of the modern portfolio-traded-as-a-share structure. It originated with what has come to be known as *portfolio trading* or *program trading*. From the late 1970s through the 1980s, program trading was the then-revolutionary ability to trade an entire portfolio, often a portfolio consisting of all the S&P 500 stocks, with a single order placed at a major brokerage firm. Similar portfolio trades were available using other indexes in Canada, Europe, and Asia. Some relatively modest advances in electronic trade entry and execution technology, and the availability of large order desks at some major investment banking firms, made these early portfolio or program trades possible. The introduction of S&P 500 index futures contracts by the Chicago Mercantile Exchange (and similar contracts in other markets) created and required an arbitrage link between the new futures contracts and portfolios of stocks. It was even possible, in a trade called an exchange of futures for physicals (EFP), to exchange a stock portfolio position, long or short, for a stock index futures position, long or short. The effect of these developments was to make portfolio trading either in cash or in futures markets an attractive activity for many trading desks and for many institutional investors. The attraction was a combination of opportunities for arbitrage profits and lower trading costs. The equity arbitrage complex is a natural consequence of these developments.

From developments that originally served only large investors, there arose interest in a readily tradable portfolio or basket product for small institutions and for individual investors. The early futures contracts were relatively large in notional size, and the variation margin requirements for carrying these futures contracts were cumbersome and relatively expensive for a small investor. The need for a low-price-point security (i.e., an SEC-regulated portfolio product) that could be used by individual investors was increasingly apparent. The first such products in the United States were index participation shares (IPS).

Index Participation Shares (IPS)

Index participation shares were a relatively simple, totally synthetic proxy for the S&P 500 index. While other indexes were also available, S&P 500 IPS began trading on the American Stock Exchange (Amex) and the Philadelphia Stock Exchange in 1989. A federal court in Chicago quickly ruled that the IPS were futures contracts and had to be traded on a futures exchange, if they were to be traded at all. The stock exchanges had to close down IPS trading. This would not have been an issue in most other countries. Outside the United States, securities and futures are typically overseen by the same regulator, and there is less legal distinction between a security and a futures contract.

While a number of efforts to find a replacement product for IPS that would pass muster as a security were underway in the United States, Toronto Index Participation Securities (TIPs) were introduced in Canada.

Toronto Index Participation Securities (TIPs)

TIPs were a warehouse receipt-based instrument designed to track the TSE-35 index and, later, the TSE-100 index as well. TIPs traded actively and attracted substantial investment from Canadians and from international indexing investors. The ability of the trustee to lend out the stocks in the TIPs portfolios for a fee led to a negative expense ratio at times. However, the TIPs proved costly for the Toronto Stock Exchange and for some of its members who, because of the simple (noncommercial) TIPs structure, were unable to recover their costs from investors. Early in 2000, the Toronto Stock Exchange decided to get out of the portfolio share business, and TIPs positions were liquidated or, at the option of the TIPs holder, rolled into a fund now known as the iShares CDN LargeCap 60. This fund had assets of about C$12 billion at the end of 2009.

Meanwhile, two other portfolio-in-a-share products were under development in the United States: SuperTrust and SPDRs.

SuperTrust and Supershares

The SuperTrust and Supershares were a product complex using both a trust and a mutual fund structure—one inside the other. Supershares were a high-cost product. The complexity of the product, which permitted division of the Supershares into a variety of components, some with option and option-like characteristics, made sales presentations long and confusing for many customers. The Supershares were developed by Leland, O'Brien, Rubinstein Associates, the folks behind portfolio insurance. The SuperTrust securities never traded actively, and the trust was eventually liquidated. This product failure stemmed from higher costs and greater complexity than investors were prepared for in the early 1990s. The failure was unrelated to portfolio insurance.

Standard & Poor's Depositary Receipts (SPDRs)

Standard & Poor's depositary receipts (SPDRs, pronounced "spiders") were developed as a trading vehicle by the American Stock Exchange, approximately in parallel with the SuperTrust. The original SPDRs are a unit trust with an S&P 500 portfolio that, unlike the portfolios of most U.S. unit trusts, can be changed as the index composition changes. The reason for using the unit trust structure was the Amex's concern for costs. A mutual fund must pay the costs of a board of directors, even if the fund is very small. The Amex was uncertain of the demand for SPDRs and did not want to build a more costly infrastructure than was necessary. Only a few other ETFs (e.g., the MidCap SPDRs, the NASDAQ-100 QQQs, and the DIAMONDS, based on the Dow Jones Industrial Average) use the unit trust structure. Most ETFs introduced since 2000 use a modified version of the mutual fund investment company structure. Nonetheless, the S&P 500 SPDRs remain the largest ETF and the largest consumer equity investment product in the United States and the world, with assets of nearly $85 billion at the end of 2009.

SPDRs traded reasonably well on the Amex in their early years, but only in the late 1990s did SPDRs' trading volume and asset growth take off, as investors began to look past the somewhat esoteric in-kind share creation and redemption process, and focus on the investment characteristics and tax efficiency of the SPDRs themselves. It is difficult to ascribe the phenomenal success of the SPDR and subsequent ETFs to a small list of factors, but certainly among the contributing features to the SPDRs' success were: (1) extremely tight and aggressive market making by the specialist team at Spear, Leeds & Kellogg; (2) the fact that the Amex was able to get the SPDRs' expense ratio below the expense ratio of the Vanguard 500 mutual fund, the SPDRs' principal competitor; and (3) the steady growth of interest in the tax efficiency of exchange-traded funds, which usually permits the holder of this type of ETF to defer all capital gains taxation until the shares are sold. Note that these features all reflect the importance of cost reduction in the success of a new product.

World Equity Benchmark Shares (WEBS, Renamed iShares MSCI Series) and Other Investment Company Shares

The World Equity Benchmark Shares (WEBS) are important for two reasons. First, they are foreign index exchange-traded funds—that is, funds holding stocks issued by non-U.S.–based firms. Second, they are some of the earliest exchange-traded fund products to use a management investment company (mutual fund) structure as opposed to a unit trust structure. If you are going to create a large number of similar products, a mutual fund series structure can be much less costly to maintain than a separate unit trust for each product.

Another family of foreign index funds designed to compete with the WEBS was introduced on the NYSE at about the same time that WEBS appeared on the Amex. For a variety of reasons, the most important of which were structural flaws in the product, these country baskets failed, and the trust was liquidated.

The sector SPDRs were the first ETFs with domestic stock portfolios in a mutual fund structure similar to the WEBS. They were introduced in late 1998, and their assets have grown more consistently than most other specialized ETFs.

Other brands for ETFs and similarly traded products have included:

- Ameristock
- BLDRS (Baskets of Listed Depositary Receipts)
- Claymore
- Fidelity
- First Trust
- FocusShares
- HealthShares
- HOLDRS (Holding Company Depositary Receipts)
- MacroShares
- PowerShares
- ProShares
- Realty Funds
- Rydex
- SPA ETF Europe Ltd.
- State Street SPDRs
- StreetTracks
- TDAX Independence Funds
- VanEck
- Vanguard
- Victoria Bay
- Wisdom Tree

with new brands added frequently. Many of the same brands are represented in ETF markets outside the United States, and, of course, some firms offer funds in just one country or a small number of countries. At the end of 2009, there were more than 1,907 ETFs trading on 39 exchanges around the world with total assets of USD 1 trillion (Fuhr, 2009).

ETFs Not Operating under the Investment Company Act of 1940

The unit trust structure of the SPDRs, and the managed investment company structure of the WEBS, sector SPDRs, and other true funds launched after 2000 in the United States, are subject to the Investment Company Act of 1940, the legislation that covers the operation of mutual funds. In addition to these true funds, there are a number of other products under a broader definition of an ETF that are organized as a grantor trust, as another type of trust, or as an open-end exchange-traded note. These products exist because some portfolio products cannot be issued under the Investment Company Act of 1940. The Investment Company Act and related tax statutes restrict the type of financial instruments that can be held by an investment company and the type of income it can receive. As is their wont, financial engineers have developed a wide range of products that mesh with the securities laws in appropriate ways to package portfolios of securities, commodities, and derivatives for delivery in a convenient package that is not encumbered by some of the restrictions imposed by the Investment Company Act. Some of these are grantor trusts with pass-through of the incidents of ownership to the holders of shares in the trust. Others are in the form of limited partnerships, necessitating the distribution of K-1 tax reports to each investor in the United States.

Still others are relatively simple exchange-traded notes, which are open-ended to provide for expansion and contraction in a manner similar to the creation and redemption mechanism of the investment company ETFs. ETFs, in the broadest sense, have been an arena for significant financial engineering innovation, and there is no reason to expect the pace of innovation to decline. Nevertheless, one cannot help speculating that some of the low-hanging financial engineering fruit has been plucked and that the most fruitful area for innovation going forward will involve modifying the structure and operation of open-end portfolio ETFs.

Open-End Portfolio ETFs Subject to the Investment Company Act of 1940

The open-end ETFs based on the SPDR model (both unit trust and mutual fund structures) have a number of fundamental characteristics that have made this new generation of funds a worthy model for further development by financial engineers. These open-end ETFs do not have shareholder accounting expenses at the fund level, and they have few, if any, embedded marketing expenses. In a sense, they are like mutual funds stripped of some costly historical baggage. These expense-reducing features, and the fact that these fund shares are traded like stocks rather than like mutual fund shares, usually make ETFs more costly than no-load mutual funds to buy and sell, but nearly always less costly to hold than comparable mutual funds. Some early investors in ETFs were attracted by the fact that the ETFs were low-cost index funds. However, today's index funds—ETFs and mutual funds—are not always the low-cost portfolios their owners thought they were buying.

From a financial engineering perspective, it is useful to focus on two important characteristics of the SPDR-style ETF that were, in some respects, serendipitous. Because these characteristics have helped attract investors, they have been important in the early success of ETFs. These characteristics also provide a basis for development of the SPDR-style ETF model well beyond its impressive beginnings. Not everyone attaches as much significance as we do to these two features, but we are convinced that they hold the key to the development of better funds. The two key features of most existing SPDR-style ETFs are shareholder protection and tax efficiency.

SHAREHOLDER PROTECTION

The material described in the next few paragraphs is widely known, but not frequently discussed. A recent comprehensive description of mutual fund pricing over the years is available in Swenson (2005).[4]

In 1968 (that year again), the Securities and Exchange Commission (SEC) implemented Rule 22(c)(1), which required mutual fund share transactions to be priced at the net asset value[5] (NAV) *next determined* by the fund. This meant that anyone entering an order after the close of business on day 1 would purchase or sell fund shares at the net asset value determined at the close on day 2.

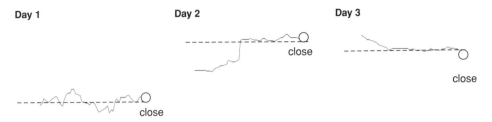

Exhibit 6.6 Since 1968—Buying and Selling Mutual Fund Shares at the Net Asset Value Next Determined

Correspondingly, someone entering an order to purchase or sell shares after the close on day 2 would be accommodated at the net asset value determined at the close on day 3. This process is illustrated in Exhibit 6.6.

There is a transaction fairness problem for fund investors with Rule 22(c)(1) in place.[6] That problem is illustrated in Exhibit 6.7.

By pricing all transactions in the mutual fund's shares *at the net asset value next determined*, as required by Rule 22(c)(1), the fund provides free liquidity to investors entering and leaving the fund. All the shareholders in the fund pay the cost of providing this liquidity. As Exhibit 6.7 illustrates, anyone purchasing mutual fund shares for cash gets a share of the securities positions already held by the fund and priced at net asset value. The new investor typically pays no transaction costs at the time of the share purchase. All the shareholders of the fund share the transaction costs associated with investing the new investor's cash in portfolio securities. Similarly, when an investor departs the mutual fund, that investor receives cash equal to the net asset value of the shares when the NAV is next calculated. All the shareholders in the fund bear the cost of selling portfolio securities to provide this liquidity. To the entering or leaving shareholder, liquidity is essentially free. To the ongoing shareholders of the fund, the liquidity given to transacting shareholders is costly. Over time, the cost of providing this free liquidity to entering and leaving shareholders is a perennial drag on a mutual fund's performance.

Exhibit 6.8 shows that exchange-traded funds handle the costs of accommodating entering and leaving shareholders differently from mutual funds. For exchange-traded funds, creations and redemptions of shares are typically made *in-kind*. Baskets of portfolio securities are deposited with the fund in exchange for fund shares in a creation. In a redemption, fund shares are turned in to the fund in exchange for a basket of portfolio securities. The creating or redeeming

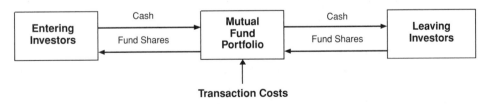

Exhibit 6.7 Cash Moves In and Out of a Mutual Fund: The Fund Trades Securities to Invest Incoming Cash or to Raise Cash for Redemptions

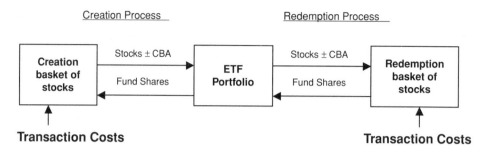

All securities transfers are priced at the net asset value next calculated
CBA = Cash Balancing Amount

Exhibit 6.8 ETF Creation and Redemption Is In-Kind: Transaction Costs Are Paid by Entering and Leaving Investors

investor—often a market maker in the ETF shares—is responsible for the costs of investing in the portfolio securities for deposit, and the cost of disposing of portfolio securities received in the redemption of outstanding fund shares. The market makers even pay a modest creation or redemption fee to cover the fund's administrative expenses. The market maker expects to pass these transaction costs on to investors when the market maker trades fund shares on the exchange. The cost of entering and leaving a fund varies, depending on the level of fund share trading activity and the nature of the securities in the fund's portfolio. For example, the cost of trading in small-cap stocks can be much greater than the cost of trading in large-cap stocks.

SPDR-type ETFs are different from mutual funds in the way they accommodate shareholder entry and exit in at least two important ways. (1) As illustrated, the trading costs associated with ETF shareholder entries and exits are ultimately borne by the entering and exiting investors, not by the fund. Furthermore, (2) unlike a mutual fund, an exchange-traded fund does not have to hold cash balances to provide for cash redemptions. An ETF can stay fully invested at all times. As a result of these differences, the performance experienced by ongoing shareholders in an ETF should, over time, handily surpass the performance experienced by ongoing shareholders of a conventional mutual fund using the same investment process. Ironically, even though the exchange-traded fund was designed to be traded throughout the trading day on an exchange, it is a much better product than a conventional fund for the shareholder *who does not want to trade*. As any mutual fund market timer will tell you, a mutual fund is a much better product to trade than an ETF because the mutual fund pays the timer's trading costs. Any reader interested in more detailed information on the ETF creation and redemption process should read a fund's prospectus and statement of additional information (SAI) for a more complete description of the process. We particularly recommend the prospectus for the original SPDR for its clarity and detail.

The mutual fund structure that provides free liquidity to investors who enter and leave the fund is responsible for the problems of late trading and market timing that provoked the mutual fund scandals of 2003 and 2004. The SEC has spent a great deal of time, effort, and (ultimately) investors' money trying to deal with the problem of market timing trades in mutual funds, without eliminating the free liquidity that ongoing shareholders in mutual funds give entering and leaving shareholders. This effort has not been successful. A variety of operational patches have been made by some mutual fund companies as they attempt to restrict market timing trades. The SEC now requires a complex and costly fund share transaction reporting structure with nearly mandatory redemption fees on mutual fund purchases that are closed out within a week. In the final analysis, the elimination of free liquidity—most easily through the exchange-traded fund in-kind creation and redemption process—is the only way to eliminate market timing without imposing unnecessary costs on all fund investors. Even if there is no such thing as a market timer in the future, long-term investors will fare better in funds that protect them from the costs of other investors entering and leaving the fund.

TAX EFFICIENCY

One of the most frequently discussed advantages of exchange-traded funds is tax efficiency. Tax efficiency benefits some taxable investors profoundly, but it has value to tax-exempt investors as well. The tax efficiency of ETFs is essentially tax deferral until the investor chooses to sell fund shares. This deferral is a natural result of subchapter M of the Internal Revenue Code, which permits fund share redemptions in-kind (delivering portfolio securities to departing fund shareholders) without tax impact inside the fund. An ETF (or mutual fund) share redemption in-kind does not give rise to a capital gain that is distributable to shareholders of the fund. For more details on ETF tax efficiency, see Gastineau (2005) or Gastineau (2010).

This kind of tax efficiency also benefits tax-exempt investors in the fund because it prevents the buildup of unrealized gains inside an ETF portfolio. The buildup of unrealized gains in a mutual fund portfolio can lead to portfolio management decisions that adversely affect tax-exempt shareholders. When the choice facing a portfolio manager is (1) to realize gains on appreciated portfolio securities and distribute taxable capital gains to the fund's shareholders or (2) to hold overvalued securities and avoid realizing capital gains, the portfolio manager faces a conflict between the interests of tax-exempt and taxable investors.

With exchange-traded funds, the decision to change the portfolio can be based solely on investment considerations, not on the tax basis of portfolio securities. Any conflict between taxable and tax-exempt shareholders disappears because the achievement of tax efficiency in ETFs is largely a matter of careful designation of tax lots, so that the lowest-cost lots of a security are distributed in-kind in redemptions, and high-cost lots are sold to realize losses inside the fund when a sale is necessary or appropriate.

Exchange-traded funds grow by exchanging new fund shares for portfolio securities deposited with the fund. Redemptions are also largely in-kind. Investors sell their fund shares on the exchange rather than redeeming them directly with the fund. If a fund has more shares outstanding than investors want to hold, dealers buy fund shares and turn them in to the fund in exchange for portfolio securities. This process serendipitously lets ETF managers take full advantage of the redemption in-kind provision of the Internal Revenue Code. The early developers of exchange-traded funds were aware of this tax treatment, but the tax deferral it gives holders of these ETFs was by no means a significant objective in the early development of ETFs. It is largely serendipitous that most well-managed exchange-traded funds will not distribute taxable capital gains to their shareholders. Creation and redemption in-kind not only transfers the cost of entering and leaving the fund to the entering and leaving shareholders; it also defers capital gains taxes until a shareholder chooses to sell his or her fund shares.

The in-kind creation and redemption of exchange-traded fund shares is a simple, nondiscriminatory way to allocate the costs of entry and exit of fund shareholders appropriately and to eliminate any portfolio management conflict of interest between taxable and tax-exempt shareholders. This in-kind ETF creation/ redemption process is an efficient, even elegant, solution to several of the obvious problems that continue to plague the mutual fund industry. A growing number of fund industry experts believe that the exchange-traded fund structure should replace conventional mutual funds. To make that happen, however, the serendipity of early ETF development needs to be harnessed through creative financial engineering to overcome weaknesses in the index ETF structure and extend the best ETF features to a wider range of portfolios.

THOUGHTS ON IMPROVING ETFs

It is time to look at some new ETF features that will improve these funds' performance. If *any* fund is going to serve the interests of its shareholders, the portfolio manager needs to implement portfolio changes without revealing the fund's ongoing trading plans. Whether a fund is attempting to replicate an index or to follow an active portfolio selection or allocation process, portfolio composition changes cannot be made efficiently if traders in the market know what changes a fund will make in its portfolio before the fund completes its trades. A number of recent studies have highlighted an index composition change problem that many of indexing's strong supporters have been aware of for some time: Benchmark indexes like the S&P 500 and the Russell 2000 do not make efficient portfolio templates. Investors in index funds based on any transparent index are disadvantaged by the fact that anyone who cares will know what changes the fund must make before the fund's portfolio manager makes them. These problems are discussed at length in Chen, Noronha, and Singal (2006). When transparency means that someone can earn an arbitrage profit by front-running a fund's trades, transparency is neither desirable nor acceptable. For a comprehensive discussion of the cost of trading transparency, a problem for all index funds and other funds afflicted with trading transparency, see Gastineau (2008).

For ETFs to dominate all segments of the fund business and to replace mutual funds as the repository for most pooled investments in the United States, ETFs must be freed of the burden of trading transparency. The limited delay in portfolio disclosure in the SEC's initial approval of limited-function actively managed ETFs is not an adequate answer. These recently launched funds must announce the changes in their portfolio composition before the market opens on the day after the changes are made. The full degree of trading and portfolio composition confidentiality that is available to mutual funds must be available to ETFs.

Because they were created to have something to trade on the American Stock Exchange, ETFs have been locked into the revelation of the value of their portfolios every 15 seconds and the revelation of the composition of the portfolio every morning. These features, which have been deemed necessary for the kind of secondary market trading chosen for the initial ETFs, are inconsistent with the features an ETF must have to realize its full potential to deliver good performance to investors.

Intraday trading in ETFs is useful to many investors, but portfolio transparency is a fatal flaw in the ETF trading process. If the portfolio does not track a popular index or if trading in the fund shares is light, the cost to trade in the intraday market will be high and difficult to calculate, even after the trade is completed. In addition, market makers and other large traders may have an intraday trading advantage over individual investors who are less able to monitor market activity and intraday fund price and value relationships. To state this problem in another way, there is inappropriate asymmetry in the amount and kind of information available to large traders on one hand, and small investors on the other hand.

Many individual investors have a stake in being able to make small, periodic purchases or sales in their mutual fund share accounts. The prototypical investor of this type is the 401(k) investor who invests a small amount in his or her defined contribution retirement plan every payroll period. The mutual fund industry has developed an elaborate system that permits small orders for a large number of investors to be handled at a reasonable cost and at net asset value. There are ways to modify ETF procedures so that these investors, while paying a little more than they have paid in the past to cover the transaction costs of their mutual fund entries and exits, will still be accommodated in ETFs at a similarly low cost. The snowballing rush to greater transparency in the economics of defined contribution accounts like 401(k) plans will make fund cost and performance comparisons easier—to the advantage of ETFs. Transparency in costs is as desirable from the investor's perspective as transparency in portfolio changes is undesirable.

We believe that the best solution to problems that stem from today's intraday trading in ETFs is to change the focus for most ETFs away from trading at a price close to an intraday net asset value proxy, to trading for settlement at or relative to the official net asset value calculated for the fund based on closing prices in the securities markets. NAV-based secondary market trading can be made available for existing ETFs, new actively managed ETFs, and improved index ETFs using the funds' end-of-day official NAV calculation as the focus for trading.

To clarify how NAV-based secondary market trading will work, there can be two ways to trade most ETFs. The first way is the familiar intraday ETF trading at prices determined simply by supply and demand, facilitated by periodic updates of a proxy value for the ETF portfolio. The updated proxy values will be disseminated less frequently for nontransparent ETFs (full-function, actively managed, and improved index funds) and continue to be disseminated every 15 seconds for benchmark index ETFs. In addition to the current intraday, "just like a stock" trading method, investors will be able to enter orders throughout the trading day to commit to execution *at the end-of-day NAV* as calculated by the fund, *or at a specified premium to, or discount from, the end-of-day NAV*.

A different symbol—a new three- or four-character symbol bearing no necessary relationship to the fund's current symbol, or an extension modifying the current symbol—will probably be used for the new trading process. Alternatively, the present trading symbol with a different FIX tag may be used. To illustrate two possibilities, the intraday trading symbol for the SPDR is SPY. The NAV-based transaction symbol for the SPDR might be XXP or it might be SPY.NV. In any event, it will be clear to investors which trading mechanism they are using. Trades relative to NAV will be possible throughout the trading day. Orders will be entered, and trades will be executed in terms of a base number, say 100.00. A bid, offer, or execution at 100.01 will be for settlement at the 4:00 P.M. net asset value calculation for the fund *plus one cent per share.* An execution at 99.99 will be for settlement at the 4:00 P.M. net asset value *minus one cent per share.*

The traditional ETF intraday trading process and the NAV-based transaction process will co-exist and interact. The existence of the NAV-based transaction system will assure all investors that it will be possible for them to execute an ETF trade at or close to the day's closing net asset value at any time they wish to increase or reduce their ETF position. The NAV trading process is reminiscent of the way conventional mutual fund shares have been traded. One major difference is that liquidity in the new NAV-based transaction process will be provided by other investors and by market makers, not by the fund and its shareholders. These transactions, in contrast to transactions in conventional mutual funds, will be secondary market transactions. *They will not be trades with the fund.*

With secondary market NAV-based trading in ETFs, fund share traders can receive value for something they have been giving away: the time value of the order. Buyers and sellers of conventional mutual fund shares have essentially been giving away an option to profit from the fact that they are entering an order hours earlier to be executed at the end-of-day net asset value. A secondary market order that is entered at 10:00 A.M. to buy shares at or close to the end-of-day NAV will have value to some market participants. An ETF market maker might agree to sell shares at 10:00 A.M. with the transaction priced at a penny a share *below* the 4:00 P.M. net asset value because the transaction reduces the market maker's inventory. Laying off a position or acquiring shares at or near the end-of-day NAV can be a lower-cost way for a market maker to adjust inventory than creating or redeeming shares in a trade with the fund.

Individual and institutional investors who are interested in buying or selling fund shares cannot be confident that their up-to-the-second market information is as good as the information available to market makers. These investors might prefer to trade—as they have done with conventional mutual funds—at or at a price related to and determined by the fund's end-of-day net asset value. Buyers and sellers of fund shares will be able to trade in the NAV-based ETF market throughout the trading day. All trades will take place at NAV or at a slight premium to or slight discount from the 4:00 P.M. NAV. All parties can participate in NAV-based trading with confidence that it would be extremely difficult for any market participant to have a significant impact on the fund's net asset value calculation.

There are similarities and differences between secondary market NAV-based trading for exchange-traded funds and the purchase or sale of conventional mutual fund shares at NAV in transactions with the fund. Both mechanisms give investors assurance that they can trade on the same terms as other market participants. However, as Exhibit 6.7 illustrates, the mutual fund portfolio absorbs the cost of mutual fund share trading. A hallmark of the exchange-traded funds offered today is that every investor entering or leaving the fund (including an investor purchasing or selling ETF shares in the secondary market) pays the costs associated with his or her transactions (Exhibit 6.8). This principle will be in full force with ETF NAV-based secondary-market trading.

One of the important advantages of secondary-market NAV-based trading is that an investor buying or selling the fund shares in this secondary market will be able to measure very precisely the transaction costs associated with the purchase or sale. The transaction costs are essentially any price difference between the execution price and the net asset value, plus any commission payment. Furthermore, no one, neither a very large investor nor a very small one, will have any particular knowledge of where the net asset value will be—or the ability to affect the net asset value in a significant way.

The availability of NAV-based trading is not the only requirement for full-function actively managed ETFs. Another feature will be a formal early cutoff time for the commitment to create or redeem ETF shares. The purpose of the early cutoff is to permit the fund portfolio manager to trade positions in the creation and redemption basket that are not part of the fund portfolio, and to trade in the portfolio to achieve a target portfolio at the end of the day. Transactions between the creation/redemption cutoff time and the market close will effectively pass the cost of entry and exit to the investors who are entering or leaving the ETF. Everyone who trades in the fund shares will have access to information on the expected magnitude of the trading costs associated with creation and redemption transactions of various sizes. This knowledge will permit all investors to trade fairly and effectively in the NAV-based secondary market with no more exposure to changes in the value of the fund portfolio than they would have with a conventional mutual fund. The transaction cost disclosure will also give market makers a good indication of the magnitude of the transaction costs they will have to recover to earn a profit from their market transactions with investors.

There are other characteristics of this new generation of ETFs that will make them unique in a number of ways, but this brief preview provides a general idea of how improved, actively managed, and nontransparent index exchange-traded funds can work.

NOTES

1. For more information on derivatives valuation, see Kolb (2009) and Hull (2008).

2. Globally, it is not uncommon for multiple options exchanges to share a common clearinghouse. For example, all equity options exchanges in the United States share the same clearinghouse. This is the Option Clearing Corporation (OCC), which is based in Chicago. There are several advantages to this. First, there are enormous economies of scale in clearing operations, such that it is far more cost effective to have one large clearinghouse than numerous small ones. Second, by employing the same clearinghouse, an option position can be put on through a trade made at one exchange and then offset (i.e., closed out) by a transaction made on a different exchange.

3. The CBOT was acquired by the CME in 2007.

4. The illustration depicts a no-load fund. A sales load would complicate the discussion without changing the conclusion.

5. The net asset value is reported on a per share basis. NAV is calculated as the total market value of the assets held by the fund, less any accrued liabilities. This is then divided by the number of fund shares outstanding to arrive at the NAV per share.

6. There was an even greater fairness problem before 1968 because fund transactions were priced in arrears. Specifically, a buyer or seller got the previous day's net asset value until today's close. The problems this created on a few occasions are of only historic interest today.

REFERENCES

Chen, Honghui, Gregory Noronha, and Vijay Singal. 2006. "Index Changes and Losses to Index Fund Investors." *Financial Analysts Journal* (July–August): 31–47.

Fuhr, Deborah. 2009. *ETF Landscape, Industry Preview.* (November): 3. http://www.exchange-handbook.co.uk/index.cfm?section=news&action=detail&id=87442.

Gastineau, Gary L. 2005. *Someone Will Make Money on Your Funds—Why Not You? A Better Way to Pick Mutual and Exchange-Traded Funds.* Hoboken, NJ: John Wiley & Sons.

Gastineau, Gary L. 2008. " The Cost of Trading Transparency: What We Know, What We Don't Know and How We Will Know." *Journal of Portfolio Management* (Fall): 72–81.

Gastineau, Gary L. 2010. *The Exchange-Traded Funds Manual.* 2nd ed. Hoboken, NJ: John Wiley & Sons.

Hull, John. 2008. *Options, Futures, and Other Derivatives*, Seventh Ed. Upper Saddle River, NJ: Prentice-Hall.

Kolb, Robert, and Overdahl, James A. 2009. *Financial Derivatives: Pricing and Risk Management.* Hoboken, NJ: John Wiley & Sons.

Swenson, David F. 2005. *Unconventional Success: A Fundamental Approach to Personal Investment.* New York: Free Press.

ABOUT THE AUTHORS

Gary L. Gastineau is the principal of ETF Consultants, a firm providing specialized exchange-traded fund consulting services. He is also a managing member and co-founder of Managed ETFs, a firm that developed new ETF trading techniques and procedures for actively managed ETFs. A new edition of his book, *The Exchange-Traded Funds Manual*, is available from John Wiley & Sons. Gary is also the author of *Someone Will Make Money on Your Funds—Why Not You?* (John Wiley & Sons, 2005), *The Options Manual* (McGraw-Hill, 3rd ed. 1988), and co-author of the *Dictionary of Financial Risk Management* (Fabozzi, 1999), as well as numerous journal articles. He received the Bernstein Fabozzi/Jacobs Levy Award for an outstanding article in the *Journal of Portfolio Management*. Gary serves on the editorial boards of the *Journal of Portfolio Management*, the *Journal of Derivatives*, and the *Journal of Indexes*. He is a member of the Review Board for the Research Foundation of the CFA Institute. Gary is an honors graduate of Harvard College and Harvard Business School.

John F. Marshall is an expert in derivatives and their applications in financial engineering. He has worn a number of hats in his 35 years in finance, often at the same time. He served on the faculties of Stony Brook University, St. John's University, Moscow Institute of Physics and Technology, and Polytechnic Institute of New York University. At the latter he held the position professor of financial engineering. Jack is also the senior partner of a financial engineering and derivatives consulting firm that served many of the world's leading financial institutions for almost 20 years. He is credited by some as the person who, in the 1980s, first identified financial engineering as an emerging new profession and, in 1991, he co-founded the International Association of Financial Engineers. He has authored more than a dozen books and numerous journal articles. He earned a BS in Biology/Chemistry from Fordham University, an MBA in Finance from St. John's University, an MA in Quantitative Economics, and a PhD in Financial Economics from Stony Brook University while also a dissertation fellow of Columbia University.

CHAPTER 7

The Foreign Exchange Market

LAURENT L. JACQUE
The Fletcher School (Tufts University) and HEC School of Management, France

Foreign Exchange Market Snapshot

History: Since time immemorial, foreign exchange trading was conducted almost solely for the purpose of enabling international trade in goods and services. However, with the breakdown of the Bretton Woods system of fixed exchange rates in 1971, the foreign exchange (forex, FX) market has experienced exponential growth powered by improved technology, the unrelenting dismantling of foreign exchange controls, the accelerating pace of economic globalization, and the design of powerful algorithmic trading models. It is now an asset class in its own right.

Size: The over-the-counter foreign exchange derivatives market has grown from $18 trillion in 1998 to $49 trillion in 2009. The exchange-traded market, which is exceptionally smaller than the OTC market, has increased from $81 billion in 1998 to $311 billion in 2009.

Products: Major foreign exchange products include spot and forward contracts, as well as currency swaps, options, and swaptions. Exchange-traded currency futures and options are also widely-used instruments.

First Usage: The first widely-publicized OTC foreign exchange derivative was a currency swap that was executed in 1979, when IBM and the World Bank agreed to exchange interest payments on debt denominated in different currencies—the Swiss franc and German mark from IBM were exchanged for U.S. dollars from the World Bank.

Selection of Major Forex Derivative Debacles

1987: Volkswagen AG, the German car manufacturer, had a policy of keeping itself fully hedged against foreign exchange risk. However, managers who were responsible for forex risk management failed to put on the appropriate currency hedges. When exchange rates moved against the firm, employees hid their failure to put on and maintain appropriate hedges by falsifying documents to indicate that they did have the necessary hedging contracts in place. Later, when senior management sought to enforce these contracts they discovered that the contracts did not exist. The forgery of the contracts was discovered by the National Bank of Hungary and eventually led Volkswagen to recognize losses of $259 million.

1991: Allied-Lyons—better known for its tea bags than for its forays into the currency market—announced a stunning $269 million forex loss (approximately 20 percent of its projected profits for 1991). Facing a sluggish economy, its treasury had elaborated a sophisticated scheme that gambled not so much on the absolute level of the dollar/sterling rate as on its volatility. This gamble was achieved by writing deep-in-the-money currency options in combinations, known as straddles and strangles, that in this particular case would have produced profits had the exchange rate turned out to be less volatile than the option premium implied. This ingenious scheme was implemented at the beginning of the Gulf War. However, when the allies launched their air offensive, the initial uncertainty as to the outcome did not reduce the option volatility—at least not soon enough for Allied-Lyons to see its speculative gambit succeed and it was forced by its bankers to liquidate its options position at a considerable loss.

1993: Showa Shell Sekiyu KK, a large oil refinery in Japan, expected the U.S. dollar to rise against the Japanese yen, and thus started to buy currency forwards in 1989 to hedge its dollar-denominated oil bill. However, the dollar fell against the yen, thus engendering enormous exchange rate losses for the company. The situation deteriorated when the treasury department of the firm tried to conceal the losses by rolling over its positions (with the tacit cooperation of its counterparty banks), eventually accumulating losses of $1.5 billion.

2002: Allfirst Bank, a former subsidiary of Allied Irish Banks, Ireland's second-largest bank, hired a trader in 1993 named John Rusnak, who took long positions in Japanese yen by purchasing currency forward contracts. However, as the yen continued to appreciate, Rusnak faced losses on his unhedged positions. In order to cover up his losses, Rusnak wrote pairs of bogus put and call options, which were deceitfully entered into the Bank's systems to give the impression that his positions had been hedged. Rusnak opened up a prime brokerage account and continued betting on a rise in the yen until his scheme was discovered by the parent bank. His total losses amounted to $691 million.

Best Providers (as of 2009): Deutsche Bank was nominated by *Global Finance* magazine as the Best FX Derivatives Provider in North America, Europe, and Asia.

Applications: Participants in the forex markets use foreign exchange contracts and derivatives to execute cross-border commercial transactions, to hedge currency exposures, to engage in various forms of arbitrage and carry trades, and to speculate on currency exchange movements.

Users: The forex customer market refers to the market for end users of foreign exchange. Customers would include importers and exporters, multinational corporations, central banks intervening in the forex market or simply managing their currency reserves, commercial banks, insurance companies, investment banks' proprietary trading, and hedge funds involved in carry trades or other forms of high-frequency algorithmic trading.

INTRODUCTION

If there were a single world currency there would be no need for a foreign exchange market. At its simplest, the raison d'être of the foreign exchange market is to enable the transfer of purchasing power from one currency into another arising from the international exchange of goods, services, and financial securities. Trade carried over great distances is probably as old as mankind and has long been a source of economic power for the nations that embraced it. Indeed, international trade seems to have been at the vanguard of human progress and civilization: Phoenicians, Greeks, and Romans were all great traders whose activities were facilitated by marketplaces and money changers that set fixed places and fixed times for exchanging goods. Indeed, from time immemorial, traders have been faced with several problems: how to pay for and finance the physical transportation of merchandise from point A to point B (perhaps several hundred or thousands of miles away and weeks or months away), how to insure the cargo (risk of being lost at sea or to pirates), and last, how to protect against price fluctuations in the value of the cargo across space (from point A to point B) and over time (between shipping and delivery time). In many ways the history of foreign exchange and its derivative contracts parallels the increasingly innovative remedies that traders devised in coping with their predicament.

Long confined to enabling international trade, foreign direct investment, and their financing, foreign exchange has recently emerged as an asset class in its own right. This largely explains the recent surge of money flowing through the foreign exchange (forex) market. Catalyzed by improved technology, the unrelenting dismantling of foreign exchange controls, the accelerating pace of economic globalization, and the design of powerful algorithmic trading models, the daily turnover in the forex market now exceeds $3 trillion, thus dwarfing equities and fixed-income securities markets. Surprisingly, though, the international trade of goods and services accounts for only 5 percent of trading.

This chapter first describes the institutional framework within which forex transactions are carried out, emphasizing how Internet-based electronic automation has overhauled the market microstructure. Second, it maps the rules of the game that determine the price—foreign exchange rate—at which such transactions are completed. Third and last, it shows how the 1971 breakdown of the Bretton Woods system of fixed exchange rates, that had long provided free-of-charge risk-avoidance services to market participants, spurred the engineering of risk management products—namely, futures, options, and swaps: In effect, central banks had privatized risk management.

HOW FOREX IS TRADED: THE INSTITUTIONAL FRAMEWORK

The forex market is by far the oldest and largest market in the world. Unlike the New York Stock Exchange, the Paris Bourse, or the Chicago Board of Trade, which are physically organized and centralized exchanges for trading stocks, bonds, commodities, and their derivatives, the foreign exchange market is made up of a network of trading rooms found mostly in commercial banks, foreign exchange dealers, and brokerage firms—hence its description as an *interbank market.* It is

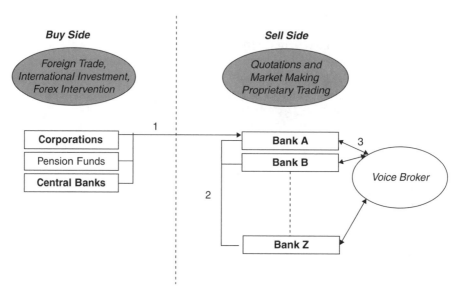

Exhibit 7.1   The Phone-Forex Market (until the Early 1990s)

largely dominated by approximately 20 major banks, which trade via their branches physically dispersed throughout the major financial centers of the world—London, New York, Tokyo, Singapore, Zurich, Hong Kong, Paris, and so on.

In the 1960s, foreign exchange trading rooms were linked by telephones (and later telexes), which allowed for very fast communication (but not quasi-instantaneous as today, with computer terminals and the Internet) in this *over-the-counter* market. Each currency trader would have "before him a special telephone that links the trading room by direct wire to the foreign exchange brokers, the cable companies, the most important commercial customers. . . . The connections are so arranged that several of the bank's traders can 'listen in' on the same call." (Holmes and Scott, 1965) See Exhibit 7.1.

Today foreign exchange trading rooms are linked electronically, with traditional means of telecommunications such as telephone, telex, and facsimile machine playing a subsidiary role: Computer terminals have established themselves as the undisputed medium of transaction, as they allow for instantaneous communication in this over-the-counter market. Foreign exchange traders with display monitors on their desks are able to execute trades at prices they see on their screens by simply punching their orders on a keyboard.

Indeed, the new computerized system offers currency traders the opportunity to enter orders that are then automatically matched with other outstanding orders already in the system. This globally reaching and linking trading system substantially cuts the time and cost of matching and settling trades and, more importantly, provides the foreign exchange market with the ticker tape to record the actual prices at which foreign exchange transactions are carried out. It should be emphasized that this information has, so far, never been made public, since foreign exchange markets' biggest traders have profitably kept this secret to themselves.

This ethereal, ubiquitous, electronic foreign exchange market is trading literally around the clock. At any time during a 24-hour cycle, forex traders are buying and selling, say, pounds for yen somewhere in the world. By the time the New York foreign exchange market starts trading at 8:00 A.M. ET, major European financial centers have been in full swing for four or five hours. San Francisco and Los Angeles extend U.S. forex trading activities by three hours, and by dinnertime on the West Coast, Far Eastern markets, principally Tokyo, Hong Kong, and Singapore, will begin trading. As these market trading activities draw to a close, Bombay and Bahrain will have been open for a couple of hours, and Western European markets will be about to start trading.

One major implication of a 24-hour currency market is that exchange rates may change at any time in response to any new information. Thus, foreign exchange traders must be light sleepers ready to work the night shift if necessary since they may need to act on news resulting in a very sharp exchange rate movement that occurs on another continent in the middle of the night.

Products

There are four major types of products traded in the forex market: spot contracts, forward contracts, forex swaps, and currency swaps. In all cases contracts are tailor-made[1] —that is, negotiated by the two counterparties in amounts of no less than $1 million.

1. *Spot* contracts are transactions for the purchase or sale of currency for currency at today's price for settlement within two business days (one day if both parties are domiciled in the same time zone, such as U.S. dollar for Canadian dollar or Mexican peso).

2. *Forward* contracts are agreements in terms of delivery date, price, and amount set today to purchase or sell currency for currency. Delivery date at some time in the future (anytime between one week and 12 months for the most part), at a price agreed upon today, and known as the forward rate. If the forward contract is not matched with a spot transaction it is known as an *outright forward*.

3. *Forex swaps.* If combined with a spot transaction, a forward contract is referred to as a *swap*. More specifically, foreign exchange swaps combine two transactions of equal amount, mismatched maturity, and opposite direction; for example, the bundling of the *spot purchase* of €10 million for U.S. dollars at today's price of $1.50 = €1 with the 60-day *forward sale* of the same amount of €10 million at the forward rate[2] of $1.48 = €1 would constitute a foreign exchange swap.

4. *Currency swaps* and *cross-currency swaps*, which should not be confused with FOREX swaps above, are similar in structure to interest rate swaps. One leg typically pays interest on a given quantity of notional principal in one currency, and the other leg pays interest on a given quantity of notional principal in a different currency. As a practical matter, it is often only the difference between the two payments that is actually paid by the higher paying counterparty to the lower-paying counterparty. These sorts of swap

contracts do not necessarily require the actual exchange of currencies either at the beginning or the end of the contract's life.

According to the most recent triennial survey by the Bank for International Settlements' Triennal survey (2010), the forex market averaged $3.2 trillion of trading per day in April 2007, with one-third accounted for by spot transactions (for comparison, Wall Street has a daily turnover of approximately $75 billion). The U.S. dollar was involved in 86 percent of all forex transactions, with the euro a distant second at 37 percent. London is the undisputed hub of forex trading with an average daily volume of $1,359 billion, followed by New York City with $661 billion during the same month of April 2007. The forex market is made up of two distinct but closely connected tiers: the *customer* market (buy side) and the *interbank* market (sell side).

Buy Side Meets Sell Side in the Forex Market[3]

The customer market refers to the market for end users of foreign exchange. Customers include importers and exporters; multinational corporations repatriating dividends, extending an intra-corporate loan to one of their foreign affiliates, or concluding a cross-border acquisition; central banks intervening in the forex market or simply managing their currency reserves; commercial banks; insurance companies; investment banks' proprietary trading; and hedge funds involved in carry trades or other forms of high-frequency algorithmic trading (see left panel of Exhibit 7.2).

Because it would be difficult for customers to find another customer counterparty directly, they would turn to their bank and declare their intention to trade. In fact, some of the largest market makers in forex trading, such as Deutsche Bank,

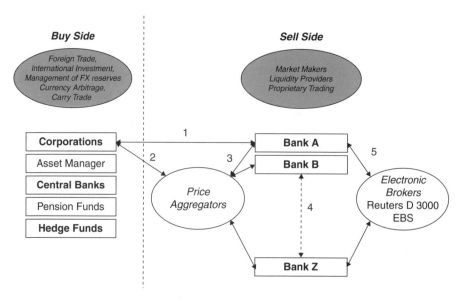

Exhibit 7.2   The e-Forex Market (from the Early 1990s to the Present)

Barclays, and UBS, have developed their own electronic trading platforms that facilitate bank-customer relationships.

Increasingly the buy side would rather access a multiple-dealer portal that functions as a price aggregator or bulletin board streaming quotes from key dealer banks and routing buy-side orders to the most cost-effective sell-side providers (Exhibit 7.2, arrow 2). Today this consumer segment would rather have direct access to an electronic communication network (ECN) such as FXall, FXconnect, or Currenex. ECNs are electronic trading systems that automatically match buy and sell orders placed by various customers. Access to ECNs is limited to subscribers, who must also have an account with a broker-dealer before their orders can be routed for execution. ECNs post orders on their systems for other subscribers to view and then automatically match orders for execution.[4]

The Interbank Market

The bank in turn will give quotes either directly to its customers, thereby acting as a market maker[5] (Exhibit 7.2, arrow 1), or via multiple-dealer portals. The bank would hope to use its existing inventory of foreign exchange to meet its customers' needs but is often unable to do so. The bank's dealer/trader will then turn to the *interbank* market to cover his customers' trades. The dealer/trader will quote buying and selling rates to another bank (bilateral trade) without revealing his real intentions (but revealing his identity) as to whether he is interested in buying or selling or how much of the currency he is interested in trading (Exhibit 7.2, arrows 2 and 3). The advantage of direct trading is that no commission would have to be paid, but there is no guarantee that the trader has secured the best bargain. Indeed, there are more than 1,000 banks trading foreign exchange and probably more than 10,000 forex traders. Direct trading is thus decentralized and fragmented since transactions amount to bilateral deals between two dealers and cannot be observed by other market participants. However, it should be noted that approximately 10 banks account for a disproportionate 50 percent share of forex trading in each currency pair. Specialization, in terms of currency pairs traded, is widely known among market participants, which facilitates bilateral direct trading. However, it is next to impossible to know, in such a physically dispersed market, if the best possible deal has been secured.

Electronic Brokers

Hence the second approach is for the bank forex trader to contact a broker (formerly referred to as a "voice broker," but more likely to be known today as an electronic broker); this is known as *indirect trading*[6] (Exhibit 7.1, arrow 4). Brokers are some-times referred to as bulletin boards. "Brokers do not make prices themselves. They gather firm prices from dealers, and then communicate those prices back to deal-ers." (Lyons 2001, p. 40.) Such broker-intermediated trading used to be conducted over the phone, but today forex brokering is channeled through two dominant computer systems—Reuters D3000[7] and Electronic Broking Services (EBS).[8]

EBS dominates trading in the three major currency pairs—dollar/euro ($/€), dollar/yen ($/¥), and euro/yen (€/¥)—whereas Reuters leads in pound (£) trading and other lesser or emerging market currencies. Both electronic platforms are in effect *electronic limit order books* akin to the electronic trading systems used by stock exchanges. A limit order book aggregates buy and sell orders for a given currency by order of priority. Dealers when entering their order will also specify the volume they intend to buy/bid or sell/ask as well as the price at which to buy or sell. The order is kept in the system until a corresponding order with matching volume and price is entered or the order is revoked/withdrawn by the original bidder. Posting limit orders through brokers will also protect the dealer's identity. Brokers serve as matchmakers and do not put their own money at risk. Through computerized quotation systems, such as Reuters D3000 or EBS, electronic brokers monitor the quotes offered by the forex trading desks of major international banks. By continuously scanning the universe of forex traders, brokers perform a very useful searching function and provide the bank's forex trader with the best possible price. Such service is provided at a cost to its user, as dealers will pay commissions to brokers with the hope of having accessed the best possible deal.

Has the human trader at major dealer banks been completely disintermediated as a result of electronic automation of forex trading? Not quite. According to several industry reports, approximately a third of all forex transactions continue to be intermediated by traditional traders. The buy side of the market is consciously channeling a significant proportion of its business to forex dealers to keep the relationships alive, as it values the advisory content of human contact with traders. This is particularly true in times of market turbulence and high price volatility, when forex traders prove to be especially useful as algorithm pricing tends to err, if not outright fail. Similarly, currencies that are more lightly traded, and the more idiosyncratic, tailor-made forex products, will benefit from the human touch.

Further strengthening the functioning of the interbank market is the newly established settlement service CLS Bank (Continuous Linked Settlements), which began operating on September 9, 2002, and links all participating countries' payment systems for real-time settlement. This eliminates or greatly reduces counterparty or default risk in the settlement of spot transactions.[9]

Algorithmic Forex Trading

Since foreign exchange is widely considered an asset class, hedge funds and other institutional investors are increasingly relying on automated trading models that seek and act instantly on market opportunities to generate alpha. As new forex quotes and news items arrive on the news feed, they are instantly incorporated in pricing and trading algorithms, which will trigger a buy or sell order on a particular currency. Banks, in turn, have built pricing algorithms to handle this new high-speed flow of forex trading, and corporations have followed suit by engineering their own hedging algorithms.

Market Efficiency

As emphasized earlier, the forex market is best described "as a multiple-dealer market. There is no physical location—or exchange—where dealers meet with customers, nor is there a screen that consolidates all dealer quotes in the market" (Lyons 2001, p. 39). Because of its idiosyncratic microstructure, the order flow of foreign exchange transactions is not nearly as transparent as it would be in other multiple-dealer markets. There are no disclosure requirements for forex trading as one would find in most bond and equity markets, where trades are disclosed within minutes by law. Because trades or order flow are generally not immediately observable, the critical information about fundamentals that would have otherwise been made available to all market participants is released more slowly, thus impairing the efficiency of the forex market.

However, electronic trading is metamorphosing the price discovery process and speeding up price dissemination to the point of becoming quasi-instantaneous. Indeed, with dealers and most customers now able to access current prices in real time, the over-the-counter forex market is gaining increasing transparency. With price discovery becoming quasi-automated and increasingly centralized, this over-the-counter market is taking on some of the characteristics of centralized exchanges. However, if increased transparency and speedy, widespread price dissemination are bolstering the informational efficiency of the forex market, it remains that intervention in the spot market by secretive central banks continues to be a major impediment.

HOW ARE EXCHANGE RATES DETERMINED?

The breakdown of the international monetary system of fixed exchange rates that had prevailed until 1971 under the Bretton Woods agreement, ushered the world economy into uncharted territories. The new international financial order that has emerged in its stead is commonly characterized as a system of floating exchange rates. Such a characterization, however, is misleading since it applies to only a handful of major currencies that float independently, such as the U.S. dollar ($), the Japanese yen (¥), and the euro (€). Most other currencies are actually closely managed by their respective central banks when they are not actually pegged to or tightly stabilized vis-à-vis the U.S. dollar, the euro, or a basket of currencies. This section develops a framework for understanding how exchange rates are determined and how different exchange rate regimes have evolved in each country: it provides a theoretical backdrop against which the operational framework for forex trading presented in the first part of this chapter should be understood.

First Principles about Exchange Rate Determination

International transactions have one common element that makes them different from domestic transactions—namely, one of the parties involved must deal in a foreign currency. When an American consumer—admittedly well-heeled—imports a British-made Aston Martin, the car buyer pays in either dollars or British pounds. If the buyer pays in dollars, the British manufacturer must convert the dollars into pounds. If Aston Martin receives payment in pounds, the American buyer must first exchange his or her dollars for pounds. Thus, at some stage in the chain of transactions between the American buyer and the British seller, dollars must be converted into pounds. The medium through which this can be achieved is the foreign exchange market. The basic function of such a market is thus to transfer purchasing power from the U.S. dollar into the British pound.

Examples analogous to the preceding case of an import transaction could be multiplied. Generally, the demand for pounds arises primarily in the course

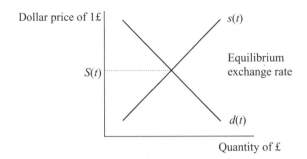

Exhibit 7.3   Equilibrium Exchange Rate

of importing British goods and services such as shipping or insurance, as well as making investments in sterling-denominated stocks and bonds or extending loans to the United Kingdom. Conversely, the supply of pounds results from exporting/selling U.S. goods, services, and securities to the United Kingdom, as well as receiving investments and loans from British institutions. The interaction between supply $s(t)$ of and demand $d(t)$ for pounds thus sets the price at which dollars are going to be exchanged for pounds for immediate delivery (within one or two business days); it is defined as the spot exchange rate $S(t)$.

The free interplay of demand for and supply of pounds thus determines the equilibrium rate of exchange. At this rate of exchange and at no other rate, the market is cleared, as illustrated in Exhibit 7.3. The pound, like any other commodity, has thus a price at which it can be bought or sold. As an illustration, assume that on December 1, 2009, the dollar price of one pound is US$1.71 for spot or immediate delivery (that is, within one or two business days). Clearly, the United States deals with a multitude of countries besides the United Kingdom, and for each conceivable pair of countries (United States, country i), there will exist a foreign exchange market allowing the purchasing power of the U.S. dollar to be transferred into currency i and vice versa.

The concept of a foreign exchange market, as presented in the previous section, comes as close to the perfectly competitive model of economic theory as any market can. The product is clearly homogeneous, in that foreign currency purchased from one seller is the same as that foreign currency purchased from another. Furthermore, the market participants have nearly perfect knowledge, since it is easy to obtain exchange rate quotations from e-forex price aggregators in real time. And there are indeed a large number of buyers and sellers.

Yet the actual exchange market deviates from the model of a perfect market for two reasons: (1) the foreign exchange market is physically and geographically dispersed with no direct way for market participants to monitor the order flow of transactions,[10] and (2) central banks act as a major agent of price distortion, either by directly intervening in the foreign exchange market, and thereby impairing the flexibility of exchange rates or, indirectly, by limiting entry to the market (exchange controls), and thereby limiting the convertibility of the currency. In other words, the first source of price distortion is simply *limited flexibility*, whereas the second is *limited convertibility*. In this vein it is helpful to think of a country's exchange rate regime along the two dimensions of (1) flexibility ranging from 0 percent

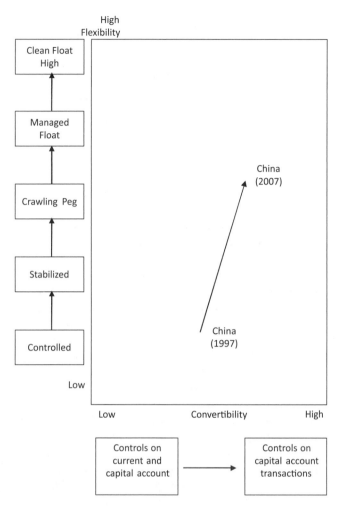

Exhibit 7.4   The Currency Flexibility x Convertibility Space

(controlled rate) to 100 percent (clean float) and (2) convertibility ranging from 0 percent (tight controls on all current and capital account transactions) to 100 percent (absence of controls on all balance-of-payments transactions). On the chart in Exhibit 7.4 we portray the story of China, which over the past 10 years has moved cautiously toward higher convertibility and since 2005 toward timid flexibility. The case of China is actually representative of many emerging market countries that are steadily moving toward more flexibility and more convertibility: Adam Smith's invisible hand is reasserting itself in Exhibit 7.4.

Indeed, central banks are unlike any other participant in the forex market: they pursue objectives of national interest guided by their fiscal and monetary policies—they are not profit-maximizing entities. Why, how, and to what extent central banks actually do limit fluctuations in market prices are major factors constraining exchange rate determination. The next section discusses *floating*, *stabilized*, and *controlled* exchange rates in ascending degrees of price manipulation by

Exhibit 7.5   Exhibit 7.5 Map of Exchange Rate Systems

Floating	
→Clean Float	U.S. dollar, Canadian dollar, Australian dollar, New Zealand dollar, British pound, Swiss franc, euro, Brazilian real,
→Dirty Float	Japanese yen, Korean won, Indian rupee, Mexican peso, Argentine peso, Malaysian ringgit, Taiwan dollar, Indonesian rupiah, Thai baht
→Crawling Peg	Chinese yuan, Vietnamese dong
Stabilized	
→Basket Peg	Russian ruble ($, €)
→Single Currency Peg	CFA Franc Zone pegged to euro, Saudi rial pegged to U.S. dollar, UAE pegged to U.S. Dollar
→Currency Board	Hong Kong Dollar, pegged to U.S. Dollar
Controlled	Venezuelan bolivar
	Burmese kyat

central banks—more specifically: (1) systems of *floating* exchange rates, in which the prices of currencies are largely the result of interacting supply and demand forces with varying degrees of stabilizing interference by central banks; (2) systems of *stabilized* exchange rates (also referred to as "pegged yet adjustable"), whereby the market-determined price of currencies is constrained through central bank intervention to remain within a scheduled narrow band of price fluctuations; (3) systems of *controlled* exchange rates, in which currency prices are set by bureaucratic decisions.

Although exchange controls are most readily associated with controlled exchange rates, they are actually found in most floating and stabilized exchange rate systems as well—albeit to a much lesser degree. The sweeping deregulation that has engulfed financial systems around the world is certainly marching through the forex market, but has not yet reached its final destination; see Exhibit 7.5 for the map of current exchange rate regimes for the 25 major world economies.

Floating Exchange Rates (Clean Float)

The free interplay of supply and demand for a given foreign currency was shown earlier to determine the rate of exchange at which the market is cleared. This equilibrium exchange rate, however, is unlikely to last for very long: The continuous *random* arrival of information, such as news about latest inflation statistics, gross domestic product (GDP) growth, oil prices, and so on, will result in a modification of supply and demand conditions as market participants readjust their current needs as well as their expectations of what their future needs will be. Changing supply and demand conditions will, in turn, induce continuing shifts in supply and demand schedules until new equilibrium positions are achieved. As an illustration, fictitious supply and demand curves for British pounds (£) at times (*t*), (*t* + 1), and (*t* + 2) are depicted in Exhibit 7.6. Corresponding equilibrium exchange

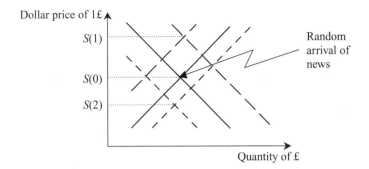

Exhibit 7.6 Shifts in Supply and Demand Curves

rates or dollar prices of one pound at times (t), $(t + 1)$, $(t + 2)$, and so on are graphed in Exhibit 7.7.

Over time, the exchange rate will fluctuate continuously or oscillate randomly around a longer-term trend, very much like the prices of securities traded on a stock exchange or of commodities traded on a commodity exchange.

In the real world, few countries have ever left the prices of their currencies free to fluctuate in the manner just described. For countries whose foreign sector (imports and exports) looms large on their domestic economic horizon, sharply fluctuating exchange rates could have devastating consequences for their orderly economic development.[11] Picture, for instance, an industrialized country that imports close to 100 percent of its energy. Abrupt fluctuations in the exchange rate would cause abrupt fluctuations in the price of energy—since energy is a significant input in nearly all economic activities whose prices are denominated in U.S. dollars—and these fluctuations would affect the prices of nearly all finished products. This means that the cost of living index, the purchasing power of consumers, and the real wages of labor would be subjected to abrupt variations.

Managed Floating Exchange Rates ("Dirty" Float)

It is then not surprising that countries that have adopted a system of floating exchange rates have generally resisted the economic uncertainty resulting from

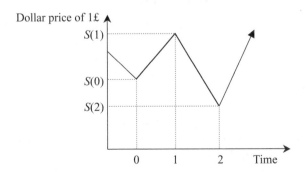

Exhibit 7.7 Oscillating Exchange Rates

a clean float. By managing or smoothing out daily exchange rate fluctuations through timely central bank interventions, they have been able to achieve short-run exchange rate stability (but not fixity) without impairing longer-term flexibility. Such a system of exchange rate determination is generally referred to as a managed or dirty float. It is the system that best approximates the handful of currently floating currencies referred to at the outset of this chapter.

Unlike central bank intervention in a stabilized exchange rate system,[12] neither the magnitude nor the timing of the monitoring agency's interference with the free interplay of supply and demand forces is known to private market participants. Furthermore, objectives pursued by central banks through their interventions in the foreign exchange market are not necessarily similar.

Clean versus Dirty Floaters

Who are the "clean" and the "not so clean" floaters? Anglo-Saxon countries, which have a long tradition of low regulation and reasonably unfettered markets, would fall into the (somewhat) clean category; since the mid-1990s the United States, the United Kingdom, Canada, Australia, New Zealand, and alpine Switzerland have resisted intervening in the forex markets. Note that these countries, with the exception of Switzerland, are common-law countries and maritime powers, and have a financial system that tends to be market- rather than bank-centered.

Yet many central banks, such as Korea's and Russia's, intervene in foreign exchange markets. The largest "dirty" floater is Japan. Between April 1991 and December 2000, for example, the Bank of Japan (acting as the agent of the Ministry of Finance) bought U.S. dollars on 168 occasions, for a cumulative amount of $304 billion, and sold U.S. dollars on 33 occasions, for a cumulative amount of $38 billion. A typical case: On Monday, April 3, 2000, the Bank of Japan purchased $13.2 billion of dollars in the foreign exchange market in an attempt to stop the more than 4 percent depreciation of the dollar against the yen that had occurred during the previous week. As a result of its aggressive interventions to stem too rapid a rise in the value of the yen, Japan's foreign reserves exceeded a trillion dollars for the first time in 2007.

—Adapted from the Federal Bank of New York

Taxonomy of Central Bank Intervention

Recent experiences with managed floats have unveiled three major classes of central bank intervention strategies. They can be described as follows:

> *Strategy 1:* At one end of the spectrum would fall countries concerned only with smoothing out daily fluctuations to promote an orderly pattern in exchange rate changes. Clearly, under such a scheme, a central bank does not resist upward or downward longer-term trends brought about by the discipline of market forces.

Strategy 2: An intermediate strategy would prevent or moderate sharp and disruptive short- and medium-term fluctuations prompted by exogenous factors recognized to be only temporary. The rationale for central bank intervention is to offset or dampen the effects of a random or nonrecurring event bound to have a serious, but only temporary, impact on the exchange rate level. That could be the case of a natural disaster, a prolonged strike, or a major crop failure, which would, in the absence of a timely intervention by the central bank in the market, result in a sharp falling of the country's exchange rate level below what is believed to be consistent with long-run fundamental trends. Such a strategy is thus primarily geared to delaying, rather than resisting, longer-term fundamental trends in the market, which is why this strategy is generally dubbed "leaning against the wind."

Strategy 3: At the other end of the spectrum, some countries have been known to resist fundamental upward or downward movements in their exchange rates for reasons that clearly transcend the economics of the foreign exchange market. For example, in 1994, the Federal Reserve Bank of New York resisted—if only briefly—the yen appreciation beyond the "traumatic" ¥100 = $1 threshold. Such a strategy of so-called unofficial pegging is, in effect, tantamount to a system of stabilized exchange rates that would not define an official par value.

Modus Operandi of Central Bank Intervention

The next question is how central banks actually intervene in the foreign exchange market. So far we have been referring, in a somewhat abstract sense, to official intervention by responsible monetary authorities in their foreign exchange markets without describing the steps that central banks actually take to manipulate exchange rate levels.

Official intervention is primarily achieved through central banks' spot purchases or sales of their own domestic currency, in exchange for the foreign currency whose price they seek to influence. Consider the following case: The Bank of England wants to moderate the depreciation of the pound (see Exhibit 7.8) from 1£ = $1.72 to 1£ = $1.67 that would result from the free interplay of market forces (clean float) over the time interval $(t, t + 1)$. Assume further that the (secret) target level—indicated by an asterisk—at which the central bank wants to maintain its

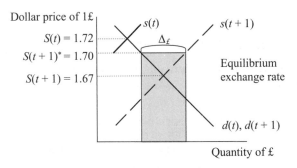

Exhibit 7.8   Modus Operandi of Central Bank Intervention

exchange rate is $S(t + 1)^* = 1.70$. From Exhibit 7.8, it can be readily seen that at the target rate of \$1.70 to a pound there is an excess supply of $(\Delta_£)$ or, equivalently, an excess demand of $[\Delta_£ \cdot S(t + 1)^*]$.

Purchasing $(\Delta £)$ exchange for the equivalent dollar amount, that is, by supplying the foreign exchange market with $[\Delta S(t + 1)^*]_\$$, the central bank will effectively stabilize at time $(t + 1)$ its exchange rate at \$1.70 rather than letting it depreciate to \$1.67.[13]

Moderation of the depreciation of the pound (strategy 2, the "leaning against the wind" type) will result in the Bank of England depleting its dollar reserves. Rigid pegging of the exchange rate at \$1.72 through large-scale central bank intervention (strategy 3, the unofficial pegging type) will result in an even steeper rate of depletion of the Bank of England's dollar reserves. In contrast, if the Bank of England limits itself to smoothing out short-run fluctuations (strategy 1) in either direction, its stock of dollar reserves will hover around a constant trend.

Tracking Central Bank Intervention

It is thus possible, on an ex post basis, to ascertain the type of objectives that the central bank pursues by tracking trends in its level of official reserves. Intervention, however, is often concealed by central banks and does not necessarily appear in official international reserve statistics. This may be due to central banks borrowing foreign currencies but reporting only gross, rather than net, reserves. In addition, the profits and losses from intervention in the foreign exchange market are generally buried in balance-of-payment accounts for interest earnings on assets.

The various possible cases are recapitulated in Exhibit 7.9.

Central Bank Intervention and Market Expectations

Finally, it should be emphasized that central bank interventions have—in addition to an obvious supply-and-demand effect—a continuing impact on market participants' *expectations*. Thus, foreign exchange market participants will interpret the clues about central bankers' attitudes by carefully analyzing the magnitude, timing, and visibility of central bank intervention. Furthermore, action to influence exchange rates is certainly not limited to direct intervention in the foreign exchange market. Equally, or perhaps more, important are domestic money market conditions and movements in short-term interest rates, which exercise a major influence on short-term capital flows that, in turn, will move the exchange rates.

Stabilized or Pegged Exchange Rates

Under a system of stabilized exchange rates, the fundamental economics of supply and demand remain as fully operative as under a system of floating exchange rates. The difference between the two systems lies in the fact that, under a system of stabilized exchange rates, central banks are openly committed not to let deviations occur in their going exchange rates for more than an agreed percentage on either side of the so-called par value.[14] This result is achieved through official central bank intervention in the foreign exchange market. The definition of par values, as well as the width of the band of exchange rate fluctuations, have varied across countries and over time. They are taken up in some detail in the balance of this

Strategy 0: *Clean float.* No intervention whatsoever by the central bank in its foreign exchange market. The level of the central bank's foreign reserves remains constant.

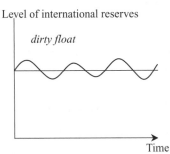

Strategy 1: *Dirty float/ intervention.* Central bank intervenes only to mitigate short-run fluctuations without resisting longer-term upward or downward trends.

Strategy 2: *Dirty float/leaning against the wind.* Central bank purports to delay a downward trend in its exchange rate by *leaning against the wind.*

Strategy 3: *Dirty float/ unofficial pegging.* Central bank resists depreciation through large-scale intervention. This is similar to *unofficial pegging.* A sharp depletion of reserve results.

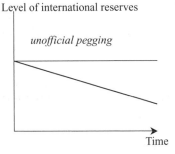

Exhibit 7.9   Taxonomy of Central Bank Intervention Strategies

section, which opens with an analytical review of the *custodian* role of central banks in a system of stabilized exchange rates.

Modus Operandi of Central Bank Intervention with Stabilized Exchange Rates
Consider the case of Malaysia, which pegged its currency, the Malaysian ringgitt (M$), to the U.S. dollar at the fixed rate of M$3.80. Whenever capital inflow or a

strong balance of trade surplus pressures the ringgitt to appreciate to, say, M$3.70 = US$1, the central bank would intervene by purchasing the excess dollars flooding the market at the fixed rate of M$3.80. We now turn to a review of current institutional implementations and variants of this general scheme of stabilized exchange rates.

Monthly Average Exchange Rates: Chinese Renminbi per U.S. Dollar

China's yuan was tightly pegged to the U.S. dollar at yuan 8.28 = $1 from 1997 to July 21, 2005. Over the period China sailed remarkably unscathed through the Asian financial crisis of July 1997 while growing at the astounding rate of better than 10 percent per year. How was China able to withstand the Asian financial crisis? To a large degree China—unlike its Asian neighbors—kept tight exchange controls on capital account transactions, which limited the mobility of short-term capital in and out of China.

On July 21, 2005, the People's Bank of China (China's central bank) announced that it was "reforming the exchange rate system by moving into a managed floating exchange rate regime based on market supply and demand with reference to a basket of currencies. The Yuan will no longer be pegged to the U.S. dollar. . . . The exchange rate of the U.S. dollar against the Yuan will be adjusted to 8.11 Yuan per U.S. dollar. . . . The daily trading price of the U.S. dollar against the Yuan will continue to be allowed to float within a band of +/–0.3 percent around the central parity published by the People's Bank of China."

—Professor Werner Antweiler, University of British Columbia,
Vancouver, BC, Canada

Pegging to an Artificial Currency Unit (Mid-1970s to the Present)
When the world's major currencies began to float independently in early 1973, most small countries initially continued to peg their currencies to the single reserve currency that they had previously used to stabilize their exchange rates (mainly the U.S. dollar, British pound, and French franc). However, the benefits of single-currency pegging were soon overshadowed by the costs of exchange rate fluctuations against other major currencies, especially as the single reserve currency such as the U.S. dollar or British pound became prone to prolonged *over-/undershooting* against other major trading currencies. Consequently, a number of countries began to manage their exchange rates systematically against key trading partners' currencies; this could be greatly facilitated by pegging the home currency to a basket of currencies—the so-called artificial currency unit (ACU) (e.g., the European Currency Unit [ECU, 1979–1999], which became the euro, or the special drawing right [SDR] issued by the International Monetary Fund—whose composition would typically reflect the country's bilateral trade flows pattern. Indeed, a great many countries have abandoned a single-currency pegging in favor of pegging against a currency basket of their own choosing).

DERIVATIVES AND THE PRIVATIZATION OF FOREX RISK MANAGEMENT

The breakdown of the Bretton Woods system of quasi-fixed exchange rates and the subsequent advent of volatile exchange rates ushered the world financial system into a new era of deregulation and financial innovation, with the introduction of currency futures, options, swaps, swaptions, and other products. As early as 1972, currency futures started to trade at the newly established International Monetary Market (IMM, a subsidiary of the Chicago Mercantile Exchange). Soon the deregulation of interest rates in the United States set in motion the introduction of interest rate derivatives, which eventually would dwarf currency and commodity derivatives. When the world became a riskier place, firms and financial institutions naturally sought safe harbors in the form of hedging with financial derivatives. With protection against volatile exchange rates no longer provided free of charge by their central banks, forex market participants resorted to private-sector solutions by engineering new insurance products, also known as derivatives. In a sense, risk mitigation had been privatized!

Indeed, derivatives are sophisticated instruments whose spiraling success over the years has largely been driven by increased price volatility in commodities, currencies, and interest rates. Derivatives facilitate efficient risk transfer from firms that are ill-equipped to bear risk and would rather not be exposed to risk to firms that have excess risk-bearing capacity and are willing to take on exposure to risk. Thanks to derivatives, risk transfer has become far more precise and efficient as its cost plunged because of breakthroughs in computer technology and financial theory. Thus derivatives allow for economic agents—households, financial institutions, and nonfinancial firms—to avail themselves of the benefits of division of labor and comparative advantage in risk bearing: But are derivatives, indeed, adequate instruments for risk avoidance and value creation? Shouldn't the major derivatives-linked disasters that are striking some of the best-managed firms in the world with predictable frequency be construed as evidence of wealth destruction rather than wealth creation? Let's now turn to the specific types of firms' exposure to foreign exchange risk before reviewing how forwards, futures, and options can be harnessed for hedging forex risk.

Transaction Risk

In the early phases of internationalization, firms are primarily exposed to foreign exchange risks of a *transactional* nature. Firms that are actively involved in exporting will find it necessary, for competitive reasons, to invoice accounts receivable in the currency of the buyer. Similarly, firms actively *sourcing* components or finished products and services from foreign companies may have to accept to be invoiced in the currency of the supplier. In other words, their accounts payable would be in a foreign currency. Either way, whether a firm buys or sells goods in a foreign currency, sizable exchange losses may be incurred from unforeseen and abrupt exchange rate movements. These currency fluctuations can wipe out profits on export sales or eliminate cost savings on foreign procurement.

Transaction Exposure in the Trading Room: Citibank Forex Losses[15]

We are periodically reminded of the "treachery" involved in measuring—let alone managing—transaction exposure in the forex "trading room." The recent (January 2008) $7.5 billion loss incurred by the almighty Société Générale at the hands of a junior trader, because of unchecked speculation on DAX and Euro Stoxx futures, is only the latest incident.

Witness how Citibank incurred an $8 million loss in June 1965, the heyday of the supposedly tranquil Bretton Woods system of pegged exchange rates. A Belgian trader, working on salary rather than commissions, elaborated a sophisticated speculative scheme based on his conviction that the pound sterling would not be devalued from its par value of $2.80 against the U.S. dollar, in spite of mounting balance of payments pressure to do so.

As early as September 1964, the trader started to accumulate long (asset) sterling positions at a significant forward discount, betting that the spot pound would remain within the range of $2.78–$2.82. Since traders are expected to report "square" positions of all outstanding forward contracts at the end of the trading day, the long sterling position had to be disguised by entering into a string of short-term forward sale contracts. Unfortunately, the short-term contracts were maturing at a loss (cash outflow) that ultimately exposed the scheme to senior managers, who hurriedly, and mistakenly (as it turned out), liquidated the long sterling positions before maturity at a large loss.

Square positions, by netting asset and liability positions regardless of maturity, hide deceptive speculative positions. Back-office operations are advised to maintain independent and unforgiving scrutiny of any transactions that are cleared for the front-office traders.

Translation Risk

Multinational corporations are required to report their worldwide performance to their shareholders on a quarterly basis in the form of simple statistics—consolidated earnings and the much awaited and closely studied earnings per share (EPS). This periodic translation process will lead to exchange losses or gains.

Pressures from a somewhat myopic investment community on multinational corporations to more fully disclose and account for exchange losses (or gains) are clearly compelling treasurers to pay close attention to translation risk. Accordingly, the suboptimal objective of smoothing the pattern of consolidated earnings between accounting periods tends to substitute itself for the sounder one of net cash flow maximization. Is it a good idea?

At the core of the translation risk hedging debate is the fact that translation losses or gains—however large they may be—are unrealized noncash flows in nature and without tax implications. Yet we know that value creation is driven by cash flows—not by accounting profits. Is it then legitimate for sophisticated multinational corporations to concern themselves with translation exposure hedging? It would seem that such activity is, at best, an attempt to deceive investors through accounting gimmickry rather than being motivated by value creation, unless it can be shown that hedging translation exposure by modifying/lowering the risk profile of the firm is, indeed, resulting in higher stock prices, which in turn lowers the cost of equity capital. In capital markets that are truly efficient that will not be the case. In financial markets that are not quite fully efficient, investors will reward firms that are producing smoother earnings streams. In this case, hedging translation exposure is value creating. There are two special situations where hedging translation exposure will have more direct cash flow implications:

1. *Loan covenants.* If the firm has to satisfy a loan covenant that requires that a threshold metric, such as debt-to-equity ratio, not be crossed because of unchecked translation losses to the cumulative translation losses account, then direct cash flow implications may result in the form of a higher cost of debt. Failure to meet such loan covenants may lower or reduce the firm's credit rating or its borrowing capacity, or force it to renegotiate lending conditions at less favorable terms.
2. *Credit rating.* A debt-to-equity ratio unduly impacted by a string of translation losses may result in a firm's debt rating being downgraded and therefore an increased cost of debt financing.

After reviewing the long-established forward contract, we turn next to a detailed review of forex derivatives, which have been engineered since 1971.

Forward Contracts

A forward exchange contract is a commitment to buy or sell a certain quantity of foreign currency on a certain date in the future (maturity of the contract) at a price (forward exchange rate) agreed upon today when the contract is signed. Clearly it is important to understand that a forward contract, when signed, is an exchange of irrevocable and legally binding promises (with no cash changing hands), obligating the two parties to go through with the actual transaction at maturity and deliver the respective currencies (or cash settlement) regardless of the state of the world—that is, regardless of the spot exchange rate at the time of contract settlement. Forward exchange contracts had been available for decades, but it was not until the breakdown of the Bretton Woods system of fixed exchange rates, and the resulting heightened volatility in currency prices, that new foreign exchange risk management products started to appear. Futures contracts on foreign exchange were first introduced in May 1972, when the International Monetary Market of the Chicago Mercantile Exchange began trading contracts on the British pound, Canadian dollar, Deutsche mark, Japanese yen, and Swiss franc.

Currency Futures

A currency futures contract is *traditionally* defined as a legally binding agreement with an organized exchange to buy (or sell) *today* a set amount of foreign currency for delivery at a specified date in the *future*. As such, a currency future does not appear terribly different from the old-fashioned forward contract, except for the fact that such contracts are entered into with organized (and generally regulated) exchanges—a fact that has far-reaching implications for *credit risk* (counterparty risk). There are, however, a number of additional differences between futures and forwards, which we address next.

Contract Standardization

To promote accessibility, trading, and liquidity, futures contracts specify a standardized face value, maturity date, and minimum price movement. Consider, for example, the euro (€) futures contract as traded on the International Monetary Market (IMM) of the Chicago Mercantile Exchange: It specifies a standardized face value of €125,000 with delivery date set for the third Wednesday of March, June, September, or December, as well as the minimum price movement, or tick size, which is set at $12.50 per contract (or $0.0001 per €). On December 1, 2009, the March 2010 contract closed at $1.4715 per €. By contrast, the reader will recall that forwards are tailor-made contracts negotiated directly by the two parties involved, with the amount transacted starting at $1 million and maturity dates generally stretching in multiples of 30 days.

Marking-to-Market and the Elimination of Credit Risk

In order to minimize the risk of *default* (*counterparty risk*), a futures exchange such as the IMM takes at least two precautionary measures for every contract it enters into: (1) it requires the buyer to set up an *initial margin* (a surety bond of sorts) that, at the minimum, should be equal to the maximum allowed daily price fluctuation; and (2) it forces the contract holder to settle immediately any daily losses resulting from adverse movement in the value of the futures contract. This is the practice of forcing the contract holder to a daily *marking-to-market*, which effectively reduces credit risk to a daily performance period with daily gains/losses added/subtracted from the margin account. To avoid a depleted margin account (which essentially means that the surety bond has become worthless), the futures trader is obligated to replenish his or her margin account (so-called *margin call*) should it fall below a preset threshold known as the *maintenance margin*. One practical question is, of course: How are the initial margin and the maintenance margin determined? The initial margin should protect the clearinghouse against default by the futures contract holder, and will therefore well exceed the maximum daily allowance; but ultimately it will be on a case-by-case basis reflecting, in part, historical volatility of the currency price—let's say 5 percent of the face value of the contract or $0.05 \times €125,000 = \$6,250$. The maintenance margin typically would be set as a percentage of the initial margin—let's say 75 percent of $6,250 = \$4,687$.

Currency Option

A currency option gives the *buyer* the right (without the obligation) to buy (*call* contract) or to sell (*put* contract) a specified amount of foreign currency at an agreed price (*strike* or *exercise price*) for exercise on the expiration date (European option) or on or before the expiration date (American option).[16] For such a right, the option buyer/holder pays to the option seller (called the *option writer*) a cash premium at the inception of the contract. A European option whose exercise price is the forward rate is said to be an *at-the-money* option;[17] if it is profitable to exercise the option immediately (disregarding the cash premium), the option is said to be an *in-the-money* option; and conversely, if it is not profitable to exercise the option immediately, the option is said to be an *out-of-the-money option*. As expected, in-the-money options command higher premiums than out-of-the-money options. When held to maturity, the option will be exercised if it expires in-the-money and abandoned when it expires out-of-the-money. Currency options can be negotiated over-the-counter with features (face value, strike price, and maturity) tailor-made to the special needs of the buyer, who is responsible for evaluating the counterparty risk (that is, the likelihood of the option writer delivering if the option is exercised at maturity). Of practical interest is the trade-off between strike price and premium: The further in-the-money the strike price is, the more expensive the option becomes (i.e., the higher the premium), and conversely, the further out-of-the-money, the less expensive it is. Standardized option contracts available from organized exchanges such as the Philadelphia Stock Exchange are practically devoid of counterparty risk, since a well-capitalized clearinghouse[18] serves as a guarantor of the contracts; however, the option buyer is limited to a relatively small set of ready-made products directly available off the shelf.

Options Strategies

There are many speculative options strategies, ranging from the simple (e.g., writing covered options) to more complex strategies known under such colorful names as *straddle, strangle, butterfly, condor,* and *bull price spread,* to name a few. After reviewing the mechanics of writing covered options, this section considers the straddle strategy, whose payoff at expiry depends on the volatility, rather than on the absolute level, of the exchange rate.

Writing Covered Options

By writing *naked* (uncovered) call options on sterling, one clearly speculates by accepting an up-front payment (premium) in exchange for a potentially unlimited loss if sterling were to appreciate against the dollar. (See line 1 in Exhibit 7.10.) It would stand to reason that if the call option writer were to hold a forward asset position in sterling (Exhibit 7.10, line 2), the writer would have effectively covered the selling of a naked call option—hence the reference to writing a *covered call* option. In fact, this is misleading, since a covered call option is nothing more than writing a *naked put* option on sterling, as illustrated in Exhibit 7.10 by line 3, which is constructed as the algebraic sum of lines 1 and 2.

Options Straddles

A straddle is defined as the simultaneous purchase of put and call options of the same strike price and maturity. This strategy is especially attractive when one anticipates high exchange rate volatility but is hard-pressed to forecast the direction of the future spot exchange rate. Exhibit 7.11 superimposes the purchase of a 90-day call option (line 1) on the purchase of a 90-day put option (line 2) at the same

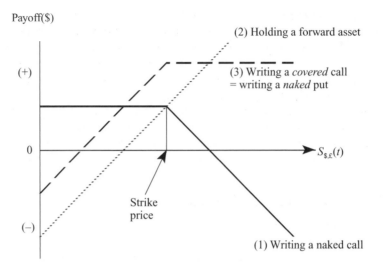

Exhibit 7.10   Writing a Covered Call Option

strike price, denoted here by $E(90)$, to create a straddle (line 3, which appears as a V in the graph of the algebraic sum of lines 1 and 2). Of interest are the break-even exchange rates (labeled A and B in Exhibit 7.11), which are symmetrical vis-à-vis the strike price, with:

$$S(90)^A = E(90) - [p(0)^c + p(0)^p]$$

and:

$$S(90)^B = E(90) + [p(0)^c + p(0)^p]$$

where $p(0)^c$ and $p(0)^p$ are the premium paid on the call and put options, respectively.

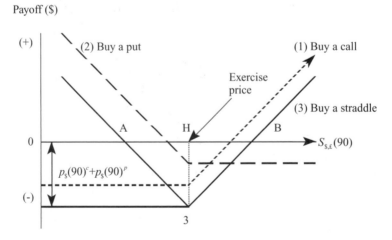

Exhibit 7.11   Buying a Straddle

If the future spot rate $S(90)$ turns out to be very volatile and escapes the AB band, the straddle will be profitable, as shown by the positive portion of line 3 in Exhibit 7.11. Conversely, if the exchange rate were to move within the narrow AB range, the buyer of the straddle may lose as much as $p(0)^c + p(0)^p$ which, graphically, is the line segment H3, also equivalent to $1/2$ the length of line AB. Importantly, this is the most the buyer could lose.

Inversely, the writer (seller) of a straddle bets on low volatility of the end exchange rate by writing both put and call options with the same exercise price. However, were this bet to be wrong, the writer's loss would be unlimited. The most that the writer would stand to gain would be the sum of the two option premiums sold.

Put-Call Forward Parity Theorem

We now turn to the powerful arbitrage relationship that binds the options market to the forward exchange market. A 90-day forward purchase contract can always be replicated by simultaneously buying a 90-day call option and selling a 90-day European put option at the same strike price, $E(90)$. Superimposing put and call options in Exhibit 7.12 shows that for the call option holder the unlimited portion of the profit function (adjusted correspondingly by the option premium) is equivalent to the unlimited profit portion of the foreign currency forward purchase contract—or, conversely, the unlimited loss portion of the same forward purchase contract corresponds to the unlimited loss of the put option writer (similarly adjusted by the option premium). Thus, in the option market it is easy to create synthetic forward contracts whose prices can be readily compared to prevailing rates in the forward

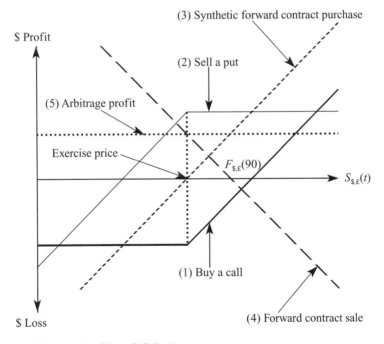

Exhibit 7.12 International Put-Call Parity

market. This fundamental equivalence between the option and forward markets drives the constant arbitrage activity between the two markets and is known as the *put-call forward exchange parity*.

By combining the purchase of a call option (Exhibit 7.12, line 1) with the writing of a put option (Exhibit 7.12, line 2) at the same exercise price, $E(90)$, one effectively purchases forward the foreign currency at the options' exercise price (Exhibit 7.12, line 3, which is the graphical sum of lines 1 and 2). The same amount of foreign currency can be immediately sold on the forward market at the forward rate of $F(90)$ (Exhibit 7.12, line 4). However, the synthetic forward contract created by buying a call and selling a put at the same strike price will cost the difference between the premium $p(0)^c$ paid for buying the call and the income generated from writing the put, $p(0)^p$. Accounting for the fact that this difference is paid (received) when the option contract is entered into rather than exercised, the total cost or terminal value of buying synthetically the foreign currency forward is:

$$E(90) + [p(0)^c - p(0)^p] \cdot (1 + i_{us}) \qquad (7.1)$$

where i_{us} is the interest rate over the 90-day period. Thus, by buying the currency synthetically at the price given by Equation 7.1 and selling it at the prevailing forward exchange rate of $F(90)$, the arbitrageur is generating a risk-free profit of:

$$F(90) - E(0) - [p(0)^c - p(0)^p] \cdot (1 + i_{us}) > 0 \qquad (7.2)$$

Allied-Lyons's Deadly Game[19]

Allied-Lyons—better known for its tea bags than for its forays into the currency market—announced a stunning $269 million forex loss (approximately 20 percent of its projected profits for 1991). Facing a sluggish economy, its treasury had elaborated a sophisticated scheme that gambled not so much on the absolute level of the dollar/sterling rate as on its volatility. This gamble was achieved through a combination of currency options known as straddles and strangles that in this particular case would have produced profits had the exchange rate turned out to be less volatile than the option premium implied.

This ingenious scheme was elaborated at the beginning of the Gulf War when the relatively high price of option premiums (due to heavy buying from hedgers) convinced Allied-Lyons that it was propitious to place an attractive short-term bet that volatilities would decrease as soon as hostilities started. Thus Allied-Lyons wrote deep-in-the-money options in straddle/strangle combinations, thereby netting hefty cash premiums. However, when the allies launched their air offensive, the initial uncertainty as to the outcome did not reduce the option volatility—at least not soon enough for Allied-Lyons to see its speculation gambit succeed. Indeed, it took another month for the ground offensive to appease the forex market, by which time it was already too late for Allied-Lyons, which had been forced by its bankers to liquidate its options position at a great loss.

shown as line 5 (line 3 plus line 4) in Exhibit 7.12. This disequilibrium will set arbitrage forces into motion as the price of the call option is bid up and the price of the put option is bid down, until the risk-free profit disappears and *parity* prevails. As arbitrageurs construct synthetic forward purchase contracts, its rate will be driven up. Simultaneously, by selling at the higher prevailing forward rate, arbitrageurs will depress the price of forward contracts, $F(90)$, thereby forcing inequality 7.2 toward equality.

Zero-Premium Options

The limitation of the forward contract is that while it gives 100 percent protection against an adverse movement in the future exchange rate, it also eliminates any opportunity for gain from a subsequent movement in the exchange rate; such a potential missed gain is generally referred to as an opportunity cost. Currency options, in contrast, allow full participation in this upside potential, though at a substantial up-front cash flow cost that discourages many would-be users. Of the many forex derivative products that have appeared recently, two products that allow participation in those potential gains—without incurring the up-front cash expenses—are of particular interest to corporate treasurers: (1) *forward range agreements* and (2) *forward participation agreements*. Both products are based on the simple idea of combining writing an option whose premium finances the purchase of another option so as to create, when superimposed on the underlying naked exposure, the desired risk profile.

Forward Range Agreements and Currency Collars

Like forwards, forward range contracts will lock in a worst-case exchange rate; unlike forwards, though, forward range contracts allow the hedger the opportunity to benefit from an upside market move delineated by a *range* of forward rates. Assuming an underlying sterling asset position a(90), the user would structure a sterling forward range agreement by first buying, for example, a sterling put option at a strike price of $E(90) = 1.8450$ (the defensive option is represented by line 1 in Exhibit 7.13) while offsetting all of the up-front cost by selling a sterling call option at a strike price of $E(90)^* = 1.9000$ (the financing option is represented by line 2 in Exhibit 7.13).[20] Note, however, that the financing option will bound the upside potential of the defensive option resulting from a favorable currency move. Typically, the user will set an exercise price $E(90)$ lower than the forward rate at which the user is buying the put option while selling a call at an exercise price $E(90)^* > E(90)$ so that the premium received from the call option $p(0)^*$ equals the premium paid on the put option $p(0)$. By entering into such a contract, the user would lock in the worst-case exchange rate, $E(90)$, while retaining the opportunity to benefit from a sterling appreciation favorable to the underlying sterling asset position (Exhibit 7.13, line 3). Thus the risks of an open foreign exchange position are eliminated, while the magnitude of opportunity is limited to the top of a range $E(90)^*$. Typically, a forward range contract is defined as a range $E(90)$, $E(90)^*$ bracketing the forward exchange rate $F(90)$ and thereby establishing a tunnel within which the hedger accepts the exchange risk exposure, but outside of which the hedger is

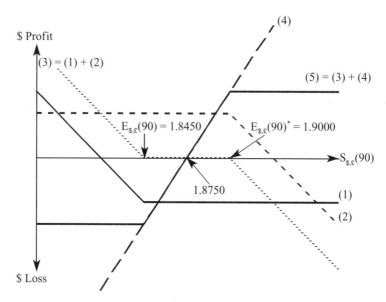

Exhibit 7.13   Forward Range Agreement

protected or restricted by the lower/upper bound of the range. The resulting risk profile is represented by line 5 in Exhibit 7.13, which is the graphical sum of lines $(1) + (2) + (4) = (5)$. As can be seen in the exhibit:

- If the actual end-of-the-period exchange rate falls below the protection level $E(90)$, the user will exercise the put option and sell sterling at $E(90)$.
- If the actual end-of-the-period exchange rate falls within the protection range $E(90)$, $E(90)^*$, the user will benefit from the actual spot exchange rate $S(90)$ and receive $a(90)S(90)$.
- If the actual end-of-the-period exchange rate exceeds the upper bound of the range $E(90)^*$, the user is limited to receiving $a(90)E(90)^*$ as the call option is exercised by the bank that sold the forward range contract.

In a *currency collar*, the hedger is willing to pay a *reduced* premium (as opposed to a *zero* premium in the case of a forward range agreement) to enjoy a wider range, $E(90)$, $E(90)^*$, or greater profit potential. This is achieved by writing a defensive call option that generates less premium income; that is, it does not fully finance the purchase of the put option.

Forward Participation Agreements

This type of protection contract shares certain characteristics with the forward range agreement in that there is no up-front fee and the user has the flexibility to set the downside protection level. However, unlike the forward range agreement, where the maximum opportunity gain is capped at a prearranged level, the forward participation agreement allows its user to share in the upside potential by receiving a fixed percentage (the participation rate) of any favorable currency move irrespective of magnitude. The user will purchase a put option whose premium $p(0)^p$ is partially financed by writing a call option, thereby generating a net revenue of $p(0)^c - p(0)^p$. Instead of restituting the difference, $p(0)^c - p(0)^p$, the bank allows the user to partake in the upside potential to the tune of α percent. Specifically, the downside protection level is tied to the participation rate, to be negotiated with the bank:

- If the actual exchange rate falls below the protection level $E(90)$, the user will exercise the put option.
- If the actual exchange rate exceeds the protection level, $S(90) > E(90)$, the user will participate [participation rate α is a function of the level of $E(90)$] and receive a rate of:

$$E(90) + \alpha[S(90) - E(90)]$$

As hinted in the introduction, financial engineering has shown tremendous ingenuity in the past decade, with far too many exotic options to include in the present chapter.

The forex market also has undergone major changes over the past decade. The interbank market has largely evolved from direct/bilateral dealing and voice brokering to electronic trading via Internet-based deal-matching systems. As a result, the microstructure of the forex market is less fragmented and points toward greater transparency, as the price discovery process is faster thanks to powerful electronic price-aggregator platforms. Similarly, the macroeconomics of the forex market points toward a lesser role for central banks due to reduced intervention in currency markets, more flexibility in exchange rates, and greater convertibility for many currencies. As central banks disengaged themselves from the risk mitigation business, the private sector filled the gap by engineering derivatives, enabling market participants to transfer among themselves exposures to forex risk in an increasingly efficient manner.

NOTES

1. Foreign exchange derivative products, in the form of currency futures and options, are also traded as standardized products on organized exchanges such as the International Money Market (IMM) in Chicago. See the last section of this chapter for further discussion.

2. The forward rate is agreed upon today and binding 60 days later when the sale is consummated regardless of what the spot rate may be on that day. The forward rate is set according to the interest rate parity formula.

3. *Buy side* refers to consumers and *sell side* to merchants. The buy side would, for example, purchase euros (selling dollars) while the sell side is selling euros (buying dollars). Because of the nature of forex trading, both buy and sell sides are buying one currency and selling the other.

4. See Bank for International Settlements (2001) and Rime, Dagfinn (2003).

5. Market makers are dealers—generally based at bank trading desks—ready to quote buy and sell prices on request. The market maker provides liquidity to the market and is compensated by the spread between buy and sell rates.

6. Voice brokers used to work through closed telephone networks, whereas electronic brokers today use Reuters D3000 or EBS.

7. Reuters introduced the Reuters Market Data Service (RMDS) as early as 1981, which allowed for the exchange of information over computer screens but no actual trading. In 1989 Reuters Dealing 2000-1 replaced RMDS and allowed computer-based forex trading, displacing telephone (and human) trading. The platform was updated in 1992 with Reuters D2000-2 and again in 2006 with Reuters D3000.

8. To counter the dominance of Reuters, the Electronic Broking System (EBS) was created in 1993 by a consortium of large banks—ABN Amro, Bank of America, Barclays, Chemical Bank, Citibank, Commerzbank, Credit Suisse, Lehman Brothers, Midland, J.P. Morgan, NatWest, Swiss Bancorp, and Union Bank of Switzerland.

9. In 1974 the default of Bankhaus Herstatt sent shock waves through the foreign exchange market, giving new meaning to counterparty and settlement risk.

10. See section on forex trading.

11. This is particularly the case in a smaller developed country, such as the Netherlands, Belgium, Denmark, or New Zealand, whose foreign sector often accounts for over 30 percent of gross national product (GNP).

12. Central bank intervention within the context of stabilized exchange rates is discussed at some length in the following section (see Dominguez, Kathryn M., and Jeffrey Frankel, 1993). It essentially results from a public commitment to maintain exchange rate variations within a narrow band of fluctuations whose ceiling and floor are unambiguously known to market participants (see Mayer, 1974).

13. The reader will remember that the supply curve of £ is nothing other than the demand curve for $. Similarly, the demand curve for £ is the supply of $.

14. Official exchange rate prevailing between a given currency and the dollar.

15. See Chapter 3 in Jacque (2010).

16. The terminology of the American or European option does not refer to the location where the option contract is traded. Both European and American option contracts are traded on both continents, as well as in the Far East.

17. American options' exercise prices are generally compared to the spot rate (rather than forward rate), with similar definitions of at-, in-, or out-of-the-money applicable since they can be exercised immediately.

18. The clearinghouse is the Option Clearing Corporation (OCC), which also clears exchange-traded equity options. OCC is jointly owned by all U.S. equity options exchanges.

19. See Chapter 8 in Jacque (2010).

20. By necessity, such products require European options.

REFERENCES

Bank for International Settlements. 2001. "The Implications of Electronic Trading in Financial Markets." (January). www.bis.org/publ/cgfs16.htm.

Bank for International Settlements. 2007. "Triennial Central Bank Survey of Foreign Exchange and Derivatives Market Activity in 2007." www.bis.org/publ/rpfxf07t.htm.

Dominguez, Kathryn M., and Jeffrey Frankel. 1993. *Does Foreign Exchange Intervention Work?* Washington, DC: Institute for International Economics.

Holmes, A. R., and F. H. Scott. 1965. *The New York Foreign Exchange Market*. Federal Reserve Bank of New York: New York.

Jacque, Laurent L. 2010. *Global Derivative Debacles: From Theory to Malpractice*. Singapore: World Scientific Publishing Co.

Kubarych, Roger M. 1983. *Foreign Exchange Markets in the United States*, 2nd ed. New York: Federal Reserve Bank.

Lyons, R. K. 2001. *The Micro-Structure Approach to the Foreign Exchange Market*. Cambridge, MA: MIT Press.

Mayer, Helmut W. 1974. "The anatomy of official exchange rate intervention systems." *Essays in International Finance* 104. Princeton, NJ: Princeton University.

Rime, Dagfinn. 2003. "New electronic trading systems in foreign exchange markets." In Derek C. Jones, ed. *New Economy Handbook*, Chapter 21. Salt Lake City: Academic Press.

Root, Franklin R. 1994. *International Trade and Investment*. 7th ed. Cincinnati: South Western Publishing.

Sarno, Lucio, and Mark P. Taylor. 2001. "The Microstructure of the Foreign Exchange Market: A Selective Survey of the Literature." *Princeton Studies in International Economics*, 89 (May).

Taylor, Dean. 1982. "Official Intervention in the Foreign Exchange Market; or, Bet Against the Central Bank." *Journal of Political Economy* 90:2 (April), 356–368.

ABOUT THE AUTHOR

Laurent L. Jacque is the Walter B. Wriston professor of international finance and banking at the Fletcher School of Law and Diplomacy (Tufts University) and director of its International Business Studies Program. From 2004 to 2007 he was the academic dean of the Fletcher School and engineered the successful launch of the Master of International Business Program. Since 1990 he has also held a secondary appointment at the HEC School of Management (France). He is the author of two books, *Management and Control of Foreign Exchange Risk* and *Management of Foreign Exchange Risk: Theory and Praxis*, as well as more than 25 refereed articles on risk management, insurance, and international finance; his latest book, *Global Derivative Debacles: From Theory to Malpractice*. He served as an adviser to Wharton Econometrics Forecasting Associates and as a director of Water Technologies Inc. A native of France, Jacque graduated from HEC (Paris) and received his Ph from the Wharton School (University of Pennsylvania), where he taught for 11 years.

CHAPTER 8

The Commodity Market

HELEN LU
Princeton University SBCC Group

CARA M. MARSHALL
Queens College of the City University of New York

Commodity Market Snapshot

History: Commodity markets pre-date recorded history, and their evolution was critical to the development of modern civilization. Early barter trades evolved into loosely organized markets, which then evolved into more organized markets. Today we have highly efficient cash and derivatives markets for most major commodities. The latter include both exchange-traded components and over-the-counter components. These markets continue to evolve with new electronic platforms rapidly replacing traditional open outcry.

Size: The growth in trading volume for both exchange-traded and OTC commodity derivatives has been impressive. The size of the exchange-traded markets, principally futures, is most often measured in terms of contract volume and contract open interest. The size of the OTC derivatives markets is most often measured in notional principals outstanding and gross market values. Notional principal in the OTC commodity derivatives markets grew from under $1 trillion in 1998 to almost $18 trillion 10 years later.

Products: The markets trade an array of products ranging from physical commodities for immediate delivery, to highly standardized exchange-traded products, such as futures and options on futures, that allow individuals and institutions to enter and exit positions quickly and efficiently. Customized derivative products are also available in the form of swaps and options. These products can be tailored to satisfy a host of end user needs.

First Usage: The first recorded futures trade was in rice contracts, developed in Japan during the seventeenth century. The over-the-counter commodity market developed during the 1980s when the first oil swap was introduced in 1986, with Chase Manhattan Bank as the intermediary in the transaction.

Selection of Famous Events:
Early seventeenth century: The first tulip bulbs were brought to Holland in 1559. A market that was dominated by the wealthy Dutch soon developed. However, by the 1630s, the middle-class of Dutch society began seeking out this coveted flower, resulting in escalating tulip

bulb prices. The market ranged from those who purchased the flower for simple enjoyment to those who accumulated bulbs for the purpose of resale and generating profits. Prices reached their peak in 1636, and people began to liquidate their tulip holdings. Eventually, panic resulted and the tulip bubble burst, with prices declining by at least 90 percent within six weeks.

1993: Metallgesellschaft AG (MG), a German industrial conglomerate, revealed losses of $1.5 billion from its New York–based subsidiary, MG Refining and Marketing Inc. (MGRM). MGRM went long in energy futures and entered into OTC energy swap agreements to receive floating and pay fixed energy prices. However, a decline in energy prices, coupled with MG lacking sufficient funds to maintain their hedging positions, resulted in significant losses. Today, it is now a part of GEA Group AG, one of the largest system providers for food and energy processes.

2006: Amaranth Advisors, a Greenwich, Connecticut, hedge fund, made futures bets on natural gas prices to rise and leveraged those bets by borrowing money. Although the firm profited from the same speculative positions in the previous year, natural gas prices fell in 2006, causing Amaranth to lose about $6 billion.

Best Providers (as of 2009)

North America and Europe: Morgan Stanley.

Asia: Standard Chartered.

Applications: Some of the ways that investors may use commodity derivatives include hedging, short-term speculation, arbitrage, long-term investing, portfolio diversification, and building structured products.

Users: Commercial interests, including both producers and consumers of commodities, are active market participants. Increasingly, investors looking for alternative asset classes are being drawn to commodities as well.

HISTORICAL PERSPECTIVE

Commodities are at the heart of our very existence. We live in homes made of wood and brick. We wear clothes made of cotton and other fibers. We eat a breakfast of eggs, bacon, orange juice, coffee, and milk. We drive to work in a car made of a variety of metals and plastics and powered by gasoline or electricity. The commodities that we consume in our daily lives are ubiquitous; so much so that we simply take them for granted without giving them much thought.

Commodity markets have an extremely long history; indeed, they pre-date any written records. They were the first markets, existing even before there was money—at least, as we understand the concept of money today. Without trade in commodities, civilizations would not have developed and life as we know it today would not be possible. The earliest transactions in commodities took place tens, perhaps hundreds, of thousands of years ago and undoubtedly took the form of barter transactions between individuals of the same tribal band or between tribal bands that occasionally interacted. I might have caught a lot of fish; more than I can consume before the fish go bad. You might have killed some game and have more animal skins than you can wear. These situations, and hundreds like them, lend themselves to barter. Perhaps we can agree that 10 fish are worth 1 deer skin. So a trade is made.

The development of markets, initially through barter, but later using money, replaced the more brutal approach of taking what you want from others by force. As such, the development of commodity markets played a key role in the evolution of civilization. In time, people began to specialize in the commodities they produced, simply because people had different sorts of skills and preferences for the types of work they did. A good hunter is not necessarily a good fisherman. A good fisherman is not necessarily a good farmer. Thus people began to concentrate on producing those things wherein they had a comparative advantage and then traded their production for the production of others. The introduction of money, itself just a standardized commodity, greatly improved the efficiency of these early commercial transactions. Indeed, the introduction of money, in itself, was a truly astounding financial innovation.

Over time, markets became more organized. This might have taken the form of different tribal bands meeting annually at specific locations to trade with one another. In time, a merchant class began to develop, and they found that they could maximize their transactional volume and minimize their cost of transporting their goods, and thereby maximize their profit, by positioning themselves along natural trade routes. This pattern was repeated throughout history and explains why most of the world's major commodity markets are located where they are. Chicago, for one, was well positioned to become a center for trade in grains and related commodities because of its position on Lake Michigan and its proximity to the lush agricultural region known as the grain belt.

With the progression of time, merchants began to organize themselves into guilds. The guilds established rules of conduct that all members of the guild were expected to obey. These guilds, in turn, established more organized markets than had previously existed. They would set the times of market operation, develop standardized weights and measures, and designate trading and delivery locations. Because money (cash) was exchanged for commodities with immediate delivery expected, these markets became known as cash markets, though they are also known today as spot markets, actuals markets, and physicals markets.

As commercial interests grew in size and became more sophisticated, new needs emerged. For example, a miller might need 10,000 bushels of wheat to mill into flour every month because he has contracted to deliver that quantity of flour to a baker. But the cash market for wheat is only bountiful in supply at the time of harvest, and the miller does not have the resources to purchase a whole year's supply of wheat at one time, nor the storage capacity to warehouse that quantity of wheat. In response to these sorts of situations, grain merchants with access to storage would agree to sell wheat today for delivery at specific later dates; that is, dates "more forward" than were considered immediate. These contracts became known as forward contracts, and the early markets in them were made by some of the same merchants who marketed grains for immediate delivery.

Forward contracts were the precursors of futures contracts, but they were not supplanted by futures contracts. Instead, forward contracts and futures contracts co-exist as each has its advantages and its disadvantages. Most people believe that the Chicago Board of Trade (CBOT) was the first futures market, but it was not. The CBOT was established by grain merchants in 1848 and began trading futures in the 1860s. In fact, a futures market in rice had earlier existed in Osaka, Japan.[1] It was known as the Dojima rice market, and it traded standardized futures-like contracts in the eighteenth century. Despite the fact that the Dojima rice market employed many of the same processes as were later employed by the CBOT, there is no evidence that the founders of the CBOT had any knowledge of this earlier rice market and its practices. Thus, futures trading, as an innovation, has occurred independently more than once. This speaks to the fact that a good idea is a good idea no matter who comes up with it. Today, futures markets exist throughout the world and employ similar structures and trading rules.

As commodity markets grew larger, they began to attract the attention of governments. When occasional shortages occurred, often due to the vagaries of weather, sharp increases in prices would result. Similarly, when the stars were aligned and Mother Nature cooperated, a bumper crop would bring so much supply to the market that prices would plunge. The former angered consumers, and the latter angered producers. Both sides would insist that speculators were manipulating the prices. Typically, they would refuse to accept that these price swings are natural market responses to imbalances in supply and demand and that they are the invisible hand that guides production and consumption. Such complaints, however ill-founded they might have been, eventually led to government oversight of these organized markets, which eventually became known as "exchanges" in some countries and "bourses" in others.

In the early days of futures trading, trading was confined to agricultural commodities—mostly grains and oilseeds, such as wheat, corn oats, and soybeans. In time, futures trading was extended to agricultural commodities other than grains and oil seeds. These included goods like coffee, cocoa, sugar, and cotton, and livestock products such as live cattle, pork bellies, and lean hogs. Still later, futures trading in non-agricultural commodities, such as industrial metals (e.g., nickel, aluminum, copper, lead, and tin) and precious metals (e.g., gold, silver, palladium, and platinum) were introduced. In more recent years, futures trading in a host of energy products, ranging from crude oil to natural gas to ethanol, was introduced. In time, it was realized that there was no real need to have a provision for physical delivery on a futures contract if acceptable and transparent cash settlement rules could be developed and enforced. This led to the introduction of non-deliverable (or cash settled) futures on both non-traditional commodities, such as freight rates and electricity, but also to futures on things that are clearly not commodities at all, such as stock indexes and interest rates.

In the 1980s, a number of important new developments occurred in the commodities markets, with two events standing out in particular. One was the introduction of exchange-traded options on futures, and the other was the introduction of commodity swaps and options. The former, like futures, are highly standardized contracts that trade on designated futures exchanges. The latter are over-the-counter (OTC) products that can be tailor-made (i.e., customized) to serve the specific commercial needs of end users. Some of the differences between exchange-traded and OTC commodity derivatives are important and will be discussed shortly.

Historically, few individual investors thought of commodities as "investment assets" except in the context of purchasing shares in commodity-producing companies. Physical commodities are, in most cases, simply too bulky to store and often have very limited life spans before they spoil. Futures, of course, represented an alternative way to take investment positions in commodities, but only a small segment of the investing community ever did so. Few had any real understanding of futures and futures market mechanics, and many of those who did feared the leverage built into these contracts. They were also often put off by the fact that most commodity futures have a relatively short life. In very recent years, however, portfolio managers and investment advisors have come to see commodities as an investable asset class—quite distinct from equities, fixed income, foreign exchange, and credit. In response to this growing acceptance of the concept of commodities as investments, and some clever financial engineering, a number of structured investment products have been introduced that any investor can use to gain exposure to commodities. Important among these are commodity-linked notes and commodity-focused exchange-traded funds. For wealthier investors, there are also "hedge fund"–like vehicles that specialize in commodities. These are known as commodity pools, commodity funds, and managed futures funds. Importantly, not all managed futures funds trade futures on commodities. Some trade futures on stock indexes, interest rates, and other non-commodity underlyings. In the United States, persons who run commodity pools must register with the Commodity Futures Trading Commission as commodity pool operators (CPOs) and persons who advise others on trading in commodities and who run individually managed commodity accounts on behalf of others must register as commodity trading advisors (CTAs). Both commodity pools and individually managed futures accounts are generally open only to investors who meet stringent criteria.

Collectively, these various engineered products have helped satisfy investors' growing interest in commodities as investments in recent years. This new interest is driven, in part, by the view that commodities can be a good inflation hedge; in part by the fact that the inclusion of commodities in the investment asset class mix can improve diversification; and, in part, by the view that rapid economic growth in developing countries will continue to drive growth in demand that will, in turn, drive commodity prices higher.

EXCHANGE-TRADED VERSUS OTC COMMODITY PRODUCTS

It is common practice to divide commodity markets into "cash markets" and "derivatives markets." The cash markets represent the markets where commodities can and are physically delivered following a transaction. The delivery may be immediate (immediacy is defined in the context of the specific market), or it can be for a period more forward than what is understood to be immediate. Contracts are negotiated directly between the buyer and the seller with all contract specifications spelled out in each contract drafted. These specifications include such things as the specific grade of commodity, the quantity of the commodity, the delivery date, the delivery location and mechanism, and the price, among other things.

The derivatives markets, which include both exchange-traded products and over-the-counter products, may or may not provide for physical delivery, and, in most cases where physical delivery is permitted, the contracts can be terminated without physical delivery, by either engaging in an offsetting transaction or negotiating a cancellation. The former include commodity futures and options on futures; the latter include swaps, cash-settled forwards, and OTC commodity options.

FUTURES CONTRACTS

Futures contracts only trade on designated futures exchanges. The exchange specifies all of the contract terms—everything except the price. Thus, the only thing that needs to be determined through the trading process is the price. The futures will be available in two or more delivery months. For example, there might be a June contract, a September contract, and a December contract. A person who wishes to buy a contract would contact his commodity broker and give appropriate instructions. He can place a variety of different types of orders but would most commonly use either a "market order" or a "limit order." For example, a customer might say to his broker, "Buy 10 June gold at market." Each of these contracts covers 100 ounces of gold, but prices are quoted in dollars per ounce. So his request translates to "buy for my account 10 June delivery gold futures contracts each covering 100 ounces of gold," and he is willing to pay whatever current market conditions dictate. This is a market order because he is willing to pay the current market price. In this case, the current market price would be the best ask price (also known as an offer price) currently available. Had he specified the maximum price he is willing to pay, it would have been a limit order and the broker must get the limit price or a better price. If the broker cannot get the limit price or a better price, the trade does not occur. The same process works when selling a futures contract. For example, a customer might say, "Sell 5 June gold at $1275.40." This is a limit order to sell five gold contracts, and the broker must get the customer a price of $1275.40 (or better) per ounce covered by the contracts. Importantly, one does not need to own a futures contract to sell one. The act of selling a futures contract creates a short position for the seller.

Both buyers and sellers of futures have to post margin with their brokers. Margin is typically 5 to 10 percent of the notional value of the contract, but the margin rules can vary depending on what other positions the customer simultaneously holds. If the price moves against the customer, he or she will be asked to post additional margin. If the price moves in the customer's favor (i.e., up for longs and down for shorts), the customer can withdraw money from his or her margin account.

Futures trading is symmetric in that there are exactly the same number of contracts held long as held short (i.e., one person's long position is another person's short position). Thus, the profits earned by one person come at the expense of losses to the other person. In the language of economics, this makes futures trading a "zero sum game." Importantly, it is only a zero sum game in a "monetary profit/loss" sense. In terms of economic "utility," futures trading can be win-win for both parties.

A customer can get out of a futures position with ease. If he is long a contract, he simply sells a contract of the same delivery month, and he is out. If he is short a contract, he simply buys a contract of the same delivery month, and he is out. This ease of entry and exit is made possible because of the standardization of contract terms and the intermediation of the clearinghouse.

Affiliated with every futures exchange, but still distinct from the exchange itself, is a clearinghouse. The clearinghouse becomes the counterparty to the customer on every trade he does, no matter with whom he traded. That is, the customer who buys a contract is "long to the clearinghouse" and the "clearinghouse is short to the customer." By the same token, a customer who sells a contract is "short to the clearinghouse," and the "clearinghouse is long to the customer." Thus, if a customer initially bought 10 June gold futures, he is long 10 contracts to the clearinghouse. If he later sells 10 June gold futures, he is then short 10 contracts to the clearinghouse. Because his counterparty in both cases is the clearinghouse, his positions cancel. He is left with the gain or loss that results from the difference between the price at which he bought and the price at which he sold. Those prices were determined on the exchange when the transactions were made.

The employment of clearinghouses and the posting of margin are key elements of futures market mechanics. The clearinghouse is protected from market risk because it is always long and short the same number of each contract. It is protected from credit risk by the margins posted by the position holders. Because of the relatively small amount of margin posted by customers, futures afford traders enormous leverage. For example, if the margin requirement is 5 percent of the notional value of the contract, the customer has leverage of 20 to 1. This is great when markets move in your favor but can prove devastating when prices move against you—hence the phrase, "leverage is a double-edged sword."

Participants in the futures markets include members of the exchange and the trading public. Here we refer to the latter as customers. Included among the members of the exchange are market makers. These exchange members offer to buy futures contracts at one price and to sell the same contracts at a slightly higher price. They are the principal, but not the only, source of market liquidity. They look to profit from the small difference between their bid (buying) price and slightly higher ask (selling) price. As noted earlier, ask prices are also known as offer prices. Other exchange members try to earn their livings by exploiting short-term trends in the price or by spotting and exploiting inefficiencies in contract pricing. Customers, and those are our real interest here, may be individuals, commercial entities such as corporations, or investment pools of various sorts. Some are short-term speculators, others are longer-term investors (the dividing line between speculators and investors is completely arbitrary), some are hedgers, and others are arbitrageurs. Speculators and investors attempt to profit by correctly predicting the direction of the market price and then positioning themselves to profit from the coming price change. Hedgers, in contrast, take positions in futures to offset the risks associated with other positions they presently hold or anticipate that they will later acquire. For example, a feedlot operator who has contracted to buy 500 calves, with delivery to be made a few months after the next birthing cycle, knows that he will need a certain amount of corn as feed to raise the calves before slaughter. His fear is that the cost of corn may go up before he takes delivery of the calves—thereby increasing his production costs. To hedge himself, he buys futures now with delivery dates after the point where he would take delivery of the calves. When he takes delivery of the calves, he goes into the cash corn market, purchases the physical corn that will be used to feed the calves, and simultaneously terminates his long futures positions by offsetting transactions. He may wind up paying more or less than he originally anticipated for the cash corn, but this unanticipated loss or gain is offset by the profit or loss on the futures contracts he used to hedge his anticipated future corn needs. Notice that he did not need to take delivery on the futures for the hedge to work, provided that the spot price of corn and the futures price of corn are sufficiently highly correlated.

Arbitrageurs seek to earn profits by exploiting perceived price discrepancies in markets. As a simple example, suppose that in August, an arbitrageur observes that the current spot price of corn is \$3.80 per bushel. He also observes that the November corn futures price is \$3.95 per bushel. He knows that it will cost him \$0.02 a month per bushel to store corn for a total of \$0.06 in storage costs. He will also have to absorb \$0.03 per bushel to transport the corn and \$0.03 per bushel to finance his holdings of the physical corn. Thus, he can buy the physical corn for \$3.80, absorb total costs of \$0.12 for storage, transport, and financing for a total all-in cost of \$3.92. Simultaneously, he sells futures at \$3.95, thereby locking in a riskless profit of \$0.03 a bushel. There are many other types of arbitrage scenarios; some, like this one, are conceptually simple, while others are far more complex. But do not be fooled; futures markets are highly efficient, and true arbitrage opportunities are very rare.

Historically, futures trading was conducted on the floors of large futures exchanges in what are called "trading pits." Each pit traded futures in one commodity but in multiple delivery months. Trading was conducted through a combination of voice and complex hand signals. Because pits take up a lot of room, the number of commodities that could be traded was limited by the size of the trading floor. Over the last few decades, futures trading has moved into the electronic age. The transition from physically meeting on a trading floor to meeting and trading in cyberspace was traumatic for many of the exchange members, and many resisted the transformation. But, the old does, sometimes reluctantly, make way for the new, and today most futures trading is conducted electronically. Indeed, some futures exchanges have completely retired their trading floors, and others are destined to eventually do so. This transition itself was an exercise in financial engineering, and it brought both greater speed to execution and a reduction in trading errors (i.e., miscommunications between buyers and sellers). It also made it possible to introduce futures on many additional commodities and non-commodities, as floor space became less of an issue.

Options on futures work the same way that equity options work, which are discussed in other chapters of this book, so we will not elaborate on them here, except to say that options on futures come in both call and put varieties and the "deliverable" is the specified underlying futures contract. Delivery of the futures contract would only take place if the option contract is exercised. The buyer of the contract pays a "premium" up front to the option writer (i.e., the seller) for the right that the option conveys. Specific option pricing models have been developed for options on futures. These models are similar to, but still not the same as, the models used for valuing equity options. The drivers of an option's value include the current price of the underlying, the volatility of the price of the underlying, the strike price of the option, the life of the option (i.e., the amount of time before the option expires), and the level of interest rates.

RISK MANAGEMENT WITH COMMODITY FUTURES/OPTIONS

There is a long literature on the use of commodity futures and, to a lesser extent, options on futures as risk management tools. Risk management is a science, a subset, so to speak, of the field of financial engineering, and it takes considerable study to do it well. Nothing illustrates this point better than a commodities hedging disaster that, in 1993, befell Metallgesellschaft AG (MG), a German industrial conglomerate. In that year, the company revealed that it had suffered losses of $1.5 billion on hedged positions in energy futures. Essentially, the company had sold over-the-counter energy derivatives and then hedged those positions by going long energy futures. Unfortunately, the correlation of the energy futures prices to those employed in the OTC market was less than expected, and, when oil prices plunged, MG was faced with massive margin calls. MG is an important case study in many university risk management and financial engineering programs precisely because it made a series of mistakes in both structuring its hedges and in managing those hedges.

COMMODITY SWAPS

Commodity swaps are an excellent example of how an innovation in one market can be recycled and become an innovation in another market. The first true swap (as distinct from earlier transactions that had similar cash flows but different contractual and legal structures) was a currency swap. This was done in 1979. The first interest rate swap was done in 1981. These early swap markets were "brokered" markets in which a bank, acting in the capacity of a broker, would match two counterparties having similar but opposite requirements. In exchange for its services, the bank would collect a commission from both end user counterparties. This commission was often referred to as "structuring fee." At first, these markets grew slowly, but when the broker banks realized that they could greatly facilitate swap transactions by transforming themselves from brokers to dealers, the swaps market took off. By 1986, the dealer market structure was well established, and, in that year, financial engineers (though that term had not yet been coined) at Chase Manhattan Bank (now part of JPMorgan Chase) realized that there was no apparent economic reason why a similar swap structure could not be applied to commodities. Typically, today, one counterparty to a commodity swap is a dealer and the other is an end user, but both parties can be dealers, and both parties can be end users. End users are parties other than dealers who have some commercial purpose for doing a swap.

In a plain vanilla commodity swap, one counterparty agrees to pay a fixed price per unit on some notional quantity of commodity. For example, consider an oil company in Texas that pumps 300,000 barrels of a specific grade of crude oil per month at the rate of 10,000 barrels per day. Each day, the company is credited with that day's spot price for its grade of oil for all the oil it pumped into the pipeline that day. Suppose now that the current spot price for the company's grade of oil is $70.50 per barrel. Its production costs are $55 per barrel. Management's worst fear, of course, is that the oil price might decline below the company's production cost, forcing the company to shut down its wells. Unfortunately, if the company

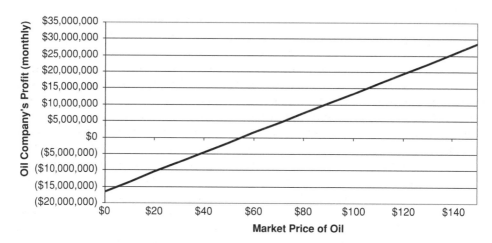

Exhibit 8.1   Profit Diagram or Risk Profile

shuts down its wells, it may not be able to start them up again, potentially forcing the company to pump at a loss until it is bankrupt. The company's monthly profit diagram or risk profile, with respect to the price of oil, is depicted in Exhibit 8.1.

To remove this risk, the company's risk manager decides to enter into a two-year oil swap, in which the company will receive a fixed price of $70.50 per barrel once a month on 300,000 notional barrels of oil, from a swap dealer, at which time it will pay to the swap dealer the "average spot price over the prior 30 days" on the same notional quantity of oil.[2] The oil swap together with the cash market transactions are depicted in Exhibit 8.2.

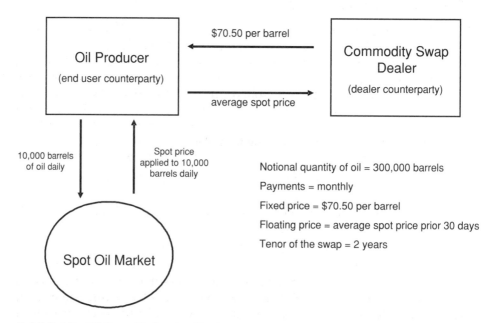

Exhibit 8.2   Oil Swap Hedge Application

It should be plainly obvious that this commodity swap is structured a little differently from most interest rate and currency swaps that you may have seen. Those types of swaps typically make one observation per payment period on the floating leg side. In this swap, the floating side takes the form of the "average spot price" from daily observations on the market price for oil. It is this average that is paid monthly on the 300,000 barrels. We could, of course, have simply made one single observation on the spot price of oil on a specific day of the month—the first business day of the month, the 15th of the month, or the last business day of the month. But, because the oil producer sells its output daily, none of these would give it a perfect hedge. That is, the single monthly observation could be more than it received or less than it received, on average, for its oil over the course of the month. By averaging the observed spot price over the course of the month, the correlation between what the company received in the cash market for oil and what it pays out on the swap will be much higher. The higher the correlation, the more effective the hedge. With this structure, the oil company can be confident of netting $15.50 per barrel profit on each of its 300,000 barrels of monthly production. That is, it has locked in a monthly profit of $4,650,000 for the next two years. The principal cost to the company is that it has also traded away the "upside," which is the potential to make even greater profits if the price of oil were to rise from its current $70.50 level.

These swaps can also be used to speculate and to invest, and also can be used as inputs in the construction of a variety of structured products and strategies. We will see several applications of this later. Importantly, the same banks that make markets in commodity swaps also, typically, make markets in commodity forward contracts.

COMMODITY OPTIONS

Many of the same dealers who make markets in commodity swaps also make markets in commodity options. Like options on futures, these can be calls or puts. They can be structured to be physically deliverable or cash settled. We will assume cash settlement for purposes of this discussion. Consider a call on oil. An end user buying the call would agree up front on the option's strike price, the notional quantity of oil, the settlement date, and the method and timing of observing the spot price for purposes of calculating the final settlement. The option will "pay off" at expiration based on the following formula:

$$\text{Payoff} = \max[S - X, 0] \times NQ$$

Had the option been a put, the payoff formula would have been:

$$\text{Payoff} = \max[X - S, 0] \times NQ$$

Where *max* is the maximum function and denotes the larger of the possible value of the term in brackets. S denotes the spot price observed in the manner agreed upon, X denotes the strike price of the option, and NQ denotes the notional quantity of oil (i.e., the number of barrels the contract is written on).

The call will "pay out" at the end if and only if it is in-the-money at its expiration. This would require that S > X. Otherwise, the call will pay out nothing. Similarly, the put will "pay out" at the end if and only if it is in-the-money at its expiration. This would require that S < X. The purchaser of either option will pay the dealer a premium up front and may lose some or all of this premium. But in no case will the option purchaser lose more on the option than the premium paid.

Using the same oil company described earlier in the swap hedging example, we will this time hedge the oil producer's risk exposure using an option. For the moment, we will assume that the oil company only wishes to hedge one month's production.

As noted earlier, the spot price of oil happens to be $70.50. The oil company, again, does not wish to take the risk of a decline in the price of oil, but doesn't want to hedge its risk with a commodity swap because, by so doing, it surrenders the opportunity to profit even more if the price of oil were to rise.

So, the company's risk manager approaches the commodity option dealer, and the dealer prices up a put option hedge on oil. They agree that the notional quantity of oil will be 300,000 barrels. They further agree that the option will pay off in precisely one month based on an average of the daily observations of the spot oil price— just as could have been done with the swap. They further agree that the strike price of the option will be $70.50. For this option, the dealer wants an up front premium of $2.00 per barrel covered, which means the option will cost the oil company $600,000. The structure, for just the one month life of the option, is depicted in Exhibit 8.3.

Now suppose that the average spot price of oil over the course of the month turns out to be $60.50 a barrel. The oil producer earns $1,650,000 from its transactions in the cash market. This is calculated by taking the price $60.50 that it received for its oil in the cash market, deducting the company's production costs of $55.00

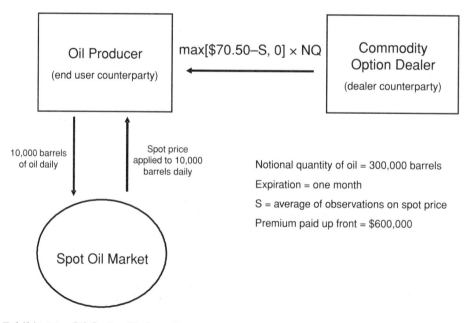

Exhibit 8.3 Oil Option Hedge—Put

per barrel, and multiplying by 300,000 barrels. But, at the same time, the company's option pays off because the put is in-the-money. The payoff is $3,000,000. However, because the company paid $600,000 up front for the put option, its profit on the option is only $2,400,000. Combining the profit of $1,650,000 earned in the cash market with the $2,400,000 profit earned on the option, the company's hedged profit for the month is $4,050,000. This is the company's worst case scenario and its overall profit would have been exactly the same at any oil price at or below $70.50. The reader is asked to verify this on his or her own. The beauty of the option hedge becomes obvious if the price of oil rises rather than falls. Suppose, for example, that the spot price of oil averages $78.50 over the course of the month. Then the company's overall profit for the month would have been $6,450,000; and if the price of oil had averaged $82.50 over the course of the month, the company's overall profit would have been $7,650,000. Again, the reader is invited to verify these numbers on his or her own (don't forget to deduct the premium paid for the option).

The oil company's profit diagram using the option hedge is contrasted to the oil company's profit diagram using the swap hedge (but just for the first month) in Exhibit 8.4. These should be compared to the profit diagram/risk profile with no hedge depicted in Exhibit 8.1. More experienced readers will notice that the profit diagram associated with the option hedge resembles the payoff profile of a call option, even though we employed a put as the hedging instrument. This is a manifestation of what is known in the option literature as "put/call parity."

Before closing this section, consider how the oil company might have hedged its production of oil out to a full two years as it did with the swap. The company could have purchased a series of 24 separate put options. The first would have a one-month expiry and would pay off based on the average spot price observed in the first month; the second would have a two-month expiry and would pay off based on the average spot price in the second month, and so on. Each of these options would command its own up-front premium. All other things being equal, the longer the time to expiry, the more expensive the option will be. But rather

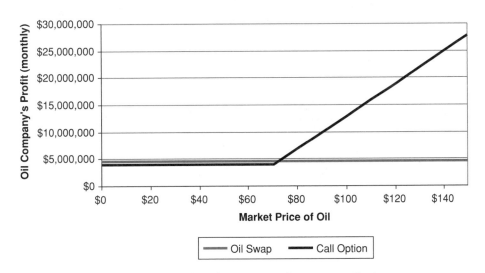

Exhibit 8.4 Comparative Hedged Profit Diagrams: Swap versus Option

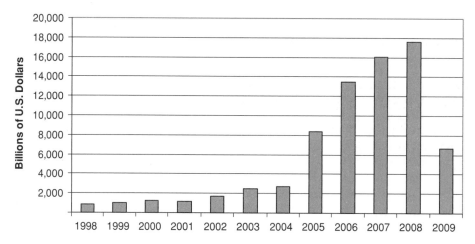

Exhibit 8.5   OTC Commodity Derivatives Notional Amounts Outstanding

than purchase 24 separate options, each with a different expiry, and each for a different premium, dealers will offer a pre-packaged multiperiod option called a "commodity floor" that accomplishes the same thing at the same up-front cost. A floor is simply a portfolio of individual puts. The individual puts, in which the floor can be decomposed, are known in the trade as "floorlets." While not shown here, the same is true for calls. A package of commodity calls structured to pay off at regular intervals over a period of time is called a "commodity cap," and the individual option components of the cap are called "caplets."

It is interesting to consider how the OTC commodity derivatives markets have grown. As indicated in Exhibit 8.5, total notional principal outstanding grew from less than $1 trillion in 1998 to almost $18 trillion in 2008, before declining sharply in 2009. It is also interesting to compare the makeup of the notional principal in terms of the percentage that is represented by options and the percentage that is represented by swaps. The swap figure also includes forwards (which can be viewed as a subset of swaps). This is depicted for select years in Exhibit 8.6. All

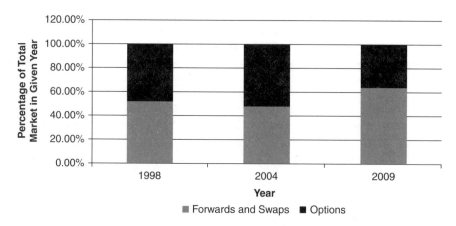

Exhibit 8.6   Over-the-Counter Commodity Derivative Market by Instrument (1998–2009)
Source: All data provided by Bank of International Settlements (BIS).

data included in Exhibits 8.5 and 8.6 is drawn from the Bank for International Settlements (BIS).

FINANCIAL ENGINEERING IN COMMODITIES MARKETS

All the products we have looked at, as well as the commercial strategies that employed them, represented, at one time or another, financial innovations by financial engineers. The people who thought up these products did not use the term "financial engineer" to describe themselves, as that term came later. They just saw themselves as thinking creatively and outside of the box. We will now consider some recent financial engineering used to create commodity-based investment products.

Investment Products

As noted earlier, one of the first commodity-based investment products, other than futures contracts themselves and the holding of physical commodities, were managed futures funds, also known as commodity pools. These did not begin to become popular until after 1974. As a general rule, they are only opened to sophisticated investors, defined loosely as those with significant net worth or significant income. Generally, in the United States, investors must be either "accredited," as that term is defined by the SEC, or a "qualified eligible person," as that term is defined by the CFTC, in order to qualify for participation in a commodity pool.

The commodity pool operator may take a technical approach to the trading of commodities, a fundamental approach, attempt to engage in arbitrage, or some combination of these. Early commodity pools tended to take a technical approach, and most still do. By technical approach, we mean they use technical analysis that depends on past patterns of price behavior to anticipate future price behavior.[3] This approach is heavily focused on spotting trends, and then positioning the pool on the right side of a trend. Typically, the commodity pool will hold positions in many different commodity futures simultaneously and may be long on some commodities while short on others. This diversification gives the pool some benefit in the form of risk reduction. Effectively managing a commodity pool requires that attention be paid to the management of cash. This is necessitated by the considerable leverage these funds employ and the need to meet daily margin requirements.

One of the great attractions to introducing commodities into an investment asset allocation plan is that commodities, as a group, tend to have relatively low degrees of correlation with more traditional asset classes, such as stocks and bonds. It is well understood that diversification, as a risk reduction tool, only works well when the assets that are collectively held have relatively low correlations with one another. Indeed, for many, this is the single biggest attraction for considering commodities as an investment.

Commodity-Linked Notes

We will focus here on exchange-traded commodity-linked notes. These are a subset of both exchange-traded notes and structured notes. (Structured notes will be discussed more broadly in other chapters of this book.) Importantly, not all exchange-traded notes or structured notes have a commodity component, but some do. When they do, they are said to be commodity-linked.

Exchange-traded commodity-linked notes trade, oddly enough, in equity markets, in exactly the same way as stocks trade. While the trading mechanics are identical, the tax and accounting rules can be quite different, and the investor needs to be aware of that. These notes are, most often, issued by highly rated banks. They typically take the form of a non-interest bearing bond that pays off at maturity based on the performance of a given commodity or a given commodity index. Most often, they are principal protected, so that the investor is guaranteed to recover the par value of the note at maturity, but they don't have to be. The principal guarantee is achieved by, essentially, coupling a zero coupon bond with a commodity option. These products typically have a life of a few years, three to seven being most common, but there are similar products with much shorter maturities as well.

The commodity-linked note can be structured to reward an investor who believes that a particular commodity will rise in value over the life of the note or fall in value over the life of the note. That is, they come in varieties that allow investors to express both bullish and bearish views on commodity prices. We'll consider one of each.

Suppose that a particular AA+ rated bank would like to raise some capital by tapping into investors' interest in commodities as an investment. Suppose further, that the bank has determined that there are many investors who are bullish on gold, and who would like to gain some exposure to gold, but who do not want downside risk. Similarly, the bank has determined that there are also some investors who are bearish on gold and who would also like to gain exposure to gold (from the short side), but who also do not want the downside risk. So the bank tasks its financial engineering department (which can go under many different labels) to engineer products to satisfy these two groups. Suppose the bank wishes to raise $200 million from "bullish on gold" investors and $100 million from "bearish on gold" investors. Suppose further, that the bank would like three-year funding and is prepared to pay 3.228 percent per annum, compounded annually. That is equivalent to 10 percent over three years when the compounding is taken into consideration.

To satisfy the bullish-on-gold investors, the financial engineers realize that all they need to do is have the bank purchase an appropriately structured three-year gold option. Suppose that the current price of gold is $1250 an ounce. The bank buys a three-year cash-settled gold call on 160,000 ounces of gold. This would be purchased from an OTC commodities derivatives dealer. The number of ounces of gold was determined by dividing the total to be raised, $200,000,000, by the current price per ounce, $1250. This option will pay off at the end of the three-year period based on the spot price of gold at that time. In order to be certain that the bank does not pay more than 10 percent of the funds to be raised (i.e., $20,000,000) for the option, they need to do a few calculations. First, on a plain vanilla $200 million zero coupon bond, the interest of $20,000,000 would have been paid three-years out.[4] But the option premium must be paid up front. Therefore, the $20,000,000 must be discounted to its present value. Discounting at a flat 10 percent, this is $18,181,818. Next, divide this by 160,000, which is the number of ounces of gold covered by the option. The result is $113.64. The trick is now to find the strike price for a three-year gold call that will result in a per ounce option premium of $113.64.

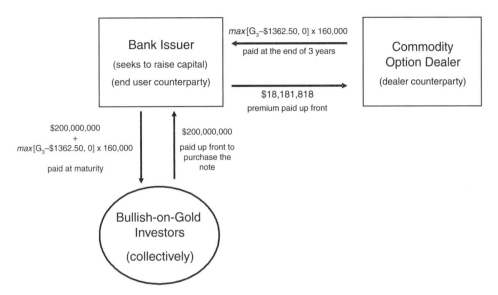

Exhibit 8.7   Structure Underlying a Bullish-on-Gold Commodity-Linked Note

All other things being equal, the higher the strike price, the lower the premium paid for a call option. However, other factors, such as gold-price volatility, will also play a role. Let's suppose that if the strike price is set at $1362.50, the option can be obtained for $113.64.

The bank then issues a $200,000,000 non-interest bearing note that guarantees to pay the sum of $200,000,000 + (max[$G_3$ − $1362.50, 0] × 160,000), where G_3 denotes the spot price of gold at the maturity of the note, to the collective holders of the note at maturity. The option that the bank purchased is simply a hedge against its promise to redeem the note at maturity for a sum that includes appreciation, if any, in the gold's price beyond $1362.50. The structure is depicted in Exhibit 8.7.

While the total note issuance is for $200,000,000, the note is actually sold in small denominations, which we will refer to here as units. Suppose that these are $10 each. Each unit entitles the holder to a pro-rata share of the final payoff at maturity. The note would likely be described, in the prospectus or offering circular, a bit differently than we described it here for ease of investor comprehension. For example, instead of working in dollars per ounce of gold, we could do the following: Since the current price of gold is $1250 and the option strike price is $1362.50, the price of gold would have to rise by 9 percent from its price at the time of the note's issuance before the gold-linkage contributes to the redemption payout. Thus, the investor would be told that, for each unit owned, he or she will receive, at the note's maturity, a sum given by: $10 +(max[A% − 9%, 0] × $10). The investor will receive no coupon interest, but will benefit from a significant rise in the price of gold without any risk to his or her principal. A payoff diagram at maturity is typically included in the prospectus so that the investor can better understand, at a more intuitive level, his final payoff. This is depicted is Exhibit 8.8.

In this example, the issuer achieved its objective of raising capital at the targeted rate of 3.228 percent per annum with no risk to the bank from a change in the price

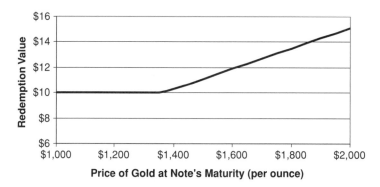

Exhibit 8.8   Redemption Value at Bullish-on-Gold Note Maturity per $10 Invested

of gold, despite the fact that it had embedded a gold call in its note. This was possible only because the note issuer is fully hedged with respect to gold. Both parties are pleased with the outcome.

Importantly, as the recent financial crisis that racked the global banking community so clearly demonstrates, well-rated bank issuers can get themselves into serious difficulty in a remarkably short period of time. Lehman Brothers and Bear Stearns were both big issuers of these sorts of notes. Lehman Brothers' note investors are creditors of the bank, and it is doubtful that they will recover the full par value of their investment as that company winds its way through bankruptcy proceedings. This, however, is a manifestation of credit risk and has nothing whatsoever to do with the structure of the commodity-linked note.

Just as our bank issuer tapped into a desire by some bullish-on-gold investors to express their view on gold without taking downside risk, so too can we structure a note to appeal to bearish-on-gold investors. This would require that the bank issuer hedge with a put option, rather than a call option, and then embed a gold put into the note it issues. Recall that the bank sought to raise $100,000,000 from this latter group. Assuming, for simplicity, that the appropriate strike price for the gold put is $1145 in order to hedge the dealer and achieve a funding cost of 3.228 percent per annum, the dealer would promise a per unit redemption (assuming an issuance price of $10 per unit) given by:

$$\text{Redemption} = \$10 + (\max[8.4\% - A\%, 0] \times \$10)$$

From the bank's perspective, the structure of the overall note (not on a per unit basis) is given in Exhibit 8.9. The notation used in Exhibit 8.9 should be interpreted in an identical fashion to that used in Exhibit 8.7.

The payoff to the bearish-on-gold investors at redemption would be illustrated in the prospectus and would look something like that depicted in Exhibit 8.10.

Importantly, the financial engineering we did here in order to help our issuing bank raise the capital it needs could be expanded to include oil-linked notes, or silver-linked notes, or even an index-of-commodities-linked note. Consider, for a moment, the latter. There are a number of important commodities indexes that could be used. Two of the most popularly quoted are the Dow Jones-UBS Commodity Indexes and the CRB Commodity Index (CRB denotes the Commodity

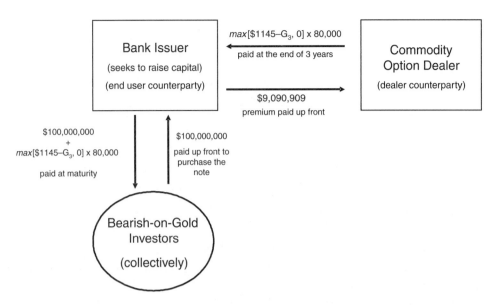

Exhibit 8.9   Structure Underlying a Bearish-on-Gold Commodity-Linked Note

Research Bureau). We build notes linked to an index by hedging in index-linked call or put options from a commodity options dealer.

We could also get more exotic, if we wished, by combining different options to create more unique commodity-linked payoffs at redemption. For example, we could structure bullish-on-gold-linked notes that employ a "gold collar" rather than a simple call. Or we could structure a note that paid off at redemption based on the "better performing" of several different commodities by using basket or rainbow options to hedge the issuer's exposure. More complex structured notes and the options used to hedge them are discussed elsewhere in this book, so we will say no more here on the subject.

From the bank's perspective, each investor's desire to express his or her view represents a "liquidity bucket." The more of these liquidity buckets a bank can tap into, the easier it is to raise capital cost effectively. Investors are generally willing to accept a slightly lower implicit rate of interest in order to get a structure that fits their investment view, and the bank is rewarded by lower overall-funding costs.

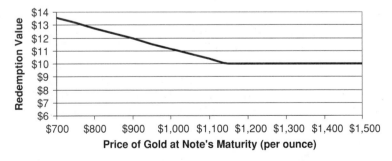

Exhibit 8.10   Redemption Value at Bearish-on-Gold Note Maturity per $10 Invested

COMMODITY ETFs

As a final thought on financially engineered vehicles that can be used by investors, small investors, in particular, (often referred to as retail investors or individual investors) may consider an exchange-traded fund (ETF) approach. Exchange-traded funds, which are discussed in considerable detail elsewhere in this book, were first introduced in 1993 to make available to the public a simple cost-effective and tax-efficient vehicle for investing in the broad market. The first ETFs were based on the S&P 500 index and are generally known as "spiders." When an investor buys a share of spiders, he or she has, effectively purchased an interest in the entire S&P 500. Later innovations include an ETF on the Dow Jones Industrial Average, known as "DIAMONDS," and an ETF on the Nasdaq 100, known as "Qs" (because of the ticker symbol). Later, sector-specific ETFs began to appear, which held only stocks representing a specific industrial sector. Since their debut in 1993, literally hundreds of ETFs have been introduced and today, trading in shares ETFs represents a very high percentage of total daily stock trading volume.

Over the past few years, financial engineers have extended the concept of an ETF to commodities. There are some commodity ETFs that are broad-based, similar to an index of commodities, and others that are single-commodity based. Without a doubt, the single largest of this latter segment are gold ETFs, which come in several different forms. Behind many ETFs is a "trust structure" that issues "units," that investors can trade with both long and short positions. The units represent undivided claims in the pool of assets held by the trust—similar in that sense to a mutual fund. While there are several different legal structures that can underlie an ETF, all ETFs work in basically this way. In the case of gold ETFs, there are some that hold physical gold bullion, with the units representing indirect claims on this bullion, and others that hold stock in gold mining companies and, in that sense, are similar to sector-specific equity ETFs.

There is no doubt that ETFs are one of the most popular financially-engineered products. Commodity ETFs are particularly appealing to smaller investors who are unsuited to use futures markets and who have no interest in taking on the credit risk associated with commodity-linked notes, but who still want to express a commodity view.

REGULATION OF COMMODITY MARKETS

While regulation will vary from country to country, in most countries futures markets are regulated by the same governmental entity that regulates securities markets. For example, in the U.K., this is the Financial Services Authority (FSA). But in the United States, futures trading has its own regulator, the Commodity Futures Trading Commission (CFTC), which is separate and distinct from the principal regulator of securities markets, the Securities and Exchange Commission (SEC). Irrespective of this difference, futures markets, wherever they occur, are highly regulated. OTC commodity derivatives markets, on the other hand, are not as heavily regulated. Further, the degree of regulation of the OTC commodity derivatives markets varies considerably from country to country.

A FINANCIAL ENGINEERING EXERCISE: SYNTHESIZING BARTER

In an odd twist on history, financial engineers have demonstrated how commodity derivatives, particularly commodity swaps, can be used to create synthetic barter.[5] The simplest structures, applicable when the two commodities trade in the same currency, can be achieved by combining two plain vanilla commodity swaps that have been properly "sized" so that the fixed-pay legs cancel. The payments on the floating legs are then used to offset the floating prices (i.e., spot prices) paid or received for the commodities in their respective cash markets. When the currencies in which the commodities trade are different, the solution becomes more complicated. In these cases, a fixed-for-fixed currency swap (i.e., a "cross-currency swap") must be added to the mix. These transactions can be beneficial when a country is heavily dependent on the export of a particular commodity—such as oil in the Middle East.

The irony here is that we have come full circle. Commercial transactions began with barter. But barter was not efficient. Yet, through properly structured (i.e., engineered) commodity derivatives we can replicate or synthesize barter. And, as has been shown by those same financial engineers, though it is not shown here, the swap-synthesized barter solution ameliorates the problems associated with actual barter. The reader is encouraged to try to synthesize barter by appropriately labeling the arrows in Exhibit 8.11. Think of Country X as your client.

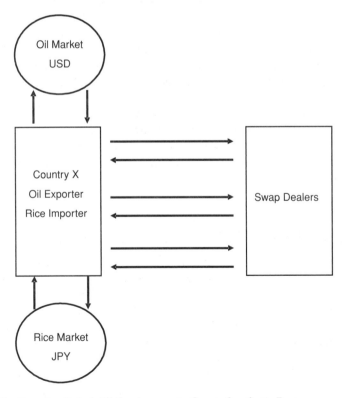

Exhibit 8.11   Exercise: Label All the Arrows to Create Synthetic Barter

Scenario: Your client, County X, is an exporter of oil and an importer of rice. The oil is sold in the world's oil markets for U.S dollars. The rice is purchased in Japan for yen. Country X is exposed to three different market risks: the price of oil in dollars, the price of rice in yen, and the price of dollars in yen (i.e., exchange rate risk). Country X wants to lock in a fixed price for rice in terms of a fixed quantity of oil, such that the same amount of oil will be required to acquire the same amount of rice each month for the next five years. You have been asked to structure a synthetic barter arrangement that accomplishes this objective. In structuring your solution, don't worry about the actual prices of oil, rice, or the exchange rate. Just map out the set of transactions, on behalf of your client, that would be necessary to achieve an outcome equivalent to a given quantity of oil for a given quantity of rice. Importantly, the two parties would buy and sell their actual oil and rice in those commodities respective cash markets. They would not exchange oil directly for rice. After you have completed this exercise, you might want to read the reference noted in this section to check how you did.

NOTES

1. For a history of futures trading in Japan, see Hauser (1974).
2. We often use the term "notional quantity" to refer to the number of units that a commodity derivative is written on. Most people prefer to measure the size in terms of notional principal. The notional principal is simply the market price times the notional quantity. Notional quantity is used here for ease of exposition.
3. Technical analysts often employ more than just past price behavior in their effort to identify the future direction of an asset's price. They often employ volume, open interest, and other "transactional" data.
4. If an analogy were being made to zero coupon Treasury bonds, the bonds would be thought of as having a face value of $220 million and sold at issuance for the discounted price of $200 million. At maturity (i.e., redemption) the investors would collect the $220 million.
5. Marshall and Wynne (1996).

REFERENCES

APX, Inc. 2008. "Creating a Trusted Environmental Commodity." www.apx.com/documents/APX-Trusted-Environmental-Commodities.pdf.

Benhamou, Eric, and Grigorios Mamalis. 2010. "Commodity markets (overview)." *Book Articles: Forthcoming in the Encyclopedia of Financial Engineering and Risk Management.* www.ericbenhamou.net/documents/Encyclo/commodity%20markets%20_overview_.pdf.

Celent. 2009. " Commodity Markets: New Rules for a New Game." www.celent.com/124_1103.htm.

Commodity Online India Limited. n.d. "What Is a Commodity Market?" *Learning Center.* www.commodityonline.com/learning_sub.php?id=5.

DeCovny, Sherree. 2010. "Commodities on the Rebound." *Market View: A Magazine for the Exchange Industry,* June 22. www.nasdaqomx.com/whatwedo/markettechnology/marketview/marketview_2010_2/commodities_rebounding/.

Doyle, Emmet, Jonathan Hill, and Ian Jack. 2007. "Growth in Commodity Invest-ment: Risks and Challenges for Commodity Market Participants." *FSA Markets*

Infrastructure Department. Financial Services Authority, March. www.fsa.gov.uk/pubs/other/commodity_invest.pdf.

Futures Technology. "History of the Commodity Markets." 2010. *History of Commodities*, April 9. www.futurestech.net/history.htm.

Garner, Carley. 2010. *A Trader's First Book on Commodities*. Upper Saddle River, NJ: Pearson.

Hauser, W. B. 1974. *Economic Institutional Change in Tokugawa Japan*. London: Cambridge University Press.

Holmes, Frank. 2010. "The Case for Commodities in 2010 (and beyond)." *Resource Investor*, January 25. www.resourceinvestor.com/News/2010/1/Pages/The-case-for-commodities-in-2010.aspx.

Investopedia ULC, 1999. *Investopedia*. www.investopedia.com.

Marshall, John F. and Kevin J. Wynne. 1996. "Synthetic Barter: Simulating Countertrade Solutions with Swaps." *Global Finance Journal*. 7: 1, 1–12.

Mlost, Karol. 2007. "Commodities futures pricing and approximation of convenience yield for Brent and WTI crude oils." Master's Thesis. Wyzsza Szkola Biznesu–National-Louis University.

Oxford Futures, Inc. 2009. "A Brief History of Commodities." *Futures Fundamentals*. www.oxfordfutures.com/futures-education/futures-fundamentals/brief-history.htm.

"Semiannual OTC Derivatives Statistics at End-December 2009." *BIS Statistics*. Bank of International Settlements. www.bis.org/statistics/.

Thinking Finance. 2009. "Commodity Market Overview." *ThinkingFinance.net*. www.thinkingfinance.net/commodities/56-commodity-market-overview.html.

U.S. Department of the Treasury. 2009. "Administration's Regulatory Reform Agenda Reaches New Milestone: Final Piece of Legislative Language Delivered to Capitol Hill." *Press Room: U.S. Department of the Treasury*. www.treas.gov/press/releases/tg261.htm.

United Futures Trading Company, Inc. 1997. "The Basics of Commodity Futures Trading." *United Futures Trading*. www.unitedfutures.com/commodities-trade.htm.

United Nations. 2010. "Recent developments in key commodity markets: trends and challenges." *United Nations Conference on Trade and Development*, January 12. http://www.unctad.org/en/docs/cimem2d7_en.pdf.

Ward, Kurtis J. n.d. "The Futures Industry: From Commodities to the Over-the-Counter Derivatives Market." *KIS Futures*. www.kisfutures.com/pdf/FUTURESINDUSTRYlawpaperKurtisWard.pdf.

ABOUT THE AUTHORS

Helen Lu is currently a second-year undergraduate student at Princeton University and plans to pursue a BA degree in Economics with a Certificate in Finance. Her academic interests include economic history, focusing especially on significant financial losses, and analyses of the recent global financial crisis. She has been working with the financial advisory firm, SBCC Group, on various financial engineering research projects that focus on risk management and on the history of financial engineering and financial institutions. She has also been involved in organizations intended to educate young women in smart and practical investment strategies in the financial markets.

Cara M. Marshall is a professor of finance at Queens College of the City University of New York. Cara holds a Ph in Financial Economics from Fordham University and an MBA with a focus on Quantitative Analysis from St. John's University. Her research interests focus on financial engineering, risk management, and derivatives, as well as behavioral and experimental methods in finance. Cara's Ph dissertation examined the pricing of volatility on U.S. options exchanges. Prior to academia, Cara worked in internet engineering, developing websites and a platform for online course delivery. She has also worked as a marketing manager for a conference and training company. Over the years, Cara has consulted to several investment banks as a trainer. In this role, she taught financial modeling to bank employees in New York, London, and Singapore. Cara has also performed analysis for hedge funds and for firms in other industries.

CHAPTER 9

Credit Markets

FRANK IACONO
Riverside Risk Advisors LLC*

Credit Market Snapshot

History: The largest components of the credit derivatives market today are
the credit default swaps (CDS) and the closely related synthetic collateralized debt obligations (CDOs). Many assume that the credit derivatives
market began with the introduction of CDS in the mid 1990s, but earlier,
predecessor products, including letters of credit, bond insurance policies,
and certain types of total return swaps had existed for some time and
serve many of the same purposes. Nevertheless, the advent of CDS was a
watershed event. The earliest CDS allowed commercial banks to transfer
the credit risk associated with their loan portfolios to third parties. By the
early 2000s, the CDS market was expanding rapidly, driven in large part by
standardization, advances in computational power, and evolved thinking
on the management of credit risk. During the past decade, CDS have been
used to create several varieties of structured products, to arbitrage capital market inefficiencies, and to both hedge and speculate on corporate,
municipal, and government fiscal health. They were also used to create exposure to the mortgage market and to protect holders of mortgage-backed
securities. CDS became the focus of considerable interest with the onset of
the credit crisis of 2007–2009.

Size: Prior to 2004, the market was of trivial size in comparison to the markets
for other types of derivatives. But from a size of $6.4 trillion in notional
amount in 2004, it grew to over $60 trillion by the end of 2007, before falling
back to $32.7 trillion in 2009. Approximately half of the growth was driven
by index trades.

Products: The most basic and widely-traded credit derivatives are credit default swaps (CDS). Other common structures include credit spread options,
bond options, total return swaps, index swaps, basket default swaps, synthetic collateralized debt obligations, and credit-linked notes (which are
not derivatives themselves, but, rather, are securities that contain embedded credit derivatives).

---

*The author would like to thank his colleagues at Riverside Risk Advisors, and especially
Yuan Zhou, for their valuable comments and assistance.

First Usage: It is reported that the first credit default swap was written in 1994 between J.P. Morgan (now JPMorgan Chase) and the European Bank for Reconstruction and Development (EBRD). The contract was written to shift the credit risk on a $4.8 billion Exxon line of credit from J.P. Morgan to the EBRD. At the time, J.P. Morgan was concerned about the financial impact on Exxon from the 1989 Exxon Valdez oil spill.

Selection of Significant Events

1992: Bankers Trust leads the way in emerging market credit spread options. Though these transactions pre-date the first CDS contracts, they fit squarely within the definition of credit derivatives, as they were documented as ISDA contracts and provided for payments based on the credit spreads of the reference assets. Some transactions were based on the spreads between Brady Bonds and U.S. Treasury securities, others on the relative spreads of Brady Bonds and local-currency securities issued by the same sovereigns. Deals were done in "unfunded" derivative and credit-linked note form.

1997: J.P. Morgan closes its First BISTRO transaction.[1]

1998: The Financial Accounting Standards Board publishes FAS 133, which requires reporting entities to record most derivatives contracts at fair value on their balance sheets and to record changes in fair value in their income statements. The resulting disconnect between the accounting treatment of CDS and instruments with similar economic features (e.g., corporate bonds and loans, funded CDOs) serves as a source of structuring challenges and opportunities and an impediment to growth at the margin.

1998: TRS (total return swaps), already an important source of financing for hedge funds, become a source of interbank financing during the LTCM (Long-Term Capital Management) crisis. This was largely the result of the ease of execution, accounting, and regulatory capital advantages of TRS relative to comparable sources of financing (e.g., secured loans, repo). One of my first significant transactions upon joining the credit derivatives desk was arranging a TRS facility for an American bank, provided by a major European bank.

1999: Several major banks begin making markets in single-name corporate CDS.

2000: The first bespoke synthetic CDOs are traded.

2001–2002: Enron and WorldCom file for bankruptcy.

2003: ISDA publishes the 2003 Credit Derivatives Definitions.

2005: Market-implied correlation declines sharply, especially at the equity level of the capital structure, as a result of the downgrade and corresponding spread widening of GM and Ford.

2007: Market-implied correlation increases sharply, especially at the senior levels of the capital structure, as a result of the failure of the Canadian asset-backed commercial paper ("ABCP") market. The Canadian conduits that issued the ABCP were large sellers of protection on the "super senior" tranches of corporate synthetic CDOs. On a fundamental level, the failure of the Canadian ABCP market serves a reminder of the interconnectedness of markets, especially in times of stress. The spike in correlation, however, is more driven by a technical concern—the prospect of hundreds of billions of super senior risk coming back to the banks.

2008: Losses on ABS CDOs, especially those with significant exposure to the mezzanine tranches of sub-prime securitizations, puts into motion the demise of several of the largest insurance companies in the United States. The downgrade of AIG triggers collateral-posting requirements that it was unable to meet, leading to a government bailout. Monoline insurers including MBIA and Ambac are also downgraded, but without a short-term liquidity crisis, as their downgrade-contingent collateral requirements are limited.

2009: MBIA and Ambac, with the support of their regulators, are each split in two, pursuant to "good bank/bad bank" restructurings.

2008–2010: Litigation filed within the Lehman Brothers bankruptcy proceeding raises legal questions with significant potential impact on the derivatives markets generally, and the credit derivatives markets in particular. Two points of contention are the assessment of early termination values for portfolios of credit derivatives and the enforceability of default-contingent subordination of a swap counterparty's claims.

2010: The Dodd–Frank Wall Street Reform and Consumer Protection Act is enacted, effecting sweeping changes on the financial markets. Subject to details to be determined by regulation, the act will have a major impact on derivatives products and markets.

Best Providers (as of 2009): J.P. Morgan was named by *Global Finance* magazine as the best Credit Derivatives Provider in North America and Europe, while Deutsche Bank received the same rank in Asia. Other dealers who have maintained a significant presence through and after the financial crisis of 2007–2009 include Morgan Stanley, Barclays, and BNP Paribas.

Applications: Credit derivatives can be used for hedging company-specific credit risk or market-wide credit spread movements, to effect outright shorts, to diversify exposure, to enhance portfolio yields, to engage in arbitrage and relative value strategies, and to access new asset classes.

Users: Major buyers and sellers of credit derivatives include banks, securities firms, insurance companies, and hedge funds. Participation by pension funds, non-financial corporations, and mutual funds has been limited.

INTRODUCTION

As recently as early 2007, most Americans had never heard the terms "credit derivative" or "credit default swap," despite the fact that the estimated size of the global credit derivatives market stood at more than $40 trillion in notional amount, more than the size of the global markets for corporate, municipal, and sovereign debt combined. As shown in Exhibit 9.1, the market would go on to peak in size at about $60 trillion at the end of 2007.

Early on, I can recall in conversations having to say "credit derivatives" at least twice, and depending on the age and career background of the person I was talking to, describing them as "virtual bonds" or "bankruptcy insurance" (always being sure to add that for legal and regulatory purposes derivatives are not insurance).

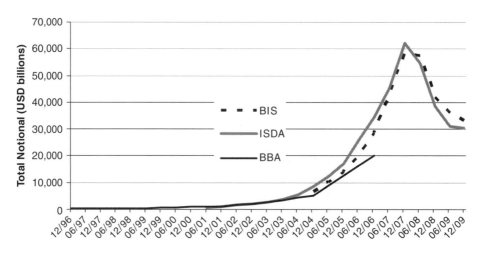

Exhibit 9.1 Size of the Credit Derivatives Market
Sources: International Swaps and Derivatives Association (ISDA), British Bankers Associations (BBA), and Bank for International Settlements (BIS).

By late 2008, however, when the topic of what I did came up in conversation, almost every lay person was able to identify credit derivatives as the "weapons of mass destruction"[2] that "wrecked the economy," caused people to lose their homes, and enriched a few "greedy Wall Street manipulators" at the expense of everyone else.

Regrettably, such perceptions inform much of what we hear about credit derivatives from the media, business leaders, and political leaders. *Newsweek*, for example, called credit derivatives "The Monster That Ate Wall Street."[3] As of the time of this writing, even the Wikipedia entry states "in plain language, a credit derivative is a wager ... [s]imilar to placing a bet at the racetrack." Sometimes the stories provide a distinction between the "good" credit derivatives, which are used by banks to manage risk and the "bad" ones, which apparently are the trades where AIG or some other major institution lost money. Sometimes no such distinction is provided. Congresswoman Maxine Waters, for example, in advocating a ban of credit derivatives trading, said that "preventing all credit-default swaps is essential to bringing stability to the market."

The purpose of this chapter is to describe in more detail the history, major developments, product innovations, and applications of credit derivatives over the past 15 years. It is written from the perspective of someone who began structuring credit derivatives products in 1998, who traded the products on both the buy side and sell side, and who continues, at the time of this writing, to work in the area as an independent advisor. The discussion is almost entirely focused on corporate credit derivatives and tends to focus on synthetic collateralized debt obligations (CDOs), which have been a critical contributor to the growth of the more liquid and single-name CDS products. One key goal of this chapter is to give the reader a clear understanding that credit derivative technology serves an important function in allowing for an unprecedented ability to manage and distribute credit risk and in providing valuable price information. While policy changes aimed at improving transparency and reducing systemic risks involved in trading large volumes of the standardized products may help the stability of the financial system, if and only if done correctly, proposals aimed at stifling innovation, or even worse, turning back the clock by banning the basic products, are not likely to help.

The next section illustrates that contracts resembling credit derivatives have a long history. Two predecessor products are discussed, with a discussion of the key differences that distinguish the modern instruments known as credit derivatives. Following that, I discuss applications, with an emphasis on risk transfer across financial institutions. Later I discuss first- and second-generation products, respectively, with some anecdotes weaved in. The chapter concludes with some thoughts on where the market for this product might be going.

PREDECESSOR PRODUCTS

Letters of Credit

The letter of credit (LC) is a traditional commercial banking product known to exist at the turn of the twentieth century. Under an LC, an insured debtor pays a bank a periodic fee in exchange for the bank's promise to make payments under a debt, purchase, or other obligation on behalf of the debtor, should the debtor fail to do so. LCs are used as credit support where financial markets or commercial practices require a very high degree of credit quality (such as trade finance or the commercial paper market) or where it is impractical for trade or financial creditors to perform an independent credit analysis of the issuer.

Municipal Bond Insurance

Municipal bond insurance, also known as financial guaranty insurance, is a product that bears significant economic similarity to a credit derivative. Under a typical contract, the issuer pays a premium to an insurance company in exchange for its commitment to provide scheduled interest and principal repayments on the bond in the event of the failure of the issuer to do so.

The business of insuring municipal bond investors began, for all practical purposes, in 1971 with the formation of AMBAC.[4] MBIA[5] was formed two years later, and by the mid 1980s the other two of the big four monoline insurers, FGIC[6] and FSA,[7] were up and running. By the time ISDA-documented corporate credit derivatives began their growth cycle in the late 1990s, MBIA and AMBAC together were insuring more than $400 billion of municipal bonds and just under $200 billion of other risk, mostly mortgages.

As with letters of credit, a key justification for the existence of municipal bond insurance is the impracticality and large costs associated with each participant in the municipal bond market performing independent credit analysis on multitudes of municipal issuers. Since the advent of the financial crisis of 2007–2009, which among other things, brought on the failure or near-failure of many of the traditional municipal bond insurers, it has been argued that perhaps the primary purpose of municipal bond insurance is the comfort value of knowing that a highly-rated insurer with a staff of capable municipal credit analysts has underwritten a bond and stands to suffer a significant loss of its capital if the issuer fails.

Modern Credit Derivatives versus Predecessors
Although the predecessor products described above bear economic similarity to
the credit derivative products of the last 15 years, there are important differences.
Perhaps three of most significant are as follows:

1. Standardization: Credit derivatives have always been transacted under doc-
    umentation produced by the International Swaps and Derivatives Associ-
    ation (ISDA). Though customization has never disappeared, the growth of
    the marketplace was facilitated by the creation and refinement of docu-
    mentation standards. The first Credit Derivative Definitions published in
    1999 gave the marketplace enough standardization to support the begin-
    nings of an actively traded market. The publication of ISDA's expanded
    2003 Credit Derivative Definitions and the birth of the index product in
    that same year further advanced the process, providing the infrastruc-
    ture necessary to support the growth that would take place over the next
    four years.
2. Lack of an "insurable interest" or other relationship between the protec-
    tion provider and the subject of the contract: Documentation terms do not
    require that the purchaser of credit protection hold a position in the under-
    lying reference entity or reference obligation. Thus, credit derivatives can be
    used to effect outright shorts, capital structure arbitrage (e.g., long equity,
    short debt) or relative value plays (long Ford, short GM). The cash credit
    markets have little to no ability to short credit.
3. Regulatory status: Credit derivatives are not considered insurance policies
    and are not regulated as such. Proposals to regulate credit derivatives as
    insurance contracts[8] did not receive broad support during the recent fi-
    nancial reform debates and have been pre-empted by the Dodd-Frank Act.
    The Act does, however, have the potential to significantly impact the credit
    derivatives marketplace. Most likely certain credit derivatives will be re-
    quired to be traded on an exchange or through a clearinghouse, and there
    will be regulatory requirements with respect to initial and ongoing mar-
    gin (i.e., collateral), disclosure and reporting, and capital for certain market
    participants. It is generally believed that LCs and bond insurance will not
    be subject to comparable regulation.

Each of the preceding factors contributed to the growth of an active market.

APPLICATIONS

Separation of Funding and Credit Risk

The development of the credit derivatives market[9] has allowed market participants
to separately price and manage funding requirements and credit risk to an extent
not possible before. No longer is the holder of a physical asset, such as a bank loan
or a bond, required to retain the credit risk of the issuer's default, and no longer
is physical ownership of a security required for an investor to earn the returns
associated with taking default risk. Put another way, credit derivatives allow for a

separation of the decisions with respect to funding and credit risk, allowing those participants who can most efficiently bear liquidity risk to do so while mitigating credit default risk, and allowing those in the best position to bear credit default risk to do so without the need to fund an asset.[10]

This point is well illustrated by the classic example of a bank purchasing credit default swap (CDS) protection on the borrower under a revolving credit (RC) facility. The typical revolving credit facility for an investment grade borrower starts out as an unfunded commitment on the part of the bank to lend should the borrower require funding during the term of the commitment. In many cases, the expectation is that there will be little to no drawings on the facility as the borrower has access to the commercial paper markets, but unforeseen circumstances, such as an inability to replace commercial paper funding, may create an unanticipated funding need. The commitment fee paid to the bank is often a single-digit number of basis points per annum on the total amount of the commitment. If the facility is drawn upon by the borrower, interest is typically paid at LIBOR plus a utilization spread, which is higher than the commitment fee.

The typical RC facility is a loss-leader for a bank. The commitment fee is typically less than the market spread for the borrower's credit risk in a stand-alone transaction. The utilization spread may be in line with the borrower's credit spread at the time the facility closes, but in states of the world where the borrower draws, one can expect the borrower's credit spread to be higher elsewhere.[11] Moreover, even after full syndication, RCs often leave banks with large single-issuer concentrations, which are undesirable from a risk management standpoint and can necessitate large amounts of regulatory and economic capital. Add to this the operational costs and risks of managing a facility in which funds can potentially be drawn upon and repaid frequently. Despite these less-than-compelling economics, commercial banks offer back-up RC facilities to their high-grade customers as part of an overall relationship, in which it is expected that the bank will be compensated by the borrower with more profitable business such as stock and bond issuances, M&A advisory, derivatives, and asset management.

A liquid and transparent market for credit risk gives banks the opportunity to reduce credit exposures while continuing to perform the function of providing liquidity for corporate borrowers. And the CDS pricing mechanism allows banks to rationally evaluate whether particular customer relationships are truly profitable when taken as a whole.

Distribution of Risk to the Capital Markets

On a more macro level, credit derivatives have allowed banks to distribute large amounts of credit risk to other participants in the capital markets. For example, starting in 2000, the banks were large buyers of protection on Enron and WorldCom, two corporate borrowers with large syndicated loan facilities that went bankrupt in 2001 and 2002, respectively. These two issuers had large amounts of bank debt concentrated in the portfolios of the largest U.S. banks. In the world before banks used credit derivatives as a risk management tool, the back-to-back defaults of Enron and WorldCom might have meant a significant capital impairment for one or more major banks. This was noted by then-Chairman of the Federal Reserve

System, Alan Greenspan, in 2002. Speaking on the topic again in 2004, Greenspan had the following to say:

> [N]ot only has a significant part of the credit risks of an admittedly few large U.S. banks been shifted to other U.S. and foreign banks and to insurance and reinsurance firms here and abroad, but such risks also have been shifted to pension funds, to hedge funds, and to other organizations with diffuse long-term liabilities or no liabilities at all. Most of the credit-risk transfers were made early in the credit-granting process; but in the late 1990s and early in this decade, significant exposures to telecommunication firms were laid off through credit default swaps, collateralized debt obligations, and other financial instruments. Other risk transfers reflected later sales at discount prices as specific credits became riskier and banks rebalanced their portfolios. Some of these sales were at substantial concessions to entice buyers to accept substantial risk. Whether done as part of the original credit decision or in response to changing conditions, these transactions represent a new paradigm of active credit management and are a major part of the explanation of the banking system's strength during the most recent period of stress. Even the largest corporate defaults in history (WorldCom and Enron) and the largest sovereign default in history (Argentina) have not significantly impaired the capital of any major U.S. financial intermediary.[12]

To get a rough sense of how much risk had been transferred, one can look to the results of the BBA credit derivative surveys from 2000 to 2006. The BBA reports protection buyers and sellers, as a percentage of total notional outstanding, as depicted in Exhibits 9.2 and 9.3.

By implication, the net buyers and sellers of protection, as measured by notional amount,[13] are depicted in Exhibit 9.4.

Applying these net percentages to the aggregate notional amounts estimated by the BBA, it would appear that, as of the end of 2006, the banking sector was a net purchaser of protection in an amount of approximately $3 trillion in notional (15 percent multiplied by a total $20 trillion of notional outstanding). But this figure is missing at least two important parts of the story. Much of the activity within the banking sector is made up of risk transfer from the global "money center" banks, which originate risk to national and regional banks, mostly outside the United States, which were large risk takers through credit derivatives and structured products based on credit derivatives (e.g., investment-grade-rated credit linked notes). This factor represents a distribution of risk not captured by the sector groupings.

Exhibit 9.2   Buyers of Protection by Institution Type

	2000	2002	2004	2006
Banks (including securities firms)	81	73	67	59
Insurers	7	6	7	6
Hedge Funds	3	12	16	28
Pension Funds	1	1	3	2
Mutual Funds	1	2	3	2
Corporates	6	4	3	2
Other	1	2	1	1

Source: British Bankers Associations (BBA), 2006.

Exhibit 9.3 Sellers of Protection by Institution Type

	2000	2002	2004	2006
Banks (including securities firms)	63	55	54	44
Insurers	23	33	20	17
Hedge Funds	5	5	15	32
Pension Funds	3	2	4	4
Mutual Funds	2	3	4	3
Corporates	3	2	2	1
Other	1	0	1	1

Source: British Bankers Associations (BBA), 2006.

The second significant factor is the degree to which the monoline insurers represent the net protection sale (i.e., long credit risk) side of the equation. The monolines are highly-leveraged entities that sold protection primarily on the AAA-rated tranches of CDOs and synthetic CDOs. Under typical documentation terms, the monolines generally do not post collateral (their AAA ratings were seen as a substitute for collateral), and there are generally very limited circumstances under which the monolines' counterparties can terminate transactions prior to maturity with the benefit of a mark-to-market based termination payment. It has since become clear to the marketplace that given the leverage, documentation structure, and "systemic" nature of the risk taken by the monolines, the monolines are not, and never actually were, the "perfect" counterparties for most of the transactions under which the banks bought protection.[14] This is especially true for entities buying protection on corporate CDOs.

Put very simply, given a macro default scenario in which one AAA rated corporate CDO suffers a loss, it's likely that many others will also suffer losses. In this scenario, the limited capital base will become overwhelmed with loss claims, and counterparties can expect to recover only a fraction of what they are owed. Put another way, the counterparties of a monoline are exposed to the performance risk of a protection provider with a small capital base in relation to protection written, and the protection contracts written are all very highly correlated.

The upshot of this second factor is that the banking sector actually transferred much less risk than one might infer from the notional amounts of the contracts.

Exhibit 9.4 Net Buyers (Sellers) of Protection Institution by Type

	2000	2002	2004	2006
Banks (including securities firms)	18	18	13	15
Insurers	−16	−27	−13	−11
Hedge Funds	−2	7	1	−4
Pension Funds	−2	−1	−1	−2
Mutual Funds	−1	−1	−1	−1
Corporates	3	2	1	1
Other	0	2	0	0

Source: British Bankers Associations (BBA), 2006.

If a protection seller has the resources to cover only a fraction of the potential losses, then the notional amount of the contract represents a multiple of the risk transferred. In assessing the overall degree to which credit derivatives have truly resulted in better distribution of risk, this caveat cannot be ignored. But what we are talking about here is better characterized as an error made by the users of the product, rather than an inherent defect in the product itself.

The Ability to Go Short

As noted previously, a key difference between modern credit derivatives and predecessor products, such as bond insurance, is the absence of an "insurable interest" requirement. As a matter of fact, there are no requirements that any relationship exist between either of the parties to the contract and the reference entity that is the subject of the contract. It is this feature, in particular, that has elicited some of the harshest, and in the view of many market participants, most misguided, criticisms of credit derivatives.

Most of the arguments for restricting the ability to establish short positions through credit derivatives are the same as the arguments in favor of restrictions on the ability to short stocks. Some critics seem to believe that an unrestricted ability to go short allows "speculators" unchecked power to destroy otherwise sound companies. Others argue that short sellers destabilize markets. What's new about credit derivatives is that there is, in theory, no limit to how large the short interest can be, whereas with stock there is an effective limit created by the availability of stock for short sellers to borrow. Therefore, if you don't like the ability to short equities, you really don't like the tools that credit derivatives provide short sellers.

Those in favor of the ability to short question how allowing the expression of only the favorable or neutral view, while censoring the negative view, promotes long-term stability and efficient allocation of capital in the economy. Others argue that short selling is a necessary counter to the large and rising presence of index funds, whose mission is essentially to be long on everything. Closer to home, others point to the unraveling of the subprime market in 2007 as an argument in favor of shorting. The senior tranche on the BBB ABX, a CDS index based on the BBB-rated, subordinated mezzanine classes of ABS transactions, started to decline in price some time before senior ABS CDO spreads widened. By sending this price signal to the market, CDS arguably hastened the demise of ABS CDOs, and therefore caused new subprime mortgage origination to grind to a halt sooner than it would have otherwise, potentially avoiding the creation of tens or even hundreds of billions of dollars of additional bad product.

Much of the discussion focuses on the outright shorts, but this misses a very important part of the picture. In addition to outright shorts, other strategies involving a protection purchase without an "insurable interest" allow market participants to express relative value views that promote the efficient allocation of capital and send important risk-pricing information to the marketplace. One such strategy is a long/short pairing of two companies in the same industry. For example, suppose that IBM and Dell trade at the same credit spread but some market participants believe that Dell is a better credit. Suppose further, that some such market participants do not have a strong conviction that Dell bonds offer good value on an absolute basis, or are generally concerned about the short-term direction of credit spreads in the tech sector, or in the market generally. The view is one of relative value, not absolute value. The ability to express such a view without credit derivatives is limited. With credit derivatives it's easy: sell credit protection on Dell, buy credit protection on IBM. If enough market participants have this view, the credit spread of Dell will tighten relative to the credit spread of IBM. This will ultimately affect the borrowing costs of both companies, putting Dell at a funding advantage relative to IBM.

Another example is capital structure "arbitrage," which is actually a bit of a misnomer. A more correct term is perhaps capital structure "relative value." Under such a strategy, an investor typically uses CDS to purchase protection on a relatively rich part of a reference entity's capital structure and purchases the relatively cheap security. A popular strategy is to simultaneously purchase CDS protection on the debt (i.e., synthetically sell the debt short via CDS) and purchase the equity of a highly-leveraged financial firm. The rationale is that if the firm is levered enough in most scenarios where the equity takes a big loss of market value, the debt is also likely to suffer a big loss (corresponding to a big gain on the CDS). But in a positive environment, the equity stands to increase in value significantly while, at worst, the value of the credit protection can go to zero (with the investor losing the value of the CDS premium only). The net effect of investors executing this strategy is to drive credit spreads on the reference entity's debt to a level that reflects its downside risk relative to the equity and lower the cost of the reference entity's equity financing to reflect its upside potential.

FIRST-GENERATION PRODUCTS: 1992–2000

Asset Swaps

An asset swap involves the exchange of the cash flows of a given asset for a different set of cash flows. In the context of credit derivatives an asset swap is the combination of a credit-sensitive asset, typically a bond, with a corresponding swap that transforms the cash flows of the non-par bond, into a par bond. Asset swaps typically transform fixed-rate bonds into par floaters, resulting in an all-in coupon of LIBOR plus a spread. The resulting spread to LIBOR can be seen as the combined price of issuer default risk and term funding for the asset.

Single-Name CDS

The single-name credit default swap is the basic building block of most of the second-generation products, including the index products and the bespoke tranches. A credit default swap (CDS) is an agreement between two parties (the "counterparties") in which the counterparties exchange the risk of default of a third party (the "reference entity"). The protection buyer pays a periodic premium to the protection seller in exchange for the protection seller's commitment to pay the protection buyer the amount of loss resulting from a credit event affecting the reference entity. Through this mechanism, the protection buyer transfers to the

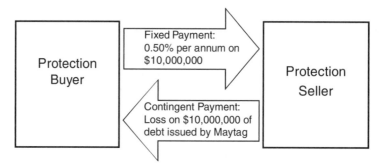

Exhibit 9.5   Single-name CDS

protection seller credit exposure to the reference entity without the exchange of an actual debt instrument. Exhibit 9.5 illustrates a hypothetical CDS with Maytag Corp. as the Reference Entity and a $10,000,000 notional amount.

The above definition begs two key questions:

1. What is a Credit Event?
2. How is the protection buyer "paid" should a "Credit Event" occur?

The short answer to both is "however the parties to the contract so provide," and in the early days of the credit derivatives market the time spent figuring out the answers to those questions was quite high in relation to the trading volume. The 1999 ISDA credit derivatives definitions represented the first significant step toward developing market-standard answers. As can be expected, the market standards have evolved over time, and customized provisions have never disappeared. That said, the dominant practices in the marketplaces have been as described next.

Credit Events

The credit events most often used in traded CDS contracts are the following:

- Bankruptcy: Bankruptcy, receivership, insolvency or other similar proceeding; dissolution (other than merger or acquisition).
- Failure to Pay: After the expiration of any applicable grace period, failure to make a payment on any debt obligation, subject to a materiality threshold.
- Restructuring: Modification of the "money terms" of a debt obligation, where such modification is adverse to the creditors and is the result of a deterioration of the creditworthiness of the reference entity.
- Obligation Acceleration: The acceleration of any debt obligation, subject to a materiality threshold, resulting from a non-payment default.
- Repudiation/Moratorium: A failure to pay or restructuring (not subject to a materiality threshold) closely following a statement by the reference entity repudiating or declaring a moratorium on a debt obligation, subject to a materiality threshold.

As for settlement, there are two broad options:

1. Physical Settlement: The protection buyer delivers a security issued or guaranteed by the reference entity and meeting the deliverable obligation criteria, and the protection seller pays par value.
2. Cash Settlement: Protection buyer identifies (but does not deliver) a security issued or guaranteed by the reference entity and meeting the deliverable obligation criteria, and the protection seller pays the difference between par value and the market value of the obligation.

For the majority of single-name CDS, deliverable obligations are senior unsecured obligations, denominated in a major global currency (e.g., USD, EUR, GBP, CHF, JPY), with no "exotic" coupon or redemption features, and having a maturity of 30 years or less. For some reference entities, most often financial institutions, there are CDS traded under which a subordinated reference obligation may be delivered.

The traded market also includes CDS under which the deliverable obligation must be senior secured loans. The reference entities are almost all non-investment grade issuers of broadly-syndicated loans. Such contracts are referred to as Loan CDS or simply LCDS. Despite the prevalence of loan-based CDS in the first-generation CDS products, LCDS did not become broadly traded until 2006, and trading volumes never came close to those of senior unsecured CDS, even in relation to the underlying debt outstanding.

Loan Total Return Swaps

Under a loan total return swap (TRS) the total return receiver takes a synthetic long position in an individual loan or portfolio of bank loans. It is effectively a credit line that gives the investor all the cash flow benefits of a loan without actually holding the asset. The investor receives the total rate of return of the loan, in exchange for which it typically makes ongoing payments based on LIBOR plus a fixed spread.

Loan TRSs are used primarily by end users to: obtain leverage on a portfolio of bank loans; as a means to outsource loan operations or physical settlement; as a vehicle to gain access and exposure to assets that might not otherwise be readily available (e.g., due to eligibility restrictions in credit agreements).

Bank loan TRSs go back at least as far as 1995. In that year, Chase began offering TRS to institutional investors and hedge fund clients who purchased Chase's syndicated leveraged loans. At the time, other banks offered TRS structures based on leveraged loans, but the growth of Chase's program relative to others was driven largely by an innovative structure called the Chase Secured Loan Trust, or "CSLT." The CSLT structure involved the creation of a special purpose vehicle (SPV) which:

- Entered into a TRS with Chase referencing the loan portfolio.
- Issued a note to investors in a par amount equal to about 20 percent of the par amount of the underlying loans.
- Invested the proceeds of the note issuance in a high-quality, highly-liquid asset, which served as collateral, first to satisfy the SPV's obligations under

the TRS with Chase, and second, to make payments of interest and principal on the note issued by the SPV.

- The note was typically rated BBB by Fitch. Assuming losses in the loan portfolio remained at historical averages, the investor would earn a coupon equal to LIBOR plus a spread of approximately 200 basis points and would receive a return of its principal at maturity (typically 10–12 years), plus an equity-like "upside" payment as described below.

The above describes an early example of what later became widely known as a synthetic CDO or credit-linked note structure: the SPV enters into a credit deriva-tive, issues a rated security, and pays a floating coupon and return of principal, provided losses on the reference portfolio remain below certain tolerance levels. This basic structure would be used again and again.

But what was particularly innovative about Chase's CSLT structure was that it used an excess spread account to provide a loss cushion to protect the rated cash flows of the issued notes. The excess spread came from the difference between the spreads earned on the reference loans, the sum of the above-LIBOR financing spread paid to Chase under the TRS, the portfolio manager's base fee, and the above-LIBOR coupon paid to the noteholder.

For example, if the average coupon on the loans was LIBOR plus 275 basis points, the funding cost under the TRS was LIBOR plus 75 basis points, the man-ager's base fee was 35 basis points per annum, and the note coupon was LIBOR plus 200 basis points (paid on 20 percent of the notional amount of the loans) then the excess spread is 125 basis points [i.e., $275 - 75 - 35 - (200 \times 20\%)$]. Assuming a 2 percent annual default rate on the loans and a 70 percent recovery —standard collat-eralized loan obligation (CLO) assumptions up until the 2007 financial crisis—the excess spread covered more than two times expected annual default losses. At the end of the transaction most funds remaining in the excess spread account were distributed to the investor,[15] creating the possibility for returns as high as LIBOR plus 800 basis points.

According to Fitch's rating models at the time, the risk of default losses over a 10-year period exceeding two times the expectation was low enough to merit a BBB rating on the notes. In all, the CSLT structure allowed an investor to take a five times leveraged position in a portfolio of BB and B rated loans with the benefit of a BBB rating on the instrument purchased. Many of the investors were insurance companies who found the relatively low regulatory capital requirements particularly compelling.

Looking back now, and admittedly with the benefit of having seen leveraged loan price volatility during the down markets of 1998–1999, 2002, and 2008–2009, there were some important risks that were arguably not given sufficient consider-ation in the rating analysis. Besides the question of whether the stressed levels of default and recovery were severe enough to support an investment-grade rating for the notes, there was the risk that the portfolio manager would not be able to acquire and maintain a portfolio earning the assumed spread over LIBOR, and the potential for losses on loans sold at a discount to par, especially at the maturity of the transaction or in the scenario where Chase terminated the TRS transaction for insufficient asset value coverage.[16]

Chase's CSLT program was discontinued in 1998 and the transactions were later restructured to more closely resemble standard cash-flow CLOs. This was done for reasons having nothing to do with the flaws in the rating methodology. Imperfections and all, the CSLT was a ground-breaking structure, and many of its features would be reutilized, with revisions and enhancements, throughout the growth of the credit derivatives market.[17]

First-to-Default (FTD) baskets

One can think of first-to-default baskets as the predecessor to "arbitrage" or "bespoke" synthetic CDOs. Though FTD baskets never became a very large component of the overall CDS marketplace, the modeling and risk management techniques developed for the product laid the groundwork for the growth of the synthetic CDO product.

In a first-to-default basket, the protection seller takes exposure to the first default in a small basket of identified reference entities, typically between 4 and 10. Most commonly, each reference entity has the same notional amount, and the premium is expressed in basis points per annum on the notional for a single-name. Losses can be either cash or physically settled.

The fair premium for an FTD basket has to be no lower than the highest premium of the reference entities (the seller of protection is exposed to the risk of any name defaulting, including the worst one, of course), and no higher than the sum of the spreads of the reference entities (the first-to-default position can't possibly suffer more losses than the entire basket). The correlation between the defaults determines where the spread fits within these bounds.

Exhibit 9.6 illustrates a result that was counterintuitive to some in the early days of correlation products, namely, that, all else equal, the first-to-default position (or more generally, the equity position) of a basket of assets is better off if the basket is less diversified. One explanation that makes the intuition clear is that the first to default position suffers a loss if one reference entity defaults, and after that

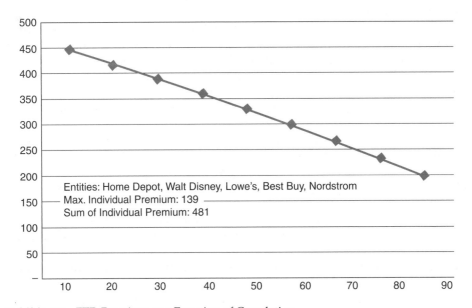

Exhibit 9.6 FTD Premium as a Function of Correlation

is no worse off if others default. Therefore, for a given set of reference-entity default probabilities, the first-to-default investor would prefer if all the credits either default or survive together.

Synthetic CDOs: Bank Balance Sheet

The first synthetic CDOs were bank balance sheet transactions, meaning that the reference portfolios were based on loans that resided in the loan portfolio of a sponsoring bank. In order to understand a synthetic CDO it's helpful to first understand CDOs. A CDO, or collateralized debt obligation, is a securitization in which the assets held as collateral are either corporate debt instruments, or are themselves tranches of a securitization (e.g., credit card debt or another corporate CDO). In a typical transaction, a special purpose vehicle is formed for the purpose of purchasing debt securities. The purchase is financed through the issuance of various classes of securities (called "tranches"), each of which has a security interest in the assets purchased by the SPV. The tranche with the first-priority security interest is typically called the "Class A." The tranche with the second-priority security interest is typically called the "Class B." The risk of each class increases as one goes down the capital structure of the CDO, with the senior-most-class, or the one with the first-priority security interest, representing the least amount of risk and lowest promised return. The most subordinated class is commonly referred to as the equity, the residual, or the first loss. The classes subordinated to the first-priority and senior to the equity are typically referred to as the mezzanine classes.

A synthetic CDO involves tranching the risk of a portfolio of credit derivatives, rather than the securitization of a pool of funded assets. In a typical transaction, the losses on a portfolio of CDS are allocated among various protection sellers (i.e., the takers of credit risk) according to specified priorities. The equity or "first loss" tranche assumes first losses on the reference portfolio up to a specified limit, usually expressed in terms of a percentage of the total portfolio size. The mezzanine tranches assume losses in excess of the limit specified by the equity, up to the mezzanine loss limit. The senior tranche assumes losses in excess of the sum of the limits specified by the equity and mezzanine.

Losses are cash-settled, meaning the loss corresponding to each credit event is determined based on market prices, and the applicable protection seller makes a cash payment to the protection buyer.

One of the first balance sheet synthetic CDOs, and surely the first such transaction to receive significant press, was J.P. Morgan's BISTRO transaction (standing for "Broad Index Securitized Trust Offering"), which closed in December 1997. J.P. Morgan subsequently closed a series of BISTRO transactions, purchasing credit protection and obtaining regulatory capital not only for itself, but for several other banks as clients. Morgan described the product as follows:

> In this structure, an originating bank buys protection from J.P. Morgan on a portfolio of corporate credit exposures via a portfolio credit swap. Morgan, in turn, purchases protection on the same portfolio from an SPV.
>
> The credit protection may be subject to a "threshold" . . . relating to the aggregate level of losses which must be experienced on the reference portfolio before any payments become due to the originating bank under the portfolio credit swap. Since this threshold represents

economic risk retained by the originating bank, it is analogous to the credit enhancement or equity stake that a bank would provide in a traditional securitization using a CLO.

The BISTRO SPV is collateralized with government securities or repurchase agreements on government securities which it funds through the issuance of notes which are credit-tranched and sold into the capital markets. In a critical departure from the traditional securitization model, the BISTRO SPV issues a substantial smaller note notional, and has substantially less collateral, than the notional amount of the reference portfolio. Typically, the BISTRO collateral will amount to only 5–15 percent of the portfolio notional. Thus, only the first 5–15 percent of losses (after the threshold, if any) in a particular portfolio are funded by the vehicle, leaving the most senior risk position unfunded. The transactions are structured so that, assuming the portfolio has a reasonable amount of diversification and investment grade-average credit quality, the risk of loss exceeding the amount of BISTRO securities sold is, at most, remote, or in rating agency vernacular, better than "triple A."[18]

The BISTRO structure allowed banks to achieve significant regulatory capital relief under the Basel I regime. Put simply, Basel I rules required banks to hold capital against most corporate credit exposures equal to 8 percent of the amount of the exposure, regardless of the credit quality of the corporate borrower. Exposures to banks were given a 20 percent risk weight, reducing the effective capital requirement to 1.6 percent. By packaging a large, well-diversified portfolio of exposures into a synthetic CDO structure, it was possible to obtain investment grade ratings on tranches with subordination levels as low as 1–2 percent. Typically, an issuing bank held dollar-for-dollar capital against the first loss retained. Assuming the issuing bank retained a first loss tranche of 1.5 percent, the regulatory capital requirement would be reduced from 8 percent to just over 3 percent [i.e., 1.5% + (98.5% × 8% × 20%)].

Bank balance sheet synthetic CDOs fell out favor in 2001 and 2002 for several reasons. The first was that most sponsoring banks required the ability to change the composition of the portfolio during the course of the transaction in order to match the changing composition of credit exposures in its loan portfolio. Suppose, for example, a bank had a loan exposure to IBM that was referenced in a synthetic CDO transaction. If IBM were to pay down its loan without the bank lending under a replacement facility to IBM, the synthetic CDO would leave the bank with a short position in IBM. Since bank loan portfolios typically do not maintain open short positions, the most desirable thing to do would be to remove IBM from the synthetic CDO and replace it with another credit.

At this point a conflict arises between the interests of the sponsoring bank and the interests of the investors. Since the pricing of the transaction is already fixed and not sensitive to the quality of the replacement, it is in the bank's interest to replace IBM with the worst credit possible, while the investors would like to see the best credit possible, or even no replacement at all. The early bank balance sheet deals attempted to address this problem by creating a requirement that the replacement credit be of equal or better quality than the removed credit and that the substitution not reduce the diversity of the reference portfolio. The marketplace quickly realized that this protection was insufficient, as the reference entities' ratings tended to lag the market's perception of credit quality, and sponsoring banks tended to have better information about the condition of the borrowers in their loan portfolios.

These factors started to matter to investors as credit spreads widened and a few investment grade borrowers defaulted in late 2000 and early 2001. Around that time, a new product came on the scene. This new product addressed the substitution conflict by making the portfolio static, not relying on obscure bilateral credits that sit on the balance sheets of sponsor banks, and allowing investors much more flexibility to tailor portfolio composition, tranche attachments, maturity, and other features. For a brief while the new product was called "arbitrage BISTRO" within J.P. Morgan, then more broadly the "arbitrage synthetic CDO" or "single-tranche synthetic CDO" until the marketplace finally settled on "bespoke synthetics" or simply "bespokes."

SECOND-GENERATION PRODUCTS: 2001–2007

Bespoke Synthetic CDOs

The first bespoke synthetic CDOs were executed in 2000, and by 2001 at least five dealers were active in the space. By the end of 2006, the number of dealers had surpassed 20. A bespoke synthetic CDO is a synthetic CDO transaction in which the investor has a large degree of flexibility to select the components of the reference portfolio, the attachment and detachment points, maturity, premium structure, and other details.

Because of its flexibility, transparency, and structural simplicity, bespoke synthetics experienced rapid growth from 2001 through the first half of 2007. Beginning with the onset of the subprime crisis in August of 2007, the volume of new bespoke synthetic CDO transactions slowed down considerably and by 2009 it had ground virtually to a halt. Several developments in 2009 and 2010, which will be discussed below, make a meaningful return of this product in the short term highly unlikely.

In each year between 2001 and 2007 the CDS market roughly doubled in size, to a total of $60 trillion. Bespoke synthetic CDOs were instrumental in driving this growth. According to BBA statistics, synthetic CDOs accounted for a total of 17 percent of total credit derivative notional, while single-name CDS accounted for 33 percent of the total. Assuming an average tranche delta of one,[19] it can be inferred from this data that synthetic CDOs drove roughly half of the single-name CDS volume. For some dealers, the synthetic CDO business actually represented as much as 80 percent of the "protection buy" side of the trading book.

The Gaussian Copula Model and Correlation Trading

In light of the significant contribution made by the bespoke synthetic CDO product to the growth of the overall credit derivatives market, it is particularly useful to understand the technology that made the product possible. In 1999, David Li of J.P. Morgan's RiskMetrics group, published a seminal paper describing the Gaussian copula modeling approach to the valuation and risk measurement of synthetic CDOs.[20] It has become an industry standard, in much the same way as the Black-Scholes model is the industry standard for pricing equity options, due to its simplicity and ease of implementation.

The Gaussian copula model starts with the assumption of risk-neutral pricing of the underlying single-name CDS (i.e., that the expected present value of the premium equals the expected present value of default loss payments). The objective of the model is to determine the fair premium for any bespoke synthetic CDO, or the level that equates present value of the premium payments to the present value of the expected losses on the CDO tranche. For each reference entity, given the term structure of its CDS spreads, a recovery assumption and the term structure of interest rates, a probability distribution of the time-to-default can be derived. The Gaussian copula model provides a framework to specify the joint distribution of the reference entities, thereby producing a probability distribution of losses for the entire portfolio at each point in time. Put simply, the "copula" is the framework by which default correlation between the reference entities is modeled, and for simplicity one can think of the model as using the standard Gaussian, or normal distribution, to correlate the "asset values" of the reference entities.[21] As noted in Li's paper, the model "introduces a few techniques used in survival analysis. These techniques have been widely applied to other areas, such as life contingencies in actuarial science and industry life testing in reliability studies."

Similar to the Black-Scholes model for equity options, the Gaussian copula model can also be used to calculate risk measures. For example, one of the measures is single name "credit 01," which captures the change in the value of a bespoke CDO value with respect to a one-basis-point shift of the CDS curve for each individual name in the portfolio. The credit 01 can then be used to determine a delta, or hedge ratio, for each reference entity in the bespoke portfolio.

While the use of this model for the valuation of synthetic CDOs has been the market standard since 2001, the specifics of how market participants have used the model have evolved in response to major market events.

One such event was the development of a correlation "skew" in the standardized tranches of broad CDS market indices. As early as 2002, J.P. Morgan and Morgan Stanley began efforts to create market-standard CDS indices. The upshot of these efforts was the creation of two highly important indices: Markit "CDX" indices in the US and the iTraxx indices in Europe and Asia. The first investment grade (IG) CDX Series, for example, began trading in October of 2003. The IG CDX is an index of 125 investment grade reference entities whose CDS contracts are actively traded. A new series of the index is created every six months, with changes to the index being driven by:

- Downgrades of reference entities to non-investment grade (e.g., Ford and GM were in the earlier series but were excluded from IG CDX series 5, which began trading in September, 2005, because both had been downgraded to non-investment grade in May of 2005).
- Defaults of reference entities (e.g., Lehman Brothers was a member of the on-the-run index when it filed for bankruptcy in September of 2008).
- Mergers (e.g., Wyeth).
- A drop in trading activity of the single-name CDS.

In late 2003, the market also began trading standardized tranches of the IG CDX as depicted in Exhibit 9.7.

A large part of the initial impetus for trading standardized tranches was for dealers to have an observable market in credit default correlation. This was necessary to provide a basis for the valuation of bespoke synthetic CDOs, which by 2003 had become a large business at several of the major global banks and investment banks.

Exhibit 9.7 Seniority Structure of IG CDX Tranches

Tranche	Attachment	Detachment	Width
Super Senior	30%	100%	70%
Senior Mezzanine	15%	30%	15%
"AAA" Mezzanine	10%	15%	5%
Mezzanine	7%	10%	3%
Subordinated Mezzanine	3%	7%	4%
Equity	0%	3%	3%

Prior to the advent of the index tranche market, dealers generally marked their credit correlation books based on historical correlations, either from stock prices or CDS spreads, and took large reserves. Average historical correlations were in the 25 percent range and reserves were in the +/− 10 percent range. For example, a long equity or short senior position might be marked at 15 percent correlation, and long senior or short equity position might be marked at 35 percent correlation.

Initially, the traded market for correlation, as reflected by the index tranches, was more or less in line with the correlation levels at which dealers were marking their books. Over time, however, a correlation "skew" developed, under which the correlation implied by index tranche prices varied depending upon the attachment point. This correlation skew is analogous to the volatility skew, or "smile" or "frown" observed in equity option pricing.

The correlation skew has tended to slope upward, meaning that implied correlations at the more senior attachments are higher. This general behavior has both a technical "supply and demand" explanation and a fundamental explanation. The technical explanation is that during the years when new bespoke issuance was active, the strongest investor demand was for the investment-grade rated mezzanine tranches, generally corresponding to the 3 percent and 15 percent attachments of the IG CDX. The tranches were attractive largely because they paid credit spreads well in excess of spreads available on single-name CDS for reference entities of comparable ratings. In addition, the existence of subordination equal to 2 to 8 times historical default loss averages, which were in part responsible for the ratings, gave investors comfort that even if there were a few unexpected credit events in the reference portfolio, the investment could still come out whole.

Equity tranches, on the other hand, do not generally have ratings and are exposed to the first loss in the reference portfolio. Two or three bad calls out of 100 or more reference entities could result in a losing investment. Lastly for tranches attaching above approximately 15 percent, there was plenty of loss cushion, at least in relation to historical averages. As a result, spreads were too low to make the investment worthwhile to most types of investors. For any given CDS spreads on the reference entities, stronger technical demand for the mezzanine compresses mezzanine spreads and "pushes" spread into the senior and equity classes. This, in turn, raises implied correlation at senior attachments and lowers implied correlation for the equity.

As for the fundamental explanation, the notion of low to moderate default rates corresponding to low correlation, and high default rates corresponding to high correlation makes intuitive sense, at least where correlation is measured under a normal (or Gaussian) distribution. Put another way, if we were to observe, say, that two investment-grade reference entities out of 125 default over a five-year period, one would expect that those defaults were the result of idiosyncratic or at most industry-specific factors. If, on the other hand, 25 out of 125 investment-grade borrowers were to default, or more than 10 times historical averages (the type of scenario it would take to reach a 15 percent attachment assuming 25 percent average recovery), one would expect that this would have been caused by a systemic economic disaster comparable to the Great Depression. Even the sustained period of recession and weak economic growth which began in 2008 is not expected to come close to such a level of corporate default.

One of the defining events in the development of the CDS market was the dislocation of the credit correlation market in May of 2005. Since late 2003, the correlation skew had been steadily steepening. In May of 2005, S&P downgraded GM and Ford to non-investment grade, or "junk" status. As expected, this caused a significant widening of the credit spreads for these two issuers, but not necessarily due to any fundamental news reported to the market by the downgrade.[22] The move was driven more by the technical effect of investment grade funds having to sell out of Ford and GM. In addition, because the investment grade funds had to replace these issuers with others, the remaining investment grade universe tightened a bit. Lastly, because the high-yield funds had to "make room" for Ford and GM, the rest of the high-yield universe widened.

The downgrade of Ford and GM was a significant decoupling event. Even without any move in correlation, the equity tranches of the IG CDX would have suffered a deterioration in value. But this deterioration was made much larger by a new concern surrounding the potential for future idiosyncratic or industry-specific events. Correlation at the 3 percent attachment point and 5-year maturity fell into the single digits, the lowest levels that had ever been seen, and generally stayed at 15 percent or lower until the first credit-market dislocation in the summer of 2007.

CDS Benchmark Indices and Tranches

As noted above, the IG CDX and iTraxx indices, and tranches on those indices, began active trading in late 2003. Since then other indices began active trading, including a U.S. high-yield index (HY CDX), "crossover" indices (XO CDX and iTraxx) and an index of loan-only CDS (LCDX). The indices are used by dealers, hedge funds, and other market participants to quickly and cost-effectively establish market long or short positions, with the particular index chosen to provide the best proxy for the type of market benchmark desired. For example, a U.S. high-yield bond asset manager with a short-term bearish market view might express this view by purchasing protection on the HY CDX. This would allow the manager to hedge his or her core long portfolio, or even establish a net short position, until such time as his or her view changed to neutral or bullish, without incurring the large bid-offer costs, and risking a potential inability to re-establish a portfolio of desired issuers.

For a while there was active trading of tranches of the HY CDX and the LCDX, but with the slowdown of bespoke tranche activity beginning in 2007, trading in these tranches dropped off significantly. At the time of this writing, the "on-the-run" series of each index is number 13 or 14, established some time in 2010. But for tranches, the only actively traded series are series 9 of the IG CDX and iTraxx, which went effective in September 2007 and March 2008, respectively.

CDS Swaptions

A CDS swaption is an option to either purchase or sell credit protection on a particular reference entity or index at a prespecified premium level. Like stock options, FX options and interest rate swaptions, CDS swaptions create a market in volatility. In the case of CDS swaptions, the relevant volatility is that of the credit spread. The first attempts to create a traded market in CDS swaptions go back to the beginnings of the CDS market itself. After a slow start, a real market in CDS swaptions began to emerge in 2007, and CDS swaptions on the indices are actively traded at the time of this writing.

GOING FORWARD

In some ways, the present time for credit derivatives is similar to 1994 for interest rate derivatives. What was a nascent market more or less 10 years ago has witnessed several years of, literally, exponential growth. Product innovation in some cases reached beyond the point of usefulness, and some market participants took meaningful losses as a result of poorly-understood risks and excessive leverage. Of course in many important ways, the comparison breaks down. The players who took big well-publicized losses in interest rate products in 1994 (e.g., Orange County, P&G, and MBS funds) were not systemically critical, and some suffered no material impact to their business. There was no systemic crisis comparable to that of 2007–2009, and interest rate derivatives weren't generally believed to have actually caused the rate volatility that led to the losses.

But, as with interest rate derivatives in 1994, some today believe that credit derivatives have outlived their usefulness and we are now on our way to a return to the old ways of managing risk. As with interest rate derivatives in 1994, I do not hold this view of credit derivatives today. Has the technology been misunderstood, misused, and mismanaged, with catastrophic consequences for some? Absolutely. But I believe just as strongly that the technology is just too useful to simply disappear from the landscape of global finance. This was what I thought of interest rate derivatives in 1994, and it's what I think about credit derivatives today.

Global banks are still large originators of risk and not only in their loan portfolios. Interest rate and currency derivatives, which thankfully are not the subject of public scorn at the moment, are a big source of credit risk for the banks. Commodity derivatives are likely to become another meaningful source. It appears likely that corporate clients who use interest rate, currency, and commodity derivatives to manage exposures will be exempt from the margin requirements of the Dodd-Frank Act.[23] At the same time, banks are becoming more disciplined in their management of counterparty risk, and proposed Basel rules will increase the capital charges associated with such risk. For these reasons, credit derivatives still have an important place in the risk management strategies of the global banks. And depending on a number of factors, we may see a new generation of standardized products to trade such risks, a new generation of customized "bank balance sheet" structures, or both.

Moreover, some other types of organizations who have not heretofore been big protection buyers should continue to have access to the product because, sooner or later, the potential applications will become apparent to them. One such organization type are the non-financial corporate entities, who may consider using the product to manage credit exposures to trade debtors or to the banks that provide liquidity facilities; to hedge risks and enhance yields in their pension funds; or to hedge anticipated borrowing costs. Another type are the federal, state, and local governments who may consider using the product to manage the risk of various financial guarantees issued and other credit exposures taken, to business ventures ranging from environmentally-friendly energy projects to sports teams.

The need is clearly there and, if anything, the desire to use the product as a protection buyer should increase. The challenge will be in finding the protection sellers.

The marketplace for the time being has lost perhaps the single most important vehicle—the bespoke synthetic CDOs. A number of factors make it unlikely that bespoke CDOs will return in meaningful size any time soon. These factors include:

- No obvious home for the senior-most classes. As discussed above, the monolines were big protection sellers, but due to their limited ability to pay, the banks ended up as the de facto holders of this risk. This is not likely to happen again.[24]
- New rating agency rules have raised the subordination levels required at all rating categories.
- Proposed BIS rules will double or triple the regulatory capital requirements of dealers making markets in synthetic CDOs.
- Regulatory capital requirements for many investors are up too, especially at non-dealer banks and insurance companies.
- New accounting rules force investors to recognize mark-to-market volatility of performing synthetic CDOs purchased in note form.

So, who will be the new protection sellers? Two types of players, who have heretofore been virtually absent, could step in, depending in large part on the regulatory environment. The first are the "real money" investors, and especially pension funds and investment companies. The second is individual investors in the United States high net worth and traditional "retail." Both these types of investors are, for different reasons, potentially good takers of risk through credit derivatives products.

Among real money investors, life insurance companies have to some extent used credit derivatives as an alternative means of taking long-term credit exposure to corporate issuers. Mutual funds and pension funds can also benefit from the diversification and yield-enhancement strategies that credit derivatives make possible. To date, however, their participation has been limited, in part due to lack of clarity with respect to how such investments are treated under applicable regulation. Realistically, there is little short-term prospect of the rules changing in such a way that opens the door for these investors to meaningfully participate in the space, but one can hold out hope for the longer term.

Moreover individual investors, subject to proper disclosure and suitability standards, could be good takers of the senior-most, systemic risk in a CDO or synthetic CDO structure. Such investments would be considered part of the "less liquid" or "long term" component of the investment portfolio, and would most likely be made through managed funds rather than directly. Individuals arguably take greater risks (in terms of likelihood and severity of loss) by purchasing stocks, traditional corporate bonds, and municipal bonds (either directly or through ETFs and mutual funds). Individual investors are not subject to accounting rules that arbitrarily identify some assets and risks for mark-to-market treatment and others for, essentially, accrual-based treatment. They are therefore in a better position to make a rational choice with respect to tolerance for price volatility. Lastly, like it or not, individuals, as taxpayers, are already exposed to the systemic risk represented by the senior tranches of CDOs and synthetic CDOs, be it through federal deposit insurance, GSEs, or programs such as TARP and TALF. Assurances to contrary, including the "anti-bailout" provisions of the Dodd-Frank Act are simply not credible. There's an argument that it would be more transparent and economically efficient if they took more of such risk through choices made with respect to their investment portfolios and less through the political process.

Thankfully, credit derivatives have thus far survived misguided attempts to ban them by legislation. There should be concern, however, that the current environment may produce rules that single out credit derivatives for more restrictive treatment than the treatment applicable to comparable products (as the accounting rules already do). If these cases can be kept to a minimum and market participants are left relatively free to engineer new products and applications, credit derivatives should continue to serve the important functions of risk management, distribution, and pricing to the benefit of the capital markets as a whole.

NOTES

1. Discussed in the chapter.
2. The use of this term to describe derivatives products was first attributed to Warren Buffett, Chairman and CEO of Berkshire Hathaway. Interestingly, Berkshire Hathaway is known to have been a large uncollateralized risk taker through credit and equity derivatives (as a seller of protection on the equity tranches of synthetic CDOs and writer of put options on the S&P 500).
3. www.newsweek.com/2008/09/26/the-monster-that-ate-wall-street.html.
4. AMBAC is Ambac Financial Group, Inc.
5. MBIA is MBIA, Inc.
6. FGIC is Financial Guaranty Insurance Company.
7. FSA is Financial Security Assurance, Inc.
8. Eric Dinallo, the New York State superintendent of insurance, stated on November 20, 2008, at the U.S. House of Representatives Committee on Agriculture, that he was withdrawing his earlier proposal to regulate credit default swaps under New York insurance law in light of the federal government's expressed interest in bringing federal regulation to the market.
9. As well as securitization.
10. Or, for that matter, to take on the costs of origination and relationship management or bear the operational burdens and risks.
11. Otherwise, the borrowers would likely seek funding from another source.
12. Remarks by Chairman Alan Greenspan at the American Bankers Association Annual Convention, New York, October 5, 2004.

13. It should be noted that not all notional is created equal. Risk transferred can vary in credit spread, maturity, and leverage. Simple notional does not measure these factors.

14. It was always understood that the monolines were imperfect counterparties, and pricing reflected this imperfection. Through mid-2007 monolines were generally paid approximately 50 to 80 percent of the premium that would have been paid to, say, a AA financial institution with daily collateral calls.

15. With a portion, typically 20 percent, paid to the portfolio manager as an incentive fee.

16. In order to protect its position as the de facto lender to the CSLT, Chase had the right to unwind the structure by selling loans out of the KZH if the value of the loans reached approximately 85 percent of par. In such a scenario, note investors would lose most or all of their investment.

17. For example, the excess spread feature was utilized again by Chase in a "balance sheet" structure called LANCE, which also featured loan portfolio equity rated BBB by Fitch. LANCE was based on CDS, which matured on the same day the notes matured, rather than on TRS. Moreover, there was no asset value coverage test. For these reasons, the rating of LANCE was less subject to extraneous risks.

    Moving forward to 2002, Lehman Brothers developed an excess spread structure in which a first-loss security obtained a rating of A3 from Moody's. This was made possible by the general credit spread widening caused by fear of "corporate governance" scandals.

    Though economics nearly identical to those of an excess spread structure could be replicated by combining rated mezzanine and unrated equity, traditional CDO investors seemed to favor the pricing transparency of the excess spread structure.

18. See J.P. Morgan and RiskMetrics Group (1999).

19. See discussion of the Gaussian Copula model in Li (1999).

20. Ibid.

21. In reality, the default rate for a group of credits tends to be higher in a recession and lower when the economy is growing. This implies that each credit is subject to the same macroeconomic environment, and that there exists some form of positive dependence among the credits. To capture the description in the simplest and most convenient mathematical term, one factor Gaussian copula is introduced. In brief, it is a multivariate normal joint distribution defined on the n-dimensional unit cube $[0, 1]n$ such that every marginal distribution is uniform on the interval $[0, 1]$ assuming a single correlation parameter. More specifically, each individual credit in the portfolio is modeled as an asset combining two independent components; one is a systemic component, which can be thought of as the state of the general economy, and the correlation of the credits in the portfolio is captured through the sensitivity to this macro factor only; the other component is an idiosyncratic component, which is specific to each individual name. In the Gaussian copula framework, both components are normally distributed, which implies the asset itself is normally distributed. Moreover, the distribution of the asset value is mapped to each corresponding time to default distribution indicated above, thus providing a complete description of the joint portfolio loss distribution, which enables us to compute the expected loss and premium payments for the entire portfolio.

22. It's well understood that credit ratings tend to lag changes in credit spreads, though the rating agencies have done much to improve the response time of corporate ratings in recent years.

23. The Act itself does not create such an exemption to the collateral rules, but given the clear intent conveyed in the Dodd-Lincoln letter, it would be surprising if the CFTC and SEC were to force a significant change to the status quo for corporate end-users.

24. Or if it does, it won't be in the same form.

REFERENCES

J.P. Morgan and RiskMetrics Group. 1999. *The J.P. Morgan Guide to Credit Derivatives.* www.defaultrisk.com/pp_crdrv121.htm.

Li, David X. 1999. " On Default Correlation: A Copula Function Approach." *Journal of Fixed Income* 9:4, 43–54.

ABOUT THE AUTHOR

Frank Iacono is a partner at Riverside Risk Advisors LLC, an advisory firm specializing in the structuring, execution, and risk management of interest rate, currency, and structured credit derivatives transactions. He has over 15 years of experience with derivatives and structured products as a trader, structurer, manager, and advisor. From 2006 to 2008 Frank was CEO of Cournot Financial Products LLC, a AAA rated Credit Derivatives Product Company sponsored by Morgan Stanley. From 2001 to 2006, Frank worked with Lehman Brothers as the senior executive responsible for the corporate-structured credit business in New York. From 1998 to 2001, Frank worked with Chase as a vice president in the Credit Derivatives Group. From 1994 to 1998, Frank worked at Capital Market Risk Advisors, a consulting firm specializing in structured products and risk management. Frank holds a BS in Applied Math (summa cum laude) from Yale University and a JD (cum laude) from Harvard Law School. Frank is a licensed attorney in the State of New York.

PART III

Key Applications of Financial Engineering

CHAPTER 10

Securitized Products

KONSTANTIN BRAUN
Smart Energy Capital

INTRODUCTION

Securitization is defined as a sale of assets to a bankruptcy-remote special purpose entity with a concurrent sale of interests in the entity in the capital markets. The most basic objective of a securitization is to separate the credit risk of the originator of assets from the credit risk inherent with the assets. The bankruptcy-remote special entities are called special purpose entities (SPEs) or special purpose vehicles (SPVs). The interests in such entities that are sold in the capital markets are known as asset-backed securities (ABS). Securitization began in the 1970s when government agencies issued securities backed by home mortgages. Later, commercial mortgages, credit card receivables, auto loans, student loans, and many other financial (and, later, nonfinancial) assets were securitized. While securitization itself is just a few decades old, its roots lie in an age-old practice of collateralized borrowing.

Securitization is focused on legal isolation of assets and is a legal technique at its core. However, we will not address legal or tax aspects of securitization in this chapter. Instead, we will focus on the structuring and analytical aspects of transactions, as well as market history and trends. In a number of cases, we will rely on numerical examples to illustrate key concepts. We will use simplified examples with a deliberate goal of forging broad intuitive understanding of securitization.

ORIGINS OF SECURITIZATION

The use of securitization as a financing tool has grown rapidly since its inception. In its most basic form, securitization is simply a legal technique for isolating assets from the originator of those assets or from their current owner. In a securitization, the assets are transferred to a special purpose entity (SPE) in such a way that the legal ownership of the assets is transferred from the original owner to the SPE (see Exhibit 10.1). The SPE then issues ABS (also known as asset-backed bonds or asset-backed debt) backed solely by the collateral it owns. This allows investors to analyze the credit quality of the securitized assets separately from the credit quality of the originator, making risks relatively transparent.

Under this arrangement, if the originator were to file for bankruptcy, its creditors would have no claims on the assets in the SPE. Similarly, if the cash flows

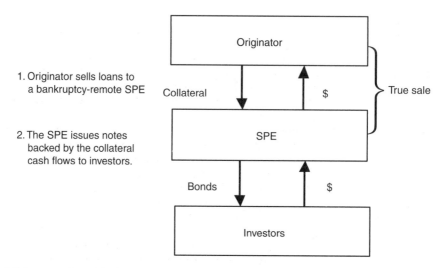

Exhibit 10.1 Simplified Diagram of a Securitization

generated by the collateral are insufficient to pay back all the ABS investors, they do not have a claim on the originator. This bankruptcy remoteness is the heart of the securitized products market.

MARKET SIZE AND SEGMENTS

Asset-backed securities are often categorized by collateral asset types. It is customary to subdivide the market into two broad segments: mortgage-backed securities and asset-backed securities.

Mortgage-backed securities (MBS) include U.S. government agency issues: the Government National Mortgage Association (GNMA, Ginnie Mae); the Federal National Mortgage Association (FNMA, Fannie Mae); and the Federal Home Loan Mortgage Corporation (FHLMC, Freddie Mac); as well as securities backed by pools of nonconforming high-grade residential mortgages. Commercial mortgage-backed securities (CMBS) are backed by mortgage loans related to commercial properties. Commercial mortgage-backed securities are often included within the MBS category for the purposes of market statistics. Over the past two decades, the size of the MBS market has outpaced the size of the U.S. Treasury market as well as the size of the U.S. corporate debt market. According to the Securities Industry and Financial Markets Association (SIFMA), outstanding MBS was in excess of $9.2 trillion as of Q2 2009. The size of the market has nearly tripled since 2000.

Asset-backed securities (ABS) include bonds backed by a wide variety of collateral types. Most common collateral types include credit card receivables, auto loans and leases, student loans, equipment leases, dealer floor plan loans, and collateralized debt obligations (CDOs). It is customary to include securities backed by subprime mortgage loans in the ABS category, rather than grouping the subprime with MBS. In part, this underscores the consumer credit nature of this product as opposed to its housing-related character. Boat loans, consumer lines of credit, manufactured housing loans, motorcycle loans, subprime auto loans,

Exhibit 10.2   Key Parties to a Securitization

Key Party	Description
Issuer/Trust	Legal entity that issues the securities to investors. The sole obligor of the liabilities that are created by the securitization.
Seller/Originator	The entity that originates and/or sells the underlying receivables that are securitized.
Transferor	A bankruptcy-remote entity required between the seller/originator and the SPE in order to protect the receivables from the originator's insolvency and to characterize the transaction as a true sale for legal (bankruptcy) purposes.
Servicer	An entity that is responsible for servicing the receivables pursuant to its standard servicing and collection procedures.
Indenture Trustee	Trustee for the ABS note holders.
Rating Agencies	The nationally recognized statistical rating organizations that assign debt ratings to the securities that are issued by the SPE.

aircraft leases, railcar leases, recreational vehicle loans, small business loans, truck loans and leases, franchise loans, lottery awards, rental car fleet leases, franchise and pharmaceutical royalties, stranded cost receivables, tax liens, and time-share loans are among the less common ABS collateral types. According to SIFMA, total outstandings of the U.S. ABS market grew from about $1 trillion in 2000 to $3.65 trillion as of Q3 2009. In the first half of 2010, new ABS issuances in the United States totaled $64.8 billion.[1] ABS issuance volume peaked in 2006 at $753.9 billion. Since 2006, issuance volume has steadily declined, primarily driven by the decline in issuance of subprime mortgage ABS.

Key Parties

Each securitization is comprised of various parties that are involved in the transaction. (See Exhibit 10.2.)

SPE Sources and Uses of Funds

The SPE or SPV can be viewed as an ongoing business entity that has various sources of funds that are used to pay its obligations.

Excess spread (the funds remaining after payment of the SPE's operating expenses and debt service expenses) forms the first layer of credit protection. Excess spread is normally used to:

- Pay down the securities, thereby creating overcollateralization (the amount by which the balance of the receivables exceeds the balance of securities).
- Pay down the securities to eliminate collateral deficiency caused by losses experienced by the collateral pool (i.e., eliminate negative overcollateralization).
- Fund a reserve account until it reaches a specified level.

See Exhibits 10.3 and 10.4.

Exhibit 10.3   Sources of Funds of a Securitization

Sources of Funds	Description
Scheduled payments on the receivables	Scheduled interest and principal collections.
Prepayments on the receivables	Full or partial prepayments.
Servicer advances	Advances made by the servicer with respect to delinquent receivables. These "loans" are made only to the extent the servicer expects to be repaid from subsequent payments.
Liquidation proceeds	Any proceeds received on a defaulted receivable, including insurance proceeds and sale proceeds from the disposition of collateral.
Amounts on deposit in reserve account	The reserve account can be funded from a deposit by the seller and/or excess spread and is used to cover shortfalls in the SPE's available funds needed to pay interest and principal on the securities.
Other	In a transaction that involves assets other than loans, a SPV's assets may generate rental payments, royalties, lottery winnings, and so on.

Funds get allocated based on a predefined priority of payments, also known as a *cash flow waterfall*. Exhibit 10.5 illustrates a basic waterfall of a hypothetical auto loan securitization.

Credit Enhancement

Credit enhancement is required to achieve the desired rating on the securities. As discussed later in more detail, the rating agencies work with a number of cash flow scenarios, in which they stress defaults, prepayments, and a number of other factors to determine the required enhancement level consistent with the desired rating.

Credit enhancement for a basic ABS transaction may take several forms:

- Excess spread.
- Cash reserve account (initial deposit or built from excess spread).
- Overcollateralization (initial deposit or built from excess spread).
- Subordination of principal.

Exhibit 10.4   Uses of Funds of a Securitization

Use of Funds	Description
Servicing fee	Fee paid to the servicer as compensation for administering and servicing the assets.
Reimbursement of servicer advances	Repayment of previous liquidity advances made by servicer.
Interest payments	Interest due on securities.
Principal payments	Repayment of the principal amount of the securities.
Deposits to the reserve account	Funds required to be deposited into the reserve account if its balance is below the required level.

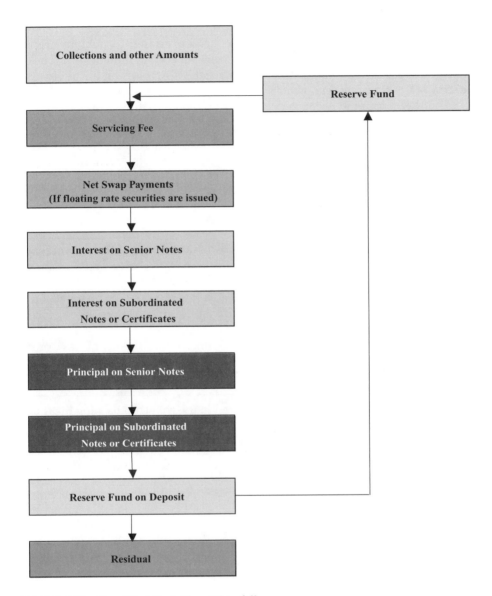

Exhibit 10.5 Simplified Cash Flow Waterfall

These methods of enhancing a transaction can be used in combination to achieve the desired transaction characteristics.

Excess Spread
If the interest rate earned on a loan pool is greater than that owed to pay ABS bondholders and servicing fees, the excess is generally available to cover losses on the collateral.

Cash Reserve Accounts
Cash reserve accounts are conceptually the simplest form of enhancement. Generally, cash reserve accounts are utilized in combination with subordination or

overcollateralization in most automobile loan ABS structures. The cash portion of the enhancement is required by the rating agencies to address liquidity concerns. Cash is deposited into the reserve account by the seller and/or built up over time by depositing excess spread into the account. In most cases, losses on the receivables in excess of the excess spread and any overcollateralization are reimbursed from draws on this account in order to protect the note holders from loss. Cash in the reserve account is generally restricted by the rating agencies to liquid, highly rated eligible investments such as A-1+/P-1 commercial paper. Since the rate earned on these investments is low relative to the seller's cost of capital, the seller experiences *negative carry* (i.e., the difference between the rate earned and the cost of capital) on the balance in the reserve account. As a result, efficient structures seek to minimize the cash reserve account requirements.

Overcollateralization

Overcollateralization is defined as the excess of the collateral pool balance over the outstanding securities balance. Overcollateralization can be structured initially or built from excess spread over time.

- Initial overcollateralization is created by depositing collateral into the trust in excess of the par amount of securities to be issued.
- Overcollateralization can be built over time by "turboing" excess spread (i.e., using excess spread in addition to normal principal collections) to retire bond principal until target overcollateralization levels are achieved.

Overcollateralization is effectively invested in the collateral backing the transaction, and therefore avoids the negative carry associated with a reserve account.

Subordination

While reserve accounts and overcollateralization normally support the entirety of issued securities, it is also possible to have assets behind one or more classes of lower-rated securities provide credit support. Subordination of one or more classes is accomplished by defining the payment priority of the trust to favor certain classes over others in receipt of principal cash flows. Subordination requires no additional cash or receivables, but does have an effect on execution, since some securities receive lower ratings due to the lower likelihood of ultimate receipt of principal. Simpler structures may use only two levels of subordination—for example, a single-A class supporting a triple-A class or classes.

Motivation

Loan and lease originators require access to capital in order to engage in loan and lease production. Commercial banks and other institutions with significant balance sheet capacity and a low cost of financing, often choose to retain assets they originate and fund them with deposits or unsecured debt. Securitization presents an alternative source of asset financing. Independent finance companies typically do not have the balance sheet and ratings to finance receivables economically through unsecured debt. They sell loans into securitizations and retain a first loss piece (also known as *securitization residual* or *securitization equity*). There are

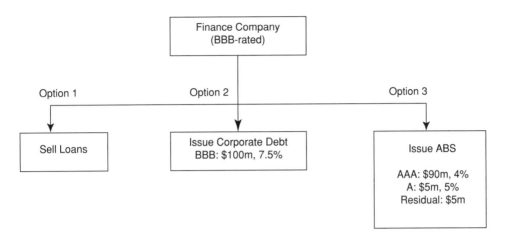

Exhibit 10.6 Simplified Funding Options

multiple reasons for asset originators to securitize their assets. For many, the biggest benefit is a lower cost of funds. The bankruptcy remoteness of the SPE can, and often does, result in a credit rating for the ABS that is higher than that of the originator itself.

Let's consider the example presented in Exhibit 10.6. A finance company with a BBB rating has a pool of loans and needs additional funds to originate new loans. Broadly speaking, the finance company has three funding options:

1. *Sell loans.* The company could sell its existing portfolio of loans. A pool of assets may either be offered for competitive bidding or be sold to a specific buyer on prearranged terms as part of a larger arrangement. While this would generate cash, it does have several drawbacks. First, the originator would need to find a buyer for the loans who is looking for assets that match the specific duration and credit risk profile of the loans themselves. Let's say we are dealing with a $100 million pool of retail auto loans with a weighted average remaining term of 48 months, weighted average interest rate of 6 percent, weighted average FICO score of 690, significant share of used vehicles, and so on. In this case, the target investor pool would be constrained by a lack of credit rating and the fairly unique nature of the credit risk that this pool would present. Such uniqueness limits the number of possible investors and drives up the cost of capital, driving down the sale price. Furthermore, if the originator chooses to sell the receivables, the company forgoes any upside in the assets' performance. If the assets perform better than expected, the originator does not benefit (the converse is also true—if they perform worse than expected, then there is no additional loss to the originator).

2. *Issue corporate debt.* The company could issue corporate debt. The issuer would retain any upside if the assets perform better than expected. The company would also retain any downside if the assets' performance is worse than expected. The cost of funding the assets would be the marginal cost of funds to the company. For purposes of the example that follows, we will assume this cost to be 7.50 percent.

3. *Issue ABS.* By issuing ABS, the company could obtain financing with weighted average cost of 4.05 percent, which means savings of 3.45 percent relative to the cost of issuing corporate debt. Additionally, by retaining the equity or first loss piece, the company retains any upside from better than expected collateral performance. Similarly, if the assets perform worse than expected, the company's losses are capped at its retained exposure (5 percent of the collateral pool in our example).

In our example, issuing ABS is the superior financing option. In reaching this conclusion, we are comparing 7.5 percent cost of corporate debt with 4.05 percent weighted average cost of ABS debt (assuming pro rata amortization of all ABS tranches). While this comparison makes sense for $95 million of debt out of a $100 million loan pool, our conclusion fails to take into account the fact that the entire $100 million needs to be financed. Under the third option, the incremental $5 million is a highly levered piece that is likely to carry a high assumed cost of funds and would move the weighted average cost of funds above the level of 4.05 percent.

Cost of equity is often an important consideration in choosing between options 1 and 3. Let's assume that after marketing this pool of loans to a range of prospective buyers, the owner has ended up with the best level of $101 million for the $100 million pool of loans. The owner now needs to compare this execution with results under option 3. The owner knows that the pool can generate $95 million from the sale of ABS. However, putting $101 million side by side with $95 million is not a fair comparison since the owner would derive an incremental value from the ownership of the securitization residual under option 3. Thus, $95 million needs to be supplemented with the value of the residual. The value of a residual piece is typically computed as a present value of projected cash flows under a certain loan pool performance scenario. Exhibit 10.7 shows simplified collateral, bond, and residual cash flows for a $100 million retail auto loan pool. Total cash flow to the residual stands at $8.9 million. Assuming a 15 percent discount rate, net present value of the residual stands at $6.7 million. Combined with ABS cash proceeds of $95 million, the total pool value stands at $101.7 million and exceeds the market level of $101 million, pointing to option 3 for the owner of the pool. Let's change the discount rate assumption to 25 percent. In this case, net present value of the residual would drop to $5.75 million, leading to total transaction value of $100.75 million and pointing to option 1.

Needless to say, in real life these choices are driven by a variety of additional considerations such as accounting treatment, rating agency treatment, and transaction fees.

Securitization has multiple additional benefits. As discussed earlier, the ability to secure higher ratings on certain bonds than the issuer itself is rated can result in a lower cost of funds. This is particularly true for lower-rated issuers or collateral pools of higher-quality assets. As a general rule, the funding cost advantage declines as an issuer's rating improves and/or the asset quality declines. We highlight a few additional benefits of securitization:

- *Diversification of funding.* Securitization increases the range of financing options for an originator, particularly for lower-rated issuers that may have more limited access to the capital markets.

Exhibit 10.7 Simplified Sell versus Securitize Analysis

	Retail Auto Loan Pool				Class A, AAA-rated ABS			Class B, A-rated ABS			
Year	Beginning Balance	Loan Interest	Loan Principal	Loan Loss	Beginning Balance	Class A Interest	Class A Principal	Beginning Balance	Class B Interest	Class B Principal	Equity
1	100.0	7.0	24.0	1.0	90.0	3.6	22.5	5.0	0.3	1.3	3.4
2	75.0	5.3	24.0	1.0	67.5	2.7	22.5	3.8	0.2	1.3	2.6
3	50.0	3.5	24.0	1.0	45.0	1.8	22.5	2.5	0.1	1.3	1.8
4	25.0	1.8	24.0	1.0	22.5	0.9	22.5	1.3	0.1	1.3	1.0
Total		17.5	96.0	4.0		9.0	90.0		0.6	5.0	8.9

- *Asset-liability management.* Securitizing a pool of assets can help reduce or eliminate interest rate and duration mismatches on an originator's balance sheet.
- *Risk management.* By securitizing a pool of loans and retaining the residual or first loss piece, the issuer retains any upside from better than expected collateral performance. The potential losses are also limited to retained portions of the securitization.

TRANSACTION PROCESS

Loan originators hire investment banks to structure and sell securities. Debt underwriting is largely a fee business for investment banks. Banks may or may not provide firm commitments to sell bonds at certain spread levels, depending on circumstances. Typically, a group of banks is picked to do a transaction. Among many considerations, originators tend to choose based on indicative or guaranteed pricing, reputation, and strength of institutional relationship. Within a group of banks picked to execute a transaction there are lead managers who take a primary role and co-managers. Typically, one of the lead managers is in charge of structuring the deal.

As a first step, the structuring bank comes up with multiple structural alternatives and shares economics in each alternative with the client. Once the optimal structure is chosen, bankers work with rating agencies to get credit ratings and with lawyers to prepare necessary offering documents. Marketing and sale of bonds to investors conclude the transaction process. If necessary, the investment bank brings other parties into a deal. For instance, a deal may benefit from a derivative product (such as an interest rate swap or interest rate cap).

CREDIT RATINGS

Rating agencies evaluate deals and assign credit ratings based on estimated creditworthiness of individual securities. Although credit ratings are not intended as recommendations to buy or sell specific securities, on most occasions bond investors take ratings into account in their investment process. While some investors may find rating agency analysis helpful, others are simply required to take ratings into account due to the institutional role that ratings play. Over decades, credit ratings have made their way into investment guidelines, capital adequacy rules, and all sorts of regulations.

In assigning credit ratings, rating agencies study various aspects of a securitization. Rating analysts dedicate significant effort to studying the legal framework of any given deal with a goal of ensuring legal isolation of assets sold to an SPE and continuation of harvesting of such assets for the benefit of bondholders in case of bankruptcy of a seller of assets. On a quantitative front, rating agencies engage in extensive analysis of bond performance under a variety of collateral scenarios. Let's perform a simplified rating agency analysis using auto loan securitization as an example. As a first step, rating agencies would study the collateral pool and develop a view with regard to future collateral performance. Projected portfolio credit loss rates are a function of projected default rates and projected loss severity rates. Historically, auto loan default rates have been primarily driven by the state of the labor market. The main factors that drive auto loan loss severity are the economic environment, new vehicle incentives, used car supply from fleet leases, and general availability of credit, as well as credit terms. In analyzing collateral performance, rating agency analysts would also focus on a variety of factors, including historical performance of assets originated by the same entity, loan prepayment rate expectations, credit scores, geographic concentrations, loan seasoning, and so forth.

Then, using their knowledge of the collateral as a starting point, the agencies would come up with multiple collateral performance cases in order to assess the strength of a proposed capital structure. Fundamentally, there are two approaches to such analysis.

Under the first approach, which is known as *deterministic*, the rating analyst would come up with a small number of scenarios for each rating category and would evaluate bond performance under each scenario in order to make sure that each bond with a targeted rating X is able to pay full interest and repay full principal in stress scenarios associated with such rating. For example, let's assume an analyst has come up with the following base case and stress scenarios for the auto loan pool described earlier in the chapter. (See Exhibit 10.8.)

Assuming a weighted average life of this collateral pool at two years and using a simplified back-of-the-envelope approach to debt sizing, the analysis will yield bond sizes shown in the last column on the right. Using an AAA-rated Class A bond as an example, the rating agency guideline requires that Class A be sized to survive a loss of 16.5 percent of the collateral pool. With excess spread covering losses of approximately 6.3 percent of the collateral pool, the rest needs to come from excess collateral (subordination and overcollateralization) and, as such, drives the sizing of Class A to 89.8 percent. In reality, detailed bond cash flow analysis is necessary to derive bond sizes in each rating scenario. Among many things, in a detailed cash flow run, higher loss rates and faster prepayment rates relative to the expected case will reduce the amount of excess spread. Therefore, since the yield on the assets itself is subject to curtailments due to defaults and prepayments, the rating agencies will give credit for only a fraction of the excess available as credit enhancement. In some cases, more credit will be given to the excess spread by the rating agencies if the excess spread is trapped in a reserve account or used early on to build overcollateralization by paying down principal on the securities.

The second analytical approach deals with a large number of simulated collateral performance scenarios. After setting base case assumptions for any given collateral pool, rating agency analysts would estimate statistical distributions for each

Exhibit 10.8 Simplified ABS Debt Sizing

Rating Category	Base Case Loss Multiple	Cumulative Loss %	Annual Excess Interest	Cumulative Excess Interest	ABS Sizes
AAA	5.50x	16.5%	3.2%	6.3%	89.8%
AA	4.50x	13.5%	3.2%	6.3%	3.0%
A	3.50x	10.5%	3.2%	6.3%	3.0%
BBB	2.50x	7.5%	3.2%	6.3%	3.0%
Base Case	1.00x	3.0%	3.2%	6.3%	

variable. Using distribution parameters as inputs, rating agency models would produce thousands of performance scenarios and measure bond performance in each. Bond ratings are derived by comparing average bond performance with a benchmark performance set for a particular rating category.

Whether bond sizes are determined based on a small number of well-defined scenarios with a goal of achieving full timely payment of interest and principal, or based on a large number of simulated collateral scenarios with a targeted average performance for each security, the key challenge from a rating agency perspective remains in identifying input parameters for stress testing for different rating categories. The agencies run internal processes that require extensive collateral research followed by committee approvals of stress scenarios and collateral assumptions. It is not uncommon for different rating agencies to come out with dissimilar views on a particular deal, resulting in different credit ratings for the same bond.

Recent Events

Banks typically have large deposit bases and low cost of funds. However, they also prefer to lend to high-credit-quality borrowers. In contrast, much of the lending to medium- to lower-credit-quality borrowers is done by finance companies with smaller balance sheets. The ABS market allows these lenders to originate, securitize, and use the proceeds to fund new lending. The development of the "originate and sell" model, rather than the "originate and hold" model, has helped spur the growth of credit available to consumers and firms alike, as well as lowered the cost of that credit. Issuers also don't have to raise new debt, or wait for existing receivables to pay down if they want to grow their business. From the mid-1990s to 2007, this phenomenon led to the emergence of lenders that relied almost exclusively on securitization for funding their lending businesses. These lenders had very limited balance sheets of their own. Their loan origination policies and pricing were driven by ABS investor and rating agency requirements. By early 2007, investors had become concerned with exposure embedded in certain types of real estate–related securitizations. With investor appetite waning, many independent finance companies lost their primary funding source and were forced to shut down in the period from 2007 to 2009, leaving a significant segment of the population without access to borrowing and without ability to refinance existing loans. This led to increased consumer defaults, which in turn led to actual and expected deterioration in ABS collateral pools, leading to further loss of investor appetite and creating a vicious circle. Plunging bond prices crippled the balance sheets of even large financial institutions. This led to further widespread credit contraction that affected business confidence and undermined employment.

In early 2007, ABS issuance was running at a strong $70 billion to $80 billion per month. Approximately 65 to 75 percent of that total was subprime and ABS CDOs. As the residential credit crisis started to appear, investor appetite for subprime assets quickly evaporated and issuance rapidly declined. By August 2007, total subprime and ABS CDO issuance had fallen to less than $10 billion, and by the fall of that year it had fallen virtually to zero. By early 2008, ABS issuance had shrunk to just $10 billion to $15 billion a month and consumer ABS (autos, credit cards, and student loans) made up about 95 percent of the total.

In order to revive consumer lending, which had become increasingly dependent on ABS funding over the years, the Federal Reserve Bank and the U.S. Treasury introduced the Term Asset-Backed Lending Facility (TALF) in early 2009 with an aim to restart the new-issue ABS market. The TALF program allowed investors to borrow from the Federal Reserve against newly issued ABS debt, and the leverage provided significant returns to the investor, creating huge incentives for hedge funds and other nontraditional ABS investors to invest in new issues. Although the TALF program got off to a slow start due to initial confusion over the terms of the program, investors gradually got more comfortable, and by mid-2009 new issuance in the U.S. ABS markets had increased back to $10 billion to $15 billion a month, largely driven by auto loan and credit card securitizations.

By the end of 2009, the recovery in the ABS markets was fully underway with spreads on traditional ABS issuances (auto loans and credit cards) having come in dramatically tighter than the highs seen at the peak of the credit crisis, although still wider than pre-credit-crisis levels.

Fundamental collateral credit concerns were at the core of the investor panic in 2008. However, aside from credit considerations, there are other potential issues that affect ABS valuations, bond performance, and issuer risks.

Credit versus Liquidity: The Student Loan Example

The Federal Family Education Loan Program (FFELP) student loan ABS provides an excellent example of the importance of liquidity in credit spreads. Both principal and accrued interest (from 95 percent to 100 percent, depending on the year of origination) on FFELP student loans are guaranteed by the U.S. government. In fact, unlike agency debentures, the guarantee is explicit, not implied. One might have thought FFELP student loan ABS would benefit from the general flight to quality that took place during the credit crisis. In fact, the opposite occurred as spreads on FFELP student loan ABS widened to unprecedented levels in 2008. Investors chose to flee into liquid U.S. Treasury securities, seeing ABS spreads as an insufficient premium for lower liquidity.

Breaching Triggers

Triggers could cut off cash flow to subordinate bondholders and the residual holder. Triggers are a credit enhancement mechanism and are often used to redirect cash flow away from subordinate tranches to senior tranches in the event that collateral performance is worse than expected. Breaching a collateral trigger can have two effects on subordinate bondholders. The first is an extension of the bond's weighted average life. If principal payments on a subordinate bond are redirected to pay down the senior classes, the bond will extend. Investors who thought they had purchased a bond with a certain duration will find themselves holding a bond with a potentially much longer duration. The extension may also cause the loss profile of the bond to increase. For example, if a bond is paying pro rata with a senior bond and a trigger is breached that causes the waterfall to switch to sequential, then principal payments will cease, exposing the bondholders to a greater potential write-down.

Triggers can also be problematic for the issuer. Many issuers retain the residual pieces to their securitizations. To the extent that they are relying on ABS residual cash flows to provide working capital to the company or to originate new loans, a breach of a trigger that cuts off residual cash flows could lead to liquidity problems. This problem becomes even more acute if the issuer's transactions are cross-collateralized. When trusts are cross-collateralized, a breach of a trigger in one trust may cause all cross-collateralized trusts to redirect cash flows. Cross-collateralization typically leads to lower subordination levels, lowering the issuer's cost of capital, but doing so at the expense of increased exposure to deteriorating collateral.

Duration Mismatch

Another issue that has emerged is funding long-term assets with short-term liabilities. The turmoil in the auction-rate securities market is a good example of this. Many student loan originators issued auction-rate securities tranches in some of their ABS trusts. The use of auction-rate securities in student loan ABS was most common among municipal agency issuers, although most major issuers, including the Student Loan Marketing Association (SLMA, Sallie Mae), the National Education Loan Network (Nelnet), and First Marblehead, all issued auction-rate securities in certain deals. Auction-rate notes are often issued in 7-day, 14-day, and 28-day periods. At the end of each period, a Dutch auction is held to determine the rate for the next period. If new investors cannot be found, then the auction is said to have failed and existing note holders retain their securities, usually with a step-up in the coupon. In March 2008, as the credit crisis froze much of the capital markets, auctions failed at record levels, leaving many auction-rate security holders stuck at their maximum rates with what they assumed were short-dated securities. Unless issuers choose to refinance these securities (at higher costs), many auction-rate investors will be holding these securities for a substantial period of time. Given the spreads these securities traded at, it is clear that investors and issuers had not properly priced the option component of these securities.

■ ■ ■

Although the ABS markets have revived again, there are some fundamental changes that have taken place as fallout from the credit crisis and the resulting buyer's market:

- Rating agencies, which were seen as primary contributors to the subprime fallout due to their flawed methodologies for providing AAA ratings to highly leveraged subprime ABS and CDO offerings, have become more conservative in their ratings process and have raised the requirements for issuers to obtain the highest ratings on their ABS issuances.
- Investors are now demanding more information disclosure on underlying assets from ABS issuers and are spending more time performing their own credit analysis with lesser reliance on credit ratings obtained by the issuers. More frequently, for nontraditional assets, transactions are being initiated on the basis of reverse inquiries from investors, or being executed as private placements with a small group of investors who negotiate not only the terms at which they would buy the debt, but also some of the key structural features they would require in the transaction.

- The absence of monoline insurers from the ABS markets has made it more expensive for many issuers to fund their assets through securitization, as the bonds now have to be rated based on actual credit enhancement in the transaction; this holds true especially for securitizations backed by operating assets such as rental car/truck fleets, aircraft and container leases, and restaurant franchise royalties, among others, which historically have been structured and sold largely with external credit enhancement provided by the monoline insurers.
- Regulators continue to work on a wide range of new and revised rules, including capital adequacy rules, which may significantly affect attractiveness of securitization in the future.
- It remains to be seen if these changes are a temporary response due to the supply/demand imbalance in the credit markets, and if the ways of the market will return to the pre–credit crisis days as regulations settle down, deleveraging stops, and as the demand for credit and the risk appetite increase.

NOTE

1. Data provided by CNBC and Thomson Reuters.

ABOUT THE AUTHOR

Konstantin Braun is a managing partner at Smart Energy Capital, a finance and investment company focused on the North American solar photovoltaic industry. He has 15 years of structured finance and financial engineering experience; he structured, rated, and marketed over $100 billion of transactions, including securitizations for Citibank, Sallie Mae, Ford, Public Service Electric and Gas (PSE&G), Dunkin' Donuts, International Lease Finance Corporation (ILFC), Hertz, Crown Castle, and many others. Formerly a managing director at Lehman Brothers, most recently head of ABS/MBS structuring, he provided debt structuring expertise in connection with the origination and execution of asset-backed securities collateralized by a wide range of asset types; in addition, he provided loan pricing and funding for Lehman's proprietary, nonmortgage consumer finance origination and securitization platforms. Konstantin holds an MA in international economics from Yale University and a BS in economics/mathematics from Moscow University.

CHAPTER 11

Structured Products

TIMOTHY A. DAY
Guggenheim Securities, LLC

INTRODUCTION

The term *structured products* is sometimes used to connote anything new and innovative in the financial markets. However, more narrowly, structured products are defined as products that are based on an underlying security (e.g., single securities or indexes such as stocks, baskets of stocks, commodities, debt issuances, or foreign currencies). Indeed, after a review of the ways in which the term has been used in the vernacular, one is tempted to loosen the definition even further: a structured product is *anything that varies in any meaningful way away from some original underlying instrument*. Now, this is purposely vague in order to highlight the fact that virtually anything and everything can be described as a structured product. Therefore, we begin with a conceptual discussion of structured products, including various examples of what are and what are not considered structured products and why or why not this is the case.

This chapter is intended to provide an overview of structured products and their applications with a specific focus on equities and credit. It is in the interest of brevity that we do not include summary sections on commodities or interest rate and forex structured products. Those are covered elsewhere in this book.

A Note on Derivatives

The growth in structured products occurred as an extension of the growth in the derivatives market as a whole; in fact, separating the one from the other today is impossible. The growth of both has been extraordinary. While there has been no shortage of negative press—for example, Enron's bankruptcy in 2001 and the credit crisis that began in 2007—the benefits outweigh the risks.

An early driver of the derivatives markets was the need to hedge pricing risk. An illustration is the farmer who seeks to immunize himself from mark-to-market volatility in order, say, to ensure the sale price of a crop. It was not much of a stretch to see the introduction of contracts to enable delivery to occur on behalf of another party, and the subsequent formations of exchanges and such, to promote the efficient clearing of these contracts.

Soon, there were contracts not only on corn and wheat, but also on cotton, coffee, cacao, and other commodities. Moreover, contracts spread to almost anything that could have a deliverable. This extended beyond commodities and into monetary contracts, Eurobonds, and so forth.

Now a market participant could not only manage price exposure, but could also engage in a secondary exposure to an asset class without actually engaging in the risk of holding the underlying asset. This is generally referred to as taking synthetic or derivative exposure.

The advent of derivative exposure has both widened ports of access to individual asset classes and increased the number of asset classes that are available. In short, derivatives increased liquidity in the underlying asset classes and, thereby, increased the number of market participants.

We proceed with a summary of the history of structured products and then describe the structured products' life cycles, including roles of the various participants, and the role structured products play in systemic risk distribution.

A HISTORY

Structured products have existed in Europe for four decades and were created in response to investor demand for achieving investors' risk-return objectives (for example, principal protection) or an issuer's risk distribution needs. Only more recently have structured products become popular as investment vehicles in the United States and Asia.

Once upon a time, the financial product lexicon consisted of a well-defined universe of products divided into segments with which we are still familiar today: equity, fixed income, foreign exchange, interest rates, and commodities, among others. However, with the advent of the age of the financial engineer, a veritable bloom of structured products arose in the financial seas. It was the financial engineer who noted that investors desired risk-return characteristics to fit a variety of investment needs or to take specific views on the performance of any of a wide variety of asset classes. In such a way, a traditional security could be combined with a derivative in order to meet specific investor demand.

As new variants on the product increased (and investment bankers began to realize fees on the creation of these products) so too did the breadth of structured products. Structured products began to move from the convertible bond space until each product area had its very own enclave of structured products. Today, structured products include a host of instruments.

As mentioned in the preceding, the building blocks for many structured products consist of a note and a derivative component. The note component may consist of either the individual security (or swap in the case of a synthetic transaction) or index of securities (or swaps). The derivative component may consist of any of a variety of various options, swaps, or, less frequently, futures, forwards, and the like. In combination, these, and the legal framework of the vehicle used for purposes of the execution of a specific trade, comprise the transaction structure.

The motivations of the various parties are key to the formulation of the structure. Each party seeks to achieve the most favorable terms possible, as constrained by the wants and needs of the other parties, especially pertaining to the economic feasibility of the overall transaction. It is this latter element that the banker for the transaction is most concerned with, and, under the banker's purview, an orchestration is performed that consists of various balancing acts to achieve the twin aims of profitability and client satisfaction.

EQUITIES

If we must pick the product that symbolizes the birth of the structured product, then we might as well start with the convertible bond. This instrument represents a departure from the cozy and staid condition that the financial products lexicon had found itself in. In a convertible bond, an investor is willing to accept a lower rate of interest in exchange for a higher possible return if the equity value increases. As this already represented a note with an embedded option to convert to equity, it was a simple extension for investment bankers to bundle in other features, such as principal protection or limited conversion rights.

With respect to equities, the note component can be considered to be either a stock or an index (i.e., a portfolio of stocks). There are a variety of regulatory issues that one must consider when dealing with stocks and indexes. These include various corporate and securities law issues—dilution, dividend, borrowing, and exchange issues—and the role of constituent documents.

Corporate and securities laws regulate the issuance and subsequent trading of individual stocks and securities. Naturally, these regimes differ according to geographic and national boundaries, as well as the specific type of stock or security under consideration. The regulatory constraints pursuant to applicable corporate and securities laws are not only important for the individual security, but come into play with the equity derivative as well. Therefore, when considering a structured product, one must consider the ways in which these laws might interact with the provisions of the law governing the entity responsible for issuing the structured note, as well as the securities laws that may be relevant to the issuance of the structured note.

Dilution is a particularly interesting issue with respect to the interplay among stock, derivative, and structured notes. Dilution occurs when the firm issues more stock, or a derivative may directly be responsible for dilution when the firm issues call options (e.g., a convertible bond issuance). Derivatives that reference the stock will be affected by this through the change in the stock price.

The dividend is a particularly vexing issue in the valuation of any equity derivative and, hence, any structured note that contains an equity derivative component. A dividend, by design, has an unknown timing and payoff profile, not to mention raising accounting and tax treatment issues.

Borrowing stock is mainly required when one undertakes a short-selling strategy. One's ability to borrow may be influenced by the overall liquidity in the market.

Exchange trading considerations must also be taken into account. The exchange rules will determine variously how a stock may or may not be traded, as well as influence the trading costs associated with specific transactions.

Last, we must consider the firm's constituent documents that govern the actions that may be undertaken with respect to a firm's stock. This will clearly impact the equity derivative as well as those that reference the stock directly. One must consider the impact of this on the structured note.

Strategies that relate to indexes are prone to all of these issues as well as various others. Indexes are constructed to resemble either existing indexes—for example, the Standard & Poor's (S&P) 500 index or the Dow Jones Industrial Average (DJIA)—and structured notes on these allow the investor to synthetically replicate exposure to the underlying index.

Various products have been created to simulate exposure to indexes such as the S&P 500 or the DJIA. This evolution began when exchange-traded funds (ETFs) were created in 1993 on the back of the birth of program trading. Structured notes referencing indexes have substantially impacted trading and liquidity in the underlying equity markets and generally are seen to have enhanced the price discovery mechanism. To be fair, the creation of indexes and the ease of trading in and out of these instruments has also led to a large amount of technical trading, which may or may not be considered a useful element in price discovery. This point is geared toward the difference between valuation and price and is the subject of a later section within this chapter.

Index creation has allowed for a far greater degree of short selling, as well as increased flexibility with respect to the ability to leverage various positions, track intraday price movements, and assist in trading strategies. These strategies may be directional or volatility based, or may be strictly of an arbitrage nature. Index strategies may also be layered onto other positions either as a partial hedge or to create new complex positions.

The purposes behind equity derivatives strategies are varied but may be generally classified along three dimensions: (1) asset allocation, (2) transaction cost management, and (3) return enhancement.

Asset allocation refers to an investment strategy that involves a manager's prediction for a market or market segment as opposed to more traditional single-stock-picking strategies. This technique has gained favor in tandem with the growth in the depth and breadth of equity derivatives and structured equity product offerings. Asset allocation allows for specific trades to be structured that, for example, make a play on the relative value of a specific stock or a basket of stocks.

Transaction costs come increasingly into play as more stocks are considered for a specific trading strategy. Thanks to various scale economies, one can reduce costs through employing index strategies.

Index strategies are also important, in that they allow the investor to take part in fractional trades; that is, the amount of an investment in a specific index may result in owning only a fraction of some shares. This partially removes an important barrier to entry: the individual stock price. This is an added benefit for liquidity in those underlying stocks, as the market maker can then act as an intermediary for small investors who may wish to partake in high-priced stocks. This further enhances liquidity in the underlying stock as well.

Returns are also more easily enhanced through the employment of index strategies. Bankers are more apt to provide leverage on a basket of securities than they are on a specific security. Additionally, management of exchange rate risk and other risks inherent in direct foreign investment may be incorporated into a product, thereby allowing for cross-border diversification strategies divorced from direct foreign exchange rate considerations.

Structured equity is also integral to equity capital management (i.e., the firm's ability to manage the capital structure). The company may do this on a variety of levels, including the management of equity price risk, in order to lower the cost of capital, manage equity positions, or manage equity risk as it pertains to mergers and acquisitions (M&A) transactions.

Since structured equity products allow for access to hard-to-access securities and separation of specific risk components (e.g., rate risk) from the market component, it should come as no surprise that structured equity is integral to many alpha-generation strategies. These are strategies that seek to maximize return to investors through generation of returns not explained by the market factor. As we will find in the following sections on other asset classes, this is a common theme in structured products and continues to serve as a prime driver for new product creation.

CREDIT

The fixed-income arena has been one of the strongest engines of growth in structured products for the past decade as a result of the burgeoning credit derivatives market. The credit derivatives market is primarily composed of total return swaps and credit default swaps. From these, in turn, a variety of products are structured to employ various strategies on—for example, the forward curve of credit spreads or the probability of various default/recovery events on credit baskets.

Total return swaps replicate the performance of a loan or bond whereby the investor takes on all the risk of the underlying assets. The bank pays all the payments (whether interest or principal) on the underlying asset while the investor makes a payment (essentially the funding cost). The investor additionally takes on all mark-to-market (MTM) risk associated with the underlying through a series of periodic payments over the life of the transaction. The bank pays the investor the MTM difference to the extent the value of the bond rises, and the investor pays the bank to the extent the value of the bond falls.

The advantages of this structure are similar to those outlined in the equity section and include the capacity to short sell, funding cost advantages, and leverage capability.

However, a total return swap differs in that it is an off-balance-sheet transaction. This, combined with the potential funding cost advantages, allows entities with lower credit ratings to gain access to the credit market without having to build out the infrastructure necessary for trading and settlement of credit securities.

Due to the lack of direct alignment of interests between the underlying borrower and the end investor, certain issues may arise surrounding confidentiality and dispute resolution in the event of default (especially in the case of loans). This is one of the many documentation issues faced when investing in these products and should be scrutinized carefully.

Credit default swaps divorce specific bonds from the process altogether in an attempt to arrive at a price for the underlying credit risk associated with debt issued at a specific point in a company's capital structure.[1] The protection buyer pays a spread (premium) to the seller, who is obligated to make payments upon the event of default in an amount equal to the difference between the nominal amount and the recovery amount on, generally, the cheapest-to-deliver security in the relevant point of the capital structure.

It should be clear from the preceding that credit derivatives are a highly documentation-intensive enterprise. The International Swaps and Derivatives Association (ISDA) has standardized the documentation for these transactions. The standard is, of course, always evolving, but it is of note that the industry has weathered several defaults (e.g., Enron, WorldCom, etc.) without severe incident. This is in large part due to the counterparties involved—that is, large qualified institutional buyer (QIB) type institutions—and may vary as less sophisticated investors venture into the territory. The main elements of concern are settlement issues that constitute an event of default.

Events of default (EODs) determine under what conditions the protection seller is to pay the protection buyer. The main EODs are bankruptcy, failure to pay, obligation acceleration, repudiation or debt moratorium, and restructuring. Other EODs can be specified in the contract and may be appropriate based on the nature of the underlying referenced entity, but this can result in a substantial liquidity premium. The discussion of each of these is beyond the scope of this chapter. It is interesting to note that restructuring, in particular, is geographically variant, with specific modifications put in place to better serve the terms of European entities.

Settlement issues are of paramount importance in credit derivative transactions whether total return swaps or credit default swaps. Settlement may be specified as either cash or physical and varies from agreement to agreement. In cash settlement, valuation dates are specified to determine the price of the bond, whereas in physical settlement the actual bond is delivered. The advantage of the cash settlement process is that one need not necessarily have the bond itself in hand to conduct the required auction pursuant to the valuation process. In such ways the credit markets are made more accessible to investors.

Parallel to the equity market, there are a variety of indexes in the credit derivative universe that are used for the same purpose of enhancing liquidity in the underlying asset and enabling an overall reduction in transaction costs. There are a multitude of other specifications regarding the reference obligation, deliverable obligation, and delivery process, which are beyond the scope of this chapter.

The credit derivatives market has developed rapidly to include a number of products such as credit default swap options and various fixed recovery credit default swaps.

Credit default swap options allow the buyer of protection to enter into a credit default swap at a specific date at a specified strike price. This may allow investors to protect themselves against a corporate default only to the extent that the default risk had exceeded a certain amount by a certain date—an arrangement we might easily imagine would save one's job under certain circumstances and certainly would allow for the elimination of some worry that might otherwise remain latent.

Fixed recovery default swaps eliminate the recovery risk. These swaps are generally less liquid and therefore demand a premium that would seem to be out of line with the proper valuation of such a security. Therefore, the question arises: "Why would one enter into such a trade?" The answer has to do with the regulatory capital treatment of such debt. Credit default swaps normally are triggered when there is a default on any debt of the referenced entity, but the deliverable is generally senior, and this debt is often treated as a 20 percent risk-weighted asset. Therefore, there is the possibility to obtain exposure to subordinated debt at a capital charge less than that of purchasing the subordinated debt separately.

The credit derivatives market also includes several standardized indexes that are divided into investment-grade corporate debt, high-yield corporate debt, loans, and several subsets thereof. These indexes serve a similar purpose to that of equity indexes in terms of providing liquidity and enhancing price transparency.

There are a variety of products that result from the index technology. All major investment banks and an increasing number of other parties utilize this technology to make structured bets on when assets default relative to various market segments or the likelihood of a specified amount of loss on a portfolio. These products are very similar in concept to collateralized debt obligations and afford a dizzying array of variants.

First-to-default swaps are swaps where the seller of protection provides default protection on the first asset to default among a basket of reference entities. Here, buyers of protection can pay substantially less than they would for protection on the assets individually while protecting themselves against the first entity to default among a pool of assets. This might be particularly useful when one is concerned, say, about a small number of corporations in a specific industry sector and one wants to partially hedge the risk associated with a default event in this sector. Credit default swap protection has also been increasingly employed to hedge the credit risk inherent to other derivative instruments (e.g., interest rate swaps). This usually is an attempt to hedge out the counterparty risk inherent to the payment of any number of legs of a particular set of derivatives. To consider any swap, forward, or option position, one must take into account that both the timing and the notional amount will vary at each point in time. To write protection on such swaps, one must consider the mark-to-market of the position at the time of the default on the credit-linked notes and collateralized debt obligations.

Credit-Linked Notes and Collateralized Debt Obligations

It seems only natural at this point to discuss products that combine fixed-income securities with a derivative to enable an investor to replicate exposure to a security without the purchase of the actual securities. A credit-linked note is, essentially, functionally similar to a funded credit default swap and may be written either on a single name, or on a basket, or a portfolio of names. Interest in credit-linked notes stems from both the seller and the buyer of risk.

While most corporate debt capital is raised by debt issuance in the capital markets, lending by banks and other financial institutions remains a vital component of financial intermediation. These banks and other financial institutions, then, are fundamentally long credit risk. As credit derivatives technologies have expanded, the ability of banks (and other institutions) to measure and evaluate their credit risk on a portfolio basis has increased. Risk managers, duly noting this, have encouraged greater credit-risk portfolio management activities, such as the purchase of credit protection vis-à-vis credit-linked notes.

Meanwhile, investors are driven to purchase these notes to diversify their holdings and to put cash to work. However, they may have various regulatory or administrative issues:

- In terms of diversification, the credit-linked note market has been a boon to investors. As part of the issued bond market, corporate risk represents only a fraction of the issuance when compared to government/sovereign debt issuance.
- Investors often need to put cash to work in order to satisfy various portfolio yield targets.
- Regulations may prohibit various parties from entering into credit derivatives transactions.
- Administrative issues exist with the documentation, recording, valuation, and tax and accounting issues associated with credit derivatives.

The nature of the protection seller is the main limiting factor in the advancement of the credit derivatives market. The bank's main concern as a net issuer and holder of credit risk is that sellers of protection have certain characteristics in order to allow the bank to obtain regulatory capital relief and to increase the quality of their credit exposure to outside counterparties. This means, in practice, that not only does the seller generally need to have a credit quality higher than that of the referenced entity, but that the seller must be a bank or sovereign institution. To top it off, a bank's credit department will want to have assurances that there is a low default correlation between the seller and the reference entity.

Investor demand for access to the credit market has also been a factor in the advancement of credit-linked note technology. The credit market outside the credit-linked note market has been difficult for investors to access as a result of regulatory concerns. Examples of these regulatory concerns include determining whether investments are even allowed in the product, and dealing with the various complexities in obtaining approval to invest in these securities directly. Additionally, settlement difficulties and relatively high transaction costs have encumbered the expansion in direct corporate investment. Over the past several decades, as governments reduced their debt, investors were left with more and more free cash. Given the existence of various diversification requirements, investor demand for products that would allow access to credit markets increased.

This combination of regulatory and transactional difficulty and free cash translated into a ripe market for product development and promulgated the credit-linked note market. Bankers were able to work with existing documentation standards and utilize their balance sheets (e.g., through medium-term note programs or specially set up special purpose vehicles in the Caymans, Dutch Antilles, or other tax-advantaged jurisdictions). Advantages of setting up notes through such programs include the ability to reduce the legal complexities associated with direct investment in the underlying corporate debt and the flexibility to tailor the specific terms to the investor (as these often differed from the original issuer-driven terms).

The possibilities for tailoring debt issuance to investor needs have led to immense growth in credit-linked notes:

- The currency of the offered note may differ from that of the referenced security.
- Minimum denominations may vary. This allows investors to more easily allocate credit risk across any number of funds.
- The specified interest rate may be changed to accommodate specific investor needs whether on an absolute basis or from fixed to floating.
- Various degrees of principal protection can be realized. The note seller (protection buyer) accomplishes the issuance by combining a zero coupon bond of similar maturity (usually from the government market) with the corporate debt. The purchaser (seller of protection) does not see the specific mechanics of this, instead only seeing the resultant terms.
- Ease of investing in previously unavailable assets (foreign bonds).

Such notes may be constructed not only to replicate credit derivatives but also to replicate total return swaps or first to default notes. Another interesting application that we have not yet addressed is repackaging.

In the repackaging of an asset, the bank can achieve a true sale of an existing security into a special purpose vehicle, and then the cash flows and credit risk are recombined by entering into various credit derivatives transactions with the arranger (dealer).

Collateralized Debt Obligations

Collateralized debt obligation (CDO) is a generalized concept used to describe any form of credit-based securitization. The first types of assets that were securitized in such a manner were loans and bonds. Soon, as the advantages of these structures became clear to the sponsor banks, the banks began using them to securitize a variety of assets that were difficult for the bank on an economic level.

The first CDOs were therefore largely arranged by banks seeking to reduce their balance sheet exposures to any of a number of assets or derivatives that were often difficult to value. Additionally, the credit risk associated with the sponsor bank would also often be removed and replaced with various collateral assets. The bank could thereby benefit from the removal of credit risk from its balance sheet, and the investor could invest in specific risk divorced from the risk of the sponsor bank.

The transition from securitizing loans and bonds to pooling multitudinous assets was accomplished through the employment of the credit-linked note structure as described in the preceding section. This allowed derivatives and other assets that were difficult to securitize directly to be referenced in a CDO portfolio.

The CDO technology benefited investors greatly by allowing them not only to specify the type of asset classes in which they would like to invest, thus enabling the relative value plays and other asset allocation discussed previously, but also to specify the level of credit risk associated with those referenced asset classes. This was accomplished through the tranching of the risk.

The traditional cash flow CDO may best be thought of as a miniature bank. The CDO has both an asset component and a liability component. On the asset side, the CDO invests in any of a wide array of assets and, generally, enters into various derivative agreements to hedge out market, currency, and other risks in order to isolate the credit risk component. The CDO may then be analyzed as a company with specific asset cash flows.

In order to fund the purchase of the assets, as well as the required derivatives, the CDO then issues liabilities to investors. These liabilities are issued in credit risk slices (or tranches), the legal characterization of which ranges from equity and preference shares (at the highest risk layer) to investment-grade and high-yield debt.

While the needs of the sponsor banks were the primary motivating force behind the first CDOs to be issued, investor demand quickly increased in importance. This fundamental shift from balance sheet to arbitrage transactions changed the role of the sponsor bank from one of risk provider to that of structuring agent.

Structuring CDOs requires the matching of investor demands with the bank's ability to source risk at levels such that the associated parties to a transaction might be paid and investors left with suitable cash flow so as to warrant the investment. The main parties to a transaction range from investors, lawyers, rating agencies, and bankers to auditors and trustees.

Synthetic CDOs utilize the same technology as the CDO just described. However, instead of purchasing entire portfolios of specific assets, the CDO may purchase only a portion of the credit risk associated with a portfolio. This vastly reduces the number of securities that are required to be sold, greatly easing the ability to engage in credit risk management. Synthetic CDOs, however, do not achieve balance sheet reduction as there is no transfer of assets. They do substantially reduce funding costs associated with traditional CDOs as they do not require funding for a large portion of the transaction. This latter point, coupled with the significant reduction in required securities' placement, significantly enhances the viability of large portfolio management techniques from the sponsor bank's perspective.

From the investor perspective, the same versatility of design associated with credit-linked notes is available. For example, one may remove prepayment risk, foreign exchange risk, the implementation of static run-off structures, and leveraged returns on asset classes. Leveraging is an especially important feature, in that investors are able to enhance returns on high-grade assets or difficult-to-access asset classes (e.g., life insurance-based products).

There are a number of features that are employed in CDO technology to divert cash flows to protect senior note holders and align the interests of a manager of the asset pool (if one exists) with that of the end investor(s).

Collateralized debt obligations have served an important function as cleanup tools in times of crisis. They help achieve a transfer or reduction of risk in order to free up a business to proceed in new business ventures. As such, they may be deemed a catalyst for change.

Pricing transparency is accomplished in this space through the construction of various tranches of risk that trade and allow investors to hedge risk on a correlation basis. Essentially each tranche represents a layer of risk. As there are fairly standardized markets in various tranches for each of the indexes, these allow the investor to individually hedge portfolio exposures at specific debt levels.

Securitizations and Structured Finance Structures

Securitizations predate CDOs in occurrence but may likewise be thought of as a subset of CDO technology. Securitizations exist to finance pools of certain assets and are specialized to the particular characteristics of their respectively referenced asset class that include but certainly are not limited to automobiles, credit cards, residential mortgages, commercial mortgages, student loans, and small business loans.

There are a number of specialty structures that have been developed as a result of the boom in CDO and securitization technologies. Of late, acronyms such as SIV (structured investment vehicle) and CDPC (credit derivative products company) have come to join the vernacular along with terms such as the now ubiquitous CDO, asset-backed security (ABS), residential mortgage-backed security (RMBS), and commercial mortgage-backed security (CMBS). SIVs and CDPCs, however, are two important classes of structured finance operating companies (SFOCs), which utilize specified sets of operating principles that are reviewed by the rating agencies in order to obtain specific ratings.

Risk Assessment

As we have seen, the tools of the financial engineer encompass almost any financial product. The objectives of the issuer and the investor work in concert to motivate an idea in the mind of the structurer, who will then employ these tools. However, the structure cannot be complete without some glue. That glue is a combination of the legal and corporate structure that is required to achieve the economic purpose of the transaction.

The corporate structure used is determined not only by the structure's purpose, but also by the legal, accounting, regulatory, and ratings requirements. These structures can range from characterizations of derivatives as notes, as we saw in the case of the credit-linked note, to specific structures designed under operating guidelines, as in the case of SFOCs.

The risks that therefore exist in a specific structure will include the risks of the underlying notes and derivatives, as well as those of the corporate structure. Many of the most important and under-analyzed risks relate to the interaction of termination provisions in the underlying derivatives and, at the corporate level, the event of default (EOD) provisions and subsequent termination or liquidation provisions.

Events of default are defined in the indenture to the transaction, this being a document between the trustee and the securities' issuer. The EODs generally include the following standard provisions:

- Bankruptcy
- Obligation acceleration
- Obligation default
- Failure to pay
- Repudiation/moratorium
- Restructuring

There may be other provisions that require some interpretation. For example, starting in approximately 2005, ABS CDO indentures began to include EODs that were triggered based on various structural triggers, some of whose measurements were, from time to time, calculated for purposes of determining an EOD alone differently than otherwise in the transaction documentation. This meant that in certain cases a transaction would be in EOD despite the fact that no tests, as described in the usual marketing materials, were breached.

There are, however, even more concerns. As a result of the often substantial documentation in these transactions, there is the possibility for differing interpretations of the same concept and even outright contradiction between various areas of documentation. Further, the rules surrounding each party's obligations under various circumstances may be vague or may not have been well communicated by the presented marketing materials (for example, the rules surrounding early redemption or liquidation). This can lead to difficulties in pricing and substantial legal disagreements between parties.

In addition to the aforementioned risks, one must take into account the interaction of the various products employed in the construction of the structure, as well as various moral hazard issues that can arise with multiple parties to a transaction.

These include the alignment of all parties' interests—for example, the alignment of a manager's incentives to the protection of the debt holders in a CDO or the obligation of the trustee to conduct auctions that protect the note holders' interests in a liquidation scenario.

Valuation and Hedging

An accurate assessment of the risks associated with a given security is essential to the risk management of that security, whether it be the monthly valuation, liquidity assessment, or hedge position. The assessment of risk should consider:

- A summary of all parties to a transaction.
- A breakdown of the responsibilities of each party.
- The risk drivers to the transaction.
- Structural features of the transaction.
- Tax and regulatory considerations.

The list of transaction parties is imperative to ensure that one establishes the relevant entity responsibilities. Without such a list, it is rather easy to overlook particulars that may well lead to a different view of the probability of a specific action occurring. Consider the liquidation of a special purpose entity. Here, we would need a careful construction of the rights and responsibilities of the various note holders, trustees, swap counterparties, rating agencies, and so on. A senior note holder oftentimes will have voting rights with respect to the liquidation of the transaction, but there may be other provisions that determine the extent of these rights (e.g., the consent of a swap counterparty may be required).

The risk drivers of the transaction determine the instruments used in the hedging of the transaction. Specifically, all the cash flows of a transaction must be determined in order to understand the risks of these drivers. Examples of these include:

- Which asset classes are represented?
- Are rates fixed or floating?
- Are rates linked to an index?
- What are the day-count conventions used?
- Are there funding components to the transaction?

We alluded to the structural features of the transaction previously in a brief example concerning liquidation. However, there are a number of structural features that impact the direction of cash flows to a transaction as well. As a result of this complication in cash flow, with each addition to the structure it becomes more difficult to predict cash flows under each and every scenario. More importantly, it is also difficult to determine the likelihood of each of these scenarios. Even to the extent that one becomes comfortable with the level of certainty, it is clear that due to this variability there would be costs imposed on any hedging strategy for a specific transaction.

CONCLUSION

The past several decades have seen a surge in the number and variety of structured products created to capitalize on the increased appetite for new asset classes or to allow participation in heretofore difficult-to-access asset classes. The array of products that now exist range from variations on traditional stocks to special purpose entities whose structures are motivated by desires to arbitrage market inefficiencies and generally distribute asset classes to a broader array of investors. As has been seen throughout the unfolding of the credit crisis of 2007–2010, it is now clearer than ever that an accurate assessment of risk is necessary. The risks in a given product may or may not be obvious. The only way in which one reduces the risk of omission is to conduct a thorough analysis of the various components of a given product, from the parties involved to the underlying assets referenced by the product. As investors continue to focus on novel ways to outpace the competition, it is likely that risk management requirements for structured products will increase. This may in the short run decrease product innovation. However, as the desire to improve returns continues unabated, we will no doubt see in the future new innovations in the structured product space to give those who can better assess risk the ability to create alpha-generating returns.

NOTE

1. By specific point in the company's capital structure, we are referring to the debt issue's standing in terms of the issuer's credit hierarchy, that is secured bank loans, senior bonds, subordinate bonds, and so on.

ABOUT THE AUTHOR

Timothy A. Day is director of the Financial Securitizations Group at Guggenheim Securities, LLC. From 2001 to 2007, he worked at UBS Securities LLC, where he focused on corporate synthetic transactions. Prior to that, he worked in CLO/CDO origination at J.P. Morgan Securities LLC. In addition, he was previously employed by Lexam Capital LLC and Capital Market Risk Advisors, Inc. Mr. Day graduated from the University of Chicago, where he specialized in economics and mathematics.

CHAPTER 12

Thoughts on Retooling Risk Management

TANYA BEDER AND SPENCER JONES
SBCC Group Inc.

INTRODUCTION

Risk Management is one of the largest academic and practitioner fields within financial engineering. Broad and specialty roles—and often complete departments that focus on risk—exist in tens of thousands of financial and non-financial firms around the world. Areas of practice and, indeed, whole firms have been established to service the risk management community. These include consultants, specialty advisors in accounting firms and law firms, software providers, data vendors, broad stream and specialty media firms, and educational organizations from universities to executive education and conference providers. Risk management draws on core theoretical principles in pure and applied mathematics, finance, economics, accounting, law, psychology, behavioral finance, and the physical sciences, among others. Not only has risk management established itself as a large, permanent field, but also it often takes center stage during times of crisis.

Analysis and discussion of how risk management practices may have contributed to the financial crisis are inevitable. Why were so many firms and customers allowed to become so highly leveraged? How were some lending standards allowed to slip to enable subprime or other loans without proper documentation? How did some banks and broker dealers, and the financial services industry as a whole, become so exposed to single risk factors such as house price inflation? Risk Management practices find themselves in the spotlight outside the financial world as well. Was the BP Gulf oil spill avoidable? Were risk calculations incorrect, or were risk management practices weakened? Were building codes ignored, or were there flawed assumptions or sign-offs that contributed to the loss of life in major earthquakes or mud slides in places such as Haiti and China? The postmortem is necessary both to assess the damage caused as well as to provide valuable lessons for the future.

Major risk incidents do not necessarily point to a major failure in risk measurement or risk management. It is natural for managers and executives to seek a culprit. Risk model flaws, policy weaknesses, mistaken assumptions, over-leveraging, greed, and myopia were named as culprits in other crises ranging from the savings and loan crisis to the 1987 stock market crash to the bursting of the dot.com bubble to the Asian currency crisis to the unwinding of LTCM. The need for geographically diversified backup and failover facilities plus detailed disaster plans were "unforeseen" culprits after the September 11th terrorist attack in the United States; this was despite the fact that such preparation is well-embedded in other countries in the Middle East and the United Kingdom. Regulators, supervisors, and others cited their own culprits, such as procyclicality of accounting treatment and risk management benchmarking.

On many occasions risk managers spoke up about issues, only to find that their warnings were not heeded. Examples have been featured in the mainstream media regarding whistleblowers at companies such as Lehman Brothers Holdings, Inc., Fannie Mae, HBOS, Wells Fargo, Citigroup, Bernard L. Madoff Investment Securities LLC, Washington Mutual, and Royal Bank of Scotland to name a few.[1] In some cases, whistle-blowing staff, and even those that resisted transactions they perceived to have excessive or insufficiently compensated risk, have found themselves shunned, silenced and—in several cases—forced to leave the firm (either by the firm or through their own moral standing). One high-profile case has been that of Matthew Lee, a Lehman Brothers employee who went to extensive lengths to report his concerns regarding "repo 105"; a practice in which the firm reported overnight security transactions as short-term loans, reducing the leverage appearing in financial statements.

In other circumstances, Boards of Directors and Supervisors during post-loss reviews were shocked to find that, upon review, common sense had been cast aside and that "stress" tests were far from stressful. It is common human nature to relax—perhaps for risk oversight to wane—during prolonged good times of growth and wealth. Alan Greenspan's "Irrational Exuberance" was aided and abetted by the relaxation of risk controls. For example, many banks are currently in the process of liquidating their private equity, residential mortgage, or commercial real estate portfolios at significant haircuts. These portfolios were built up on the basis of generating solid returns. The banks wanted to have their own large returns, in some cases believing that an equity stake in a deal or the equity tranche of a structured note might increase their chances of providing loan facilities or additional services to the firms. To enable this, some banks adjusted their risk appetite policy to allow them to increase level 3 (illiquid) asset holdings in light of the projected earnings potential.

In July 2007, Chuck Prince, CEO of Citigroup, famously spoke on the topic of subprime mortgages. "When the music stops, in terms of liquidity, things will be complicated. But as long as the music is playing, you've got to get up and dance. We're still dancing." This quote has unsurprisingly increased in profile over the intervening years as the concern forming the basis of the question proved to be prescient. Interestingly the second part of Mr. Prince's response to the *Financial Times* journalist has not gained a similar profile. "The depth of the pools of liquidity is so much larger than it used to be that a disruptive event now needs to be much more disruptive than it used to be. At some point, the disruptive event will be so significant that instead of liquidity filling in, the liquidity will go the other way. I don't think we're at that point."[2]

From this one quote and subsequent coverage we gain a valuable insight and reflection on how risk control and management operated at Citigroup at the time. It seems that someone may have raised concerns regarding the market, specifically liquidity; be that liquidity in the origination and distribution part of the market, or in the secondary market for trading holdings. Also, it seems the concerns may have reached business executives (or that the executives had concerns of their own), at least in some capacity. An important question is whether these concerns carried less weight than other drivers to do business (for example, a desire to create asset growth, market share, or earnings). The "Tone at the Top" of an organization is critical to answer such questions. The Citigroup story is not unique. As the post-mortem of the financial crisis continues, ever increasing numbers of risk managers and others who tried to express concerns are identified.

It is within this context of lessons learned from the credit crisis that we approach the questions of whether and how to retool risk management. Some lessons are new while others may only be described sadly as history repeating itself. It is apparent that even where things went right—for example, some identified and tried to speak up about the Madoff fraud, others challenged questionable accounting practices or spoke up to insist levels of risk in some mortgages and CDOs far outweighed the "additional" yield—things still wound up going horribly wrong. In such cases the risk managers were not caught off guard by these events; tragically, they could not get their own organizations or others to heed their warnings. Yet in other cases, risk models and frameworks succeeded in providing warning signals, some of which resulted in reformative action.

In this chapter we describe three actions that we see firms taking now to retool risk management:

1. Revisit the Tone at the Top of the Organization
2. Conduct a Board Level Review of VaR and Stress Testing
3. Add Warning Labels to Risk Reports

As we discuss, all three of these actions can provide valuable results for financial and non-financial firms alike.

REVISITING THE TONE AT THE TOP OF THE ORGANIZATION

In any organization there are few people who share the experience of the board of directors. The role of the board necessitates a wealth of experience. The board's position and existence offer the opportunity to set the tone at the top of the organization. The credit crisis has underscored the need to do so for many. In the board's discussion of the "tone at the top," common questions around the globe have been: Did our firm set overly aggressive targets? Did our firm allow overly lenient accounting treatment? Did our firm miss or ignore important warning signals? What could our firm have done to avoid losses? Did we ignore excessive profits or growth that preceded losses? How can the board work more effectively with the management and the risk management of the organization? Did the firm's compensation practices encourage or facilitate poor decision making on a risk-adjusted basis? What changes do we need to make going forward?

During the credit crisis, there have been ample cases where individuals have either chosen to back down, left a firm, or found themselves forced out (either literally, or by sudden reassignment). As these have come to light, boards have asked the additional question of whether this happened in their firm. Clear action plans for approaching these cases are required to ensure that any and all concerns reach the appropriate audience before being addressed, closed down (i.e., do not have merit), or escalated as set down by the tone at the top.

Important questions that drive the organization benefit from the board's role. For example, "once in a hundred year" events are observed to occur in the financial markets every year. Should a large financial firm operate with the expectation that each and every year it will need to have capital on hand to weather 100-year storms, or should the firm operate assuming such events are rare? Should the firm have a risk appetite statement? If the firm has someone in the role of chief risk officer or head of enterprise risk management, should this individual play only an oversight role or a larger strategic and advisory role? Should the risk appetite and risk procedures, practices, and controls be approved by the board?

The tone at the top is also critical to provide continuity where necessary in firms. Individual career paths have increased in their transiency between roles and firms. Given this context of shifting levels of experience, combined with the increased appointment of individuals with very specific specialist skills in the quantitative finance field, risk management functions can benefit greatly from the extensive perspective and experience of both senior management and the board. The tone at the top is also critical to guard against the human and organizational tendency to focus on the most recent issues at hand.

The Centre for the Study of Financial Innovation (CSFI)[3] produces a biennial report, titled "Banking Banana Skins," that focuses on the main risks facing financial Institutions. From a survey of bankers, regulators, and industry observers, the report compiles a list of the top risks facing the global banking industry. Over the past decade, outside of the stable years (2004–2007), it is not uncommon to see new risks come into the spotlight as the report's major focus. For example, business continuity became a high priority in 2002 in the wake of the September 11th terrorist attacks. More recently, liquidity (2008) and political interference (2010) became the highest priorities, with credit spreads also placing high on the list. None of these risks had placed among the top 30 risks in previous surveys. The behaviors in the "risk concerns list" reflect a scare-of-the-moment mentality. Following the collapse of Barings Bank in 1995, all institutions reinforced their efforts to place safeguards against rogue traders. However, within a few years, rogue trading dropped to a level of low concern or did not appear on the list of top risks by respondents. Seven years later, when rogue traders had become a minor concern for risk divisions relative to items such as business continuity, Allied Irish Bank suffered a large loss from a rogue trader. Risk managers then again elevated rogue trading to a high concern, only to later let it again slip down the list. A further seven years passed, and Jerome Kerviel of Société Générale was discovered to have committed the largest rogue trader event to date. The tone at the top leads the organization not only in the ethics and business practices of the firm, but also in the firm's risk management focus. It is up to the board to set the tone as to whether material potential risks are to be less actively or no longer monitored—or whether new material potential risks are to be taken—without raising these to the board.

The tone at the top is equally important to limit rash decisions to exit activities that may accompany unexpected loss-taking. Given the events in the subprime meltdown, analysis of losses may be used by some to argue for an exit from the market for all securitized or financially engineered products. For financial institutions to continue to perform and manage risk well, some form of market for securitized products and asset-backed (including mortgage-backed) securities is likely to remain. Continuing activity in these markets with appropriate risk controls and risk-adjusted return measures may be preferable to limiting the firm's competitiveness.

The inverse of this situation is also true—the tone at the top is critical to limit risk-taking decisions made solely on the basis of good experiences. This has the potential to cause financial downside, compared to the opportunity cost from the restrictive alternative. Experiences that have worked out well for the organization can result in rapid expansion into a market that is not appropriate, extending relationships into areas to which the organization is not well suited, or to increasing risk limits to accommodate larger transactions with clients who have enjoyed success on a smaller scale.

The tone at the top communicated by the board is necessarily different on many dimensions for every senior management team and risk department. While most firms have some inherent capacity to bear many risk types, skill, available capital, regulatory restrictions, risk appetite, and organizational strength will vary. Said another way, different firms can extract a better return on equity from certain risk types and this method of assessment can assist them in focusing on that objective. Such self-analysis and review is critical to the tone at the top discussions. Further, discussions should separate owned risks from those that the institution may actively choose to seek in the future. An organization can then assess new risks as to how they fit into the picture—are these risks we would like to add to our profile? Over time the owned risk profile can be morphed. For example, a previous decision to have 20 percent of assets as prime residential mortgages cannot immediately be removed, but the process for further lending can be adjusted to lower the overall exposure over time. Alternately, business units may be divested or acquired. New risks that may be considered can vary significantly, with the only clear similarity being that the firm can choose whether or not to take each risk on as part of their risk profile.

The tone at the top also sets other important dimensions of the firm's operations. Media attention has been focused upon the compensation structures within financial and non-financial firms alike. Some CEOs and staff were paid millions in bonus payments as recently as 2007, with the firms unable to recoup any of these payments when the business conducted at that time cost billions of dollars in losses in later years. Governments in the United States, the U.K. and elsewhere have taken steps to adjust the compensation structure. For example, the United States inaugurated a "Pay Tsar" for banks supported by the Troubled Asset Relief Program (TARP) and inserted compensation into the Financial Reform Act, whereas the U.K. implemented new taxes to redirect high bonuses to the taxpayer.

CONDUCT A BOARD-LEVEL REVIEW OF VaR AND STRESS TESTING

Value at Risk (VaR) gained huge acceptance as a risk measure, particularly after Riskmetrics[4] facilitated the provision of key data after 1994. Providing an estimate of maximum potential loss over a given time period, for a given confidence level (the probability of occurrence), the metric provided both suitable rigor for many risk managers and simplicity embraced by many regulators and senior managers. VaR typically was bolstered via stress testing. The stress testing encompassed changing key assumptions, testing outcomes under historically dire market environments, testing outcomes under other scenarios expected to be painful, and evaluating liquidity assumptions among others. Common goals were to determine both how much key assumptions and/or the asset/liability mix could change prior to causing unacceptable forecast losses, and which assumptions, given a small change, might cause a substantial increase in VaR and/or a substantial drain on the liquidity position. With time, VaR was incorporated into many risk management processes; for example, by establishing VaR levels that were to trigger immediate reductions in existing risk positions.

VaR's weaknesses were well-known during the boom period that preceded the crisis.[5] As the markets grew increasingly illiquid, VaR-based triggers to exit positions could not be attained. In such cases the assumptions made to calculate a liquidity-stressed VaR had failed. As the markets displayed more and more "highly rare" moves, stress tests were found to be lacking in the degree of stress they forecast. In such cases, the hazards of employing the normal distribution in quantitative finance, given that once-in-a-hundred-year events occur several times each year, returned to the forefront. As stress tests of key assumptions—for example, volatility levels—were reviewed, overconfidence in extended periods of low volatility and easy monetary policy came to the limelight. During the fall of 2008 volatility, as measured by the VIX, almost quadrupled to 80 percent and maintained an unprecedented sustained level above 50 percent for weeks. The behavior of the VIX from January 1998 to September 2010 is depicted in Exhibit 12.1. The trend line depicts the average.

Within the financial crisis we witnessed the collapse of Lehman Brothers, AIG, Ambac, the bailout of Fannie Mae and Freddie Mac, the bailout of Citigroup and General Motors, a TED spread[6] that increased by over 900 percent, the failure

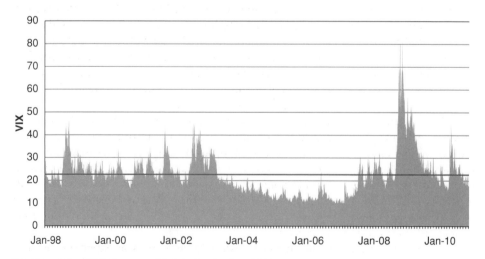

Exhibit 12.1   VIX: January 1998 to September 2010
Source: Bloomberg Finance L.P.

of many auction markets and the evaporation of short-term credit. Not only were each of these risks considered an extreme outside-odds hazard, but they transpired within a matter of weeks of each other. There are so many major risk events just in 2008 that the experience of $4 gas as oil reached $147/barrel rarely warrants a mention.[7]

There exists a natural inclination for people to assume a lower probability of rare events than can be justified by statistical analysis. Anecdotal evidence of this can be provided in the form of the hole-in-one gang from the early 1990s.[8] A group of British golf fanatics set about placing a number of bets on a hole-in-one occurring during a tournament. Bookmakers, specialists on creating odds for gamblers, provided odds of 20–1 and higher on such an event not occurring. This means that they assumed a maximum of only one hole-in-one event in twenty-one tournaments or less than a 5 percent probability. (Some bookmakers assigned odds of less than 1 percent.) The advantage that the gamblers had over the bookmakers was having performed thorough analysis, rather than trying to arbitrarily place odds on a perceived outside chance. The analysis had shown that the likelihood of a hole-in-one in a major tournament was nearer to even odds. By recognizing the bookmakers inclination to consider certain items less probable than their true chance, the gang earned hundreds of thousands on their gambling (in 1991, three of the four major tournaments had a hole-in-one).

Risk Managers have known for years to ask the question, *"When the 99 percent confidence risk level does not hold, how much can we expect to lose?"* When the risk figure is breached, as it inherently forecasts will happen, how bad can we expect the event to be?

By way of illustration we can take the example of General Electric ("GE"). As a firm, GE embraced the structure and methodology surrounding VaR with the implementation of Six Sigma to the vast majority of their processes (a form of Total Quality Management). We can consider the assortment of VaR-like models that exist within the firm. For one area, a six sigma, 1 percent, risk event can be a faulty refrigerator. To another area it could be design error that results in an aircraft engine failure, as used on a Boeing 747. Or, as GE experienced in 2008, the 1 percent outside of VaR took the form of extensive losses within their Real Estate division that ultimately required a $3 billion private investor recapitalization. While it is unlikely that these divisions of GE would have a similar VaR dollar amount, it is clear that the scale of the 1 percent events exist on a far more extreme level also. The scale of the extreme event risk can also vary significantly from the level provided within VaR; a one-in-a-million event of aircraft engine failure can result in a very low VaR level, but a very high extreme loss situation.

Methods and approaches do exist for both assessing and controlling the tail risk within portfolios. And these advance both in theory and in practice. For example, Extreme Value Theory (EVT) has typically been applied in areas where extreme, low probability events need to be assessed. This is a common technique for assessing natural disasters, but has made some progress into financial risk measurement. Further improvement is necessary as it has become an annual event, if not more frequent, to hear about the occurrence of a once in twenty-, fifty-, or one-hundred year event within financial markets.

The use of Extreme Value Theory to estimate tail events or expected shortfall within financial events has been the subject of academic papers and incorporated into risk analysis over the past decade. Using a Generalized Pareto Distribution to

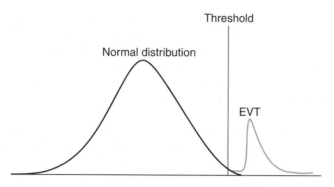

Exhibit 12.2   Normal Distribution with Extreme Event Distribution Overlay

create a fat-tailed structure to estimate excess distributions, a density function is applied beyond a threshold to distribute the tail losses (see Exhibit 12.2).

With the increasing number of tail-events, and the subsequent increased focus of executives to become more comfortable and aware of such circumstances, risk managers are presented with an opportunity to bring EVT and other techniques to the table for consideration.

Vineer Bhansali of Pimco has authored a number of strategies designed to remove tail risk within a portfolio while achieving similar expected returns to a default portfolio.[9] The approach, conceived in the context of an equities portfolio, is designed to take increased risk on the investment portfolio sufficient to produce enough extra expected return to finance the hedging of tail risk via the purchase of an out-of-the-money put option on the portfolio. The portfolio is then hedged, to a level, against extreme events by the option. Bhansali's approach to Tail Risk Hedging is not that the option will come into the money, but rather that the occurrence of a tail risk event will dramatically increase volatility. This movement in the volatility surface will increase the value of the out-of-the-money option significantly relative to the premium paid at purchase, whereupon the hedging party will sell out of the hedge.

Extreme Value Theory and Bahnsali's approach to address tail events are but two of the many approaches that exist for risk managers and firms to consider in managing tail risk. Additional approaches are discussed in published studies, such as those by the Board of Mathematical Sciences and Their Applications at the National Academies: "Technical Capabilities Necessary for Systemic Risk Regulation: Summary of a Workshop" and "New Directions for Understanding Systemic Risk: A Report on a Conference Co-sponsored by the Federal Reserve Bank of New York and the National Academy of Sciences," among others.

With respect to VaR and stress testing, one action that can be taken immediately by firms is to ask the board of directors to conduct a review of risk management practices with or without the help of outside advisors. One useful standard is to ask that this review be conducted at the same level of rigor as that used during a review of important forecasts, budgets, and business plans. During such reviews, directors often question key inputs, such as the assumed cost of materials, assumed manufacturing costs, assumed employee costs (including benefits and pension expenses). Directors often challenge key drivers of the outcome such as sales growth, the forecast timing, and degree of success for expansion plans into new markets or geographies, or the assumed synergies that will benefit the bottom line after an acquisition. As new approaches emerge, directors often question whether these are included in the forecast, budget, or business plan. Examples are the advent of new technologies, new hedging techniques, or new providers for items critical to the success of the business. Substantial debate is the norm in board rooms regarding forecasts, budgets, and business plans. Often, the wisdom of board members provides valuable input and improvements to the adopted version of forecasts, budgets, and business plans. VaR and stress testing should be reviewed under similar challenge and debate prior to being approved on an annual basis. Further, VaR and stress testing should be re-reviewed whenever a large unexpected result occurs—whether good or bad.

As the mortgage business accelerated over the half-decade leading up to the crisis, the defined neutrality of non-executive directors reviewing major assumptions within models might have provided the support required for changes. Many risk managers would have recognized that assumptions providing only a 5 percent probability of any downturn in housing were overly optimistic. A policy defining the importance of such assumptions and requiring their approval and discussion by the risk committee could have provided the support risk managers required. Non-executive directors lie outside the earnings-motivated business structure and would bring their knowledge of house prices in the 1990s and previous international collapses (e.g., Japan, United Kingdom).

This wider experience can provide an excellent test of context for any assumptions or stress testing. Stresses of credit spreads within models can be placed in a more historical context. Stresses that seem large in the context of recent history can be scaled to accommodate longer time-frames that more extensive experience can easily recall. Combination scenarios from prior downturns will be better incorporated and tested. Involvement of the risk committee in defining the stresses and assumptions within the models employed should motivate executives to be more involved and in touch with the risk figures that are presented. Involvement throughout the process will enable management to be better placed to ask questions on risk reports and be familiar with the context in which they are provided.

Incorporating the board and executives more fully into the process of risk definition and testing can provide a strong positive feedback loop for risk management. While requiring greater scrutiny and discussion on risk inputs, assumptions, and parameters, developing involvement at the highest level will enable greater understanding of risk reporting and the benefit of experience to complement that held by individuals within risk management. Further, it brings variety to the thought process, benefiting risk managers with the wider perspective provided by the varied experiences of the senior team, while revealing revenue or asset or other growth drivers so these may be agreed at the highest level of the firm.

ADDING WARNING LABELS TO RISK REPORTS

Interpretation is a fact of life for most risk calculations as well as their inputs. What does a "mark-to-market" ("MTM") price mean? In one firm, instruments may be simple—for example, just-issued sovereign debt or round lots of highly liquid equities traded on major global exchanges, such as the NYSE, FTSE, and NIKKEI—so

MTM may be assumed to be close to values at which the instruments may be bought or sold. At another firm, instruments may be more complex—for example exotic custom derivatives, large block positions or private equity investments in emerging market companies—here, MTM begins and ends with numerous assumptions and may be far from values at which these instruments may be bought or sold. As many firms learned as markets plunged in the crisis, the ability to earn profit without realization can be hazardous for the allocation of risk capital. Assets held under MTM delivered strong "earnings" but turned out to be driven by MTM appreciation in markets where liquidity evaporated and sent MTM prices spiraling downward. In the case of many subprime real-estate-linked instruments, as the participants increased, so did MTM values, as demand for these instruments rose. Prices inflated, asset bubbles were created and, for many, cash was not realized while income was booked. IMF studies have identified empirical evidence that MTM accounting encourages procyclicality within banks.[10] The "originate loans to distribute/sell the loans" model is an entire business area where numerous regulators and supervisors—as well as the mainstream press—correctly observe that accounting policy and profit motives can collide to encourage subpar risk practices.

As a second example, consider the question, "What does a 'AAA rating' mean?" For some instruments it has the widely expected meaning that default risk is remote. Yet in other cases this is not so. For example, the "AAA" tranches of many CDOs defaulted without progressing through interim ratings downgrades, and Auction Rate Securities became illiquid and lost substantial value. These and other instruments did not behave the way many assumed AAA investments behave. Once sought-after investments in "agency" paper went awry as Freddie Mac, Fannie Mae, and other government-sponsored entities tanked and had to be bailed out.

The reliance on the ability to manufacture AAA paper became a core part of some business models. Securitization facilitated a create-to-distribute business model. This model could only work under the assumption that the product would be distributable. Should the assets need to be held on the balance sheet, the risks would remain within the firm. Financial firms reliant on securitizing a production stream found themselves unable to distribute as liquidity vanished over quality concerns by investors. If the firms had not considered this eventuality, they were either forced to immediately reduce lending, or worse, try to sustain increased short-term funding during the liquidity crisis at great expense. Even firms that had operated with caution, had prime quality assets in the pipeline for securitization, or operated using a covered bond program, found that they could not access the market.[11] The assumption that the distribution model would continue to operate came at an expense for many firms and for taxpayers. For some firms, the failure of the distribution model came at the expense of their independence or even existence.

As a third example, consider transactions with what were broadly believed to be reliable, credit-worthy counterparties. Many of these turned out differently as firms defaulted and banks got into serious trouble in Iceland, Ireland, the United States, and elsewhere. Many large organizations were impacted by difficulties in identifying their exposure to Lehman Brothers, Bear Stearns, and AIG, among others. Many executives and managers who believed their firms could identify total exposures to major trading parties were almost instantaneously shocked to discover otherwise. As a consequence of understandable difficulties relating to data granularity, location, offsetting transactions, and secondary effects, the necessity for a better alternative compounded. In these cases, counterparty risk manifested at a higher magnitude and greater complexity than projected.

The complexity in counterparty risk was evident in the uncovering of the Madoff Ponzi scheme in 2009,[12] highlighting the difficulty of identifying full exposures within the shadow banking system and secondary market funds. Even with a database of counterparty exposures a firm may have significantly underestimated its exposure to Madoff. It is now understood that the numerous feeder funds to Madoff were unlikely to be captured with the first assessment of exposure, with numerous entities operating as a storefront for the fund. Such realities demonstrate a complexity through cross-holdings, fund of fund investments, and numerous other paths to possible exposures. Several fund of hedge funds themselves found they had a similar complexity of potential exposures to untangle.

Yet many risk reports *start* with such information—MTM, rating, counterparty exposure, among many others—merely as *inputs* to risk calculations that go on from there. Layer upon layer of assumptions are routinely made—for example, regarding liquidity, volatility, and correlation—in order to produce everything from VaR to stress test results to liquidity and counterparty risk reports. With risk measures based around a framework of probability distributions and consideration of multiple events, the necessary assumptions continue and grow even more complex. Further, as the importance of risk factors change, additional assumptions may be layered on.

With regulatory risk likely to be one of the major risks of the forthcoming decade, single-number risk estimates based on regulatory capital may not be well aligned to the businesses executives will be leading. Such estimates may even be more problematic at times of tight credit or liquidity stress in the capital markets. Based on such changes it is an excellent time to perform a review of such underlying factors to the risk management process.

Sometimes, large organizations are able to perform functions better than smaller ones. Global customer relationship management, increased service through distribution networks, the ability to provide better pricing, and a balance sheet that can accommodate larger, more complex transactions are common examples. Of course, there are also areas where scale has been proven to be disadvantageous, typically in the sphere of certain trading strategies where increased capital serves to decrease returns. Perhaps somewhat counter-intuitively, risk management also falls under the category of areas that may become weakened by scale.

Risk managers, data analysts, and technology professionals are all too familiar with the extensive data processing required to produce timely risk reporting. This is a separate area of yet even more assumptions in the overall risk process. Large-scale business activities, across geographies, time zones, systems, products (from simple to complex), maturities, and counterparties, rapidly become a vast sea of data. Irrespective of the limitations of these base data, the sheer volume of transactions held by an organization at any one time presents enormous challenges.

The complexity and scale of portfolios creates a necessary trade-off for risk management and reporting; to report risk positions expeditiously, such as an end-of-day risk report, data must be mapped through a process of stratification, correlation, and simplification. To provide more accurate reporting (i.e., to incorporate less simplification of the data) often requires substantial additional expense and takes significantly longer, with technology presenting tradeoffs as to the cost and speed at which a risk assessment can be completed. Further, trade-offs made at one time—for example huge simplifications made at a time that a certain activity of the firm was small—may need to be revised to continue to provide accurate risk reports.

However, the issue of operating with summarized data streams is not an issue exclusive to larger organizations. With ever-increasing complexity within securities, the analysis of a single security portfolio can itself force assumptions in correlations, stratification, and mapping. Holding a mortgage-backed security necessitates assumptions on single-loan behaviors based on region, credit score, prepayment behavior, quality of the underlying documentation, and other metrics. A CDO increases the scope and scale of these assumptions by a factor. In assessing the risks within CDO^2 (also known as a "CDO squared," or a CDO within a CDO), synthetic CDOs with substitution rights, tranches with accelerated repayments, the necessity and complexity of assumptions and mappings to be made increase rapidly. In larger organizations, the difficulties of data mapping are compounded when working with these complex securities, with correlations on top of correlation matrices, and with credit spreads simplified and then amalgamated further.

It is critical that the user of risk reports have an understanding as to where simplifying assumptions have been made and how these may impact the quality of the results. Risk departments frequently begin with a careful review of available data, modeling, and assumptions. Data hierarchies, model risk policies, and discussions of the Achilles heel in specific quantitative approaches are often heated debates with productive results within risk management departments. Clearly, successful Risk Officers must determine the right balance of complexity versus simplifying assumptions in the approach. A trade-off exists between a model seeking to be roughly right and precisely wrong. There is a point where assumptions made within the model become a more significant component of the output of the model than the actual exposure being evaluated. Other trade-offs exist as well. Some simplifying assumptions may seem theoretically fine but may create dangerous results in practice. For example, the use of a report that includes output from a model that has a closed-form solution may be expedient for certain theoretical estimates, but may cause losses if used for other purposes.

A common technique employed, as greater and greater assumptions have been agreed and implemented, is to implement mark-to-model reserves. Simply explained, mark-to-model reserves try to estimate how far off results may be, given the assumptions required to use a particular model. As the reader can imagine, this may be difficult not only to evaluate a single model—for example, the model used to estimate the mark-to-market value for a given CDO—but grows increasingly difficult as the results of multiple models are combined to produce results such as for VaR and stress tests.

One action that can be taken immediately by firms is to include warning labels within risk reports. Similar to the practice followed in prescription drug labeling, these would include how the risk report's figures are recommended for use, and dangerous potential applications or interpretations would be clearly displayed. Some risks cannot be successfully combined and therefore should not be combined, nor presented in a manner that will imply that they can. While some of this may be communicated via presentations or in discussions with senior management and the board, labeling may serve to address the types of issues that have been common since the outset of the credit crisis. In particular, questions over whether the limitations of the risk reporting were well understood.

CONCLUSION AND AN ENDNOTE

Based on all of the above, it is our recommendation that organizations (1) revisit the tone at the top, (2) conduct board-level review of VaR and stress testing, and (3) add warning labels to risk reports. These suggestions also may assist in addressing two additional items of heightened concerns in the risk arena: coping with procyclical rules and contagion.

Coping with Procyclical Rules

A shared problem for both risk management and the executives within firms is the procyclical nature of much of the regulatory environment in which they must operate. While Basel III is moving to develop methods to protect against procyclicality, it is unlikely that the committee will reflect the risk potential to the degree that is perceived by many practitioners or management. With management not wanting to deliver boom-and-bust cycles to investors, they can be expected to seek to minimize loss events by developing protection against procyclical behavior. This will likely form the basis of a major component of forward-thinking discussions.

Fighting procyclical behavior is, in part, trying to enforce rules that are contrary to human nature. Buying into asset bubbles in larger volumes is natural if more capital can be made available, as profitable markets are difficult for firms to resist (and in conflict with much of their purpose). Risk management already has numerous tools that can help contend with procyclical behavior. Risk models operating on a long-term investment basis, using Monte Carlo simulations and stress scenarios, can capture the potential risk. For short-term, liquid investments risk management's argument is more difficult and is often contended. More often than not, the side battling to enter the procyclical market wins, with the opportunity to make profit proving seductive.

The IMF recommendations to address the procyclicality include full fair value accounting (to avoid cherry picking of assets), consensus pricing, and reclassification committees for moving assets in and out of held-to-maturity status. The debate over procyclical accounting policy will certainly involve these factors, but will also benefit from risk involvement in other control mechanisms. The Pandora's Box of mark-to-market accounting has been opened, and remains the best identified accounting policy for financial firms at present. Decision rules on fair value adjustments and the method of any circuit breakers applied will involve extensive input from risk management. While Finance will present the opinion of accountancy, the business area will encourage behavior that paints it in the best light. Risk management should develop a role for itself in presenting the risks associated with the reclassification of the assets.

Contagion

An understanding of risk contagion is likely to have a significant influence on how a firm chooses to build its risk profile. Once contagion concerns are taken into consideration, the selection of new assets and risks will adjust to reflect the potential exogenous risks that the firm will become exposed to. The contagious nature of risk is well illustrated by the subprime mortgage debacle. It moved from hedge funds performing repo, to American banks sourcing liquidity, and then on to insurance companies and European banks with minimal subprime exposure. The contagion transcended sectors and borders. IMF studies using Extreme Value Theory have indicated statistically-supportable levels of contagion within U.K. banks from international and domestic stresses.[13] The analysis of risk contagion has become an active area in finance research, with the Bank of International Settlements and other authorities assessing contagion within banking, sovereign debt, and other markets.

Consideration of risk contagion could motivate an organization to avert speculative bubbles. If liquidity is managed and monitored well, the risk contagion factors of many competitors holding large asset portfolios that are similar in characteristics would be of concern. In 2006, as the mortgage market was at its height, the threat of risk contagion as a result of the mortgage market was high; banks, the shadow banking system, and insurance firms all had extraordinary exposures to housing. With an ability to capture and monitor the market for contagious risks, a firm would (hopefully) be able to notice this trend and seek to reduce its own position in the market. In effect, through monitoring and controlling the exposure to risk contagion, the firm is seeking to diversify itself from its peers.

The diversification from other institutions by way of the type of assets and positions that are held will better enable firms to ride through financial storms. Awareness of the level of exposures that create systemic exposure within the organization could become a valuable component for setting and evaluating risk appetite. Managing the risk of contagion to the firm alongside exercising judicious control of liquidity will best enable an organization to continue in normal business through difficult periods, without having to significantly adjust the business model applied.

The proposals for Basel III, currently in draft regulation form, seek to incorporate considerations of leverage, counter-cyclicality, counterparty risks, and liquidity provisions. Though the expansion to recognize increased numbers of risk factors is welcomed, financial risk managers must be wary of repeating past errors and focusing only on the regulated risk factors. They need to consider all factors, regulated and unregulated, that present risk to the organization.

The critical component of this proposed approach to risk management is that risk management does not need to be torn down and completely rebuilt. The capacity, ability, and methodologies applied within the vast majority of firms to manage risk successfully exist already. Further, many of the models within these institutions perform well at their defined task. Instead, the focus should be placed on where no models are defined. This may be a result of a lapse in communication such that management is not specifically clear on the coverage provided by the risk models and the reports that currently exist. It certainly exists in areas that have not been fully analyzed, or perhaps have not ever been analyzed at all.

As organizations begin to work towards achieving improved transparency (both in reporting, assumptions, and risk measurement), risk experts can work with the risk committee to ensure that assumptions are reviewed by appropriate parties. Many assumptions will remain under localized control, where risk experts are the appropriate individuals to consider the variables. Key drivers of the risk picture and risk profile of the firm, however, would benefit from the involvement of directors.

NOTES

1. See Corkery (2010), Overby (2010), Prenesti (2009), BBC News (2009), Hudson (2010), Wilchins (2010), Chernoff (2009), Gordon (2010), and Bremer (2009).
2. See Nakamoto and Wighton (2007).
3. The CSFI is a London-based think tank established in 1993.
4. RiskMetrics is a risk subsidiary that was rolled out from J.P. Morgan to market its Value at Risk modeling and advisory.
5. See Beder (1995).
6. The Treasury to LIBOR differential for similar maturities.
7. We also fail to mention Goldman Sachs and Morgan Stanley becoming bank holding companies, GE requiring a private bail out, the bankruptcy of 43 companies with over $1bn in assets. See Altman and Karlin (2010).
8. See Carter and Simons (1993).
9. See Bhansali (2010).
10. See Novoa, Scarlata, and Solé (2009).
11. Covered Bond Programs are an alternative to securitization where the assets are ring fenced but remain on the balance sheet of the firm rather than being transferred to an SPV. While not providing capital relief like the securitized alternative, the Covered Bond provides liquidity to fund mortgage issuance. The buyer of covered bonds has the explicit support of the balance sheet of the firm, providing more assurance.
12. The Madoff scheme was uncovered in late 2008, but the full extent of it was not understood until 2009.
13. See Chan-Lau, Mitra, and Ong (2007).

REFERENCES

Altman, Edward I., and Brenda Karlin. 2010. "Special Report on Defaults and Returns in the High -Yield Bond and Distressed Debt Market: The Year 2009 in Review and Outlook." Working paper, February 8.

Beder, Tanya. 1995. "Value at Risk: Seductive but Dangerous." *Financial Analysts Journal* (September–October): 12–24.

Bhansali, Vineer, and Joshua Davis. 2010. "Offensive Risk Management: Can Tail Risk Hedging Be Profitable?" *PIMCO*, (April): 1–14.

Bhansali, Vineer, and Joshua Davis. 2010. "Offensive Risk Management II: The Case for Active Tail Risk Hedging." *Journal of Portfolio Management* 37:1, 78–91.

Bremer, Jack. 2009. "RBS executives claim they were intimidated." *The First Post*, March 23. www.thefirstpost.co.uk/46802,business,rbs-executives-claim-they-were-intimidated.

Carter, John, and Paul Simons. 1993. *Hole-in-One Gang*. Monrovia, MD: Yellow Brick Publishers.

Chan-Lau, Jorge A, Srobona, Mitra, and Li Lian Ong. 2007. "Contagion Risk in the International Banking System and Implications for London as a Global Financial Center." Working Paper 07/74, International Monetary Fund.

Chernoff, Allan. 2009. "Madoff whistleblower blasts SEC." *CNN Money*, February 4.

Corkery, Michael. 2010. "Lehman Whistle-Blower's Fate: Fired." *Wall Street Journal*, March 15.

Gordon, Marcy. 2010. "Risk officers say they tried to warn WaMu of risky mortgages." *USA Today*, April 13.

"HBOS whistleblower probe demanded." 2009. *BBC News*, February 11.

Hudson, Michael W. 2010. "Mortgage Meltdown: How Banks Silenced Whistleblowers." *ABC News*, May 11.

Nakamoto, Michiyo and David Wighton. 2007. "Citigroup Chief Stays Bullish on Buy-Outs." *Financial Times*, July 9.

Novoa, Alicia, Jodi Scarlata, and Juan Solé. 2009. "Procyclicality and Fair Value Accounting." Working Paper 09/39, International Monetary Fund.

Overby, Peter. 2010. "Consultant: Federal Aid Program Failing Homeowners." *National Public Radio*, August 6.

Prenesti, Frank. 2009. "HBOS whistleblower threatens more disclosure-report." *Reuters*, February 15.

Wilchins, Dan. 2010. "Former Citi Manager's Testimony Helps Lawyers." *Reuters*, April 9.

ABOUT THE AUTHORS

Tanya Beder is currently chairman of SBCC in New York and SBCC Group Inc. in Connecticut. SBCC, founded in 1987, has a broad base of hedge fund, private equity, traditional investment management, financial services, and corporate clients. From 2004 to 2006, Tanya was CEO of Tribeca Global Management LLC, Citigroup's USD 3 billion multi-strategy hedge fund, and from 1999 to 2004 was managing director of Caxton Associates LLC, a USD 10 billion investment management firm. She serves on the National Board of Mathematics and their Applications as well as on the boards of a major mutual fund complex and family office. Tanya has taught courses atYale University's School of Management, Columbia University's Graduate School of Business and Financial Engineering, and the New York Institute of Finance. She has published in the *Journal of Portfolio Management*, *Financial Analysts Journal*, *Harvard Business Review*, and the *Journal of Financial Engineering*. She holds an MBA in finance from Harvard University and a BA in mathematics from Yale University.

Spencer Jones is currently an associate at SBCC Group, where he has worked on projects including bank restructuring, structured credit portfolio analysis, and municipal risk management. From 2005 to 2007 he was a risk manager in Barclays Treasury, responsible for risk management across two divisions of the bank, including two M&A projects. From 2000 to 2004 he was an Analyst with HBOS, working in Asset & Liability Management developing risk models. He received an MBA, with distinction, from New York University and an MA in Economics with First Class Honours from the University of Edinburgh.

CHAPTER 13

Financial Engineering and Macroeconomic Innovation

CARA M. MARSHALL
Queens College, City University of New York

JOHN H. O'CONNELL
Financial Integration, LLC

INTRODUCTION

The credit crisis of 2007–2009 and the recessionary aftermath have sparked considerable, often heated, debate with respect to policy issues—both fiscal and monetary. The crisis led to the introduction of a number of new central bank monetary policy tools and an aggressive expansion of the monetary base in Europe and Japan. But nowhere has monetary policy been more accommodative than in the United States. While classic monetarist theory would hold that this is inflationary foolishness, the dominant concern among many economists (and some notable hedge fund managers) is for deflation, not inflation.

On another front, the recession stressed corporate cash flows, particularly in cyclically sensitive industries, leading to a sharp decline in employment. State and local governments too have been stressed as their tax bases shrank while the demands on their services simultaneously expanded. This has, once again, brought home the cyclically sensitive nature of municipal coffers. Unlike the private sector, municipalities are typically loath to shrink their work forces and reduce services until they reach a crisis stage. Not surprisingly, this has led to a general decline in the perceived quality of municipal debt and to the outright bankruptcy of some municipalities. These macroeconomic stresses on corporations and municipalities alike have sparked renewed interest in macroeconomic derivatives. It is a pity that the barn door so often seems to close only after the horse has left.

In this chapter, we are going to look at several things. They are only related to one another in that they involve macroeconomic innovation at some level. Specifically, we are going to provide a brief refresher on monetary policy and how it works; touch on the tools of monetary policy, including some recent innovations (central bank financial engineering if you will); strategies investors can employ to deal with inflationary and deflationary beasts; and take a look at macroeconomic derivatives and how they might be used to forestall future municipal (and, by extension, corporate) crises.

A REFRESHER ON MONETARY POLICY

Monetary policy refers to the actions taken by a central bank to influence the availability and the cost of money and credit. The purpose of monetary policy is to promote national economic goals. Most often these include the two, sometimes contradictory, goals of price stability and full employment. While not always made explicit, a third goal is often to influence the value of the nation's currency vis-à-vis other currencies (i.e., foreign exchange rates). In the U.K. monetary policy is the responsibility of the Bank of England (BOE), in the Eurozone it lies with the European Central Bank (ECB), in Japan it is the purview of the Bank of Japan (BOJ), and in the United States it rests with the Federal Reserve System (the Fed). By its nature, monetary policy is highly susceptible to politicization. For this reason, many countries have taken steps to insulate their central bankers from political pressures, though it is questionable how well these insular devices actually work without a strong figure at the head of the central bank.[1]

All of the central banks noted above have engaged in a policy of quantitative easing over the past several years. In the case of Japan, this policy has actually been in place for nearly two decades. "Quantitative easing" is central banker jargon for an aggressive expansion of the monetary base. It is this aggressive expansion of the monetary base that had led many to fear the possibility of an inflationary spiral a few years further down the road. But others argue that it is not so simple. While central banks do indeed control their nation's monetary base, they do not have full control over their nation's money supply. (As a side note, there are several different definitions of the money supply depending on how narrowly or how broadly one chooses to define it. For purposes of this chapter, the distinction is not important. We will occasionally make reference to M1, which is a narrow definition.) The aggregate decisions of thousands of individual bankers take us from the monetary base to the money supply (often called the "money stock") by way of a metric called the money multiplier. Finally, the equation of exchange takes us from the money supply to economic activity—including both price and output levels. Here, too, the central banks have limited influence. The equation of exchange is driven, in part, by the velocity of money. The velocity of money is not under the direct control of any central bank—rather, it is the end result of the individual decisions of millions of individual consumers and businesses.

We will take a brief look at the three basic equations: the money multiplier, the money supply, and the equation of exchange. These relationships are essentially the same in every economy, but the parameters can vary dramatically from country to country. Note that we are using the term "bank" generically to include all types of depository institutions whether technically classified as a bank or not. The term "bank" should not be confused with the term "central bank."

The Monetary Base

The monetary base, which we will denote B, is the sum of currency (both coins and paper money) in circulation and bank reserves.[2] Bank reserves represent the fraction of a bank's deposits that a bank turns over to its central bank to be held there on behalf of the bank. Banks can also keep some of their reserves in the form of vault cash, but this is such a small component of overall reserves that it does not merit further discussion. Banks hold two kinds of reserves: those that are required (called required reserves) and those that are not required (called excess reserves).

The Money Supply

The money supply, or money stock, is the sum of money a nation has created. It is related to the monetary base by the money multiplier. The money multiplier is simply a multiple of the monetary base. We denote the money supply by M and the money multiplier by m. The relationship is:

$$M = m \times B \qquad \text{Money Supply}$$

So, for example, if the money multiplier is 3.99 and the monetary base is 100 currency units (e.g., dollars, yen, euros, etc.) the money supply is 399 currency units.

The Money Multiplier

The money multiplier, in turn, is determined by several factors including the currency drain ratio (c), the required reserve ratio (r), and the excess reserve ratio (e). The required reserve ratio is discussed below, the excess reserve ratio is the percentage of deposits held as reserves in *excess* of that which are required, and the currency drain ratio is money held as currency outside the banking system (cash in the pocket so to speak). The relationship between the money multiplier and its drivers is given by the following money multiplier equation:

$$m = \frac{(1+c)}{(r+e+c)} \qquad \text{Money Multiplier}$$

So, for example, suppose that the reserve requirement ratio is 20 percent, that the excess reserves are 5 percent, and that the currency drain ratio is 0.1 percent. Then the money multiplier is:

$$m = (1 + .001)/(0.20 + 0.05 + .001) = 3.99$$

This basically says that for every one currency unit increase in the monetary base, there will be a 3.99 currency unit increase in the money supply.

The central bank sets the reserve requirement ratio, and through this ratio it attempts to control the money multiplier. But this control is weakened by the fact that the central bank does not control the individual banks' decisions with respect to excess reserves, or people's individual decisions with respect to how much currency they hold outside the banking system.

Equation of Exchange

Now consider the fundamental relationship between the money supply and real economic activity. This relationship is known as the "equation of exchange."

$$P \times Q = V \times M \qquad \text{Equation of Exchange}$$

Here, P is the aggregate price level, as measured by some price index scaled to reflect the average price of the average good; Q is the quantity of real output of goods and services (real economic output), and you can loosely think of this as real GDP measured in units of output; V is the velocity of money, which means the number of times the average currency unit is used to make a transaction in a given year, and M is the money supply.

Clearly, assuming that velocity is constant, increasing the money supply on the right hand side of the equation will show up as an increase in the price level or an increase in real output or both.[3] Increases in real output represent real GDP growth. When the economy is in a recessionary state, such that there are unemployed factors of production, including labor, with the result that production is well below capacity, increases in the money supply often lead to economic expansion. But, when the economy is near full utilization of its resources, any increase in the money supply must translate into inflation (i.e., the price level rising). It is this latter fact that led Milton Friedman to unequivocally argue that inflation is a monetary phenomenon. At the time of this writing, many of the world's economies are well below full utilization of their resources (labor being just one of those resources). So it would *seem* that an expansionary monetary policy—expansion of the monetary base—should lead to increases in economic activity, growth, and employment. Indeed, an unusually aggressive expansion of their monetary bases by the central banks noted in the introduction to this chapter has been policy for some time now. Yet, these same countries have seen very little economic growth.

POLICY TOOLS OF CENTRAL BANKS

Irrespective of what they call them, central banks have, essentially, three policy tools with which to influence their country's monetary base, and through the monetary base, the money supply. The central bank can change its required reserve ratio, which would, in theory, alter the money multiplier. Lowering the reserve ratio should increase the multiplier and raising it should lower the multiplier. Whether this will actually work depends on how banks choose to respond with respect to their excess reserves. For example, suppose that banks choose not to lend out their excess reserves and, instead, allow their excess reserve ratio to rise. This voluntary expansion of the excess reserve ratio would tend to mitigate the effects on the multiplier of lowering the required reserve ratio.

The second tool is to change the rate that the central bank lends to its nation's banks. This rate is, in many countries, called the discount rate. By lending to a bank, the central bank directly increases the borrowing bank's reserves because the loan is made by simply crediting the borrowing bank's reserve account. The central bank can encourage banks to borrow more by lowering their discount rate. This, of course, assumes that banks want to borrow. This tool becomes moot when interest rates reach zero—as they did in some countries in the aftermath of the credit crisis.

The third tool is to engage in open market operations. This refers to the buying and selling of securities in the open market. Most often, central banks purchase or sell their own government's securities. So the BOJ buys or sells Japanese government bonds (JGBs), the BOE buys or sells British government bonds (Gilts), and the Fed buys or sells U.S. government bonds (Treasuries). When a central bank buys securities, it pays for them by crediting the selling dealer-bank's reserves, thereby expanding the monetary base. When a central bank sells securities, it gets paid for them by debiting the selling dealer-bank's reserves, thereby shrinking the monetary base. These purchases and sales lead to excess reserves and reserve deficiencies, respectively, for the banks. The banks can lend their excess reserves out to other banks, or they can use them to make loans. The rate at which banks lend their excess reserves to other banks is an important indicator of monetary policy and the central bank's intentions. Indeed, this rate is often "targeted" as part of the monetary policy process. In the United States this rate is called the "federal funds rate" or simply the "fed funds rate."

While the tools are rather straightforward, there remains a great deal of uncertainty. The recent experience of the United States illustrates the situation quite well, so we will focus on the U.S. experience for the remainder of this discussion—but the issues and problems are common to central banking.

THE FEDERAL RESERVE AND THE LIQUIDITY CRISIS

The credit crisis that began in 2007 resulted in a sudden and massive disappearance of liquidity across the entire universe of financial institutions. This was largely, but not entirely, due to a sudden collapse in the values of many mortgage-backed securities and other "hard to price" financial assets, and the disappearance of bidders, making valuations exceedingly difficult. The crisis, as crises often do, fed on itself, and the situation grew progressively worse at an alarming rate. The Fed responded to the crisis by using its tools, primarily open market operations, to dramatically expand the monetary base. It did this by buying up literally hundreds of billions of dollars of securities—eventually reaching into the trillions. These included both agency MBS and Treasuries. Indeed, over just three years, the Fed's balance sheet ballooned by some $2 trillion. The explosive growth of the monetary base can be seen in Exhibit 13.1.

Beginning in December 2007, the Federal Reserve sequentially introduced a number of new, *temporary*, monetary policy tools in an effort to restore liquidity to financial institutions. These tools represented "innovation on the fly." Three of these tools were the Term Auction Facility (TAF), the Term Securities Lending Facility (TSLF), and the Primary Dealer Credit Facility (PDCF). All of these have now expired, but they are worth a brief mention as they, or programs like them, could be brought back in short order.

The TAF was a credit facility that allowed banks to borrow from the Fed for periods of 28 days using a wide variety of collateral. When the Fed lends in this way, it credits the borrowing institution's reserves (a liability for the Fed) while

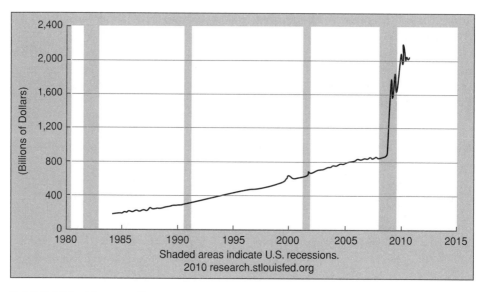

Exhibit 13.1 Monetary Base
Source: Federal Reserve Bank of St. Louis.

simultaneously adding the collateral to the Fed's assets. While Fed lending against collateral increases both the Fed's assets and liabilities by equal amounts, it also has the effect of increasing the monetary base by increasing bank reserves. If the Fed does not wish to see the monetary base expand, it can counteract the effect through open market operations.

The TSLF program allowed prime dealers to borrow Treasuries from the Fed in exchange for less liquid collateral, such as mortgage-backed securities. It was a sort of bond-for-bond swap of securities that did not increase or decrease reserves but did help to restore liquidity to certain key financial institutions. These bond swaps were, like TAF, for periods of up to 28 days.

The PDCF was a cash-for-bonds program that provided funding for prime dealers for up to 120 days. The program accepted a wide variety of collateral. Like TAF, these loans against collateral increased both the Fed's assets and liabilities. They also added to bank reserves. Again, if the Fed did not wish these loans to increase the monetary base, it could take offsetting actions through open market operations.

A fourth tool amounted to the extension of open market operations to include the purchase of agency MBS (i.e., issuances of Ginnie Mae, Fannie Mae, and Freddie Mac) in much the same manner as the purchase of Treasuries. This program is separate and distinct from the U.S. Treasury's Troubled Asset Relief Program or TARP. TARP is not, technically, a Federal Reserve policy tool. It is a program of the U.S. Treasury department that allows the Treasury, in consultation with the Fed and with timely notice to various congressional committees, to purchase troubled assets—primarily residential and commercial mortgage-backed securities. The goals behind the TARP program were to allow banks to get these troubled assets off their balance sheets, restore liquidity to this segment of the financial markets, and to encourage banks to begin lending again. Clearly, these are goals the Fed shared.

As the mortgage-backed securities that the Fed holds have gradually paid down (i.e., principal returned), the Fed has stated that it may reinvest the proceeds into Treasuries. This concerns many economists as it represents a monetization of the national debt with serious long-term inflationary potential.

So What Is It: Inflation or Deflation?

Despite the fact that there is near universal agreement among economists with respect to all three of the key monetary equations noted earlier in this paper and repeated below, economists still disagree as to whether the developed world is headed down an inflationary or a deflationary path. Oddly both are distinct possibilities.

$$\text{Money Multiplier Equation:} \quad m = \frac{(1+c)}{(r+e+c)}$$

$$\text{Money Supply Equation:} \quad M = m \times B$$

$$\text{Equation of Exchange:} \quad P \times Q = V \times M$$

To see how this can be so, consider the equation for the money multiplier. The money multiplier declines if banks choose not to lend so that their excess reserves (e in the money multiplier equation) rise. It is no secret that banks have become skittish and have dramatically reduced their willingness to lend and have raised their lending standards. The latter is not necessarily a bad thing; it is certainly preferable to making uncollectible loans, but it does reduce the money multiplier. Indeed, as of this writing, U.S. bank excess reserves have reached an unprecedented level of $1 trillion. All other things being equal, a reduction in the money multiplier will reduce the money supply for any given monetary base. As a consequence, even though the U.S. monetary base has grown at an explosive rate (ranging from 20 percent to about 100 percent per annum) over the past few years the actual money supply, as measured by M1, has grown at a much slower rate (ranging from 0 percent to about 17 percent per annum) over the same period. Will this continue? Not indefinitely, of course, but for how long is open to debate. The dramatic decline in the money multiplier over the past few years is evident from Exhibit 13.2.

While you might argue that the Fed can compensate by increasing the monetary base further, that is actually very difficult to do. Increasing the monetary base in part requires that banks be incentivized to expand their reserves. The Fed would normally accomplish this by lowering interest rates (i.e., its target Fed funds rate and/or the discount rate). But with the target Fed funds rate nearly zero, there is little more that the Fed can do without literally giving away money. Thus, banks' reluctance to lend can, in the short run, bring about a shrinkage, or at least very slow growth, in the money supply even as the monetary base continues to expand. This shrinkage in money supply can bring on a bout of deflation. In the longer term, however, when banks do finally begin to lend aggressively and the excess reserve ratio trends back toward zero, the money multiplier can be expected to

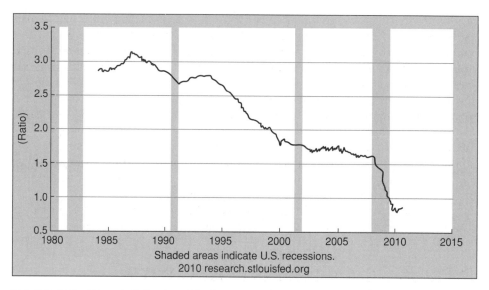

Exhibit 13.2   Historic Behavior of the Money Multiplier
Source: Federal Reserve Bank of St. Louis.

rise dramatically. This in turn could bring about a rapid expansion of the money supply and, eventually, a serious bout of inflation.

Now consider the equation of exchange. In our earlier discussion of the effect of an expansion of the money supply on the price level and/or real GDP, we assumed that the velocity of money is constant. But, in fact, it is not. It is very much influenced by how people feel about their personal wealth status, their employment prospects, and their perceptions of future prices. Specifically, when people feel "poorer" they tend to dispense with some of their discretionary spending, increasing their savings rate, and thereby reducing velocity. When unemployment rates rise or are high, people also slow down their spending due to job insecurity concerns. This, too, contributes to a decrease in the velocity of money. Finally, if people believe that prices will decline, they tend to postpone consumption in order to get a better price later. This also decreases the velocity of money. Of course, the opposite is also true—as people feel wealthier, as unemployment rates fall or remain low, and as inflationary expectations rise, the velocity of money increases.

Given that at least two of these velocity drivers have been driving velocity lower; that is, people feel poorer due to declines in real estate values and stock portfolios and employment prospects are bleak, we would expect the velocity of money to have declined even if people have no opinion about future prices. Their view on future prices could either mitigate or reinforce these velocity effects. Indeed, in recent years, the velocity of money has been trending downward: between 2008 and early 2010, the velocity of M1 declined by more than 20 percent. The trend in velocity has recently turned modestly upward, but it is as yet unclear if this is the start of a new trend or if the downward trend will resume.

So now consider the implications of a flat money supply despite a rising monetary base and a simultaneously declining velocity of money. If output, that is, real GDP, grows, price levels must fall and a bout of deflation is most likely. If output declines, it could absorb some of the pressure on prices, but it would also likely result in a further exacerbation of the unemployment rate, and this, in turn, could further slow the velocity of money. In other words, a downward spiral in the price level becomes a distinct possibility with further increases in unemployment. This is the classic liquidity trap.

On the other hand, sooner or later it can be expected that the economy will return to its long-term growth path—though this is far from certain as foolish government "fixes" can actually prolong the problems. When this happens the money multiplier will rise dramatically thereby increasing the money supply from a now very high base, and consumers would likely return to their old spending habits with a concurrent increase in velocity. Unless the Fed is able to shrink the bloated monetary base, potent inflation would then be in the offing.

The conclusion is—it could go either way. But deflation seems a more likely shorter-term scenario while inflation seems a more likely longer-term scenario.

EXPRESSING A VIEW: INVESTING WITH PRICE INSTABILITY

How can one position oneself to benefit from his or her monetary outlook? Consider first the prospect of inflation. Here there are several old standbys. During inflationary periods, durable commodities tend to hold their value quite well. This is especially true for precious metals like platinum, gold, and silver. In September 2010 gold hit an all-time historic high, suggesting clearly that not all the world foresees deflation. Even if an investor expects a period of deflation to be followed by serious prolonged inflation, gold and other hard commodities would be a viable hedge. Adding a little leverage changes the outcome, if the view proves right, from a purchasing-power hedge to a very rewarding investment. A number of well-known hedge fund managers, including George Soros, Leon Cooperman, John Paulson, and Erich Mindich, have all purchased gold bullion and/or gold ETFs for their funds, such as SPDR Gold Shares (GLD).

A different approach would be to buy financially-engineered securities specifically designed as a hedge against inflation. Certain types of structured securities serve this purpose well. Examples would be inflation-indexed notes and bonds. The Treasury version, called Treasury Inflation Protected Securities (TIPS), do have some hidden tax traps caused by phantom income, but they offer the credit safety of Treasuries. Corporate inflation-linked bonds and notes do not, generally, suffer from the phantom income problem, and they offer higher yields because they carry greater credit risk. In both cases, however, these products can be shown to be a combination of a traditional bond and a macroeconomic derivative (discussed later). For aggressive investors, new ETF products couple the inflation-indexed products with leverage, allowing them to truly profit from inflation, not just protect their wealth from a loss of purchasing power.

In a serious inflationary environment, interest rates eventually rise dramatically. This causes bonds with fixed coupon rates to lose value. Thus, an inflationary view can be expressed by shorting bonds or, equivalently, by buying a bond ETF specifically structured to be bearish on fixed coupon bonds. This is accomplished with a little financial engineering.

For those with a deflationary outlook, all of the aforesaid strategies can be reversed. However, given how low bond yields have fallen, it is doubtful that there is much upside in an investment-grade long bond position unless considerable leverage is applied. But, that is, of course, what hedge funds tend to do. Paul Broyhill, who runs Affinity, took that approach. Some large hedge funds have, in recent months, been buying up high yield (i.e., junk) bonds, reasoning that those bond yields have further to fall if the deflationary scenario comes to pass—as they expect. One example of this mindset is David Tepper, who runs Appaloosa Management.

MACROECONOMIC DERIVATIVES

Perhaps a purer approach to playing the inflation/deflation views, as well as other novel economic scenarios, is to structure appropriate macroeconomic derivatives (sometimes called economic derivatives).[4] These sorts of products were proposed by a number of financial theorists/practitioners over the years including Marshall et al. (1992) and Shiller (1993). But it wasn't until a decade later that derivatives dealers and derivatives exchanges began making markets in these novel products.[5]

A macroeconomic derivative is a derivative instrument (i.e., swap, option, forward, or futures) contract that is linked to a macroeconomic index of some sort. One could argue that certain commodities have such a broad impact on economic activity that they could be considered macroeconomic indexes. Some would feel this way about the price of crude oil and, therefore, oil futures and oil swaps would be macroeconomic derivatives. Here, however, we take the definition a bit more literally to include only those derivatives written on macroeconomic indexes. These indexes would include such things as inflation rates, unemployment rates, non-farm payrolls, GDP growth rates, real estate indexes, and so on.

While macroeconomic derivatives have not yet attracted a great deal of attention and the market is still in its infancy, they nevertheless have interesting theoretical and practical applications. Indeed, some of the more popular financially-engineered products, such as inflation indexed bonds, can be shown to be a combination of a straight bond and a macroeconomic swap—specifically, an inflation swap. Suppose, for example, that a bond issuer prefers to issue a straight bond (i.e., fixed coupon, fixed maturity, no embedded optionality) but knows that there is a strong demand on the part of investors for inflation-protected debt products. Specifically, consider the issuer in Exhibit 13.3. It enters into an inflation swap to convert its fixed rate to an inflation-linked rate. The inflation-indexed bond costs the issuer a fixed rate of 4.5 percent per annum: 2 percent is paid to the swap dealer in exchange for the inflation rate, which, in turn, is given to the investor along with an additional fixed rate component of 2.5 percent.

These sorts of structures run the risk of negative inflation (i.e., deflation) so that the change in the CPI component could be negative. Indeed, if the deflation rate were to exceed 2.5 percent, the coupon to the investor would be negative. This can be avoided by embedding an option in the swap and in the note so that the CPI would have a floor of −2.5 percent. (This would likely entail some reduction in the fixed rate component of the note to pay for the option.) This is the same process by which various types of principal-protected equity-linked notes and commodity-linked notes are created.

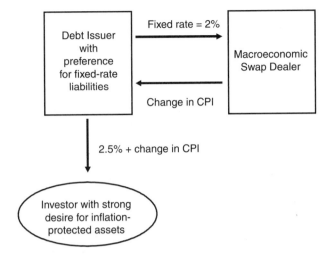

Exhibit 13.3 Engineering an Inflation-Linked Bond

Alternatively, in an environment such as the present in which views are strongly split between inflation and deflation, we could have an issuer issue two bonds: one indexed to play the inflation view and one reverse indexed to play the deflation view. This is depicted in Exhibit 13.4. From the investor's perspective, one has an inflation-biased product and the other a deflation-biased product. But from the issuer's perspective, the aggregate issuance is fixed rate.

While not shown here, the principal can be protected on each of these notes, using an appropriately structured option, and leverage can be added if the investors so desire. For example, the note could pay a fixed rate plus/minus some multiple of the change in the CPI.

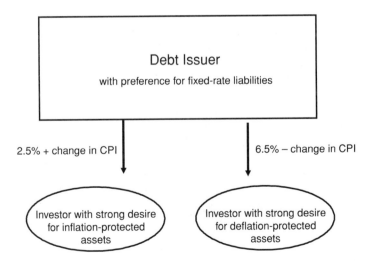

Exhibit 13.4 Issuer with Offsetting Bonds

Cyclically Sensitive Municipalities (and Corporations)

At the end of August 2010, the city of Harrisburg, announced that it expected to default on its debt by missing a $3.9 million interest payment. Harrisburg is the capital of the Commonwealth of Pennsylvania. Actual default was averted, at least temporarily, when the Commonwealth of Pennsylvania announced a week or so later that it would accelerate some grants and other payments to the city to allow Harrisburg to meet its upcoming debt service. The bonds are insured by a municipal bond insurance company, so investors were not at significant risk, but a default would drive up Harrisburg's, and other municipalities', future funding costs. At the time of this writing, the cities of Detroit, Michigan, and San Diego, California are in similar straits.

The problem for these three municipalities, and almost all others as well, is that any economic slowdown will cause a decline in their tax revenues while increased community needs will make greater demands on the expenditure side. Almost all municipalities are cyclically sensitive. But the degree of cyclicality varies considerably from locale to locale. A city that is home to many cyclically sensitive businesses will itself be particularly cyclically sensitive. A city that is dominated by colleges and universities will be less impacted, at least for a time, by economic stress.

Given this cyclical sensitivity, one might be inclined to think the solution is simple: Municipalities should build reserves during expansionary periods in order to have a rainy day fund to draw on during periods of contraction. But history proves that few municipalities can do this. Politicians are always under pressure to show the voter that they are conscious of the voters' concerns—especially with respect to taxes. Surpluses are hard to justify as they lead to pressure to either (1) increase spending, (2) cut taxes, or (3) some combination of the two.

Macroeconomic derivatives could easily represent a powerful, albeit partial, solution to this problem. Using historic data, a city like Harrisburg should be able to determine how changes in national or regional GDP growth impact its cash flows. Alternatively, it might do the analysis using the national or a regional growth rate in non-farm payrolls. The city could then enter into a GDP or non-farm payroll swap. We will use the GDP swap to illustrate the process.

Let's suppose that a city's risk management committee (RMC) knows from experience that the municipality's budget is balanced when the real economy grows at 2.7 percent—which is the official estimate of the long-term real GDP growth rate. The RMC (or an outside expert hired for that purpose) has further determined that a one percent change in GDP translates into $20 million of net cash flow for the city. That is, for every one percent increase in GDP the city will have an annual extra $20 million of net cash flow. (Net cash flow is the difference between revenues received and the sum of budgeted and unbudgeted expenditures.) Conversely, for every one percent decrease in GDP, the city will suffer an annual $20 million decrease in net cash flow. When the city is in a cash surplus state, it experiences pressure from special interest groups to spend more and from taxpayers to cut rates. When the city is in a cash deficit state, pressure mounts to raise taxes (always politically unpopular), spend more on social safety net programs, and borrow in the capital markets. The goal is to keep the city's budget balanced in all economic climates.

So the city enters into a 10-year GDP-swap with a macroeconomic swap dealer that uses the same estimate of 2.7 percent long-term real economic growth as measured by GDP. This growth estimate is used to price the swap. Suppose that they structure the swap such that the city pays the swap dealer the actual annual growth rate in GDP on notionals of $2 billion and the swap dealer pays the city an annual fixed rate of 2.7 percent on the same $2 billion of notionals. Note two things: First, the notional principal is not real money, and no one gives this to the other—it only exists for purposes of calculating the later periodic payments. Second, in practice, there would be a spread, measured in basis points, on the GDP leg to compensate the dealer for its role in the swap, but we will ignore that in this example. The structure of the swap, together with the municipality's cash flows from taxes and expenditures, is depicted in Exhibit 13.5.

The beauty of the swap solution is that the city is now insulated (i.e., hedged) against a large portion of its macroeconomic (a form of systemic) risk stemming from the cyclicality of the city's cash flows. Importantly, the city would not want the swap to have a very long tenor because a city's internal dynamics change over time and the degree of cyclicality may be impacted by that change. To see that the swap works, suppose that the economy's growth rate increases to 3.7 percent. Then, under the terms of the swap, the municipality would pay the dealer $74 million (i.e., 3.7 percent × $2 billion), and the swap dealer would pay the city $54 million (i.e., 2.7 percent × $2 billion). In a swap, only the net is exchanged with the higher paying party paying the lower paying party the difference. So, in this case, the city pays the swap dealer $20 million—which is precisely the size of its surplus for the year. On the other hand, suppose that the following year the economy sinks into a recession and GDP growth becomes negative, say –1.3 percent. Then, the swap dealer will pay the city $26 million on the GDP leg. (This is because the payment on

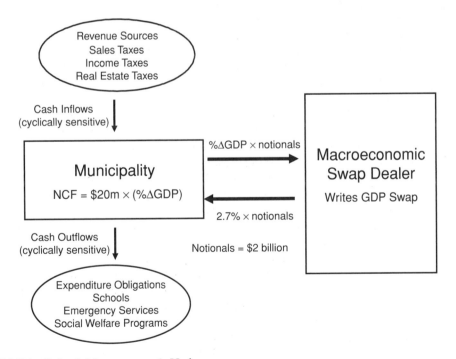

Exhibit 13.5   A Macroeconomic Hedge

the GDP leg is negative, so it goes in the opposite direction.) And the swap dealer also pays the city $54 million on the fixed leg. Thus, the city receives an infusion of $80 million from the swap dealer thereby offsetting its cash flow shortfall caused by the decline in GDP (i.e., the recession).

One of the beautiful things about this solution to a municipality's cyclical macroeconomic risk is that it would likely remove much of the political pressure to increase spending in good economic times and decrease pressure to raise taxes and cut services during poor economic times. Thus, it fosters an environment of stability, which facilitates long-term municipal planning.

Macroeconomic swaps (and other macroeconomic derivatives) are not as easily constructed as we might have led you to believe. In the swap market, dealers act as intermediaries between end users. To function well in this capacity, there needs to be a two-way market. Of course, there are far more corporations and municipalities that are cyclical than counter-cyclical, so one might argue that the market cannot work. But, there are ways around this problem as has been demonstrated by the Case-Shiller real estate indexes. These indexes became the basis of futures contracts and swap dealers can hedge in the futures. It only requires that there be sufficient speculative interest on the other side of the futures contracts. There are, of course, other problems with swaps of this nature, such as how to handle revisions in the GDP number, which can happen several calendar quarters out. But those sorts of issues are resolvable by employing appropriate lags.

Another solution, which really involves an embedded swap, very much the same way that the inflation-indexed bonds involve an embedded swap, is to structure municipal debt offerings with a floating coupon such that it is tied inversely to the growth rate of GDP. For example suppose that, under current market conditions, our aforementioned city could issue a 10-year note paying a fixed rate of 5 percent. Instead, suppose they issue a note paying 2.3 percent plus the growth rate of real GDP. If the long-term growth rate of GDP turns out to be 2.7 percent, then on average, the city has paid an annual coupon of 5 percent over the 10 years. But in years when GDP is above its long-term estimated growth rate, they pay more and in years when GDP is below its long-term estimated growth rate, they pay less. This sort of debt financing would have negated the need for the city of Harrisburg to announce that it was going to miss an interest payment. Indeed, this sort of debt financing would likely lead to a long-run increase in the debt rating of the city. Rating agencies would see the city's finances as more economically stable. This, in turn could lead to an even lower fixed rate component. For example, the coupon might be 2.1 percent plus the GDP growth rate.

In concluding this chapter, we hope that we have demonstrated that there is lots more room for financial innovation and financial engineering. If done right, it can help address systemic problems that have plagued municipalities and corporations alike since the birth of the modern state.

NOTES

1. The importance of a strong figure at the helm of a central bank is well documented in Ahamed (2009).

2. The monetary base is also known as base money, high-powered money, and reserve money.

3. Of course, it is possible for an increase in the money supply, assuming velocity is constant, to show up as a decline in P or Q but a more than offsetting increase in Q or P.

4. We prefer the term *macroeconomic derivative* to economic derivative. In a sense, all derivatives serve an economic purpose and could therefore be loosely called economic derivatives, but not all derivatives can be macroeconomic in nature. For example, a futures contract on a commodity price is "economic" in nature, as the prices of all commodities are determined by the laws of supply and demand. This would generally be "microeconomic" but still economic. The term *macroeconomic derivatives* makes clear that we are talking about a derivative on a macroeconomic variable. Admittedly, it is sometimes difficult to draw the line between what is microeconomic and what is macroeconomic.

5. In the early 2000s, Deutsche Bank and Goldman Sachs collaborated in creating a market in over-the-counter macroeconomic derivatives. Similarly, several futures exchanges have introduced macroeconomic index based futures contracts.

REFERENCES

Ahamed, Liaquat. 2009. *The Lords of Finance.* London: Penguin Press.

Bansal, Vipul K., J. F. Marshall, and R. P. Yuyuenyongwatana. 1995. "Macroeconomic Derivatives: More Viable than First Thought!" *Global Finance Journal* 6:2, 101–110.

Blaise Gadanecz, R. Moessner, and C. Upper. 2007. "Economic Derivatives." Bank for International Settlements, *BIS Quarterly Review*, March.

Gurkaynak, Refet, and J. Wolfers. 2006. "Macroeconomic Derivatives: An Initial Analysis of Market-Based Macro Forecasts, Uncertainty, and Risk." NBER Working Paper No. 11929.

Marshall, John, F. V. Bansal, A. F. Herbst, and A. L. Tucker. 1992. "Hedging Business Cycle Risk with Macro Swaps and Options." *Continental Bank Journal of Applied Corporate Finance* 4:4, 103–108.

Shiller, Robert. J., 1993. *Macro Markets: Creating Institutions for Managing Society's Largest Financial Risks.* New York: Oxford University Press.

ABOUT THE AUTHORS

Cara M. Marshall is a professor of finance at Queens College of the City University of New York. Cara holds a PhD in Financial Economics from Fordham University and an MBA with a focus on Quantitative Analysis from St. John's University. Her research interests focus on financial engineering, risk management, and derivatives, as well as behavioral and experimental methods in finance. Cara's PhD dissertation examined the pricing of volatility on U.S. options exchanges. Prior to academia, Cara worked in internet engineering, developing websites, and a platform for online course delivery. She has also worked as a marketing manager for a conference and training company. Over the years, Cara has consulted to several investment banks as a trainer. In this role, she taught financial modeling to bank employees in New York, London, and Singapore. Cara has also performed analysis for hedge funds and for firms in other industries.

John H. O'Connell is managing director of Financial Integration, LLC, a New York-based provider of training programs to leading financial institutions, which he founded in 2003. John brings considerable practical experience to the classroom with over 24 years of Wall Street experience. John started his career in finance at

Refco as a floor broker on the New York Mercantile Exchange and later organized and conducted intensive derivatives training and marketing programs on behalf of Refco for commercial hedgers in Europe, Latin America, and Asia. Subsequently, he managed Refco's New York research department and international client education programs. In 1996 John joined Morgan Stanley where he served as executive director for global financial product training. While at Morgan Stanley, he designed and implemented educational programs for new hires, clients, and senior traders. John is a CFA and holds an MBA in Finance from the Stern School of Business at NYU. He is a frequently requested speaker and has published in a number of industry outlets including *Euromoney* and *Futures and Options Magazine*. John came to finance after serving as an officer in the United States Army.

CHAPTER 14

Independent Valuation for Financially-Engineered Products

CINDY W. MA AND ANDREW MACNAMARA
Houlihan Lokey

INTRODUCTION

Financial engineering has led to the creation of a wide variety of financial vehicles. Many of these are complex, making the analysis and risk management of these products more difficult than "plain-vanilla" investments. However, there are many situations that call for valuation, including portfolio management (whether to buy or sell an investment at a given value), financial reporting (including net asset value calculation), and dispute resolution. In these circumstances, it is often critical to develop a thoughtful, flexible valuation model backed up with well-researched input assumptions, and to present an analysis of multiple potential scenarios. Because of the complexity of these tasks and the amount of judgment required to analyze financially-engineered products, it is often advisable to seek an independent party (i.e., other than the portfolio managers or the members of the deal team) to help provide valuation advice. While some larger institutions have the resources to develop an internal group that provides independent views, third-party support can provide both small and large institutions with needed analytical support and independence.

Transparency has been a key issue for market participants throughout the financial crisis that started in 2007. Whether decrying the complexity of relationships between giant financial institutions or implementing rules meant to increase disclosure requirements, both investors and regulators have indicated that transparency is critical. For example, the recent Dodd-Frank Wall Street Reform and Consumer Protection Act requires central clearing of certain over-the-counter derivatives, along with data collection and publication in a section appropriately titled "Wall Street Transparency and Accountability." Indeed, financially-engineered products are often esoteric, bespoke, or complex. Independent valuations can be one element of a strategy designed to improve the price transparency for these instruments.

In this chapter, we investigate the world of financial engineering, giving some examples of these kinds of products along with various analytical methods and considerations for valuation and risk management. Finally, we argue that the complexity of many financially engineered products, and the amount of judgment required in evaluating the choice and application of valuation models, suggest that third parties can provide independence and transparency to the valuation process, which is critical in many circumstances.

THE UNIVERSE OF FINANCIALLY ENGINEERED PRODUCTS

What are financially-engineered products? Let us first examine the field of financial engineering. According to the International Association of Financial Engineers (IAFE), "financial engineering is the application of mathematical methods to the solution of problems in finance." This statement gives a sense of the breadth of topics the field covers. While the categorization of "financially engineered products" may be disputed, some of the papers that appear on the IAFE's website discuss such products as credit derivatives, collateralized debt obligations (CDOs), insurance, and commodity derivatives. In addition, other topics that have been addressed include systemic, market, and liquidity risk, as well as hedge fund return attribution.

Accounting standards have been trending toward greater use of market data in financial reporting for some time. While Accounting Standards Codification (ASC) Topic 820, "Fair Value Measurement," has generated a significant amount of press coverage, it introduces relatively few new concepts.[1] ASC Topic 820 does not prescribe when assets or liabilities should be measured at fair value, but it does define fair value. It also gives a framework as to how fair value should be measured and requires certain additional disclosures. Therefore, ASC Topic 820 is a key source document for financial reporting and valuation issues.

ASC Topic 820 defines fair value as "the price that would be received to sell an asset or paid to transfer a liability in an orderly transaction between market participants at the measurement date." It clarifies that the price should not represent a distressed liquidation or other forced transaction, and contemplates a "usual and customary" exposure to the market to allow for marketing activities. "Market participants" are buyers and sellers who are independent of the reporting entity, have a reasonable knowledge of the asset or liability, and are both willing and able to transact for the asset or liability.

THE FAIR VALUE HIERARCHY

ASC Topic 820 requires the measurement of assets and liabilities using three hierarchical levels of input assumptions:

> **Level 1 Inputs.** Quoted prices in active markets for identical assets or liabilities. Exchange-traded instruments or securities normally fall under Level 1. Liquid exchange trading prices generally provide the most reliable evidence of fair value and should be used when available.
> Examples:
> - Shares of IBM common stock trade on the New York Stock Exchange.
> - Heating oil futures contracts trade on the New York Mercantile Exchange (NYMEX).

Level 2 Inputs. When Level 1 prices are unavailable, ASC Topic 820 requires the use of Level 2 inputs, which include quoted prices for similar assets or liabilities in active markets, quoted prices for identical assets or liabilities in illiquid markets, inputs other than quoted prices that are observable for the asset or liability (e.g., interest rate curves and volatilities), and inputs that are derived principally from or corroborated by observable market data.

Examples:

- Consider a one-year swaption on heating oil. Although this over-the-counter derivative contract is not publicly traded, standard valuation models exist, and the input assumptions to value this derivative contract can be derived from market-observable data without significant judgment or adjustments. For example, key input assumptions used to value these instruments include the future prices of heating oil and expected heating oil volatility; both can be derived from the heating oil futures and options contracts traded on the NYMEX. Since one-year options on heating oil are traded and can give meaningful estimates of implied future volatility, these input assumptions are considered Level 2.
- Consider a corporate bond that is not quoted by brokers and is exempt from registration under Rule 144A. The bond does not trade publicly because it is not registered, and it is not quoted over the counter, so the security cannot be considered Level 1.[2] However, the same corporation may have issued a registered, publicly-traded bond with substantially similar terms and maturity date as the unregistered debenture. Assuming that the publicly-traded bond has traded recently and an implied yield can be extracted, this and other inputs and assumptions (e.g., benchmark interest rates) would likely be considered Level 2 inputs.

Level 3 Inputs. Unobservable inputs based on assets and liabilities that are not actively traded and must be estimated, using assumptions that market participants would use when pricing the asset or liability. Level 3 assets and liabilities are those that trade so infrequently that there is no reliable market price. It is important to note that even when using management's estimates or inputs, the objective of estimating the "exit price" based on inputs and assumptions that market participants would use remains the same.

Examples:

- Level 3 inputs include unobservable interest rates for a long-dated currency swap, volatility estimates for long-term equity options, or a financial forecast based on management's assumptions when there is no information reasonably available to suggest that market participants would use different assumptions.
- Ten-year heating oil swaptions are an example of an investment that would require Level 3 input assumptions. The models used in valuation are the same as a one-year heating oil swaption contract, but since 10-year heating oil futures and options contracts are not publicly traded on NYMEX, the derivation of the 10-year future heating oil prices and corresponding expected volatility requires judgment. As such, they are considered to be Level 3 inputs.

Exhibit 14.1　Fair Value Hierarchy

	Level 1 Marking-to-Market	Level 2 Marking-to-Matrix	Level 3 Marking-to-Model
Description	Assets with observable market pricing.	Assets with inputs based on observable market prices.	Not based on market prices, but rather management estimates of market participants' assumptions.
Examples	Listed equity/fixed income securities traded on an active exchange. Exchange-traded derivatives.	Infrequently traded bonds. Structured notes. OTC derivatives with values based on observable LIBOR forward interest rate curves.	Real estate and private equity investments. Long-dated financial instruments. Illiquid asset-backed securities. Intangible assets.
Valuation Precision	**Most**	**Less**	**Least**

As shown in Exhibit 14.1, Level 1 deals with assets with observable market pricing while Level 3 is the most subjective. As such, the valuation precision generally decreases as the level increases.

Valuation of financially engineered products involves many different types of mathematical analytical techniques. For example, according to a model described by Hull and White,[3] the valuation of a credit default swap (CDS) involves estimating expected probabilities of default based on bonds issued by the reference entity and then computing the present value of the expected payments and payoffs on the swap. On the other hand, valuing traditional CDOs can involve simulations based on copulas, which model the joint distributions of several variables (in this case, the probabilities of default of the underlying bonds). In addition, derivatives valuation procedures today often incorporate a credit value adjustment,[4] which is intended to capture the risk that the counterparty to the transaction will not make good on its commitments. Many financially engineered products, especially highly complex, bespoke instruments, would fall under the Level 3 category for valuation purposes under ASC Topic 820.

Valuing financially engineered products can be challenging. First, financially engineered products are often esoteric or bespoke; they often are not well-covered by academic research, and as a result the models used to value them may not capture certain relevant features or may break down under certain market conditions. Second, much of the valuation technology developed to analyze these products involves models that contain simplifying assumptions designed to allow traders to obtain valuations quickly; however, these "black box" models can sometimes obscure important modeling assumptions that should be considered carefully in the context of a valuation. As a result, analyzing these products requires a careful evaluation of the facts and circumstances surrounding the product to see whether and how standard modeling practices can be applied and where they fall short.

MODELING ALTERNATIVES: CDOs

One example of the importance of scrutinizing accepted valuation models involves CDOs. These products were developed in the late 1980s. In general, a CDO raises capital in the form of debt and equity and invests it in a portfolio of financial securities. Conceptually, CDOs redistribute the risks and returns on a portfolio of collateral according to certain structural rules. Initially, CDOs focused on funding the purchase of portfolios of corporate debt, but as the product matured, other forms of collateral were used, including corporate loans, commercial real estate, and trust-preferred securities. Structured finance or asset-backed security CDOs (SF CDOs or ABS CDOs) invest in portfolios of securitized products, including mortgage-backed securities of different kinds, and sometimes liabilities, or "tranches," issued by other CDOs.

Like other forms of securitizations, CDOs usually contain provisions designed to allocate credit risk (i.e., minimize the risk of principal loss to the most senior tranches). One of these provisions is structural subordination—in general, senior tranches receive principal before junior tranches, and junior tranches absorb losses before senior tranches. Exhibit 14.2 illustrates structural subordination and another credit risk protection used in other securitized products, overcollateralization,[5] in a generic asset-backed structure.

These charts illustrate structural subordination (left) and overcollateralization (right). The different CDO liabilities are labeled with different names that correspond to differing levels of seniority: for instance, the Class A1 notes are shown as senior to the Class A2 notes and so on. The "R" class denotes the residual, or equity of the deal, which is usually structured to receive any excess cash flow generated by the assets.

In addition, CDOs often include trigger tests, which can affect the distribution of cash flows among tranches and, in so doing, provide additional protection to senior tranches. For ABS CDOs, these are often in the form of overcollateralization (OC) tests and interest coverage (IC) tests. OC tests are defined at the tranche level and measure (in general) the ratio of the par amount of non-defaulted collateral to the par amount of outstanding debt for a given tranche.[6] The higher the ratio,

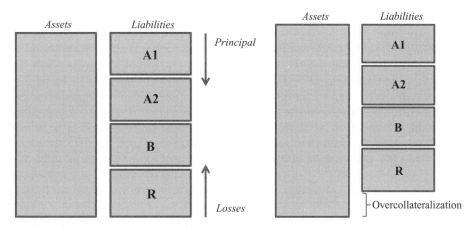

Exhibit 14.2 Structural Subordination and Overcollateralization Provide Credit Support

the more note holders are protected from credit loss.[7] IC tests are also measured at the tranche level and compare the ratio of the scheduled interest due on the underlying collateral to the scheduled interest due on the given tranche and all tranches senior to that tranche. Again, the higher the ratio, the more protection the senior note holders have. These ratios are periodically tested against predefined trigger levels. If the ratio does not meet the trigger, interest proceeds from the collateral are diverted; instead of paying interest on junior tranches, the interest that would have been paid on those tranches is used to pay principal on the senior tranches. Since the interest is not paid in cash on the junior tranches, they are sometimes referred to as pay-in-kind tranches.[8]

In general, the more junior tranches of a CDO are more risky, since they bear losses before the more senior tranches and can also have interest paid in-kind instead of in cash. For the equity in a CDO, the risk may be more nuanced. CDO equity cash flows can be concentrated toward the end of the life of the deal; once the principal of the debt tranches is paid off from the amortization of collateral assets, the equity is entitled to the remaining collateral value, including any excess spread that has built up over the life of the deal (of course, CDO equity is also the first to bear losses on the collateral).

Traditional modeling techniques for CDOs focused on assessing the probabilities of default of individual collateral assets and the correlations of those defaults. For example, many market participants use a Gaussian copula model for estimating the probabilities of default of the CDO portfolio and, in turn, the CDO tranches themselves. Extensions of this concept include the use of "base" correlation mapping, which infers a correlation parameter from observable market data in a similar way that implied volatilities are calculated for traded options based on the Black-Scholes option pricing model. However, this technique has seen much negative publicity in the wake of the financial crisis starting in 2007. It is argued that some of the simplifying assumptions of the model itself, like the normal distribution assumption, do not reflect reality and lead to dramatic underpricing of risk because the model does not give sufficient weight to the incidence of highly-correlated, elevated default rates in times of market stress.

How can an analyst reconcile the elegance and market-wide use of these mathematical models with a fundamental understanding of the shortcomings of the model? One important first step is to return to basics: understand the key assumptions of the model, under what circumstances they can make the model results less useful, and how critical they are. Once this understanding is established, additional steps can be taken to evaluate or mitigate the model's shortcomings. For example, the distribution of defaults between similar assets could be measured, and the chances of a severe downturn that would cause highly-correlated, elevated defaults estimated. A more rigorous investigation would involve the construction of different models that do not rely on the same modeling assumptions; valuation results should be corroborated by these models.

Valuation Methodologies: Cash Flow Analysis

For example, one alternative to copula models that has been used by many analysts of CDOs (especially ABS CDOs) is a discounted cash flow (DCF) model. One of the key valuation steps in performing a DCF analysis of securitized products is developing reasonable assumptions about the expected future cash flow characteristics of the underlying assets. The cash flow characteristics of a pool of securitized assets are generally affected by factors such as prepayment rates, delinquency rates, default rates, and loss severity.

Prepayment rates refer to early repayments of a loan by a borrower.[9] Prepayments are generally paid out to senior tranches before junior tranches, so an increased amount of prepayments will affect senior tranches and junior tranches differently. The more prepayments a given deal experiences, the shorter the life of the senior tranches will be; this can result in a higher value (if the bonds are already trading below par) or a lower value (if the bonds are already trading above par) based on straightforward bond mechanics. However, if a deal experiences an increased level of prepayments, junior tranches will not be able to benefit from an increased level of excess spread from those prepaid loans. Therefore, increased prepayments may in fact be detrimental to the value of junior tranches.[10]

Delinquency is the percentage of the loan pool that is late in paying scheduled payments by a certain amount of time and the loan is termed "delinquent" by a certain number of days (e.g., 30–59 days delinquent, 60–89 days delinquent, etc.).

Default rates are rates at which borrowers default, or fail to satisfy their obligations, on their loans.[11] Since defaults generally result in some recovery of principal for the loan holder when the underlying collateral is sold, defaults usually result in an early repayment of principal on the underlying collateral. However, unlike other forms of prepayments, default liquidations often result in accompanying losses if the liquidation proceeds are insufficient to repay the loan. Therefore, liquidation proceeds are usually used to pay down senior tranches while losses are applied against the credit enhancements at the lower end of the capital structure (e.g., overcollateralization and junior tranches). For a senior tranche, then, an increased level of default can result in increased principal payments in the near term, which can be beneficial to senior debt holders. However, if built-up losses exhaust the credit enhancements on a senior tranche, the principal of the tranche can be affected by losses as well; once collateral losses reach this point, increased defaults will result in lower cash flows to the senior tranches; this, in turn, may result in lower values for those tranches. Since junior tranches generally absorb losses before senior tranches and often do not receive prepayments, increasing default levels usually result in lower values for these tranches. These relationships are highly dependent on the waterfall structure of the deal.

Loss severity measures the amount of loss on a defaulted loan's principal experienced upon the liquidation of the underlying property.[12] The lower collateral values fall, the lower the amount of liquidation proceeds that are available to the trust; and consequently the higher the loss severity. Also, for loans that hold a second or higher lien on the underlying collateral, liquidation proceeds are applied to the first-lien loan before proceeds are available to pay the junior-lien loan. Therefore, loss severities are generally much higher on these junior-lien loans than on first-lien loans, often approaching 100 percent or more (e.g., costs incurred in the foreclosure process build up over time, and since they are often paid upon a liquidation of the underlying collateral before the junior-lien loans, the calculated loss severity on those junior loans can exceed 100 percent).

Significant resources have been dedicated to estimating the projected future cash flow performance of pools of securitized collateral. In the case of residential mortgage loans, analyses range from simple extrapolations of historical performance trends to state-based roll-rate models that project the probabilities of given borrowers entering different payment states (e.g., from current to paid off, or from current to 30 days delinquent) to detailed loan-level econometric models. Insights from the latter types of studies have revealed the connection between macroeconomic variables and loan performance (e.g., when interest rates decrease, voluntary prepayments tend to increase as borrowers refinance their loans early; also, when home prices decline, recovery rates on defaulted loans also decline, since the reduced proceeds from the sale of the collateral are used to satisfy the claim of the lender). Regardless of the specific projection methodology chosen, it is important to test the assumptions through comparative analysis: Are the near-term projections consistent with recent historical performance? Are the projections internally consistent (e.g., if the collateral includes a large population of delinquent loans, the default rates should be expected to increase)? Are there fundamental characteristics of the collateral being adequately captured (e.g., the projections should reflect rate resets on adjustable-rate loans)? Are macroeconomic trends or conditions being captured (e.g., loan modification programs)?

In addition to forming a reasonable set of loan pool projections, it is often helpful to incorporate multiple scenarios to capture different possible outcomes of loan performance.

Scenario Analysis

Many financially-engineered products incorporate the concept of financial leverage in their structures, either explicitly (as in the tranches of CDOs) or implicitly (derivatives positions can be used as vehicles for obtaining leveraged exposure to underlying investments). In the context of credit risk, leverage acts to increase the "tail risk" of the investment. An extreme example can be seen in a mezzanine tranche of a CDO: These subordinated tranches were often structured as very thin pieces of the capital structure. If losses erode all the credit support below a given tranche, any incremental loss may represent a large percentage write-down on the tranche, even though it may represent only a small loss relative to the size of the collateral pool as a whole. Because of this, loss outcomes can be viewed as almost "binary" for some tranches of these types of CDOs: Losses are either nonexistent, if collateral losses do not erode the credit support, or they are total, if collateral losses result in a write-off of the tranche itself.

For investments that incorporate this type of leverage, evaluating multiple scenarios is especially important. In this way, the analyst can gain an understanding of the sensitivity of the investment's potential cash flows under various plausible scenarios as well as under a worst case and a best case scenario. In some cases, the analyst will assign probabilities to each of the scenarios he or she has created, and weight the value indications from each according to its estimated probability of occurring. In addition, the range of outcomes is also important: If the performance of a leveraged investment is especially sensitive to small, plausible changes in input assumptions, an investor may require additional returns relative to a less-sensitive investment.

It may seem that we have taken a circuitous route from stochastic copula models, which incorporate various probabilities of assets defaulting, to cash flow analysis that is driven by a single set of projections, to scenario analyses, which incorporate multiple projections with different probabilities. However, it is important to remember that the reason to explore alternative models is to address potential deficiencies in existing valuation models. If a scenario-based cash-flow analysis is based on the same fundamental assumptions as the copula model, the analysis will not help address these potential deficiencies.

In addition, thinking about the valuation of a given asset in the context of a different analytical model sometimes highlights different characteristics of the asset that may not be captured well by a given model but that play an important role in valuation. This may help identify risks affecting the investment that may be measured and managed. Also, if a particular valuation model does not incorporate a given risk factor, the model cannot be used for managing the risk of the investment related to that particular factor. This is another benefit of using multiple models to analyze financially-engineered products.

INCORPORATING THE EFFECTS OF ILLIQUIDITY IN VALUATION

Another important factor to consider in valuing financially engineered products is illiquidity. Many of the more esoteric, bespoke, or complex financially engineered products would need to be evaluated using Level 3 inputs under ASC Topic 820. As discussed earlier, Level 3 input assumptions require valuation assumptions not based directly on market evidence. With financial investments whose value is dependent on a significant amount of judgment, the effects of liquidity are important to capture: the risks inherent in that judgment are amplified when the investor cannot easily sell the investment if necessary (i.e., if the investment is illiquid). Therefore, when analyzing a financially engineered product, it is important to capture the effects of the liquidity of the investment.

Liquid assets, such as equities traded on exchanges, are generally much easier to value than illiquid assets. Their worth can usually be determined based on observed transactions that occur between willing buyers and sellers. Illiquid assets are difficult to value because of the absence of transaction data. A fundamental analysis of the value of an illiquid asset is necessary. While liquidity risk is well understood and accepted, even from a common-sense standpoint, its full impact is not always recognized in valuations. For example, the term "liquidity risk" can be applied both to asset liquidity risk (i.e., the risk of not being able to sell an asset because of a lack of volume in the market) and funding liquidity risk (i.e., the risk of a company being forced to liquidate assets because of a lack of available funds). Funding liquidity risk can come into play with leveraged investments, which may draw a margin call when valuation levels fall. Faced with a margin call, an investor is forced to put up cash or sell the investment, sometimes at a considerable loss.

The Global Financial Crisis Exposed the Illiquidity Risk of Financially Engineered Products

The two forms of liquidity risk are intertwined. Declines in one form of liquidity can lead to declines in the other. This was seen vividly during the global financial crisis starting in 2007, when market participants were painfully on the "misery-go-round:" (i) asset values dropped quickly, causing an upheaval among banks, structured investment vehicles, and much of the securitization market; (ii) leveraged entities were forced to liquidate assets to meet margin calls; (iii) the resulting excess supply of assets drove down their values further; (iv) lower asset values forced further margin calls; and the misery cycle continued. Even companies that avoid leverage can face funding risk. When other counterparties cannot finance the purchase of assets through capital markets, demand for the assets can fall, leading to declines in asset values.

The value of illiquidity has been observed in many anecdotal situations throughout the recent financial crisis. Many investors that formerly purchased financially-engineered products (whether structured products, auction-rate securities, or complex, bespoke derivatives transactions) have "fled the market" and no longer invest in these products. The prices of some of these products have gone down despite low estimated credit risk, suggesting that investors value liquidity.

Exhibit 14.3 contains a chart of the historical yield spread between the 3-month AA-rated financial commercial paper and 3-month constant-maturity Treasury. This measure has been used as an indication of market-wide liquidity. During the summer of 2007, short-term debt (such as the commercial paper issued by financial institutions and structured investment vehicles) became difficult to refinance, and transaction volume in risky instruments dropped dramatically. As the financial

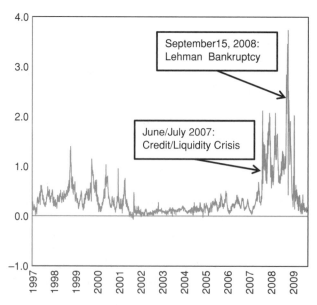

Exhibit 14.3   Spread Between 3-Month Commercial Paper and 3-Month Treasury (Percent)
Source: Board of Governors of the Federal Reserve System.

crisis unfolded, credit worries became increasingly apparent as well, with loss estimates on residential-mortgage collateral increasing significantly. In September 2008, Lehman Brothers Holdings, Inc. filed for bankruptcy protection after having failed to obtain support from the U.S. government. The failure of Lehman caused global market disruptions and pushed the illiquidity in debt markets to an extreme.

What Is Liquidity?

We often have a basic sense of what liquidity means: for example, we recognize that publicly-traded common stock is usually liquid while investments in real estate are generally not. Many recent news stories have discussed how the markets became illiquid during the global credit crisis, with market participants becoming unwilling to transact.

A definition of liquidity may include several factors, including: (1) a reasonable timeframe for transacting; (2) a minimal deviation from some fundamental measure of value; and (3) the ability to transact in large blocks without adverse price impact. Liquidity is a continuum, not a binary "liquid vs. illiquid" state of being: two different investments can be equal, slightly different, or very different in liquidity. We can often recognize liquidity. We have developed theories about what affects it, and we can observe "proxies" for liquidity that confirm our intuition about which securities are liquid and which are not. However, it is not a straightforward, easily measurable property. There are no trading data that directly demonstrate the discounts that market participants apply to completely illiquid securities—by definition, such securities do not trade!

As we have seen from recent market conditions, liquidity can vary substantially over time; it also varies with various characteristics of the subject asset. It depends on the nature of market participants (pension funds investing cash in low-risk securities value liquidity very differently from private equity funds making subordinated unsecured loans to risky creditors), and many argue it depends on the liquidity of the instrument in a portfolio context. That is, an asset that is expected to become illiquid when the rest of the investor's portfolio is also illiquid is riskier than an asset whose liquidity patterns are unrelated to the liquidity patterns of the rest of the portfolio. Thus, in valuing illiquid assets, we must be aware not only of how the level of illiquidity is related to other properties of the security (for instance, the credit ratings of a corporate bond), but also of market conditions as of the date of the analysis.

One framework for evaluating liquidity relates to the round-trip transaction cost of buying and selling a given investment. Transaction costs can be divided into three categories. The first component encompasses the explicit costs of transacting, including the bid-ask spread and any commissions charged for trading. A second component is the market impact of a trade—the amount by which a sale of the investment will drive the market price down. A third component, explored by Treynor (1981), is opportunity cost, or what opportunities are given up by waiting for the "right time" to liquidate the investment. These components are important in evaluating the quality of trading execution,[13] and have been found to be related to metrics associated with liquidity.

Both bid-ask spreads and price impact costs seem to be affected by the volume of trading and measures of turnover. With respect to opportunity costs, the less liquid the investment, the more time it may take to liquidate that investment at the right price; in this situation, the potential for lost profits increases. Opportunity costs to a particular investor may also be impacted by factors such as the investment strategy of the investor: that is, the more the investor values the ability to trade investments frequently, the more the cost of waiting to liquidate a particular position. These factors indicate that investments that are less liquid should bear higher transaction costs than investments that are more liquid.

Illiquidity across Different Asset Classes

There has been significant research into the effects of illiquidity on value across various types of investments. Some of the first lines of liquidity research investigated the effects of liquidity in the market for Treasury securities. It is a common notion that on-the-run (i.e., most-recently auctioned) Treasuries are considered more liquid than comparable off-the-run Treasuries. This notion is often attributed to the securities becoming locked up in investors' portfolios, and thus unavailable for trade.[14] Several published studies provide evidence of this, though rebuttals attribute price differences between on-the-run and off-the-run Treasuries to factors other than liquidity.[15] More recent papers have argued that measured differences can only be explained by differences in liquidity.[16]

Research on corporate debt markets has yielded much clearer evidence of a discount for illiquidity. Some researchers have tried to estimate a "proxy" for the level of liquidity of a given bond, and estimate price or yield sensitivities to these proxies.[17] Other researchers have tried to account for factors other than liquidity that affect yield and treat the "leftover" unexplained yield component as a liquidity premium.[18]

Equity markets have also been widely studied for the effects of liquidity. Whether examining sales of restricted stock (i.e., comparing the price at which restricted stock sells relative to the corresponding public market quote), studying stock sales just prior to initial public offering, or performing more complex studies that integrate liquidity factors into asset-pricing models or view liquidity with option-like characteristics, academic research has found strong support for the existence of a discount for illiquid stock.[19]

Limited Studies on Illiquidity of Derivatives

Although the literature on liquidity and derivatives is much sparser than that for equity or fixed income assets, several studies have provided evidence of a value effect on derivative instruments due to liquidity. For example, employee stock options (ESOs) are generally long-dated, non-exchange-traded options with numerous restrictions (such as non-transferability, vesting requirements, and blackout periods for exercise). As such, ESOs are generally issued at a discount to the exchange-traded options issued by the same company. Huddart and Lang (1996) provide evidence that employees exercise ESOs relatively early in the option's life (i.e., suboptimally), an effect they attribute in part to the effect of non-transferability (i.e., illiquidity) for the ESO holders.[20]

Brenner, Eldor, and Hauser (2001) studied the effect of illiquidity on the value of currency options, and found that options that are non-tradable until expiration are discounted by an average of 21 percent. Using data on exchange-traded options on U.S. stocks from 1996 to 2004, Cao and Wei (2008) confirmed the existence of a liquidity risk premium by examining differences in the option premium according to a variety of proxies for liquidity, including proportional bid-ask spread, trading volume, dollar trading volume, and others. Çetin, Jarrow and Protter (2004), Jarrow and Protter (2005), Çetin, Jarrow, Protter, and Warachka (2006), and Jarrow and Protter (2007) all worked toward constructing a theoretical closed-form framework that incorporates liquidity risk into options pricing. Modeling liquidity risk as a stochastic supply curve, these models incorporate liquidity risk into the Black-Scholes options pricing formula.

To account for the effects of illiquidity in valuing derivatives, several factors should be considered. First, if the underlying asset itself is illiquid, it may be appropriate for the valuation model to capture the liquidity-adjusted value of the asset. For example, in valuing an option on a private company's stock, the illiquid value of the stock may be used in estimating the stock value input to the option model. Also, the valuation model could be adjusted to capture any ancillary effects of illiquidity, such as exercise behavior of holders of ESOs. Finally, investor preferences for liquidity may be captured by applying an appropriate discount to the model results. Given the limited empirical studies that have been performed, it is difficult to quantify the amount of required discount.

Derivatives and other financially engineered products are often valued with models that are highly sensitive to only one major input. For example, the Black-Scholes model requires several inputs, but the most critical one is volatility. Because of this variable's importance, many options traders will provide quotes not in terms of price, but in terms of implied volatility. As noted earlier, the bid-ask spread on an asset is often thought to correspond closely with that asset's level of liquidity; therefore, it is also common to observe adjustments for illiquid options being captured through a change in the volatility used as an input to the valuation.

Looking Ahead: Quantifying the Effects of Illiquidity for Financially Engineered Products

Studies of the effects of liquidity across asset classes have found substantial evidence of an effect of liquidity on asset value: in general, the more liquid the investment, the higher the value, all else equal. While substantial effort has gone into quantifying equity and fixed-income discounts, the body of research does not reveal much about financially-engineered products—the asset classes that cause much of the trouble for today's markets. Derivatives have received some research treatment, but there are not enough research results to form an appropriate conclusion; this is an area that deserves further study.

When incorporating discounts for illiquidity into a valuation of financially-engineered products, several approaches can be taken. First, the value can be computed by assuming the investment is liquid (e.g., by using data on comparable publicly-traded investments), and then applying a discount to the resulting value. Second, an adjustment for illiquidity can be incorporated into the valuation itself—for example, through an incremental increase in a risk-adjusted discount rate for a discounted cash flow analysis. In either case, the discount applied or the adjustment made should appropriately reflect the circumstances of the invest-ment and how those circumstances would likely be valued by market participants. This could be done either through a qualitative approach, using empirical data or the results of academic studies and adjusting appropriately, or through a more quantitative approach.

It should be noted that many of the studies we have reviewed are based on data for registered, relatively liquid investments. Applying the results of these studies or methodologies to private, completely illiquid positions requires making the assumption that the findings from liquid markets can be applied to a private transaction. As always, the judgment of the valuation practitioner is required here, and this assumption should be considered carefully.

THE ROLE OF THIRD-PARTY VALUATION PROVIDERS

We have reviewed several important aspects related to the valuation of financially engineered products. From model choice and the use of alternative models to incorporating the effects of illiquidity in valuations, it is important to incorporate common sense and judgment in the process and to ensure a robust process by considering value from a number of different perspectives.

Another aspect of valuation that is critically important is the valuation process. With any valuation, biases will influence the result; in many contexts it is therefore critical to minimize these biases and mitigate any conflicts of interest that present themselves in the process.

In the market for financially engineered products there are many opportunities for these conflicts to arise. Often, one or both parties to a transaction have an incentive to minimize or maximize the transacted value of the product. In some instances, third-party advisors may be compensated based on the value of the investment, leading to a conflict of interest. Independence is therefore a critical factor in dealing with valuation risk. Independent parties can provide comfort that a model and the assumptions that are used with that model are appropriate; independent parties can also mitigate the risk of deliberate manipulation of values through complex modeling.

Large financial institutions often have dedicated groups that provide indepen-dent valuation and risk management services within the organization. However, when these internal groups disagree with business managers, political struggles can ensue. Smaller financial institutions often do not have the scale to invest in a dedicated valuation control or risk management group. In both of these situations, obtaining third-party support is an industry best practice.

Often times, third parties are engaged to provide a written opinion as to the value of a particular investment. However, not all third party opinions are equal. Different forms of opinion can include "negative assurance," "positive assurance," and full independent valuations. Negative and positive assurance opinions typ-ically make use of limited procedures, in contrast to full valuations, which are usually more comprehensive and rigorous.

In a negative assurance opinion, a third party renders the opinion that an entity's determination of value "does not appear unreasonable." In a positive assurance opinion, which is similar to a negative assurance opinion, a third party concludes that a firm's valuation "appears reasonable." In both cases, the third party generally reviews its client's own valuations, as opposed to developing its own independent opinion of value. When starting with someone else's valuation analysis, it is easy to overlook broader questions of whether a model is appropriate; also, biases can affect the evaluation of model input assumptions. A full independent valuation provides the highest degree of independence of the three forms of opinion. In addition, full independent valuation is the subject of many professional "best practice" standards: Business valuation and real estate appraisal standards are widely known. In contrast, determining whether a given valuation is "reasonable" is highly qualitative, and there are no industry standards or valuation guidance to set the scope and the boundary for reasonableness.

In recent years, with the development of complex financially engineered products and the ensuing financial crisis, transparency has become an essential component of third-party valuations. Whether for large institutions or smaller shops, independent third-party valuation can help provide the analytical support, independence, and political leverage to deliver positive, proactive results. Since portfolio managers' compensation is often tied to investment performance, the independence of the analysis becomes even more critical. When third-party opinions are used, management should take steps to understand what type of valuation is being done, and what methodologies, inputs, and assumptions are being used. Investors should also be aware of what form of valuation opinion will be delivered.

CONCLUSION

In today's investment world, the growth in financially-engineered products has made analyzing investments more challenging, while making valuation even more vital than in the past. Valuation is a key and integral part of financial organization, and will only grow in importance. As professionals involved in this market, we must be aware of the various techniques and pitfalls, and design processes that mitigate the model risk and other risks that have led to criticism in the past.

The valuation of assets and liabilities is often more art than science, especially when using unobservable data to assess the worth of illiquid investments. While rules of thumb and quantitative studies can and should be used to help guide the professional, it is also critical to incorporate human judgment and an understanding of the drivers of value into the process.

In addition, we must be aware of the valuation requirements, as independence can often be a critical element to the valuation process. When third parties are used to help with valuation analyses, it is important for the end users to understand the scope of the analysis to be performed and the types of deliverables to be presented.

NOTES

1. ASC Topic 820, formerly known as Statement of Financial Accounting Standards Number 157, was unveiled by the Financial Accounting Standards Board in 2006.

2. Some securities that are exempt from registration under Rule 144A are traded over the counter through dealers, and investors may be able to obtain quotes that would be considered Level 1 inputs.

3. See Hull and White (2000).

4. While counterparty risk was recognized before the financial crisis that started in 2007, including this factor in valuations picked up considerably during the crisis. Credit risk adjustment analysis is outside the scope of traditional derivatives modeling, and it is complicated, affected by netting arrangements and collateral agreements with counterparties.

5. Overcollateralization refers to a securitization trust containing a higher principal balance of collateral assets than the sum of the principal balances of the liabilities that finance it.

6. See Kothari (2006).

7. See Lucas, Goodman, and Fabozzi. (2006), p. 20.

8. Ibid., p. 22.

9. Repayments on a pool of loans can be scheduled or unscheduled, and unscheduled repayments can be voluntary or involuntary. Scheduled repayments represent normal amortization of collateral. Involuntary unscheduled prepayments result from a default on an underlying asset and the liquidation of the collateral to satisfy the loan. Voluntary prepayment can occur if a borrower moves, if a borrower refinances because interest rates have declined, or for a variety of other reasons.

10. Additionally, prepayments are sometimes accompanied by prepayment penalty fees, which can accrue to the trust or to specially designated tranches in the waterfall structure.

11. An event of default on a loan is generally a defined term that encompasses a breach of one or more of the terms or covenants of the loan. However, in the context of measuring and predicting loan pool performance, the term "default" can have several interpretations. When a borrower fails to pay an amount due on his or her loan, the loan is termed "delinquent" by a certain number of days (e.g., 30–59 days delinquent, 60–89 days delinquent, etc.). Some market participants classify loans at a certain level of delinquency (e.g., 60 or more days delinquent) as a default. Alternatively, some trustees report defaults only when the underlying property is liquidated and some type of resolution (e.g., a short sale, foreclosure sale, or other liquidation) is brought to the loan. If defaults are measured using anything but the latter metric, there may be a delay between the time that a loan is classified as defaulted and the time that recoveries on the loan are realized (sometimes called the "recovery lag").

12. Since servicers can advance principal and interest while a delinquent loan moves through the default process and are entitled to be repaid these advances from liquidation proceeds, the longer the period between delinquency and liquidation, the less proceeds are available to the trust, resulting in a higher loss severity, all else being equal.

13. See Maginn, et al. (2007).

14. See Pasquariello and Vega (2009).

15. For example, Amihud and Mendelson (1991) and Kamara (1994) find evidence of a liquidity premium, but Strebulaev (2002) does not, instead attributing differences in yield to differences in tax treatment of certain types of Treasury securities.

16. See Longstaff (2004).

17. For example, using a proxy proposed by Lesmond, Ogden, and Trzcinka (1999), De Jong and Driessen (2006) found evidence that bonds with lower levels of liquidity commanded yield premiums over bonds with higher levels of liquidity. Chen, Lesmond, and Wei (2007) found similar results, also incorporating the bid-ask spread as a proxy for liquidity.

18. Longstaff, Mithal, and Neis (2005) provide an example of this approach. They use credit default swap spreads to account for credit risk and Treasury yields to account for risk-free interest rates. They found that the "residual" yield was correlated with market-wide measures of liquidity.

19. For an overview of various approaches to studying the liquidity of equity markets, see Damodaran (2005).

20. See Huddart and Lang (1996).

21. Brenner, Eldor, and Hauser (2001).

REFERENCES

Amihud, Y. and H. Mendelson. 1991. "Liquidity, Maturity, and the Yield on U.S. Treasury Securities." *Journal of Finance* 46, 1411–1425.

Brenner, M., R. Eldor, and S. Hauser. 2001. "The Price of Options Illiquidity." *Journal of Finance* 56 (April): 789–805.

Cao, M. and J. Wei. 2010. "Option Market Liquidity: Commonality and Other Characteristics." *Journal of Financial Markets* 13:1, 20–48.

Çetin, U., R. Jarrow, and P. Protter. 2004. "Liquidity Risk and Arbitrage Pricing Theory." *Finance and Stochastics* 8, 311–341.

Çetin, U., R. Jarrow, P. Protter, and M. Warachka. 2006. "Pricing Options in an Extended Black-Scholes Economy with Illiquidity: Theory and Empirical Evidence." *Review of Financial Studies* 19, 493–529.

Chen, L., D. Lesmond, and J. Wei. 2007. "Corporate Yield Spreads and Bond Liquidity." *Journal of Finance* 62, 119–149.

Damodaran, A. 2005. "Marketability and Value: Measuring the Illiquidity Discount." Working Paper: New York University Stern School of Business. http://ssrn.com/abstract=841484.

De Jong, F. and J. Driessen. 2006. "Liquidity Risk Premia in Corporate Bond Markets." Social Science Research Network. http://ssrn.com/abstract=686681.

Huddart, S. and M. Lang. 1996. "Employee Stock Options Exercises: An Empirical Analysis." *Journal of Accounting and Economics* 21, 5–43.

Hull, J. and A. White. 2000. "Valuing Credit Default Swaps I: No Counterparty Default Risk." *Journal of Derivatives* 8:1, 29–40.

Jarrow, R. and P. Protter. 2005. "Liquidity Risk and Risk Measure Computation." *Review of Futures Markets* 14:1.

Jarrow, R. and P. Protter. 2007. "Liquidity Risk and Option Pricing Theory." In J. Birge and V. Linetsky, eds. *Handbooks in Operations Research and Management Science Volume 15: Financial Engineering*, 727–762. Amsterdam: Elsevier, North Holland.

Kamara, A. 1994. "Liquidity, Taxes, and Short-Term Yields." *Journal of Financial and Quantitative Analysis* 29 (September): 403–417.

Kothari, V. 2006. *Securitization: The Financial Instrument of the Future*. Hoboken, NJ: John Wiley & Sons, 439.

Lesmond, D., J. Ogden, and C. Trzcinka. 1999. "A New Estimate of Transaction Costs." *Review of Financial Studies* 12 (Winter): 1113–1141.

Longstaff, F. 2004. "The Flight-to-Liquidity Premium in U.S. Treasury Bond Prices." *Journal of Business* 77, 511–526.

Longstaff, F., S. Mithal, and E. Neis, 2005. "Corporate Yield Spreads: Default Risk or Liquidity? New Evidence from the Credit Default Swap Market." *Journal of Finance* 60 (October): 2213–2253.

Lucas, D., L. Goodman, and F. Fabozzi. 2006. *Collateralized Debt Obligations: Structures and Analysis*. 2nd ed. Hoboken, NJ: John Wiley & Sons.

Maginn, CFA, J., D. Tuttle, CFA, J. Pinto, CFA, and D. McLeavey, CFA, eds. 2007. *Managing Investment Portfolios: A Dynamic Process, 3rd ed.* Hoboken, NJ: John Wiley & Sons.

Pasquariello, P. and C. Vega. 2009. "The On-the-Run Liquidity Phenomenon." *Journal of Financial Economics* 92 (January): 1–24.

Strebulaev, I. 2002. "Liquidity and Asset Pricing: Evidence from the U.S. Treasuries Market." Working Paper: London Business School.

Treynor, J. 1981. "What Does It Take to Win the Trading Game?" *Financial Analysts Journal* (January–February).

ABOUT THE AUTHORS

Cindy W. Ma is a managing director at Houlihan Lokey, where she leads derivatives and complex securities valuation. She has extensive experience in commodities, derivatives, distressed debts, structured products, and risk management. Since the global credit crisis in July 2007, she has been focused on valuing illiquid instruments, including asset-backed securities, collateralized debt obligations, collateralized loan obligations, mortgage derivatives, auction rate securities, distressed debt instruments and private equity investments for financial reporting, transaction advisory, restructuring alternatives and litigation purposes. She has qualified and testified as an expert witness in the United States courts and arbitration proceedings. She served as a panelist in the Securities and Exchange Commission's roundtable concerning mark-to-market accounting in 2008. She graduated with honors from Columbia University with a PhD in finance and from Indiana University with a BS in accounting. She is a CFA and had a CPA license (now inactive) from the State of Colorado. She is a member of the Financial Instrument Expert Group of the International Valuation Standards Council. Dr. Ma has published numerous articles on valuation and risk management and is a frequent speaker in industry conferences.

Andrew MacNamara is a vice president in Houlihan Lokey's Financial Advisory Services group. He specializes in valuing illiquid equity, debt, and derivative investments, analyzing transactions in connection with fairness and solvency opinions, and building advanced valuation models for complex investments, including structured products, derivative investments, and auction-rate securities. He has significant experience with modeling and computer programming techniques, including Intex, Monte Carlo simulations, C/C++, R, and Perl. He earned a BS in computer science from the University at Albany, State University of New York, with Dean's List and Presidential Scholar distinctions, and graduated with distinction and Beta Gamma Sigma from the Leonard N. Stern School of Business at New York University, where he earned an MBA with specializations in finance and accounting. He received the Dean's Award and the Marcus Nadler Money Marketeers Award and was a Glucksman Fellow. He was also a co-portfolio manager for the MPSIF Value Fund, a student-run endowment fund, and was responsible for the fund's portfolio analytics function.

CHAPTER 15

Quantitative Trading in Equities

KUN GAO
Tudor Investment Corporation

INTRODUCTION

Equity trading began when the Dutch East India Company issued the first stock in 1606. During most of the more than 400 years that have followed, equity trading was treated more like a game than a science, and many of the more famous players in this game were speculators. But over the last 60 years, advances in financial theory set the stage for a more scientific approach. Together with the rapid development of computer technology and the increasingly fast speed with which information is disseminated, these theoretical advances sparked a quantitative revolution over the past 30 years. The combination of advances in financial theory, mathematics, computer technology, and informational access, together with dramatic reductions in trading costs, have inspired a new scientific approach to the trading of equities that has come to be known as *quantitative trading*.

Quantitative trading is the systematic trading of securities using rule-based models and executed through computer algorithms. These computer models, sometimes called systems, are often based on economic theory or patterns observed in the market, fully backtested using historical financial data on a large number of stocks across a long period of time, and encoded in programs to be traded automatically via computers with little or no human intervention.

Selected Key Events in Quantitative Equity Trading

1982: James Simons, a noted professor of mathematics at Stony Brook University, founds Renaissance Technologies. Prior to that, Simons set up his first investment management firm, Moemetrics, in 1977. Renaissance would later prove to be one of the most successful quant-driven hedge fund management firms of all time.

1983: Gerry Bamberger starts trading stock pairs, now known as "pairs trading," at Morgan Stanley with $500,000 and a small group of traders. Later Nunzio Tartaglia would take over the group and rename it Automated Proprietary Trading, or APT. In 1986, APT pulled in what was then an eye-popping $40 million. It pulled in another $50 million in 1987.

1986: David Shaw is hired to Tartaglia's APT group in Morgan Stanley.

1988: David Shaw starts up his own investment firm, D. E. Shaw, with $28 million in capital.

1990: After a few less-than stellar early years, Renaissance Technologies' flagship fund Medallion gains 55 percent after fees. In 1993, with $280 million in assets, Medallion was closed to new investors.

1992: Peter Muller joins Morgan Stanley. By 1994, Muller put together a team of math and computer experts known as the Process Driven Trading (PDT) group. During the late 1990s and early 2000s, PDT accounted for one-quarter of Morgan Stanley's net income.

1994: Clifford Asness joins Goldman Sachs and launches the Quantitative Research Group.

1995: Asness starts Global Alpha, a Goldman Sachs internal hedge fund. By late 1997, the Quantitative Research Group was managing $5 billion in a long-only portfolio and nearly $1 billion in Global Alpha.

1998: Asness leaves Goldman Sachs and starts his own hedge fund, AQR, with $1 billion in start-up capital. It represents one of the largest hedge fund launches on record to that point, and three times as much as the founders originally projected they could raise.

2000: The dot.com bubble begins to burst in March, and quant funds suffer huge losses. Renaissance's Medallion fund lost $250 million in three days, nearly wiping out its year-to-date profit. AQR was on life support and had to come up with $600 million of its $1 billion seed capital, in part due to investors pulling out of the fund.

2007: Quant funds experience an August meltdown. The Renaissance Institutional Equities Fund (RIEF), which managed about $26 billion in assets, was down 8.7 percent from the end of July to Aug 9, 2007—a loss of nearly $2 billion. On a percentage basis, the Medallion fund suffered worse, losing a whopping 17 percent in the same period, which translated to a loss of roughly $1 billion. Goldman's Global Alpha was down nearly 16 percent in August, a loss of about $1.5 billion. AQR and PDT lost about $500 million and $300 million, respectively on Aug 8, 2007.

—This timeline is adapted from Scott Patterson's excellent book
*The Quants: How a New Breed of Math Wizzes Conquered Wall Street
and Nearly Destroyed It* (New York: Crown Publishing, 2010).

Why do some people trade equities using highly quantitative models? The short answer is "Because these models afford benefits that are not available with less quantitative, more traditional approaches." First, quantitative models are rule-based, which means they can be backtested using historical data. Backtesting allows us to investigate the model's performance, and by implication the ideas that motivate the model, in a reproducible and, therefore, more scientific way. This has considerable appeal over more traditional methods that tend to be much more ad hoc. Second, the quantitative approach allows us to explicitly incorporate risk modeling into the backtesting regime, and this, in turn, can lead to better risk-adjusted returns. The result is that quantitatively-driven portfolios often have much lower volatilities than traditional portfolios. Third, computerized models can evaluate thousands of securities and discover market mispricing that human traders are likely to miss, thus enriching trading opportunities. Fourth, quantitative models are more disciplined, so they significantly reduce trading mistakes that often accompany bursts of human emotions such as greed and fear. Indeed, emotion-based trading by non-quantitative traders often causes behavioral anomalies in the markets that can be exploited readily by quantitative models. Lastly, quantitative models can trade more cheaply and more efficiently because of the inherent economies of scale and the lower risk of human error. Compared with more traditional investment styles, quantitative trading offers investors investment products that have moderate, but stable, returns that often have low correlation to the equity market. This low correlation itself is another benefit if the investor only partially diversifies away from more traditional equity approaches.

As already noted, the seed for quantitative equity trading lies in advances in financial theory, especially modern portfolio theory (MPT). Modern portfolio theory began with the work of Harry Markowitz who, in the early 1950s, developed the foundations of optimal portfolio selection in a mean-variance context. Markowitz's (1952) work attracted little attention at first. But over time it led to broad advances in academic research, inspiring later developments such as the capital asset pricing model (CAPM), other asset pricing models, and optimal execution strategies. Before MPT, the decision to include a particular security in a portfolio was made either on speculation or some, often crude, fundamental analysis of the firm based on the firm's financial statements and its dividend policy. Markowitz's breakthrough was his insight that the value of a security to an investor might best be evaluated by its expected future returns, its risk, and its correlation to other securities in the portfolio. Assets' expected returns are directly related to certain components of their risk. Given a group of stocks' expected returns and their full covariance matrix, Markowitz showed that one can use mathematics, specifically mean-variance optimization, to select a portfolio with the highest possible expected return for a target level of risk. Or, for a target future return, one can select a portfolio with the lowest possible risk. Investing is essentially a careful balancing act between risk and expected return. These principles are also the theoretical foundation for quantitative equity trading.

STRUCTURE OF QUANTITATIVE EQUITY MODELS

To this day, the general framework for quantitative research is a twostep process: estimation and implementation. Estimation is to find signals that forecast the key statistics as inspired by Markowitz: stock expected returns, risks, and transaction costs. Implementation is using key statistics to generate and trade portfolios that optimally balance risks and returns.

Estimate Key Statistics

Developing accurate forecasts of key statistics is the first and most critical step in the quantitative investment process. Due to the large number of stocks typically traded, it is impractical for quantitative managers to conduct detailed research on individual stocks to estimate their expected returns, risks, and costs of trading. Instead, quantitative managers heavily rely on statistical models to forecast such metrics.

Forecast Expected Returns

Expected future returns are perhaps the most important statistics to estimate. To estimate expected returns, quantitative managers first identify a set of signals that might be able to forecast future returns. Next, they backtest the performance of each signal both by itself and in combination with other signals. Finally, they blend the effective signals to generate the expected returns.

There are many starting points in the search for signals that have very little cost to the modeler. Among others, good places to start include academic papers, sell-side research reports, finance and investment books, and trader forums and blogs. Authors of trading ideas often describe their models in great details and show their backtest results. However, before trading such strategies, one needs to thoroughly test whether these ideas make intuitive sense, are free of data errors and survivorship bias, sufficiently profitable to cover all transaction costs, and profitable across a variety of economic environments and for a sufficiently broad universe of stocks. But developing a successful investment strategy requires more than just implementing other people's ideas. Successful strategies need to have their edge, which may come from original thoughts, improvements on well-known ideas, or technological advantage.

Typically, quantitative signals are most often classified as either technical or fundamental, depending on the nature of the data used to generate them. Technical strategies try to exploit opportunities in price and volume patterns. Fundamental strategies use company-reported accounting numbers to make investment decisions. Another approach to classify signals is by the way they are traded. After identifying repeating patterns in the data, quantitative managers will either bet that the patterns will reverse themselves or that they will continue. The former is often called mean reversion, and models that employ this approach are sometimes called "mean reverters" or "convergence" strategies. Strategies that take the view that a pattern will continue in the same direction are often called "momentum strategies." These are "trend following" in some sense. Mean reversion and momentum are found in both technical and fundamental data, and perhaps it is a more general way to classify quantitative signals.

Mean Reverter or Convergence Models.   From an historical perspective, mean reversion is possibly the earliest strategy that quantitative equity managers used for trading. In the 1980s, a group of quantitative traders at Morgan Stanley started to use a version of a mean reversion strategy called "pairs trading" to exploit temporary market inefficiencies. They noticed that large block trades would often significantly move the price of a stock, while the price of another stock in the same industry group barely changed. For example, Coca-Cola and Pepsi stocks often move in tandem. If a large buy order on Coca-Cola hits the market its stock price will increase while Pepsi's price will most likely stay about the same. This temporarily elevates the typical spread between the two stock prices. A mean reversion strategy could benefit by buying Pepsi and selling Coca-Cola simultaneously and waiting for the prices of the two to converge to their more normal state. Since this enlarged spread is caused by temporary liquidity imbalance in the market, it usually reverts back quickly, and a profit is earned in the process. Other examples of pairs trading include dual-listed stocks that are traded in more than one locale. The most famous example of pairs trading, however, is the spread between Royal Dutch and Shell. Prior to 2005, Royal Dutch Petroleum and Shell Transport and Trading were two companies that jointly owned the Royal Dutch/Shell entity. The two companies shared the cash flows generated by their jointly owned entity at a contractually-fixed ratio, but the two companies were separately traded on two different exchanges, London and Amsterdam. Therefore, when the prices of these stocks differed due to different liquidity conditions at the two exchanges, pairs trading algorithms would buy the cheaper one and sell the more expensive one to earn a profit when the market corrected.

Mean reversion is also observed in fundamental data. For example, Fama and French (1992, 1998) found that value stocks—which have high book-to-price, earnings-to-price, and cash flow-to-price ratios—often outperform growth stocks (which have much lower ratios). They found that, over time, there was a tendency for these ratios to revert to the mean ratio for the group as a whole. The mean ratio is the average of the same ratio (such as book-to-price) for a group of companies in the same industry. Thus, one would tend to buy those stocks with high ratios and sell those stocks with low ratios. When prices adjust and the spreads narrow, a profit should be earned. There is no guarantee that mean reversion, if it occurs at all, will happen in any specific period of time, so patience is often necessary.

A key characteristic of mean reversion strategies is that they do not aim to price the stock in absolute terms. Instead, they try to identify stocks' attractiveness relative to each other, and then form portfolios that go long on the most attractive stocks and short on the least attractive ones. The goal is to capture the relative inefficiency between the long and short positions. For this reason, these strategies are often viewed as subsets of a broader type of strategy called relative value arbitrage. A long–short portfolio often has a negligible beta and therefore minimal exposure to the market. Indeed, some managers carefully weight the components of these long-short portfolios in such a way that the overall beta is exactly zero. Such portfolios are called "beta neutral" or "market neutral." As you would expect, the returns from market neutral strategies can be completely uncorrelated with market returns.

The advantage of relative value arbitrage is that it avoids the difficult task of determining the true values of stocks. Theoretical equity pricing models, such as dividend discount models, require predictions of a company's future earnings, payout ratios, interest rates, and so forth. All these statistics are time-varying and thus are very difficult to estimate. Further, small estimation errors often lead to significant changes in the final values obtained. Relative value arbitrage attempts to resolve this difficulty by comparing the prices of securities that have similar characteristics. By the law of one price, regardless of whether the market overestimates or underestimates the general level of stock prices, the large spreads between similar stocks are likely to diminish as prices converge.

Why does mean reversion exist in the equity market? Over short time spans, as illustrated in the earlier block trading example, price distortions could be caused by the fact that buyers and sellers come to the market place at random times, thus causing temporary supply and demand imbalances. Market forces gradually correct these aberrations. Over longer time spans, distortions may occur because one company gains a technological edge over its industry competitors. Given time, competitive pressures force the other companies to innovate as well. This can easily explain, for example, why value companies tend to catch up over time to growth companies. Even if growth companies continue to do well, they may acquire value companies, and thus the value spread will still be reduced.

In recent years, behavioral economists have suggested that price distortions may be caused by human traders' overreaction to events. In many ways this theory is at odds with the efficient market theory, which maintains that, collectively, human beings always respond appropriately to events. In the decades after it was introduced in 1970s, the efficient market theory became a cornerstone of academic thought on the subject of market pricing. The theory is predicated on the assumption that people behave rationally at all times—if not individually, then collectively. But more and more evidence has been unearthed over the past twenty years to indicate that while rational behavior may be the norm, there are, at times, significant deviations from rational behavior as a direct consequence of our biological evolution and our psychological imprinting. These departures from the assumption of rationality are such that they can explain a number of behavioral phenomena that can lead to market distortions. The well documented "herd instinct" is probably the simplest of these behavioral traits that is at odds with rational behavior.

But, even without human behavioral errors, "noise" alone might be sufficient for mean reversion to exist in the equity market. Mean reversion strategies provide liquidity to the market place by selling stocks at times when many people want to buy, and by buying stocks at times when many people want to sell. In the short term they can often buy at the bid and sell at the ask, thus capturing the visible bid-ask spread. In the longer term they capture the invisible spreads that markets reward to liquidity providers.

Momentum or Trend-Following Models.   In contrast to mean reverter models, momentum models try to detect signals that indicate a price trend in a stock. They then take a position on the side of the trend: long for up-trending stocks and short for down-trending stocks. One rationale behind the approach is that some people have access to information before others. As the information gradually becomes known to more people, the new recipients of the information push the price further. For example, if a stock's price is rising faster than its peers, it is likely that it is being driven up by traders armed with new bullish information. By positioning themselves on the side of the trend, they will win as long as the trend remains intact. Critical to such strategies is the ability to recognize when the trend has ended in order to exit the position before the profit dissipates.

Such trending activities are common in human behavior in areas other than finance. In many situations, following other people is not a bad strategy. For example, it is difficult for one person, on his own, to spot a grizzly bear in Yellow Stone National Park because they are rare and too well camouflaged. However, if he is willing to go where he sees other people gather, the chance that he will find a grizzly bear will greatly increase.

In the book, *The Wisdom of Crowds: Why the Many Are Smarter than the Few and How Collective Wisdom Shapes Business, Economies, Societies and Nations*, the author points out that "under the right circumstances, groups are remarkably intelligent, and are often smarter than the smartest people in them" (Surowiecki 2004, XIII).

The right circumstances are (1) diversity of opinion; (2) independence of members from one another; (3) decentralization; and (4) a good method for aggregating opinions. In other words, if randomly selected individuals with independent judgments and diverse information sources choose the same action, such actions should be respected and perhaps be followed. If these conditions are not met, it will be the blind leading the blind, and the ditch is but a little way on.

Momentum is widely observed in both technical data and fundamental data. For example, even though price reversion is often observed over very short and very long time spans, in the intermediate term prices often exhibit momentum. Jegadeesh and Titman (1993, 2001) were among the first to document price momentum in the intermediate time frame. They find that momentum strategies that buy stocks with high returns over the previous 3 to 12 months and sell stocks with low returns over this same time period perform well over the following 12 months. On the fundamental front, well documented post-earnings announcement drift is an example of the momentum phenomenon. Research has shown that stocks that announce earnings that beat expectations continue to outperform stocks that miss expectations. Expected earnings also exhibit momentum when a leading analyst revises up or down the forecast of a company's earnings and other analysts gradually follow suit.

Momentum models try to capture the persistence of local trends while reversal models seek to identify the inversion of local trends, such as price reversals. They coexist in both the technical data and the fundamental data for different stocks and over different time horizons. Together, momentum and reversal models are the most widely used modeling techniques. They also perform differently in different market conditions. Mean reversion works well under normal market conditions so that "what goes up will come down." Momentum strategies work best when markets experience large up or down trends. To some degree, mean-reversion is similar to valuation-based strategies while momentum relates more to human psychology. A successful quantitative strategy needs to have both flavors in order to survive all market conditions.

Forecast Risk

Risk is the second key statistic suggested by modern portfolio theory. In Markowitz's mean-variance framework, the risk associated with an equity portfolio is measured as the variance of the portfolio's return. This, in turn, is derived from the variances of the individual stocks' returns and the covariances of the returns among the different stocks included in the portfolio. (Note that the same results can be obtained using correlations rather than covariances.) The variance of a return gauges the range and likelihood of possible values that the return can assume. A small variance indicates a narrow potential range and therefore lower risk. A large variance indicates a broader potential range and therefore greater risk. Covariance measures the co-movements of returns among stocks. Asset return covariance matrices are key inputs to portfolio optimization algorithms used for asset allocation and active portfolio management.

In practice, quantitative managers rarely estimate the full covariance matrix directly because the number of individual elements is too large to be estimated precisely. Factor models have become pervasive in risk modeling because they offer a parsimonious way to estimate risk without a large and unreliable security covariance matrix. A factor model decomposes an asset's return into factors common to all assets and an asset-specific factor. The common factors are interpreted as the systematic risk components, and the factor model quantifies an asset's sensitivities to these risk factors.

The first, and still the most famous, factor model is the capital asset pricing model (CAPM), which was developed by financial researchers extending Markowitz's mean-variance portfolio theory. One of its creators, William Sharpe, was a student of Markowitz. They later shared the 1990 Nobel Prize in Economic Science for their contributions.[1]

CAPM answers the question left behind by Modern Portfolio Theory: How do you measure an asset's expected return and risk? The model demonstrates that, when in equilibrium under the assumptions of Modern Portfolio Theory, the expected excess return of an asset is equal to its sensitivity to the market risk times the market's expected excess return. Excess returns are defined as returns in excess of the risk-free return. This sensitivity to the market is called a stock's beta, and it cannot be eliminated through diversification. The risk associated with a single asset is then the sum of its non-diversifiable market risk and its specific risk. Further, the covariance between two assets is the product of their betas with market risk. Thus, CAPM was the first single-factor model capable of measuring both return and risk.

Today's risk models may all be viewed as extensions of the CAPM model. However, instead of using market return as the single explanatory factor, most practical risk models use multiple risk factors and measure an asset's exposures to those risks. For instance, it is logical to assume that the risk associated with a stock would also be influenced by the risk of the sector it operates in, its leverage, and its sensitivity to interest rates, and so on. Depending on the source of the risk factors, multifactor risk models are of three main types: (1) macroeconomic risk models; (2) fundamental risk models; and (3) statistical risk models.

Macroeconomic risk models use observable economic time series, such as interest rates and inflation, as measures of pervasive or common risk factors contributing to asset returns. CAPM is a special case of such a model. Another famous macroeconomic model was developed by Chen, Roll, and Ross (1986). They found that factors such as surprises in inflation, surprises in GNP, surprises in investor confidence as measured by the corporate bond risk premium, and shifts in the yield curve work well in explaining stock risks. In contrast to macroeconomic models, fundamental factor models use observable firm- or asset-specific attributes such as firm size, earnings yield, and industry classification to determine common factors in asset returns. An example of commercially available models of this type is BARRA.[2] Statistical risk models treat the common factors as unobservable or latent factors, and are estimated using statistical methods such as factor analysis and principal components analysis.

Fundamental and macroeconomic risk models have the advantages that all risk factors are easy to understand and less subject to excessive data mining and spurious price patterns. Their disadvantages include potentially correlated risk factors, and slow reaction to changing market conditions. For example, volatility and company leverage are often used as explanatory variables in fundamental risk models. Financial theory shows that companies with high leverage have high volatility, therefore these two risk factors are correlated with each other. However, they are not completely redundant, because a stock's volatility also depends on the nature of the company's business and firm specific news. Unfortunately, using correlated risk factors to estimate risk exposures will cause high estimation errors.

Statistical risk models have the advantage that they are easy to implement, and have good statistical properties such as uncorrelated risk factors. If done carefully, they are more adaptive to market conditions, and thus are more likely to capture risk factors that fundamental models may miss. On the downside, they operate like a black box, and it is hard to interpret the practical meanings of the risk factors. Additionally, the user is more likely to be accused of excessive data mining and more likely to have data errors.

Forecast Transaction Costs

Transactions incur both explicit and implicit costs. Explicit costs include commissions and infrastructure charges. Implicit costs are often called market impact (or slippage), which is the price concession traders must pay to liquidity providers who accommodate their trades—particularly when those trades are large.

Explicit costs are easy to measure and tend to be relatively small. This is because employers of quantitative strategies often use only the brokers' infrastructure to go to the market. Once brokers already build the infrastructure, the marginal cost for facilitating more trades is minimal. Market impact is often measured as "implementation shortfall," which is the difference between the price that triggers the trading signal and the average execution price of the entire order. This is often described as measuring trading costs relative to an arrival price benchmark. Forecasting market impact is more difficult because researchers observe prices only for completed trades. They cannot determine what a stock's price would have been without these trades. In other words, they cannot step in the same river twice. Further, market impact depends on the way the orders are executed. The faster the orders are executed, the larger the market impact will tend to be, and vice versa. In practice market impact costs are much larger than the explicit costs. According to Investment Technology Group (ITG), in 2009 the average commission-related explicit cost for U.S. stocks was 9 basis point (bps), while the average market impact cost was 48 bps, more than 5 times the explicit cost.

Transaction cost estimation is an often overlooked, but very important, subject in quantitative trading. This is especially true for institutional managers who manage much larger portfolios than individual investors. To see how important transaction costs are, Coppejans and Madhavan (2007) show that, assuming a moderate 40 basis points transaction costs and 200 percent annual turnover, a typical fund's information ratio[3] is halved when transaction costs are taken into account. The authors also show that a strategy's information ratio is partially determined by the correlation between predicted and realized costs, which underpins the importance of transaction cost modeling to a strategy's realized performance.

Most transaction cost models measure market impact as two components: temporary impact and permanent impact. Temporary impact is caused by orders taking liquidity out of the order book but do not bring fundamental news that alters the market's long-term view. In this case, a buy order will temporarily increase a stock's price, and a sell order will temporarily decrease its price, but the disturbance is short-lived, and the market will revert to its original state quickly. Permanent impact, on the other hand, occurs when an order's private information is leaked to the market via the act of trading, and thus changes the market's long-term view of the stock. It is closely related to the academic research on strategic trader models, which study how informed traders hide behind the flow of "noise" traders, and how market makers infer the informational content of trades from order flow. By definition, permanent impact is nontransient, and it impacts subsequent executions and valuations.

A typical transaction cost model uses such inputs as relative order size, market capitalization, stock volatility, and spreads to estimate transaction costs. Many quantitative managers estimate transaction costs using the experience of their own trades. This approach is ideal because different trading styles have different market impact patterns. For example, mean-reversion types of strategies provide liquidity and thus have less market impact than momentum types of strategies, which take liquidity. Strategies that trade large cap stocks have less trading costs than those that trade small cap stocks because large cap stocks are less volatile and their average daily volumes are higher. For these reasons, it is preferable to use the trader's own trades when developing proprietary transaction cost models.

Implementation

Implementation is the process of translating key statistics into investment profits. It includes portfolio construction and trade execution. Portfolio construction takes the key statistics, namely expected returns, covariance estimates, transactions cost estimates, and the current portfolio as inputs, and generates an output for a target portfolio driven by the investor's objective function. Trade execution is the process of moving the current portfolio to the target portfolio. Both portfolio construction and trade execution involve careful balancing of risk and return. The trade-off between risk and return is the central feature of both academic and practitioner finance. Investment managers need to measure risks, model the relationship between risk and return, and decide which risks to take and how much of them to take.

In practice, portfolio construction can range anywhere from simple and straightforward to mathematically complicated and computationally intensive. An example of a simple portfolio construction methodology is stratification. In this approach, a few mutually exclusive and collectively exhaustive risk factors, such as size and industry group, are identified. Then stocks with similar risk profiles are grouped together. For example, large cap energy stocks will be in one group, and small cap retailers will be in another. Within each group, stocks are sorted by their signals. Stocks ranked the highest in each group are bought long and stocks ranked the lowest in each group are sold shorts. Despite its simplicity, stratification allows a strategy to concentrate on capturing the mispricings indicated by its signals while eliminating exposure to outside risks, such as sector risk and capitalization bias, by taking both long and short positions within the same risk bucket. The disadvantages of stratification are also readily apparent. For example, it does not allow managers to explicitly control for trading costs, and it ignores the magnitude of the signals.

A more general way to construct a portfolio for quantitative managers is portfolio optimization, which is the classic framework for portfolio construction pioneered by Markowitz. Portfolio optimization uses computer algorithms to find a set of optimal weights that maximize a portfolio's expected future returns after transaction costs for a target risk level. Unlike stratification, portfolio optimization takes all the information about alpha, such as risks and magnitude of signals, into account, and it is very convenient to incorporate trading cost controls and other investment constraints in the optimization criteria.

In general, portfolio optimization works better than simpler methods partly because it uses more information. However, more information is a double-edged sword. If not used appropriately, it may hurt the performance of an optimizer. For example, researchers have long found that the original mean-variance optimizer is very sensitive to estimation errors of returns and risks, which are almost unavoidable in practice. As a result, unbounded mean-variance optimized portfolios are often dominated by the equal weighting alternative.

There are a couple of ways to mitigate these problems. The simplest ad hoc solution is to incorporate constraints. Constraints limit the maximum weight assigned to any single stock, and force the optimizer to spread out weights to more stocks. The second method is called portfolio resampling, which uses Monte Carlo simulation to resample the data and create a mean-variance optimized portfolio for each sample. The final weights are the average weights of all simulations, which is usually more stable than the plain vanilla mean-variance optimizer that uses only one realization of data history. The third approach is to use Bayesian theory. The Black-Litterman (1992) model is the best known within this category. It starts with the market capitalization equilibrium portfolio as a prior, then uses Bayesian techniques to adjust the portfolio to reflect the investor's signals in proportion to their informational contents. Since the market capitalization equilibrium portfolio is the benchmark portfolio and it acts as a center of gravity, the resulting portfolio weights will be more robust to estimation errors.

Transaction costs link the two implementation components together. To reduce transaction costs, quantitative managers should reduce unnecessary turnovers in the portfolio construction stage and trade smarter in the trade execution stage. In the portfolio construction stage, turnover can be either specified in the objective function or as a constraint. Most commercial optimizers can handle overall turnover limit, and some of them can handle sector-specific turnover limits.

Trade execution is, itself, essentially an optimization problem. In principle, traders want to trade as quickly as possible after they acquire new information so that they can profit from it before anyone else has it. However, they cannot trade too quickly as orders executed over a short period of time will have a greater market impact cost. Orders executed in multiple smaller lots but over a longer period of time may have a lesser market impact, and therefore smaller expected cost, but are more risky, since the asset's price can vary greatly over longer periods of time and the trader's information may become stale. Therefore, to trade a list of stocks efficiently, investors must strike the right balance between trading costs and execution risk. The tradeoff here is quite similar to the risk/return tradeoff in modern portfolio theory.

Two popular benchmarks for trade execution are the previous day's closing price and the current trade date's opening price. Actual trade prices are compared against the benchmark prices, and the difference is the implementation shortfall, which captures the variable part of transaction costs. Practical execution algorithms follow the mean-variance approach to minimize the expected value of implementation shortfall for a given variance of implementation shortfall.

Among passive investors, another popular benchmark is "volume weighted average price," commonly called the VWAP. In this execution approach, traders split their orders for the target trading horizon in proportion to market volume in the same horizon. Thus it aims to achieve the average execution price. The VWAP strategy is easy to implement and requires less mathematical complicacy. However, the estimation of market impact in this approach is very crude and it ignores the importance of opportunity costs. Further, it is only suitable for trades that are relatively small compared with total trading volume over the trading periods. For larger traders, the trades themselves will distort the benchmark.

Due to the large number of stocks and the frequency with which quantitative managers trade, most of their orders are executed electronically. Besides traditional exchanges, quantitative traders increasingly use alternative trading venues such as electronic communication networks (ECNs) through some form of direct market access (DMA) provided by their brokers. An ECN is a computer system that facilitates trading of financial products outside of stock exchanges. Since the Securities and Exchange Commission first authorized their creation in 1998, ECNs have becoming increasing popular due to their liquidity and automated direct matching of buyers and sellers. ECNs provide traders more anonymity and more control over their order flows. ECNs tend to be better for traders who are not in a hurry, since they pay liquidity providers for their order flow while they charge liquidity takers for their order flow (in order to pay the liquidity providers).

Most of the published research on trade execution is in the area of market microstructure, which studies the detailed mechanisms of how markets work and prices are formed. Interest in microstructure and trading is not new, but the market crash in October 1987 spurred vast new interest in this area. Recent literature is characterized by more theoretical rigor and extensive empirical investigation using new databases. It remains an active field in financial research.

OUTLOOK

Building a successful trading strategy is not an easy task. Numerous studies, for example, Malkiel (1990), have shown that the majority of professional money managers have been unable to beat the market on a risk-adjusted basis. Does that imply that the market is always efficient and that there is no need to waste one's time to find trading opportunities? Perhaps not. Grossman (1976) and Grossman and Stiglitz (1980) convincingly demonstrate that perfectly efficient markets are an impossibility. This is because if markets are perfectly efficient, then the return for gathering information is zero, in which case there would be little reason to trade. Consequently markets have no reason to exist. A more practical version of an efficient market, as suggested by Lo and MacKinlay (1999), is a market with occasional excess profit opportunities on average and over time. However, it is not possible to earn such profits consistently without some type of competitive advantage.

In his article "What Does It Take to Win the Trading Game?" Jack Treynor (1981) argues that there are two ways traders can make profits in the stock market: Either the trader uses superior information, or the trader applies superior reasoning to existing information. These are the general guidelines to find good trading opportunities for both quantitative and more traditional managers.

For quantitative managers, superior information either comes from the possession of new data sources or quicker access to useful data than others have. Historically, before standardized fundamental data became commercially available, traders who acquired such data through their own research would have a competitive advantage over those who did not. Quicker access to data has been one key to market success throughout stock market history. In 1815, for example, the London banker Nathan Rothschild made a huge profit in the stock market because he got advanced news of the outcome of the battle of Waterloo. Today many quantitative funds, especially the high frequency trading funds, invest heavily in technology in order to acquire information and trade on that information just a few fractions of a second before other market participants.

Superior analysis is the other key ingredient in successful quantitative investment. In "How I Helped to Make Fischer Black Wealthier," Jay Ritter (1996), a professor and ex-futures trader described how Fischer Black made a profit from him by correctly pricing Value Line futures contracts. In that trade, both parties were well versed in financial theory, but Fischer conducted superior analysis by noticing that the Value Line Index is a geometric average rather than an arithmetic average, and thus should be priced differently from the textbook model.

Superior analysis can be conducted throughout the process of quantitative investment as discussed above, and this is what many quantitative researchers strive to achieve. For example, in an effort to forecast expected returns, some quantitative researchers try to apply chaos theory and neural network models to handle the nonlinear patterns in data. In risk modeling, many develop new methods to estimate covariance matrices using tick-by-tick data. In portfolio and trade optimization, the original Markowitz normality assumptions are often relaxed, and more robust optimization techniques are applied.

The quantitative trading business, with quantitative models as its products, is just like any other business. In the long run, no company can survive with just one magic product that works under all market conditions at all times. Likewise, quantitative funds need to keep improving existing models, inventing new models, and enhancing their technology in order to keep pace with the market and with their competitors. Any quantitative fund can be made obsolescent by a failure to keep up with the competition or by bad management, and, of course, these things are no less true for companies in other industries. But the quantitative trading business will likely continue because there will always be those who innovate.

NOTES

1. See Sharpe (1964).
2. The BARRA Integrated Model is a multiasset class model for forecasting the asset and portfolio level risk of global equities, bonds, and currencies. The model is now owned by a subsidiary of Morgan Stanley.
3. The information ratio is one of the measures of risk-adjusted return. It is defined as the ratio of the portfolio's active return (i.e., alpha) to the portfolio's tracking error, where tracking error is the standard deviation of the active return.

REFERENCES

Black, F., and R. Litterman. 1992. "Global Portfolio Optimization." *Financial Analysts Journal* 48 (September/October): 28–43.

Chen, Nai-Fu, Richard Roll, and Stephen Ross. 1986. "Economic Forces and the Stock Market." *Journal of Business* 59:3, 383–403.

Coppejans, M., and A. Madhavan. 2007. "The Value of Transaction Cost Forecasts: Another Source of Alpha." *Journal of Investment Management* 5:165–78.

Fama, E., and K. French. 1992. "The Cross-Section of Expected Stock Returns." *Journal of Finance* 47:2, 427–465.

Fama, E., and K. French. 1998. "Value versus Growth: The International Evidence." *Journal of Finance* 53:6, 1975–1991.

Grossman, S. 1976. "On the Efficiency of Competitive Stock Markets where Trades Have Diverse Information." *Journal of Finance* 31:1, 573–585.

Grossman, S., and J. Stiglitz. 1980. "On the Impossibility of Informationally Efficient Markets." *American Economic Review* 70:393–408.

Investment Technology Group. 2010. "Global Trading Cost Review." www.itg.com/news_events/papers/ITGGlobalTradingCostReview_2009Q4.pdf.

Jegadeesh, N., and S. Titman. 1993. "Returns to Buying Winners and Selling Losers: Implications for Stock Market Efficiency." *Journal of Finance* 48:1, 65–91.

Jegadeesh, N., and S. Titman. 2001. "Profitability of Momentum Strategies: An Evaluation of Alternative Explanations." *Journal of Finance* 56:2, 699–720.

Lo, A. and C. MacKinlay. 1999. *A Non-Random Walk Down Wall Street.* Princeton, NJ: Princeton University Press.

Markowitz, H. M. (1952). "Portfolio Selection." *Journal of Finance* 7:1, 77–91.

Malkiel, B. 1990. *A Random Walk Down Wall Street.* New York: W. W. Norton & Company.

Patterson, Scott. 2010. *The Quants: How a New Breed of Math Wizzes Conquered Wall Street and Nearly Destroyed It.* New York: Crown Publishing.

Ritter, J. R. 1996. "How I Helped to Make Fischer Black Wealthier." *Financial Management* 25:4, 104–107.

Sharpe, W. F. 1964. "Capital Asset Prices—A Theory of Market Equilibrium Under Conditions of Risk." *Journal of Finance* 19:3, 425–42.

Surowiecki, James. 2004. *The Wisdom of Crowds: Why the Many Are Smarter than the Few and How Collective Wisdom Shapes Business, Economies, Societies and Nations.* New York: Doubleday.

Treynor, J. L. 1981. "What Does It Take to Win the Trading Game?" *Financial Analysts Journal* 37:1, 55–60.

ABOUT THE AUTHOR

Kun Gao recently joined Tudor Investment Corporation ("Tudor") as a Research Portfolio Manager in the firm's quantitative trading group where he researches and develops portfolio management systems. Tudor is part of the Tudor Group, a group of affiliated companies engaged in trading in the fixed income, equity, currency, and commodity markets headquartered in Greenwich, Connecticut. Prior to joining Tudor, Kun was a portfolio manager at WorldQuant LLC, a quantitative hedge fund based in Old Greenwich, Connecticut. He also had extensive trading and research experience in quantitative equity strategies at Morgan Stanley and Caxton. He received a Ph. in statistics from Yale University.

CHAPTER 16

Systematic Trading in Foreign Exchange

CHRIS ATTFIELD AND MEL MAYNE
Par Asset Management LLP

We can define systematic trading as a process or discipline that employs a mechanical set of rules, called a trading model, for determining market entry and exit points based on a pre-established and predefined plan. However, like most other aspects of trading, everyone has their own interpretation. Many traders refer to themselves as "rules based" rather than "systematic" as this allows them to have some discretion over their trading. We are taking a broad church approach in this chapter, which we believe will provide a wider-ranging introduction to the subject as well as allow the reader to adapt what he or she may find appropriate to suit his or her own style of trading.

INTRODUCTION

The aim of this chapter is to provide an introduction to systematic trading and its benefits and limitations. Nevertheless, it is important to first examine the growth in systematic trading that has taken place over the past 10 years or so and the associated impact of electronic trading technology on the foreign exchange (FX) industry in general.

Although the FX markets have developed at an impressive pace since the end of the Bretton Woods agreement in the early 1970s; the technological advances that have occurred over the past 10 years have transformed the industry in a way that was unimaginable a decade earlier. This transformation, when viewed in conjunction with the parallel growth in the derivatives markets, has accounted for what can only be described as a revolution in the way risk and liquidity are priced in the market today.

The principal liquidity providers of FX have traditionally been the major international banks who need to provide their clients with spot and forward pricing to facilitate their international trade. In the mid 1990s some of these banks recognized that the banking industry was about to undergo a major change that was being driven by the technological revolution taking place in commerce and banking. The banks that invested early in the technology saw their share of this expanding market grow dramatically. In addition, over the past few decades, an intensive period of mergers and acquisitions within the banking sector has resulted in a concentration of flow of business to a few dominant players (data from Euromoney Survey). This investment in technology also allowed these banks to improve operating margins with the replacement of labor-intensive activities with electronic systems, which proved both more efficient and more cost-effective.

With this concentration of order flow have come economies of scale and the recognition that machines could be more efficient at determining price and at capturing the value inherent in client order flows. There was also a realization by software and system engineers that markets have some of the attributes associated with physical systems and that price moves and customer demand could be accurately forecast and predicted in a way that was not possible before. The application of these systems resulted in a significant increase in revenues from order flow for the banks that developed them. These banks recognized that high and ultra–high frequency trading strategies, which had previously been employed in the equities markets, could also be used in the FX markets to generate and capture value in price generation.

The introduction of multicurrency cash settlement systems such as those provided by the CLS Group, meant that banks were able to facilitate substantially larger daily volumes while simultaneously decreasing their counterparty risk. With the increased share of the market came the opportunity to generate revenues from trading and liquidity provision that was thought unimaginable in the 1990s. This was accomplished without taking significant proprietary trading risk.

The top five banks in FX, as measured by the 2010 Euromoney Poll, now account for over 55 percent of the turnover in the industry. See Exhibit 16.1.

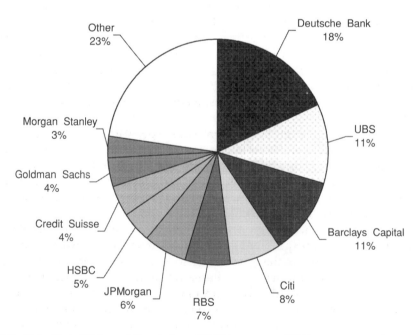

Exhibit 16.1   Data Table and Graph from 2010 Euromoney FX Survey
Source: Euromoney FX Survey 2010.

When one considers that many of the remaining banks in the business "white label" one or more of the top five's FX platforms to their own clients, we can see how dominant the top five players have actually become. Those banks that failed to recognize the change have been left behind, and the technological and infrastructure costs of rebuilding their businesses are now too prohibitive for most of them to contemplate re-entry into the top tier. Many have slipped into niche roles or have developed products that are designed to help their clients manage risk, as opposed to providing liquidity.

The FX market has seen the emergence of independent electronic trading platforms, such as EBS (ICAP Group), FXall, and HotspotFX, that provide liquidity to the market. Recently, these platforms have reported a growth in business-to-business transactions thereby bypassing the banks. In some instances this accounts for over 50 percent of the platform's turnover. Smaller niche providers, such as FrontierFX, have targeted the professional market, and this sector looks set to continue to grow.

One of the positive aspects of this revolution in the industry has been that foreign exchange, as a traded market, has become much more egalitarian in nature. The dissemination of news and information, that was formerly the province of the privileged few, is now available instantly over the Web. As a result, the major institutions now have little temporal advantage with respect to information. More importantly, there has been a dramatic fall in transaction costs in the industry in recent years. This has been driven primarily by the advent of electronic trading, which has encouraged competition and liquidity provision. But it has also coincided with the growth in speculative retail trading platforms that have allowed the smaller investor access to a market that was previously only available to the professional investor. The entry of these new participants in the sector has provided the market makers with new sources of liquidity and revenue.

FX is now viewed as an "asset class" by many speculators and investors that had previously confined their investments to stocks and bonds. The dramatic increase in volatility in these traditional markets following the credit crisis has led investors to look at alternatives, and FX has been a significant beneficiary in terms of risk allocation and turnover. The increase in volume is clearly evident in Exhibit 16.2.

Perhaps the biggest contributor to growth in speculative FX trading has been in the area of systematic and algorithmic trading. A decade earlier, trading of this kind was seen as a minority activity and was mainly confined to a few hedge funds and sophisticated treasury operations. The majority of traders were discretionary, and what short-term trading there was remained mainly confined to proprietary trading within the banking industry.

One of the catalysts for this growth in systematic trading was the availability of accurate, reliable, and inexpensive high-frequency data. This allowed anyone who could handle a spreadsheet the opportunity to test and develop trading systems. Many saw this style of trading as an alternative to discretionary trading—which required a skill set that could only be acquired through years of trading experience. This increased availability of data coincided with a reduction in the cost of transacting in FX and with the growth of margin-based trading platforms offering multi-product electronic trading. The result was that many new speculators were attracted to the market.

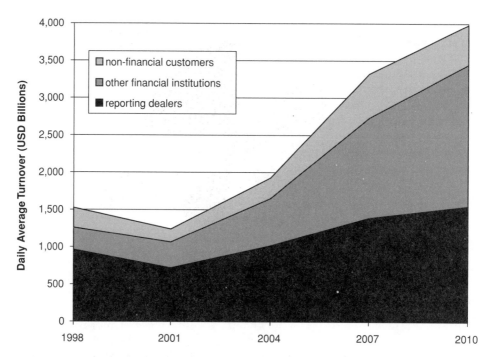

Exhibit 16.2   Global Foreign Exchange Market Turnover by Counterparty
Source: BIS Triennial Central Bank Survey of Foreign Exchange and Derivatives Market Activity, April 2010.

One of the fastest areas of growth has come from commodity trading advisors (CTAs), quantitatively driven managed futures funds, and hedge funds that have adapted trading systems that had earlier been proven in equities and fixed income markets. Many of these funds have developed high or ultra–high frequency trading systems that now account for a significant percentage of daily turnover in the FX markets. These new entrants wish to trade electronically. Only those banks that had developed their own proprietary electronic trading systems were positioned to benefit from the business. The BIS triennial data (see Exhibit 16.2) has shown, for the first time, that the turnover from non-financial institutions now exceeds that of the banking sector for the first time.

The Euromoney data in Exhibit 16.3 shows that leveraged funds make up a significant proportion of this sector, and the concentration of flow to banks servicing it is significant both in terms of profitability and information.

IS SYSTEMATIC TRADING JUST FOR GEEKS AND QUANTS?

Although some areas of systematic trading require a strong mathematical background, this is by no means true of the sector in general. Systematic trading can

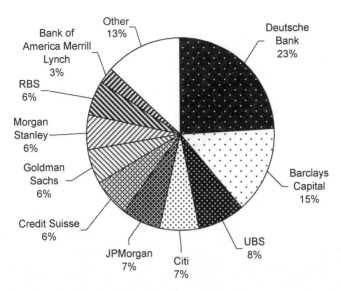

Exhibit 16.3   Leveraged Fund Market Share
Source: Euromoney FX Survey 2010.

be as simple or as complex as one wants to make it. What systematic trading does provide is the opportunity to conduct detailed analysis of trading strategies and risk management. This is a fundamental and ongoing part of successful trading. Relying on a selective memory is, unfortunately, no substitute for cold facts.

All successful traders are systematic and disciplined in their approach to trading. The shelves of bookshops around the world are loaded with acres of books selling advice on how to become a successful trader. As many have found to their detriment, speculating successfully in any market requires more than the accumulation of these weighty tomes and blindly following someone else's "trading system." Doing so will invariably result in trading losses or worse. This is because:

- Having not tested the strategy yourself over a suitable period of time, it is difficult to satisfy yourself that it actually works.
- Faith in the system will begin to erode during a significant drawdown (i.e., a period of losses), and there is a temptation to stop trading the strategy(s) and thereby lock in losses.
- There is the temptation to employ some discretionary overlay to the strategy that is untested, subjective, and driven by emotions.

However, if we look beyond the hyperbole surrounding these systems, we find that the common theme behind all successful trading approaches is a structured and disciplined application of the system in question. If fact, many experienced traders believe that it is the *way* a position is managed and not the position itself that is important in trading.

All traders employ approaches that make sense to them. These have generally been developed over a number of years and are the culmination of different experiences gained from trading in the market. Whatever system one uses, it is important that it be based on a rational analysis of the market or on some behavioral aspect of its participants. However, beyond that, there are as many ways to trade markets, as there are traders. It is helpful if the strategy can be tested in some way to validate the assumptions and the clearly defined rules that make it work. Many of the most successful traders employ this process religiously during every trade in order to keep subjective decisions to a minimum.

Becoming a successful trader is the process of developing a disciplined approach that works well over a significant period of time. If we accept that all successful traders are systematic to some significant degree, we need to examine how best to develop and employ a systematic approach to trading FX and to examine the benefits and limitations of such an approach. Although there is no substitute for actual experience, live trading can be a very expensive way to test ideas. Paper trading is a logical and less expensive substitute; but it still requires the benefit of time to observe and fine-tune the approach. On the downside, paper traders are prone to employ subjective ex post rationalizations.

Testing simple logical ideas and examining the outcomes can be a very rewarding and informative process. It has been the bedrock of modern scientific thinking for the past 300 years and has its role to play in trading markets. All that is needed initially is a reliable data set for the market traded and some basic spreadsheet skills. Although many traders associate trading success with complex systems, the opposite is more often true. This chapter is not intended to provide the reader with a "how to guide" to model building. There are a plethora of books available on that subject. We are more concerned here with describing the benefits, as well as the limitations, of testing and employing systematic trading models. Importantly, we are not advocating a complete change for those of you who employ a discretionary approach. Although some systematic zealots would disagree, being systematic does not preclude the use of discretion or judgment in decision making. However we would suggest that this is best employed in a non-emotive and, if possible, predetermined way to take into account extraordinary events.

One further word of caution with regard to testing in financial markets: It is helpful to remember that markets are essentially social and not physical systems and are made up of all the participants in the market at any one time. All social systems are subject to sudden behavioral changes. Such behavioral changes can be at odds with the assumptions we made when we were developing our model. As recent events have shown us, markets can behave in a chaotic manner, and models tend to perform poorly in such environments.

WHAT CAN SYSTEMATIC TRADING ANALYSIS DO FOR ME?

You learn most from your mistakes, not your successes. You have to handle getting your butt kicked and learn from it.

—Paul Tudor Jones

Learning from your mistakes is a good place to start, and one of the real benefits afforded to systematic traders is that they can analyze their trading history in some detail. It is very difficult to avoid the effects of selective memory when conducting an objective appraisal of trading success. For the discretionary trader, this is also a good place to start. Many successful traders keep a detailed record of all of their trades including not only the entry and exit points, but also the rationale behind each trade. The more information we have, the better the analysis.

What can analyzing a trading history reveal?

1. Your ratio of winning and losing trades:
   - Winning and losing sequences go on longer than you would expect.
   - This is especially true of trend traders.
2. The average size of your wins and losses (as a percentage of the value of the position):
   - An average of 0.550 percent on wins and –0.45 percent on losses over time would be excellent.
3. Winning and losing trades by strategy/market:
   - There is a tendency to trade markets we are most comfortable with. This is not always the most profitable use of resources.
4. The average holding period of your trades:
   - There is a direct relationship between volatility and time. The longer you hold a trade, the bigger the P&L swings.

Systematically analyzing a trading history can reveal a great deal about the trader and his or her approach. The more information we have the more detailed and useful the analysis. Top athletes analyze their game on an ongoing basis, trying to identify areas of strength and weakness. The trader should be no different.

ADVANTAGES AND LIMITATIONS OF SYSTEMATIC TRADING

For many traders, distilling their trading approach into a couple of simple rules can be a difficult process that they do not wish to attempt. However, doing so is a worthwhile activity: The cathartic process of defining a trading approach can be extremely revealing to both systematic and discretionary traders alike. Patterns that we believe we have discerned from the market are often illusory.

Advantages of a Systematic Approach

Removing the emotion from trading decisions: Trading is very emotional, as anyone who has experienced the euphoria of having a position go right will testify. Unfortunately, the flip side of that experience is the "fight or flight" reaction that is triggered when you are losing money. This type of reaction is very useful when running away from predators, but often counterproductive in a market context. Research has shown that this type of reaction shuts down the parts of the brain responsible for logic and reasoning. Losing money is an inescapable part of trading, so the emotional response to "escape" from a losing position can be very harmful. Having a trading system means that one can dispassionately make decisions in advance about how positions are to be managed. In essence, it can override the instinctive and counterproductive response in those fight or flight moments.

In-built trading discipline: One thing most top traders will agree on is that discipline is vital to trading success. Adopting a disciplined approach is hard work. One advantage of creating systems is that they can enforce discipline in the form of stop-loss levels and prompt entry to trades (the least obvious trades are sometimes the most profitable).

It is testable: This is the biggest single advantage. Market literature and accumulated folklore are overflowing with indicators, technical levels, fundamental drivers, candlestick patterns, and what have you, all claiming to tell you whether the market is going up or down. The majority of these will fail to live up to their promise. As humanity learned some time ago, the best way to distinguish between superstition and reality is to test.

Of course, even gut feeling trading can be tested. With a long enough history of trades, you can work out when your gut feel has worked and when it hasn't. However, if someone comes to you with a new trading idea today, how can you evaluate it? If the idea can be written down with enough clarity to form a series of rules, it can be tested—in fact, just seeing if it can be stated clearly in this way is a good test of whether it has any merit.

Although it is not a substitute for an actual trading history, testing is an extremely valuable way to see if the claimed approach works. Essentially, if you have market data for a sufficiently long period, say 10 years, and a trading idea that can be stated as a set of rules, you can create an artificial "trading history" complete with trade entries, exits, and P&L that would have been experienced by someone mechanically following your rules during those years. This approach is called backtesting, and we will say more about it later.

The emphasis on testing might strike some as unnecessary. If a pattern in the market is obvious to the eye, why bother? The answer was given by physicist Richard Feynman, albeit in a different context:

The first principle is that you must not fool yourself, and you are the easiest person to fool.[1]

The human mind is very good at pattern-matching, but the penalty for that is that we can get a lot of false positives. Take the example of pareidolia, where human faces are seen in a variety of entirely natural objects such as the surface of the moon or burnt tortillas. We are very good at recognizing faces—so good that we will even see them where they do not exist. Another example is the canals on Mars, which were extensively mapped in the nineteenth century, until an experiment in 1903 showed them to be an optical illusion caused by our tendency to "join the dots" of craters when seeing a blurry image. The only defense against fooling ourselves in this way is to test in a non-emotional and non-subjective manner.

Why Systematic Trading Is Not a Magic Bullet

It may seem perverse to include a section on the drawbacks and problems of systematic trading, but like most powerful techniques it has its dangers, and is easy to misuse. The trouble is that many of the misuses of trading systems will not be immediately apparent: the tested performance will look very good, and no problems come to light until the system is traded live.

The truth is that a lot more trading ideas look as though they work than do actually work. Backtesting is great for instilling confidence that an idea is genuine, and, armed with a simulated "equity curve," it is easy to think that you have come up with a foolproof moneymaking machine. An equity curve depicts the cumulative percentage change in the trader's equity over time as a consequence of trading. Good-looking equity curves are both beguiling and remarkably easy to produce. Unfortunately, although all good ideas backtest well, a lot of bad ideas do too, and it is a truism of systematic trading that backtests invariably look better than real trading performance. It is a fallacy to think that this can be overcome by just making the backtested performance worse in some way, such as by reducing the return. For a bad model the actual trading results can be unrecognizable from the backtested equity curve. Why is this?

Fitting the Noise, Not the Data

Market data is noisy—it contains a lot of "random" ups and downs, along with the signal that your system is trying to extract and profit from (of course, exactly what is "signal" and what is "noise" depends on what the system is, and its timescale). What you would like the test to do is tell you whether the signal your system is trying to exploit is a real recurring pattern in the historical data. However, the test is actually answering the question "Is there any way at all I can make this work?" It is very easy for random, unrepeatable price action to accidentally give positive P&L, and any attempt to search for the right parameters to use will highlight these "lucky" accidents. This may seem unlikely, but bear in mind the Pareto principle that 80 percent of your P&L comes from 20 percent of your trades. Good luck has a lot more impact than you might expect.

Over-Optimization

In backtesting, it is very common to vary the system parameters to find the "best" value. A parameter is any input that you can vary. For example, in a simple moving average, the number of days over which you "look-back" is a parameter. If the system is traded once per day, then the time of day you execute is also a parameter. The more complex a trading system is, the more parameters it will require, and the more tests you have to do to find the best values for those parameters. For example, if there is only one parameter, then you may wish to try 20 different values for that parameter to see which gives the best results. If you have two parameters and you would like to try 20 possible values for each, then you will be searching through $20 \times 20 = 400$ different combinations of parameter values. For three parameters it will be 8,000. It is relatively simple to get a computer to search all values of these parameters, but the more tests you do, the more likely you are to find "something" where nothing actually exists (this is known in statistics as the "multiple comparisons problem"). By the time you get to four parameters, even *random* trading signals can generate an excellent equity curve with double-digit returns and a good risk/return ratio—all purely by chance. This is illustrated in Exhibit 16.4.

For any given trading algorithm requiring parameter selection (and all algorithms will require some form of parameter selection), you will end up with an equity curve that looks as good as it can possibly look over the historic period used to develop the model.

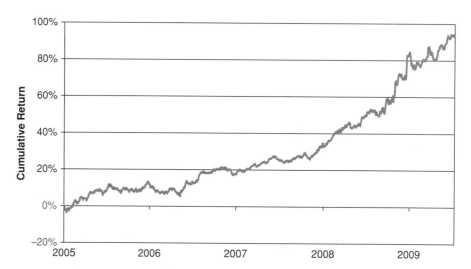

Exhibit 16.4   The Effect of Change: Random Trading in EUR–USD (the best result of 160,000 equity curves)

Parameter Choice

When trading a model out-of-sample—that is, into the unknown future, not with the same data you used to determine the parameters—it is very unlikely that the parameters chosen will be the perfect parameters for the new period. The best case is that they are still good. The worst case is that they are completely inappropriate. It may be that the trading rules would still work, but only with a different set of parameters that you could not possibly have chosen in advance. This is the difference between a model that is robust and one that is brittle. Ultimately, a system that has parameters that are impossible to specify in advance is useless. It will always backtest well, but never perform well out-of-sample.

Past as Prologue—Or Not

Even if you have found a genuine effect in your backtest, the market is ever-evolving. It may be that the model trades successfully for some time out-of-sample, but a systemic shock or other change in the way the market trades could eliminate the anomaly that you were relying on. It is likely that all models have "lifetimes." What separates a robust approach from a brittle one is the length of time for which the parameters or algorithm can be relied upon for successful trading.

Position Management

Even good trading signals are no substitute for good trading discipline and position management. It might be assumed that the directional signals generated are of primary importance, and that position management is only a second-order effect, but this is unlikely to be true. Consider the following equity curves depicted in Exhibit 16.5. These were generated from a momentum-based trend-following model using two different exit rules. In one case, the model employed a rule requiring that profits be taken if, and when, a specified positive P&L level was reached. This version did not employ a stop-loss, so losses could run. In the other case, a stop-loss rule was employed at a loss level that mirrored the P&L level of

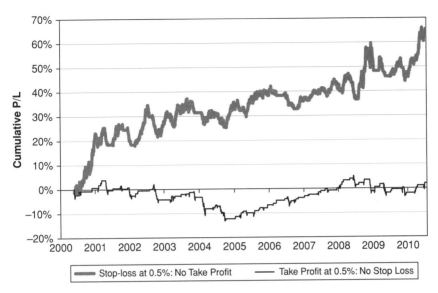

Exhibit 16.5 Effect of Position Management (EUR–USD trend trading)

the first rule. This version did not take profits at a target level so profits could run. It is worth noting that taking profit early and running losses is characteristic of undisciplined, emotional trading behavior—our brains are wired to see stop-losses as a "punishment" and take-profits as a "reward," so we tend to seek the latter and avoid the former. Backtesting shows how damaging this is to performance!

How Can These Mistakes Be Avoided?

It is impossible to say with certainty that a model is robust, but it is possible to weed out a lot of candidates by rigorous testing. It is very difficult to walk away from a model that looks profitable on paper, but this can often be the wisest course of action. The important thing to be wary of is *confirmation bias*, which is the tendency to seek out supportive evidence and dismiss the negative. You must be your own worst critic. You must actively seek out evidence that your system does not work and identify the failure modes that could cause it to lose money. Unless you have seen how badly it can perform, you have no grounds for confidence—and remember, backtesting will systematically sweep the flaws under the carpet. Testing on other data sources is not always possible, but is a good idea, as it guards against overfitting to random fluctuations in the original data set.

The question of how sensitive the model is to changes in its parameters is very important (see following). A useful warning sign is that all its profit has come from one or two short periods in history. Lastly, and very importantly, is the model *code* itself correct? That is, if a model is a candidate for live trading, it is wise to have it independently rebuilt from scratch using only a specification of the algorithm.

WHAT IS NECESSARY FOR A SYSTEM TO WORK?

Any list such as this can only ever be "necessary, but not sufficient." Having said that, any model that has the following is more likely to be valid:

A clearly defined rationale: This should be explicitly decided and preferably written down prior to constructing the system itself. Every model has an underlying market behavior that it is trying to exploit. The best models express this clearly and simply. Some corollaries to this are:

- **Don't tinker**: It has been said that exceptions make bad laws, and this is also true of rule-based trading. Putting multiple exceptions into your code just overfits history, and leads to a multitude of parameters, which will guarantee a good-looking, but meaningless, equity curve.
- **Don't post-rationalize**: Explanations of model behavior after it has produced a good equity curve always sound convincing, but are rarely useful. It should be borne in mind that your system's performance *cannot* be evidence in favor of an *ex post* rationalization as to why it works. If your post-rationalization can be tested, you can determine if it is valid; if not, it's a nice-sounding explanation that may make for good marketing copy, but nothing more.

Entry and exit conditions: This may sound obvious, but it is surprising how many well known "trading systems" are out there that consist entirely of entry signals. Such a "system" is in fact only half a system: it cannot be tested because the exit signals are crucial in determining its profitability or otherwise. Systems that trade continuously and reverse position are fine, but otherwise the exit signals must be part of the specification.

A small number of parameters: These must be specifiable with some confidence. We have already established that large numbers of parameters make good results much less significant. It is also likely that in a many-parameter model, the parameters will not be independent; that is, the values of one parameter will depend on the values of the other parameters. This means that rather than getting the values of the individual parameters right independently, you must get the combination exactly right—a much harder task.

To some extent this is inevitable, but it can also signal that your parameters perform a similar or overlapping function in your trading system, and that the rules should be simplified to reduce the two overlapping parameters to a single one. Note that this simplification will always make the backtest look worse! Ideally you should have a feel for what the parameters should be prior to searching, thus transforming a data-mining exercise akin to flipping a coin many times into a real test of whether reasonable parameters perform acceptably. It is much easier if your parameters have meaning, that is, correspond to measurable things like market volatility or an average day's move.

WHAT CAN I REASONABLY EXPECT?
Risk/Return Ratio

The trade-off between the risk and the return associated with a strategy is commonly measured via the Sharpe ratio. The Sharpe ratio is the annualized excess return of a strategy divided by its annualized volatility (i.e., risk).[2] By *excess return* we mean that we deduct the risk-free rate of interest from the strategy return.

Because return is in the numerator and risk is in the denominator, the higher the Sharpe ratio, the better. The major driver of volatility for a system that can trade no more than once a day is the underlying market volatility. So for a market volatility of 10 percent, a system with a Sharpe ratio of 1.0 would have an annualized excess return of 10 percent. Backtests can easily give Sharpe ratios of 2.0 or more, but, as noted earlier, backtests always exaggerate performance. Over the long-term, a Sharpe of 1.0 is good, and 0.5 is about average. Quoting Sharpe ratios for periods shorter than one year gives nonsensical results and should be avoided. Note that the preceding figures exclude ultra–high frequency (UHF) trading systems: such systems trade much more frequently, and can have very high Sharpe ratios. For such systems, the true risk is not market volatility leading to P&L fluctuations, but systemic breakdown of the trading methodology, which typically leads to sudden unprecedented large losses. The equity curve for UHF trading generally does not give a good representation of the real risk, which can be hard to quantify.

Maximum Drawdown

Maximum drawdown (MDD) is a measure of how far the portfolio's cumulative P&L has fallen below a previous high water mark. MDD is measured as the difference between the highest equity attained and the subsequent low point, and calculated on a daily basis. It is a popular measure because it is perceived by many as a "worst-case-loss scenario," that is, the experience of the unluckiest investor in a program who joins immediately before the largest sustained loss. In practice, MDDs measured from backtests tend to be optimistic. Backtests are always rose-tinted, and large drawdowns are necessarily rare by virtue of being extreme events. Maximum drawdowns can only increase with increasing length of track record: a short track record with a low MDD merely means that nothing has gone wrong *yet*. MDD scales as volatility, in that a model with a 20-volatility rating (possibly due to trading at greater leverage) will have twice the expected MDD of a 10-volatility model. But, in the high volatility case, the MDD is more *uncertain*—the worst-case could be a lot worse in the high volatility model. The ratio of return to MDD is called the Calmar ratio[3] and is sometimes reported along with the MDD. Over a realistic timeframe, a Calmar ratio of 1.0 is considered good, and anything higher probably understates the MDD risk or overstates the return.

Win Ratio

The win:loss trade ratio is highly strategy-dependent, but if we consider it on a per-day basis there is a clear, linear relationship with the Sharpe ratio. This can be tested with a dummy "trading model" that has daily signals with a user-specified win ratio, using real market data. Using results from this model, it can be seen that a Sharpe of 1.0 corresponds to a daily win:lose ratio of 54:46 (assuming you're not getting all the big days wrong). By contrast, a win:lose ratio of 70:30 would give a Sharpe of 5, which is very unrealistic unless trading in an ultra–high frequency system.

Industry Comparisons

There are various hedge fund indices available against which a trading strategy's performance may be benchmarked. Obviously, it only makes sense to do this with out-of-sample performance results as opposed to backtest performance results. Regrettably, there are some problems endemic in the industry when it comes to reporting results. The index may contain backtested "performance" figures, as performance is usually self-certified by the data providers (i.e., the hedge fund managers) themselves. The differences between backtest performance and real trading performance may be ignored in the published index. It is also common practice to remove the track record of funds that have ceased trading (usually due to unsatisfactory performance) from the entire index, historical and future. This creates a huge *survivor bias* in the reporting: it is perfectly possible to get a good-looking index from random data if the losing results can be excluded! This survivor bias (often called *survivorship bias*) can have a huge effect, and has led some industry figures to speculate whether the hedge fund sector as a whole may have negligible returns net of fees if these effects were corrected for.[4]

USES OF SYSTEMATIC TRADING METHODS

A trading model gives a directional signal for a particular market. This may incorporate strength of signal (anywhere between 0 and 100 percent) or be digital in nature: long, short, or neutral. Although trading signals are necessary for any systematic trading program, we need to consider how these signals are used in practice. We will then look at the two main applications of systematic trading: speculative trading and hedging programs.

Construction of a Systematic Trading Portfolio

In stock trading, a portfolio is a collection of stocks, which may be held in different quantities, which are thought of as a unit in the expectation of a reduction in volatility and improved risk/reward ratio when compared to trading single stocks. This principle also applies to systematic FX trading. But, as the number of relevant currency pairs is small in number compared to the number of publicly traded stocks, diversification is achieved by trading different models, as well as different currency pairs.

In order for this to be of any benefit, the models must offer returns with a low correlation. We can summarize the different forms of diversification as follows:

1. **Diversification across markets:** This form of diversification is the most similar to the stock analogy. It aims to produce uncorrelated returns by trading many different currency pairs. If different currencies are driven by different underlying factors, the patterns and price action exhibited by different currency pairs will have little to do with each other, and thus the same model traded in different markets will produce a different pattern of returns. This is most pronounced when the currency pairs do not share a currency in common. For example, although EUR–USD and GBP–USD will offer some diversification, they share exposure to USD factors. It would

be reasonable to assume that EUR–JPY and GBP–USD would have lower correlation.

2. **Diversification across models**: Different trading models earn their returns based on different market behaviors. The simplest example is trend following, which aims to profit from sustained directional moves. On the other hand, mean reversion trading aims to profit from the opposite type of behavior, where a move is reversed rather than extended. These two systems would be expected to have a very low, or even negative, correlation, leading to good portfolio effect.

3. **Diversification across time-scales:** Surprisingly, running two similar models in the same currency pair can yield diversification if one model is long-term and the other is short-term. In the example of two trend-followers, one might aim to profit from moves in the one-week time horizon, whereas the other may be looking for longer term-moves of a month or more. Although they will have the same position in the face of a long-term trend, their signals will offset each other for a significant proportion of the time, especially when the signal is not clear.

Unfortunately, portfolios designed with diversification in mind can fail to deliver the expected benefits. Some of the most important factors affecting them are:

1. **Illusion of diversification**: It may appear that EUR–JPY has nothing to do with AUD–USD, but since September 2008, their average 1-month rolling correlation has been 0.69, with a peak of 0.97. More importantly from a trader's perspective, the direction and timing of trends looks very similar when viewed on a chart. See Exhibit 16.6. If the market currently views both these currency pairs as "risk trades," an outbreak of risk-aversion would affect both of them in a similar fashion. This is especially true for

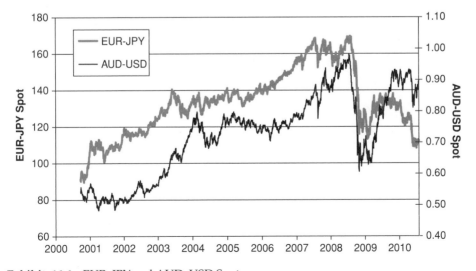

Exhibit 16.6 EUR–JPY and AUD–USD Spot

U.S. dollar–based currency pairs, where the dollar can easily be the driving factor, and the expected diversification largely evaporates. It should be remembered that in a strongly directional market, there is only one way to make money, and those models whose signals line up on the right side of the market are doing their jobs correctly—but won't be adding diversification.

2. **Dilution of returns:** It turns out that it is remarkably easy to diversify away returns as well as risk. For example, imagine trading both a trend-following system and a mean-reversion system at the same time to gain diversification. If the two models have similar time-scales, it is highly likely that what one model makes, the other one will lose—excellent diversification, but no profit! It is normally argued that if the expected return from each model is positive, the expected outcome will be positive, but this overlooks the fact that the models are not independent. In a given year, a strongly trending market is very likely to give poor, or even negative, returns for the mean-reverter, and likewise a market full of reversals will cause the trend-follower to lose money. This can easily mean that the "average case" becomes the best case, and the actual returns are far smaller than envisaged.

3. **Correlation increases during market shocks**: Even currency pairs that are uncorrelated under normal market conditions can have the same reaction to an extreme event. Global news events can have traders "fleeing to quality," with the result that any currency seen as overly risky suffers a move in the same direction (see Exhibit 16.7). These shock moves are typically against the prevailing trend (especially if the trend is in favor of the carry trade, which is almost always vulnerable to these events). Thus, all models that are currently profitable are liable to suffer a drastic reversal of fortune at the same time. These sorts of breakdowns in historic correlation are typically accompanied by market moves in the "fat tails regions." This can lead to a double-whammy effect that can put incautious traders out of business. The difference between the average case and the worst case for a large portfolio tends to be substantial, and shock events can make the worst case much more likely than a naïve treatment of risk would suppose.

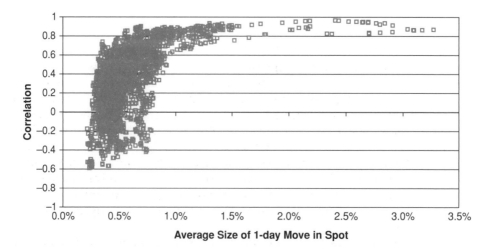

Exhibit 16.7   EUR–JPY and AUD–USD (Correlation versus Size of Daily Move)

Considerations in Portfolio Design

So, what makes for a well-diversified, robust portfolio? A great deal has been written on this issue including some of the most important financial theory—most notably what is now called Modern Portfolio Theory, which we will discuss shortly. For the moment, however, there are some common-sense considerations that must be applied to any allocation decision. The question is, in essence, extremely simple: "What amounts should I trade in each of my trading models in order to maximize my projected return for a given level of risk?"

The first thing to note is that, in order to achieve a reduction in volatility compared to trading a single model, it is necessary to have meaningful amounts trading in more than one model. Diversification happens when the P&L from one set of models partially offsets the P&L from another set. If the allocations are such that a single model, or subset of models, has an overwhelming allocation of capital, then not much offset is possible and little risk reduction is achieved.

Conclusion: Portfolio weights must be roughly evenly balanced for maximum risk reduction through diversification.

The second thing to note is that not all models and not all markets are equal. Some are more risky than others. Volatility is the standard measure of risk, and can be thought of as a measure of the average size of move that can be expected. Double the volatility and you would expect market moves of twice the size. As the events of 2008 and beyond showed, the assumption that foreign exchange market volatility is roughly constant at 10 percent is invalid, even if some currency pairs have now re-entered that regime. The credit crunch caused some markets to triple or even quadruple their volatilities in under a month. This dramatic increase in volatility, however, was not experienced to the same extent by every currency pair, causing large risk disparities.

Conclusion: Portfolio weights must take account of risk, and must be periodically re-balanced to allow for the changing risk profile of different markets.

It is worth noting, in passing, that varying risk levels cause a problem in the overall level of risk in the portfolio, as well as the relative weights of individual models. This relates to the total position size, or leverage, of the portfolio, and will be addressed later.

Two Portfolio Design Approaches

Modern Portfolio Theory (MPT) Approach

Despite its name, MPT dates from 1952.[5] The central concept is that knowledge of how the various portfolio components correlate (represented by a correlation matrix), together with their expected returns (usually derived from historical performance), allows one to calculate the optimal weightings that will give the best answer to the question posed earlier; that is, "What weighting scheme will maximize return for a given level of risk?" Different levels of specified risk will be associated with different levels of maximum expected return. And associated with each of these risk/return points is some corresponding portfolio composition (i.e., weighting scheme). Collectively, these risk/return points make up the so-called *efficient frontier*.

MPT is mathematically elegant and provides well-defined solutions to the problem of portfolio weights. But any model is only as good as its assumptions.

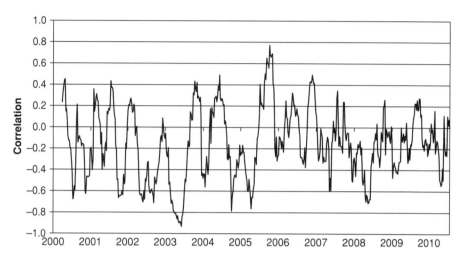

Exhibit 16.8   EUR–GBP and USD–JPY 3-Month Correlation (Weekly Data)

Critical to MPT is the assumption that correlations are stable and that expected returns are estimable. So, one needs to ask "How stable are the correlations between the different models, and how well can we estimate the expected returns?" Correlation is a famously slippery concept. By changing the historical period used in the calculation, one can derive widely differing correlation coefficients. This is illustrated for the EUR–GBP and USD–JPY currency pairs in the Exhibit 16.8.

MPT results are sensitive to changes in the correlation inputs. Given the variability in historical correlations, it is no surprise that future correlations may differ widely from those expected. The second problem is in estimating historical returns. Although this is simpler, it still assumes that the future P&L of a model is well represented by the average P&L over a long period. In practice, even a well-performing model can have poor years, and similarly a poor-performing model may have some exceptionally good years. This means that the P&L for any given model with a realistic risk/return profile may differ greatly from the average case, which in turn means that the "optimal" portfolio weights employed may be far from optimal in any given year.

The net result of these two uncertainties, smuggled into the assumptions of MPT, is that there is a great deal of uncertainty in the optimized portfolio weights it generates, which lays it open to charges of over-optimization. There is also the problem that, for any given portfolio, the component weightings may be far from equal simply because of a correlation between two trading models that arose by chance (sometimes called "spurious correlation"). As soon as this chance effect breaks down, the weights that were calculated become invalid. The results of a MPT optimization are liable, therefore, to be brittle rather than robust. For this reason, the process should be used with caution, and heavily constrained to ensure a sensible answer.

"Old School" Approach

This approach eschews any form of optimized solution in favor of the simple maxim of equal weights for everything. Although this may seem primitive, it has a number of advantages. As the weights aren't optimized, there is no danger of over-optimization based on history that may not be repeated. Very few assumptions are made about relative performance levels, and the main challenge is setting the overall leverage of the portfolio.

The problems associated with this approach come from the failure of the assumption that all models and markets are created equal. For example, a model trading GBP–USD may have half the P&L volatility of the same model trading GBP–JPY, but this approach would weight them the same. A modification of this approach, weighting things equally *by risk*, rather than by face amount, goes a long way toward solving this problem.

It is worth noting that employing conservative assumptions for correlation and knowledge of future returns in an MPT analysis often gives results very similar to this "Old School" approach.

Leverage and Margin Trading

Having decided on the relative amounts (i.e., weightings) that will be applied in a portfolio of trading models, one must next decide how much to allocate to the portfolio in total. This is normally decided with reference to either an investment amount or a risk budget—or, more commonly, a combination of both.

In a traditional hedge fund structure, the investment amount is defined as the capital (including reinvestment) that the investors have placed in the fund structure. Here, the leverage is defined as the ratio of total position size to that investment amount. If the two are the same, the fund is said to be unleveraged (or running at one-times leverage). Running at higher levels of leverage implies a larger total position size, engendering both more volatility and higher potential return.

Systematic trading is commonly done via margin trading—in fact, some of the first systematic traders were the so-called commodity trading advisors (CTAs), which traded managed futures funds (sometimes called commodity pools) using on-exchange margin trading. Margin trading has the advantage that you do not have to deposit the whole investment amount on day one (which can be very cash inefficient). Instead, the margin account must be sufficiently funded to cover all projected trading losses—an amount that can be as little as 10 percent of the equivalent investment amount. The notion of an "investment amount" is largely hypothetical in margin trading, which can make it difficult to compare returns between managed futures funds and conventional funds. Sometimes margin traders will quote returns as a percentage of margin, which can result in some very large and misleading percentage figures for return and risk. The only valid way to compare different funds is to compare return per unit risk, which is commonly done by the Sharpe ratio.

The Sharpe ratio is the most commonly used risk-adjusted return measure. It is nearly universally employed in the hedge fund and CTA worlds. As previously noted, it is defined as the annualized excess return divided by the annualized volatility of those returns, normally measured from daily return data. To obtain the excess return, the risk-free rate on any funds deposited must be deducted from the trader's return.[6] As the Sharpe ratio is annualized, the minimum acceptable period over which to calculate it would be one year. Calculating the Sharpe ratio over a short period of good performance will result in a misleadingly high ratio that may bear little relationship to longer-term performance.

Risk targeting is commonly done using either maximum drawdown (discussed earlier) or volatility measures. Any margin trading system must ensure that sufficient margin is available to cover a maximum drawdown event. The problem with MDD as a risk measure is that it is often taken as a "maximum loss limit," whereas in fact it can only increase over time. MDD events are by definition rare, so relying on them as a true indicator of the risk to which a portfolio is exposed is dangerous. Volatility is a more reliable risk measure, although it does not have the direct relationship to margin that makes MDD popular. Funds are commonly described by either their volatility target or the leverage they employ. As volatility can be highly variable, this targeting can only be approximated using any of a number of possible techniques to estimate current and future portfolio volatility.

Currency Alpha and Beta

The Capital Asset Pricing Model (CAPM) was introduced over the period 1961–1966, and classified stock returns as alpha and beta.[7] The beta return of a stock is the portion of its return that is explained by movements in the market index or by the market as a whole. A stock with a beta of 1 would be expected to produce returns equal, on average, to those of the market as a whole. Beta, in this context, is often said to represent the "systemic" risk exposure of the stock. The alpha is the portion of the stock's return that is *not* explained by the market as a whole, and therefore represents "pure" or uncorrelated return.

The application of alpha and beta to currency markets is not immediately obvious. There is no "market" as a whole that can be invested in, and every purchase of a currency is *ipso facto* the sale of a different currency. However, from the perspective of a stock investor, the returns from currency trading would represent "pure alpha," as they have been largely, or even entirely, uncorrelated to the stock market (i.e., zero beta). It has thus become customary to refer to currency trading returns as providing "currency alpha."

In the last few years, it has been increasingly common to hear currency referred to as an "asset class." To quote the Yale Endowment in 2005, "The definition of an asset class is quite subjective, requiring precise distinctions where none exist." This sort of language was first adopted by large investment banks seeking to sell foreign exchange products to conventional asset managers, so it may be suspected that this was an attempt to co-opt the language of asset management to sell trading products that asset managers might not otherwise consider within their remit. The truth is that foreign exchange contracts and stocks have both similarities and differences. The similarities chiefly relate to the fact that they can both be traded in a liquid market. It may be more accurate to say that foreign exchange is a *risk* class rather than an *asset* class: It is an arena in which market risk may be taken in order to earn an expected return. The difference between this and a conventional stock market is that "buy and hold" in FX is not a strategy with which anyone should expect to make money long term.

Some practitioners have taken the analogy between FX trading returns and conventional CAPM modeling further. It is not uncommon now to see "currency beta" products offered, some of which have been securitized. These define beta as the systematic exposure to artificial indices associated with different styles of trading. By using mathematical techniques, such as multivariate regression, and fitting them to various industry performance benchmarks, they calculate standard strategies that represent "pure" trend trading, carry trading, and mean reversion. An individual manager's performance may be compared to the performance of these strategies and a beta calculated in the same way that a stock beta is calculated with reference to the stock index's performance.

These "pure beta" strategies are now offered as trading products by a number of leading institutions. Whether such an approach has any validity depends largely on the way in which the products are used. Many asset managers seeking to diversify into the hedge fund arena seek to gain exposure to different styles of trading, but are obliged, by absence of choice, to invest in a "fund of funds" to do so. The disadvantages of this approach are many, including the potential for style drift and a double layer of performance fees. If all that is desired is to gain exposure to a typical pattern of, say, trend trading, then a "pure trend beta" product offers a cheaper and more transparent alternative—free from problems of individual manager misjudgment or style drift. If the individual manager wishes to buy and sell "trend" as a commodity (in much the same way that the VIX secondary market allows people to buy and sell volatility), then this is an ideal vehicle. If, on the other hand, the asset manager wishes to buy and hold a portfolio of beta strategies, the analogy to the stock market collapses, as there is a paucity of evidence that this approach will produce positive returns over the long term. Viewed in this way, "currency beta" strategies are just simplistic trading systems designed to look like everyone else rather than to make money.

Systematic Hedging

Hedging systematically has a long history. For many companies, it is common practice to cover their exposures using a program of trades, such as rolling forward cover or a strip of options. Although these are systematic, they are passive and in no way attempt to follow or react to the market, and therefore fall outside our purposes in this chapter.

However, a more active approach to hedging has been followed by some companies and financial institutions. In the same way that a speculator takes a view on the market and goes long or short to express that view, a hedger may increase or decrease a hedge to express the same view. The actions will be different depending on whether the underlying exposure is short or long for the currency pair in question, but the signals can be identical. The hedger is much more constrained than the trader: in order to qualify as hedging, the positions taken must always be against the underlying position, and cannot be a greater size than it. Also, the hedger does not have the freedom to specify which markets they wish to trade, but must only take positions in those markets in which the institution has exposure.

Example of Hedging Using Directional Signals

Imagine now Company A, which is domiciled in the United States and has net assets in Germany worth EUR 100m. In order to hedge its balance sheet exposure, the company's management decides to sell EUR forward versus the USD. They start by placing a forward hedge (the "constant cover") for half the amount, that is,

EUR 50m. The remaining EUR 50m is traded according to a systematic long-term directional program.

Suppose now that the system (i.e., directional program) generates a long signal. This would be in favor of the underlying exposure. The EUR 50m associated with the trading system is bought, offsetting the 50 percent constant cover hedge. The net hedge amount is therefore zero, and the company benefits in full from any appreciation in the EUR.

Alternatively, suppose that the system generates a short signal. This would be against the underlying exposure. Then the actively-traded EUR 50m is sold, adding to the forward hedge that is already in place, thereby hedging 100 percent of the underlying exposure. Company A is now fully protected from any weakening of the EUR.

Finally, suppose the system generates a neutral signal, implying no opinion on the direction of the EUR. Then the actively-traded part of the hedge is neutralized, leaving just the EUR 50m constant cover. The company is now partially hedged and will experience half the benefit or loss of any movement in EUR-USD.

Note that, in all of these cases, the actions taken with respect to the active portion of the hedge are *identical* to the actions that would be taken by a speculator trading EUR-USD with a EUR 50m position size. Thus, any speculative system generating trading signals may also be used for the purpose of hedging, although for practical reasons very high-frequency systems are generally unsuitable. As a side note, I would point out that, in some countries, adding a speculative component to a hedging program might result in the loss of the right to use hedge accounting, and this can have implications for the volatility of P&L. We will return to this point later.

Benchmarking and Risk Appetite

Depending on a company's risk tolerance level, sometimes called its "risk appetite," several variations on hedging with the directional signals theme are possible. The risk appetite determines the company's "default hedge position," which can be thought of as how much of their exposure they would hedge if they had no view on the direction of the relevant currency (i.e., the constant cover). In our prior example, the constant cover was 50 percent of the exposure, and it could vary from 0 percent to 100 percent depending on the directional system's indications. Now consider a company that has very little risk appetite and employs a constant cover of 90 percent, allowing itself a downward departure of only 10 percent when its directional system indicates the EUR will rise, but never going beyond its maximum cover of 100 percent when it thinks the EUR will fall. Thus, for the same size exposure as in our prior example, the company's hedge would vary from EUR 100m to EUR 80m, but would never go below EUR 80m.

Of course a company's constant cover could be anywhere between 100 percent (an entirely passive hedge) and 0 percent (entirely unhedged). For example, it might be 75 percent. In this case, with a similar exposure to the company above, management might wish to hedge EUR 75m as constant cover, and actively trade the remaining EUR 25m. This would result in a maximum hedge ratio of 100 percent as in the previous example, but a minimum hedge ratio of 50 percent. In this case, even when the signal is long, the company is still partially hedged. Although this may lead to hedge losses (if the signal is correct!), the P&L volatility and risk are constrained. It would also be possible to revert to a 100 percent hedge given a neutral signal, biasing the system further in favor of the full hedge. As this approach is fully hedged by default, and risk is measured as the deviation from that position, so Company A would be said to have a "fully-hedged benchmark."

Importantly, the cash requirements associated with hedging can be substantial and may not correspond to actual receivables—as in the case of balance sheet hedging in the examples above. To avoid excessive P&L volatility and to preserve competitiveness against unhedged competitors, a company might choose an unhedged benchmark. This is the inverse of the above: by adopting, for example, a EUR 25m constant cover and actively trading EUR 25m, the maximum hedge ratio is 50 percent, and the minimum zero. It should be noted that the active portion of the hedging program is unchanged in this example from the fully hedged case: all that has changed is the magnitude of the constant cover hedge.

A balanced (symmetric) benchmark is also possible and would correspond to the EUR 50m constant cover hedge in the original example. However, there is nothing obliging Company A to actively trade the entire remainder. It would be possible to trade only 25m actively, giving a maximum hedge of 75 percent and a minimum of 25 percent.

In all of the above cases, the size of the actively traded portion defines the size of the deviations from the benchmark: in the symmetric case, by $+/-$ the amount, and in the fully-hedged–unhedged cases, by twice the amount. The size of the active portion, therefore, should be related to the company's risk appetite—risk here being defined as deviation from the benchmark. In the limiting lower case (no active trading), this then defaults to being the passive benchmark strategy. The upper limit is as given in the original example, with maximum and minimum hedge ratios of 100 percent and zero.

Currency Overlay

Currency overlay is the outsourcing of currency risk management. A "risk discovery" exercise is performed to identify and quantify the nature of a company or institution's exposures. After the benchmark and risk appetite of the client has been determined, the overlay company trades the hedging program on behalf of the client, usually by a margin account/power of attorney arrangement similar to an investment management agreement for a CTA. The manager is normally incentivized by a flat fee. Performance fees are only appropriate in the case of a balanced benchmark, as otherwise the manager is penalized for reverting to the benchmark position, even when it is in the client's best interest. In any case, performance fees represent an incentive to overtrade.

Some overlay providers have been criticized for a "smoke and mirrors" approach, promising currency alpha plus a reduction in risk while ignoring the introduction of substantial tracking error, and sometimes overstating the performance of their actively traded component. The truth is that it is quite hard for overlay providers to add value. The choice of currency pair is not theirs to make, and it is rare for a trading system to work equally well in all currency pairs. They can only add value in one direction, unless the benchmark is symmetrical (overlay providers are much more in favor of this approach than most institutions), and the actively traded portion may only be a fraction of the total exposure to meet the client's risk appetite. Against this, some clients can display confusion as to the purpose of overlay: some may want to disguise a speculative program as a hedge, and be disappointed that the above constraints make it underperform.

Advantages and Disadvantages of Systematic Hedging

1. **Quantify the "known unknowns"**: A great advantage of systematic hedging is that expected performance and risk can be quantified in advance. Although there is still the unknown risk of systemic change leading to model failure, systematic trading allows future hedge performance to be forecast much better than with discretionary management.

2. **Discipline: Best practice**: With many companies and financial institutions employing consultants who demand a level of rigor in execution, systematic hedging allows the hedging processes to be certified and benchmarked, with the benchmark built into the strategy itself.

3. **No trading by committee**: The alternative to a program of hedges might well be macroscopic decisions made by the board in infrequent meetings. Trading by committee rarely has market-beating outcomes, as consensus is usually only achieved when a move is so obvious that the boat has already been missed.

4. **Limited trading portfolio**: As noted earlier, with most trading approaches, some currency pairs trade better than others. Hedging is limited to longer-term approaches and heavily biased in favor of trend-following: increasing a long hedge in a falling market can be difficult to justify when it goes wrong! If your company has exposure to unpredictably trending markets, your trading system may not add value.

5. **Effectiveness and suitability as a hedge**: Today, hedges have to be judged suitable and effective by accounting auditors, or they will be treated as speculative positions with negative tax and P&L accounting implications. Some trading programs, especially short-term or mean-reversion based systems, may not meet that requirement.

6. **Intrinsically speculative**: The active portion of a systematic hedging system is by its nature speculative. It may be determined by a company's board that this is inappropriate, and that the additional model risk is not justified by the perceived benefits the systematic hedging system affords. In this case, a completely passive program would be more suitable.

EVALUATION OF SYSTEMATIC TRADING IDEAS AND PRODUCTS

Most people, of course, do not want to trade for themselves or become professional money managers who run funds or otherwise trade for others. Yet they might want to invest some of their own money or some of their client's money in a systematic trading program—either an account managed by someone else on their behalf or a fund in which they would invest. In closing this chapter, we ask, "What would

I want to know about a manager and his trading systems before I entrust him or her with my money?"

Shedding Some Light On the Black Boxes

It is customary for prospective investors in hedge funds and managed futures funds to do "due diligence" on the fund managers. In addition to the usual checks for legal and financial soundness, the investigation usually encompasses the trading methodologies employed. Any such due diligence process will usually run up against the problem that the algorithms at the heart of their trading system are proprietary, and they will be understandably reluctant to divulge something that could allow their entire trading product to be duplicated.

However, this may be less of a problem than it first appears. Unless the prospective client is very experienced in the design and analysis of trading algorithms, it is questionable how much value is added by disclosing them: judgments on their validity will be highly subjective. In any case, other sources of information will be available that largely render this unnecessary to make a proper evaluation of a manager.

In practice, doing due diligence on an investment manager, particularly a systematic trader, greatly benefits from having experience in the field, as the tacit knowledge that comes from working with trading models first-hand is irreplaceable. The checklist below is not intended as a replacement for that skill and knowledge, but as a supplement to ensure that the important areas are covered. It can also be used as an auditing checklist for internal evaluation of trading systems, where disclosure is not an issue. In a lot of cases, the important thing is that the manager has thought about the questions and does have answers.

The purpose of due diligence is twofold: (1) evaluation of the manager's trading success via track record, and (2) evaluation of the manager's trading process. For both of these, a lot of information will be available that is very pertinent without having to look inside the "black box" of their trading algorithms. We will consider each in turn.

Track Record Criteria

Does the Track Record Represent Real Trading, Out-of-Sample or Backtest?
As discussed earlier, in-sample (backtested) results have little validity when it comes to evaluating the real-world performance of a trading approach. The manager should be clear about what, if any, parts of his track record are in-sample. You should not have to ask. If any parts are in-sample, the manager should be able to provide justification, such as "they haven't started trading yet."

The track record may also be simulated, but out-of-sample. This is an important distinction, as hindsight bias only affects in-sample returns. However, selection bias is not as easily dismissed. For example, would you be seeing these returns if they were negative? Real track records cannot be so easily hidden. If the portfolio is claimed as out-of-sample, find out if it has been changed since the start of the history, and for what reason.

Simulation also can give rise to errors due to the assumptions made in the calculations. Ask about the magnitude of trading costs, and how order fills were modeled. High-low data is somewhat unreliable in FX as no central exchange is involved, so the true ranges might be different and a fill might be difficult to achieve without a lot of slippage. Open-close data is a lot more reliable and less prone to data errors.

Daily versus Monthly Track Record

Many managers now provide their performance data at daily frequency. This can tell you a lot more than monthly frequency data. For example, it is unlikely that the worst one-month period fell exactly on calendar boundaries. Likewise, the daily maximum drawdown is very likely to be worse than a monthly measure. Any stress testing or VaR analysis you do will also need daily data. It is worth repeating what was previously mentioned about track records and what sorts of performance are reasonable. If the risk shown in the track record is inconsistent with the manager's stated approach, then one or more of the problems of selection bias, in-sample returns, and over-optimization is probably present. Alternatively, the track record might be too short to show any significant drawdowns.

More Questions You Should Ask

- What was their worst period of actual trading? How did they cope?

  Comment: Openness and honesty are good signs, as is the fact that they have had a serious drawdown in the past—if not, then it's waiting to happen, and you don't know how they'll cope. Changing approach or style should be proactive decisions, not reactive in the face of a drawdown. Is the amount of discretionary intervention in line with their stated aims?

- How successful have they been at meeting their stated targets for volatility and return?

  Comment: Volatility is a tough metric to target as it is itself unstable. How has their process responded to market shocks? Have they replaced the leverage in good order after the shock has passed? Are they overcautious, leading to systematic under-leverage?

- Is their Sharpe ratio realistic and how do they feel about it?

  Comment: Refer to our earlier discussion for what are reasonable Sharpe ratios. Most experienced market practitioners will be happy to get double-digit return in a 10 volatility environment. Realistic expectations on both the manager's and the client's part are essential for a good working relationship.

- What was the reason for any flat spots (i.e., periods in which the equity curve was flat)?

  Comment: Do the flat spots correspond to poor performance in the rest of the manager's portfolio? A simple correlation analysis will not pick up this type of effect.

Process Criteria

Ideally, you would have full divulgence of all processes and trading systems allowing your quants to re-create the entire trading history with independent data sources. Needless to say, this is hardly ever realistic. So, you should aim to validate their process using the following criteria:

How do they generate signals?

- What is their trading approach? The main schools of thought in systematic trading are trend-following, mean reversion trading, pattern-matching (including neural net approaches), and the carry trade.
- What timescale do they operate on? Is it intra-day or daily, and what is their average and maximum trading frequency and holding period? It is also useful to find out whether the signals are generated with reference to any data sets other than that of the traded currency pair (extrinsic signals).

Comments:

- Does the timescale match your needs? Higher-frequency trading can make, or lose, money faster than long-term trading, which is limited by market volatility.
- Have they suffered style drift? Have they compromised their original ideas, and if so, do you believe their reasons or have they just tinkered?

Model Management

- Do they have a process for researching new models and retiring old ones?
- When is it no longer appropriate to trade a model?
- Are new models traded pari passu with existing approaches?

Comments:

- Is their process more discretionary than their marketing makes out?
- How quickly do they recognize that a new approach isn't living up to expectations?

Portfolio Construction

- Are the models equally weighted, risk weighted, or optimized (MPT)?
- When do the weights change, and on what criteria?

Comments:

- How certain is the manager that his portfolio weights are correct?
- Is the "portfolio" critically dependent on a subset of approaches/currencies because of deficiencies in risk weighting?
- Are the weights constrained at all to prevent risk-weighting deficiencies from happening in the future, even if it isn't the case now?

Risk Management

- What is the fund's typical and maximum leverage?
- How does the manager respond to changes in market volatility?
  - Stress test: How did the system cope with the 2008 shock?
  - Did this occasion intervention?
  - Did the trading process change as a result?
- How does the manager cope with model failure?
- Does the manager employ portfolio-level or model-level risk management?
  - What does the portfolio look like without this intervention?

Comments:

- Is the approach robust with respect to market volatility shocks and other secular changes? What would cause the manager's approach to fail?
- Does the manager over-leverage in low volatility environments? This may take the form of trading too much on the entire portfolio, or may result in the portfolio becoming unbalanced with respect to a particular currency pair or trading model.
- Are the manager's expectations of model failure realistic?
- Would the manager stop trading under any circumstances, and if so, what are they?
- While it can be hard to insist on answers, financial history is replete with tragic losses as a consequence of failure to ask the right questions and do the appropriate due diligence.

NOTES

1. Caltech commencement address given in 1974.
2. Because return is in the numerator and risk is in the denominator, some people would describe the Sharpe ratio as a return/risk measure. While, of course this is technically correct, the custom has always been to talk of risk/return ratios even when it is really a return/risk ratio. This semantic confusion is actually an artifact of the earliest measures of risk/return that did use risk in the numerator and return in the denominator. The Sharpe ratio is named for William Sharpe, who proposed it in 1966. See Sharpe (1966).
3. The term Calmar ratio was introduced by Young (1991). Calmar is an acronym for California Managed Accounts Reports, which is the name of Terry Young's company.
4. See, for example, Wilson (2010), who summarizes some recent literature on survivorship bias in hedge funds.
5. Modern portfolio theory began with the work of Markowitz (1952).
6. Importantly, a lot of "margin" trading is actually done on a line of credit, so the Sharpe ratio must be redefined accordingly.
7. The CAPM is the culmination of the work of a number of contributors including Sharpe (1964), Lintner (1965), and Mossin (1966). Treynor (1961, 1962) also contributed to the foundations of the CAPM. While Treynor circulated his work in the early 1960s, he did not publish his work on the subject until much later. Nevertheless, his unpublished work inspired others.

REFERENCES

Lintner, J. 1965. "The Valuation of Risk Assets and the Selection of Risky Investments in Stock Portfolios and Capital Budgets." *Review of Economics and Statistics* 47:1, 13–37.

Markowitz, H. 1952. "Portfolio Selection." *Journal of Finance* 7:1, 77–91.

Mossin, J. 1966. "Equilibrium in a Capital Asset Market." *Econometrica* 34:4, 768–783.

Sharpe, W. F. 1964. "Capital Asset Prices: A Theory of Market Equilibrium under Conditions of Risk," *Journal of Finance* 19:3, 425–442.

Sharpe, W. F. 1966. "Mutual Fund Performance." *Journal of Business* 39:S1, 119–138.

Treynor, J. 1961. "Market Value, Time, and Risk." Unpublished manuscript.

Treynor, J. 1962. "Toward a Theory of Market Value of Risky Assets." Unpublished Manuscript (later published in 1999).

Young, T. 1991. "Calmar Ratio: A Smoother Tool." *Futures Magazine*, October 5.

Wilson, D. 2010. " Hedge Fund Returns Dragged Down by 'Hidden Bias.'" *Bloomberg*. March 31.

ABOUT THE AUTHORS

Mel Mayne has 25 years' experience in the Foreign Exchange markets. He has traded fixed income and FX products for Chemical Bank, UBS, Chase Manhattan, and First Chicago where he was head of trading and sales for Europe, Middle East, and Africa.

After leaving First Chicago he set up a currency fund in 2000; he was joined by Chris Attfield when he set up PaR Asset Management as senior partner in 2003. He has a successful track record in developing and trading short- and medium-term models in the FX markets and is currently involved in developing portfolio risk systems for his own portfolio.

Chris Attfield has 15 years' experience in the foreign exchange market. Starting in FX and option sales, he was a founder member of the Strategic Risk Management group at First Chicago, which pioneered VaR, balance sheet simulation, and systematic trading solutions for their clients, and launched their currency overlay subsidiary. After leaving First Chicago (then Bank One) in 2002, he joined Mel Mayne as a partner in PaR Asset Management LLP. There he was responsible for trading system research and development including model backtesting and portfolio-level risk control. Chris has a BSc in Chemistry from Bristol University.

PART IV

Case Studies in Financial Engineering: The Good, the Bad, and the Ugly

CHAPTER 17

Case Studies Introduction

PENNY CAGAN
Algorithmics/Fitch Group

INTRODUCTION

This part of this book, which consists of this short introductory chapter and the next five chapters, examines major cases involving some form of operational failure. While success is always preferable to failure, it is often easier to learn important lessons from an examination of failure than from an examination of success. In the following chapters, we will look at a total of eleven cases that have been logically grouped based on some commonality. Specifically, we will look at mortgage case studies, derivatives case studies, fixed income case studies, funds case studies, and credit derivatives cases studies.

At the core of these case studies is the concept of *fiduciary duty*. Financial institutions are obligated to put client interests above their own. This holds true in both the retail and the institutional sectors and includes the selling of mortgages; providing advice to mutual, pension, and government funds; and executing trades on behalf of others. There is no other industry, with the exception of health care, that is obligated to put a client's interests above its own. For example, when a consumer buys a computer from a computer company, there is no obligation to sell "the best computer at the best price" in the same way that a brokerage is obligated to "execute the best trade at the best price." It is, of course, good business practice on the part of the computer manufacturer to provide the best computer at a competitive price, but there is no fiduciary duty, as mandated by laws and regulations, to do so.

A variety of operational risk issues surface in the series of case studies we examine, but fiduciary duty as an obligation can be found at the heart of most of them. Countrywide Financial, for example, had a duty to sell the most suitable mortgage to its retail clients at the best interest rate available. Once the firm started relying on securitizing mortgages, however, its business model changed to one that favored volume over creditworthiness. The securitization of its mortgage origina-tions moved the credit risk off the books of Countrywide. Once freed of credit risk, the company then concentrated on initiating a high volume of subprime mortgages that were favored in the secondary markets because they had higher payoffs. As Countrywide financed an ever-growing proportion of its lending business from the securitization market, it no longer placed the interests of its retail clients, and what mortgages were most suitable for them, first.

The board of the state of Florida's money market fund compromised its fiduciary duty to the state and its employees and citizens when it shifted how it compensated portfolio managers. Its money managers were given pay incentives in exchange for bringing in above-average returns. This led the money managers to purchase instruments that would act as kickers in their portfolios—specifically, mortgage-backed securities (MBS). The problem with this strategy is that providing incentives to money managers to increase yield led to investment in riskier securities, while the mandate of the fund was to have cash on hand to finance government business. When the mortgage-backed securities market froze up, the fund no longer had this ready source of cash and the money managers had compromised their mission to manage the funds with a low-risk strategy that afforded ready access to cash.

Unauthorized trading events are often triggered by the behavior of traders who sustain losses from one trade and then find themselves in a downward spiral in an effort to trade their way back to profitability. This behavior, while possibly inherent in the personality profile of traders in general, is able to express itself as a result of control factors that are not functioning properly. Such outsized trading misdeeds often occur in environments that tolerate breaches of trading limits, and where management often does not take a long, hard look at where profits are coming from. This lax control environment, which often exists in organizations that experience such large unauthorized trading events, results in a breach of fiduciary duty to the bank's clients, employees, and, most importantly, shareholders; it is the shareholders who are last in line when an institution suffers a liquidity crisis and who often are left with the largest losses.

The concept of fiduciary duty to shareholders is key in all organizations but becomes especially important in financial organizations. This is because a financial institution must have the courage to resist entering sectors or engaging in practices that could put it at risk for regulatory or client troubles later on. Financial institutions that enter into questionable market practices because of pressure to bring in certain returns also put shareholders at risk if they find themselves with large losses later on, due to conflict of interest, regulatory violations, and a failure to put client interests first. It takes a strong management to say, "We don't like this practice, and we, as an institution, are not going to engage in it," when such a practice is earning great returns for its competitors. That very same management, however, will be in much better shape to weather the next tide of market practice investigations or market turmoil than its competitors. And it will have much happier shareholders and stakeholders of all types.

Finally, all of the outsized case studies provided have another key element in common: They occurred during periods of market volatility and at the end of periods of exuberance when controls may have become especially lax. The operating environment of financial institutions often becomes more fluid during boom times, and high-risk activities are more readily tolerated. There is a credit risk maxim that says that mistakes are made during good times rather than bad times. All of these cases involve certain control oversights, and a certain amount of hubris, associated with the amount of profits that could be made without regard to the associated risk, which ultimately ended up costing the institutions close to everything they owned. Again, it takes an act of courage for management to take a step back and make sure its controls are functioning during the good times.

Markets are cyclical and, ultimately, the goal of a financial institution should be to have the resilience to survive tough times.

ABOUT THE AUTHOR

Penny Cagan is a managing director with the Operational Risk division of Algorithmics/Fitch Group. She has over 25 years' experience in the field of financial services research. She currently manages the First and Opdata operational risk loss event databases and is head of research for the group. She has published numerous articles on the topic of operational risk in *Risk* magazine, *Operational Risk* newsletter, *Futures and Options World* (FOW), and the *John Liner Review*. She is a highly regarded and frequently requested speaker on operational risk and has given many keynote presentations on the topic.

Penny developed the case study approach to operational risk based on external events, and was the first person to go to market with an operational risk case study database. She has established the best practice standard for examining and analyzing case studies and has managed the First database for the past seven years under three different owners. Earlier in her career, she served as head of research for Deutsche Bank's North American Business Information Services division and as head of reference services with PaineWebber's investment banking division.

Penny holds an MLS in library science and a BA and MFA in English literature and creative writing.

CHAPTER 18

Mortgage Case Studies: Countrywide and Northern Rock

ALGORITHMICS SOFTWARE LLC*

CASE STUDY ONE: COUNTRYWIDE FINANCIAL[1]

Event Summary

Countrywide Financial, the largest home lender in the United States, found itself under liquidity pressure in August 2007 when the markets experienced extreme volatility as a result of rising defaults in the subprime mortgage market. Countrywide first tapped into an $11.5 billion credit line and then accepted $2 billion in financing from Bank of America. The lender later announced, on January 11, 2008, that it had agreed to be fully acquired by Bank of America for about $4 billion in stock, or approximately $6.90 per share. Countrywide's shares had been selling for $42 per share in January 2007. The value of the deal was later reduced to $2.8 billion.

Countrywide's troubles triggered a class action lawsuit that contends that the lender issued "materially false and misleading statements regarding the company's business and financial results" during the period from January 31, 2006, through August 9, 2007. In addition, the firm was accused of perpetuating predatory business practices in its emphasis on selling loans with high associated fees to consumers. Countrywide announced a $1.2 billion third-quarter loss on October 26, 2007; this was its first reported loss in 25 years.

Event Details

In 2007, Countrywide had $408 billion in mortgage originations and a servicing portfolio of about $1.5 trillion with 9 million loans. Rumors that Countrywide was in trouble contributed to extreme volatility in the markets during the month of August 2007. Countrywide had issued an alert the previous month indicating that its earnings were likely to be down as a result of defaults in the lower end of the

---

*This information is the sole property of Algorithmics Software LLC and may not be reprinted or replicated in any way without permission.

home equity sector. The loans that were not performing optimally were its home equity lines of credit, subprime mortgage loans, and closed-end second lien loans. This led Countrywide to announce that it was putting aside $388 million to cover risks associated with these loans. The company's CEO, Angelo Mozilo, further scared the markets when he commented that "we are experiencing home-price depreciation almost like never before, with the exception of the Great Depression" (McClean and Nocera 2010).

Among the problems suffered by Countrywide was a run on the bank on August 20, 2007, when customers lined up at its offices in several U.S. cities in order to inquire about their deposits and withdraw funds. This caused worry among analysts, because Countrywide had already stated that it planned to use its banking unit as a source of funding for home loans. A run on the lender's certificates of deposit, for instance, would mean that it would be unable to fund its lending business.

In addition to its credit problems, concern was expressed about the company's business practices. The *New York Times* reported (8/26/2007) that Countrywide's entire profit structure was predicated on earning fees that were higher than industry averages on loan issuance and servicing. The mortgage lender's sales team received higher commissions if they sold loans that carried prepayment penalties with longer terms than the average, or loans that reset after a short period of time at higher than average rates. Sales executives were also compensated if they convinced borrowers to take out home equity loans at the same time as primary mortgages. One former unnamed sales representative told the *New York Times* that "the whole commission structure in both prime and subprime was designed to reward salespeople for pushing whatever programs Countrywide made the most money on in the secondary markets."

Countrywide's reliance on bundling and selling mortgages in the secondary markets was believed to be at the core of its problems, because it encouraged what could be deemed predatory selling behavior among its sales team, and lax lending standards among loan underwriters. For instance, subprime mortgages were especially lucrative for Countrywide because they were favored by investors in the secondary market for the higher returns they yielded. This was a self-perpetrating loop that led to the payment of higher commissions to sales executives who sold higher-priced mortgages to borrowers who might have qualified for lower rates.

The *New York Times* (8/23/2007) reported that what added to the pressure on Countrywide was its alleged "quiet promise" to investors in its loans in the secondary markets that it would repurchase any mortgages that failed to perform. According to the *New York Times*, Countrywide's loan modification agreements cover about $122 billion worth of mortgages that were sold to investors between 2004 and April 1, 2007. A Countrywide spokesperson, however, contended that the amount of loans that can be modified in any mortgage pool that it has sold in the secondary markets is limited to 5 percent.

Countrywide announced on August 20, 2007, that it was planning to eliminate 500 jobs from its Full Spectrum and wholesale lending divisions. Full Spectrum specialized in subprime and Alt-A loans, which often have no-documentation attributes. The wholesale division arranged loans primarily through brokers. Countrywide at the time employed a workforce in the range of 60,000. Approximately

25 percent of the subprime loans serviced by Countrywide were in default as of June 2007, compared with 15 percent for the same period during the prior year.

Countrywide was the largest originator of home loans in the United States with a 17 percent market share. The number two lender was Wells Fargo, with 10.5 percent. With the acquisition of Countrywide, Bank of America now became the largest home loan lender, with a 25 percent market share. Bank of America has low exposure to the subprime sector; it exited the business in 2001 when its newly appointed CEO, Kenneth Lewis, deemed the business too risky. In addition, Bank of America relies on its substantial pool of retail deposits, rather than the securitization of mortgages, to finance its lending activities.

Countrywide's troubles triggered a class action lawsuit alleging that Countrywide issued "materially false and misleading statements regarding the company's business and financial results" during the period from January 31, 2006, through August 9, 2007. Such shareholder lawsuits are not uncommon when a company experiences financial difficulties. The American Federation of State, County and Municipal Employees' pension fund, which holds shares in Countrywide, called for CEO Mozilo's ouster and cited a long list of grievances.

Three U.S. states filed lawsuits against Countrywide during the month of June 2008. The states of California and Illinois filed lawsuits contending that the mortgage lender engaged in improper sales practices and sold mass-produced risky mortgages to thousands of home owners. Both states allege that as a result of Countrywide's sales practices, their local economies and housing markets have suffered irrevocable damage. California State Attorney General Jerry Brown (now governor) called Countrywide "a mass-production loan factory" that produced "ever-increasing streams of debt without regard for borrowers." He also commented, "Countrywide exploited the American dream of homeownership and then sold its mortgages for huge profits on the secondary market" (2008). Washington State also filed a lawsuit against Countrywide, contending that the mortgage lender engaged in discriminatory lending practices in addition to the selling of unsuitable loans. The state analyzed over 600 Countrywide loans and found 50 instances where minority borrowers received "less favorable" loans than others. The study found that in instances where minority and non-minority borrowers had similar credit scores and loan-to-value ratios on their purchased properties, the minority borrowers received loans with higher interest payments and less advantageous terms. The state is seeking to suspend Countrywide's license in the state and fine the lender $1 million.

Control Failings and Contributory Factors

Corporate/Market Conditions

Market conditions for all financial institutions and lenders became so precarious during August 2007 that the Federal Reserve stepped in to add liquidity to the markets. The Federal Reserve last provided cash to the banking system in 1998 during the collapse of Long-Term Capital Management. This suggests that conditions that led to Countrywide's troubles were at least a once-in-10-years event. When the Federal Reserve moved to cut the discount borrowing rate, it released a statement saying that risk in the markets had increased "appreciably." Jan Hatzius, chief U.S. economist for Goldman Sachs, commented: "In Fed-speak, things are either 'slightly' or 'somewhat.' Saying that the risks have increased 'appreciably' is a pretty strong statement for them."

Improper Management Practices

The *New York Times* (8/26/2007) reported that Countrywide's businesses, which include lending, servicing, and closing divisions, were designed to squeeze from consumers every possible dollar in fees. The newspaper reported that the mortgage lender was not necessarily living up to its promise of "the best loan possible," and that, in some cases, it did not count certain streams of income, such as cash reserves, in order to justify issuing higher-cost loans to borrowers. This strategy allegedly influenced how mortgage brokers and sales executives were compensated. They were paid higher commissions for loans with lengthier-than-average prepayment terms, and for loans that reset after a short period of time with higher-than-average rates. In addition, sales personnel earned higher commissions if they convinced a borrower to take out a home equity loan at the same time as a primary mortgage.

Compensation

The *New York Times* (8/26/2007) criticized Countrywide's CEO for being "a huge seller" of his company's stock during the prior few years and for not buying a single share in the company since 1987. The *Times* contended that as subprime troubles unfolded, Mr. Mozilo's selling of Countrywide's shares accelerated. During a 12-month period ending in late August 2007 he made $129 million from selling Countrywide shares. He continued to hold 1.4 million shares in Countrywide, or 24 percent of the company, which were estimated to be worth $29.4 million. A company spokesperson commented that Mr. Mozilo was simply diversifying his portfolio as he approached retirement. An unidentified source, quoted by several publications on October 18, 2007, disclosed that Mozilo's stock sales were being informally investigated by the Securities and Exchange Commission (SEC). Mr. Mozilo was not expected to have a role in the newly combined organization.

Undertook Excessive Risks

The *New York Times* reported that Countrywide issued certain risky loans even after some of the problems in the subprime market emerged. For instance, Countrywide allegedly issued loans that required no money down through March 2007, and no-documentation loans that required only 5 percent down, through February 2007. The lender issued loans through late July 2007 in amounts up to $500,000 to borrowers with credit scores as low as 500 if they put down 30 percent deposits.

Conflict of Interest

The *Wall Street Journal* reported in several articles that a group of individuals nicknamed "Friends of Angelo" were able to obtain loans at favorable rates and with laxer than average lending standards as the result of Mr. Mozilo's intercession. These individuals included retired professional athletes, two senators, and two former CEOs of mortgage-acquirer Fannie Mae. Mr. Mozilo allegedly continued to intercede in securing loans for his "friends" even after the mortgage sector started to exhibit increased defaults.

Corrective Actions and Management Response

Countrywide ran newspaper ads in major cities on August 20, 2007, assuring clients that their deposits were safe. The advertisements sought to reassure Countrywide's investors and customers by declaring that its "future is bright." Countrywide offered the high rate of a 5.65 percent yield on its 12-month certificates of deposit. In addition, Countrywide stated that it would originate only loans that could be sold off to Fannie Mae or Freddie Mac; this would preclude the lender from originating jumbo loans in the near future.

Countrywide announced on August 16, 2007, that it had tapped its entire $11.5 billion line of credit with a group of 40 banks in an effort to "navigate" difficult markets. The lender said that it would tighten credit standards for all types of loans that it originates. David Sambol, the company's president and chief operating officer, said in this announcement, "Countrywide has taken decisive steps which we believe will address the challenges arising in this environment and enable the company to meet its funding needs and continue growing its franchise." Some of these changes included a restructuring that would shift the lender's mortgage business into its banking subsidiary, Countrywide Bank.

Countrywide announced on October 23, 2007, that it was planning to refinance nearly $16 billion of debt for more than 52,000 subprime borrowers who had adjustable-rate mortgages scheduled to reset in the next 14 months. This was an effort by Countrywide to stave off a flood of additional foreclosures on borrowers' properties. It was a strategy that other mortgage lenders have deployed as well; Washington Mutual announced that it pledged $2 billion to a program that will convert subprime mortgages into traditional 30-year fixed-rate loans.

Lessons Learned

The rapid descent into a cash crunch for the country's largest mortgage lender demonstrates the complexity of the operating environment in August 2007. Guy Cecala, publisher of the *Inside Mortgage Finance* newsletter, commented that he was "shocked" by Countrywide's troubles and added that "there is no question that we've never seen this kind of panic going on. The panic has cleared out all sources of financing." He characterized Countrywide as the "face of the U.S. mortgage industry" and added: "to have them fail would have a huge impact on the U.S. economy and send huge repercussions around the world."

If Countrywide was the "face of the U.S. mortgage industry" at one time, it has also been touted as the "face" of credit-related excess in the United States. *BusinessWeek* reported (1/14/2008) that "every go-go period on Wall Street has a spectacular flame-out that comes to symbolize the excesses of the day, from Sam Insull's Middle West Utilities during the Great Depression to Pets.com in the dot-com era. Now it's Countrywide Financial's turn."

Aftermath of Event

Fitch, the ratings agency, downgraded Countrywide's issuer default ratings after the announcement that the mortgage lender had drawn down its $11.5 billion credit line. The rating agency called this "a clear sign that liquidity pressure was mounting." Fitch also stated that while the decision was cause for concern, it also relieved some pressure on Countrywide in the near term and blamed the lender's problems on "unprecedented disruption in the capital markets" rather than "a fundamental breakdown of the company's financing plan or strategy." Fitch commented that the company's outlook "hinges on the return of normal secondary market conditions" and noted that Countrywide was safer than others because it had a thrift charter, which provides access to a significant deposit base and Federal Home Loan Bank funding.

In the first report on earnings after Countrywide's credit problems emerged, the lender announced on October 26, 2007, that it had suffered a $1.2 billion loss for the third quarter of 2007. This was Countrywide's first reported loss in 25 years. The lender, however, said that as a result of restructuring, it expected to report profitable earnings for the fourth quarter of 2007 and in 2008. Countrywide's chairman attributed the loss to "unprecedented disruptions" in the mortgage and housing sectors. Fitch responded to Countrywide's earnings announcement by stating that it would continue to review the lender's rating, which was BBB+.

According to American Banker (1/14/2008), Bank of America's $2.8 billion stock purchase of Countrywide would allow the bank "to accomplish its goal of becoming a mortgage powerhouse quickly without paying anything close to premium." The transaction was done at a steep discount: Countrywide's market value was estimated at about $30 billion one year earlier. Bank of America's CEO said he would undertake a review in order to determine whether Bank of America will retain the Countrywide brand and name in the near future. The integration of Countrywide and Bank of America is expected to result in the loss of 7,500 jobs.

CASE STUDY TWO: NORTHERN ROCK[2]

Event Summary

In a reflection of jittery nerves concerning market conditions, hordes of Northern Rock PLC's customers lined up in front of the mortgage lender's branches on September 14, 2007, in an attempt to withdraw money from savings accounts. The run on the bank occurred shortly after the Bank of England announced that it would provide emergency cash to the third-largest mortgage lender in the United Kingdom. The bailout, which was the first of its kind since 1995, was necessary after Northern Rock announced that it was unable to issue new loans to borrowers. Northern Rock ultimately borrowed an estimated £25 billion from the Bank of England. Two serious bids were later filed to acquire the bank, but in the end it was nationalized by the British government. Two years later the U.K. government proposed a plan to split the bank into "good" and "bad" banks, and to sell the profitable entity to a potential acquirer.

Event Details

Northern Rock was the third-largest mortgage lender in the United Kingdom, with 1.4 million retail deposit accounts, 76 bank branches, and 800,000 mortgage borrowers. By 11 A.M. on September 14, 2007, depositors were lined up outside branches in London. By the next day, Northern Rock had seen an estimated $2 billion flow out of its accounts. This followed on the heels of a previous run on a mortgage lender's savings bank that was experienced in California by Countrywide Financial.

Northern Rock was the first major British financial institution to find itself in a liquidity crunch since the start of the subprime credit crisis in the summer of 2007. Some of its troubles were attributed to reliance on funding from the capital markets—both through securitizing mortgage loans and through borrowing money from the issuance of short-term debt. The bank was not considered to be a reckless lender. It had a good credit record with only 0.47 percent of its loans in arrears. This was about one-half the average rate for British mortgage lenders. At the same time, the bank was known for issuing mortgages for 130 percent of the value of the underlying property; this allowed first-time buyers to enter the housing market but also exposed the lender to unsecured loans.

It was Northern Rock's growth strategy, with a reliance on capital market financing rather than funding based on customer deposits, that led to difficulties. Most banks balance their funding more equally between customer deposit accounts and capital markets. The bank was well diversified in its capital market sources of funding; its major vulnerability was associated with the unlikely prospect of an entire shutdown of the wholesale lending markets. Unfortunately, Northern Rock faced these unusual conditions in the summer of 2007.

Northern Rock had launched its securitization program in 1999 as a way of boosting its share of the U.K. mortgage market through a program named Granite. Granite was designed to raise money by securitizing Northern Rock's loans and to provide liquidity and funding so that it could finance new mortgages. The Granite program was at the heart of Northern Rock's problems. The Granite strategy involved the bundling of mortgages and the subsequent issuing of bonds. Funds flowed into Granite from what Northern Rock collected in interest payments from its mortgage customers.

Northern Rock's reliance on securitization allowed it to initiate a greater number of mortgages than if it relied more heavily on its modest depositor base. When the market for such securitized products dried up in the summer of 2007, Northern Rock found it difficult to continue writing new mortgages. And without the ability to issue new mortgages, Northern Rock was unable to continue financing Granite, which relied on the interest income from mortgage payments to pay out securitized notes as they came due. And if the trust was not provided with sufficient funding from new mortgages, certain triggers could be hit that were designed to protect borrowers. By the end of June 2007, Granite contained £47.8 billion in mortgages.

Once news of Northern Rock's troubles led to a run on its bank, the Bank of England, the government, and the lender quickly assured all those impacted that their funds were safe. All three parties moved to explain that a liquidity crunch and difficulty with obtaining short-term cash is very different from actual insolvency. The news of Northern Rock's bailout led to a 33 percent drop in the company's share price at the closing of the day on September 14, 2007. By Monday, September 17, the bank's shares plunged another 35 percent. The bank's market value on September 17, 2007, was estimated to be £1.1 billion. It had been estimated to be worth £5.2 billion in the spring of 2007.

Northern Rock was believed to be a takeover candidate. By the weekend of September 22, 2007, the media reported that at least 12 European banks were approached concerning an acquisition of Northern Rock; all the approached banks allegedly declined to make an offer. The banks that were approached were reportedly hesitant to take Northern Rock's £100 billion in mortgages onto their own books. Richard Branson and a consortium of financiers approached Northern Rock in October 2007 with a proposal to invest US$2 billion in the failing bank and rename it Virgin Money.

By late October 2007, the Bank of England had lent Northern Rock an estimated £25 billion. This would make any future acquisitions difficult. The Bank of England's loan to Northern Rock was at a "punitive rate" in order to protect against any moral hazard associated with a bailout. Northern Rock's additional option included a gradual winding down with a transfer of deposits to other banks. It was possible that if circumstances became dire enough, a token sale would be organized, as was the case with Barings PLC in March 1995. The Bank of England later suggested a plan to swap the loan for bonds that could be issued to the public.

In the end, only the Virgin-led consortium and a group comprised of the bank's board of directors and management team filed official offers for Northern Rock. The U.K. government determined in February 2008 that neither offer was in the best interest of the bank, its customers, and the British taxpayer. The bank was nationalized on February 17, 2008.

Northern Rock's shareholders lost the entire value of their holdings after the bank was nationalized. A group of aggrieved shareholders sought compensation from the British government for losses associated with their Northern Rock investments. The lawsuit, which was filed on behalf of SRM Global, RAB Capital PLC, and a group of private investors, was dismissed by a Court of Appeals in London in July 2009. The group of former Northern Rock shareholders said that they intend to file an appeal with the House of Lords. SRM was Northern Rock's largest shareholder and held 11.5 percent of outstanding common shares, while RAB held 8.2 percent.

Control Failings and Contributory Factors

Corporate/Market Conditions

Northern Rock was alleged to have been "unusually reliant" upon bond markets in order to raise money for underwriting new mortgages. In the aftermath of the collapse of the U.S. subprime market, it became increasingly difficult for mortgage lenders such as Northern Rock to borrow money from global debt markets. This led to difficulty with funding newly underwritten mortgages and to the Bank of England's emergency bailout.

Undertook Excessive Risks

Analysts conjectured that Northern Rock's overreliance on the bond markets in order to finance mortgage lending activities was a high-risk strategy. *BusinessWeek* (2007) commented that Northern Rock "thrived on—and then was brought down by—its innovative business model," which relied on securitization of its underwritten mortgages, and capital markets financing, to grow its business. It obtained an estimated 77 percent of its financing from the capital markets. It was more typical for large lenders to obtain closer to 50 percent of their financing in this way. By June 2007, the former Newcastle Building Society had an approximately 19 percent market share of the British mortgage sector. But by September 2007, its various strategies to finance those mortgages were failing at seemingly the same time.

Corrective Actions and Management Response

In a conference call held on September 14, 2007, Northern Rock CEO Adam Applegarth stated, "Frankly, life changed on August 9th, virtually like snapping a finger. Watching liquidity disappear on a global basis has been astonishing." He further commented that when he was faced with a liquidity crunch, "it was the entirely logical thing to approach the Bank of England." Mr. Applegarth resigned from Northern Rock in November 2007; his £760,000 contractual payout and £2.6 million pension came under criticism at the time. Some critics characterized the payments as a "reward for failure."

The bailout would "help Northern Rock to fund its operations during the current period of turbulence in financial markets," the Bank of England, the U.K. Treasury, and the Financial Services Authority (FSA) said in a joint statement. The bailout came just days after Bank of England Governor Mervyn King said in a letter to the Treasury Committee of the House of Commons that any such pumping of cash into the system "undermines the efficient pricing of risk by providing ex-post insurance for risky behavior." He warned of the possible moral hazard involved with such bailouts when he said they "encourage excessive risk-taking and sow the seeds of a future financial crisis."

The Bank of England relented from its strong abhorrence of bailouts when it rescued Northern Rock, due to the lender's size and importance to the markets. The bank released a statement saying that it decided to lend funds to Northern Rock because "the failure of such a bank would lead to serious economic damage." The bank further stated that the prospect of "moral hazard" was mitigated by the charging of a "penalty rate" attached to the funds it lent to Northern Rock. The Bank of England further noted that despite its concern for "excessive risk-taking," it continued to be the lender of last resort for troubled banks.

Northern Rock did not move to stem the run on deposits by enforcing withdrawal limits on customers immediately following the Bank of England's announcement that it would provide liquidity to the mortgage lender. The Financial Services Authority, in an extremely rare public comment, said, "If we believed Northern Rock was not solvent, we would not have allowed it to remain open for business" (2007).

Northern Rock's new management team, under the guidance of CEO Ron Sandler, issued a provisional reorganization plan in late March 2008 that emphasized three goals: repayment of the Bank of England loan, release of the government's guarantee agreements, and, ultimately, a return to the private sector. During what the bank called its temporary public ownership status, it pledged to maintain competitive practices, including refraining from promoting government guarantee arrangements, and limiting its market share to levels below what they historically had been (as the number three mortgage lender in the U.K. market).

Lessons Learned

Some analysts speculated that a run on a bank of the type that was experienced in September 2007 by Northern Rock was inherently bad for the system, because it created "jitters" concerning the stability of all banks. *BusinessWeek* (2007) commented that the run on the bank "can only damage confidence in the previously solid British economy." Simon Adamson, an analyst with Credit Sights, commented that this was "an alarming development—this is not a small niche institution." Adamson also stated in the article that it would be prudent to investigate which other banks and lenders rely so heavily on the capital markets for their liquidity. Northern Rock obtained 77 percent of its financing from the capital markets; its competitor Bradford & Bingley obtained 58 percent of its funds in this way.

The United Kingdom was potentially more vulnerable to bank runs than the United States, due to the fact that a smaller portion of customer assets was protected if a financial institution became insolvent. Deposits were insured by the Financial Services Compensation Scheme, which protected up to £31,700. The first £2,000 was covered completely, while 90 percent of the next £33,000 was insured. In the United States, the Federal Deposit Insurance Corporation (FDIC) insures $100,000 per customer account (up to $250,000 through 2013). The U.K. government later offered to guarantee 100 percent of up to £35,000 in new deposits held with Northern Rock.

Chancellor of the Exchequer, Alistair Darling, said at a Labor Party conference that there were "lessons to be learned" associated with global supervision of financial institutions (2007). The British Bankers' Association offered pragmatic advice when it commented: "Everyone should calm down and refrain from making simplistic comments in a very complex area which just causes unnecessary worry and concern" (Hosking et al. 2007).

The Financial Services Authority came under criticism for the role it played in regulating and supervising Northern Rock. The FSA released what the *Economist* (3/28/2008) called a "surprisingly frank report on its own manifold shortcomings in supervising Northern Rock." The report, which was released on March 26, 2008, covers the months before Northern Rock collapsed and delineates a series of supervisory lapses. The lapses included a failure to keep records of meetings, and a group of supervisors who oversaw Northern Rock that reported into the FSA's insurance department. Over the course of three years, the team moved a number of times, and overall responsibility for supervision of Northern Rock changed three times. The report calls for a number of reforms in how the FSA supervises entities.

Aftermath of Event

The *Financial Times* reported in July 2009—almost two years after Northern Rock initially failed—that it was operating with capital ratios below the minimum that are required by regulators. The bank said that it planned to address the deficiency through a recapitalization plan that would split it into a "good bank" and a " bad bank." The bad bank would serve as a holding entity for non-performing mortgage loans, while the good bank would hold £20 billion of retail deposits and healthy loans. The good bank is likely to be sold to an acquirer. Richard Branson expressed continuing interest in acquiring Northern Rock on behalf of his Virgin Money subsidiary. The plan is subject to approval by the European Commission, which has voiced concern about the "aid measures included in the new restructuring plan" and their "compatibility with the common market."

The *Financial Times* reported in May 2009 that a group of regulators in the U.K., including the Financial Services Authority, the Bank of England, and the

Treasury, conducted secret "war games" in 2004 with the mission of determining how vulnerable banks were to systemic risk. Northern Rock and HBOS were identified as potentially susceptible if foreign banks withdrew funding from the wholesale lending markets that they relied upon. The *Financial Times* reported that although the regulators reached the conclusion that both banks were reliant on inherently risky business models, they lacked the power to "force the lenders to change their practices." The problem appeared to go unaddressed until the wholesale lending markets dried up in 2007 and "the war game's findings proved eerily prescient."

NOTES

1. Algo First database of operational risk case studies.
2. Ibid.

ABOUT THE AUTHOR

Algorithmics Software LLC (www.algorithmics.com) is the world leader in enterprise risk solutions, dedicated to helping financial institutions understand and manage risk. Its innovative software, content, and advisory services provide a consistent, enterprise-wide view of risk management to help firms make better business decisions and increase shareholder value.

CHAPTER 19

Derivatives Case Studies: SocGen, Barings, and Allied Irish/Allfirst

ALGORITHMICS SOFTWARE LLC[*]

CASE STUDY ONE: SOCIÉTÉ GÉNÉRALE[1]

Event Summary

In what the *Wall Street Journal* (1/24/2008) called a "singular feat in the world of finance," Société Générale (SocGen) announced a €4.9 billion (US$7.2 billion) loss on January 24, 2008, as a result of the misdeeds of a single rogue trader. The bank characterized the largest rogue trading event to date as the result of "elaborate fictitious transactions" that allowed the 31-year-old trader to circumvent a series of internal controls. The trades in question involved the arbitrage of plain vanilla stock index futures.

The trader previously worked in a back office function for the bank and gained knowledge of how to circumvent the bank's systems through this prior position. He was initially characterized by the governor of the Bank of France as a "computer genius," but over time came to be known as an unexceptional employee who worked very hard to conceal unauthorized trading positions. SocGen estimated that the value of Jérôme Kerviel's positions was €50 billion (US$73.26 billion). A report published by the French Finance Ministry said that Kerviel's rogue trading started in 2005; he was allegedly given a warning at the time concerning trading above set limits.

In addition to the €4.9 billion trading loss, the French Banking Commission levied a €4 million fine against Société Générale on July 4, 2008; this brings the total loss amount in this case to €4,904,000,000.

Event Details

Jérôme Kerviel was a 31-year-old trader with Société Générale's Paris office who earned approximately €100,000 per year in base salary. He joined the French bank

---

[*]This information is the sole property of Algorithmics Software LLC and may not be reprinted or replicated in any way without permission.

in August 2000. He worked for three years in a middle office function before being promoted to the bank's Delta One proprietary trading desk. According to the *Financial Times* (1/25/2008), Mr. Kerviel was the beneficiary of the bank's initiative to promote talented back and middle office employees. He was tasked with futures hedging on European equity market indexes. His bonus for 2006 was €60,000. He requested a €600,000 bonus for 2007 and was granted €300,000; the bonus information was gleaned from an investigatory report published on February 20, 2008, by Société Générale entitled "Mission Green."

The bank said that winding down the trades resulted in a €4.9 billion charge—the largest to date as the result of a rogue trading event. SocGen commented that the "exceptional fraud" involved the purchase of massive positions in futures that were beyond Kerviel's limits. At least one individual was identified as having known about Kerviel's trades, but the bank stated that it could not draw any suppositions concerning Kerviel's supervisors as a result of "judicial inquiries currently under way." The individual is an unnamed trading assistant who helped execute the trades. In its second Mission Green report, published in May 2008, the bank characterized the trading assistant as someone who should have acted as an independent agent and who reported directly into the middle office.

The head of the Bank of France, Christian Noyer, said that Mr. Kerviel managed to breach "five levels of controls." The controls were identified in the earlier Mission Green report and consisted of canceled or modified transactions, transactions with deferred dates, technical (internal) counterparties, nominal (non-netted exposures), and intramonth cash flows. In addition, the second and more detailed Mission Green report identified a host of supervisory lapses, organizational gaps, and warning signs that were never heeded.

A report released by French Finance Minister Christine Lagarde identified three areas where controls failed within the bank: the assignment of an employee to the trading floor who had spent time in the back office; security problems with the internal computer system; and the lack of an escalation process for alerting management of abnormal trades.

The Mission Green reports stated that Kerviel began taking "directional" (as opposed to arbitrage) positions starting in 2005 for relatively small amounts. These small unauthorized directional trades continued through 2006. The size of the directional positions had grown substantially by March 2007. Kerviel's trades lost money from March 2007 through July 2007, but turned profitable for the remainder of the year. They turned vastly unprofitable in early 2008. It is estimated that by July 2007 his trades resulted in €30 billion in unhedged exposure for the bank.

Kerviel was faced with a problem in early 2008; he had realized more than €1 billion in gains from unauthorized trading during the latter part of the previous year, and needed to find a way to report profits from trades that were beyond his allowed limits. He concocted a plan to enter a fictitious counterparty trade onto the books in an attempt to explain the gain. He listed a small German brokerage as the counterparty; the bank became suspicious because the size of the trade was larger than the market value of the German firm. A trader alerted the bank's management of this anomaly and, when questioned, Kerviel said that he had entered the wrong counterparty onto the book and that, in actuality, it was Deutsche Bank. Deutsche Bank was contacted in order to confirm the trade. It was quickly discovered that the trade did not exist. The bank interviewed and suspended Mr. Kerviel, who initially assisted with the investigation.

Mr. Kerviel told investigators that one of his earliest wins was a bet placed on insurer Allianz during the summer of 2005. He was betting that the European markets would fall. After the London transport system suffered a terrorism attack in July 2005, his trade earned the bank €500,000. He was interrogated before a special committee at the time and warned that if he overrode his limits in the future he would be fired. Kerviel, despite the warning, continued to break the rules during the next 18 months and placed increasingly larger bets. In one example, he placed a bet in January 2007 that the German DAX index would fall. Instead, the index increased, and he sustained a loss. He told prosecutors that the loss went unnoticed at the bank because during that period of the year "there is no cross-checking control within SocGen."

In November 2007 the surveillance team at Eurex, the deriviatives exchange run by Deutsche Boerse, sent an inquiry to Société Générale concerning the volume of trades it was receiving from Mr. Kerviel. When confronted about the trades, he said that any comments would reveal his trading strategy to competitors. Société Générale responded to Eurex by saying that it had engaged in after-hours trading as a result of volatility in the markets. Eurex officers were unhappy with the explanation and contacted the bank a second time. Mr. Kerviel eventually produced a response that satisfied the bank and the exchange, and the matter was dropped the following month.

Mr. Kerviel was in essence an arbitrage trader—he was tasked with exploiting differences in the prices of futures contracts based on European stock indexes. In this capacity he was supposed to match long positions in futures contracts with corresponding short positions. The price discrepancies are often small, but can result in significant returns when arbitrage trades are executed through volume. It is the volume and size of such transactions that some industry experts have targeted as problematic, as there are continuous backlogs in settling such trades at banks.

Mr. Kerviel bought bets on the direction of European stock markets through the purchase of futures on indexes tracking the U.K. and German markets and the Euro Stoxx 50. SocGen's head of investment banking said that "every two or three days, he was changing his position. He would input a transaction that would trigger a control in three days and before that happened he would replace it with a different one." It was Kerviel's knowledge of how control processes worked that allowed him to understand the mechanics and timing of when they are triggered.

When SocGen's executives started examining what Kerviel had been doing, they were shocked to discover that he was not hedging his positions and had accumulated nearly €50 billion in exposure to European stock indexes. Instead, he was faking the hedging contracts and accumulating large unhedged positions. It appeared that he was taking a bet that the indexes would rise sharply. However, they started moving in the opposite direction and left Société Générale heavily exposed. Most of his unauthorized positions were executed through the purchase of securities with a deferred start date, futures transactions with a pending counterparty, or forward transactions with an internal counterparty.

Mr. Kerviel was able to circumvent internal controls by using passwords and accounts that belonged to other employees. He then logged into the bank's systems and approved his fictitious trades. He understood how this worked from his prior middle office position. Jean-Pierre Mustier, the head of SocGen's investment banking division, spent the weekend of January 19 interviewing Mr. Kerviel in an attempt to unravel what had happened. Mr. Mustier commented that Jérôme Kerviel seemed "confused" about the impact of what he had done and that he thought "he had discovered a new trading technique which was performing very well."

Société Générale knew about the rogue trades over the weekend of January 19, 2008, but said that it waited to inform the markets until it completed unwinding the positions. By the time it discovered the fraud, Kerviel's losses were already in the range of €1.5 billion. However, it unwound the trades in very difficult conditions, and the losses continued to increase. By the time the trades were unwound, the bank's losses from the positions were €4.9 billion. SocGen said that it kept its trades to about 10 percent of the total volume on the exchanges where it traded, so as not to negatively impact the markets when it unwound the trades.

Société Générale unwound the trades on Monday, January 21, 2008—a day when global markets were sharply down on speculation of an economic slowdown and following Fitch Ratings' downgrade of bond insurer Ambac the preceding Friday. The U.S. markets were closed that day for the annual Martin Luther King Jr. holiday. There was fear that the U.S. markets would open downward the following day—Tuesday, January 22, 2008—and continue to fall sharply as a result of mounting bad news concerning the economy, the housing sector, and the worsening subprime mortgage crisis.

The U.S. Federal Reserve announced, before the open of markets on January 22, the unusual decision to cut interest rates by three-fourths of a percentage point. This was the sharpest cut since the 1980s. It has been conjectured that the unwinding of the rogue trades may have contributed to the steep drop in world markets on January 21. Société Générale has said that the unwinding of the trades did not impact the direction of the market. The U.S. Federal Reserve said publicly that it did not know about the unwinding of SocGen's trades the previous day but that it remained comfortable with its decision to cut rates.

News of the rogue trading incident came on the same day that Société Générale announced a €2.05 billion write-down in assets related to subprime exposure. The news also came at a time when the banking sector was struggling to raise capital and was suffering from an implosion in the capital markets. Market conditions could not have been worse for the unwinding of such large positions. SocGen announced that it would turn to the capital markets in order to raise €5.5 billion in the following weeks.

Société Générale is considered a well-managed institution with strong risk controls and has won awards for the quality of its derivatives trading capability. Nicolas Rutsaert, an analyst who covers European banks for Dexia, said that Société Générale "was a leader in derivatives and was considered one of the best risk managers in the world." SocGen was voted the best equity derivatives house by Euromoney in July 2007. It also won accolades for its equity derivatives trading strategy from *Risk* magazine in 2008.

The comparisons between this event and the quintessential unauthorized trading event that led to the dissolution of Barings PLC (discussed later in the chapter) are difficult to ignore. Both events involved traders that originally worked in back office positions and had knowledge of how risk and control systems worked. Both events involved derivatives and futures positions and relatively young and inexperienced traders. They both used their knowledge of bank processes to hide escalating trading losses.

There are also significant differences between the events. Kerviel's loss appears to have accumulated much faster than Leeson's (of Barings PLC), and he worked for a bank with very sophisticated risk management systems. Kerviel also worked on a trading desk at his bank's headquarters, as opposed to Leeson, who worked in the Singapore branch. There was a strong reporting structure at Société Générale, while at Barings it was uncertain who was in charge of directly supervising Leeson. Most importantly, Kerviel was not tasked with settling his own trades as Leeson was. However, by overriding the bank's systems and using his colleagues' passwords and accounts, in essence that is exactly what Kerviel did.

One key difference between the two events is the possible impact on markets—especially during very volatile times. Société Générale's unwinding of such large positions could have possibly had an influence on the severity of the downward trajectory of the markets; Leeson did not have the same impact on the markets. Another key difference between the two events is that Barings did not survive its unauthorized trading event and was rescued by ING Group for the token amount of one pound. Société Générale, although weakened and mentioned as a takeover candidate, was expected to recapitalize and survive.

This case surfaced just a few weeks before a high-profile trial was scheduled to begin in France. SocGen CEO Daniel Bouton was scheduled to testify at a trial that accused the bank of failing to comply with money laundering regulations. At the same time, the U.S. Securities and Exchange Commission announced that it was investigating the sale of a SocGen board member's shares of the bank's stock just before the announcement of the rogue trading event and the bank's subprime losses.

Control Failings and Contributory Factors

Lack of Internal Controls/Failure to Set or Enforce Proper Limits
Société Générale's co-chief executive, Philippe Citerne, said that Mr. Kerviel was able to place such large bets on stock index futures contracts through the circumvention of the firm's computer systems and controls. There was also a breakdown in processes that police limits, as he was trading above his allowable authority for several years. Mr. Kerviel said during the investigation that he regularly "flouted" rules concerning trading limits and that it was not unusual for his trading colleagues to do so.

Employee Misdeeds
The bank commented that Kerviel knew how to circumvent his limits because of knowledge he had of how controls operate, from the three years he worked in a middle office function. The bank said that one of the reasons he was able to succeed with overriding limits was because he "knew intimately the bank's risk controls, and swiftly shifted positions to evade detection at each level of control." According to the bank, "Each time he [Kerviel] took a position one way, he would enter a

fictitious trade in the opposite direction to mask the real one." The bank identified 947 transactions where Kerviel "set the parameters of these transactions in such a manner as to use them to cover the fraudulent positions actually taken." Price-waterhouseCoopers (PwC)'s final report on the control environment surrounding the incident listed three categories of concealment measures that were deployed by Kerviel: the entry and subsequent cancellation of trades ahead of the period when controls would kick in; entries of pairs of fictitious reverse trades; and booking of intramonthly provisions that would cancel out earnings from the concealed activities.

Inadequate Due Diligence
This fraud was unraveled once the bank detected a fictitious counterparty trade. The counterparty was contacted, and it was quickly determined that the trade did not exist. This act of manually checking a trade suggests that a process for confirming trades through a counterparty contact could result in more accurate and timely detection—particularly for transactions over a certain size or frequency.

Failure to Reconcile Daily Cash Flows
While it may have been possible for Kerviel to trick risk management systems by fraudulently approving his own trades, it is still unclear why the large number of unsettled trades were not detected earlier by the bank's accounting and finance departments. However, it is not uncommon for there to be a backlog in investigating unsettled trades, given the huge volume of the derivatives business. One unidentified trader said that the process to settle trades is laborious and conducive to being tampered with by someone who really understands back office processes. French Finance Minister Christine Lagarde said in her report on the event that the bank should have done a better job monitoring the nominal, rather than just the net, value of Mr. Kerviel's trades.

Failure to Question Above-Market Returns
The *Financial Times* (1/25/2008) asked whether the bank's accounting department had the authority or wherewithal to question the profitable derivatives trading desk. In addition, there is evidence that Mr. Kerviel's trades were profitable during the second half of 2007 and it appears that the source of his profits may not have been closely examined. In fact, at one point in late 2007 his trades were so profitable that he had to manufacture a transaction in order to account for a €500 million gain. Société Générale stated in its May 2008 Mission Green report that despite Kerviel's declared earnings, which constituted 27 percent of the earnings of Delta One in 2007, and 59 percent of the earnings of his assigned desk, there was "no detailed examination of his activity that was carried out or required by his hierarchy."

Insufficient Compliance Measures
Mr. Kerviel was reported to have taken only four days of vacation during 2007; the failure of a trader to take a holiday, which is often in breech of banking rules that require a certain amount of consecutive days off, can be considered a red flag. When questioned by supervisors, Mr. Kerviel said that he was too depressed to take time off because his father had recently died. In reality, with all the effort required

to regularly delete and reenter fake trades, it would have been difficult to continue covering up his activities if he took time off. This behavior is not unknown in unauthorized trading events; John Rusnak, who was responsible for a $690 million rogue trading event while with Allied Irish's Allfirst subsidiary (discussed later in the chapter), rarely took a day off and often traded from home.

Lack of Management Escalation Process

French investigators and Société Générale disclosed that Eurex, the largest European derivatives exchange, expressed concern in November 2007 of positions taken by Mr. Kerviel. The exchange did not comment on who at SocGen was notified of the problem, but the Mission Green report later said that Kerviel's direct supervisor failed to act on the information. The Paris public prosecutor commented that Mr. Kerviel said during the course of the investigation that after Eurex questioned his trades he produced false documents in order to document his positions. There is evidence that Kerviel's rogue trading behavior was flagged by the bank in 2005. The Finance Ministry mentioned in its report on the incident that the lack of a management escalation process was a key failing. The May 2008 Mission Green report cited "a lack of attention and reactivity when faced with numerous alerts, which denotes a lack of sensitivity to the risk of fraud at the Front Office Level."

Corporate Governance

Often behind such events, which appear to be the results of one bad employee, is a corporate culture that encourages high-risk-taking behavior through compensation, incentives, pressure to deliver certain results, and idolization of star traders. Strong and sophisticated risk departments can exist in such organizations, but it is much more difficult to impact a bank's risk culture when it is at odds with an ethos to drive profits. The *New York Times* reported (2/5/2008) that the bank allowed a "culture of risk to flourish" which in turn "enabled the rogue trader's activities to go undetected."

Undertook Excessive Risks

Société Générale was known for its appetite to take large risks with its own funds. Revenue from proprietary trading became an increasingly substantial share of profits realized by its investment bank. In 2004, proprietary trading (as opposed to market making) accounted for 29 percent of profits for the division; this grew to 35 percent by the middle of 2007.

Omissions

The trading activity that Kerviel engaged in was viewed as having relatively low risk by the bank. He was tasked with purchasing an index of stocks while selling, at the same time, a similar portfolio. The bank made a small gain from the price differentiation between the two. The supposition was that the portfolios offset each other through arbitrage trading and resulted in little underlying risk. This may have led to an underestimation by the bank of the risk inherent in the activities undertaken by the Delta One trading team, and a failure to fully consider the business unit's risk—particularly operational risk.

Employee Omissions

An additional omission was the failure of the bank's management to question the documentation that Kerviel supplied when his trades raised red flags. The Mission Green report stated that the bank's internal control system generated 75 alerts by Kerviel starting in 2006. When questioned, Kerviel supplied documentation that was not scrutinized very closely. The report said that even when these reports "lacked plausibility," Kerviel's supervisors were not alerted. The report credited this pattern of behavior to a "lack of initiative" on the part of its compliance staff. The report also said that the staff members were not thorough enough in their checks—including, in eight cases, where there were "anomalies" present in Kerviel's e-mail.

Failure to Test for Data Accuracy

The PricewaterhouseCoopers report on this incident targeted a failure by the trader's managers and supervisors to "perform the necessary analyses of existing data schedules (detailing positions, valuations, earnings, or cash flows) that would have revealed the true nature of the trader's activities."

Organizational Gaps/Organizational Structure

PricewaterhouseCoopers highlighted gaps with the hierarchical structure of reporting lines above Kerviel's position. For instance, the report targeted a "fragmentation of controls between several units, with an insufficiently precise division of tasks, [and] lack of systematic centralization of reports, and of feedback to the appropriate hierarchical level." This fragmentation led to a "lack of a systematic procedure for centralizing and escalating red flags to the appropriate level in the organization."

Failure to Supervise

PricewaterhouseCoopers characterized Kerviel's immediate supervisor as lacking "trading experience" and a "sufficient degree of support in his role." He was new to the role, but the bank allegedly failed to offer mentoring or proper support. The supervisor, whom the bank says it cannot interview directly because he is no longer an employee, allegedly failed to monitor interday directional positions of the department he managed. Société Générale echoed this sentiment in its Mission Green report published in May 2008: "Supervision of JK proves to have been weak, above all since 2007, despite several alerts generating grounds for vigilance or for investigation." Jérôme Kerviel had no immediate supervisor during the period of January 12, 2007, through April 1, 2007, after the desk manager for the Delta One unit resigned. The bank identified this as a period when Kerviel began "to build up his massive fraudulent and concealed positions on index futures."

Inadequate Technology Planning

At the heart of this event was the issue of volume and the bank's struggle to keep abreast of the rapidly growing volume of trading in its equities division. The PricewaterhouseCoopers report characterized this as a "difference between the growth in the means (including information systems) available to control and support services and the very strong growth in transaction volumes." The consulting firm identified a "mismatch between the resources allocated to support and control functions and the level of front office activities." In addition, PwC cited the bank's "information systems," which were "unable to keep pace with the growing complexity of the general trading environment." As a result, there was a "heavy reliance on manual processing." The May 2008 Mission Green report said that the operating environment was "rendered difficult by strong, rapid growth in the division, with numerous signals revealing a deterioration in the operational situation, in particular in the Middle Office." This rapid growth included a doubling of volume in a one-year period, front office employee numbers that grew from 4 to 23 in two years, and an understaffed compliance department.

Corporate/Market Conditions

The announcement of SocGen's rogue trading incident came on the same day that the bank announced a €2.05 billion write-down related to its subprime exposure. The trading loss was announced during extremely volatile conditions, with the markets swinging wildly on both an interday and intraday basis. CEO Daniel Bouton said that the loss from the unauthorized trade was exaggerated by market conditions. This is the second unauthorized trading event of notable size that has been publicly revealed in France since the start of the credit crisis in 2007. Credit Agricole also experienced a €230 million loss from such an event.

Corrective Actions and Management Response

The bank announced a decision to raise €5.5 billion in the capital markets and that it already had interest from potential investors. The rights issue for preferred shares was underwritten by J.P. Morgan and Morgan Stanley. The bank assured investors that "the capital increase is fully guaranteed, and will offset the loss generated by the fraud."

SocGen's chairman and CEO at the time, Daniel Bouton, apologized to shareholders on January 24, 2008. He announced that he would forgo regular salary payments through June 2008. Mr. Bouton offered to step aside, but the bank's board of directors initially rejected his resignation. In March 2008 the bank's chief financial officer, Frederic Oudea, was promoted to deputy chief executive; this was the first shift in management since the announcement of the rogue trading incident. In a later shift, Daniel Bouton announced on April 17, 2008, that he would relinquish his role as CEO to Mr. Oudea. Mr. Bouton retained his chairman position.

Société Générale announced on May 2, 2008, that Michel Peretie has replaced Jean-Pierre Mustier as head of the bank's corporate and investment banking division. Mr. Mustier will take another position within the bank. *Les Echos* (6/2/2008) reported that the "departure of Mr. Mustier has been thought inevitable."

Mr. Kerviel and up to five supervisors above him were terminated by the bank. Société Générale said that it lodged a complaint with French prosecutors against the rogue trader. The allegations include fraud, falsification of bank records, and fraudulent use of bank documentation and computer systems. The bank also said that the fraud remained undetected for some period of time because Mr. Kerviel had an "intimate and malicious" knowledge of SocGen's controls.

Société Générale formed a special committee that investigated the incident and released the first Mission Green report on February 20, 2008. A more in-depth report was later released in May 2008. The committee, which consisted of more than

40 employees, was tasked with uncovering the chronology of events, identifying relevant control failings, analyzing possible underlying motives, and searching for additional evidence of fraud. PricewaterhouseCoopers was hired to work with the committee and released a report of its own in May 2008.

The special committee also announced a three-pronged improvement plan that included strengthening of information technology (IT) security and adoption of a biometric identification system, reinforcement of the management of controls and the associated reporting process, so that relevant information can be shared among management and business units, and strengthening of the bank's operational risk function, so that it operates cross-functionally in an effort to better manage the risk of fraud.

The French Finance Ministry released a report on the rogue trading event on February 4, 2008. The Ministry made the following recommendations: enhanced surveillance of notional positions; a mandatory audit trail for every transaction; tracking, analyzing, and collating of information related to canceled transactions; trades verified through reconciling of accounts and contacting counterparties; documentation of terms and conditions reached with counterparties; and enhanced operational risk-reporting requirements. Société Générale responded to the findings in the Ministry's report by releasing a statement indicating that it would take the recommendations into account.

The bank announced in April 2008 that it intended to invest between €50 million and €100 million in order to improve its risk management systems, which included an investment in enhanced trade monitoring. The bank also established an independent internal fraud investigation unit comprising approximately 20 people.

The French Banking Commission fined Société Générale €4 million on July 4, 2008, and cited weak internal controls for the action. The commission mentioned poor supervision as a contributory factor in this event. The commission said that "failures, particularly in the hierarchical controls, continued over a long period and the control system neither detected nor corrected them. These shortcomings went beyond simple repeated individual failures. They enabled the development of the fraud and its grave financial consequences."

The Banking Commission also cited problems with separation of duties between trading and control staff and said that as a result Société Générale "infringed several essential rules on internal banking controls." According to the *Financial Times* (7/5/2008), the €4 million fine is the largest penalty levied by the Banking Commission for risk control lapses to date.

Lessons Learned

This outsized fraud resulted in the usual call for more regulation. It also raised some concern that the regulators themselves are unable to police such large potential events. The Bank of France said that it would examine how the "process malfunctioned and look into whether the internal controls were sufficient." The bank said that once it determined what had gone wrong it would consider whether a tightening of regulations is necessary in France.

Christian Noyer, the governor of the Bank of France, commented: "We need to learn what happened at Société Générale to make sure this cannot happen again." He also said that the Bank of France did not consider this event to represent a failure of control on its part to properly supervise SocGen. Mr. Noyer added: "We can't have a controller behind every trader at every bank in the country at every moment. Even the best laws and the best police can't always stop someone who is determined to defraud the system" (Moore 2008).

The European Central Bank called for stronger controls at all financial institutions. "The lesson to be drawn, as in the case of previous frauds of this magnitude [is the] ... absolute necessity of substantially reinforcing internal controls and internal risk controls in all establishments," said chief banker Jean-Claude Trichet. CEO Bouton himself said that while the derivatives business was growing so exponentially, the bank's risk systems could not keep up (2008).

SocGen is considered a well-run bank with a strong risk management department. One analyst commented that, given how strong the bank's derivatives and risk functions were, at first he thought news of the rogue event was a "joke." A loss this large sparked debate on how effective risk management can be if, in the words of Mr. Noyer, you cannot put a controller behind every trader in every bank.

Axel Pierron, an analyst with Celent, said that one of the problems with risk management systems is that those who work with them eventually learn how to circumvent them. He commented: "Banks, despite the implementation of sophisticated risk management solutions, are still under the threat that an employee with a good understanding of the risk management processes can get round them to (hide) his losses."

In the end, even the most robust controls will fail if one clever person with malicious intent manages to find loopholes in a bank's systems and processes. The lesson of unauthorized trading events is that in the end, severe losses can result from the misdeeds of a single individual.

CASE STUDY TWO: BARINGS[2]

Event Summary

Barings PLC, a venerable institution with roots going back 233 years, suffered a catastrophic loss in February 1995 that has become a benchmark case for operational risk. The bank's US$1.4 billion (£830 million) unauthorized trading loss was precipitated by a Singapore-based trader with a hotshot reputation who eventually pleaded guilty to two counts of fraud and was sentenced to a six-and-a-half-year jail term.

The $1.4 billion loss was larger than the bank's entire capital base and reserves, and created an extreme liquidity crisis. Barings was forced to declare bankruptcy and was later purchased by the Dutch bank ING Group for the token amount of one pound, and an agreement to assume the fallen bank's substantial debts. This event shook the world's financial markets, and ultimately led to an increased awareness on the part of financial institutions and regulatory agencies of inherent operational risks.

Event Details

When the Bank of England embarked on its investigation into the incident, it was seeking the answer to two questions: How did the massive losses at Barings happen, and why were the responsible trader's positions not detected earlier? The central bank eventually arrived at the following conclusion: The incident was caused by a series of concealed unauthorized derivatives trades, and those trades were not uncovered sooner due to "serious failure of controls and managerial confusion within Barings."

Nicholas Leeson, the 28-year-old trader with Baring Futures Singapore who was held responsible for the unauthorized trading loss, was missing from his desk in Singapore on February 23, 1995, when Barings's senior management in London first realized the magnitude of the incident. Leeson, a trader from a humble background who had emerged as a star in the rough-and-tumble derivatives world, was granted a great deal of autonomy by Barings's management. He had worked in Singapore since 1992 and had registered significant profits on the bank's books by placing bets on the future direction of the Nikkei index.

The Bank of England discovered that Leeson had been acting in an unauthorized capacity in a variety of circumstances: He violated his intraday trading limits on a consistent basis and traded in futures and options despite the fact that he did not have the authority to do so. He ultimately hid his losses in a special account, numbered 88888, which was opened shortly after he showed up for work in Singapore. He engaged in options trading and breaches of his limits on a continuous basis, and by December 31, 1994, he was responsible for accumulating losses of $208 million. Throughout this entire period, he represented to his management that he was making profits on his trades and was characterized as a star.

The use of account 88888 played a central role in the concealment of Leeson's unauthorized trades. By February 27, 1995, he had rolled about £830 million of losses into this account. The existence of the account was "suppressed" from Barings's management in London and reported only in margin files that did not elicit scrutiny from the head office. In addition, falsified reports were submitted to the head office that misrepresented Leeson's trades and hedges.

By December 1994, with $512 million in losses already under his belt, Leeson bet heavily on Tokyo's stock index. When it did not rise as expected, and Japan's post-bubble economy continued on its downward path, Leeson continued to buy Japanese futures contracts. The country was recovering from the devastating Kobe earthquake, and Leeson bet that the rebuilding effort would help boost the Japanese economy. Instead, Japan's economy continued to head downward. Over a period of three months, Leeson had bought more than 20,000 futures contracts in hopes he would recoup his accumulating losses. Three-quarters of the $1.3 billion that Barings eventually lost can be traced to these trades.

The Bank of England was unable to determine Leeson's motive, besides the obvious fact that he received over a million dollars annually in salary and bonus based on the revenue that he allegedly generated.

Control Failings and Contributing Factors

Failure to Question Above-Market Returns

No one looked very closely at the nature of Leeson's profits—either because derivatives trades appeared too exotic to be understood by senior management in the early 1990s, or because Barings was thrilled to register Leeson's spectacular trading gains. What has since become apparent is that Leeson was not a wunderkind; instead of generating substantial profits, he was losing money.

Lack of Dual Control/Lack of Proper Segregation

Leeson violated a central tenet of good operational risk best practices: the importance of dual controls and checks and balances. He was the acting settlement manager for both the back office and the front office, and was able to hide his accumulating losses for more than two years. It is speculated that Leeson was given these dual duties by Barings as a cost-cutting measure. The lack of segregation of duties was first identified in February 1994 as a serious problem by the group treasurer of the bank, and was included in an internal audit report that was sent to management; although the report made specific recommendations concerning separation of duties, they were not implemented.

Slow Reaction to Mandate

Senior management, including the bank's CEO, CFO, treasurer, head of risk, and chief operating officer, received the audit report. Yet the recommendations to segregate Leeson's control of both the front and back offices were never acted upon. Most of the individuals who received the report and were later interviewed by the Bank of England said that they considered it to be the responsibility of management in Singapore to implement the recommendations. This, of course, never happened, and by the time the massive loss was realized in February 1995, Leeson was still responsible for front and back offices in Singapore. The Bank of England determined that "the points raised by the report on segregation of duties were of such importance that we consider that it was necessary for checks to have been made to ensure that they had been implemented."

Failure to Supervise/Organizational Gaps/Unclear Reporting Structure/Unclear Organizational Structure

An additional control failing cited by the Bank of England was lack of supervision and the failure of the head office to properly supervise Leeson's activities in Singapore. The Singapore office was operated almost entirely by Leeson alone, and his staff was relatively junior and simply followed most of his orders. There were no clearly defined reporting lines for Leeson, and although he was partially supervised by the bank's head of capital markets in Japan, this was not fully understood or delineated for any of the parties involved. In fact, the Japanese manager had very little knowledge of Leeson's trading positions. The reporting lines were determined by a complicated matrix structure, which the Bank of England contends can be effective only if proper controls are in place and a clear understanding of responsibilities exists with open hubs of communication; this, of course, was not the case here.

Management Actions/Inactions

While Leeson is the obvious culprit in this fiasco, Barings's management is also responsible. The internal audit report warned of the dangers involved with having Leeson manage both the front and back office settlement process. The Singapore International Monetary Authority (SIMEX) also cautioned Barings about the inherent dangers of this arrangement. There is no record of the bank having acted on this information—in fact, it continued to finance Leeson's trades. And many of those trades were not properly reconciled, nor were there controls in place governing the reconciliation process in Singapore.

Lack of Internal Controls

In its consideration of the role Barings's management played in this incident, the Bank of England concluded that the failure of controls was "absolute" in the Singapore operation. This is an opinion that was shared by Barings's chairman at the time, Peter Baring. The Bank of England concluded in its study that it was "this lack of effective controls which provided the opportunity for Leeson to undertake his unauthorized trading activities and reduced the likelihood of their detection."

Omissions

The central bank further stated, "we consider that those with direct executive responsibility for establishing effective controls must bear much of the blame" (Eisenhammer and Brown 1995). What was remarkable about this case was that it demonstrated clearly and coherently that a lack of control structure and management omissions in terms of operational risk best practices were directly responsible for the failure of a business.

Corrective Actions and Management Response

Several months after ING took over as the owner of the failed Barings, the Dutch bank fired 21 executives who had "functional responsibility" for the trading of derivatives in Singapore, through either direct or indirect responsibilities. ING released a statement that called the unauthorized trading incident "extraordinary" and "not endemic." The executives who were dismissed included the head of investment banking and the head of financial products, who were the most senior executives at the top of Leeson's reporting matrix. Additional officers who were dismissed included the chief operating officer, the finance director, the head of settlements, the head of futures and options settlement, the treasurer, the head of group treasury and risk, the head of the bank group, the manager of market risk, and the global head of equity derivatives. The two highest-ranking executives at the bank, the chairman and deputy chairman, had already resigned prior to the May 1995 dismissals.

Lessons Learned

Ultimately, Barings's losses left the banking community a noteworthy legacy in the form of lessons learned and the emerging attentiveness to operational risk issues. The general sentiment in the banking community is that a Barings type of event should never happen again.

Aftermath of Event

The uncovered loss of £830 million led to a liquidity crisis for the bank, and it was immediately placed in administration. The majority of its assets and liabilities were purchased by ING for the token amount of a single pound. This allowed for the protection of the bank's depositors and creditors. Shareholders, however, suffered the brunt of the loss.

Mr. Leeson spent several years in a Singapore jail for his fraud and published a memoir in 1996. He continues to owe £100 million to the liquidators of Barings. He returned to England in 1999 after serving about four years of his six-and-a-half-year sentence and after being diagnosed with colon cancer; he has appeared actively on the speaking circuit discussing "what went wrong" during his time in Singapore.

CASE STUDY THREE: ALLIED IRISH/ALLFIRST[3]

Event Summary

In what the *Financial Times* (2/7/2002) has called "another chapter in the cult of the rogue trader," and the largest such case since Nick Leeson managed to topple Barings Bank, Ireland's largest bank revealed on February 6, 2002, that a currency trader had disappeared after defrauding a U.S.-based subsidiary of $691.2 million. John Rusnak was identified as the rogue trader who initially went into hiding after the event was made public. Mr. Rusnak pleaded guilty to one count of bank fraud on October 24, 2002, and was sentenced to a prison term of seven and a half years in January 2003.

Event Details

John Rusnak was employed by Allied Irish Bank (AIB)'s Allfirst subsidiary in Maryland, and earned a base salary in the US$100,000 range, with annual bonus payments ranging between $122,000 and $220,000 during the years 1998 to 2001. Eugene Ludwig, the former U.S. comptroller of the currency, completed an internal investigation over the course of a month. The bank released his findings to the public in early March 2002 via its web site (www.aibgroup.com).

Mr. Rusnak was charged with seven counts of fraud on June 5, 2002, one of which he pleaded guilty to four months later. The indictment claimed that Rusnak was paid $850,000 over the course of five years as a result of fraudulent trades and confirmations. The indictment also provided an indication of the great lengths he went to hide his trades. For instance, he rented a postal box from Mailboxes Etc. in New York under the fictitious name of David Russell. He had Allfirst send trade confirmations to this address, where he would retrieve the notifications, sign David Russell's name, and return them to his employer.

Eugene Ludwig found no evidence of collusion in his report, except for mild criticism of two U.S. banks over their prime brokerage arrangements with Allfirst. However, Rusnak has agreed to cooperate with prosecutors in determining whether others were involved in the fraud. There is also no evidence that Mr. Rusnak undertook any of these trades for personal gain—except perhaps to the extent that they contributed to his annual bonus number. Rather, it appears from the Ludwig report that the trader was caught in a downward cycle of trying to veil trading losses and of accumulating ever-increasing losses as he tried to compensate for his losing trading strategy.

What is clear is that Rusnak was in significant violation of his trading limits, and that this lapse went undetected within the bank for five years—with most of the losses and trading violations occurring during the years 2000 and 2001. Rusnak transacted trades as large as $150 million, even though his assigned limit was $2.5 million. It took a great deal of close attention to complex details in order to perpetuate this sham for over five years.

The long litany of transgressions that Mr. Rusnak enacted, and the bank itself failed to uncover, are remarkable in terms of their number and complexity. Mr. Rusnak employed various techniques. One involved the use of a strategy that a committee of currency market executives and representatives of the Federal Reserve Bank of New York had warned against as early as 1991. This practice is known as "historic rate rollover" and involves the extension of a currency contract when it comes due.

A 1991 Federal Reserve document warned that "a dealer who routinely offers to roll over his customers' maturing contracts at historical rates could unwittingly participate in efforts to conceal losses, evade taxes, or defraud his or another trading institution." It is still unclear why the alleged use of such a large number of rollover contracts—and a multitude of other items—did not trigger the attention of the bank's management. Rollovers allow a trader who might have realized losses to extend the terms of a currency contract in hopes that the exchange rates will improve in the trader's favor during the extended terms. The downside is that the losses can deepen, as they apparently did in Rusnak's case.

At the heart of this remarkable loss is a losing trading strategy: Mr. Rusnak bought a large quantity of yen and other currencies under the assumption that they would rise in value. Instead they fell in value and resulted in significant losses for trades that were already above his set limits. Common practice would have required Mr. Rusnak to purchase contracts that hedged against the possibility of currency price movements. These are typically options contracts that give a trader the option of buying or selling a currency at a targeted future price.

According to passages of the Ludwig report, Mr. Rusnak was so protected by his management that irregularities were often not questioned as they surfaced on a variety of occasions. And to further ensure the veil of respectability, his trades were backed by agreements from both Bank of America and Citibank in their capacity as prime brokers. Under the prime brokerage relationship, when Rusnak made a trade with other banks these agreements would appear in Allfirst's computer system as a Bank of America or Citibank trade. This meant that there were fewer banks to deal with during the trade confirmation process, and Mr. Rusnak had more credibility in the markets in order to execute large trades. At one point, his managers were questioned about the nature of these prime broker agreements, but the arrangements were explained away as being "cost effective."

Control Failings and Contributory Factors

Lack of Dual Control/Lack of Proper Segregation/Failure to Question Above-Market Returns

Mr. Rusnak entered false hedges into the books that were never consummated and offered no coverage against accumulating losses. It is standard practice to have all trades reviewed by someone else at the bank. Not only did this not happen, but when Mr. Rusnak's strategies—including the size of his trades and the use of the bank's balance sheet—were questioned, he was aggressively defended by his managers. His management, in fact, out of fear that bank profits would walk out the door with Mr. Rusnak, expressed on more than one occasion that any scrutiny of his behavior and strategies might encourage him to leave.

Failure to Supervise/Failure to Reconcile Daily Cash Flows/Omissions/ Lack of Internal Controls

There were early signs that there was something amiss with Mr. Rusnak—particularly in terms of his behavior toward the compliance staff, who are characterized in the Ludwig report as inexperienced and unsupervised. In a remarkable instance, it was discovered by a supervisor that Rusnak's Asian trades were not being confirmed even though it was the policy at Allfirst to confirm all trades. It had been argued—and accepted by the compliance staff—that Rusnak's trades offset each other and thus did not require confirmation. No one seemed to pay attention to the fact that the trades had different expiration dates and hence could not offset each other, until a supervisor inadvertently spotted unconfirmed trading tickets on a junior staff member's desk in early December 2001. This policy of not confirming such trades had been going on for at least 18 months before this date. The supervisor directed the employee to confirm all trades. And yet, when he checked back in late January 2002—almost eight weeks later—Mr. Rusnak's Asian trades continued to be unconfirmed.

Strategy Flaw/Staff Selection and Compensation/Failure to Comply with Established Policies and Procedures

The failure to routinely confirm Mr. Rusnak's trades—which has been explained by his alleged "bullying" of the inexperienced back office staff and a general lack of understanding on the part of his managers of what he was actually doing—is an example of how one control after another failed Allfirst. In fact, the Ludwig report described an institution whose entire trading and risk control architecture was flawed—including the fact that it was involved in proprietary trading activities that could not have been profitable for an institution the size of Allfirst, with its limited resources and market clout. Aggressive compensation schemes and the fact the Mr. Rusnak was allowed to trade alone were all cited as problems inherent in the bank's structure. And although he applied devious methods in his circumvention of the bank's controls, many of those controls were dysfunctional in the first place.

Employee Misdeeds/Inadequate Stress Testing/Failure to Test for Data Accuracy

Mr. Rusnak himself is characterized in the Ludwig report as "unusually clever and devious." He devised elaborate schemes for hiding his accumulating losses, including downloading and manipulating historic foreign exchange prices. This was exacerbated by the fact that the bank ignored its own rules for independent sources of market prices, because it did not want to pay Reuters an estimated $10,000 for its service. Rusnak also manipulated the inputs into the bank's value at risk (VaR) models and minimized the visible riskiness of his trading strategy. In fact, the Ludwig report cited Allfirst as being too reliant on VaR measures in lieu of utilizing additional strategies, such as stress testing and scenario analysis, which might have alerted the bank to the inherent risk in so-called long tail events.

Corrective Actions and Management Response

This incident created an enormous public relations crisis for Allied Irish Bank. Its management team flew over to the United States from Dublin in order to assure worried analysts that it could continue to operate as a viable entity and was not in danger of going under as Barings Bank had done in 1995. In addition, the bank's risk management procedures and controls came under attack, and the bank's Tier 1 ratio fell to a less desirable level. The Irish bank's stock price was hammered in the markets, with a $1.66 billion reduction in its market value on February 6, 2002. It was believed after the Barings event that this sort of rogue trading incident could never occur again and that the banking community had tightened its controls in general. Now there was expected to be increased scrutiny of the industry's controls and supervisory procedures.

The Allfirst incident led Allied Irish to dramatically overhaul its risk management structure. Fitch Ratings credited Allied Irish in the aftermath of the event with significantly improving its risk culture. In a July 2004 report, the rating agency concluded that the fraud "led to a re-evaluation of AIB's risk management structure." Fitch further reported that the bank was expected to "further strengthen existing systems to reinforce its conservative approach to risk."

On April 24, 2006, the U.S. Federal Reserve prohibited two former AIB executives from working in the U.S. banking industry. David Cronin, the former treasurer at Allfirst and former boss of Rusnak, and Robert Ray, a former senior vice president of treasury funds management and Rusnak's immediate superior, were both barred from "participating in any manner" with an insured depository institution, bank, or savings association holding company. According to the Federal Reserve, the orders were based on "alleged unsafe and unsound practices in connection with [Cronin's] supervision of a subordinate." However, the orders do not constitute admissions of guilt by Mr. Cronin or Mr. Ray. AIB fired Mr. Cronin, Mr. Ray, and several others in early 2002, after Rusnak's activities were revealed. The Federal Reserve determined that Mr. Cronin was the "key weak link" in the control process and that both he and Mr. Ray had "missed the big picture" in their failure to understand the details of Rusnak's activities.

Lessons Learned

The fact that trades could have occurred at a small regional subsidiary of Allied Irish Bank that must have been in the billions of dollars, as indicated by the size of the actual loss, has stimulated awareness of how the over-the-counter markets regulate themselves. These losses usually occur when there are inadequate dual controls in place, or lack of separation of responsibilities between the traders and settlement staff. After Barings, the general feeling in the industry was that these types of controls were applied uniformly across all trading organizations. These assumptions were questioned by analysts and investors at a time when the markets were suffering from a lack of confidence on the part of individual and institutional investors.

The lessons learned in this case also include the realization that organizations have to scrutinize the risk profiles of their nontraditional or noncore business lines very carefully. They will need to undertake assessments of businesses, such as proprietary trading, and determine whether they have the appetite for potential losses, and the deep pockets for the required investments in risk systems and risk experts. Another major lesson is one that also emerged from the Barings case: A rogue trader can succeed in his over-the-limits dance only if he is partnered with an institution with lax or absent risk controls.

Aftermath of Event

In an aftermath to this case, Allied Irish sold the Allfirst unit to M&T Bank in September 2002 for $3.1 billion. It retains a 22.5 percent stake in the combined operations.

NOTES

1. Algo First database of operational risk case studies.
2. Ibid.
3. Ibid.

ABOUT THE AUTHOR

Algorithmics Software LLC (www.algorithmics.com) is the world leader in enterprise risk solutions, dedicated to helping financial institutions understand and manage risk. Its innovative software, content, and advisory services provide a consistent, enterprise-wide view of risk management to help firms make better business decisions and increase shareholder value.

CHAPTER 20

Fixed Income Case Study, Swap Market: The Allstate Corporation

ALGORITHMICS SOFTWARE LLC*

THE ALLSTATE CORPORATION[1]

Event Summary

On February 6, 2009, it was announced that a $250 million catastrophe (cat) bond, Willow Re, issued by Allstate in 2007 and backed by Lehman Brothers, had defaulted on an interest payment. Allstate Corporation was the ceding insurer of Willow Re—one of four cat bonds that had Lehman Brothers Special Financing Inc. listed as their counterparty in a total return swap. The swap was terminated due to the collapse of Lehman Brothers in September 2008. The bond, due to mature in 2010, was issued to cover potential exposure to storms in the northeastern United States.

Event Details

Catastrophe (cat) bonds are a type of insurance-linked security used to manage exposures to natural disasters. Investors in a catastrophe bond receive coupon payments, but can lose some or all of their principal if a specific type of natural disaster occurs in a particular region and claims are made. The bonds were first developed in the 1990s. Cat bonds became well known after Hurricane Katrina devastated New Orleans in 2005. The catastrophic hurricane led to payments totaling $190 million that were paid out by Kamp Re to cover claims against Zurich Financial Services. Kamp Re was the first catastrophe bond to suffer a publicly acknowledged total loss of principal, although there may have been earlier wipeouts that were not disclosed to the public.

Willow Re was issued in 2007 by Allstate Corporation to protect the auto and home insurer from claims linked to windstorms in New York, New Jersey, and Connecticut. The bond was to mature in 2010. Cat bonds are backed by a pool of

---

*This information is the sole property of Algorithmics Software LLC and may not be reprinted or replicated in any way without permission.

collateral that is held to make sure that interest and principal payments can be made if a disaster triggers claims. The value of the collateral pool is guaranteed or topped up by a total return swap; the swap transaction is designed to compensate for any decline in the value of the collateral.

In the case of Willow Re, as well as three other cat bonds (Ajax Re, Carillon, and Newton Re), the swap counterparty was Lehman Brothers Special Financing Inc., a unit of Lehman Brothers, which collapsed in September 2008. At that time Lehman was involved in protecting about 4.4 percent of the cat bond market, according to an industry expert. Lehman's collapse terminated Willow's total return swap and left note holders with exposure to the collateral pool and credit risk. Rating agencies sharply downgraded the bonds; the implication was that they faced a greater probability of default given that it was unlikely Willow Re would find a replacement counterparty for Lehman and the market value of collateral in the pool was uncertain.

Control Failings and Contributory Factors

Undertook Excessive Risk

The sudden collapse of its total return swap counterparty—a unit of Lehman Brothers—left Willow Re exposed to credit and market risk in the fall of 2008. Cat bonds were marketed as being a "pure insurance play" that was exempt from such risks.

Corporate/Market Conditions

Uncertainty as to the market value of collateral securing the bond also led to problems with making a scheduled interest payment in February 2009.

Corrective Actions and Management Response

Willow Re defaulted on a scheduled interest payment on February 6, 2009. A spokesperson for Allstate Corporation said that Willow Re had paid 95 percent of the scheduled interest payment and that it would continue to meet its reinsurance obligations. "The default of Willow Re does not create any contractual obligations for Allstate," the company said.

Despite the default on the interest payment, the reinsurance contract between Willow and Allstate remained in effect: Allstate continued to pay its reinsurance premium, and Willow paid out every quarter to note holders, who also received any revenue on assets in the collateral account. If a qualifying catastrophe were to occur before the bond matures and damage claims were to reach a specific threshold amount, the value of any payment made to Allstate would depend on the value of the pooled collateral.

Lessons Learned

The problems incurred by several cat bonds that had Lehman Brothers as total return swap counterparty show that investors in such bonds may face credit and market risk in addition to insurance risk. On December 10, 2008, Reuters quoted a research note issued by Lane Financial LLC, a broker-dealer that specializes in risk transfer between insurance companies and capital markets: "The [insurance-linked securities] market was founded on the idea that it was a pure insurance play, invulnerable to nasty things like credit risk. It has not lived up to its own rhetoric." As of May 2009, a second Lehman-backed cat bond, Ajax Re, was reported to have defaulted on interest payments.

Exposure to Lehman Brothers was a common weak link in four catastrophe bonds and led to calls for improved transparency and stricter controls on collateral quality. The issuance of new catastrophe bonds fell from 27 bonds worth $7.3 billion issued in 2007 to 13 bonds worth $2.7 billion in 2008.

The collapse of Lehman Brothers is widely considered to have dampened enthusiasm for such products. In 2009, investors in such bonds began to require stricter controls against credit risk in the management of collateral held against the bonds; this includes a requirement that collateral be held in U.S. Treasuries or similar high-grade collateral, rather than illiquid or long-term securities.

A report by Fitch Ratings on March 9, 2009, suggested that new structures were being added to encourage investors to return to the cat bond market. These enhancements included asset portfolios invested in more liquid securities, such as government-backed securities, with shorter maturities matched to those of the bonds. Similarly, enhanced cat bonds would also feature greater disclosure of the assets owned, more frequent marking to market, and topping up of market value declines by the swap counterparties.

NOTE

1. Algo First database of operational risk case studies.

ABOUT THE AUTHOR

Algorithmics Software LLC (www.algorithmics.com) is the world leader in enterprise risk solutions, dedicated to helping financial institutions understand and manage risk. Its innovative software, content, and advisory services provide a consistent, enterprise-wide view of risk management to help firms make better business decisions and increase shareholder value.

CHAPTER 21

Lessons from Funds: LTCM, Florida, and Orange County

ALGORITHMICS SOFTWARE LLC*

CASE STUDY ONE: LONG-TERM CAPITAL MANAGEMENT[1]

Event Summary

The significance of the events surrounding the collapse of Long-Term Capital Management (LTCM), and its subsequent loss of $4.4 billion, should not be underestimated. The breakdowns at LTCM include an overexposure to several types of risk: leverage, sovereign, model, liquidity, and volatility risk. In addition, the firm lacked the diverse revenue streams of the Wall Street investment banks to which it liked to compare itself. Overall, the fiasco portrays a failure of the firm to implement a broad-based risk management strategy and to properly stress test its models.

Event Details

Long-Term Capital Management was founded in 1994 and held a prestigious position in the unregulated hedge fund sector as a result of the reputations of its senior management, which included Nobel Prize winners Robert Merton and Myron Scholes. The hedge fund was founded by John Meriwether, who was previously head of fixed-income trading at Salomon Brothers until the firm was implicated in a government securities scandal. Meriwether brought some of the best minds with him to Long-Term Capital. The hedge fund's investors included many of the most prominent names in the financial services industry.

LTCM distinguished itself from the start with several years of above-average returns, which it earned from positions on interest rate spreads and market price volatilities. It used highly sophisticated models in order to target pricing inefficiencies in the markets. According to Federal Reserve Chairman Alan Greenspan's testimony before the U.S. Congress, these models were efficient as long as the markets behaved in the same way in the present and the future that they had in

---

the past. In addition, once the models targeted where profits could be made from pricing anomalies, certain efficiencies were created and the opportunity no longer existed to achieve higher-than-average returns.

In short, the pricing models that were used by LTCM, and increasingly its competitors, were so efficient that they worked to close any gaps that could have resulted in above-average returns. In order to compensate for this trading cycle of diminishing returns, LTCM's trading strategies took on more leverage and risk. LTCM's timing was less than optimal, and it took on increased risk at the very time that the markets became more volatile. This resulted in what some have characterized as an overall failure of risk management at the firm.

An additional risk factor at LTCM was the use of leverage by a fund that garnered a great deal of credibility on Wall Street as a result of its highly respected management team. It was able to borrow 100 percent of the value of collateral and use the borrowed funds to purchase additional securities, which it would post as collateral in order to borrow more money. The hedge fund was involved in a cycle of borrowing and leveraging collateral. This partially resulted from the respect it had in the markets and the failure of any of its counterparties to question very deeply whether the fund had taken on too much risk and whether it could meet its obligations. In its first two years in business, LTCM earned 43 percent and 41 percent return on equity as a result of its strategy to finance and leverage its collateral. Its leverage multiple was on average in the range of 25. This is what a fully diversified investment bank might assume, but not a ratio that a market-neutral hedge fund would be expected to take on.

LTCM also faced an additional strategic issue: It was hard for its models to be effective and for the firm to have a competitive advantage when its trades were copied by most of the major players on Wall Street. LTCM raised funds from the big Wall Street firms: Morgan Stanley, Merrill Lynch, and Goldman Sachs. But with the funding came the request for transparency and a disclosure of its trading positions. This ultimately led to a shadowing of LTCM's trades on Wall Street. And the firm's models failed to account for this shadowing effect, and what it meant if all the firms that were copying its trades moved to dispose of their positions at the same time. What occurred is what could have been predicted: price deflation of the disposed assets and a liquidity crisis.

LTCM's troubles began to surface on July 17, 1998, when Salomon Brothers started liquidating its dollar interest arbitrage positions; in essence, Salomon started selling many of the assets that LTCM owned. This brought down the prices of these positions. The next important piece in the unraveling of LTCM was the government of Russia's announcement on August 17, 1998, that it was "restructuring" its debt, or lengthening the terms of the payout on short-term bonds. In actuality, this comprised a default event, and the markets, with a newly acquired suspicion of all sovereign instruments, witnessed a mass unwinding of credit risk positions.

The strategists at Long-Term Capital remained convinced that their mathematical models would hold up under the stress, and that the markets would behave as they had done in the past. LTCM predicted that the markets could go down by only a certain percentage before they would correct themselves within an assumed time frame. This did not happen.

On one day alone, August 21, 1998, the firm lost $550 million. Half of that money was lost in a single trade: a short position in five-year equity options.

LTCM's prime broker and clearing agent, Bear Stearns, increased its demand for collateral, which in turn depleted the fund's available reserves. The fund was on the verge of liquidation in mid-September, and the fear was that this would cause a large chain reaction through very significant market disruption as major broker-dealers moved to cover derivative trades with LTCM. There was an additional fear that the amount of leverage on LTCM's books was unknown.

Control Failings and Contributory Actions

Corporate/Market Conditions

The chairman of the Federal Reserve, Alan Greenspan, testified before congress that a number of market conditions contributed to the central bank's decision to step in and arrange for an industry bailout of the hedge fund; these conditions included "financial market participants" that were already "unsettled by global events" and elevated credit spreads that were placing downward pressure on asset prices. Mr. Greenspan further elaborated that the "plight of LTCM might scarcely have caused a ripple" in the near past, but under present "fragile" market conditions there was a risk of a "severe drying up of market liquidity" (*New York Times* 1998).

Undertook Excessive Risks

LTCM's models created efficiencies in the markets over time that hampered the hedge fund's ability to earn above-average returns. In order to compensate for the diminishing returns, the hedge fund revised its trading strategy to take on more risk and leverage; this occurred at the very time when the markets were becoming more volatile and investors more risk averse. At the same time, market conditions did not follow past patterns, and LTCM's models—which were predicated on historical cycles repeating themselves—did not perform very well.

Inadequate Stress Testing

LTCM model's were not properly tested for changing market conditions and, in particular, for conditions where investors would turn so risk averse and dump all assets—no matter their performance—at the same time. This was an irrational market condition that had not been witnessed before; in previous times there was a flight to quality with investors fleeing to safe and liquid assets. During 1998 investors started fleeing from *all* assets. It was at this very moment that LTCM found itself with large losses and the need to unwind its portfolio. Alan Greenspan testified that unwinding a portfolio at this time and in "such market conditions amounts to conducting a fire sale" (Federal Reserve Board 1998).

Strategy Flaw

One of LTCM's largest problems was the shadowing of its trades. This meant that it could no longer achieve returns based on market inefficiencies. It also meant that when the time came to unwind its positions, there would be many more sellers than buyers for the assets it was unloading, and an associated downward price pressure. LTCM opened its books to all the major Wall Street firms in its effort to grow quickly and raise cash; this also meant that it revealed its trading strategy to these same firms.

Corrective Actions and Management Response

The effect on the market of LTCM's unwinding its portfolio was so enormous that the Federal Reserve Bank, in a historic move, initiated a bailout of the hedge fund. On September 23, 1998, the Federal Reserve organized a consortium of 14 banks, which injected $3.6 billion into the fund in exchange for a 90 percent ownership stake. Of the $4.4 billion ultimately lost, $1.9 billion belonged to the LTCM partners and the rest to other investors. And of that $4.4 billion, $3 billion came from two types of complex trades: sophisticated interest rate swaps and long-term options in the stock market. Control of the hedge fund passed to a committee comprised of investors.

Alan Greenspan defended the Federal Reserve's decision to step in and arrange for a rescue of LTCM as a result of the fact that the hedge fund was unwinding its complex portfolio at a time when all assets were being sold at fire sale prices. The concern was that downward pressure on all assets—no matter how safe they appeared in the past—would result in "severe, widespread and prolonged disruptions to financial market activity." In addition, the Federal Reserve Bank of New York expressed the opinion that the act of unwinding LTCM's portfolio in a "forced liquidation" would lead to a "set of cascading cross defaults" (U.S. House of Representatives 1998).

Lessons Learned

Federal Reserve Chairman Alan Greenspan testified that the rescue agreement reached by the consortium of banks was never a bailout and did not involve public funds. He positioned the agreement as something that was a good investment to the rescue committee if they were able to sell its assets over time instead of under pressure in a forced liquidation scenario. Greenspan stated, however, that "whenever there is public involvement that softens the private-sector losses—even obliquely as in this episode—the issue of moral hazard arises." He further elaborated that any government involvement can have the impact of raising "the threshold of risks market participants will presumably subsequently choose to take."

Mr. Greenspan justified the Federal Reserve's rescue effort by claiming: "Had the failure of LTCM triggered the seizing up of markets, substantial damage could have been inflicted on many market participants, including some not directly involved with the firm, and could have potentially impaired the economies of many nations, including our own." In the end, he reached the conclusion that the Federal Reserve acted in the way it did not to protect LTCM's stakeholders, but to "avoid the market distortions through contagion." Additional financial institutions would suffer losses in this case (Federal Reserve Board 1998).

CASE STUDY TWO: FLORIDA STATE BOARD OF ADMINISTRATION[2]

Event Summary

Florida's State Board of Administration (SBA) experienced the equivalent of a run on the bank in November 2007 that was characterized as one of the largest in history; $16.5 billion in assets was withdrawn from the $27 billion fund during the month of November 2007. The outflows followed disclosure that the Local Government Investment Fund (LGIF) was heavily invested in mortgage-backed securities (MBS). The severity of the problem escalated when the fund sold off its higher-quality investments in order to meet its obligations. This left the fund with a larger percentage of troubled securities in the remaining portfolio. The fund later halted all outflows while it restructured and created a separate vehicle for the distressed securities.

Event Details

The Local Government Investment Fund was run by the State Board of Administration as a money market fund for the state of Florida's local agencies, municipalities, and education system. The fund was the largest of its kind in the United States and managed assets for approximately 1,000 state participants. Funds such as the Local Government Investment Fund are required to invest in short-term and safe securities; the Florida fund strayed from this mandate over a few years in an attempt to gain higher yields during a period of relatively low interest rates. This led to the acquisition of more exotic instruments, such as collateralized mortgage obligations (CMOs) and structured products.

The State Board of Administration announced on November 29, 2007, that it would "temporarily not accept or process deposit or withdrawal requests." The Local Government Investment Fund reopened to investors on December 7, 2007, following a restructuring that placed the "bad paper" into a fund called Fund B that prohibited withdrawals. Fund B primarily consisted of structured investment vehicles (SIVs) that had been devalued by subprime-related market issues.

The state of Florida was now left with a portfolio of securities that it might not be able to sell for a long time. An estimated 14 percent of the LGIF's portfolio was invested in distressed securities. About 86 percent of the portfolio was invested in investment-grade and liquid holdings. The troubled portion of the portfolio was now quarantined in Fund B, which represented about $2 billion in assets. The remaining $12 billion in healthy assets resided in Fund A.

The freezing of redemptions from the Local Government Investment Fund between November 29, 2007, and December 7, 2007, left many schools and local communities scrambling to pay their bills; they relied on the LGIF for access to liquid assets. News of problems with the LGIF led to lines at the state's school districts, with fear emanating from employees that they would not receive monthly paychecks. One local school district met its obligation to employees but canceled $700,000 in payments to external vendors.

The chief financial officer for the northwest Florida school district said on December 1, 2007, that the district "kept all our surplus cash in that pool and now we cannot get access to it." He added that "we are now flat broke." He further stated that the district kept its funds in the LGIF after the state's chief financial officer issued a statement indicating that the fund was healthy. The school districts and municipalities that decided to keep their money in the fund in order to avoid "hysteria" now said they felt misled by state officials (*Financial Times* 2007).

One of the agency's largest municipal banking clients, Hillsborough County, threatened to sue. The run on the bank and subsequent sale of healthy assets left the county with approximately $112 million, or 14 percent, of its $800 million investment in the LGIF exposed to SIVs. Hillsborough requested that counties in Florida that withdrew their funds, such as Orange County, should be required to send the money back. Florida's Orange County had withdrawn $370 million of its holdings from the fund without suffering a loss.

The State Board of Administration came under additional criticism for how it revealed its subprime exposure to constituents. The SBA issued a statement on October 31, 2007, indicating that its investment funds did not contain subprime-related mortgage bonds. However, the report did indicate that the funds had holdings in "less than prime" mortgage-backed securities, which had been downgraded to below investment-grade levels and as a result presented liquidity problems.

A limit on withdrawals of 15 percent of the total value of investments restricted outflows from Fund A. This cap was expected to remain in place until at least March 2008. A review of current investors conducted in December 2007 found that at least one-third had pulled out funds up to the 15 percent limit. The fund was also facing difficulty attracting new investors. One money manager said that his board "is not comfortable with sending any more funds to SBA while they have a lockdown on our investments."

Florida's State Board of Administration has more than $170 billion of assets under management, including approximately $138 billion belonging to the state's pension system and hurricane fund. It also allegedly has notable holdings in mortgage-backed securities in both Citizens Property Insurance and the Florida Hurricane Catastrophe Fund. A fund director stated that any holdings related to subprime mortgages would be traded out of the funds before hurricane season hit Florida in the summer of 2008. However, it may have been difficult, given valuation and liquidity issues, to sell the holdings by then.

Control Failings and Contributory Factors

Insufficient Compliance Measures
Hillsborough officials requested that the state of Florida roll back the clock to a date before the run on the bank and require counties that withdrew funds to return the illiquid portions. A clerk for the county cited Chapter 218 of the Florida statute as justification for this claim, which requires the State Board of Administration to "purchase investments for a pooled investment account in which all participants may share pro rata, as determined by rule of the board, in the capital gains, income, or losses, subject to any penalties for early withdrawal." In addition, according to the state clerk, "an order or warrant may not be issued upon any account for a larger amount than the share of the particular account to which it applies; and if such order or warrant is used, the responsible official shall be personally liable under his or her bond for the entire overdraft."

Undertook Excessive Risks
States, pension funds, and local governments began accumulating riskier securities during a period when interest rates were relatively low. They were consequently able to earn higher yields, but also took on higher risk. In this case, the state of Florida continued to acquire subprime-related securities in the months after it was clear that there was a problem; Bear Stearns announced that two of its hedge funds had lost over 90 percent of their value in July 2007, and Countrywide Financial

faced a liquidity crisis in August 2007. The state of Florida continued to purchase investment stakes related to subprime mortgages as late as August 2007 and held on to its holdings through October 2007.

Compensation

The former director of the State Board of Administration, Coleman Stipanovich, was encouraged to take on risk through his compensation agreement. He was provided with financial incentives of up to 8 percent of his annual salary if he increased returns for the state's pension fund. The manager of the Local Government Investment Fund was provided with similar incentives. This drive for return, and encouragement through incentives to bring in returns without the consideration of risk, has led to many operational risk blowups in the past. It can be argued that in Florida's case, it encouraged the state's senior managers to invest in securities that would boost yield, but also led to a substantial increase of risk in what should have been a safely invested money market fund.

Corporate/Market Conditions

Market conditions for all financial institutions and lenders became so precarious during August 2007 that the Federal Reserve stepped in to add liquidity to the markets. The Federal Reserve had last provided cash to the banking system in 1998 during the collapse of Long-Term Capital Management. This suggests that conditions that led to Florida's troubles are at least a once-in-10-years event. When the Federal Reserve moved to cut the discount borrowing rate, it released a statement saying that risk in the markets increased "appreciably." Jan Hatzius, chief U.S. economist for Goldman Sachs, commented: "In Fed-speak, things are either 'slightly' or 'somewhat.' Saying that the risks have increased 'appreciably' is a pretty strong statement for them" (Gosselin 2007).

Corrective Actions and Management Response

The state of Florida pulled Bob Milligan out of retirement in order to function as the State Board of Administration's interim executive director. He replaced former executive director Coleman Stipanovich, who resigned on December 4, 2007. Mr. Milligan had been comptroller for the state of Florida from 1995 through 2003. At the same time, the state of Florida brought in New York–based BlackRock to help restructure the troubled Local Government Investment Fund.

Mr. Milligan found a problem when he showed up for work in his interim role: Too many people were attempting to manage the crisis, and as a result BlackRock was being given conflicting directions from state executives. Mr. Milligan stated that one of his first tasks was to make it "very clear to them [BlackRock] who they report to and who they are working for, and the lines of communications I want to be followed both in terms of routine things that occur and any extraordinary things that may occur."

Mr. Milligan, who was 75 years old, said he was putting a system in place for his successor. One recommendation was to hire an experienced money manager and offer an annual salary in the $300,000 to $350,000 range. His predecessor, Mr. Stipanovich, earned approximately $180,000 per year. Mr. Milligan said that the next head of the agency should have private-sector experience running large funds. At least one trustee of the fund commented that the recommended salary level for the next head of the fund sounded too high, and public sector employees should expect to earn less in exchange for the "opportunity to serve."

Lessons Learned

A peripheral concern in this case is the fees that BlackRock charged as a money manager that was brought in to restructure the troubled state fund. According to the *Orlando Sentinel* (12/18/2007), local governments were attracted to the LGIF originally because its management fees were relatively low. However, there was concern that BlackRock's fees were too high; they were about 26 times higher than what the state charged. Others contend that the fees were appropriate given the crisis situation that faced the fund. BlackRock was charging a two-tier fee structure, with a higher fee charged for Fund B than for Fund A.

Part of the concern for BlackRock's fees is for what it was charging for Fund B, given that the fund manager advised to let the fund sit for a year or so without any notable active buying or selling of assets. BlackRock argued that the extra fees were necessary because of the complexity of analyzing the securities involved and determining the best time to attempt to sell off some of the assets.

In addition, investment banks that sold mortgage-backed securities to Florida and other states are coming under criticism for fiduciary issues. Lehman Brothers sold the state of Florida $842 million of mortgage-backed debt in July and August 2007—just a few months before the revelation that the state's money market fund held the securities. *Bloomberg* alleged (12/18/2007) that the investment banks were attempting to offload securities that they knew were distressed to states, which were in search of higher yields and were willing buyers. The states are likely to take the Wall Street firms to court over allegations that they breached their duty to less sophisticated public investment funds.

Counties that left their funds in the LGIF have been placed at odds with counties that pulled out their investments in November 2007. Counties such as Hillsborough argue that the state should have halted all withdrawals when it became apparent that the mortgage-related investments were becoming impaired and were suffering from a lack of market liquidity. This increased the risk for counties such as Hillsborough, which saw its exposure to mortgage-backed securities grow from 3.4 percent of its entire investment to over 14 percent.

A clerk for the county said that he did not want to withdraw his investment at the time because he thought it would "just add to the panic and hurt in the long run." He added that he was not "worried about 3 percent." However, the state proceeded to sell off its liquid assets in order to meet its obligations to the counties that were actively withdrawing funds, and as a result counties that decided to stay found that troubled assets now comprised a larger portion of their investments.

CASE STUDY THREE: ORANGE COUNTY MARKET RISK EVENT[3]

Event Summary

In December 1994, Orange County in Southern California announced publicly that its investment pool had suffered a $1.6 billion loss. This was the largest investment loss ever registered by a municipality, and led to bankruptcy and the mass layoffs of municipal employees. At the center of the case was the county's treasurer, Robert Citron, who was responsible for investing the county's money in interest rate derivatives in order to boost returns for the investment pool that he managed. The Federal Reserve, however, raised interest rates multiple times in 1994, which resulted in significant losses for Citron's investment strategy. Through the purchase of interest rate derivatives, Citron had placed bets that interest rates would fall rather than rise.

Event Details

The $1.6 billion loss was blamed on the unsupervised investment strategy of Robert Citron. Mr. Citron portrayed himself at the time of his trial as an unsophisticated investor who was misled by Merrill Lynch investment advisers, and did not fully understand the risks involved with the recommended strategy to purchase interest rate derivatives. Orange County argued in court that since Mr. Citron had exceeded his authority by leveraging his investment pool by a ratio of 13 to 1, the investment advisers were ultimately responsible for the loss.

Citron placed a bet through the purchase of reverse repurchase agreements that interest rates would fall or stay low, and reinvested his earnings in new securities that were mostly five-year notes issued by government agencies. Mr. Citron's strategy worked until February 1994, when the Federal Reserve undertook a series of six interest-rate hikes that generated significant losses for the fund. The county was forced to liquidate Citron's managed investment fund in December 1994, and suffered a loss of $1.6 billion. A county that was among the most affluent in the United States filed for Chapter 9 bankruptcy, and was forced to put large projects and expansion plans on hold.

Also playing a role in Orange County's bankruptcy were Merrill Lynch and its ex-Marine broker, Michael Stamenson. A training tape that featured Mr. Stamenson was presented as evidence in a lawsuit brought by Orange County against the brokerage firm. In the tape, Mr. Stamenson coaches new brokers that they need the "tenacity of a rattlesnake, the heart of a black widow spider, and the hide of an alligator." In the end, Merrill's dealings with the county cost the brokerage over $480 million.

In 1998 the Los Angeles District Court upheld Citron's authority to invest in derivative securities, despite the fact that he made "grave errors" and "imprudent decisions." It was difficult for Citron to represent himself as an "inexperienced investor" and "lay person" after he testified that he had more than 20 years' experience in the investment industry. Evidence was presented that demonstrated Citron's influence: When Goldman Sachs criticized his high-risk strategy in 1993, he advised the firm to avoid seeking business opportunities with the county in the future.

The group of brokerage firms that were later sued in court for the role they played in the event argued that this was not the posture of an "inexperienced lay person." Citron had delivered returns that were 2 percent higher than other municipal pools in the state of California, and was viewed as a "wizard" who obtained better-than-average returns in difficult market conditions. He enjoyed his near-celebrity status until December 1994 when everything unraveled and the county declared bankruptcy. Ultimately, Mr. Citron pleaded guilty to six felonies.

Control Failings and Contributory Factors

Employee Misdeeds/Undertook Excessive Risks
Mr. Citron originally portrayed himself as an unsophisticated investor who was misled by Wall Street brokers. However, he eventually pleaded guilty to a variety of misdeeds, including making false statements in order to sell securities to schools and local agencies that had invested in Orange County's investment pool, falsifying financial documents, and failing to pay proper levels of interest to participants in the investment pool.

Failure to Supervise
Mr. Citron appeared to have engaged in his risk-taking strategy without supervision from the county's management. The *Wall Street Journal* (6/4/1996) reported that the county's supervisors referred to the investment pool as "Citron's portfolio" and hired a lawyer who concluded that they were not responsible for supervising Mr. Citron. Matt Raabe testified that authorization to sell the securities in the portfolio might have been interpreted as an acknowledgment that the board had some responsibility for the loss. The *Wall Street Journal* contended that this was part of the general pattern within Orange County: "The county's elected leaders washed their hands of responsibility for the county's finances."

Corrective Measures and Management Response

Orange County declared bankruptcy on December 6, 1994, after it discovered that Mr. Citron's leveraged interest rate bet had produced $1.5 billion in paper losses. The portfolio was later liquidated and resulted in a $1.63 billion real loss.

Orange County's prosecutor sought a seven-year sentence for Robert Citron and a $400,000 fine. Instead, he was sentenced to a one-year jail sentence and a $100,000 fine. He never actually served time in jail; instead, he worked in a clerical position on a work-release program that allowed him to return to his home each evening.

Lessons Learned

It is worth noting that, according to Professor Philippe Jorion in his case study on Orange County,[4] a huge opportunity was lost when interest rates started falling shortly after the liquidation of the fund, and a potential gain of $1.4 billion based on Citron's interest rate strategy was never realized. He found the county most guilty of "bad timing."

Nobel Prize winner Merton Miller also questioned whether liquidation of Orange County's portfolio was the right strategy; he argued that the county had enough money on hand to continue operations and could have recouped its losses within one or two years. According to the *Wall Street Journal* (6/4/1996), several Wall Street firms were allegedly standing by in an attempt to buy portions of the investment pool. But for legal reasons the county decided to declare bankruptcy despite the fact that some experts, including Mr. Miller, contended that there were other options.

The lessons learned from this debacle include the lack of employment of classic risk management techniques by Citron and his investors, including the use of value at risk (VaR), and the lack of honest analysis of how the county was managing to realize above-market returns.

NOTES

1. Algo First database of operational risk case studies.

2. Ibid.

3. Ibid.

4. Jorion, Philippe. 1995. *Big Bets Gone Bad: Derivatives and Bankruptcy in Orange County.* Orlando, FL: Academic Press.

REFERENCE

Gosselin, Peter G. 2007. "Fed Gets Message, Lowers Key Rate," *Los Angeles Times.* August 18.

ABOUT THE AUTHOR

Algorithmics Software LLC (www.algorithmics.com) is the world leader in enterprise risk solutions, dedicated to helping financial institutions understand and manage risk. Its innovative software, content, and advisory services provide a consistent, enterprise-wide view of risk management to help firms make better business decisions and increase shareholder value.

CHAPTER 22

Credit Derivatives Case Studies: AIG and Merrill Lynch

ALGORITHMICS SOFTWARE LLC*

CASE STUDY ONE: AMERICAN INTERNATIONAL GROUP (AIG)[1]

Event Summary

The U.S. Federal Reserve, under the guidance of the Treasury Department, took control of American International Group (AIG) with an $85 billion bailout on September 16, 2008. The rescue left the U.S. government holding 80 percent of the largest insurance company in the world until the company can be recapitalized. The recapitalization was expected to occur through a sale of the insurance company's assets. A significant portion of AIG's problems were attributed to credit derivative losses suffered by its financial products division. The firm was found to have taken on too much risk, and to have not had the resources to meet calls for additional collateral, when the value of reference collateralized debt obligations (CDOs) that it had insured started plummeting. New York State Attorney General Andrew Cuomo is investigating payouts the firm made to a series of counterparties who demanded additional collateral. AIG's disclosure statements involving the collateral calls are also being investigated.

AIG's underwriting businesses were deemed essentially healthy and believed to be of interest to a variety of possible acquirers. Hank Greenberg, the founder and former chief executive of AIG, was mentioned as a possible buyer for some of the company's assets. At least one pension fund sued AIG for "gross imprudent risk taking."

Event Details

It was unprecedented for the U.S. Federal Reserve to intervene in the rescue of an insurance company, but the decision reflects concern for how intertwined the company was with financial markets and the risk of an even larger systemic failure if the insurer was allowed to go under. Just days before the Federal Reserve stepped

---

*This information is the sole property of Algorithmics Software LLC and may not be reprinted or replicated in any way without permission.

in to rescue AIG, it allowed Lehman Brothers to go under rather than provide financial backing. The failure to rescue Lehman Brothers was surprising, because the Federal Reserve had earlier stepped in to rescue Bear Stearns in March 2008; circumstances, however, had changed since March, and the U.S. government came under political pressure to resist appearing to be saving Wall Street while Main Street (or Middle America) suffered from the economic downturn. In the case of AIG, the Federal Reserve said that a "disorderly failure of AIG could add to already significant levels of financial market fragility." AIG's takeover followed the September 7, 2008, government rescue of Freddie Mac and Fannie Mae.

AIG's cash shortage, which became evident by the weekend of September 6, 2008, was attributed to its financial products division, which was exposed to credit default swap (CDS) contracts, including those that insured mortgage-backed securities (MBS). Credit default swaps provide investors with a type of credit insurance in the event of a default; credit default swaps are triggered by credit events, including a bankruptcy filing. Besides AIG's importance as the largest insurer in the global markets and its book of corporate and personal insurance policies, there was worry that if the company was allowed to file for bankruptcy a new round of credit protection contracts would have been triggered, and a downward spiral would have been created, if the entities that would have to honor contracts on AIG went under and triggered a new round of payouts. The *New York Times* (9/18/2008) reported that while the company's core business was underwriting insurance contracts and selling annuities, it was "deeply involved in the risky, opaque market for derivatives and other complicated financial instruments that operate largely outside regulation."

Unwinding AIG's portfolio of derivatives contracts is perhaps the largest task ahead for a senior management team that was facing many challenges. It was estimated that AIG provided $440 billion of credit insurance on debt products. Payouts on such transactions and requests for additional collateral dramatically increased since subprime mortgages, which underlie many of these complex debt securities, lost value following the market disruptions of August 2007. AIG was a counterparty to billions of dollars' worth of other types of derivatives. There was also concern that if AIG filed for bankruptcy a series of credit default swaps tagged to its debt would have been triggered. For this reason, the government's description of the rescue used specific language that was designed to avoid triggering a credit event.

The *Financial Times* reported (9/18/2008) that AIG got caught in what was essentially a game of "regulatory arbitrage." Global banks were able to use credit default swaps to offset the amount of capital they had put aside to cover certain credit risks. The banks that entered into default contracts with AIG were able to claim that they were offsetting the risk that a certain underlying credit asset would default. They were allowed to hold less cash in reserve as a result of entering these contracts. The cost of these contracts was less than the cost of holding regulatory capital. AIG advertised the credit protection that it offered as a method for providing "regulatory capital relief rather than risk mitigation." As AIG's credit insurance business grew, it also acquired a concentration of credit risk. The *Financial Times* wrote that as the market for credit default swaps grew, "dangerous levels of counterparty risk would accumulate in institutions willing, as AIGFP [AIG financial products division] was, to write insurance on very attractive terms."

When AIG first approached the Federal Reserve for assistance, it was in the belief that it would need about $20 billion in order to continue operating. New York State allowed AIG to tap into available funds from its insurance subsidiaries in order to cover the shortfall—a commingling of funds that is usually prohibited. But it became evident after J.P. Morgan Chase, Kohlberg Kravis Roberts (KKR), and J.C. Flowers pored through AIG's books that it needed not $20 billion, but $40 billion, then $65 billion, and later at least $80 billion in order to survive. AIG received a buyout offer of $10 billion from J.C. Flowers, under the condition that it would have to retain its present credit rating. KKR and Texas-Pacific Group offered $20 billion for 50 percent of the company if the credit rating was maintained, and if additional funding was provided by Wall Street and the U.S. government. A credit rating downgrade, however, was already planned for the insurance company. The major ratings firms announced on September 15, 2008, that they had downgraded the firm. A series of credit ratings downgrades meant that AIG was required by counterparties on its swaps contracts to post an additional $13.3 billion in collateral. This increased call for additional collateral is believed to have created a cash shortage at AIG and is under investigation by Attorney General Andrew Cuomo and federal regulators.

Also being investigated is the role Joseph Cassano played at the time the collateral calls were occurring. Mr. Cassano was head of AIG's ill-fated financial products division. He told AIG shareholders, "We have, from time to time, gotten collateral calls from people. Then we say to them, 'Well, we don't agree with your numbers.'" He added that they then "go away." He made similar statements to his firm's auditors (Cohen 2010).

Documents received by *CBS News* (6/23/2009) belie Mr. Cassano's comments concerning the collateral calls; an internal memo documented 84 collateral calls received by late November 2007, totaling more than $4 billion. The same set of documents indicated that 38 calls were from Goldman Sachs, 18 margin calls were from Merrill Lynch, and 25 such calls were received from Société Générale. Despite the large number of collateral calls, CBS reported that during a December 5, 2007 conference call with investors, "AIG executives were silent about the specific number of collateral calls" and appeared to "gloss over any potential problems with its CDS portfolio." Former CEO Martin Sullivan commented on the firm's CDO portfolio during the call: "The probability that it will sustain an economic loss is close to zero." The U.S. Justice Department is allegedly investigating this period in an effort to discern whether AIG's senior executives misled investors and auditors about the health of its CDO business.

AIG was the tenth most popular stock holding in employee 401(k) plans. It was also widely held by pension funds. The City of New Orleans Employees' Retirement System announced on September 18, 2008, that it had filed a lawsuit against AIG Chief Executive Robert Willumstad and the board of directors of AIG, accusing them of mismanagement and "grossly imprudent risk taking." The pension fund seeks the return of all compensation that the firm's individual defendants earned from the company, in addition to other claims for recompense. It is also probable that the firm will be the target of additional shareholder lawsuits that will contend that it failed to properly report its true financial condition and risks. The investment banks that underwrote an AIG offering in May 2008, in an effort to raise cash, are vulnerable to lawsuits alleging fiduciary breaches associated with their role as underwriters. This type of suit has already been filed against the underwriters that assisted Fannie Mae with raising funds, even though Fannie Mae was ordered to do so by its regulator.

AIG reported losses related to write-downs on credit default swaps linked partially to subprime mortgages in the fourth quarter of 2007. The firm was also the subject of continual regulatory investigations over the prior several years, which were heightened when former New York State Attorney General Eliot Spitzer was in office. Some analysts traced the firm's troubles to the Spitzer regulatory regime, which ultimately pushed out longtime CEO Maurice Greenberg.

Control Failings and Contributory Factors

Corporate/Market Conditions

AIG was heavily exposed to asset-backed securities that had subprime mortgages as their underlying instruments through the credit derivatives market. The appetite for mortgage-backed securities dissipated after the market events of August 2007, when it became evident that subprime mortgages exposed financial markets to a great deal of credit, market, and operational risk.

Strategy Flaw

AIG was unique among insurance firms, in that it took on so much capital markets–related risk and expanded aggressively into noncore businesses, such as offering a form of credit insurance through the significant role it played in credit default swap transactions. A large part of this exposure was through offering protection for bonds linked to mortgage-backed securities. Internal memos that emerged later indicated there were problems with how these contracts were structured. The documents suggested that AIG failed to include reliable thresholds before collateral calls would be triggered (thresholds determine by what percentage reference CDOs would have to decline before the seller of protection is required to post additional collateral). The memos indicate that some of AIG's CDO contracts included no threshold, and others' thresholds were as low as 4 percent. This offered little protection against the counterparty calls for additional collateral that have been mentioned as a contributory factor to the firm's liquidity crisis in September 2008.

Failure to Disclose

Evidence presented by *CBS News* suggests that AIG had knowledge that its CDO portfolio might be in trouble before a meeting that it held with investors on December 5, 2007. This knowledge may have been reflected in the number of collateral calls it received on the portfolio during the period before the meeting. However, during what the news service called "a crucial meeting," the firm's senior management commented to investors that there was no probability that the portfolio would sustain losses.

Undertook Excessive Risk

A business model that allowed one noncore division within AIG to put the rest of the firm at risk was a highly risk-taking strategy. AIG's losses, resulting from its credit derivatives exposure, reflect the high and very opaque risk inherent in credit default swap transactions. They also represent how concentrated this type of risk became within the firm; in its core insurance underwriting businesses it is unlikely that AIG would have allowed its risk exposure to become so concentrated. The risk associated with credit default swaps can rapidly expand during volatile market conditions, when default triggers exponentially kick in. As mentioned, a lawsuit filed by a New Orleans pension fund specifically targeted AIG's "grossly imprudent risk taking."

Corrective Actions and Management Response

The terms of the rescue plan call for the issuance of a two-year bridge loan of $85 billion to AIG; in return the U.S. government takes ownership of a 79.9 percent stake in AIG. The bridge loan was granted at the high interest rate of 8.5 percentage points above the London Interbank Offered Rate (Libor) as a deterrent to any possible moral hazard. It is in AIG's interest to retire the loan as soon as possible through the sale of assets. Assuming ownership through the issuance of equity warrants was a method deployed by the government in order to prohibit shareholders from benefiting directly from the rescue of the company, which was deemed another example of potential moral hazard.

The terms of the rescue called for replacement of the firm's CEO. Edward Liddy replaced Bob Willumstad as the firm's chief executive. Mr. Liddy agreed to receive a salary of $1. In a letter to employees, Mr. Liddy, the former CEO of Allstate, indicated that he had no intention of shutting down AIG: "My intention is not to liquidate the company. Insurance operations are solid, capitalized and well funded." He also reassured the markets when he said, "the mess we're in is solvable." He announced on May 21, 2009, that he was resigning his position at AIG and would remain on the job only until a replacement could be found (Son 2008).

The estimate for AIG's breakup value was in the range of $150 billion. A number of names were mentioned as potential acquirers of AIG's businesses, including Prudential Financial, Prudential PLC, Aviva, Berkshire Hathaway, Munich Re, and Allianz. The senior management of AIG's profitable aircraft leasing business was attempting to put together financing for a management buyout.

AIG's board of directors issued the following statement on September 16, 2008: "The AIG Board has approved this transaction based on its determination that this is the best alternative for all of AIG's constituencies, including policyholders, customers, creditors, counterparties, employees and shareholders. AIG is a solid company with over $1 trillion in assets and substantial equity, but it has been recently experiencing serious liquidity issues. We believe the loan, which is backed by profitable, well-capitalized operating subsidiaries with substantial value, will protect all AIG policyholders, address rating agency concerns, and give AIG the time necessary to conduct asset sales on an orderly basis. We expect that the proceeds of these sales will be sufficient to repay the loan in full and enable AIG's businesses to continue as substantial participants in their respective markets. In return for providing this essential support, American taxpayers will receive a substantial majority ownership interest in AIG."

Lessons Learned

The rescue of AIG led to the inevitable concern for associated moral hazard. The U.S. Treasury department and Federal Reserve were also under pressure to explain why they would extend emergency financing to an insurance company when just a day earlier they failed to extend a lifeline to Lehman Brothers. The issue at the crux of the decision is how intertwined the firm is in the overall economy, and how much systemic risk it poses. The decision was made that AIG was too big to fail and too intertwined in world markets. This was the result of several facts: It is one of the most widely held stocks in portfolios of many pension funds and mutual funds, and is held by a large number of retail investors; it is heavily bound into both sides of credit default transactions; and it is the largest insurer in many markets around the world. By contrast, the failure of Lehman Brothers was predicted to be more contained.

The Federal Reserve's role in stabilizing AIG represented a shift in the regulatory landscape. The Federal Reserve morphed seemingly overnight from an entity that was primarily concerned with the stability and capitalization of the monetary and banking systems, to the role of steward of the overall economy. Some overseas analysts commented that the series of rescues that have occurred during the prior few months represent a shift away from a pure free-market economy. While maintaining that they understand why the Federal Reserve stepped in to save Fannie Mae, Freddie Mac, and AIG, they also commented that hypocrisy was possible because the U.S. government and the World Bank have in the past criticized foreign governments in growth countries that attempted to stabilize ailing private entities.

CASE STUDY TWO: MERRILL LYNCH[2]

Event Summary

Merrill Lynch & Co., Inc. filed a lawsuit against bond insurer XL Capital Assurance Inc. on March 18, 2008. The suit alleged that a bond insurance unit of XL breached its contract when it voided default protection on $3.7 billion of collateralized debt obligations (CDOs). The default protection provided by XL was in the form of credit default swaps (CDSs). On April 1, 2008, SCA countersued, defending its termination of seven CDS written for Merrill Lynch International. On July 28, 2008, SCA agreed to pay Merrill Lynch & Co., Inc., $500 million to terminate the seven CDS contracts. At around the same time, SCA was spun off from XL Capital Ltd and renamed Syncora Holdings.

Event Details

Merrill Lynch required bond insurance to protect its holdings of senior tranches of certain mortgage-backed CDOs issued since 2005. In late 2005 the insurance firm AIG, which had previously insured some mortgage-backed securities issued by Merrill, decided it would stop selling new insurance on such securities. Merrill Lynch International then entered into seven credit default swap (CDS) contracts with XL Capital Assurance, an operating subsidiary of Security Capital Assurance

Ltd. (SCA), to insure its CDOs. CDS contracts typically last for five years, although other term structures exist.

In August 2007, Merrill reportedly proposed that XL Capital Assurance insure a further $20 billion in Merrill CDOs. "Pick your deal. It's a very nice deal for XL and a big help for ML," a Merrill salesman was alleged to have told an XL employee at the time. XL declined to take on the new business, and Merrill turned to a smaller insurer, ACA Financial Guaranty.

In February and March 2008, XL Capital attempted to void seven CDS transactions that protected the original $3.7 billion in CDOs, on the grounds that Merrill breached the terms of the contract by granting "control rights" to a third party without informing XL. The third party is reported to be bond insurer MBIA Inc. Control rights include potential actions to help senior note holders in the top tranche of a defaulting CDO obtain full payment, pitting their interests against those of lower-rated note holders. At least two of the CDOs at issue in the case received event of default (EOD) notices. In March 2008, SCA recorded a charge of $632.3 million relating to the swaps in question.

Merrill filed suit against XL in federal court in New York on March 18, 2008, claiming breach of contract, and asking the court to order that the seven CDS contracts remain in force. News of the filing triggered sales in Merrill Lynch shares, which fell 8.4 percent over the day on the New York Stock Exchange on the expectation that further CDO write-downs could follow.

Security Capital Assurance then countersued Merrill Lynch in federal court on April 1, 2008, disputing Merrill's claims and defending its terminations of the CDS contracts. SCA's suit alleged that Merrill, after forecasting a $7.9 billion write-down on subprime-related assets in the third quarter of 2007, "undertook a rushed campaign to find parties willing to hedge or provide protection on its remaining (CDO) positions. . . . Determined to get these CDO risks off its books at all costs before the third quarter of 2007 closed, Merrill Lynch made the decision to blatantly ignore its prior commitments to" XL Capital. At least two of the CDS contracts signed by XL "negligently" omitted to include language specifying that XL would be granted control rights. Security Capital argued that Merrill agreed to amend the two contracts but never did so.

On April 17, 2008, Merrill Lynch announced first quarter results for 2008. The company's write-downs included "credit valuation adjustments of negative $3.0 billion related to hedges with financial guarantors, most of which related to U.S. super-senior ABS CDOs." However, it is not known whether this refers directly to the CDS contracts that are the object of the dispute in the current case.

Control Failings and Contributory Factors

Failure to Disclose
Security Capital alleged that Merrill Lynch failed to notify XL it had granted control rights in several CDO contracts to third parties, thus breaching its contract.

Corporate/Market Conditions
Increasing rates of default on residential mortgages in the United States led to a rapid deterioration in the market for asset-backed CDOs. This in turn placed pressure on companies that wrote bond insurance on such securities.

Poor Documentation

At least two of the CDS contracts signed by XL "negligently" omitted language specifying that XL would be granted control rights. SCA argued that Merrill agreed to amend the two contracts but never did so.

Corrective Actions and Management Response

On July 28, 2008, it was announced that Merrill Lynch had agreed to allow SCA to cancel $3.7 billion in credit default swaps on mortgage-related securities, ending the litigation. In exchange for the cancellation, SCA agreed to pay Merrill $500 million. The deals were brokered by New York Insurance Commissioner Eric Dinallo. The announcement of the settlement was accompanied by news that XL Capital, the Bermuda-based re-insurer that was formerly SCA's parent, had agreed to pay SCA $1.78 billion in cash, and issued 8 million shares in SCA, which was to be renamed Syncora Holdings. In June 2008, shareholders of SCA had agreed to a renaming of the company and, at around the same time as the settlement was announced, SCA was renamed Syncora Holdings.

Lessons Learned

The fast-growing CDS market remains largely unregulated despite the large volume in contracts written. The securities have not been subjected to conditions of widespread defaults, and there has been little or no litigation testing how the contracts are written. Therefore, as a J.P. Morgan analyst commented in the *Financial Times*, "Dealers that retained and hedged senior AAA CDO exposures may face greater losses if monolines are successful in shifting losses due to legal issues, or [they] may face litigation from junior investors over sloppy documentation." However, analysts also note that if a CDS dispute were to be decided in court, the standard of proof for a claim of misrepresentation would be high, given that parties on both sides qualify as sophisticated investors. However, some of these contracts are speculative investments, rather than hedges, and an unknown amount is believed to be held by highly leveraged entities with little in the way of reserves, such as hedge funds.

The well-known investor George Soros said of the instruments on April 4: "It is a totally unregulated market hanging like a Damocles' sword over the financial system. You don't know whether your counterparty is good for its payment or not." Many firms that bought CDS contracts to hedge their investment risk must discover who currently holds the insurance contract, as the insurer may have assigned the insurance contract to another party, who can then do the same. Thus, a company may not even know the identity of the counterparty against which it would obtain payment in an event of default.

According to an analysis by the *New York Times* on August 10, 2008, the agreement to settle the contracts for $500 million—about 13 percent of their face value—raised questions about the valuations of other outstanding CDS contracts. If SCA had been obliged to pay out the full value of the swaps, it is considered likely that it would have been unable to do so. Then SCA would have been placed under regulatory control and Merrill might have received little or nothing. As Commissioner Dinallo told the *New York Times*, "There was the looming threat of us sending the whole thing over to rehabilitation where it is still uncertain what happens." Under a regulatory takeover, the swaps could be considered junior to other claims on SCA. "This uncertainty presented the market clearing price for the credit default swaps," Commissioner Dinallo said, noting that at least 13 other banks had similar CDS contracts with SCA.

Mr. Dinallo pushed to have the contracts regulated as insurance products, which would require that purchasers have an "insurable interest" that the contract covers, and that sellers maintain reserves to cover the value of the contracts. Others have urged that the products (and perhaps currency and interest rate swaps, too) should be regulated as derivatives. As of November 2008, CDS contracts remain unregulated and there is no clearinghouse for the contracts.

NOTES

1. Algo First database of operational risk case studies.
2. Ibid.

REFERENCES

Cohen, William. 2010. "The Fall of AIG: The Untold Story." *Institutional Investor* April 7. http://www.iimagazine.com/article.aspx?articleID=2460649.
Son, Hugh. 2008. "AIG's Liddy Plans to Keep Company in Business, Not Liquidate." *Bloomberg* September 18. http://www.bloomberg.com/apps/news?sid=aqkraD7yNDEw&pid=newsarchive.

ABOUT THE AUTHOR

Algorithmics Software LLC (www.algorithmics.com) is the world leader in enterprise risk solutions, dedicated to helping financial institutions understand and manage risk. Its innovative software, content, and advisory services provide a consistent, enterprise-wide view of risk management to help firms make better business decisions and increase shareholder value.

PART V

Special Topics in Financial Engineering

CHAPTER 23

Performance Fees

MARK P. KRITZMAN
Windham Capital Management LLC

INTRODUCTION

This chapter explores three aspects of investment management fees, which are not commonly understood. First, performance fees for a group of funds are higher than the average of the funds' expected fees. Second, the standard deviation of returns net of performance fees understates a fund's exposure to risk. Third, typical mutual fund fees are as high as, or higher than, typical hedge fund fees. Allow me to explain.

PERFORMANCE FEES

Hedge funds typically charge a performance fee that is a percentage of profits—but not losses—relative to a benchmark along with a base fee that is a fixed percentage of assets under management. Often the base fee is deducted from the profits before the performance fee is applied. If, for example, the base fee equals 2 percent and the performance fee equals 20 percent, a hedge fund manager who produces a 7 percent return in excess of the benchmark on a $100 million portfolio will collect a $2 million base fee (2 percent × $100,000,000) and a $1 million performance fee [20% × ($7,000,000 − $2,000,000)], for a total fee of $3 million. The investor's return net of fees, therefore, is 4 percent in excess of the benchmark. Exhibit 23.1 shows fees as a function of relative performance given this particular fee arrangement.

    Exhibit 23.1 reveals that a performance fee, in which the hedge fund manager collects a share of the upside but does not pay for any downside, is tantamount to a long position in a call option on relative performance for the manager, and a short position in this option for the investor. If the investor engages several managers with performance fees, the investor is effectively short a portfolio of options as opposed to an option on a portfolio, because performance fees are paid on the individual performance of the funds, rather than on the average performance of the funds. If, for example, one fund is up and another is down by the same amount, the investor is still required to pay a performance fee on the profitable fund. This arrangement dilutes the portfolio's expected performance beyond the expected value of the fee, as I will now demonstrate.[1]

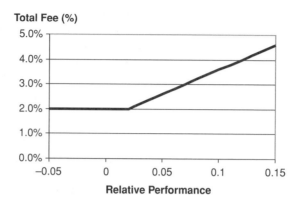

Total Fee (%)

Exhibit 23.1   Performance Fee Payoff Diagram

Impact of Asymmetry

Suppose an investor hires two managers who each charge a base fee of 2 percent, and a performance fee of 20 percent, and these managers both have expected returns in excess of the benchmark of 7 percent. The expected fee for each manager is 3 percent [2 percent + 20 percent × (7 percent − 2 percent)]; hence the investor might expect an aggregate return net of fees from these two managers equal to 4 percent. This expectation would be justified, however, only if both managers' returns exceed the base fee. If, instead, one manager produces an excess return of 25 percent and the other a −11 percent excess return, and an equal amount of capital is allocated to each manager, the investor would pay an average fee of 4.3 percent rather than 3 percent, and the average return to the investors would equal 2.7 percent rather than 4 percent, even though the managers still have an average excess return of 7 percent.

The difference between the expected return to the investor of 4 percent, and the realized return of 2.7 percent, is the drag attributable to the asymmetry of the performance fee, as I just explained. The result shown in Exhibit 23.2 is specific to the assumptions of this example, but it is easy to determine the typical asymmetry penalty given assumptions about expected excess return, standard deviation of excess return, and the average correlation of the managers' excess returns by applying Monte Carlo simulation.

Exhibit 23.2   Asymmetry Penalty Numerical Example

	Excess Return	Manager Fee	Return for Investor
Fund 1	7.0%	3.0%	4.0%
Fund 2	7.0%	3.0%	4.0%
Average	7.0%	3.0%	4.0%
Fund 1	25.0%	6.6%	18.4%
Fund 2	−11.0%	2.0%	−13.0%
Average	7.0%	4.3%	2.7%
Penalty			1.30%

Suppose, for example, we invest in 10 hedge funds, each of which has an expected excess return of 7 percent and a standard deviation of 15 percent. We will examine the impact of asymmetry under three different return correlation scenarios. These are −25 percent, 0 percent, and 25 percent. We assume, for simplicity, that all ten funds' returns are mutually correlated to the degree indicated. In order to estimate the impact of asymmetry on a collection of hedge funds we proceed as follows:

1. We first draw 1,000 returns for 10 funds, each from a multivariate normal distribution with means equal to 7 percent, standard deviations equal to 15 percent, and correlations equal to −25 percent, 0 percent, and 25 percent.
2. Then we apply the fee structure to each individual fund's returns for 1,000 trials and compute the average net return of 1,000 trials for all 10 funds.
3. We next compute the average return across 10 funds for 1,000 trials.
4. We apply the fee structure to the average return of 10 funds for 1,000 trials and compute the average net return of 1,000 trials.
5. We compute the difference in average returns from steps 2 and 4.

Exhibit 23.3 shows the results of such a simulation, assuming a base fee of 2 percent and a performance fee of 20 percent, which is applied to the excess performance after subtracting the base fee.

As we should expect, the size of the asymmetry penalty is inversely related to the correlation of the funds, because the more disparate their performance, the more likely it is that some funds will outperform while others underperform.

Asymmetry also impacts risk. Specifically, it invalidates standard deviation as a measure for estimating exposure to loss. It turns out that the standard deviation of a fund's returns net of fees is lower than the standard deviation of returns before fees, but this difference does not imply a reduction in risk. Exhibit 23.4 illustrates why standard deviation fails to capture exposure to loss.

Exhibit 23.4 shows the distribution of returns for various fee strategies. The diamonds represent the median returns, while the boxes show the 25th and 75th percentile returns. The extended lines show the maximum and minimum returns. The first plot shows the distribution assuming there are no fees. The second plot subtracts only the base fee. The third plot assumes that the performance is applied to the net return of the 10 funds, as would be the case in a multi-strategy fund. The fourth plot assumes that the performance fee is applied individually to the various funds. Finally, the fifth plot subtracts an additional base fee of 1 percent and a performance fee of 10 percent as compensation to a fund of funds manager.

Exhibit 23.3 Asymmetry Penalty Simulated Results

Correlation		
−0.25	0%	25.00%
0.80%	0.69%	0.47%
Alpha = 7%		
Expected return = 11%		
Standard deviation = 15%		

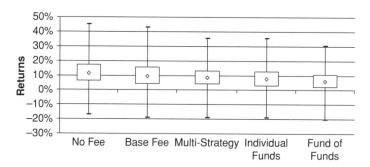

Exhibit 23.4   Upside versus Downside Volatility

Although the distribution of returns is tighter after performance fees are deducted, implying a lower standard deviation, this reduction in volatility does not
imply lower risk. The standard deviation is reduced because the performance fees
attenuate upside performance, not downside performance. The downside is just
as low or lower after deducting fees than it is before fees. Therefore, standard deviation is not a reliable indicator of exposure to loss, nor should it be used to build
efficient portfolios comprising funds that charge performance fees. Instead, we
should use downside deviation to measure risk and determine optimal allocation
to hedge funds and other funds that charge performance fees.

Optimal Allocations

Let's now explore the impact of performance fees on optimal portfolio allocations.
Suppose we wish to allocate a portfolio across stocks, bonds, and hedge funds
based on the following assumptions for stocks and bonds. Exhibit 23.5 shows
the expected return and downside deviation, given various fee arrangements and
assumptions for alpha ranging from 7 percent to 10 percent.

We can use this information to determine the optimal allocation to hedge
funds, assuming an investor starts with a 70 percent allocation to stocks, which
are expected to return 9.5 percent with a standard deviation of 20 percent, and
a 30 percent allocation to bonds, which are expected to return 8 percent with
a standard deviation of 10 percent, and assuming that stocks and bonds are
30 percent correlated.[2]

Exhibit 23.6 reveals that a 7 percent alpha is insufficient to warrant any exposure to hedge funds. If alpha is as high as 8 or 9 percent, portfolios should include
substantial allocations to hedge funds within a multi-strategy portfolio, and even
funds that charge performance fees individually; however, funds of funds are still
undesirable. It is only when alpha reaches 10 percent that a small allocation to
funds of funds makes sense.

Summary

Performance fees have a hidden cost called the asymmetry penalty, arising
from payment for outperformance without reimbursement for underperformance.

Exhibit 23.5 Return and Risk Net of Fees

Alpha = 7%, Libor = 4%

	No Fee	Base Fee	Multi-strategy	Individual Funds	Fund of Funds
Expected Return	11.00%	9.00%	7.71%	7.24%	5.52%
Downside Deviation	8.55%	8.55%	7.70%	7.70%	7.26%

Alpha = 8%, Libor = 4%

	No Fee	Base Fee	Multi-strategy	Individual Funds	Fund of Funds
Expected Return	12.00%	10.00%	8.56%	8.10%	6.30%
Downside Deviation	8.55%	8.55%	7.64%	7.69%	7.20%

Alpha = 9%, Libor = 4%

	No Fee	Base Fee	Multi-strategy	Individual Funds	Fund of Funds
Expected Return	13.00%	11.00%	9.40%	8.98%	7.10%
Downside Deviation	8.55%	8.55%	7.49%	7.63%	7.09%

Alpha = 10%, Libor = 4%

	No Fee	Base Fee	Multi-strategy	Individual Funds	Fund of Funds
Expected Return	14.00%	12.00%	10.23%	9.83%	7.86%
Downside Deviation	8.55%	8.55%	7.71%	7.85%	7.23%

Performance fees lower volatility but not risk, because they limit upside deviations. Investors in hedge funds should account for the asymmetry penalty and downside volatility when determining optimal hedge fund allocations. Investors should expect a premium of several hundred basis points to justify allocation to funds of funds.

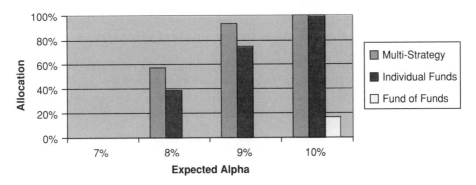

Exhibit 23.6 Optimal Hedge Fund Allocations with Asymmetry Penalty and Downside Volatility

Exhibit 23.7 Mutual Fund and Index Fund Returns and Values

	Mutual Fund		Index Fund		
Month	Return	Value	Return	Value	Alpha
		1,000,000		1,000,000	
January	0.41%	1,004,078	−1.13%	988,744	1.53%
February	6.03%	1,064,613	5.87%	1,046,783	0.16%
March	−8.30%	976,258	−8.08%	962,172	−0.22%
April	6.09%	1,035,759	6.23%	1,022,096	−0.13%
May	6.08%	1,098,733	7.03%	1,093,908	−0.95%
June	−4.74%	1,046,667	−5.66%	1,031,986	−0.92%
July	−0.95%	1,036,682	−1.85%	1,012,925	−0.89%
August	−5.83%	976,241	−4.41%	968,206	−1.42%
September	1.72%	993,060	1.59%	983,618	0.13%
October	2.49%	1,017,814	3.45%	1,017,575	−0.96%
November	−1.84%	999,069	−3.10%	985,983	1.26%
December	10.10%	1,100,000	9.54%	1,080,000	0.57%
Cumulative Return	*10.00%*		*8.00%*		*2.00%*
Standard Deviation	*19.29%*		*19.59%*		*3.23%*

HEDGE FUND VERSUS MUTUAL FUND FEES

Most investors believe that hedge fund fees are much higher than mutual fund fees. After all, the typical hedge fund charges a base fee that is much higher than the typical mutual fund fee and, on top of that, hedge funds take a substantial fraction of the profits in the form of a performance fee. Surely hedge fund fees must be higher than mutual fund fees—or perhaps not. Hedge funds, in principle, hedge out market returns and thereby produce a pure alpha; hence the term *hedge fund*. Alpha, in principle, is uncorrelated with market returns. Mutual funds, by contrast, generate returns that comprise a market component and an alpha component. The returns of mutual funds are typically more than 95 percent correlated with market returns. Taking these factors into account, it is unclear whether hedge funds or mutual funds are more expensive. The following example illustrates the relative cost of investing in hedge funds and mutual funds.

Exhibit 23.7 shows the monthly returns and values of a hypothetical mutual fund and index fund, assuming an initial investment of $1 million. The index fund serves as the benchmark for the mutual fund.

The mutual fund manager had a fairly good year. He generated a 2 percent alpha with active risk equal to 3.23 percent, for a respectable information ratio of 0.62 (alpha's cumulative return divided by alpha's standard deviation). Moreover, although not shown here, he has produced similar performance in years past. Because he has a solid long-term track record, he charges 75 basis points of the average of the beginning and ending values of the fund.

We might be tempted to hire this talented mutual fund manager, but as it turns out, he has a twin sister who is just as talented. In fact, their similarity as twins extends to their stock-picking skills, because they make the exact same active bets. She applies her skill, however, not as a mutual fund manager but as a hedge fund manager. Rather than invest in the stocks she expects to outperform the benchmark, she puts the capital to work in a short-term investment fund (STIF) that earns 4 percent. She then sells short the index fund and uses the proceeds of these short sales to purchase the stocks she expects to outperform, and she levers these exposures 12 to 1. Thus, she delivers a pure alpha stream, rather than the composite of market returns and alpha that her twin brother delivers through his mutual fund. Exhibit 23.8 shows the returns and values of her hedge fund, assuming an initial investment of $1 million.

The $1 million investment in the short-term investment fund compounds at 0.33 percent per month for a cumulative annual return of 4 percent. The initial exposure to the mutual fund equals $12 million (12:1 leverage), while the initial exposure to the index fund equals negative $12 million (again 12:1 leverage). The value of the hedge fund each period, therefore, equals the sum of the short-term investment fund position and the mutual fund and index fund positions.

Her hedge fund strategy produced an annual return of 28 percent, which equals 12 times her twin brother's 2 percent alpha plus 4 percent from the funds invested in the short-term investment fund. The annualized standard deviation of her monthly returns is slightly less than 12 times her brother's active risk, owing to her hedge fund's allocation to the short-term investment fund. Thus, she produced an information ratio of 0.79 compared to her brother's information ratio 0.62. Her performance in this year, just like her brother's performance, was consistent with her performance in years past; hence she charges a 2 percent base fee based on the average of the beginning and ending total value of the hedge fund and a performance fee equal to 20 percent of profits after netting out the income from the short-term investment fund as well as the base fee.

Although we might be justifiably impressed by her hedge fund's performance, its standard deviation of nearly 36 percent may be too much risk for us to swallow. Moreover, we may be unwilling to pay such high fees. First of all, we would have to pay a base fee of $22,800:

$$2.00\% \times (\$1,000,000 + \$1,280,002) \div 2 = \$22,800$$

Then on top of the base fee, we would have to pay a performance fee equal to $43,440, as shown in Exhibit 23.9.

The total hedge fund fee, therefore, would equal $66,240, compared to a total mutual fund fee charged by her brother of only $7,875 [0.75 percent × ($1,000,000 + $1,100,000) ÷ 2]. She charges more than eight times as much as her brother—or does she?

Remember, the mutual fund is a composite of market exposure and exposure to alpha. We could have achieved 80 percent of the mutual fund's total return by investing in a low-cost index fund. Moreover, suppose that the mutual fund returns are more than 98 percent correlated with the index fund returns. Why should we pay active fees for a product with such a large passive component?

The hedge fund, in contrast, is designed to have no market exposure, and in fact was slightly negatively correlated with the index fund returns during the period shown. We are comparing apples to oranges when we measure the fees of a hedge fund that delivers a pure alpha stream with the fees of a market-driven mutual fund. What if we combined a low-cost investment in an index fund with

Exhibit 23.8 Hedge Fund Returns and Values

Month	STIF		Mutual Fund		Index Fund		Hedge Fund	
	Return	Value	Return	Value	Return	Value	Return	Value
		1,000,000		12,000,000		−12,000,000		1,000,000
January	0.33%	1,003,274	0.41%	12,048,933	−1.13%	−11,864,929	18.73%	1,187,278
February	0.33%	1,006,558	6.03%	12,775,360	5.87%	−12,561,400	2.80%	1,220,518
March	0.33%	1,009,853	−8.30%	11,715,098	−8.08%	−11,546,068	−3.41%	1,178,883
April	0.33%	1,013,159	6.09%	12,429,110	6.23%	−12,265,152	−0.15%	1,177,118
May	0.33%	1,016,476	6.08%	13,184,899	7.03%	−13,126,891	−8.73%	1,074,385
June	0.33%	1,019,804	−4.74%	12,560,008	−5.66%	−12,383,827	11.32%	1,195,985
July	0.33%	1,023,142	−0.95%	12,440,182	−1.85%	−12,155,104	9.38%	1,308,221
August	0.33%	1,026,492	−5.83%	11,714,890	−4.41%	−11,618,472	−14.17%	1,122,910
September	0.33%	1,029,852	1.72%	11,916,718	1.59%	−11,803,419	1.80%	1,143,152
October	0.33%	1,033,224	2.49%	12,213,770	3.45%	−12,210,897	−9.36%	1,036,097
November	0.33%	1,036,606	−1.84%	11,988,828	−3.10%	−11,831,800	15.20%	1,193,634
December	0.33%	1,040,000	10.10%	13,199,999	9.54%	−12,959,998	7.24%	1,280,002
Cumulative Return	4.00%		10.00%		8.00%		28.00%	
Standard Deviation	0.00%		19.29%		19.59%		35.56%	

Exhibit 23.9 Performance Fee

Hedge Fund Gross Profit	1,280,002 − 1,000,000	280,002
STIF Profit	1,000,000 × 4%	40,000
Base Fee	2% × (1,000,000 + 1,280,002) ÷ 2	22,800
Hedge Net Profit	22,802 − 40,000 − 22,800	217,202
Performance Fee	20% × 217,202	43,440

investment in the hedge fund, instead of investing exclusively in either the mutual fund or the hedge fund? Exhibit 23.10 shows the returns and values of a 90/10 mix of the index fund and the hedge fund.

This particular mix of a $900,000 initial investment in the index fund, together with an initial investment of $100,000 in the hedge fund, produces precisely the same return as the mutual fund: 10 percent; and it achieves this result at slightly less risk: 17.39 percent versus 19.29 percent for the mutual fund. Moreover, the returns of this strategy are 99.85 percent correlated with the mutual fund returns. It is almost a perfect substitute for the mutual fund. But what does it cost?

Let's suppose the index fund charges five basis points, which is higher than what institutions typically pay for index funds. Exhibit 23.11 shows the total cost of investing in this strategy.

The total fee for this strategy is $7,092 compared to the mutual fund fee of $7,875. It is cheaper to invest in the hedge fund alongside an index fund than it is to invest in the mutual fund. This comparison is apples to apples, because the mutual fund blends market exposure with active bets, and the 90/10 strategy mimics the mutual fund strategy. In the 90/10 strategy, however, we pay active fees for active exposure and passive fees for passive exposure. In the mutual fund strategy, we pay active fees for both the active and passive exposures. The mutual

Exhibit 23.10 Returns and Values of 90/10 Mix of Index Fund and Hedge Fund

	Index Fund		Hedge Fund		90/10 Mix	
Month	Return	Value	Return	Value	Return	Value
		900,000		100,000		1,000,000
January	−1.13%	889,870	18.73%	118,728	0.86%	1,008,597
February	5.87%	942,105	2.80%	122,052	5.51%	1,064,157
March	−8.08%	865,955	−3.41%	117,888	−7.55%	983,843
April	6.23%	919,886	−0.15%	117,712	5.46%	1,037,598
May	7.03%	984,517	−8.73%	107,438	5.24%	1,091,955
June	−5.66%	928,787	11.32%	119,598	−3.99%	1,048,386
July	−1.85%	911,633	9.38%	130,822	−0.57%	1,042,455
August	−4.41%	871,385	−14.17%	112,291	−5.64%	983,676
September	1.59%	885,256	1.80%	114,315	1.62%	999,572
October	3.45%	915,817	−9.36%	103,610	1.99%	1,019,427
November	−3.10%	887,385	15.20%	119,363	−1.24%	1,006,748
December	9.54%	972,000	7.24%	128,000	9.26%	1,100,000
Cumulative Return	8.00%		28.00%		10.00%	
Standard Deviation	19.59%		35.56%		17.39%	

Exhibit 23.11   Total 90/10 Strategy Fee

Index Fund Fee	.05% × (900,000 + 972,000) ÷ 2	468
Hedge Fund Base Fee	2% × (100,000 + 128,000) ÷ 2	2,280
Hedge Fund Gross Profit	128,000 − 100,000	28,000
STIF Profit	100,000 × 4%	4,000
Hedge Net Profit	28,000 − 2,800 − 4,000	21,720
Performance Fee	20% × 21,720	4,344
Total Strategy Fee	468 + 2,280 + 4,344	7,092

fund and the 90/10 strategy both have about the same passive exposure, yet the mutual fund fee exceeds the fee for the 90/10 strategy. Therefore, the *implicit* active fee of the mutual fund is greater than the active fee of the 90/10 strategy, which is the hedge fund fee.

There are several simplifying assumptions that underlie this analysis. I assume, for example, that the income from selling securities short exactly offsets the cost of purchasing securities on margin. In practice, there are net costs associated with the long/short strategy described in my example. My example also depends on specific assumptions about return, volatility, interest rates, and fee schedules, which all conspire to produce the result you see. Nonetheless, variations in these assumptions will not alter the essence of my argument, which is that hedge fund fees and mutual fund fees are remarkably similar when measured properly. Or perhaps it is not at all remarkable, but rather what efficient markets dictate.

Summary

Explicit mutual fund fees are typically less than 1 percent of assets under management. The typical hedge fund charges a base fee of 2 percent and, on top of that, a performance fee equal to 20 percent of net profits. The preponderance of mutual fund performance is driven by passive exposure to the market, yet the fee is applied to the total fund. Hedge fund performance, by design, is independent of market performance. We can mimic a mutual fund's performance by combining an index fund, representing the mutual fund's passive component, with a hedge fund, representing the mutual fund's active component. The fee of the combined fund, comprising a low-cost index fund and a high-cost hedge fund, is remarkably close to the mutual fund fee, revealing that the *implicit* fee of the mutual fund's active component is very close to the hedge fund fee.

NOTES

1. This problem was pointed out to me by Eric Rosenfeld, who posed a problem to my students at MIT who were asked to measure the extent of this performance drag.

2. With these assumptions, a 70/30 mix is optimal for an investor with quadratic utility whose risk aversion coefficient equals 1/3.

ABOUT THE AUTHOR

Mark P. Kritzman is president and CEO of Windham Capital Management, LLC. He also serves as a senior partner of State Street Associates, and he teaches a financial engineering course at MIT's Sloan School. Mr. Kritzman serves on the boards of the Institute for Quantitative Research in Finance and the Investment Fund for Foundations, and on the editorial boards of *Emerging Markets Review*, the *Journal of Alternative Investments*, the *Journal of Asset Management*, the *Journal of Derivatives*, and the *Journal of Investment Management*. Mr. Kritzman has written numerous articles for academic and professional journals and is the author of six books, including *Puzzles of Finance* and *The Portable Financial Analyst*. He has an MBA with distinction from New York University and a CFA designation.

CHAPTER 24

Musings About Hedging

IRA KAWALLER
Kawaller & Company

This chapter is personal.

I've had the good fortune to be able to enjoy a career in finance for more than 25 years and counting. For almost all of that time, I've worked with derivative contracts of one form or another. My focus during the first half of my professional life was on exchange-traded derivatives. As the director of the New York office of the Chicago Mercantile Exchange (CME), I marketed the CME's financial contracts, including futures and options pertaining to interest rates, currencies, and equity markets. Since then, my scope has broadened to include over-the-counter derivatives as well. For the most part, however, I've stayed with pretty traditional tools: futures, forwards, options, and swaps—plain-vanilla derivatives and textbook applications.

At the end of 1998, the CME closed its New York office, and I started consulting. A niche had developed that turned out to work for me. Just about that time, the Financial Accounting Standards Board (FASB) had come out with new accounting rules for derivatives and hedging transactions. The rules were (and still are) complex and difficult to apply. The FASB appreciated this problem and recognized that questions were bound to come up. To assist in responding to these questions, the FASB established a Derivatives Implementation Group, which was tasked with advising the FASB on implementation questions being submitted by the public. I was invited to be a member of this group and, with this credential, my consulting tilted toward assisting companies with these concerns.

Shortly after leaving the CME, I also started trading futures and options for myself—something that was prohibited while I was an exchange employee. After establishing a track record, I founded the Kawaller Fund, structured as a commodity pool, and offered my services as a money manager.

I've come to appreciate that many lessons that are commonly understood and accepted by one market segment get overlooked by other market segments. Put another way, hedgers tend to see the world one way, traders see it somewhat differently, and accountants see it yet another way. The perspectives of each, however, are deserving of consideration by the others. That's what this chapter is about.

THE HEDGING ORIENTATION

Hedgers are subject to some preexisting risk, and they use derivatives as overlay positions to mitigate this risk. In my experience, most companies fail to use derivatives to their maximum advantage. The vast majority of companies tend to rely on one tool for each exposure. For instance, most companies that hedge variable interest rate debt rely exclusively on interest rate swaps for their hedging purposes. This strategy has merit, of course, but so do other strategies; and these other strategies warrant consideration, as well.

As an example, from time to time, companies may find it advantageous to use caps to provide one-sided protection against the prospect of higher variable interest rates, leaving the prospect of being able to enjoy the benefit of lower rates, should they occur. Alternatively, they might consider using collars or corridors instead of swaps.[1] Making the selection of one strategy without consideration of other alternatives is simply shortsighted. If these alternatives are categorically ignored, the potential opportunities that might otherwise be achieved would be lost.

A single-minded approach to hedging isn't unique to interest rate hedgers. In almost any market sector—pertaining to interest rates, currencies, or commodity prices—companies tend to rely on a single risk management tool with a single associated hedging objective. Different times and different conditions (i.e., different price relationships) would likely change the balance of preference for one tool over another, but you have to evaluate relative costs and benefits on an ongoing basis to be able to capitalize on opportunities when they arise.

Beyond the determination of the preferred hedging objective (and thus the appropriate derivative construction), the question of *how much* to hedge is often approached suboptimally. I favor imposing a systematic procedure that sets a specific planning horizon and ranges of hedge coverage within that horizon. For instance, consider the company with an ongoing need to buy euro-denominated goods. The company might operate with a three-year planning horizon, where its policy stipulates hedging 50 to 70 percent of the prospective euro-denominated purchases expected to occur in the first year, 30 to 50 percent of the second year's exposures, and 10 to 30 percent of the third year's exposures. The hedge positions would likely be adjusted higher as time goes by, all else remaining equal. This approach still affords considerable discretion to the hedge manager; but at the same time, it ensures that at least some risk mitigation will occur.

Presumably, the appeal of the declining coverage for the further exposures derives from the greater uncertainty for the more distant events. Any comments to the contrary notwithstanding, hedgers will likely be predisposed to hedging more of their exposures when their fear of an adverse market move is more pressing, and vice versa. Moreover, we tend to have a greater confidence in our capacity to forecast near-term versus long-term.

While this approach is common to foreign exchange (forex) hedgers, it tends *not* to be used for variable interest rate exposures. That surprises me. If the concept has appeal, why wouldn't it be applied more broadly? Beats me. The parallel hedge treatment in the context of most interest rate risk might call for applying amortizing swaps (i.e., swaps with declining notional amounts over their terms) to variable interest rate exposures; but this rarely happens. Amortizing swaps tend to be used in conjunction with amortizing principal amounts on exposures, or not at all.[2]

This determination of *how much* to hedge deserves ongoing consideration. Hedging is a process. It's not a trade. Thus, the prudent approach should track the net exposure (i.e., the unhedged portion of the company's risk) and modify the hedge coverage if and when this net exposure falls outside of an acceptable range. All too often these subsequent adjustments to the hedge position aren't considered in any sort of disciplined way.

Suppose you've put on a hedge—any market, any hedging construction—and further suppose that subsequent to putting on this hedge, the risk being hedged starts to be realized. In response to these market conditions, the hedge gains in value. Now what? Should the hedge be terminated or continued? Although there's no right answer here, the resolution should be well considered—not ad hoc. Understand that if the hedge were terminated, on the one hand, the hedge gains would, of course, be captured; but we'd no longer be protected from further adverse market moves. On the other hand, if the hedge position was maintained and the underlying price trend reversed direction, we'd necessarily have to give up the previously generated hedge gains. Clearly, our course of action should be to reflect our best judgment about the future. There's no getting around that. The only wrong response would be to ignore the situation and blindly proceed without reconsidering how much hedge coverage should be maintained.

Some companies have no regularly scheduled assessments of hedge coverage. Even so, they may (or may not) react to some precipitous market move or to some significant structural change in their organization. With such a development, they wake up to the fact that their net exposure is out of kilter and something needs to be done. A better approach would be to operate with regularly scheduled reviews, augmented by more episodic considerations in response to changes in the economic landscape.

So how frequently should these reassessments be done? Annually, quarterly, monthly, weekly, daily, hourly? I tend to believe they should be more frequent than the reporting interval, but I have no bias favoring any *particular* horizon length for this purpose. That said, my suspicion is that few hedgers would opt for hourly or daily reviews. Somehow, that frequency would seem to move us from our perch as *hedgers* into the world of *traders*. With especially frequent reassessments, it's unlikely that the aggregate gains or losses of a hedge over time will correspond to the gains or losses on the exposure over virtually any accounting horizon. This outcome might not necessarily be a bad thing, however.

Suppose the hedger imposed a hedge to protect against rising prices just before these prices moved sharply higher. Then, with prices at or around their peak and the perceived threat of *further* price increases no longer pressing, assume the hedger now terminates his or her derivative position. Clearly, if prices retrace their rise, returning to their original level, this hedger would capture the gains on the hedge with no corresponding change in the price of the hedged item. To my mind, this example is illustrative of one of the more attractive scenarios under the myriad of possible *ex post* hedge outcomes. The fact that the hedge gains don't correspond to losses for the hedged item doesn't bother me a bit.

Before moving onto the next section, I have one heretical point to make about hedging: With every application of a derivative contract, at the inception of the hedge, it's not clear that the hedge will gain or lose. Clearly, though, hedgers would have to expect the derivative to make money or else it would be unlikely that the hedge would be transacted in the first place. Put another way, we tend to put on hedges when we perceive the adverse price move to be more likely. It's all well and good to claim that, as a hedger, we don't care about whether the hedge makes or loses because the exposure would be generating the opposite effect, but it's hard to imagine a company entering into hedges with the expectation that these hedges will generate losses.

The question of expected gains or losses aside, we might still favor hedging because we expect it to foster lower income volatility, which we might expect to work to the benefit of our company's valuation. (Investors tend to reward companies with lower income volatility with higher price-earnings [P/E] ratios, all else remaining equal.) Thus, we might be prepared to lose *some* money in the short run. In the long run, however, it's not clear that this is an appropriate trade-off to make if the cost of attaining lower income volatility is reduced expected earnings.

This concern is especially vexing because, in the general case, hedges tend to cover only part of their exposures. Thus, in terms of the bottom line of the company's performance, the company is actually better off making losses on its hedging derivatives, as that would mean even greater gains on the (larger) exposure. We find ourselves in the awkward position of putting on derivative positions and then hoping that they generate losses. Weird.

THE TRADING ORIENTATION

Although there may be about as many trading styles as there are traders, I'd expect the vast majority of professional traders to agree on the following points (in no particular order):

- Financial market prices (and hence derivatives prices) exhibit considerable random variability.
- You can't reliably pick market tops and bottoms.
- To be successful, you have to limit losses—which are inevitable for active traders.
- *All* price projections deserve skepticism, but the degree of skepticism should rise with the length of the forecast horizon. (We can be more confident of near-term forecasts than we can be of longer-term forecasts.)

These four points should influence the way hedgers behave. For instance, given the decision to enter into or exit from a hedge, phasing into hedge positions rather than effecting a single transaction may be an appealing tactic. This point is especially compelling when you appreciate the typical way in which companies size their hedge portions in the first place. Except in rare circumstances, hedging need not be—and in my judgment, should not be—an all-or-nothing proposition. In the general case, when an exposure looms, most companies will decide to hedge only a portion of the exposure, rather than all of it.

In making this decision, it's useful to realize that the portion of the exposure that the entity chooses to hedge is revealing. It says something about the hedging entity's market view. Consider the foreign currency hedger exposed to the risk of a stronger foreign currency. The use of a forward contract locks up the exchange rate for some future value date. In effect, entering into this contract today (as opposed to leaving the exposure unhedged) is a bet that the exchange rate *will* move adversely, *from today*. Leaving the exposure unhedged, in contrast, is a bet that the prospective exchange rate change (by the value date) will be beneficial. The term *hedge* is somewhat of a misnomer in this instance. Fifty-fifty coverage, meaning 50 percent of the exposure is hedged and 50 percent of the exposure is left unhedged, is the only hedge position that reflects a neutral or agnostic view of the course of exchange rates. Does that mean that this 50–50 hedge ratio *should* be instituted? Not necessarily. Business judgments should be able to override, but decision makers should understand when they are taking a market view and be held responsible for deviating from the neutral standard.

A possible exception may arise in connection with companies that use derivatives to effect a spread—such as a financial intermediary that seeks to lock in a net interest margin or a commodity distributor that buys product from a supplier and sells it to a customer. In these cases, the enterprise may be largely immune to sharp changes in interest rates or commodity prices, as both revenues and expenses respond similarly to the underlying interest rate or price change. Thus, the hedges are designed to compensate for timing imbalances. Even in such situations, though, it's a rare company that operates on a fully-hedged basis. The more typical case is one where some exposure remains.

In any case, most hedgers come to the determination of how much to hedge fairly casually. Put another way, the hedge coverage is usually determined without a great deal of rigor. Usually, some fairly arbitrary portion of the exposure is selected as the amount to be hedged. For example, the person/committee tasked with the responsibility of sizing the hedge picks 50 percent for the exposure, rather than 40 percent or 60 percent. The decision is hardly the stuff of higher mathematics. It simply comes down to a business decision.

How much we hedge, though, should likely be influenced by the pricing of these derivatives, but this consideration is too frequently overlooked. Again, returning to the forex hedger considering the use of forward contracts to lock up exchange rates on prospective purchases, wouldn't it make sense to employ a process that covers some minimal portion of the exposure at the start, but where there are standing orders to add to the hedge coverage if and when opportunities arise to lock in even more attractive exchange rates?

This approach can be applied in the reverse direction if the exchange rate starts to move beneficially, as well. Notice that this adjustment process would result in buying cheap forwards and selling expensive forwards. Thus, if exchange rates fluctuated within a trading range, our practice would end up generating incremental trading gains. As always, the ever-present risk is that anything not hedged is exposed. Thus, whatever trading rule we might be tempted to apply, the original question of how much to hedge needs to be readdressed on some periodic basis, independently from any technical (i.e., trading-determined) adjustments that we might otherwise be making.

THE ACCOUNTING ORIENTATION

When it comes to derivatives accounting, it is critical to differentiate between two environments: the trading environment versus the corporate finance environment.

In a trading environment, the entity assembles a portfolio of instruments (including derivatives), and the objective is simply to generate gains through any combination of interest income, dividends, and capital gains. Here, accounting for derivatives is a trivial exercise. Derivatives are carried on the balance sheet at their market values, and gains or losses are recorded in current earnings.

It's much more complicated in a non-trading, corporate finance environment. Here, the concept of special hedge accounting is of particular relevance. For hedgers in this environment, it is logical and desirable to record the earnings impacts of derivatives concurrently with the earnings impacts of the hedged items. For instance, if a swap is being used to hedge prospective variable interest rate exposures, it's quite understandable that the hedger would want the swap's current period settlements to impact current earnings—but nothing else. That is, with the sacrosanct requirement to carry the swap on the balance sheet at its fair market value, this type of hedger would prefer *not* to record the change in present value of the swap in current earnings. The hedger would want this component of results to be deferred.[3] Unfortunately, while this desired accounting treatment *may* be available, it can't be counted upon. Special hedge accounting would preserve this pairing of the derivatives' earnings impacts with those of the hedged items, but this treatment requires specifically crafted hedge documentation, and the qualifying criteria are often difficult to satisfy. Even if these criteria are satisfied when hedging is initiated, in many cases the authority to apply hedge accounting could be terminated midway through the hedge.

It is often said that Financial Accounting Standard No. 133 (FAS 133)—the governing rules for accounting for derivatives and hedge accounting, which has since been recodified as Accounting Standard Codification (ASC) 815—is "form driven," meaning that if the documentation isn't correctly presented, that fact by itself could disallow hedge accounting. Hedgers need to appreciate that their documentation will detail much of the qualifying criteria to enable the application of hedge accounting, and they will be held to these requirements. History is replete with examples of companies specifying conditions in their documentation that they've then been unable to satisfy—often for seemingly trivial or stylistic reasons—thereby precluding the use of hedge accounting. Whether you handle this responsibility in-house or with a consultant, this responsibility needs to be in the hands of someone with specialized knowledge and experience. Too many pitfalls lie in waiting, and the consequence of getting caught could be severe.

Without hedge accounting, unrealized future gains or losses *for all prospective periods in the hedging horizon* will be recorded in current income. For example, for the variable interest rate hedger with, say, a swap having five years of remaining life, if interest rates change, the current earnings effect will include not just the most immediate settlement amount, but also gains or losses relating to all *future* settlements. In effect, if no hedge is in place, the company will realize income volatility relating to just the current period. With a hedge in place but without hedge accounting, the current period's income volatility could be many times higher.

This situation creates a dilemma for the hedge manager. If hedge accounting is tenuous, a question arises as to whether to (1) put a derivative position in place and take the risk of (substantially) higher income volatility if hedge accounting can't be applied or (2) remain unhedged, where income volatility might reasonably be expected to be less severe. All else remaining equal, those entities at risk of losing the authority to apply hedge accounting will be discouraged from hedging, and some might fail to implement prudent long-run risk management strategies in deference to this short-term consideration.

To be fair, the reader should appreciate that, as of this writing, the Financial Accounting Standards Board (i.e., the entity responsible for promulgating accounting rules) is evaluating the current accounting rules for derivatives, and changes are being considered. Philosophically, the proposed new rules would seem to be tilting toward lowering the bar in terms of hedge accounting prerequisites. That said, the devil is in the details, and I'm not at all convinced that the end results of this process will necessarily make (and keep) hedge accounting more accessible. This issue is one that deserves an ongoing watchful eye.

There is one area under the accounting rules, however, that is especially problematic and is likely to remain that way. Specifically, I'm referring to interest rate hedging where the hedged item is fixed-rate debt. Here's the problem: There are two major types of hedge accounting: cash flow hedge accounting and fair value hedge accounting. Cash flow hedge accounting applies to exposures associated with future, uncertain cash flows. Thus, by default, any exposure to fixed interest payments cannot apply cash flow hedge accounting. The only avenue available for such exposures is fair value hedge accounting.

Fair value hedge accounting requires the derivative's gain or loss to be recorded in current earnings, but so, too, is the gain or loss of the hedged item, due to the risk being hedged. A prerequisite for qualifying for this treatment is making the statement that the derivative's result is expected to (closely) offset the change in the fair value of the hedged item (i.e., the fixed-rate debt), due to the risk being hedged. The problem is that for the classic interest rate objective of swapping from fixed to floating, this outcome should *not* be expected.

Consider the case of a company that simultaneously issues five-year fixed-rate debt at par and simultaneously enters into a five-year pay floating/receive fixed swap. Assuming that the notional amount of the swap matches the principal on the debt, and the swap's accrual periods are aligned with the debt's accrual periods, this swap will perfectly serve to replace fixed interest payments with variable payments based on the variable index of the swap. There's virtually *no* chance, however, that the gains or losses on this swap will offset the change in the fair value of the debt. Remember, over the life of the debt, the change in the fair value will be zero, but the gain or loss on the swap will be the sum of the cash flows paid or received over the life of the swap. Although we don't know what this swap gain or loss will be, we can be sure it will be something other than zero!

This isn't to say that companies aren't managing to qualify for and apply fair value hedge accounting in these situations. They are—but with great difficulty.

And in fact, unless or until the FASB authorizes a significant overhaul of fair value hedging rules, it's likely that this problem will persist.

CONCLUSION

Typically, managers learn about hedging one instrument at a time. They start with their predominant risk category (e.g., interest rate risk, currency exchange rate risk, or commodity price risk), and then they identify the derivative of choice and learn how to use it. The textbook application is conceptually quite simple: Determine the amount to be hedged, and enter into a derivative with the derivative position sized to compensate for this magnitude of exposure.

This chapter strives to move to a higher step on the learning curve. It intends to highlight the fact that hedging is—or should be—a dynamic process. It recommends that hedgers review their exposures and hedges periodically and adjust their positions in type and size as market conditions vary and risk appetites evolve. It further looks to the experience of traders as a source of knowledge and experience that could be relevant in connection with tactical aspects of how hedge positions are transacted. And finally, the chapter warns that hedgers need to be fully cognizant of how their hedge positions will impact reported earnings. Unfortunately, the current accounting regime may serve to discourage hedgers from pursuing prudent risk management goals due to considerations relating to the timing of income recognition.

NOTES

1. In this context, a collar would be constructed by buying a cap and selling a floor, thereby imposing a best-case outcome and a worst-case outcome for interest expenses. A corridor involves buying a lower-strike cap and selling a higher-strike cap. This combination locks in the interest expense if the market interest rate falls between the two respective strike yields, leaving the company exposed beneficially to market interest rates below the lower strike, and exposed adversely to market rates above the upper strike.

2. It may be cumbersome to make incremental adjustments to the hedge coverage with swaps. Eurodollar futures/options, however, could serve quite conveniently for this purpose.

3. Changes in the present value of the swap are ephemeral (i.e., swaps typically have a zero present value at inception and at termination). Put another way, *ex post*, gains or losses of swaps held to term are equal to the sum of the settlements. Any gains or losses from sources other than the swap's settlements will necessarily have to be netted out over the life of the swap.

ABOUT THE AUTHOR

Ira Kawaller: Prior to founding the Kawaller Fund and Kawaller & Company—the former being a commodity pool and the latter being a consulting company that assists companies in their use of derivatives—Kawaller held positions with the Chicago Mercantile Exchange, J. Aron & Company, AT&T, and the Board of Governors of the Federal Reserve System. He received a PhD in economics from Purdue

University and has held adjunct professorships at Columbia University and the Polytechnic Institute of New York University. He is currently a board member of Hatteras Financial, a publicly traded real estate investment trust (REIT); and he has also served on a variety of professional boards and committees, including the board of the International Association of Financial Engineers and the Financial Accounting Standards Board's Derivatives Implementation Group.

CHAPTER 25

Operational Risk

MONIQUE MILLER
WR Managed Accounts LLC

INTRODUCTION AND CURRENT STATE OF KNOWLEDGE

An appropriate definition of operational risk has been debated in the financial community for decades. In the past, many have used an all-inclusive definition that classifies operational risk as any risk that is not categorized as market risk or credit risk. The Basel Committee on Banking Supervision came out with a definition of operational risk several years ago that has been generally adopted by the financial services industry, although its comprehensiveness continues to be debated. The Basel Committee, in consultation with the banking community, crafted the following definition: "Operational risk is the risk of loss resulting from inadequate or failed internal processes, people and systems or from external events. This definition includes legal risk but excludes strategic and reputational risk."[1]

No matter how it is defined, insufficient management of operational risk can be devastating to every type of organization. The highly publicized corporate scandals that led to the bankruptcies of Enron and WorldCom can be attributed in part to operational risk. Banks and trading firms spend tens of millions of dollars every year to manage and measure operational risk, and buy-side investors are demanding tighter controls and increased transparency from their investment managers in order to avoid fraud and other operations-related losses.

The emergence of more sophisticated financial products, coupled with economic and market factors such as globalization, a rise in electronic trading, and the growth of the hedge fund industry, has increased the potential for operational risk events and made it even more difficult to identify, measure, and manage risk. Complex derivative instruments, risk transfer markets, and the creation of illiquid over-the-counter products with their associated lack of transparency, contribute to increased risk and added difficulty in monitoring operational risk.

The best way for managers and investors to mitigate operational risk in this modern market environment is to recognize the warning signs for potential risk and understand that risks are interrelated. It is no longer appropriate to classify a risk event as only market-risk driven or credit-risk driven. Most loss events include an operational risk component. As financial products become more complex, so does the relationship across various risk types.

In order for an organization to measure, manage, and mitigate risks, the relationships among risk types and the interdependencies of a firm's business units must be recognized and understood. Risks within an organization should not be looked at as silos. A collaborative approach to risk management is required. Business processes should be coordinated, and staff should be well trained and have a thorough understanding of the business strategy, the market environment, and the complexity of financial instruments.

A BRIEF HISTORY OF THE BUSINESS OF OPERATIONAL RISK

As good business practice, financial institutions have always focused on efficiently managing people, processes, and procedures. The emergence of operational risk management as a business discipline arose in the 1990s as a result of some high-profile and highly publicized loss events, including the Barings Bank collapse.

In February 1995, Barings Bank, a respected institution with a long and profitable history, suffered a trading loss of US$1.3 billion, which was more than the bank's entire capital base. The bank was forced to declare bankruptcy and the trader who was responsible for the loss was sentenced to six and a half years in prison.[2]

The highly publicized collapse forced the financial community to focus on operational risk. At the time, it was unfathomable to the financial community that a single person's actions could cause such overwhelming harm to an established organization. Prior to the Barings collapse, it was unusual for management to be held responsible for tolerating loose internal controls and failing to act on warning signs for potential risks. The bank's collapse was a wake-up call for many managers to look inside their own organizations for similar deficiencies.

The loss occurred as a result of futures and options trading in the Nikkei index on the Singapore International Money Exchange by derivatives trader Nick Leeson. Leeson made unauthorized speculative trades in futures contracts that initially generated large profits for Barings. However, losses soon were incurred, and by the end of 1992 Leeson had lost £2 million. The losses escalated to over £200 million by the end of 1994.

There were many operational and management failures that contributed to the loss. One primary contributor was the lack of division of responsibilities within the bank. Because of cost-cutting measures implemented by Barings, Leeson had dual responsibility for settlements as well as trading. This enabled him to have access to the firm's operations, giving him the ability to conceal the losses over several years. Additionally, there were unclear reporting lines in the bank, and a failure to manage the trader in both his investment and noninvestment roles. Because the transactions were in derivative instruments, managers did not look into the unusual activity because of the complexity of the product. An internal audit report stated multiple deficiencies with respect to the segregation of duties, but management failed to implement the recommendations.

As a result of the Barings collapse and other loss events, financial industry professionals began to focus on the importance of operational risk and how to best manage risk in large organizations. In September 1998, the Basel Committee on Banking Supervision published a survey of 30 major banks. The following common themes arose with respect to operational risk:[3]

- *Management oversight.* Awareness of operational risk was increasing among senior management, but most felt that the primary responsibility for managing risk was with each individual business unit.
- *Risk measurement and information systems.* Awareness of operational risk as a separate risk category was just emerging at the time of the survey. Many banks were in the very early stages of developing a monitoring and measurement framework.
- *Monitoring.* Banks had monitoring processes for volume, turnover, errors, settlements, and so on, but few had taken the step of incorporating this data into formal operational risk measures.
- *Control of operational risk.* Internal controls and internal audits were seen as the most effective methods of controlling operational risk.
- *Policies and procedures.* Banks were actively reviewing their policies and procedures to see if they were adequate or could be expanded to mitigate risk.
- *View of possible role of supervisors.* There was a clear preference for qualitative management and the potential for supervisors to mitigate risk and raise awareness of potential risks across the organization.

The importance of operational risk management emerged as a priority in the banking community, and in June 1999 the Basel committee called for capital charges for operational risks as part of its proposed Capital Adequacy Framework. By the time the Basel II committee released the revised framework in November 2005, operational risk measurement had evolved into a growing discipline with an industry focus on how to best quantify risk.

In the years following the release, the international banking community made strides in improving risk management. Most large banks began using sophisticated calculations for operational risk measurement and relied on detailed databases to monitor both internal and external loss events.

Unfortunately, these measures failed in predicting and protecting against the unparalleled losses that occurred as a result of the 2007–2009 financial crisis. In fact, inadequate operational risk controls on the part of financial institutions and rating agencies contributed significantly to the crisis. Financial institutions clearly did not do enough to stress-test their internal valuation models and to monitor the size and concentration of risks on their books. Clearly, management should have done more to oversee and understand the risks being taken in their various business units.

OVERVIEW OF SUBJECT

Although the Basel II framework and the efforts leading up to the policies were helpful in focusing the industry on the importance of operational risk issues, recent history has taught us that firms need to do more to understand the sources of risk and the interdependencies across risk types. In the effort to mitigate risk, financial engineering has contributed to the establishment of risk transfer markets, hedging products, and increasingly sophisticated financial instruments. But along with this innovation, additional sources of risk and new relationships across risk types have developed. The added complexities that arise from new markets, products, and players must be addressed, and extreme scenarios must be considered when assessing potential losses.

The Joint Forum of the Basel Committee, the International Organization of Securities Commissions, and the International Association of Insurance Supervisors recognizes the new risk landscape, noting that "risk concentrations at most financial conglomerates are still chiefly identified, measured and managed within separate risk categories and within business lines."[4] The Joint Forum refers to this type of risk identification as "silo management."

The Joint Forum identifies "second order effects" that should be incorporated into a firm's risk management policy. These are "indirect effects to a firm(s) exposure(s) caused by a change in economic or financial market conditions, from a shock or change in policy. This can be within a risk category or from contagion from one risk category to another risk category."[5]

The Joint Forum acknowledges that organizations' efforts to integrate risks across business lines have led to growth in risk transfer markets (such as asset-backed securities and collateralized debt obligations), which could make identifying and measuring risk even more complex through the introduction of new risk exposures. The report goes on to note that certain risk measurement and mitigation techniques may not be adequate in stressful markets.

This became apparent during the recent credit crisis. Most risk models did not take into account the added liquidity risk that emerged as credit markets became stressed. Additionally, models failed to predict contagion across asset classes and geographic regions. As credit facilities froze in late 2007 and 2008, international stock markets also became stressed, causing additional losses.

A white paper published by Algorithmics further analyzes the relationship between risk types, specifically operational risk and market risk.[6] The paper observes that there are spikes in the number and severity of reported operational risk loss events in times of high market volatility. Operational loss events are generally recorded at the time they are discovered (which corresponds to times of high market stress), but the action that caused the loss generally takes place over a long period of time. The paper concludes that increased market volatility enhances the probability that a loss event will be detected, or may increase the severity of a loss, but does not increase the number of operational risk events. The report goes on to note that volatile market environments often lead to increased oversight and controls in financial institutions, which could also increase the likelihood that a loss would be discovered.

This was the case in identifying the Bernard Madoff Ponzi scheme. The volatility of the overall markets and investor liquidation requests contributed to exposing the fraud. Despite whistle-blower complaints to the Securities and Exchange Commission (SEC) and other regulators that it was mathematically impossible to achieve the consistent gains that Madoff reported to investors, and the contention that Madoff's three-person accounting firm would not have been able to process the high frequency of transactions made in a legitimate fund of that size, the regulators did little to investigate. The Ponzi scheme probably started in the late 1980s or early 1990s, but the fraud was not exposed until the end of 2008 when Madoff had difficulties meeting $7 billion in redemption requests.

The high-profile failure of the Bear Stearns hedge funds further illustrates the interdependence across risk types, and how market volatility can magnify operational losses. Bear Stearns had large losses in two of its hedge fund businesses. The High Grade Fund, which had $1 billion in assets, lost 5 percent in the beginning of 2007. The Enhanced Leverage Fund, which had $600 million in assets, lost 23 percent over the same time period. Both funds invested in bonds, mortgage-backed securities, collateralized debt obligations (CDOs), and hard-to-value exotic CDOs with investments backed by subprime mortgages. The Enhanced Leverage Fund, which was launched in the fall of 2006, invested in more risky tranches and took much more leverage than did the High Grade Fund.[7]

The hedge fund losses were largely attributed to market risk, credit risk, and liquidity risk factors, but operational risk factors also came into play. There were valuation issues for some of the more illiquid instruments that arose as the markets became stressed. The Algo First database of case studies reports that in a June 2007 investor letter, the fund revised its April loss from 6.5 percent to 18.97 percent. According to a *BusinessWeek* report in October 2007, many of the more illiquid instruments had historically been valued by the fund's management team "in the absence of readily ascertainable market values,"[8] but the mispricings were not reported until a severe market event occurred.

In addition, the fund's decision to use a high leverage factor when investing in high-risk assets must also be questioned. The Enhanced Leverage Fund was launched because of the initial success of the High Grade Fund, which had enjoyed 40 consecutive months of growth as of January 2007. However, the risk profiles of the two funds were very different, particularly as the markets became stressed. Not only was the leverage "enhanced," but the investments were much more exotic and illiquid in the newer fund.

As a result of the losses, in June 2007, Bear Stearns pledged $1.6 billion in loans to keep the High Grade Fund from collapsing, but did nothing to save the Enhanced Leverage fund. But the fall of the Enhanced Leverage Fund weakened the High Grade Fund, forcing both funds to file for bankruptcy in July 2007. The failure of the hedge funds caused reputational damage to Bear Stearns, which was one of many contributing factors to the firm's decline and subsequent bailout in March 2008.

MORE ON HEDGE FUNDS AND OPERATIONAL RISK

The hedge fund industry has grown precipitously in the past 20 years. There are currently more than 8,000 hedge funds with over $2 trillion in assets under management.[9] The types of investors in hedge fund products have also changed over the past decade. As the hedge fund landscape becomes more institutionalized, more pension and institutional assets are moving into alternative investments. Additionally, new registered products are being developed for retail investors.

As the industry continues to grow, risk also increases. Because hedge funds typically use more sophisticated investment strategies than mutual funds do, they are considered to have higher market risk profiles. But because the industry is currently not required to disclose strategy or business model details, there is a higher potential for operational risk events. A Capco white paper published in 2003 reports that 50 percent of hedge fund failures are due to operational risk. The study found that the most common operational shortcomings have been the misrepresentation of investments, misappropriation of funds, unauthorized trading, and inadequate resources.[10]

The Asset Managers' Committee of the President's Working Group on Financial Markets issued a best practices document in April 2008, stating:

> We sought to identify and address key areas where best practices would most effectively promote investor protection and reduce systemic risk. These areas include:
>
> **Disclosure**: *Strong disclosure practices that provide investors with the information they need to determine whether to invest in a fund, to monitor an investment, and to make a decision whether to redeem an investment;*
> **Valuation**: *Robust valuation procedures that call for a segregation of responsibilities, through written policies, oversight, and other measures for the valuation of assets, including a specific focus on hard-to-value assets;*
> **Risk management**: *Comprehensive risk management that emphasizes measuring, monitoring, and managing risk, including stress testing of portfolios for market and liquidity risk management;*
> **Trading and business operations**: *Sound and controlled operations and infrastructure, supported by adequate resources and checks and balances in operations, to enable a manager to achieve best industry practices in all other areas;*
> **Compliance, conflicts, and business practices**: *Specific practices to address conflicts of interest and promote the highest standards of professionalism and a culture of compliance.*[11]

Disclosure policies across funds vary, and, for this reason, it is often difficult for investors to interpret the information that is provided by hedge fund managers. Few funds provide position-level transparency, which makes it difficult for investors to monitor valuation policies or aggregate risk across funds. If more hedge funds continue to experience large operational losses, investors will push harder for increased transparency from their managers.

Because of this lack of transparency, many investors are moving toward managed accounts for their hedge fund investments. In a managed account structure, the hedge fund trades the strategy pari passu in a separate investor-owned account. This gives the investor greater transparency into the trading strategy, and the ability to aggregate risk exposures across investments in order to monitor guidelines. Although it is estimated that a significant amount of hedge fund growth will come from managed accounts, investors need to ensure that they are using the information effectively. It is not enough to have position-level detail if risk exposures are not properly aggregated, measured, and monitored.

Investors should scrutinize the performance differential between the benchmark fund and the separately managed account. If there is a tracking error or there are performance shortfalls in the managed account, investors should understand the source of the differences. There are cases where a hedge fund manager is unable to trade pari passu in a managed account due to capital constraints or liquidity factors. But operational risk can also arise in managed accounts in the form of broker or manager misallocations.

Whether investing in a managed account or a fund structure, proper investor due diligence is vital. While some hedge funds look more like investment banks, with significant infrastructure and large operations and technology staffs to support the varied business lines, most funds are small, and either outsource their operational functions or have small staffs to perform non-investment-related functions. Many industry groups have published due diligence questionnaires, which include recommendations for verifying processes and procedures, interviewing personnel, and ensuring that proper legal and compliance policies are in place. But investors should be aware that checking the boxes of a template is not sufficient due diligence; it is merely a starting point for more detailed examination.

Institutional investors have a fiduciary responsibility to understand the types of risks inherent in hedge funds and to ask questions to determine whether those risks are being managed to acceptable levels. Investors should be familiar with the hedge fund's structure and strategy and be able to identify inadequate resources, potential procedural shortcomings, or significant changes in operational controls. If an investor is uncomfortable with the lack of transparency in a particular fund, it may be better to pass on the investment or demand a separately managed account rather than incur the added risk.

A one-time due diligence effort is not sufficient. Investors need to periodically follow up to ensure that there is no investment style drift or change in operational processes. Investors should also be aware of material changes in personnel or third-party providers. It is an investor's responsibility to make sure that the appropriate operational controls are in place and to insist on adequate transparency and liquidity when making hedge fund investments.

MITIGATING OPERATIONAL RISK

As noted, regulators and investors have made significant efforts to identify and mitigate operational risk in recent years. But as we have seen, operational risk is often closely related to other portfolio risks and can be difficult to measure and monitor. Operational risk events have devastated large institutions as well as small investors. The challenge for managers and investors is to identify where those risks could *potentially* be present in order to limit exposure to losses.

The following list identifies the types of warning signs that managers and investors should be mindful of when assessing the potential for operational risk:

- *Large-scale growth in a particular market or industry.* Rapid growth can lead to market bubbles and infrastructure failures. In April 2008, the International Swaps and Derivatives Association, Inc. (ISDA)[12] reported that the notional growth in the credit default swap market had risen 81 percent from the year prior.[13] It is not surprising that the credit markets became stressed when there was bubble-type participation. As markets grow rapidly, it is often difficult for organizations to implement the appropriate technology, valuation processes, and infrastructure to support the business.
- *Outsized profits can often mean outsized risks.* The hedge fund Amaranth,[14] which lost over $6 billion on natural gas spread trades in 2006, reportedly had made over $1 billion in its energy trading division the prior year. The fund was up in excess of 30 percent in the first four months of 2006, significantly more than similar multi-strategy funds. When the fund closed its doors in the fall of 2006, it was the largest hedge fund failure on record at the time. One contributing factor to the fund's failure was that the firm's risk models were

unable to properly identify the unique risks inherent in trading calendar spreads in the energy markets. Risk managers should better evaluate the results of their models, and benchmark the results of several models, in order to properly assess the probability of loss in certain trading strategies.

- *New market participants add new risks.* In recent years, financial institutions have become more complex and have branched out from their traditional business lines. Hedge funds have become an important source of liquidity to international financial markets. Private equity funds are becoming increasingly involved in corporate governance, and investment banks are active in proprietary trading and in asset management. For many new entrants it takes time to develop robust infrastructure and staff to support the business functions. Operational risks can result due to lack of experience or commitment to a particular business line.

- *Market complexity.* As the field of financial engineering brings us new markets and products, often the complexity of these nascent markets can be a risk factor. Illiquidity, improper hedging, incorrect valuation, and inadequate infrastructure are all common problems when investing in new products.

- *Business strategy.* Sometimes the operational components of a particular business are in place but the overall business strategy is unsound and a source of operational risk. For example, Northern Rock's[15] growth strategy relied on capital market funding rather than on deposits. Because of the credit crisis and the dislocation in lending markets, the bank faced a major liquidity crisis.[16]

- *Changes in investment environment or business cycle.* Volatility shocks could expose operational risk events that remained hidden or were less severe in ordinary market environments.

- *Crowding into a particular investment strategy.* Often market participants have similar strategies or are invested in the same assets. In the case of a shock, there can be liquidity constraints that further magnify the impact of the event. This was the case in the summer of 2007, when there was a sharp rise in volatility in the equity markets. As many hedge funds (particularly quantitative strategies) started to unwind their positions to reduce risk, there were abnormal moves in some markets and sectors due to herding behavior and overcrowding in certain trades.

- *Deep cost-cutting efforts.* Institutions can increase operational risk by implementing cost-cutting measures. We saw in the Barings Bank case that Nick Leeson had oversight of support functions due to budgetary constraints. Very often organizations try to save money by moving operations to less expensive locations, hiring less qualified people, or failing to implement appropriate technology. This can be a costly mistake if it leads to an operational risk event.

- *Risk culture.* Particularly when making allocations to hedge funds, investors should understand and be comfortable with the risk culture of the firm. Some firms have sophisticated operational processes and understand the importance of managing risks. They apply leverage conservatively and do not take overly concentrated positions. Others do not manage their businesses to mitigate unnecessary risks. Due diligence can shed light on risk culture and help investors understand the inherent risks of the organization.

Given these risk factors, the most important tool organizations have in mitigating operational risk is a qualified and knowledgeable team. As noted, firms often try to save money on their operations by moving important business functions to remote locations or by hiring inexperienced staff to perform and manage noninvestment activities. Given the added complexity of the markets, the interdependencies of different types of risks, and the potential cost of an operational risk event, it is crucial that firms attract and train high-quality operational management and teams.

Risks across business lines are sometimes similar and should be aggregated. It is important to not silo risk exposures within particular businesses or departments. Risk managers should be familiar with the firm's strategies across all business units in order to perform comprehensive risk assessment.

It is important for firms to have robust technology and current databases to manage their business operations and their risks, but the systems are secondary to understanding how to properly use the technology and the information to evaluate risk. Risk managers use stress testing to measure what-if scenarios for market risk. Similar tests should be applied to operational risk management. But without thorough knowledge of potential risk indicators, or an understanding of the market environment, managers are unable to design the appropriate measures, ask the right questions, or recognize the warning signs of operational risk events.

Similarly, it is important that processes and procedures be documented and followed throughout the firm. However, it takes more than blindly following a procedure to mitigate operational risk. Staff should be well educated about the business in order to determine whether the processes are effective. Too often operational staff will go through the motions without thinking about why a particular procedure is being performed and how the various processes can be made better. Clerks and operational managers are in the best position to notice a rogue trading or other risk event. If staff members are not properly trained or compensated, it is unlikely that they will be proactive in helping to identify risks.

In order for firms to be effective in managing operational risk, they need to adopt the appropriate risk management culture. Risk committees with members from various departments, including some who are not investment professionals, should be formed to review the details of the business, the support infrastructure, and the risk management process. Risk management should be a priority across the entire organization, and risks should be aggregated across business lines.

It is the role of financial engineers to further develop risk methodologies, policies, and technology to appropriately measure and monitor risks in a changing market environment. As we learned from the recent market crisis, traditional risk management tools that rely on historical data are insufficient. The industry needs to move toward adaptive risk technology and analytics that utilize forward-looking measures that incorporate loss probabilities into the suite of risk measures.

NOTES

1. Basel Committee on Banking Supervision, Basel II: International Convergence of Capital Measurement and Capital Standards: A Revised Framework, November 2005.
2. Algo First database of operational risk case studies.

3. Basel Committee on Banking Supervision, Operational Risk Management, September 1998.

4. The Joint Forum, Cross-Sectoral Review of Group-Wide Identification and Management of Risk Concentrations. April 2008, 3.

5. Ibid., 4.

6. Cagan, Penny, and Yakov Lantsman, "The Cyclicality of Operational Risk: The Tracking Phenomenon Thesis: Dynamics in Number of Operational Risk Events Track Volatile Cycles in the Markets." Algorithmics white paper.

7. Algo First database of operational risk case studies.

8. Goldstein, Matthew, and David Henry. 2007. "Bear Bets Wrong: Two Bear Stearns Hedge Funds Soured by Specializing in Exotic Securities and Unorthodox Practices; Then They Imploded and Helped Set Off a Global Credit Market Meltdown." *BusinessWeek*, October 22.

9. Asset Managers' Committee. 2008. "Best Practices for the Hedge Fund Industry: Report of the Asset Managers' Committee to the President's Working Group on Financial Markets." April 15.

10. Capco. 2003. "Understanding and Mitigating Operational Risk in Hedge Fund Investments," Capco white paper (March).

11. Asset Managers' Committee, "Best Practices for the Hedge Fund Industry."

12. www.isda.org.

13. International Swaps and Derivatives Association, Inc. 2008. "Year-End 2007 Market Survey." April 16.

14. Amaranth Advisors LLC was a $9 billion multi-strategy hedge fund founded by Nicholas Maounis, which was liquidated in 2006 after large losses in energy trading.

15. Northern Rock PLC is a British bank that in September 2007 received liquidity support from the Bank of England due to losses caused by the subprime credit crisis.

16. Algo First database of operational risk case studies.

ABOUT THE AUTHOR

Monique Miller's professional experience lies in investment management, research, and risk management. She is currently the Chief Operating Officer and a Principal at WR Managed Accounts LLC, a hedge fund managed account services and risk aggregation firm. Previously she was division head of a quantitative trading business at Caxton Associates, a New York–based hedge fund. Ms. Miller is on the board of directors of the International Association of Financial Engineers (IAFE) and a co-chair of the IAFE's Operational Risk Committee.

CHAPTER 26

Legal Risk

JORDANA KROHLEY

INTRODUCTION

Legal risk is not simply a concern for lawyers. Whether you are a CEO, CFO, COO, compliance officer, supervisor or regulator, shareholder or bondholder, chances are that legal risk is more a part of your life than ever. Parties recently impacted by the realization of legal risk include investors who bought a Collateralized Debt Obligation (CDO), entered swaps to hedge an Auction-Rate Security (ARS), invested capital with Bernie Madoff, had Lehman Brothers or AIG as a counterparty, owned General Motors equity or debt, had a derivative contract with the subsidiary of a bank that was nationalized in another country, had an Icelandic credit default swap, held super senior credit default swaps "insured" by MBIA, or had a financially engineered transaction with one of the many regional banks that failed during the financial crisis. Accordingly, the analysis of legal risk is one of the critical due diligence concerns of any participant in the financial markets; a party that neglects this province may suffer civil and criminal penalties, be unable to enforce its contract against a counterparty, or discover that it has an unforeseen liability to another party.

Regrettably, the lack of consensus within the financial industry on how to define legal risk is a fitting indicator of the ambiguity and complexity that characterizes the topic. Legal risk can be conceptualized in different ways for different purposes, often overlapping with other categories of risk. To date, the Basel Committee on Banking Supervision does not define legal risk in and of itself, but rather classifies it as a subcomponent of operational risk.[1] On the other hand, legal risk is often associated with market and credit risk. When a counterparty loses a large amount of money on a transaction, reflecting market risk, they may resort to legal action as a means of recovering some of the losses. Similarly, situations of default, reflecting credit risk, invoke questions of contract enforcement, which creates legal uncertainty. Legal risk can also be seen as an environmental risk, because the legal framework in a particular jurisdiction affects the risk of doing business there, or it can be viewed as a strategic risk, affecting a company's decision to move into a particular area of business.

Regardless of the lens through which legal risk is viewed, useful definitions focus on the concept that it consists of two components. First, legal risk arises in addressing questions of *substantive law* on a transaction-specific level. Since most derivatives are bilateral contracts that derive value from changes in an underlying financial instrument, reference price, rate, or index, the legal risk often lies in the bilateral contract and the counterparties negotiating it. When a problem arises with a contract or counterparty, the determination of rights and remedies invokes questions of law. Second, is the risk that the *regulatory environment* may impede market counterparties from enforcing their derivatives contracts or impose penalties for lack of compliance with prescribed obligations. Substantive law and regulation often overlap; for example, courts have adopted concepts of financial regulation and best practice in deciding whether a number of substantive law tests have been satisfied. Thus, a useful working definition of legal risk is: the risk that a transaction will not be enforceable because of a failure in the legal framework, the documentation, or by a counterparty that results in the increased probability of loss.

Legal risks associated with financially-engineered products are typically more ambiguous than those attached to traditional commercial and investment banking products. Unlike loans, most derivatives transactions entail two-way credit exposure, meaning that both counterparties may have an incentive to litigate in the future. Yet the relative immaturity of the derivatives market, and the rapid evolution of products, means that relevant judicial precedent on how to interpret novel contract provisions is often scarce. In addition, derivatives, commonly used to eliminate the currency exposure of borrowers and investors who chose to transact overseas, can involve more cross-border issues than loans or investments. The exposure to multiple legal regimes is problematic as these frequently conflict. Furthermore, since derivatives regulation has historically lagged behind the market's evolution, the risk that the law in a given jurisdiction will change during the life of the contract is elevated.

The costs associated with legal risk are high, both for counterparties and the market as a whole. Aside from the evident burden of direct costs in the form of litigation awards, opportunity costs associated with litigation, including senior management's time, front- and back-office resources, reputational harm, and public exposure of internal policy, are similarly damaging. In many cases, financial firms choose to settle cases despite recovering only a portion of losses owed, simply to avoid the expense of litigation. For markets, legal risk poses a significant threat to overall efficiency because it adversely affects the enforceability of contractual rights and obligations, and generates uncertainty.

In his 2003 keynote address at the Derivatives and Risk Management Conference, the then Vice-Chairman and Chief Legal Officer of Lehman Brothers quoted the G30's 1993 pronouncement: "The greatest risk facing the derivatives industry is not market, credit or operational risk, but legal risk."[2] More than a decade later, as the derivative market suffers record defaults by both dealers and their customers alike, and as legal risk becomes increasingly intertwined with other types of risk, understanding it is more critical than at any other time in the market's history. This chapter provides an overview of key legal risks and legal risk mitigation, examines the chief regulatory regimes that govern financially engineered products, and reviews proposed changes to relevant legislation that will profoundly affect the way the market functions going forward.[3]

KEY LEGAL RISKS

Derivatives invoke myriad legal risks, but a useful starting point in understanding their scope is to survey issues that commonly give rise to litigation. Some of these issues, such as ambiguous documentation, will pose a perpetual risk. Others, such as characterization of products or certain aspects of insolvency, have historically been significantly mitigated by the implementation of legislation designed to improve legal certainty and promote market agility. However, as the financial crisis recalibrates policy makers' risk appetite and leads them to significantly revise legislation, these issues are likely to resurface or change shape.

Regulatory Characterizations

Historically, derivatives in the United States and the United Kingdom were subject to a common-law rule known as the "rule against difference contracts."[4] The rule permitted wagers on anything from wheat prices to interest rates but, in order for a court to enforce the wager, at least one of the parties to the wager had to hold title to the underlying instrument that was the subject of the bet. A CDS contract, for example, would only have been enforced if one of the parties actually owned the bonds (for example) on which the CDS was written. In this context, synthetic derivative transactions, in which no real dealing in the benchmarked underlying asset occurs, could be characterized as illegal gambling devices rather than legitimate derivatives transactions. Such transactions could be declared unenforceable, enabling the losing party to escape its obligations entirely. Indeed, because of authorities' concerns over the ramifications of gambling as a matter of public policy, parties to such transactions could in fact be prohibited from fulfilling their obligations even if both wished to. In recent times, these concerns were largely quelled in the United States and the United Kingdom by legislation that protects derivatives from the prohibitions of gambling laws. In mid-2010, however, these protections were partially eliminated in the United States through regulatory reforms enacted in the wake of the financial crisis, meaning that the issue may be revisited in the near future (see the section entitled *Regulatory Evolution—United States* below for more information).

Another potential pitfall attributable to the regulatory characterization of a derivative transaction is that a party may seek to avoid an obligation by arguing that the transaction, or the combined effect of several transactions, actually constitutes an alternative transaction type, such as a loan. In actions against J.P. Morgan Chase and Citigroup in 2003, for their roles in Enron's manipulation of its financial statements, the SEC based its fraud claims on the theory that both banks engaged in derivatives transactions that were structured in a deliberately complex way to mask the fact that they were, in fact, loans.[5] J.P. Morgan and Citibank agreed to pay $135 million and $120 million respectively to settle the actions.

Similarly, in a private action in England, *Mahonia Ltd. v. J.P. Morgan Chase Bank*, defendant WestLB AG sought to avoid payment on a letter of credit it issued to Mahonia by arguing that the economic effect of a series of swap transactions to which it was a party were actually a loan, and that the transactions' nature as a loan should have been disclosed prior to issuance of the letter of credit.[6] In that instance, however, the court rejected the argument, finding that the existence of price and performance risks, among other characteristics of the transactions supported their classification as "price risk management activities."

Ambiguous Documentation

Legal risk associated with papering derivatives transactions became more significant with the inception of the swap markets. Unlike exchange-traded futures, which are standardized, the essence of the over-the-counter market is to tailor contracts to the counterparty. Customizing legal documentation widens the margin for error, creating additional risk. The advent of standard documentation has been a powerful countermeasure and a driver of derivatives growth. It creates certainty and predictability about the underlying nature of the financial contract in question and improves investor confidence. Nevertheless, standard contract documentation cannot eliminate problems due to simple human error.

In April 2000, UBS bought $10 million of credit protection on Armstrong World Industries, Inc. from Deutsche Bank AG. Telephone records and the indicative terms and conditions prepared by Deutsche Bank confirmed this. However, a confirmation subsequently sent by Deutsche Bank to UBS in May of the same year referred to *Armstrong Holdings, Inc.* as the reference entity, which was the indirect holding company of Armstrong World Industries, but which did not assume any of its obligations. In December 2000, Armstrong World Industries filed for bankruptcy. When UBS delivered Credit Event Notices to Deutsche Bank, the latter refused to pay on the grounds that the confirmation related to protection on Armstrong Holdings, not Armstrong World Industries.

Commentators generally believe that UBS would have won its claim (the case, brought before the High Court of Justice in London was settled out of court without disclosure of the settlement terms) since a judge, after looking at the erroneous contract, would amend it if evidence showed that it did not reflect the true agreement between the parties. Nevertheless, the case highlighted the risk involved in faulty contract documentation and the potential losses at stake. In the wake of the case, a consortium of banks, headed by Goldman Sachs, pioneered the creation of a centralized subscriber database called the Reference Entity Database (RED) that legally verifies the relationship between reference entities and reference obligations. RED data helps to reduce errors when affirming or confirming single name or basket trades and ensures correct representation of the underlying credit risk.

Lack of Capacity or Authority

The general rule is that a party must have both the capacity and authority to enter into a transaction. An entity's *capacity* to contract depends on whether it is within the theoretical ability of the entity itself to enter into the transaction. A counterparty might not be authorized to enter into derivatives contracts if the charter governing its operations, or some other form of legal inhibition, forbids it from engaging in this activity. For example, certain entities created by statute, such as municipalities, are governed by constitutional provisions limiting their ability to create excess indebtedness. Known as the ultra vires doctrine, an entity's lack of capacity to enter into a transaction can be an excuse to renege on obligations later.

In the case of *Hazell v. Hammersmith and Fulham*, the London Borough Council, a local authority, established a capital market fund for the purpose of conducting transactions involving interest rate movements.[7] The local authority engaged in a substantial amount of derivatives transactions, including interest rates swaps. Their positions resulted in major losses as British interest rates subsequently almost doubled. The British High Court invalidated the transactions, holding that the local authority had no power to enter into them because they were inconsistent with its borrowing powers. With the contracts deemed void, the authorities were therefore not held responsible for the $178 million in losses that were, instead, absorbed by their counterparties. A parallel situation arose in the United States in the mid 1990s, when the state of West Virginia lost $280 million in interest rate swaps and sued its broker dealer, Morgan Stanley, claiming that it lacked the requisite capacity to enter into derivatives transactions.[8]

An entity's *authority* to enter into a transaction turns on whether the person who entered into it on behalf of the corporate entity had the authority to do so. If the individual who purports to enter into a transaction on behalf of the entity has no actual or ostensible authority to do so, the transaction will generally not be binding on the entity. The entity will, however, be able to ratify the transaction if it wishes to adopt it. This is particularly troubling in the context of a derivative, where the transaction might be ratified if it results in a profit but not if a loss is incurred.

Breach of Fiduciary Duty

If a party to a derivatives transaction enters into a fiduciary relationship with the counterparty but fails to comply with its fiduciary duties, it may incur liability. The principal circumstance in which a fiduciary relationship arises is when a fiduciary knowingly accepts the trust and confidence of his client to exercise his expertise and discretion on the client's behalf. Most of these relationships are unequal, because the fiduciary has specialized skills or knowledge that the other party does not have. For example, a fiduciary relationship might exist between an investment manager and an inexperienced investor such as a municipality. The law forbids the fiduciary from putting himself in a position in which his duty to the beneficiary conflicts with his duty to other customers or where his personal interests conflict with those of the beneficiary; making a profit from his fiduciary position; or using information obtained in confidence from the beneficiary for his own benefit or that of another person.

In a trading relationship, these requirements can be problematic and expose a firm to an action for breach of fiduciary duty. For example, a firm proposing to enter into an equity derivative transaction with a customer may be aware that a second customer is preparing to launch a takeover offer of the company that will likely impact the share price. The fiduciary duty requires disclosing to the derivatives customer all of the information available to the firm, but doing so would breach the firm's duty of confidentiality, exposing it to suit by the second customer.

In a corporation, the inherent risks involved in derivatives transactions expose management's practices and policies regarding these instruments to the possibility of shareholder suits for breach of fiduciary duty. Officers and directors are fiduciaries to shareholders, who are the owners of the corporation, and their main fiduciary duty is to operate the corporation in the interests of the shareholders (i.e. to maximize value). In *Drage v. Procter & Gamble*, P&G and several of its directors were the target of a shareholder derivative action to recover damages for corporate waste resulting from the defendants engaging in "concededly dangerous derivative leveraged swaps," resulting in an after-tax charge of $102 million. The complaint alleged that investing in the swaps involved an excessive level of risk, particularly in light of management's inexperience in the field, constituting a breach of the defendants' fiduciary duty. While the case was dismissed on procedural grounds, it illustrates how management's inexperience with complex financial instruments exposes it to legal risk.[9]

Fraud

A seller of financial instruments may be liable for fraud if the seller entered into the contract on the basis of a false statement that the seller knew to be untrue, and the buyer acted on that statement to his detriment. The landmark English case *Derry v. Peek* concerned a company that asserted, in its prospectus, that it had the right to operate trams by steam power rather than by horses, whereas it was, in fact, only able to use steam power if the Board of Trade authorized it to do so.[10] When permission was in fact refused, the plaintiff shareholder brought an action for fraud against the directors, but they were not held liable because they had made the statement in the prospectus in the honest belief that it was true.

By contrast, in 2008, state regulators and the SEC filed charges against UBS Securities and UBS Financial Services, accusing the Swiss bank of causing multi-billion dollar losses through fraudulent misrepresentation in the course of its sales activities.[11] The allegations centered on the sale of ARSs (shares or debt instruments for which the interest rate is reset at regular intervals), which the bank's financial advisors marketed as being safe and so liquid they were equivalent to cash. The regulators asserted that, in fact, such representations were deceptive, as the ARS market came under tremendous strain, even prompting various UBS insiders to simultaneously dispose of their own ARSs while encouraging investors to purchase them. The securities were left with mounting liquidity risks that eventually blocked thousands of customers across the United States from accessing their holdings. Regulators brought a rash of similar cases related to ARSs against approximately 30 financial institutions. Pursuant to settlement agreements, the banks agreed to buy back billions of dollars worth of ARSs from retail clients, and pay millions of dollars in civil penalties.

Closely linked to the misrepresentation of fact, and often occurring at the same time, is the purposeful failure to state material facts, which is fraudulent if the nondisclosure is misleading. In April, 2010, the SEC filed securities fraud charges against Goldman Sachs for omitting and misstating key facts in sales pitches to potential customers. In early 2007, as the U.S. housing market teetered, Goldman Sachs created and sold a synthetic CDO that hinged on the performance of residential mortgage-backed securities. The SEC claimed that Goldman failed to disclose that a large hedge fund named Paulson & Co. helped pick the underlying securities and bet against the instrument.[12] The SEC alleged that, had Goldman Sachs customers known this, they might not have bought the instrument. Even if a jury found that the customers would have bought the product with knowledge of Paulson's role, it could still find in favor of the SEC if it found that those facts were intentionally hidden. In July, 2010, Goldman Sachs acknowledged that its marketing materials contained incomplete information and agreed to pay $550 million to settle the SEC charges, the largest-ever penalty paid by a Wall Street firm.

Breach of Contract

A failure to comply with the express terms of a transaction will naturally give rise to a breach of contract claim. By way of example, in 2010, Lehman Brothers Holdings Inc. and Lehman Brothers Special Finance sued Nomura International PLC, claiming that the latter breached the parties' swap agreement by, among other things, calculating its loss in bad faith.[13] Upon LBHI filing for bankruptcy in September 2008, the contract's early termination provision was triggered, and Nomura was clearly required by the terms of the contract to calculate the settlement amount as of the date and time of that event. On the eve of LBHI's bankruptcy, Nomura had calculated the value of the swap agreement to be significantly in favor of LBSF, yet several days after LBHI declared bankruptcy, Nomura changed the calculation and claimed that that it was in fact owed payment by LBSF. Rather than obtaining market quotations from multiple independent dealers, as required by the swap agreement, Nomura instead admitted that it had calculated sums owed using its own internal models. Based on this methodology, Nomura then revised the settlement amount even higher based on a claim for payments associated with transactions relating to certain Icelandic banks that experienced defaults in November 2008. The inflated claims would deprive Lehman Brothers of hundreds of millions of dollars.

Another breach of contract claim arose in 2009 when two trusts sued MBIA Insurance Corp., a large insurance company, claiming that MBIA had sold substantially all of its assets to an affiliate, leaving MBIA with only dubious assets and their corresponding liabilities, consisting of approximately $232 billion in structured finance products.[14] Upon the announcement of this split, MBIA was downgraded by rating agencies to "deep junk" territory. The trusts argued that MBIA's behavior was especially egregious because it had sold them $400 million of notes in January of 2008 without giving notice that it intended to use the proceeds not to invest in MBIA, as was represented, but to fund its separation into good and bad parts, leaving the note holders with the securities of an insolvent company. The trusts argued that this transaction violated contractual promises made in the key agreement governing their rights that MBIA would not "sell, convey, transfer or otherwise dispose of all or substantially all of its assets" unless MBIA redeemed the notes or the transferee assumed MBIA's obligations under the notes.

While a suit for breach of contract can center on a contract provision that clearly forms a part of the contract, as in the cases above, difficulties can also arise where the obligation is not clearly contained within the document. In principle, a statement in a document selling a derivative product, or in some conversation between a trader and the counterparty, may become incorporated as a term of the contract between the parties, particularly where that term is material to the transaction and to the parties' mutual intentions. Whether such inclusion is appropriate depends on whether an objective observer would conclude that the parties intended the statement to form a part of the transaction. Therefore, legal risk can arise in the course of negotiations where verbal agreements are not accurately and fully reflected in the resulting written contract.

Insolvency

Derivatives markets have repeatedly been afflicted by severe defaults. Examples include the meltdown of Lehman Brothers, the collapse of Enron, and the illiquidity of Metallgesellschaft. If a counterparty to a derivatives transaction becomes insolvent and seeks legal protection under the bankruptcy laws or similar shelters, potential losses can be enormous and recovery of payments slow. In the wake of the collapse of Lehman Brothers in 2008, the U.K. insolvency administrators predicted that it would take many years to finally resolve the inter-company and third-party claims. Moreover, a creditor seeking recovery in the event of a counterparty's insolvency is at odds not just with the latter, but also with other creditors vying for payment. In the Lehman Brothers' action against Nomura described above, Lehman Brothers claimed that the Japanese bank's arbitrary choice of methodology for calculating amounts owed, reflected a desire to "secure a windfall" from Lehman's bankruptcy at the expense of deserving creditors.[15]

The cross-border nature of derivatives transactions poses a particularly pernicious problem, as any entity doing business in multiple markets around the globe can raise legal issues that are incapable of resolution by a single country's laws. For example, Long-Term Capital Management, a U.S. hedge fund that took on very sizeable futures positions and engaged in OTC contracts with several dozen counterparties before failing spectacularly in the late 1990s, was organized as a Delaware limited partnership, but the fund it operated, Long-Term Capital Portfolio, L.P., was organized as a Caymans Island limited partnership. While a restructuring deal orchestrated by the U.S. Federal Reserve Bank ultimately enabled LTCM to avoid filing for bankruptcy, the crisis put the bankruptcy codes of the United States and the Cayman Islands on a collision course, as it is possible that both entities would have declared bankruptcy in different jurisdictions. In the event that the LTCM fund had declared bankruptcy in its chartering jurisdiction, the Cayman Islands, there is some uncertainty as to whether the rights of its counterparties to liquidate collateral under the U.S. Bankruptcy Code would have been delayed.

More recently, the multiplicity of bankruptcy regimes governing the collapse of Lehman Brothers, which had dozens of guaranteed subsidiaries around the world, makes the LTCM scenario seem simple. The Lehman Brothers holding company that acted as the "central bank" is now subject to the U.S. Chapter 11 case, along with numerous subsidiaries; Lehman Brothers Inc. is subject to a separate liquidation proceeding supervised by the Securities Investor Protection Corporation; Lehman Brothers International (Europe) and several other British entities are in a UK administration proceeding; and other foreign subsidiaries are subject to insolvency proceedings in their own jurisdictions (for example, in Hong Kong, Australia, Singapore, Japan, the Netherlands, France, and Germany.)

In 2005 and 2006, amendments to the U.S. Bankruptcy Code were implemented with the objective of expanding bankruptcy protections to counterparties and curbing the discretion of bankruptcy judges. However, decisions in the wake of Lehman's collapse depart from the trend of legislative enhancements to the protection of swaps and derivatives under the Code. In a 2010 case, the bankruptcy court addressed a contract provision governing priority of payments to a note holder, Perpetual Trustee Company Limited, and a swap counterparty, Lehman Brothers Special Finance, that held competing interests in collateral securing certain credit-linked synthetic portfolio notes. The court found that the "flip clause" calling for a reversal in priorities in the event of bankruptcy (whereby Perpetual would be entitled to sums otherwise payable to LBSF), was an impermissible *ipso facto*[16] clause prohibited by the Code because it subordinated LBSF's right to payment solely because of its insolvency. Any attempt to enforce note holder priority would constitute a violation of the automatic stay under the Code. Interestingly, the judgment conflicted with that resulting from an earlier parallel proceeding filed in England, where the court held that the flip in priorities *was* permissible under English law.[17] The U.S. bankruptcy judge recognized that the situation called for the parties to "work in a coordinated and cooperative way to identify means to reconcile the conflicting judgments." However, it remains unclear whether harmonizing the two decisions will be workable.

MITIGATING LEGAL RISK

Legal risk mitigation is the concern of market participants, large and small. Regulatory authorities, charged with investor protection and the management of systemic risk, can mitigate legal risk by continually clarifying and amending legislation to remedy ambiguity and keep up with evolving products. Industry groups are also powerful forces in legal risk mitigation. For example, the International Swaps and Derivatives Association has developed standard documentation and instruments covering a variety of transaction types, and advanced the understanding and treatment of derivatives and risk management from public policy and regulatory capital perspectives. As a result, there has been great progress in the advancement of legal certainty for privately negotiated derivatives.

The bulk of the burden in mitigating legal risk, however, remains with investors who must ensure that they follow relevant laws, regulations, and business rules. How an organization addresses this challenge depends on its size, likely legal risks, history, and applicable industry practice. But how do firms identify and measure legal risk? The basics of mitigating legal risk are similar to those for mitigating other forms of risk; they require legal risk to be adequately understood and properly identified. However, the lack of either a common definition of legal risk, as it relates to financially-engineered products or long-established market practice, creates uncertainty. Far less ink has been spilled in providing guidance on defining and mitigating legal risk than market, credit, or operational risk. The challenge is for investors and their legal advisers to devise systems and controls that make a constructive contribution to the management of their individual legal risk.

An analysis of an enterprise's risk should naturally be conceived with the key legal issues raised in the section above in mind. The specific qualities of an entity and how it is suited to measuring and handling risk must also be considered. Below is an indicative checklist of the types of issues to be evaluated in an analysis of an entity's legal risk:

- *Corporate structure and culture:* What is the entity type? Commercial and investment banks have historically enjoyed more legal certainty as market makers in derivatives than have insurance companies. How familiar are employees with ethical issues, such as conflicts of interest and fiduciary duty? How familiar are employees with laws and procedures governing their trade? Traders and marketers entering into transactions need to be made aware that the taped telephoned conversations of their agreements to commit their institutions to a derivatives transaction are a binding verbal contract. What internal upward reporting structure is in place? What diligence practices are in place? How many past instances of misconduct exist? What were the penalties? How often does the misconduct occur in the industry? What is the frequency of government and private enforcement of this risk? When employees understand the "why" behind legal factors they more appropriately align their behavior when faced with "gray areas."

- *Corporate Resources:* What is the size and quality of the entity's legal team or resources? Entities may be subject to unexpected legal risk stemming from a simple misunderstanding of their respective rights and obligations under a contract and fail to perform as expected in times of stress as a result. The quality and breadth of legal services will also affect an entity's ability to keep abreast of developments in the law as compliance requirements evolve. What is the size of its staff? What technology does it have at its disposal? Technology is an important variable in controlling legal risk. In times of crisis, relevant contractual provisions must be identified rapidly and, where volumes are high, manual review can be too time-intensive. Institutions should have online automated access that instantly alerts them to any document that has an exception to their standard close-out policy. In addition, telephones should be equipped with recording capabilities to capture and preserve oral agreements.

- *Jurisdictional considerations.* Where do the entity and its subsidiaries operate and what is the nature of the regulatory regime in each jurisdiction? What about its counterparties? Derivatives entered into with counterparties located in the United States or the United Kingdom have historically had greater legal certainty than transactions with counterparties located in jurisdictions where the legal framework is less certain. What is the maturity and sophistication of the body of judicial decisions, administrative rulings, and regulatory interpretations in relevant jurisdictions? Should contracts be governed by the laws of England or the laws of the State of New York?

- *Documentation.* What measures are in place to ensure accurate and complete documentation? Does the entity subscribe to the Reference Entity Database?

- *Type of product.* What type of product is being traded? What regulatory restrictions and classifications are invoked? The legal risk associated with a standard currency swap, for example, is minimal, but the risk associated with a Libor-squared swap has historically been exposed to claims of lack of transparency and hidden leverage.

- *Counterparties.* How large is credit exposure to any particular counterparty? What type of entities are the counterparties? As discussed, transacting with municipalities or retail counterparties rather than large sophisticated corporations and financial institutions exposes a firm to breach of fiduciary duty allegations, and to suits based on claims of lack of authority or capacity.

THE REGULATORY LANDSCAPE

Despite different approaches to the regulation of financially-engineered products worldwide, several common public policy objectives underpin most regimes. Regulators aim to protect the integrity of capital-raising markets (e.g., discourage fraud, manipulation, and other unfair practices); manage systemic risk; protect less sophisticated persons; and oversee institutions for the public benefit (e.g., place restrictions on banks and insurance companies through capital adequacy

controls). Some jurisdictions also strive to protect against instruments that provide a speculative outlet on the price of commodities, potentially causing radical
swings in the price of those products (e.g., energy or agricultural products that a
government deems central to the functioning of the economy or expedient for political reasons), and to guard the monetary system (e.g., through foreign exchange
controls to protect the integrity of the local currency and restrict capital outflows).

Navigating derivatives regulation in any market is widely held to be a complex
and baffling business. Yet understanding different regulatory rules and schemes is
an important tool in an investor's arsenal because the cross-border nature of derivatives markets lends itself naturally to regulatory arbitrage. Financial instruments
are often purposefully engineered to combine or isolate certain characteristics in
order to achieve desired regulatory consequences. If a restrictive law is introduced
in a specific jurisdiction, the business is often transferred to another less restrictive
jurisdiction, making the first jurisdiction less competitive. Indeed, in May 1998,
when a senior regulator suggested that OTC markets should be regulated, Alan
Greenspan, chairman of the U.S. Federal Reserve Board, vigorously opposed the
initiative citing the risk that the imposition of new regulatory constraints would
stifle innovation and push coveted transactions offshore through cross-border regulatory arbitrage.

Below are case studies of the development and current framework of the
regulatory regimes in two key markets: the United States and the United Kingdom.

The United States

Unlike many jurisdictions, no single authority governs the regulation of derivatives in the United States. Derivatives regulation in the United States is essentially
a hybrid of "functional" and "institutional" regulation. First, specific types of
derivatives, namely, futures and certain options, are regulated as financial products. Second, certain institutions that are already subject to regulation (e.g., banks)
may have their derivatives activities scrutinized by their institutional supervisors.

Broadly speaking, transactions in stocks, bonds, and security-based derivatives
are regulated by the Securities and Exchange Commission (SEC), and the trading
of commodities and futures is regulated by the Commodity Futures Trading Commission (CFTC). Therefore, the regulatory treatment of a derivative instrument will
depend largely on the nature of the underlying asset or interest (equity, interest rate,
credit or fixed income, foreign exchange, or commodity derivative) and whether it
is categorized as a commodity option, or futures contract, or as a security. Where
hybrid instruments combine features of a security with those of a futures contract
or commodity option, such as a cash-settleable forward contract on a security, the
analysis is particularly complicated, because these are subject to both the securities
and commodities laws. Within the broad securities and commodities categories,
another layer of regulatory implications may be triggered depending on the manner in which the instrument is related to the underlying asset or interest; swaps,
options, forwards, and indexed or hybrid instruments may each have different
regulatory consequences.

Historically, whether an instrument was subject to the CFTC, the SEC, or both
was particularly significant because of an exclusive jurisdiction provision (arguably
preempting other applicable regulatory regimes) in the Commodity Exchange Act,

and its general prohibition on the offer and sale of futures contracts or commodities options other than on a CFTC-regulated exchange. The resulting tension between the SEC and CFTC, particularly as derivatives instruments evolved, set U.S. regulation of derivatives on a path of ad hoc reforms from the 1970s to the turn of the millennium. Notable among these was the Shad-Johnson Accord of 1983, under which the SEC was granted sole authority to regulate options on securities, certificates of deposit, and stock groups. The regulation of futures, and options on futures on exempted securities and broad-based stock indices, was left to the CFTC. The accord banned futures contracts on individual securities (other than certain exempt securities) and on narrow-based stock indices.

Against this backdrop, the passage of The Commodity Futures Modernization Act of 2000 (CFMA) signaled a radical shift in the regulatory regime, and heralded the era of deregulation commonly blamed for the financial crisis that would crystallize less than a decade after the CFMA's enactment. The CFMA amends the Shad-Johnson Act and, crucially, clarifies that certain OTC derivatives transactions are outside the jurisdiction of the CFTC. Under certain conditions, the Act allows trading of futures contracts based on single stocks and narrow-based stock indices, with oversight being shared by the CFTC and the SEC. The CFMA also preempts any state or local laws that regulate gaming or bucket shops, eliminating concerns that excluded or exempted derivatives transactions could be voided on the grounds that they violated these laws.

In addition to the functional regulation of the SEC and CFTC, banking regulators provide a layer of institutional regulatory oversight. As with functional regulation, institutional regulation has evolved through a series of piecemeal responses to developments and crises in the financial markets. Legislation designed to curb excesses by banks in securities activities in the wake of the Great Depression, principally the Glass-Steagall Act (enacted in 1933) and the Bank Holding Company Act of 1956, confined these activities to a narrow universe. Deposit-taking banks were barred from dealing in, underwriting, and purchasing securities, subject to certain exceptions. However, with the growing internationalization of financial markets, and increasing overlap between securities and banking activities in the last twenty years, banks mounted a campaign to procure greater securities powers. In 1999, Congress passed the Gramm-Leach-Bliley Act, implementing sweeping reforms that repealed long-standing Glass-Steagall restrictions on affiliations between commercial and investment banks, and established a dramatically more permissive environment for securities activities.

The evolution of the regulatory environment in which banks conduct their securities activities did little to resolve its complexity. Each entity, type of activity, or individual transaction remains potentially subject to separate bodies of banking, securities, and commodities laws. While the SEC and CFTC retain regulatory control over securities and commodities respectively, there are three federal banking regulators that may exercise significant authority over entities in a banking group: the Federal Reserve Board, the Comptroller of the Currency, and the Federal Deposit Insurance Corporation. The Gramm-Leach-Bliley Act confirms the role of the Federal Reserve Board as the "umbrella supervisor" for banks, but invokes the SEC, CFTC, and state insurance regulators to supplement regulation. This unholy marriage of regulatory schemes leads to jurisdictional and legal uncertainty, as the different bank regulators often reach conflicting conclusions on bank power issues and do not always defer to the SEC on matters pertaining to securities subsidiaries of banking groups, leading to serious asymmetries between some market participants.

The United Kingdom

While the regulatory regime for derivatives in the United Kingdom is less fragmented than in the United States, its development follows a similar trajectory. As in the United States, transactions in derivatives in the United Kingdom were traditionally constrained by the common law "rule against difference contracts." The process of dismantling this restrictive regime began when the United Kingdom passed its Financial Services Act of 1986 (FSA 1986), "modernizing" its financial laws by eliminating the old rule against difference contracts, and making derivatives, whether used for hedging or speculation, legally enforceable. The 1986 "Big Bang" constituted a wholesale reformation of the regulatory system, reorganizing regulatory agencies across industry lines, and seeking to implement a consistent philosophy of regulation.

Under FSA 1986, the offering of a broad range of instruments, called "investments," was regulated by limiting the conduct of "investment business" to authorized persons who were regulated (and certain exempt persons). The Securities Investment Board (SIB) was assigned chief responsibility for regulating the financial industry. In turn, it delegated oversight responsibilities to self-regulatory organizations (SROs) that governed different aspects of financial activity. With respect to derivatives activities, regulation was split amongst several SROs but, by 1991, after a series of mergers, the Securities and Futures Authority (SFA) was the principle regulatory body. To obtain authorization to engage in defined investment activities under FSA 1986, firms, dealers, and certain persons (e.g., compliance officers) had to join the SFA, which imposed various strict requirements, such as compliance with its conduct of business rules. Meanwhile, the Bank of England retained supervisory authority over banks. It published the London Code of Conduct, which set out principles governing the conduct of wholesale market dealing in financial products outside of the recognized investment exchanges, including derivatives. While derivatives were included in the definition of "investment" under FSA 1986, and included as financial products subject to the wholesale dealing requirements of the London Code of Conduct, they were not specially regulated in the United Kingdom as instruments in their own right.

At the turn of the millennium, Parliament enacted the Financial Services and Markets Act 2000 (FSMA 2000) that further streamlined this regulatory structure. In particular, the Act harmonized regulatory control by assigning supervision of investment and related financial services in the United Kingdom, including insurance companies, to a single regulatory authority, the Financial Services Authority (FSA), which had been created in 1997 and which now replaced the SIB. The Bank of England shed its bank regulatory and supervisory duties and was instead given new monetary powers. The FSA's *Interim Prudential Source Book: Banks* establishes the general regulatory regime for U.K. banks, which remained intact under FSMA 2000: only authorized persons (or certain exempt persons) may carry on a regulated activity ("investments" as well as insurance) in the United Kingdom. Likewise, conduct of business rules remain broadly the same under the FSMA 2000 scheme as under the FSA 1986. The definition of the various forms of financial products within the scope of FSMA 2000 are set out in The Financial Services and Markets Act (Regulated Activities) Order 2001 (ROA). The ROA defines the boundaries for regulation of derivative products. Any person conducting business in relation to any of those activities within the ROA's reach must obtain authorization from the FSA.

The FSA's role as the single supervisor of financial services markets, exchanges, and firms arguably renders the United Kingdom's system of supervision of financially-engineered products more cohesive than that of the United States. However, the FSA operates as one pillar of a tripartite system of financial regulation. The other two participants are the Bank of England, which acts as a lender of last resort and is responsible for maintaining a broad overview of the financial system as a whole, and the Treasury, responsible for the overall institutional structure of financial regulation and the legislation that governs it. In this respect, the United Kingdom is not immune to the inevitable frictions that arise from fragmented control. In the wake of the financial crisis, the tripartite system was heavily criticized for awkwardly dividing responsibilities, powers, and capabilities between competing institutions. In particular, the system was maligned for placing responsibility for prudential regulation and oversight of consumer protection and market conduct in the same organization (the FSA). Efforts to abolish the FSA, and once again overhaul the entire regulatory framework, are now underway (see the section entitled *Regulatory Evolution— Europe* below for more information).

The regulation of financial services in the United Kingdom is also subject to European Union law, effectively broadening the regulatory field. The Markets in Financial Instruments Directive (MiFID) provides harmonized regulation for investment services across the member states of the European Economic Area. To determine which firms are affected by MiFID and which are not, MiFID distinguishes between "investment services and activities" and "ancillary services." Firms covered by MiFID will be authorized and regulated in their "home state" (broadly, the country in which they have their registered office). Once a firm has been authorized, it can use the MiFID "passport" to provide services to customers in other EU member states. These services will be regulated by the member state in their home state. As discussed, in the United Kingdom, the Financial Services Authority (FSA) is currently responsible for the regulation of these firms and their activities.

International Regulatory Initiatives

The development, adoption, and successful implementation of international standards are valuable counterweights to conflicts among regulatory regimes worldwide. International standards promote financial stability by enabling better-informed investment decisions, improving market integrity, and reducing the risks of financial distress and contagion. The standard-setting groups below are among those leading the charge in formulating broad supervisory standards, guidelines, and statements of best practice in the expectation that individual supervisory authorities will take steps to implement them on a local level.

- *Bank for International Settlements* (BIS): Hosts meetings for a number of standing committees whose key objectives are promoting monetary and financial stability. Among these are two committees established by the G10 central banks: the *Basel Committee on Banking Supervision* (formulates broad supervisory standards and guidelines, and recommends statements of best practice in banking in the expectation that bank supervisory authorities will take steps to implement them) and the *Committee on Payment and Settlement Systems* (monitors and analyzes developments in domestic payment, settlement and clearing systems, as well as in cross-border and multi-currency netting schemes).

- *International Swaps and Derivative Association* (ISDA): Identifies and reduces the sources of risk in the derivatives and risk management business. Among its most notable accomplishments are: developing standard documentation, notably, the ISDA Master Agreement and related materials; producing legal opinions on the enforceability of netting and collateral arrangements; and advancing the understanding and treatment of derivatives and risk management from public policy and regulatory capital perspectives.
- *International Organization of Securities Commissions* (IOSCO): Develops and promotes standards for effective surveillance of international securities markets. Its *Technical Committee* has issued a number of papers in the area of financial derivatives regulation.

REGULATORY EVOLUTION

The predictable reaction to the global financial crisis was a call for stringent reformation of derivatives regulation in markets across the globe. In order to appreciate the direction in which new regulation is heading, it is useful to understand some of the key concerns stemming from the financial crisis that policy makers and regulators are aiming to redress. Testifying before the Financial Crisis Inquiry Commission, Gary Gensler, Chairman of the CFTC, identified and disputed several fallacies held prior to the crisis:

- *The derivatives market is an institutional marketplace, with "sophisticated" traders who do not need the same types of protections that the broader public needs when investing in the securities or futures markets.* Derivatives are complex financial instruments, and even the most sophisticated parties would benefit from protections. Markets, even amongst institutions, work better when transparency and market integrity are promoted. Transparency would enable banks to determine the liquidity of particular contracts, rather than amassing "toxic assets" that cannot be priced. Lack of information in the OTC market also substantially reduces the ability of the government and other market participants to anticipate, and possibly preempt, building market pressures, major market failures, or manipulation efforts.
- *Over-the-counter derivatives do not need regulation because the institutions dealing them are already regulated.* The banks that deal derivatives have not been expressly regulated for their derivatives business. Derivatives dealers also operate as affiliates of non-banks, such as insurance companies or investment banks, which are lightly regulated. The derivatives affiliates of AIG, Lehman Brothers and Bear Stearns had no effective regulation for capital, business conduct standards, or recordkeeping. Without capital

requirements, banks took on more risk that was backed up by less capital, adding leverage to the financial system.

- *Large, sophisticated financial institutions dealing over-the-counter derivatives, as well as their counterparties, are so expert and self-interested that the markets will discipline themselves.* The "sophisticated" participants were incentivized to assume risk in order to boost revenues. They were often unable to adequately judge the risks they were assuming due to the complexity and lack of transparency of the instruments they were trading, and the counterparty credit risk involved. In the wake of the global financial crisis, Alan Greenspan publicly confessed to Congress that he had erred in his judgment on the self-regulating power of the market.

- *Over-the-counter derivatives are not amenable to centralized trading or clearing because they are customized rather than standardized.* In the futures and securities markets, trades are cleared through well-regulated central counterparties. Each counterparty is protected from the other counterparty's default since the clearinghouse stands between the dealer and the counterparty. The lack of clearing in the swaps marketplace left the financial system dangerously interconnected. As concerns about the viability of one firm increased, risk premium had to widen for all other financial firms that may have had exposure to the first entity's problems. Derivatives have become much more standardized over the last decade, and thus more susceptible to central market structures; one Wall Street CEO testified before the CFTC that as much as 75 to 80 percent of the over-the-counter derivatives marketplace is standard enough to be centrally cleared.

Flaws in ways the market was regulated prior to the crisis are easier to identify than fix. In many countries, progress is still in the discussion phase. Reforms that have been enacted have significantly evolved from their original iterations after months of negotiations among lawmakers. And while the G20 has established an agenda for reform, there has been significant variation in national response as differences in each country's existing systems, and fallout from the financial crisis, dictate the measure of change required.

The United States

In July, 2010 President Obama signed the Dodd-Frank Wall Street Reform and Consumer Protection Act, the biggest overhaul of the American financial regulatory system since the Depression, which will fundamentally alter how end users, hedge funds, private equity firms, commodity traders, banks, and broker-dealers use and trade derivatives. In broad terms, the Act creates a comprehensive framework for the regulation of most derivatives transactions, including OTC derivatives, formerly deregulated by the Commodity Futures Modernization Act of 2000.

The most significant aspects of derivatives reform addressed by the Act are: First, it calls for mandatory clearing through regulated central clearing organizations, and mandatory trading through either regulated exchanges or swap execution facilities (in each case, subject to certain key exceptions), and provides a role for both regulators and clearinghouses to determine which contracts should be cleared. Second, the Act creates new categories of regulated market participants, including swap dealers and major swap participants. Third, the "Volcker Rule" restricts proprietary trading in swaps by a "banking entity" and prohibits Federal assistance to any "swaps entity," including banks, thereby causing banks eligible for federal assistance to "push-out" most of their swap business to a separate affiliate, ostensibly ending "too big to fail" bailouts. The Volcker Rule also prohibits a banking entity from acquiring or retaining any equity, partnership, or other ownership interest in, or sponsoring, any hedge fund or private equity fund, subject to certain exceptions and a transition period.

With respect to jurisdictional allocations, the Act largely follows the historical divisions between the CFTC and the SEC. Derivatives transactions are categorized as "swaps," which are subject to primary regulation by the CFTC, "security-based swaps," which are subject to primary regulation by the SEC, or "mixed swaps," which are subject to joint regulation by the CFTC and SEC.

The Act prohibits state gaming or bucket shop laws from invalidating security-based swaps between eligible contract participants or effected on a registered national securities exchange. Interestingly, however, the preemption from state gaming and bucket shop laws is only provided with respect to security-based swaps and not for other swaps. In fact, the provision of the Commodity Exchange Act that formerly provided a preemption for over-the-counter derivatives, previously excluded from the purview of the Commodity Exchange Act, has been deleted in the Act.

While these provisions herald a profound shift in the U.S. regulatory framework, the ultimate consequences of the Dodd-Frank bill will depend on rulemaking by federal agencies. Rules are generally required to be issued within 360 days of the Act's enactment. Much of the specific impact of the law will therefore become clear only as regulators interpret, implement, and enforce it in that period, and beyond.

The European Union

In the Spring of 2010, The European Commission reached an agreement in principle with the United States on regulation of the derivatives market. The priorities for reform included subjecting the market to substantial supervision and regulation, pushing all trading of commonly traded derivative contracts onto exchanges or other regulated trading platforms, obliging all traders of standard derivative contracts to use central counterparty clearing, and giving regulators full authority to monitor transactions, including setting position limits.

Subsequently, European governments and institutions struggled to agree on a common approach to implementing such reforms. Frustrated with the slow pace of progress, certain countries undertook unilateral initiatives to effect changes. As the Greek debt crisis triggered an increase in bets against the euro, Germany passed the July 2010, Act Aimed at Preventing Abusive Securities and Derivatives Trading Activities, that prohibits naked short selling of all shares and Eurozone government debt instruments traded on a regulated market of a German stock exchange, as well as CDS to bet against Eurozone government bonds. France also proposed legislation to curb naked short-selling. As an example of comprehensive reform on a national level, the United Kingdom issued a proposal in June 2010 to fundamentally reform its financial services regulatory structure, abolishing the tripartite system, resulting in the FSA ceasing to exist in its current form. The proposal will be subject to comments through October 2010, and the government aims to put forward a more detailed proposal in 2011, with the aim of completing primary passage of the legislation by 2012.

Meanwhile, the Committee of European Securities Regulators provided technical advice to the European Commission in the context of its review of the MiFID to improve securities markets' functioning, transparency, and investor protection. In relation to its advice on transparency in non-equity markets, some of CESR's recommendations focused on defining a phased approach for the introduction of a post-trade transparency regime for structured finance products; extending the scope to clearing eligible sovereign CDS; and enhancing post-trade transparency of derivatives markets.

In June 2010, the EU Parliament adopted a resolution on the regulation of derivatives. Broadly, the resolution called for strict rules to prevent inexperienced users and speculators from building up dangerous levels of risk; asked the European Commission to consider ways to significantly reduce the overall volume of derivatives traded; supported a ban on pure speculative trading in commodities and agricultural products, and the imposition of upper limits on trading in these markets; and stressed that central counterparty clearing facilities need to be strengthened by the introduction of compulsory regulatory standards.

In early September 2010, EU diplomats and lawmakers finally approved an overhaul of the way banks and markets in the region are supervised, set to be endorsed by EU ministers and the European Parliament. The new architecture calls for three new European Union-level watchdogs for the banking, insurance and securities markets sectors, set to be operational by January 2011. Under the proposals, these watchdogs will not supervise companies or markets directly (leaving this to national authorities), but they will be required to draw up common technical rules and standards, and could acquire additional legally binding powers, including over individual companies in "emergency situations." The European Central Bank is given a central role in assessing future risks to Europe's financial system and allows the ECB president to chair a new European Systemic Risk Council for the first five years.

While the development was hailed as an important step in closing an important gap in financial regulation, some expressed concerns about a drift in rule-making from home soil to Brussels. In London, Europe's biggest financial center, there are fears that Brussels will now attempt to give more powers to the new watchdogs though other legislative initiatives that are in the pipeline, in areas ranging from derivatives to short-selling rules, potentially helping other financial centers to take business from London. As with the United States, much work is in store for Europe before its new regulatory framework is finalized and implemented.

Other Jurisdictions

Regulatory reform efforts around the world have not always mirrored those of the United States and Europe. For example, both Japan and Canada have taken comparatively limited measures of late. Japanese regulations have been progressively tweaked since its financial meltdown of the late 1990s, giving it one of the tightest regulatory environments of any advanced industrialized economy. For its part, Canada was relatively unscathed by the U.S. subprime mortgage crisis, and its reaction to calls for reform have therefore been less acute. Practically the only developed country not to have a national securities regulator, Canada has only recently proposed the establishment of a federal securities regulator by the middle of 2011 to replace its current system of provincial regulators.

The Road Ahead

The coming year promises to be challenging for a broad range of market participants. On the one hand, much effort will be expended on backward-looking endeavors, with a focus on recovering losses sustained in the recent past. For example, investors who found themselves in an unexpected position despite having performed contract and counterparty reviews of AIG, Lehman Brothers, Bear Stearns, the Icelandic banks, and monoline insurers, among others, will continue to determine their rights and remedies under the laws of several jurisdictions. On the other hand, much effort will have to be forward-looking, carefully focused on future regulatory developments in order to retain competitiveness and compliance in a rapidly changing playing field. Below are some examples of upcoming challenges and responsibilities for key market players:

- *COOs:* The role of the COO for banks and other financial organizations will grow dramatically as legislation calls for new or enhanced controls that include review and authorization protocols, policies, procedures and standards, reengineered workflow, employee training, management training, and system controls. In addition, certain groups that were previously light on compliance professionals, relative to the more mature compliance departments at investment banks, will need to develop their own quickly and effectively. For example, the Dodd-Frank Act eliminates the private adviser exemption, previously relied upon by many hedge funds, which will have the effect of requiring a large number of currently unregistered advisers to register with the SEC.
- *Rating agencies:* Often under fire for their role in the financial crisis, rating agencies are the target of regulatory reform and will need to understand the obligations imposed on them in the coming year, such as those under the Dodd-Frank Act. In the United States, two key rating agencies, Fitch and Moody's, announced in July 2010 that they would not allow issuers to include their ratings in prospectuses or registration statements, absent clarification by the SEC on whether they would potentially be exposed to "expert" liability under section 11 of the Securities Act. Prior to the Act's passage, rating agencies had never been treated as experts under the securities laws, since ratings are inherently forward-looking and embody assumptions and predictions about future events that, by their nature, cannot be verified as facts.
- *Broker-dealers:* The Dodd-Frank Act empowers the SEC to impose a fiduciary duty upon broker-dealers when they conduct business with retail customers. The SEC Chairman stated in a speech in the summer of 2010 that she had long advocated such a uniform fiduciary standard and was pleased that the legislation provided the SEC with the rulemaking authority necessary to implement it. Broker-dealers will need to understand the

parameters of this duty and determine what their role as market-makers means in light of it.

- *Regulators:* the coming year will prove very busy for regulators shaping new laws and implementing them. In the United States, for example, there is a crucial role still to be played by regulators in enforcing the provisions of the Dodd-Frank Act. Much of the legislation is short on specifics, giving regulators broad scope to determine its impact.

- *Counterparties:* while developments in ISDA contracts and internal procedures, policies and controls have improved legal risk management in financial institutions, the crisis reveals that they are far from "well oiled" machines. Furthermore, new regulation means large institutions may have to reshuffle their businesses, such as pushing out certain derivatives activities into affiliate groups. Smaller organizations will have no choice but to examine their needs and implement technologies that can support best practices and regulatory compliance. Only automation will mitigate internal risk or appease regulators, so the need for better reconciliation and reporting is crucial, especially where the collection of information from predominantly manual processes is compiled.

- *Lawyers:* Lawyers face a lot of work as they grapple with an onslaught of new rules. In the United States, corporate lawyers, their clients, and in-house law departments are bracing for a big spike in work stemming from Dodd-Frank financial reform, much as they did in the period following the passage of the Sarbanes-Oxley bill in 2002. Similarly, in Europe, much work will have to be done to digest the new regulatory framework expected to become operational in the coming year.

NOTES

1. Basel Committee on Banking Supervision. *Basel II: International Convergence of Capital Measurement and Capital Standards: A Revised Framework.* November, 2005.

2. Thomas A. Russo. *Keynote Address at the 13th Annual Derivatives Securities and Risk Management Conference.* April 25, 2003.

3. Since derivatives contracts are commonly governed by the laws of New York state or England, these jurisdictions are the focus of discussion in this chapter.

4. Difference contracts were close cousins to futures and options; in a difference contract, the contracting parties would agree to perform by paying the difference between the contract price and the market price at the time of performance, not by actually delivering the good that was the subject of the contract. Thus a "seller" who didn't own wheat and a "buyer" who didn't want wheat might have entered a difference contract for one ton of wheat at a contract price of $1,000 per ton, to be settled in six months.

5. SEC v. J.P. Morgan Chase, SEC Litigation Release No. 18252; In the Matter of Citigroup, Inc., Securities Exchange Act of 1934 Release No. 34-48230; Accounting and Auditing Enforcement Release No. 1821; Administrative Proceeding File No. 3,11192 (July, 28, 2003).

6. Mahonia Ltd. v. J.P. Morgan Chase Bank, Court of Appeal—Commercial Court [2004] EWHC 1938 (Comm) Case No: 2001/1400.

7. Hazell v. Hammersmith and Fulham London Borough Council [1992] 2 A.C. 1, 22.

8. See State v. Morgan Stanley & Co. 459 S.E. 2d 906 (W. Va. 1995).

9. See Drage v. Procter and Gamble et al., 694 N.E. 2d 479 (Ohio Ct. App. 1997).

10. Derry v. Peek, (1889) 14 App. Cas 337.

11. SEC v. UBS Securities LLC and UBS Financial Services Inc., No. 08 CIV 10754 (S.D.N.Y. Dec 11, 2008).

12. Securities and Exchange Commission v. Goldman, Sachs & Co. and Fabrice Tourre, 10 Civ. 3229 (S.D.N.Y. April 16, 2010).

13. Lehman Brothers Holdings Inc. et al. v. Nomura Securities Co. Ltd. (Adv. Proc. No. 10-03228) and Lehman Brothers Holdings Inc. et al. v. Nomura International plc (Adv Proc. No. 10-03229) (2010).

14. Third Avenue Trust et al. v. MBIA Ins. Corp., et al., C.A. No. 4486-VCS (Del. Ch. Oct. 5, 2009).

15. In re: Lehman Brothers Special Finance v. BNY Corporate Trustee Services Ltd. No. 09-1242 (Bankr. S.D.N.Y. Jan 25, 2010).

16. *Ipso facto* clauses are provisions in executory contracts that modify or terminate a contractual right or interest in property due to the bankruptcy or financial condition of a company.

17. Perpetual Trustee Company Limited v. BNY Corporate Trustee Service Limited [2009] EWHC 1912 (Ch).

ABOUT THE AUTHOR

Jordana Krohley (née Cornish) has experience in structured finance and derivatives products, securitizations and international offerings of equity and debt securities, including Rule 144A/Regulation S transactions and private placements in the United States. She was an associate at Allen & Overy LLP in London from 2007 to 2010, working in the International Capital Markets group. The law firm was appointed principal counsel for the International Swaps and Derivatives Association (ISDA), as well as Markit Group in connection with its Reference Entity Database (RED), and Jordana's work included advisory services for both organizations. Prior to being at Allen & Overy, Jordana was a paralegal in the Litigation group at Wachtell, Lipton, Rosen & Katz in New York, from 2002 to 2004. Jordana holds a JD from Vanderbilt University Law School and a BS from Vanderbilt University and is a member of the Bar of the State of New York.

CHAPTER 27

Portable Alpha

TANYA BEDER
Chairman, SBCC Group Inc.

GIOVANNI BELIOSSI
FGS Capital LLP

INTRODUCTION

Portable alpha is a form of financial engineering used by institutional investors and others in their portfolios. Portable alpha gained popularity during the late 1990s in the aftermath of the Asian currency, Russian commodity, and the Long-Term Capital Management crises. Market conditions at the time—low volatility, flush liquidity, tight spreads, low risk premiums, and high confidence in the markets—led investors to seek new ways to boost investment returns. Portable alpha was designed to provide that extra return.

Portable alpha was considered by some to be quite a major development, and was grouped along with some of finance's greatest achievements: "Every now and then, there is a development in the world of finance that results in a major paradigm shift. Examples include the introduction of present value as a tool in financial decision making, the Modigliani-Miller hypotheses regarding capital structure and the introduction of modern portfolio theory in investing ... [and] the use of various portable alpha financial engineering techniques to raise returns, reduce portfolio volatility, and/or achieve better asset-liability matching."[1]

Portable alpha can be structured a number of ways. During its first decade of use, for most institutional investors that embraced it, portable alpha was a success story. This group included well-known asset managers at firms such as Harvard Management, John Hancock, Fidelity, Goldman Sachs, Solomon Brothers, Janus, Merrill Lynch, and Morgan Stanley. But as the credit crisis took hold in 2007, and market conditions changed to higher volatility, lower liquidity, wider spreads, higher risk premiums, and lower confidence in the markets, some institutional investors wound down their portable alpha programs, dismantled the beta portion, or purged the alpha-related leverage. These included asset managers at entities such as the California Public Employees Retirement System (CalPERS), the Pennsylvania State Employees Retirement System (SERS), the Massachusetts Public Reserves Investment Management Board (Mass PRIM), and the Fire and Police Pension Association of Colorado.[2] So, in a little over a decade, portable alpha has been through birth, grew up to receive accolades as a major development in finance, and faced death in the eyes of some important investment managers. But recently, portable alpha has experienced a rebirth. In this chapter we discuss portable alpha and some of the key pluses and minuses of portable alpha.

WHAT IS PORTABLE ALPHA?

To define "portable alpha." first we need to define "beta" and "alpha." Beta is a measure of how much an investment position moves with the market. For example, betas of 0.5, 1.0, and 2.0 imply that the position will move half as much, the same as, or twice as much as the market, respectively (whether up or down). Alpha is a measure of how much an investment activity is non-correlated and unsystematically related to the market. Hence, alpha is a measure of the degree to which an investment activity (or manager) generates returns that outperform the market for a given period of time. A natural question is "which market?" The market is defined by the investor. It may be a broad equity market index, for example the S&P 500, the Russell 1000, the FTSE, the NIKKEI, the top 100 Euro or Asian or global stocks, the top energy or top technology stocks, and so on. It may be a broad bond market index, for example the Lehman Aggregate Bond Index [now Barclays], a composite market index such as ARIX, MSCI, a hedge fund index, or a custom index, for example credit spreads. Another approach is to "strip" beta from a successful active manager's returns, thereby leaving the alpha as a residual. For example, the investor has an investment in a manager who trades a broadly diversified portfolio of U.S. equities and achieves net returns of the S&P 500 plus 200 basis points. In this case, the investor would enter an equity swap paying the S&P 500 and receiving Libor, yielding net returns of Libor +200 basis points. The investor then may combine this return with another equity swap, for example paying Libor and receiving a bond index to achieve a return of the bond index plus 200 basis points. In this example, the alpha of the equity manager (200 basis points) is ported to a bond investment.

Portable alpha is the practice of separating alpha from beta by engaging in investment activities with a return pattern that differs from the market index from which their beta is derived. The purpose is to add low correlation sources of return to a portfolio, while maintaining the desired asset allocation (systematic beta exposure). There are three common ways to implement portable alpha:

1. **Alpha Overlay**

   In this approach, the investor enters into a total return swap, typically paying a short-term interest rate in exchange for alpha performance. The alpha performance may be achieved via one or more hedge fund managers, or via an investable hedge fund index.

2. **Alpha Transport**

   In this approach, the investor enters into a derivative transaction, typically paying a market index in exchange for the performance of one or more "alpha" managers, or the performance of an investable "alpha" index.

3. **Alpha Replaces Beta**

   In this approach, the investor typically sells beta exposure and buys a pure alpha investment. In this implementation, the asset allocation of the portfolio most often changes. Rather than earning alpha on top of the systematic beta exposure, the alpha investment replaces the beta exposure.

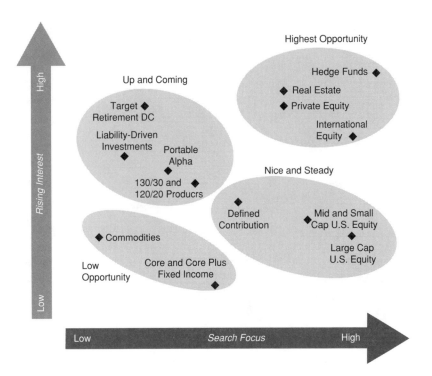

Exhibit 27.1 The 2007 Casey Quirk Search Opportunity Map

The goal is to create a non-correlated strategy designed to increase risk-adjusted returns, by increasing the expected generation of "alpha" regardless of asset class. Approaches (1) and (2) allow investors to invest in high-alpha strategies while maintaining the desired strategic asset allocation in the traditional equities and fixed income markets, among others. One common approach is to source alpha via an investment in hedge funds, fund of hedge funds, and/or investable hedge fund indices, such as those calculated and published by Hedge fund Research (HFR), Credit Suisse (CSFB), MSCI Hedge Invest Index, Standard & Poor's (S&P), FTSE, and so forth.

In their 2007 Consultant Search Forecast, covering expected trends in institutional consultant searches, Casey Quirk place Portable Alpha in the "Up and Coming" section, indicating that, although it may not represent a search focus yet, it sees "rising interest in conducting search activity." However, in their 2010 Product Opportunity Matrix, portable alpha has disappeared from Casey Quirk's categories for "Increasing Search Activity" or "Decreasing Search Activity." See Exhibits 27.1 and 27.2.

Illustration: Implementing Alpha Transport (AT)

Exhibit 27.3 illustrates a common form of the alpha transport transaction.

We now provide numerical examples to illustrate how alpha transport works. Assume that the investor places 20 percent of the notional amount of the existing portfolio into an alpha transport strategy using an investable hedge fund index. We

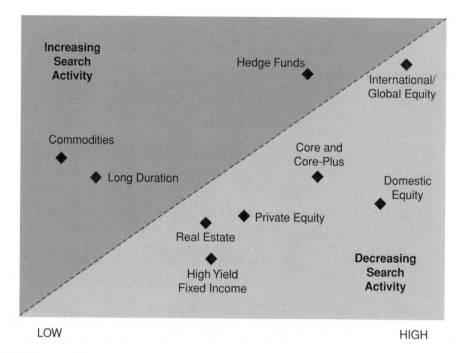

Exhibit 27.2   The 2010 Casey Quirk Product Opportunity

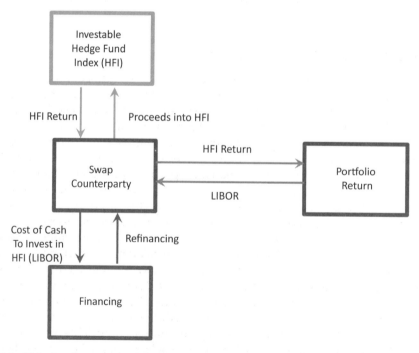

Exhibit 27.3   Implementing Alpha Transport

Exhibit 27.4 Two Hypothetical AT Performance Outcomes

	HFI > Portfolio	Portfolio > HFI
Notional invested in alpha transport strategy	20%	20%
HFI Return	10%	2%
Portfolio Return (PR)	**6%**	**6%**
Libor	3%	3%
Swap Return (HFI Return—Libor)	7%	−1%
Swap Return × Notional invested (AT)	1.4%	−0.2%
Return using alpha transport (PR + AT)	**7.4%**	**5.8%**

provide two cases, depicted in Exhibit 27.4, one in which the return of the Hedge Fund Index (HFI) exceeds the Portfolio Return and one in which the reverse is true. All other factors are held constant. The assumed returns and cost of capital are illustrated for the two cases. A note of importance—both of these examples assume that the correlation between the HFI and portfolio return is insignificant over the life of the transaction.

As the example illustrates, alpha transport is not attractive in all scenarios. The scenario on the right, which holds all assumptions constant other than reversing the relationship between the Portfolio Return and the HFI Return (PR is 4 percent lower and higher than the HFI Return, respectively, in the two scenarios), illustrates how alpha transport may in some cases lower the return of the investor's portfolio. In addition, during the credit crunch that began in 2007, some alpha transport participants found that collateral calls by the swap counterparty placed further burden on the investor.

THE APPEAL OF PORTABLE ALPHA

What is appealing in portable alpha structures in an institutional investment context? In theory, alpha overlay and alpha transport allow investment returns derived from asset classes of strategic importance to be separated from those derived from trading and portfolio management skills. From the point of view of most institutional investors, the first group of investments represents "beta"—a strategic asset allocation mix defined in the medium-long term and infrequently modified. In contrast, "alpha" involves actively-managed portfolios of assets: definitions are abundant, but a relevant one in this context is that the resulting alpha portfolios should have desirable return and risk features, with low exposure to the investor-specific set of "beta" assets. An alpha, so defined, may include assets whose underlying risk can be diversified, as in the original Sharpe (1964) notion, but also managed portfolios of "beta" assets, such as tactical assets and currency allocation programs. They could even include actively or passively managed allocations to one or more sets of assets not included in the "beta" set, such as commodities and real estate. What matters here is less what is academically pure, and more what is relevant and acceptable to each investor within the context of their asset allocation.

While many defined benefit pension plans embraced portable alpha, because it offered freedom at a targeted risk budget to select alpha where it was best or difficult to obtain (for example, commodities), many endowments shunned the concept. Endowments often budget greater volatility than pension funds and seek the best sources of return for this higher risk budget—this may not justify a portable alpha strategy.

The question is whether, for a target volatility, returns are higher with a portable alpha strategy or not. The answer may be different in a low volatility, high liquidity, low spread environment than it is in a high volatility, low liquidity, high spread environment. Further, in very strong directional markets, portable alpha may lag both on an absolute return basis and on a risk-adjusted return basis. More importantly, strategies such as portable alpha may be most challenged at times of transition from one state to the next in trading the capital markets.

The portable alpha idea is appealing, as separating these components allows for independent risk budgeting, performance attribution, and risk control of "alpha" and "beta" investments. Portable alpha depends heavily on defining the expected outcomes ex-ante (i.e., before occurrence). But if the expected ranges of volatility and ranges of correlation (i.e., volatility of volatility and volatility of correlation) are accurately predicted, sound transportable investing results. In the recent higher volatility and lower liquidity environments, it may be more difficult to formulate expected outcomes. By contrast, more traditional "commingled" alpha/beta investments, such as an actively managed long-only equity portfolio, allow only partial, and usually unsatisfactory, levels of separation through techniques such as tracking error control. This often constrains the alpha source to ensure beta exposure.

Practical Implementation Issues

In practice, even the simplest alpha structure requires attention to issues not usually encountered in more traditional portfolio management setups. Portable alpha structures usually result in additional investor exposures to assets, and/or markets that were not in the original allocation mix. A good example is provided by one of the earliest forms of portable alpha that has been used by institutional investors from as early as the mid 1980s: the replication of an active listed equity portfolio via an index portfolio or index futures contract, with a dollar-neutral long/short portfolio overlay on top (type one, or "Alpha Overlay").

This type of structure appears straightforward: in the end the weight mix of any actively managed portfolio whose performance is measured relative to a benchmark is, algebraically, the sum of the underlying benchmark plus a long/short portfolio with same-value sides (in absolute terms) by construction. As professionals familiar with this structure will know, implementing this "replicating" active equity structure requires attention to at least two additional issues.

The first issue is the potential for "net short" positions. That is, a "short" weighting in the active long/short portfolio that exceeds the corresponding "long" weighting in the benchmark, leaving the underlying investor with a net short liability. This may not be allowed or may be undesirable to the underlying investor. But eliminating it requires imposing constraints in a space, that of smaller-cap stocks, which is often where active managers seek to add value, and would ultimately re-introduce the benchmark drag that the portable alpha structure is supposed to eliminate in the first place.

The second issue is that the underlying active "alpha" manager seeks short exposure through stock borrowing and short selling. These activities involve additional technical, credit, and demand/supply exposures that would not be required in the underweight/overweight context of a traditional long portfolio. Each of them, in turn, requires proper management, and consideration needs to be paid to issues such as margining and sourcing of short names.

Additionally, it may not be possible to separate "alpha" and "beta" investments, or to obtain sufficient exposure to the long and short side of the "alpha" portion. Implementing the beta exposure via an index may be more expensive (as we have seen recently) in times of tighter liquidity, as also may be the cost of establishing swap positions to offset the requisite exposure. Thus, the economics available to direct investors, or to managers who build the strategy to offer to investors, vary significantly according to the state of the market environment. Many emerging equity markets do not allow short-selling, or limit it significantly. In these cases, it is often possible to short sell an index or futures contract against the long holdings of the portfolio, but the short-side weights are limited by the underlying index, just as in long-only benchmarked portfolios. This may be even more difficult in times of market dislocation, as we have experienced recently. Or, as until recently for real estate, and currently the case for the newer forms of alternative investments, a representative index and/or index contracts capturing the relevant "beta" may not be available separately from active management of the underlying assets.

When a solution is available it usually involves structuring by banks and, increasingly, by other specialized intermediaries. In all cases, issues of liquidity and/or counterparty/credit risk arise that need to be properly highlighted and monitored.

Critical Areas in Implementing Portable Alpha Structures

It is not difficult to show that, if properly constructed, a portable alpha structure is superior to more traditional "commingled" alternatives. It also is not difficult to show that, if the market environment changes substantially, a traditional "packaged" beta plus alpha structure may exceed the returns available via portable alpha due to the increased friction, basis risk, and transactions costs. For decades now, specialized intermediaries have been providing solutions to manage the additional exposures associated with portable alpha strategies and their associated risks. They also provide technical expertise in contract structuring. But the additional exposures nonetheless need to be identified and properly managed. These include:

- Proper identification of the beta in the investment portfolio pre-implementation of portable alpha;
- Proper identification of any beta in the alpha generator;
- Proper identification of the correlation of the preceding two items, plus stability of this correlation in different market environments;
- Legal, structuring, credit, and corporate governance of vehicles to manage the financial risk and legal liability arising from short positions;
- Liquidity and counterparty risk when alpha/beta separation is obtained via structuring through OTC, or through contract where liquidity, under

normal and stressful circumstances, is unlikely to match that requested by
the investor;

- Evaluation, monitoring, and management of additional risk exposures
  (shorting, stock lending, derivatives, margining/leverage) involved in the
  structure;
- Stability of volatility and correlations relative to predicted levels;
- Forecasting and planning for potential cash outlays under certain structures
  (for example, portable alpha structures involving swaps);
- Proper identification of embedded leverage in structures that attain beta exposure via leveraged derivatives and invest "excess" cash in alpha exposure;
- The correlation and volatility of alpha—some alpha generators provide low
  levels of alpha with small standard deviations; others provide higher levels
  of alpha with higher standard deviations—when virtually all active managers produced negative alpha during the last half of 2008, the correlation of
  these, plus the negative alpha, caused differing degrees of pain in portable
  alpha implementations; and
- Proper identification of counterparty risk.

The preceding list is far from exhaustive, but in our opinion represents a sensible starting point to identify and tackle critical implementation issues in portable
alpha, especially in a more unsettled investment environment than that experienced in the recent past.

The conclusion after the first decade of use? Successful implementation of
portable alpha has been rare. For some investors, moving from the low volatility, flush liquidity, tight spreads, low risk premiums, and high confidence in the
markets to the opposite environment that accompanied the credit crisis, was necessary to understand the leverage, credit, and cash-flow related issues discussed
in this chapter. This has contributed in no small measure to defining the concept
of portable alpha in a more robust and less simplistic way. It may be that, after
observing the full life cycle of the initial implementations of portable alpha (birth,
development, maturity, abandonment by some), we are now moving to a more
dynamic approach, where portable alpha becomes a key tool in both strategic and
tactical asset allocation.

NOTES

1. See Coates and Baumgartner.
2. See Pensions & Investments 2009.

REFERENCES

Coates, Jack, and M. Baumgartner. "Portable alpha: A Practitioner's guide, unraveling the
    hype behind the latest phenomenon." Morgan Stanley Alternative Investment Partners
    [date not included in publication].
Pensions & Investments. 2009. "Plans Dump Portable Alpha as Returns Sour."
Sharpe, William F. 1964. "Capital Asset Prices–A Theory of Market Equilibrium Under
    Conditions of Risk." *Journal of Finance* 19:3, 425–442.

ABOUT THE AUTHORS

Tanya Beder is currently chairman of SBCC in New York and SBCC Group Inc. in Connecticut. SBCC, founded in 1987, has a broad base of hedge fund, private equity, traditional investment management, financial services, and corporate clients. From 2004 to 2006, Tanya was CEO of Tribeca Global Management LLC, Citigroup's $3 billion multi-strategy hedge fund, and from 1999 to 2004 was managing director of Caxton Associates LLC, a $10 billion investment management firm. Tanya sits on several boards of directors, including a major mutual fund complex and the National Board of Mathematics and their Applications. She has taught courses at Yale University's School of Management, Columbia University's Graduate School of Business and Financial Engineering, and the New York Institute of Finance. She has published in the *Journal of Portfolio Management*, *Financial Analysts Journal*, *Harvard Business Review*, and the *Journal of Financial Engineering*. She holds an MBA in finance from Harvard University and a BA in mathematics from Yale University.

Giovanni Beliossi is currently managing partner at London-based FGS Capital LLP, where he has been CEO and responsible for portfolio management since co-founding the firm in 2002. Previously he was associate director of hedge funds at First Quadrant Ltd, also in London. His experience of managing alternative investment portfolios dates back to 1995, when he joined the firm. Prior to that he was a tenured Research Fellow with the Economics Department of the University of Bologna in Italy, and he has held appointments with BARRA International and Eastern Group PLC. Giovanni is a Board and Research Committee member of Inquire UK and Inquire Europe, and a Board member of the International Association of Financial Engineers (IAFE). He is the European Chair of the Steering Group of the Investor Risk Committee (IRC) of IAFE working on guidelines for disclosure and transparency for hedge funds. Giovanni is a CFA Charterholder.

Tanya Beder and Giovanni Beliossi served as board members of the International Association of Financial Engineers (IAFE), and they co-chair the IAFE's Investor Risk Committee (www.iafe.org).

CHAPTER 28

The No-Arbitrage Condition in Financial Engineering: Its Use and Misuse

ANDREW AZIZ
Algorithmics Incorporated

INTRODUCTION

Valuation techniques used in financial engineering typically incorporate two fundamental assumptions regarding investor behavior. The first is that investors prefer more wealth to less, and will take actions to maximize future wealth. The second is that investors have an aversion to risk, which leads them to make trade-offs between expected future wealth and uncertainty (or risk) concerning future wealth.

The "preference of more to less" assumption is analytically quite tractable. Intuitively, it seems reasonable as a broad generalization, and the notion of wealth maximization can be well defined quantitatively. In contrast, the risk aversion assumption is much less tractable. It is somewhat less appealing as a broad generalization, but, more significantly, the notion of risk aversion can neither be defined unambiguously nor measured in a straightforward manner. As a consequence, valuation techniques that are able to rely solely on the first assumption have proven to be much more effective in practice than techniques that must also rely on the second assumption.

However, as powerful as these valuation approaches have proven to be in practice, there are certain limitations to their effectiveness that tend to magnify in times of market dislocation. In addition to the investor behavior assumption, these approaches also require a range of other conditions that are associated with the efficient functioning of markets, including market completeness and the perfect capital markets assumptions. The good news is that in normal markets the valuation models have proven to be quite robust and behave *as if* these market conditions were always to hold (even if they don't actually hold in the strict sense). The bad news is that this robustness can lead to a false sense of security, and when markets move beyond a certain tolerance, the models can fail spectacularly. In times of these dislocations many of the critical assumptions, which are often forgotten, are no longer appropriate, rendering the conclusions of the models invalid.

This chapter provides an overview of a valuation framework within which the "preference of more to less" assumption can be quantitatively expressed as an optimization problem. The necessary conditions under which this single behavioral assumption is sufficient for pricing purposes are developed and illustrated with a number of examples. In addition, the chapter explores the impact on the valuation approach in the cases when the sufficient conditions do not hold, with focus on the key assumptions of frictionless and complete markets.

THE OPTIMIZATION FORMULATION

The behavioral assumption that investors prefer more to less guides the actions of arbitrageurs who seek to construct a position of holdings that produce the possibility of riskless value for zero net investment. Arbitrage profits are typically classified on the basis of two basic types, defined as *first-order* and *second-order* arbitrage.

First-order arbitrage occurs when a portfolio can be constructed that yields positive value today with no future obligations in any state of the world. Second-order arbitrage occurs when a costless portfolio can be constructed that also guarantees no future obligations but, additionally, where there is some possibility of a strictly positive value in at least one future state.

We assume a model of a market where there are n independent securities and s possible future states at time t. Each possible future state, j, at time t has a strictly positive probability of occurrence, p_{jt}. The vector P_t represents an $s \times 1$ vector of time t state probabilities. The $n \times s$ matrix M_t represents security values where m_{ijt} is the value of security i in state j at time t. Note that while the distribution of values across states for a given security can be described by various measures of dispersion, including variance, the distribution itself need not be constrained to be normal. Likewise, while the *joint* distribution of values across states for two securities can be described by various measures of co-dependence, including correlation, joint normality need not be assumed.

The market price that investors must pay for security i is equal to q_i; Q represents the $n \times 1$ vector of security prices. An investor can purchase a portfolio with holdings of security i in the amount of x_i. It is also assumed that there are no long or short constraints on the purchases of any of these securities. Thus, X, the $n \times 1$ vector of security holdings, is unconstrained. The behavior of arbitrageurs who act to maximize first-order arbitrage can be modeled as the following multistate, single-period linear program:

$$\text{minimize: } c = Q^T X$$

with respect to X

$$\text{subject to: } M_t^T X \geq 0$$

X unrestricted

where 0 represents an $m \times 1$ vector of zeros. This formulation follows the multistate, single-period, discrete model developed by Ross (1976).

In this formulation, an investor's objective to maximize arbitrage profits is re-expressed as an objective to minimize the cost, c, of purchasing a portfolio. The state constraints restrict the feasible solutions to those for which the net value over all trades is nonnegative for each state. Investors are able to buy ($x_i > 0$) or sell ($x_i < 0$) in unrestricted quantities. Given that all investors observe the same value matrix, M_t (i.e., no differential taxation or other investor-specific transaction costs), and that there are no long and short constraints, the market is assumed then to be frictionless.

POSSIBLE SOLUTIONS

Because the no-trade solution ($X = 0$) is always feasible, the cost of the optimal portfolio solving the minimization problem will always be nonpositive. However, while a solution to the problem is always feasible, it may be either *bounded* or *unbounded*.

There are three distinct possibilities to consider. In the first case, the problem is unbounded because the solution to the objective function (the cost of the portfolio) is negative infinity for a given set of security prices. This is the case of first-order arbitrage, whereby value may be extracted today with no future obligations, and can be scaled up in an unlimited manner. In the second and third cases the problem is bounded, as the solution to the objective function is equal to zero and, thus, no value can be extracted today.

In the second case at least one of the constraints is solved as a strict *in*equality. This is the case of second-order arbitrage where, given a zero initial net investment, there is *some* possibility of a strictly positive future value. In the third case, all constraints are solved as strict equalities. This solution is known as the no-arbitrage condition, since no first- or second-order arbitrage opportunities are available for a given set of security prices.

MARKET EQUILIBRIUM

In this general model, the preference of more to less is the sole assumption that guides investor behavior and, as a result, governs the equilibrium pricing of securities in markets that are frictionless and efficient. The actions of arbitrageurs as they attempt to maximize arbitrage profits therefore serve to force prices of relatively underpriced securities higher, and those of relatively overpriced securities lower, until all first- and second-order arbitrage opportunities have been eliminated.

As a result of these market dynamics, we can then assume that the security prices observable to the general investor (post the actions of arbitrageurs operating at the margin), are governed strictly by the no-arbitrage condition. This is the key conclusion of the model, and is reflected by the familiar expression, "the Law of One Price."

THE DUAL PROBLEM

Given the absence of first-order arbitrage in market equilibrium (the primal problem is bounded), the following relationship may be derived from the dual problem:

$$M_t D_t = Q \qquad (28.1)$$

and, as a consequence of the absence of second-order arbitrage (the state constraints are all solved with equality), the following relationship may also be derived:

$$D_t > 0 \tag{28.2}$$

where D_t represents the $m \times 1$ vector of dual prices with d_{jt} the dual variable associated with state j at time t. The vector of dual prices, D_t, is known commonly as the state price vector. Equations 28.1 and 28.2 represent a statement of the Fundamental Theorem of Asset Pricing (FTAP), a formal proof of which is contained in Prisman (1986).

The dual variables have the standard interpretation used in linear programming. If an investor is required to earn at least one unit of value in state j, the objective function increases by an amount d_{jt}. Accordingly, if a new security were to be defined with a value of one unit in state j at time t and zero in every other state, it must have a price equal to d_{jt}. Such an instrument is known as an Arrow-Debreu security.

When the number of independent securities, n, is equal to the number of states, s, at time t, the market is said to be complete. An important feature of a complete market is that the state values of any new security, including each of the s Arrow-Debreu securities, can be perfectly replicated by some portfolio of the original n securities, which, in order to preclude arbitrage, must be equal to the price of the replicating portfolio.

Only in the case of complete markets can *unique* prices be determined for all Arrow-Debreu securities. In markets that are incomplete, however, perfect replication is not guaranteed, and, in that case, only bounds can be placed on the prices of Arrow-Debreu securities.

PRICING RELATIONSHIPS

Assuming that the no-arbitrage condition holds in a complete market with no frictions, then the FTAP states that any arbitrary new security, z, must have the same price as a portfolio of Arrow-Debreu securities with holdings equal to the new security's value in each state as given by:

$$q_z = \sum_{j=1}^{s} = m_{zjt} \, d_{jt} \tag{28.3}$$

where m_{zjt} is the value of the new security in state j at time t. Note that Equation 28.3 is equivalent to the replication approach described in the previous section, with the only difference being that, in this case, the replicating portfolio is comprised of the s Arrow-Debreu securities rather than the n original securities.

As a specific example, the risk-free security, f, with a guaranteed value of one unit at time t, by definition has a value of one in *each* future state, and must therefore have a price, q_f, equal to:

$$q_f = \sum_{j=1}^{s} d_{jt} = d_t = e^{-r_t t} \tag{28.4}$$

where $m_{fjt} = 1$ represents the risk-free security's constant value across all j states at time t and where the new terms d_t and r_t can be defined, respectively, as the discount factor associated with time t and the continuously compounded risk-free rate over a period of length t.

Inspection of Equation 28.3 reveals that by using the FTAP, any security can be priced without knowledge of either its *expected* time t value, $E\{m_{zjt}\}$, or the individual state probabilities, p_{jt}. This is a very important result. The implication is that the pricing of securities in a complete market requires neither the explicit modeling of an investor's attitudes toward risk, nor a description of the distribution of values across states. If it were necessary to model investor attitudes toward risk, it would require incorporating this statistical information, but in the complete market case the information is entirely embedded in the prices of the Arrow-Debreu securities. As a consequence, only the assumption underlying the no-arbitrage condition, the preference of more to less, is required for valuation purposes.

The fact that knowledge of state probabilities is unnecessary for valuation purposes motivates the risk-neutral valuation approach, so called because the valuations are independent of any assumptions made about investor attitudes toward risk. If investors were truly risk-neutral, the *true* expectation of any value distribution across states at time t could be discounted at the risk-free rate. However, since investors are *not* typically risk neutral, the *true* expected values cannot generally be discounted at the risk-free rate.

Nonetheless, we can get around this point. A simple algebraic manipulation of the FTAP defines, for each state j at time t, a new variable, π_{jt} (defined such that $\sum_{j=1}^{s} \pi_{jt} = 1$), that has the characteristics of a probability. From Equations 28.1 and 28.4, the magnitude of each π_{jt} is calculated so that the pricing model can be viewed as discounting the *risk-neutral* expected value across states at time t, $M_t \pi_t$, by the continuously compounded risk-free rate to return the correct price, or:

$$Q = M_t D_t = M_t \pi_t d_t = M_t \pi_t e^{-r_t \cdot t}$$

where:

$$\pi_t = \frac{D_t}{d_t}$$

and where π_t represents the $s \times 1$ vector of risk-neutral probabilities associated with states that occur at time t. As the result stems from a simple algebraic manipulation, and given that the true probabilities are not required for pricing, then the risk-neutral approach is appropriate regardless of an investor's true attitude toward risk. From Equations 28.3 and 28.4, the new security, z, can be alternatively valued under the risk-neutral technique as:

$$q_z = \left[\sum_{j=1}^{S} \pi_{jt} m_{zjt} \right] e^{-r_t \cdot t} \tag{28.5}$$

where π_{jt} is the risk-neutral probability associated with state j at time t. In other words, we can say that the security's value is equal to the risk-neutral *expected* payment of the new security, discounted at the risk-free rate over time t.

PERFECT CAPITAL MARKETS

While the FTAP as developed in the previous sections relied explicitly on a single behavioral assumption, it also relied implicitly on three key assumptions underlying the dynamics of the market. These assumptions are described next and, along with the "preference of more to less" behavioral assumption, are typically referred to collectively as the perfect capital markets (PCM) condition. The combination of these assumptions ensures that the market operates *efficiently* from both an informational and an allocation perspective.

Frictionless Markets

Under this assumption, it is assumed that securities are perfectly divisible, meaning that they can be bought and sold in any fraction or multiple, and that there are no constraining regulations on trading, such as limits on short selling. In addition, it is also assumed that the market is free of transaction costs or taxes, although the no-taxation assumption can be relaxed if taxes are applied in a symmetrical manner, meaning that there is no differential taxation across investors.

Perfect Competition

Under this assumption, it is assumed that all investors are price takers, rather than price makers, and it ensures that no single investor can impact prices on the basis of the volume of the investor's trade. Equilibrium prices are assumed to result from the dynamics of the collective, as described by Adam Smith's "invisible hand" of market behavior. Another implication of this assumption is that there is always perfect liquidity in the market, implying that there are always as many buyers and sellers, and that prices adjust to clear the market without a liquidity premium.

Informational Efficiency

Under this assumption, it is assumed that all relevant information determining security prices is both costless and simultaneously available to all investors. In the context of the multistate framework described in the previous sections, this assumption implies that all possible future state values are known and agreed upon by all investors. Risk is modeled solely on the basis of the uncertainty of state occurrence, rather than on the uncertainty of security value given the realization of a given state.

A TWO-STATE, SINGLE-PERIOD EXAMPLE

As an illustration of the model described earlier, consider the two-state model as shown in Exhibit 28.1 whereby the realized state j occurring at time-step k over time t is given by $S\{j,k\}$. In this single time-step model, $k = 1$ for all future states over time t, while $S\{1,0\}$ represents the current state known with certainty today.

Consider two independent securities, priced today at q_1 and q_2, with state values of m_{111} and m_{211} occurring in $S\{1,1\}$ and state values of m_{121} and m_{221} occurring in $S\{1,1\}$, respectively. Given that there are as many independent securities as there are states ($n = s = 2$), the implication is that the market is complete. It is also

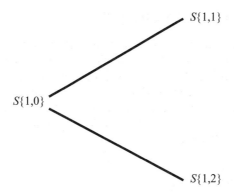

Exhibit 28.1   Two-State, Single-Time-Step Model

assumed that all assumptions underlying the PCM condition apply to this market. The state values of these securities are given in Exhibit 28.2.

Optimization Model

In this example, the behavior of arbitrageurs can be modeled by the following linear programming problem:

$$\textbf{minimize:}\ c = q_1 x_1 + q_2 x_2$$

with respect to X

$$\textbf{subject to:}\ m_{111} x_1 + m_{211} x_2 \geq 0$$

$$m_{121} x_1 + m_{221} x_2 \geq 0$$

x unrestricted

with the interpretation that the cost of a two-security portfolio is minimized, subject to the constraints that the portfolio's values must be nonnegative in each of the two future states in time-step 1. Graphically, the primal problem can be represented

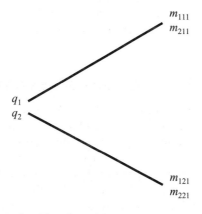

Exhibit 28.2   Complete Market: Two Securities

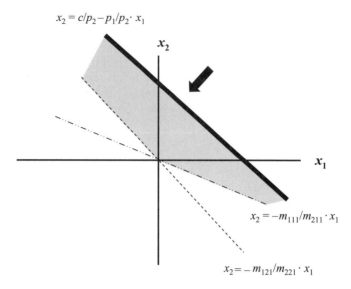

$$x_2 = c/p_2 - p_1/p_2 \cdot x_1$$

$$x_2 = -m_{111}/m_{211} \cdot x_1$$

$$x_2 = -m_{121}/m_{221} \cdot x_1$$

Exhibit 28.3 Feasible Region and Objective Function

by Exhibit 28.3, where the dashed lines represent the boundaries of the two state constraints and where the shaded region represents the intersection of feasible solutions to the optimization problem in terms of holdings x_i and x_j. The heavy line represents the slope of the objective function, and the arrow represents the direction of cost minimization. The three cases of first-order arbitrage, second-order arbitrage, and the no-arbitrage condition are determined by the relative slopes of the three lines.

In the case of first-order arbitrage, the slope of the objective function is either greater or less than the slopes of *both* of the lines representing the state constraints. In Exhibit 28.4, where $m_{121}/m_{221} > m_{111}/m_{211} > q_1/q_2$, assume that the (absolute) slope of the objective function is less than the (absolute) slopes of the constraints.

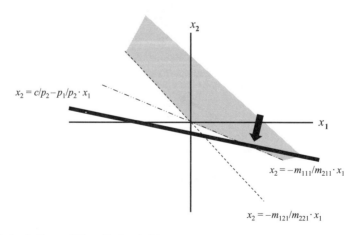

$$x_2 = c/p_2 - p_1/p_2 \cdot x_1$$

$$x_2 = -m_{111}/m_{211} \cdot x_1$$

$$x_2 = -m_{121}/m_{221} \cdot x_1$$

Exhibit 28.4 A Case of First-Order Arbitrage

In this case, the heavy line representing the objective function can be pushed infinitely beyond the origin (c becomes increasingly negative), as arbitrageurs will increasingly purchase security 1 and increasingly short-sell security 2 (x_1 becomes increasingly positive and x_2 becomes increasingly negative). The coordinates of the optimal portfolio will extend infinitely into the southeast quadrant, while the solution to the objective function is unbounded, as arbitrageurs reap unlimited first-order arbitrage unless prices readjust (i.e., unless the slope of the heavy line alters as q_1 and q_2 readjust).

In the case of second-order arbitrage, the slope of the line representing the objective function is *equal* to either of the slopes of the lines representing the state constraints. In Exhibit 28.5, where $m_{121}/m_{221} > m_{111}/m_{211} = q_1/q_2$, assume that the slope of the objective function coincides with state constraint 1.

In this case, the heavy line representing the objective function can be pushed only to the origin where the three lines intersect, and thus the solution is bounded ($c = 0$), implying that no first-order arbitrage profits are available. However, arbitrageurs can reap unlimited second-order arbitrage if state 2 were to occur, by increasingly purchasing security 1, and increasingly short-selling security 2 (x_1 becomes increasingly positive and x_2 becomes increasingly negative). The coordinates of the optimal portfolio will again extend infinitely into the southeast quadrant, this time along the coincident line of the objective function and state constraint 1 unless, once again, prices readjust.

In the case of the no-arbitrage condition, the slope of the line representing the objective function must be less than the slope of one state constraint and greater than the slope of the other. In Exhibit 28.6, where $m_{121}/m_{221} > p_1/p_2 > m_{111}/m_{211}$, assume that the slope of the objective function is less than state constraint 2 and greater than state constraint 1.

In this case, the heavy line representing the objective function can be pushed only to the origin where the three lines intersect and, thus, the solution is bounded ($c = 0$), implying that no first-order arbitrage profits are available. As the solution is solved with a single optimal portfolio ($x_1 = 0$ and $x_2 = 0$), there are also no second-order arbitrage profits available.

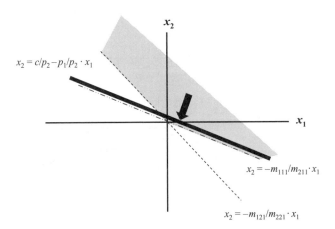

Exhibit 28.5 A Case of Second-Order Arbitrage

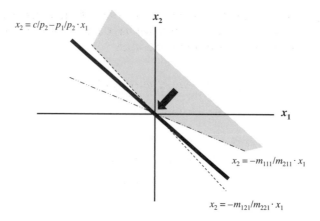

Exhibit 28.6   A Case of Market Equilibrium

The key assumption underlying almost all pricing methodologies used in financial engineering is that observable prices available to investors are such that neither first- nor second-order arbitrage opportunities are available and, thus, case 3 must hold in market equilibrium. In other words, the behavior of arbitrageurs acting at the margin will serve to ensure that prices always readjust to achieve the no-arbitrage condition in equilibrium.

Fundamental Theorem of Asset Pricing

Given both the no-arbitrage condition and the assumption of a complete market in this example, the following relationships may be derived from Equation 28.1:

$$m_{111}d_{11} + m_{121}d_{21} = q_1$$

$$m_{211}d_{11} + m_{221}d_{21} = q_2$$

where d_{11} and d_{21} represent the unique prices of the Arrow-Debreu securities corresponding to states 1 and 2, respectively, at time-step 1 and are calculated as:

$$d_{11} = \frac{q_1\, m_{221} - q_2\, m_{121}}{m_{111}\, m_{221} - m_{121}\, m_{211}}$$

$$d_{21} = \frac{q_2 - m_{211}d_{11}}{m_{221}}$$

From Equation 28.3, the price of a new security, z, with values of m_{z11} and m_{z21} over states 1 and 2 at time-step 1, can be priced as a portfolio of Arrow-Debreu securities with holdings equal to the new security's values in each state. Therefore, in order to preclude arbitrage, the equilibrium price of a new security, q_z, in market equilibrium must equal:

$$q_z = m_{z11}d_{11} + m_{z21}d_{21}$$

Applying the technique of risk-neutral valuation, the new security can also be priced by discounting its risk-neutral *expected* payment of $(m_{z11}\pi_{11} + m_{z21}\pi_{21})$ by the risk-free rate over time t, or from Equation 28.5,

$$q_z = (m_{z11}\pi_{11} + m_{z21}\pi_{21})e^{-r_t \cdot t}$$

where:

$$\pi_{11} = d_{11}/(d_{11} + d_{21})$$
$$\pi_{21} = d_{21}/(d_{11} + d_{21})$$

INCORPORATING THE EVENT OF DEFAULT

The event of default can be incorporated into this general model as an occurrence within one or more states that triggers nonpayment of an agreed-upon value by the issuer of the security. An otherwise risk-free security, z, that exhibits default risk is one that has a value of one unit in each nondefault state and some recoverable amount, expressed in terms of a rate, $0 \leq \Phi_{zjt} \leq 1$, corresponding to each default state at time t.

Assume that, of the s possible states at time-step 1, the first $j = 1, \ldots, s^*$ represent nondefault of obligor (i.e., issuer) U while the remaining $j = s^* + 1, \ldots, s$ represent obligor U default. For the moment, we also assume the market to be complete, implying the existence of $n = s$ independent securities. Given that any security in a complete market can be replicated by a portfolio of Arrow-Debreu securities, then, from Equation 28.3, the price of a new risky security, $q^u{}_z$, associated with issuer U must be:

$$q_z^u = \sum_{j=1}^{s} m_{zj1}^u d_{j1}$$

$$= \sum_{j=1}^{s^*} d_{j1} + \sum_{j=s^*+1}^{s} \Phi_{zj}\, d_{j1}$$

where $m^u{}_{zj1}$ represents the credit-risky security's payment in state j at time-step 1, which in the case of nondefault $m^u{}_{zj1} = 1$, and in the case of default $m^u{}_{zj1} = \Phi_{zj}$.

We now introduce a new variable, R_t that represents the continuously compounded *risky* discount rate associated with obligor U that can be used to price the credit-risky security over time t as:

$$q_z^u = e^{-R_t t} \tag{28.6}$$

where, in this context, the term *risky* refers to the default risk associated with obligor U.

From Equations 28.5 and 28.6, the price of the credit-risky security can be restated under the risk-neutral approach as:

$$q_z^u = \left[\sum_{j=1}^{s^*} \pi_{j1} + \sum_{j=s^*+1}^{s} \Phi_{zj} \pi_{j1} \right] e^{-r_t \cdot t} = e^{-R_t \cdot t} \tag{28.7}$$

which provides a relationship between the risk-free discount rate and the risky discount rate. If we now make the simplifying assumption that the rate of recovery is constant across all states, then Equation 28.7 can be reexpressed as:

$$q_z^u = \left[\sum_{j=1}^{s^*} \pi_{j1} + \Phi_z \sum_{j=s^*+1}^{s} \pi_{j1} \right] e^{-r_t \cdot t} = e^{-R_t \cdot t} \tag{28.8}$$

where Φ_z represents the recovery rate applicable to all default states for this security.

By now assuming a constant recovery rate, we can collapse the entire state space into just two *super*-states of default and nondefault where we can define the risk-neutral probability of default at time-step 1, π_{D1}, as:

$$\pi_{D1} = \sum_{j=s^*+1}^{s} \pi_{j1} \tag{28.9}$$

Accordingly, the risk-neutral probability of nondefault will be equal to, $1 - \pi_{D1}$, and this credit risk example can now be recast in the two-state framework as worked through in the previous section and as illustrated in Exhibit 28.7.

The advantage of the constant recovery assumption is that it now enables a complete market to be defined with only *two* independent securities required to span the default and non-default *super*-states. This can be achieved with just the risk-free and credit-risky securities as illustrated in Exhibit 28.8.

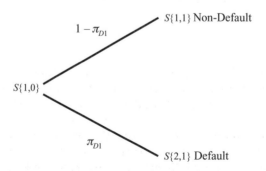

Exhibit 28.7 Two-State Model: Default and Nondefault

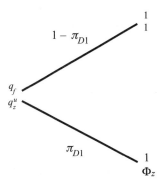

Exhibit 28.8   State Values of Risk-Free and Credit-Risky Securities

From Equations 28.8 and 28.9, the FTAP enables the price of the credit-risky security to be rewritten as:

$$q_z^u = [(1 - \pi_{D1}) + \Phi_z \cdot \pi_{D1}]e^{-r_t \cdot t}e^{-R_t \cdot t} = [1 - (1 - \Phi_z)\pi_{D1}]e^{-r_t \cdot t} = e^{-R_t \cdot t} \qquad (28.10)$$

Calculating a Credit Spread

We can define a credit spread as the difference between the risky rate and the risk-free rate, $\rho_t = R_t - r_t$, for obligor U and, thus:

$$[1 - (1 - \Phi_z)\pi_{D1}]e^{-r_t \cdot t} = e^{-(r_t + \rho_t) \cdot t}$$
$$1 - (1 - \Phi_z)\pi_{D1} = e^{-\rho_t \cdot t} \qquad (28.11)$$

and, by further rearranging Equation 28.11, the credit spread corresponding to the period $t = 1$ can be expressed as:

$$\rho_t = -\ln[1 - (1 - \Phi_z)\pi_{D1}] \qquad (28.12)$$

or, when π_D is sufficiently small, a Taylor Series expansion of Equation 28.12 allows the relationship to be more commonly defined as:

$$\rho_t \approx (1 - \Phi_z)\pi_{D1}$$

where the credit spread is shown to be a function of both the likelihood of default and the rate of recovery given default. Note that this relationship holds with respect to the *risk-neutral* probability of default as opposed to the true or statistical probability of default.

Inspection of Equation 28.10 reveals that the price of the riskless security must always be greater than that of the credit-risky security ($q_f > q_z^u$) or, alternatively, from Equation 28.12, that the credit-risky rate must always be higher than the risk-free rate ($\rho_t > 0$ or $R_t > r_t$). This observation illustrates that a credit risk premium is always required for an investment in the credit-risky security, despite the fact that neither the statistical probability of default nor investor attitudes toward risk has been explicitly incorporated into the model.

The preceding result illustrates a subtlety associated with the conventional calculation of the required credit-risky rate and the credit spread. In classical finance, it is well accepted that a risk premium over and above the risk-free rate is required to entice a *risk-averse* investor to invest in a risky security. The overall required return is calculated on the basis of the statistical expected value at time t with respect to the current market price. This definition implies that the statistical probabilities of the occurrence of each state must be known in order to determine the expected value and, ultimately, the magnitude of the risk premium.

In contrast, the required credit-risky return, as defined in Equation 28.10, is calculated solely on the basis of the FTAP. Therefore, statistical state probabilities are not required in order to determine the magnitude of the credit risk premium. As a consequence, the credit risk premium, as conventionally calculated, does not arise out of an assumed trade-off between risk and return, but simply out of the no-arbitrage relationship derived from the "preference of more to less" assumption. In fact, the credit risk premium will always be positive, even in the case when investors are truly *risk seekers*.

A MULTIPERIOD FRAMEWORK

When the number of available states at a given time horizon, t, exceeds the number of independent securities, s, the market is said to be incomplete, as unique prices for Arrow-Debreu securities cannot be found and the FTAP cannot be used to uniquely price any arbitrary new security. Without either introducing sufficient independent securities to complete the market, or invoking an additional behavioral assumption, a refinement of the state *process* over time t must be made in order to determine unique Arrow-Debreu prices.

No-arbitrage pricing in markets that are not complete over time t can still be accomplished by imposing a multistep state process such that, at each state in an *intermediate* time step, the number of available states in the *next* time-step does not exceed the number of independent securities. Given such a state process, the market is considered to be "dynamically" complete over time t through a strategy of rebalancing holdings at each state in a given time-step, such that over any next time-step the market is always complete.

The lattice in Exhibit 28.9 illustrates a two-period, two-state process that represents a complete market in the dynamic sense. Although a total of four states is possible at time t, only two states are available over the first time-step and, contingent upon the realization of a given state in the first time-step, only two states become available over the second time-step. In this particular model, the overall time period, t, is divided into $\tau = 2$ time-steps, whereby each future time-step is denoted by $k = 1, \ldots, \tau$ and where $k = 0$ represents the known state today. The realized state j occurring in time-step k is represented by $S\{j,k\}$.

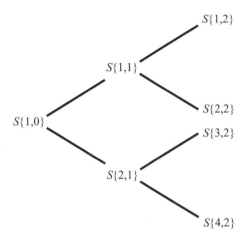

Exhibit 28.9 Two-State, Two-Time-Step Model

Extending the result of Equation 28.1, the FTAP in the multiperiod case can be expressed as follows:

$$\sum_{k=1}^{\tau} M_k D_k\{1, 0\} = Q \tag{28.13}$$

where Q still represents an $n \times 1$ vector of security prices, and where the $s_k \times 1$ vector $D_k\{1,0\}$ represents the Arrow-Debreu prices observed in $S\{1,0\}$ with future values corresponding to each state in a given time-step $k > 0$. The $n \times s_k$ matrix M_k represents realized security values across each state of time step k with each matrix component, m_{ijk}, denoting the value of security, i, in $S\{j,k\}$.

Given a dynamically completed market, the $S\{j,k\}$ observed price of an Arrow-Debreu security, with a value of one unit if state $S\{j,k + 1\}$ occurs and zero otherwise, is always unique and equal to $d_{j,k+1}\{j,k\}$. For the two-state, two-time-step framework described in Exhibit 28.9, the $S\{1,0\}$ prices of both Arrow-Debreu securities associated with the first time-step are unique and equal to $d_{1,1}\{1,0\}$ and $d_{2,1}\{1,0\}$, while the prices of the two *contingent* Arrow-Debreu securities observed in $S\{1,1\}$ associated with the second time-step are also unique, and equal to $d_{1,2}\{1,1\}$ and $d_{2,2}\{1,1\}$, respectively.

Likewise, the prices of the two contingent Arrow-Debreu securities observed in $S\{2,1\}$ associated with the second time-step are unique and equal to $d_{3,2}\{2,1\}$ and $d_{4,2}\{2,1\}$, respectively. Exhibit 28.10 illustrates the first time-step Arrow-Debreu securities and the prices of the contingent second time-step Arrow-Debreu securities associated with the framework described in Exhibit 28.9.

To preclude arbitrage in a dynamic context, the $S\{1,0\}$ price of an investment that has a value of one unit in state j of the *second* time step and zero otherwise, $d_{j,2}\{1,0\}$ must be equal to the cost of the self-financing strategy of purchasing an Arrow-Debreu security at $S\{1,0\}$ and rolling it over into the appropriate contingent Arrow-Debreu security that becomes available in $S\{j,1\}$.

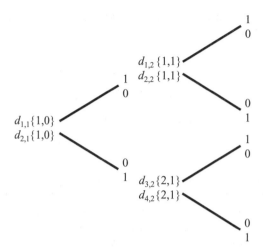

Exhibit 28.10   Contingent Prices of Arrow-Debreu Securities

The price of the Arrow-Debreu strategy, $d_{1,2}\{1,0\}$ that produces a value of 1 in $S\{1,2\}$ and zero otherwise, is achieved by purchasing $d_{1,2}\{1,1\}$ units of the Arrow-Debreu security associated with $S\{1,1\}$ today and, contingent upon $S\{1,1\}$ occurring, rolling the proceeds into one unit of the contingent Arrow-Debreu security associated with $S\{1,2\}$. The strategy is self-financing, as the $d_{1,2}\{1,1\}$ value of the investment reaped in $S\{1,1\}$ is exactly equal to the price of the contingent Arrow-Debreu security associated with $S\{1,2\}$, and thus it must be the case that $d_{1,2}\{1,0\} = d_{1,2}\{1,1\}\, d_{1,1}\{1,0\}$. Note, if instead $S\{2,1\}$ were to occur in time-step 1, the investment would expire worthless. Exhibit 28.11 illustrates the prices of each

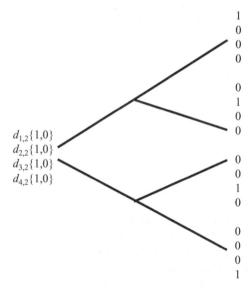

Exhibit 28.11   Prices of Arrow-Debreu Strategies

Arrow-Debreu two-step strategy associated with the available securities illustrated in Exhibit 28.10, where:

$$d_{1,2}\{1, 0\} = d_{1,2}\{1, 1\}d_{1,1}\{1, 0\}$$

$$d_{2,2}\{1, 0\} = d_{2,2}\{1, 1\}d_{1,1}\{1, 0\}$$

$$d_{3,2}\{1, 0\} = d_{3,2}\{2, 1\}d_{2,1}\{1, 0\}$$

$$d_{4,2}\{1, 0\} = d_{4,2}\{2, 1\}d_{2,1}\{1, 0\}$$

The implication is that, in a complete and arbitrage-free market, any arbitrary new security must have the same price as a portfolio of the Arrow-Debreu strategies with holdings equal to the new security's payment in each $S\{j,k\}$. From Equation 28.13, the price of a new security, z, with state values of m_{zj1} and m_{zj2} over time-steps 1 and 2, can be priced as a portfolio of Arrow-Debreu strategies with holdings equal to the new security's values associated with each state over all time-steps. Therefore, in order to preclude arbitrage, the equilibrium price of a new security, q_z, in market equilibrium must be equal to:

$$q_z = \sum_{j=1}^{s_1} m_{zj1} \, d_{j,1}\{1, 0\} + \sum_{j=2}^{s_2} m_{zj2} \, d_{j,2}\{1, 0\}$$

where, for $k = 1$, $d_{j,1}\{1,0\}$ represent the prices of the Arrow-Debreu securities analogous to a single period model and where, for $k = 2$, $d_{j,2}\{1,0\}$ represent the prices of the Arrow-Debreu strategies as defined earlier. In other words, any new security can be dynamically replicated through a series of single-step Arrow-Debreu securities.

By a simple algebraic manipulation of Equation 28.13, the risk-neutral valuation approach can be formulated for the multiperiod context in the following manner:

$$Q = \sum_{k=1}^{\tau} M_k D_k = \sum_{k=1}^{\tau} M_k \pi_k\{1, 0\} \cdot d_k\{1, 0\} = \sum_{k=1}^{\tau} M_k \pi_k\{1, 0\} \cdot e^{-r_k\{1,0\} \cdot k} \qquad (28.14)$$

where:

$$\pi_k\{1, 0\} = \frac{D_k\{1, 0\}}{d_k\{1, 0\}}$$

represents an $s_k \times 1$ vector of the risk-neutral probabilities associated with each $S\{j,k\}$ as observed in $S\{1,0\}$. The risk-neutral expected value of $M_k \pi_k\{1,0\}$ can, thus, be viewed as being discounted from each time-step k back to $S\{1,0\}$ by the continuously compounded risk-free rate, $r_k\{1,0\}$, associated with time-step k.

As a specific example, the risk-free security with a value of one unit across all states in a given time-step, k, must, therefore, have a price q_f equal to a portfolio containing one of each of the s_k Arrow-Debreu securities associated with time-step k or simply:

$$q_f = \sum_{j=1}^{s_k} d_{jk}\{1,0\} = d_k\{1,0\} = e^{-r_k\{1,0\}k} \qquad (28.15)$$

where, as before, $m_{fjk} = 1$ represents the constant value of the risk-free security across all j states in time-step k, and where the terms $d_k\{1,0\}$ and $r_k\{1,0\}$ are defined, respectively, as the discount factor associated with time-step k and the continuously compounded risk-free rate over time-step k, both observed in $S\{1,0\}$.

Term Structure of Interest Rates

Note, in a multistep framework, that an arbitrary *fixed income* security, z, which makes constant payments across all states in each time-step k for *multiple* time-steps, must have the same price as a portfolio of risk-free securities with holdings equal to the fixed income security's payment in each time-step, or as per equation 28.15:

$$q_z = \sum_{k=1}^{\tau} m_{zk} d_k\{1,0\} = \sum_{k=1}^{\tau} m_{zk} e^{-r_k\{1,0\}k}$$

where m_{zk} represents the constant payment of the fixed-income security across all states in time-step k.

If the security universe under consideration were to consist *entirely* of these fixed-income securities, then the multistep, multistate model collapses to a multistep, *single*-state model, which becomes exactly analogous to the multistate, single-*time-step* model described in the first section of the chapter. In this context, rather than solving for the prices of individual Arrow-Debreu securities for a single time-step, the no-arbitrage condition in complete markets (meaning here that the number of independent securities n equals the number of time-steps τ) enables us to solve unique discount factors for each time-step k. As the entire state space is now collapsed into a single *super*-state for each time-step, discount factors are solved for directly, rather than first solving for the prices of the Arrow-Debreu securities. This is the well-known *bootstrapping* exercise.

In a dynamically completed market (or in the *static* complete market of fixed-income securities just described), a term structure of "spot" risk-free interest rates can be defined, which, in the continuously compounded case, is expressed as:

$$r_k\{1,0\} = -\ln \frac{\left[\sum_{j=1}^{s_k} d_{j,k}\{1,0\}\right]}{k} = -\ln \frac{[d_k\{1,0\}]}{k}$$

for a given term k.

Furthermore, in a dynamically completed market (this time a complete market of fixed-income securities alone will *not* suffice), it is also possible to define a series of *contingent* risk-free securities that are observed in some future $S\{j,k > 0\}$. These securities can be priced for a given term x as observed in each future $S\{j,k > 0\}$ and will implicitly define a *state process* for the term structure of interest rates over τ time-steps such that the term structure can be expressed as:

$$r_{k+x}\{j,k\} = -\ln \frac{\left[\sum\limits_{j=1}^{s_{k+x}} d_{j,k+x}\{j,k\}\right]}{x} = -\ln \frac{[d_{k+x}\{j,k\}]}{x}$$

for a given term x.

INCORPORATING DEFAULT

The event of default can be incorporated into the multi–time-step model as an occurrence within one or more $S\{j,k > 0\}$, which triggers nonpayment of a commitment by the issuer of the security. Exhibit 28.12 illustrates the event of default for a given issuer as incorporated into the two-state, two-time-step framework described in Exhibit 28.10. Note that in this framework, default may occur immediately in step 1 or, alternatively, given that nondefault has occurred in time-step 1, it may then occur in time-step 2.

A given credit-risky security, z, issued by U, makes a fixed payment in each nondefault state and payment of some recoverable amount, $\Phi_z\{j,k\}$, expressed in terms of a proportion of the fixed payment, in each default state. Exhibit 28.13 illustrates the prices, $q^u{}_1$ and $q^u{}_2$, and future payments of two credit-risky securities, one maturing in time-step 1 and the other maturing in time-step 2.

A dash in a time-step 2 state indicates that the security has matured in a previous time-step. Note that, in addition to the possibility of defaulting at maturity, the two-time-step credit-risky security may now also default in the intermediate time-step. In this model, default is assumed to be an absorbing state as no resurrection of the two-time-step security is possible in the second time-step if default has occurred in the first time-step.

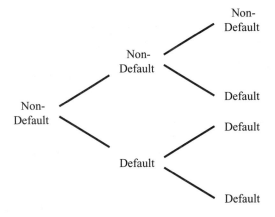

Exhibit 28.12   Default in Time-Steps 1 and 2

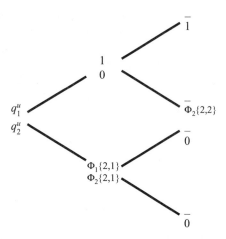

Exhibit 28.13   Payments of Credit-Risky Securities

Given that any security can be replicated by a portfolio of Arrow-Debreu securities, then, from Equation 28.13, the price of the credit-risky security maturing at time-step 1, $q^u{}_1$, associated with issuer U must be:

$$q_1^u = e^{-R_1\{1,0\}} = m_{111}d_{1,1}\{1,0\} + m_{121}d_{2,1}\{1,0\} = d_{1,1}\{1,0\} + \Phi_1\{2,1\}d_{2,1}\{1,0\}$$

where $R_1\{1,0\}$ represents the continuously compounded risky rate observed today over time-step 1.

While the pricing of the one-time-step credit-risky security is simply an application of the single-time-step model as described in the previous section, the pricing of the two-time-step credit-risky security introduces the complication of potential default prior to maturity. Again from Equation 28.13, the price of the zero coupon risky security maturing at time-step 2, $q^u{}_2$, associated with the same issuer U can be represented as:

$$q_2^u = e^{-R_2\{1,0\}2} = m_{212}d_{1,2}\{1,0\} + m_{222}d_{2,2}\{1,0\} + m_{221}d_{2,1}\{1,0\}$$
$$= d_{1,2}\{1,0\} + \Phi_2\{2,2\}d_{2,2}\{1,0\} + \Phi_2\{2,1\}d_{2,1}\{1,0\}$$

where $R_2\{1,0\}$ represents the continuously compounded risky rate observed today over time-step 2.

Risk-Neutral Valuation

From Equation 28.14, the price of the zero coupon risky security maturing at time-step 1 can be restated under the risk-neutral approach as:

$$q_1^u = e^{-R_1\{1,0\}} = [\pi_{D1}\{1,0\} + \Phi_1\{2,1\}(1 - \pi_{D1}\{1,0\})] \cdot e^{-r_1\{1,0\}}$$
$$= [\Phi_1\{2,1\} + (1 - \Phi_1\{2,1\}) \cdot \pi_{D1}\{1,0\})] \cdot e^{-r_1\{1,0\}} \qquad (28.16)$$

where $\Phi_1\{2,1\}$ is the recovery rate given default associated with $S\{2,1\}$. The term $\pi_{\overline{D1}}\{1,0\} = (1 - \pi_{D1}\{1,0\})$ represents the one-time-step risk-neutral probability of *non*default associated with $S\{1,1\}$, which can be expressed alternatively as the risk-neutral probability of *survival* until time-step 1.

Likewise, from Equation 28.14, the price of the credit-risky security maturing at time-step 2 can be restated under the risk-neutral approach as:

$$q_2^u = e^{-R_2\{1,0\}\cdot 2} = [\Phi_2\{2,1\}(1 - \pi_{D1}\{1,0\})] \cdot e^{-r_1\{1,0\}}$$
$$+ (\pi_{D2}\{1,0\} + \Phi_2\{2,2\} \cdot \pi_{D\cap D2}\{1,0\}) \cdot e^{-r_2\{1,0\}} \qquad (28.17)$$

where $\pi_{\overline{D2}}$ is the risk-neutral probability of survival until time-step 2 and where $\pi_{\overline{D}\cap D2}$ is the risk-neutral probability of time-step 1 *non*default followed by time-step 2 default. The recovery rate, $\Phi_2\{2,2\}$, is associated with time-step 2 recovery of default, given that no default occurs in time-step 1.

For analytical tractability, two typical, but perhaps unrealistic, assumptions are often made with respect to the multi-time-step case. The first is that recovery is pushed to the time-step of the anticipated payment (regardless of when default actually occurs), and the second is that the recovery rate is constant for each security issued by U and for all $S\{j,k\}$. Exhibit 28.14 illustrates the prices and values of the two credit-risky zero coupon securities resulting from these revised assumptions, where Φ represents the constant recovery rate associated with all default states at each time-step. In this context, Equation 28.17 can be simplified to produce a general relationship that resembles the specific one-time-step case of Equation 28.16:

$$q_2^u = e^{-R_2\{1,0\}} = [\pi_{\overline{D2}}\{1,0\} + \Phi(1 - \pi_{\overline{D2}}\{1,0\})] \cdot e^{-r_2\{1,0\}\cdot 2}$$
$$= [\Phi + (1 - \Phi) \cdot \pi_{\overline{D2}}\{1,0\}] \cdot e^{-r_2\{1,0\}\cdot 2} \qquad (28.18)$$

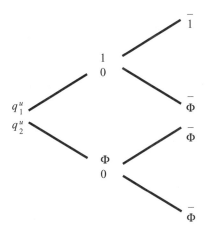

Exhibit 28.14 Impact of Recovery Assumptions

Note that it is not generally the case that the risk-neutral probability of survival over x^* time-steps, $\pi_{Dx^*}\{1,0\}$, is equal to the risk-neutral probability of survival over x time-steps (where $x^* > x$) multiplied by the conditional risk-neutral probability of survival over the next $x^* - x$ time-steps ($\pi_{Dx}\{1,0\} \cdot \pi_{Dx^*}\{\underline{D},x\}$). This observation relates to the fact that risk-neutral probabilities are simply an algebraic artifact and do not, in fact, represent true statistical probabilities. The condition that ensures equality of this relationship is *independence* of the interest rate process from the default process, which can also be satisfied by the stronger condition of nonstochastic interest rates.

Calculating the Credit Spread

The credit spread term structure, for each term $k = x$, can be defined as the difference between the credit-risky and risk-free term structures for issuer U or:

$$\rho_x\{1, 0\} = R_x\{1, 0\} - r_x\{1, 0\}$$

Given the modeling assumptions described earlier, then from Equation 28.18 the price of an x time-step credit-risky security issued by U must be:

$$e^{-\rho_x\{1,0\}} = [\Phi + (1 - \Phi) \cdot \pi_{Dx}\{1, 0\}]$$

implying that the spot credit spread for a term of x can be expressed as:

$$\rho_x\{1, 0\} = -\ln[1 - (1 - \Phi) \cdot (1 - \pi_x\{1, 0\})]$$

or when the risk-neutral probability of default over the next x time-steps is sufficiently small, by a Taylor Series expansion:

$$\rho_x\{1, 0\} \approx (1 - \Phi) \cdot (1 - \pi_x\{1, 0\})$$

The credit spread in this context can now be simplified to an analytically elegant relationship that is a function of both the risk-neutral likelihood of survival over the next x time-steps, and the *constant* rate of recovery given default. See Das and Tufano (1996) and Duffie and Singleton (1999) for detailed formulations of no-arbitrage—based models for the pricing of credit risky securities

In the context of this chapter, this exercise illustrates a typical example of the modeling trade-offs often made to achieve mathematical nicety at the expense of economic reality. In practice, these tradeoffs often prove to be acceptable under normal markets conditions, but typically are the source of model breakdown under extreme events.

CONCLUSION

No-arbitrage pricing models are the most powerful valuation techniques used in financial engineering. As illustrated in this chapter, the only behavioral assumption required is that investors prefer more to less. Observable prices are assumed to be free of arbitrage as the actions of arbitrageurs, by seeking risk-free profits, push prices to an equilibrium state whereby all arbitrage opportunities are eliminated.

The unfortunate aspect of this, however, is that most of the market conditions necessary for its use are usually not present in the real world. Markets are rarely complete in the strict sense, and the required perfect capital markets (PCM) assumptions do not typically hold in practice. In addition, many other simplifying yet unrealistic assumptions (such as the constant recovery assumption used in the examples of this chapter) are often deployed for analytical tractability. Economic reality is often sacrificed to achieve mathematical elegance for modeling purposes.

Nonetheless, in competitive markets with appropriate liquidity and enough breadth to span a wide range of possible future states, no-arbitrage pricing models usually prove to be quite robust. By appropriately collapsing the entire state space into *super*-states (as illustrated in the bootstrapping and single-period credit spread examples), and by imposing exogenously defined state processes into the model (as illustrated in the multiperiod credit spread example), complete markets can be defined in a localized sense. Critical in all of this, though, is the appropriate specification of the securities' joint value distributions across future states, capturing both the dispersion for each security and the co-dependence across securities.

The key challenge in the practical use of no-arbitrage pricing models is to understand when the underlying assumptions are appropriate and when they are not. In *normal* markets, where liquidity is plentiful and where the projected joint distributions across securities can be calibrated with confidence to the relevant past, the models usually behave quite well. In market dislocations, however, when liquidity can dry up and when correlations can converge to one, the underlying modeling assumptions must be reassessed or the models can fail dramatically.

In many cases, financial innovation in the markets has progressed faster than the mathematical tools required to adequately value new products, which is only magnified in times of market turmoil. While financial engineering has evolved significantly over the years by borrowing its mathematical techniques liberally from the physical sciences, the financial system is exposed to significant model risk if we ignore the fact that finance is fundamentally a behavioral science and not a physical science.

REFERENCES

Das, S., and P. Tufano. 1996. "Pricing Credit Sensitive Debt when Interest Rates, Credit Ratings, and Credit Spreads Are Stochastic." *Journal of Financial Engineering* 5:2, 161–198.

Duffie, D., and K. Singleton. 1999. "Modeling Term Structures of Defaultable Bonds." *Review of Financial Studies* 12:4, 687–720.

Prisman, E. Z. 1986. "Valuation of Risky Assets in Arbitrage Free Economies with Frictions." *Journal of Finance* 41:3, 545–556.

Ross, S. 1976. "Risk, return, and arbitrage." In *Risk and Return in Finance*, I. Friend and J. Bicksler, eds., 189–218. Cambridge, MA: Ballinger.

ABOUT THE AUTHOR

Andrew Aziz is executive vice president of Risk Solutions at Algorithmics, leading the firm's Buy-Side and Risk Analytics business lines. Andy has held a number of senior positions at Algorithmics, including vice president of products, vice president of professional services, and executive director of financial engineering. In addition, he currently teaches in the Financial Engineering Program at the Schulich School of Business in Toronto, Canada. Andy holds a number of degrees, including a PhD in finance from York University, an MBA in finance from Queens University, and a BSc (Honors) in chemistry from McMaster University.

CHAPTER 29

Influencing Financial Innovation: The Management of Systemic Risks and the Role of the Public Sector

TODD GROOME[*]
Alternative Investment Management Association

JOHN KIFF AND PAUL MILLS
International Monetary Fund

INTRODUCTION

This chapter discusses the limits to market-based risk transfer and risk mitigation instruments, and the implications for the management of systemic long-term risks. Instruments or markets to transfer and better manage such risks across institutions and sectors are, as yet, either nascent or nonexistent. As such, the chapter investigates why these markets remain incomplete. It also explores a range of options by which policy makers may encourage financial innovation and the development of markets as part of governments' broader role as a risk manager.

We start by showing that, while financial markets have demonstrated significant innovation regarding the management of a variety of nontraditional risks, little activity is occurring with regard to some of the most significant longer-term risks. However, we show that some innovations may provide the building blocks for further advances in risk management instruments and markets. In addition, we discuss the important structural impediments to further growth in the size and scope of certain markets, including data availability, regulatory frameworks, rating agency treatment, tax and accounting policies, and market structure.

We next outline the principal long-term systemic risks, focusing on certain long-gestation, often-accumulating risks, which may have a potentially significant impact on national economies and financial markets. In particular, we evaluate pension savings and related challenges, including longevity risk, health-care costs

[*]The views expressed herein are those of the authors and should not be attributed to the IMF, its Executive Board, or its management.

and related liabilities, and house price risk (particularly as it relates to household retirement savings). We then explore why risk transfer activity is largely absent or, to date, ineffective in these areas. The chapter highlights the ability of public authorities to influence market development and risk management practices, which may encourage greater innovation in a variety of alternative risk transfer markets. Government policies may often help to improve the measurement of risks, and therefore the management and potential transfer of risks to institutions or persons better suited to manage particular risks.

Finally, the chapter makes a case for governments to act as a macro risk manager by taking a long-term, broad-based, and proactive approach to the management of such risks across sectors. Three complementary policy approaches are highlighted: (1) governments may use the many different policy levers at their disposal to encourage private-sector and market-based solutions to foster more complete markets; (2) governments may determine, in some cases, that the least costly or most efficient approach is to use their own balance sheets, acting as the insurer of last resort; and (3) governments may determine that households, as the ultimate shareholders of the system, are best positioned to manage these risks themselves.

By seeking at an early stage to influence private-sector initiatives and innovations to pursue policies designed to develop additional risk management tools, governments (and their various constituencies) may be better able to develop and evaluate public policy initiatives, as well as to better monitor and measure policy performance. In this sense, efforts to develop greater public- and private-sector market risk management activities may produce a virtuous circle.

FINANCIAL MARKET INNOVATION

Thus far, most financial innovations that help to identify, measure, and manage systemically important risks have been applied to more traditional insurance risks, such as peak mortality and natural catastrophe (CAT) risks. Although these innovative markets are small, they are expanding, and important lessons can be learned and applied to better measure and manage long-term systemic risks.

Many of the financial innovations recently developed to measure and manage credit risks are increasingly finding application in the insurance sector. Some of the recent innovations highlight features critical to the development of insurance-oriented risk management tools, including: (1) the capability to define, isolate, and measure risk exposures more precisely; (2) the ability to model and project the evolution of risk; (3) the ability to mitigate moral hazard in the reporting of risk events and data construction; (4) regulatory and rating agency recognition of risk mitigation strategies and techniques; and (5) the structuring of such risks to attract global investment capital and thus expand existing coverage and address new and emerging perils.

Many of these characteristics are evident in recently developed market-based risk management instruments that have been well received by market participants, as discussed later. Such instruments may be broadly divided into three groups, based on how the contingent payments are triggered by the occurrence of the covered risk.

- *Parametric* instruments base the contingent payments on objective data and modeling customized to, and correlated with, the underlying events related to the potential losses of the issuer or insured party.
- Contingent payments of *index* instruments are linked to more generic industry-wide and/or geographic indices that are (more broadly) correlated with the events triggering the covered risks. They are simpler to execute than parametric instruments, although both expose ceders (e.g., reinsured parties) to basis risk (i.e., the risk that the insurance coverage does not exactly match actual losses).
- By contrast, *indemnity* instruments base the contingent payments on the issuer's actual loss experience, which makes them a close substitute for a reinsurance contract.

The use of parametric and index products is growing rapidly. These instruments, while presenting certain basis risks, allow payments to be made quickly to the insured party after a loss has occurred, and tend to attract a wider and diverse investor capital base.

Application of Recent Innovations to Insurance Risk Management

Life insurance securitizations are often based on standardized and well-defined actuarial risk measurements, which should allow for better understanding and modeling of life risk, similar in some respects to mortgage securitizations and auto insurance risk. Life insurance securitization increased from near zero in 1997 to about $7 billion in 2007.[1] During the same period, non–life insurance securitization increased from about $1 billion to about $9 billion. These transactions have been spread among approximately 20 insurance and reinsurance firms, and primarily relate to natural catastrophe risks, although some of the transactions also involve auto and industrial accident insurance. (See Exhibit 29.1.)

Issuance volumes in both sectors have fallen off sharply since 2007. Life insurance securitization volumes have declined largely due to a lack of investor appetite

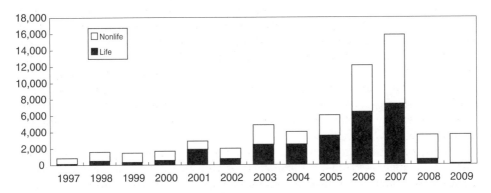

Exhibit 29.1 Insurance Securitization (In Billions of U.S. dollars)
Data source: Goldman Sachs.

for transactions wrapped with monoline insurer guarantees (see later discussion). Non-life insurance securitization fell off in early 2008, on account of a surplus of traditional reinsurance capacity, and dried up completely after the collapse of Lehman Brothers in September 2008. A number of CAT risk bonds were backed by poor-quality collateral supposedly protected by credit derivative contracts with Lehman.[2] When these bonds were sharply downgraded, investors stepped back on fears that other CAT bonds were similarly exposed to credit risk. However, these markets restarted in February 2009, as issuers introduced more conservative collateralization procedures and reinsurance markets tightened. Volumes have since bounced back smartly, although not to the 2007 peak volume levels. But even at those peak activity levels, the amount of insurance-related risk transfer activity represented only a small fraction of the potential underlying exposure.[3]

The securitization of peak mortality exposures, primarily related to pandemic-type risks and relying on parametric triggers, has illustrated the importance of identifying and measuring precisely the specific risk, including the use, where possible, of an index constructed by an independent agent.[4] The index is based on mortality rates in populations to which the insurer is exposed, and payouts from the bond are triggered upon breaches of prespecified levels. Indeed, the development of robust indices may be a key factor in the growth of insurance securitizations or related capital market insurance products, as well as related risk management tools.

A significant motivation for insurance companies to transfer risk concerns economic and regulatory capital considerations. For instance, a large volume of securitizations by U.S. life insurers has been motivated by Regulation XXX, which became effective in 2000. This regulation requires insurers to set aside statutory reserves against term life insurance policies that are generally viewed as higher than economically warranted by current actuarial experience and data. By shifting some of their risk to capital markets, such securitizations allow insurers to hold fewer reserves than required by Regulation XXX.[5] According to Goldman Sachs, of the $27 billion in life insurance–linked bonds issued globally since 1997, $13 billion were motivated purely by Regulation XXX and capital management objectives. However, Regulation XXX securitizations depend on monoline wraps to achieve the AAA ratings that investors expect, so with the monoline insurers facing their own financial challenges, the primary market has effectively been closed since 2007. Liquidity and funding considerations have also been a driver of so-called embedded value insurance securitizations, of which about $13 billion have been issued since 1997. The primary purpose of these indemnity-type transactions is to monetize expected future profits (the embedded value) on blocks of life insurance policies, since the associated expenses and regulatory reserves tend to be front-loaded, whereas the profits accrue over the life of the policy.[6]

Non-life exposures (e.g., natural catastrophes) are considered more difficult to precisely measure and model, and the amount of natural CAT risk sold in the capital markets to date has been a small fraction of the total amount of insured CAT exposure.[7] Nevertheless, the growth of CAT bonds and risks covered shows how innovation is often very dependent on data and modeling developments, in order to assess risks with the required level of confidence. Although both parametric and indemnity-type instruments are used to cover or transfer such risks, insured parties and investors increasingly prefer parametric issues, while regulators prefer indemnity instruments.

Natural CAT and peak mortality bond transactions are now applying structuring techniques typically seen in credit markets. For example, the $300 million Bay Haven transaction launched in 2006 was structured very much like a traditional collateralized debt obligation (CDO), in that it is comprised of multiple tranches that expose investors to a graduated variety of insurance risks (e.g., a relatively high-risk, first-loss or equity tranche, up to a much lower-risk senior tranche that absorbs only the most remote referenced losses). The $310 million Gamut Re "collateralized risk obligation," launched in 2007 involved an actively managed pool of underlying natural CAT risks, and the $200 million Freemantle and $1,138 million Merna transactions both included AAA-rated tranches. Some peak mortality bond issues have included tranches that are wrapped with monoline insurer guarantees so that they could be rated AAA by Moody's Investors Service and Standard & Poor's (S&P). But those without wraps have been rated no higher than AA–, with most being rated from BBB to A–. The investor base for CAT bonds has previously comprised specialized hedge funds and reinsurers, so it is notable that the senior tranches of these CDO-like transactions have attracted life insurers and other money managers.[8]

Natural CAT risks are also being transferred via CAT swaps and industry loss warranties (ILWs)—both relatively new instruments. CAT swaps have typically involved two reinsurers seeking diversification benefits (i.e., by type and/or location of peril—for example, Japanese earthquake for European windstorm risks). More recently, hedge funds and other institutional investors are showing interest in these markets. Hedge funds are also involved in the market for ILWs, which are reinsurance contracts that incorporate derivative-like features.[9]

Hedge funds have also formed reinsurance companies during periods of rising premiums, and are increasingly supporting primary insurance market activity. For example, from 2005 to the end of June 2009, in Bermuda, hedge funds and private equity firms raised about $24 billion of new reinsurance capital, including about $9 billion structured as sidecars.[10] A *sidecar* is a limited-purpose reinsurance vehicle with a finite life, typically established to do business with a single reinsurance client and/or to underwrite a particular risk.[11] Such activity has dropped off since 2007, as premiums have fallen from the record highs of 2006, and credit rating agencies have tightened their criteria for reinsurance start-ups.

Private-Sector Innovations for Managing Slow-Burn Risks

Encouraged by the increased public debate regarding pensions funding in the United Kingdom, investor interest has grown, and financial market initiatives have been launched to transfer pension-related risks. For example, private equity–style funds (buyout funds) have been established in the United Kingdom and elsewhere, seeking to acquire the assets and liabilities of closed defined-benefit pension plans, including their exposure to longevity risk. Along with a few existing insurance companies, such funds seek to purchase and subsequently manage this risk in the financial and reinsurance markets, which may stimulate further market innovation.

Broader investor interest in markets for long-term systemic risks will likely require better and timelier data to provide greater certainty of pricing and payment.[12] In addition, index design may play an important role, such as the U.S. house price index futures that began trading on the Chicago Mercantile Exchange (CME) in

2006. The CME is trading contracts for 10 U.S. metropolitan areas, and settlement is based on the values of corresponding S&P/Case-Shiller Home Price Indices, which are published monthly.[13] For health-care costs, the Milliman Medical Index, first published in 2006, focuses on medical costs based on employer-sponsored managed-care accounts in the United States.[14] This index, which is available for 14 major metropolitan areas, reflects actual medical care expenditures (not insurance premiums), and is designed to track employee medical spending on a yearly basis. However, the infrequent updating of the Milliman index (i.e., annually) may hamper its ability to serve as an effective hedging tool for health-care providers and insurers. Nevertheless, these are important financial market developments, which provide a greater ability to measure and potentially to manage a number of important economic risks.[15]

As discussed in the following pages, key challenges to expanding nontraditional risk management tools include regulatory and supervisory frameworks, as well as rating agency expertise, and support for recent and continuing financial innovations. For these and other reasons (e.g., investor knowledge, accounting treatment, and market structure), markets to better manage a variety of important risks remain incomplete.

Application of Recent Innovations to Public-Sector Risk Management

Public-sector use of risk management tools and risk transfer markets has not been significant thus far, with only a few sovereigns looking to insure or otherwise hedge various risks, including in the capital markets and the issuance of CAT bonds. However, in 2006 Mexico issued a CAT bond covering earthquake risk, and agricultural and livestock insurance is becoming more widely available (Boxes 1 and 2). Such transactions highlight the growing attraction of insurance and hedging instruments, including contingent-capital–type instruments. Increasingly, these public-sector transactions include parametric and index features, providing greater certainty regarding trigger events, and faster payments to the insured parties.

Box 1: Mexican Earthquake CAT Bond

In May 2006, Fondo de Desastres Naturales (FONDEN), a Mexican government agency created to provide emergency relief for natural disasters, issued a $160 million parametric CAT bond to reduce the potential fiscal impact of an earthquake of similar or greater magnitude to the one that killed 10,000 people in 1985 (i.e., 7.5 or more on the Richter scale).[1] The bonds were part of a $450 million three-year insurance transaction.

The rationale for a sovereign to issue CAT bonds includes diversification of insurance coverage, which often improves the coverage and pricing of the overall insured peril. CAT coverage may be particularly relevant for middle-income countries, for whom self-insurance may be less of an option and where coverage is seen as affordable, relatively efficient (i.e., in scope of coverage and

(Continued)

Box 1: Mexican Earthquake CAT Bond (*Continued*)

timeliness of payment), and complementary to traditional relief or donor funds. (See Exhibit 29.2.)

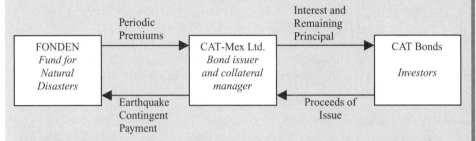

Exhibit 29.2 Mexican CAT Bond Structure

The bonds were rated by Standard & Poor's, and investors receive a floating-rate coupon. Should there be an earthquake that meets the trigger criteria, FONDEN immediately receives the full principal amount from CAT-Mex Ltd., and the bonds are canceled. In October 2009, FONDEN followed up with a similar $290 million "MultiCat" bond that covered both earthquake and hurricane risk.[2]

[1]More specifically, the payout is triggered by a 7.5 magnitude earthquake in and around Mexico City and/or an 8.0 magnitude earthquake in one of two Pacific Coast areas.
[2]The "MultiCat" issuance platform was developed by the World Bank to offer a standardized product to member countries that uses a common legal structure and documentation, while being flexible in terms of types of risks covered.

Box 2: Financial Innovations Supporting Humanitarian Aid

A large number of natural catastrophes occur in emerging-market and low-income countries, with international agencies and charities typically covering most of the costs of recovery and reconstruction. CAT-like financial instruments may provide an additional source of capital to support such traditional assistance.

For example, in March 2006, the United Nations World Food Program (WFP) insured Ethiopian drought risk (covering the period from March to October 2006) via a derivative transaction with a French insurer.[1] The WFP contracted for the insurer to pay specified amounts if a predefined Ethiopian drought index rose above an agreed trigger point. Whereas conventional aid can take many months to arrive and insurance settlements usually occur only after a lengthy

(*Continued*)

Box 2: Financial Innovations Supporting
Humanitarian Aid (*Continued*)

verification and loss-adjustment process, this transaction structure delivers the contingent payment within weeks of the trigger being breached.

The World Bank, which was involved in the Ethiopian transaction, has also developed a pilot project to provide Mongolian livestock herders with index-based peak livestock (cattle and yak) mortality protection. It features a tranched structure, whereby commercial insurers will cover losses for mortality rates between 7 and 25 or 30 percent per species, and the Mongolian government will cover losses in excess of 30 percent. Herders pay premiums for the 7 to 30 percent protection, based on the value of their herds, which will encourage risk mitigation efforts.[2]

Projects like these serve as important starting points and initiatives for the development of market-based insurance solutions for developing countries and the coverage of a potentially wider variety of risks or perils.

---

[1]See Syroka (2006). A similar program has been in operation in India since 2003 (see World Bank 2005).
[2]See Mahul and Skees (2006).

There are several significant economic risks facing industrial countries (and many developing economies) in the medium to long term, which have the potential to produce severe economic costs and possibly financial instability. Given their systemic importance, such events can have material GDP, real economy, and welfare impacts. Some of the most significant risks relate to global demographic trends and aging populations, such as pension and health care provision, which are expected to put tremendous pressure on public and private finances in the medium term, causing some countries to rethink the role and scope of the welfare state. An additional, and somewhat related factor, is that many countries have to rethink or develop energy and even food strategies, in light of tighter supply-demand dynamics in these important commodity markets. Moreover, in each case, the potential adverse economic and financial stability impacts of these developing risks are likely to be more significant the longer policy makers delay actions designed to mitigate or to better manage such risks and related effects.

G-10 policy makers recognize that these longer-term risks present major challenges to public and private finances during upcoming decades. However, a number of countries have indicated that necessary reforms to entitlement systems, subsidies, tariffs, and other policy constraints possibly needed to address these challenges are politically difficult to implement, and may be delayed or lead to undesirable compromises. Of course, markets dislike uncertainty, and these growing long-term risks will serve only to increase market uncertainty. Moreover, the financial crisis of 2007–2009 has only served to further stretch government balance sheets and intensify fiscal pressures. Therefore, at some point, possibly before government actions are taken, as the financial markets act to more clearly measure and anticipate the economic effects of these challenges, the resulting impact and subsequent adjustments could be disorderly.[16]

Governments have a variety of options, including tax increases and benefits reductions, particularly when addressing risks such as health care and pensions. In some countries, the public sector has assumed many of these longer-term risks, yet current government accounting standards often do not require the quantification, reporting, or funding of such future obligations.[17] Consequently, finance ministries frequently do not face a binding requirement, or have strong incentives, to proactively manage growing pension or health-care exposures. Going forward, government accountability for longer-term risk management may require improved public accounting and reporting standards, more robust fiscal frameworks, explicit estimates of contingent liabilities, and increased portfolio risk management by finance ministries. Until that happens, public-sector use of capital market-based risk transfer tools may remain limited.

Other Recent Innovative Risk Transfer Activity

The financial crisis of 2007–2009 has dampened innovation in a number of additional areas of risk transfer while highlighting its potential benefits. For instance, pure macroeconomic risk transfer mechanisms (e.g., GDP futures and swaps) are only intermittently transacted on a bilateral basis. However, the crisis has accelerated the development and trading of sovereign credit default swaps (CDS), which tend to be transacted more as a macro hedge against exposure to a country or a banking system rather than as protection purely against a credit event applying to the sovereign borrower. For instance, observers point out that buying credit protection on the U.S. government is a somewhat bizarre concept since, in the event of default by the United States, there is little likelihood that the counterparty selling protection (or the collateral) would be in existence to meet the obligation. However, this ignores the macro hedging use to which sovereign CDS are put to provide protection against sovereign downgrades or banking sector collapse.

In another area, the policy thrust toward cap-and-trade mechanisms to curb carbon emissions, the trading of CO_2 emissions permits and futures, is now an important element in the efficient pricing and distribution of the burden of emissions reduction. Such futures contracts are actively traded on bespoke exchanges and brokered markets where cap-and-trade schemes are operational (notably within the European Union, with some trading occurring in some states within the United States). However, the liquidity and robustness of such markets depend heavily on the reliability of the policy-making framework for permit supply and allocation, as well as careful design features within the schemes (e.g., bankability of permits between allocation periods). Policy errors in these areas in the recent past in the EU scheme have hampered the market's development.[18]

INCOMPLETE MARKETS FOR INSURANCE RISK

This section focuses on the potential reasons why capital market–based solutions for managing insurance risks may remain relatively undeveloped compared, for instance, to those used by banks to manage credit risk. Some reasons may reflect the fundamental nature and characteristics of particular risks, as well as their degree of insurability or transferability (see Box 3). Others may reflect institutional momentum, in that, historically, insurance companies have often warehoused many of the risks discussed in this chapter, rather than seeking (or being encouraged) to more proactively manage such risks.

The following are some of the key influences on market behavior, risk management practices, and financial innovation: (1) regulation and supervision, (2) rating agencies, (3) accounting and tax policies, (4) market structure, (5) data availability and quality, and (6) risk-sharing arrangements.[19] This section focuses on how these influences may explain why certain markets remain incomplete, and suggest potential public policy responses in order to complete certain incomplete markets.

Regulatory Influences

The Basel regulatory framework created incentives for banks to increasingly focus on risk measurement and management. Policy makers in industrial countries, as expressed in Basel regulatory principles, determined that banks should be encouraged through risk-based capital guidelines to better measure and more actively manage different credit and balance sheet risks, and thereby increase the resilience of their balance sheets for a given level of capital. This led to significant capital market innovations, including increased risk transfer. In short, the Basel framework spurred the development of more active and innovative risk management practices.

Similar regulatory influences on insurance companies' risk management practices have generally not been forthcoming. Indeed, insurance regulators have often been ambiguous, or even ambivalent, as to whether insurers should seek additional methods to manage and transfer their insurance risks via the capital markets rather than remaining the ultimate holders of such risk (i.e., warehousers of risk). Traditionally, insurance regulation has focused primarily on consumer protection and often-prescriptive rules related to asset portfolio management, rather than on more macro prudential and financial stability considerations, or related efforts to improve risk management practices. Consequently, insurance supervisors may often assume that insurers act (or should act) as risk repositories or warehousers of risk, and, therefore, that dedicated reserves are required to ring-fence each of the distinct risks that insurers underwrite. Moreover, reserves are often ring-fenced with their underwritten risks, and rarely viewed by some supervisors as the economic equivalent of capital, to be managed and available to address a variety of risk exposures. Based on this view of insurance regulation, reserve requirements typically are not adjusted if risk is actively managed, transferred, or hedged via the capital markets. Likewise, traditional reinsurance arrangements typically attract reserve relief only if the risk is transferred in its entirety (e.g., on an indemnity basis), which usually requires dedicated reserves from the reinsurer to be held in the covered jurisdiction (often referred to within the industry as "trapped" capital).

Of course, it can be, and has been, argued that such regulatory capital regimes are more stable and safe than the more dynamic or market risk management approaches. We understand that argument, but believe that this traditional regulatory approach seems less likely to attract new capital or encourage better risk management practices. In our judgment, both more capital and better risk management and measurement practices are needed on a systemwide or marketwide basis if we are to effectively address some of the long-term and accumulating risks in the global economy. In fact, in some markets (e.g., retail-oriented coverage) insurance capital and capacity have been reduced in recent years, due in part to political interference in the pricing and/or scope of coverage (e.g., Florida property and casualty), as well as considerations related to trapped capital. While remaining focused on macro prudential and consumer regulatory protection, policy makers need to attract more capital, not less, to a variety of broadly defined insurance risks.

Box 3: What Makes a Risk Insurable, and Possibly Transferable or Tradable?

The degree of insurability of various risks, and thus the manner which they may be managed or possibly transferred, depends on a number of considerations. In general, insurability is enhanced when a risk is assessable in terms of both its frequency and its severity, when insured events are independent of one another and losses relatively uncorrelated, and when risks may be mitigated by seeking diversification benefits through pooling or other means. In addition, transferring risks in the financial markets depends on the ability to identify, measure, and isolate specific risk characteristics, ideally using independent assessments (e.g., by rating agencies or specialized risk modeling firms).

Perceptions about the types of risk that can be intermediated change over time due to financial innovation. Moreover, such innovations are very often influenced by regulatory frameworks and technological advances, particularly with regard to the ability to better measure and decompose complex risk exposures.

Financial innovation acts to expand the boundaries of risk insurability and transferability, as most clearly illustrated by the management of credit and interest rate risks. Advances in financial market techniques allow risks that were previously considered uninsurable to be more precisely measured and proactively managed, and thus made insurable. One method by which insurers approach these issues and classify risks is by considering whether a risk exposure reflects a one-sided or a two-sided market. The latter typically involves counterparties with offsetting initial exposures (e.g., currency risks) who clearly benefit from trade. As such, two-sided risks are considered most amenable to market-based risk management activity. By contrast, one-sided risks affect exposed parties in broadly similar ways (e.g., natural catastrophes and longevity), and far fewer, if any, natural counterparties exist. Therefore, managing one-sided risks has traditionally involved pooling by (re)insurers, and charging a premium to warehouse such risks for a period of time. In addition, and very importantly, (re)insurers often also rely on the ability to periodically reprice insured risks (usually annually), which helps to adjust or limit their exposure and results in insurance customers sharing in the costs of an increase in insurance losses.

(Continued)

Box 3: What Makes a Risk Insurable, and Possibly Transferable or Tradable? (*Continued*)

Interestingly, some risks, previously perceived as one-sided, may become more two-sided, and thereafter may be transferred to a broader group of investors as new technologies and financial instruments are developed. By creating a market price for these risks, such innovations enable insurers and other market participants to more accurately measure and manage their exposures, thereby further increasing the likelihood of one-sided risks becoming tradable.

In the absence of a clear approach or regulatory framework regarding the role of insurers, only a few of the largest and most innovative insurance companies have pursued market-based risk management techniques. These insurers have been motivated in part by economic capital, capacity, and broader balance sheet and return objectives. Insurance companies can face significant difficulty in obtaining regulatory capital relief for such activities.[1] For example, while U.S. insurers can deduct the cost of reinsurance from their gross premiums for the purpose of calculating risk-based capital requirements, they generally cannot do so when securitizing risks transferred in the capital markets. In some cases, supervisors cite concerns about residual basis risk from capital market transactions (e.g., which may exist with nonindemnity structures, as noted earlier) that are not considered present with typical reinsurance arrangements. Consequently, risk reduction methods with payoffs based on indemnity triggers are more likely to be granted full capital relief, whereas the regulatory treatment of structures with payoffs based on indices or parametric triggers is typically less certain and less favorable. Relative to bank regulatory treatment, insurers in most countries get little or no regulatory credit for partial hedges or dynamic hedging strategies (e.g., transactions with term mismatches), a factor that acts to discourage proactive risk management strategies in the insurance area.

---

[1]For example, whether regulatory capital relief or benefit was given for the Fonds Commun de Créances (FCC SPARC), a French auto securitization transaction remains unclear to outside observers (see IMF 2006, Box 2.3). However, it is broadly assumed that the insurer received no regulatory capital benefit.

However, a number of insurance regulators have started to develop more comprehensive risk-based capital requirements, which recognize the benefits of reinsurance, securitization, and diversification within the risk portfolio. For example, Switzerland implemented a principles-based supervisory framework, seeking to promote a greater focus on risk and capital management and to provide insurers with regulatory capital relief for market securitizations.[20] In the Netherlands, the authorities have strengthened the regulation of pensions, particularly through more risk-based supervision, which encourages pension fund managers to focus more on risk management and asset-liability management. The U.K. Financial Services Authority also signaled its willingness to promote insurance risk transfer markets through insurance special purpose vehicles, thereby building on its new risk- and principles-based approach to insurers' capital adequacy.[21] In Asia, some regulators (e.g., the Monetary Authority of Singapore) have also encouraged more proactive risk management practices in the insurance industry.[22]

A risk-based approach is also encompassed in the EU's Solvency II framework, and in the parallel work being conducted by the International Association of Insurance Supervisors. Solvency II is a major initiative to strengthen risk management practices in the European insurance industry. By promoting greater capital management discipline, it should enable EU regulators to better align regulatory capital requirements with economic capital models.

Despite these initiatives, some market participants express doubts regarding the potential for significant cross-border regulatory coordination in the insurance sector. They see the traditional consumer-protection versus risk-based approaches, as outlined earlier, as difficult to reconcile and unlikely to lead to more common or coordinated international standards.[23] Therefore, the impact of Solvency II and related efforts remains difficult to predict.[24]

Rating Agency Clarity

Like regulators, rating agencies have not been viewed as a driving force in promoting or supporting the use of market-based risk management tools by insurers. Once again, in contrast to the credit markets, where rating agencies have had a material influence on credit risk analysis and management, the agencies have not thus far displayed the leadership or expertise needed to support the development of market-based risk management tools in the insurance area. In addition, and similar to the regulators, their recognition of any risk mitigation benefit to an insurer generally depends on the structure of risk transfer mechanism used. Consequently, reinsurance arrangements (i.e., indemnity policies) are typically recognized (although some allowance may be given for counterparty risk), whereas in contrast, no (or only partial) relief may be granted for parametric and indexed structures (favored by the insured parties and capital market investors for their clarity), due to the potential basis risk.

In light of the criticism and increased scrutiny and regulation that rating agencies are likely to encounter going forward, they may not act in the near term to further recognize or look to expand the credit given to insurers for risk transfer activity. However, the major rating agencies have been revising their rating methodologies for insurance risks, including the use of insurers' in-house capital and risk management models, and, together with the larger insurers, may contribute to the development of insurance-risk indices.[25] Such developments may provide insurers with greater incentives to consider market-based risk management practices, and may attract a broader group of market participants and additional capital to the insurance market and new types of risks.

Accounting Policies

Under current accounting rules, transactions with the same economic effect or result are not always treated the same, which may hinder the use of market-based risk management techniques by insurers. Also, current hedge accounting standards can produce disincentives for insurers to use market-based risk management instruments, especially compared with the treatment given to reinsurance contracts. Indeed, current standards may not recognize any of the economic benefits from less-than-perfect hedges (e.g., index-based instruments), and may act to increase reported earnings and balance sheet volatility. Yet such higher volatility may be inconsistent with the underlying economic reality. Rating agencies have also suggested that hedge (and regulatory) accounting standards have dissuaded them from providing a clear ratings benefit to market-based risk management techniques compared with reinsurance coverage, as financial reporting volatility may produce increased market volatility for a company's securities.

More broadly, while the shift to fair-value accounting principles in many jurisdictions may bring more focus to insurance and pension fund financial reporting, it is not clear that the volatility associated with fair-value accounting measures properly focuses insurance companies or pension funds on effective risk management objectives.[26] Therefore, policy makers may also consider whether broader disclosure of the asset and liability structures (including the maturity profile of liabilities, and market and interest rate sensitivities) may provide investors and beneficiaries with more useful information.

Market Structure

It has also been suggested that shareholder pressure to maximize returns on capital in the insurance industry may be relatively less significant than that in the banking sector, which may contribute to making risk transfer activity less urgent in the insurance industry. In addition, in some jurisdictions the prevalence of mutual insurers may act to reduce returns on capital.[27] Market participants also highlight the relative ease with which (non-life) reinsurers are able to raise capital, especially following a large catastrophe, when premiums are expected to rise. Consequently, industry participants and observers state repeatedly that the industry is not capital constrained.

On the demand side of the equation, the absence of well-established benchmarks or indices and rating agency guidance, as well as a general lack of familiarity with insurance-type risks, have made it difficult to develop a broad and diverse investor base for many insurance-type risks, despite potential portfolio diversification benefits. To date, much of the investor demand has come from other insurers and similar specialists already familiar with such risks. Similar to developments in other markets, the diversification and dispersion of risk created, even within this specialist market, would likely enhance financial stability. Moreover, improved primary market liquidity for more risks may trigger a virtuous circle, whereby the availability of liquid market indices may emerge and attract new, diverse sources of capital.

Finally, ongoing consolidation among (re)insurers may eventually limit their ability to increase capacity through traditional risk management practices, such as portfolio risk pooling or warehousing risk, and may lead to increased market-based efforts to disperse risk and attract new capital.[28] Moreover, the systemic importance of these institutions is likely to increase as fewer and fewer insurers play increasingly significant roles related to certain risks, such as retirement and health-care needs. This trend may, in turn, lead authorities to reconsider prudential regulation of insurers, and possibly encourage risk transfer beyond the insurance industry to reduce risk concentrations or systemic exposure to any one company or group of companies, and to attract more capital to a variety of additional risks.

Going forward, there is significant potential for a broader capital and investor base (and related risk management capacity) in the insurance industry, together with a more return-oriented approach to capital utilization. The recently increased presence of investors, such as private equity and hedge funds, including shareholders and owners of (re)insurers, may reflect the beginning of such a change.

Data Availability

Reliable data are critical for the development of market-based risk management solutions. Indeed, market participants often cite the inadequate availability, reliability, granularity, and timeliness of data as reasons for the absence or slow development of markets to manage longevity, health-care costs, and other risks. Data are needed to support the pricing and trading of risks, the development of risk models, and the construction of benchmarks or indices. Although the underlying data typically exist (e.g., hospital records, death statistics), they are often not systematically compiled or widely disseminated on a timely basis.

Long-term risks, such as retirement and health-care costs, are often difficult to measure because the underlying drivers of these costs may be inherently unpredictable, and because forecasts and related risk assessments may be possible only infrequently and with long time lags. For example, market participants emphasize that the pricing of annuity products is materially constrained by the lack of high-quality data on mortality for higher age categories (e.g., 85 to 90+ years), or beyond a 15- to 20-year period for most annuitants (i.e., typically aged 60 to 70 years). Consequently, the absence of adequate data increases the uncertainty associated with extreme longevity risk, resulting in higher capital requirements. Market participants have stated that approximately 20 to 25 percent of the value at risk of annuities sold to 65-year-old men in the United Kingdom relates to their potential to live beyond 90 years (see also Box 4).

For each type of risk, increasing data availability should create opportunities for better risk management. For example, to develop relevant and useful house price index contracts, the underlying data need to reflect local market conditions, and to support market liquidity such data should be published or updated on a relatively frequent basis. In this regard, although underlying house price data is published monthly, the low turnover and liquidity of the Chicago Mercantile Exchange house price futures contracts have proved disappointing. Another example is the health care sector, where the lack of data aggravates the fragmented and local nature of the delivery system (e.g., a variety of specialized health-care providers and insurers' nonstandardized systems).[29] These factors make it difficult to compile comparable health-care data on a broad basis, and thus deter the development of market-based risk measures and risk management tools.

Governments may have a comparative advantage and interest in improving the availability, reliability, and timeliness of certain data necessary for the development of markets to better manage various risks. Indeed, data provision may be a relatively low-cost method of supporting market-based solutions. For example, weather data are now relatively easy to collect cost-effectively and reliably, and can be used to facilitate the provision of agricultural insurance in middle- and low-income countries. Nevertheless, market participants cite the absence of comparable health-care data, the unreliability and out-of-date nature of mortality information, and the lack of reliable local data on house price movements as reasons risk management tools have been slow to develop, or are altogether absent from financial market analysis.[30] Such government initiatives may only need to be temporary, until a growing market demand leads to data collection and dissemination by the private sector.

The U.K. commercial property index derivatives market provides an example of the importance of the combination of regulatory, tax, and data considerations. The development of this market has been based on: (1) the existence of reliable and comprehensive commercial property indices, on which contracts-for-difference and swaps are based; (2) a ruling by the U.K. Financial Services Authority (FSA) in November 2002 that allowed property derivatives to qualify as admissible assets for life insurers, thereby counting toward their regulatory solvency ratios (in addition, the ability to hedge underlying positions in a property index enables insurers to save capital in the FSA's risk-based capital regime); and (3) a tax change in September 2004 that gave property derivatives the same treatment as other derivatives. As a result, transactions have grown significantly since early 2005 and exceeded £8 billion in 2007.[31]

Box 4: Annuity Obligations and Longevity Risk

Annuities provide individuals with the opportunity to hedge longevity risk—the risk of outliving one's assets. In its simplest form, a *life annuity* provides a guaranteed income flow throughout the annuitant's lifetime, thereby hedging the individual's longevity exposure.[1] However, annuity providers face the challenge of hedging the aggregate longevity risk associated with annuitant cohorts, because a number of exogenous factors (e.g., medical advances) result in the relatively high correlation of the longevity of cohort members.

The contracted rate of return to the recipient of an individual annuity consists of a market return plus a *mortality credit* from pooling. This mortality credit is a source of risk for the annuity provider that cannot be easily hedged. For example, in a fixed-income annuity pool of 65-year-old males, in which about 2 percent would be expected not to survive the first year, pooling provides a one-year mortality credit of about 214 basis points if the rate of return is 5 percent.[2] The value of this credit rises with the age of the pool of annuitants. For example, it reaches about 1,853 basis points for a group of 90-year-old males, of whom 15 percent would not be expected to survive a year. However, if the actual 90-year-old male mortality rate were only 14 percent, the available funds to pay the mortality credit would be reduced by 144 basis points, and the annuity provider would have to make up the difference. Indeed, projections of cohort mortality have typically understated future life expectancy and, as illustrated in Exhibit 29.3, there is a great deal of uncertainty about future longevity trends.[3] Given that the increase in longevity, as well as the uncertainty of projections, af-

(Continued)

Box 4: Annuity Obligations and Longevity Risk

(*Continued*)

fects all annuitants in broadly equivalent ways, it is largely nondiversifiable, and results in relatively more capital being required to cover the annuity providers' risk exposure to extreme longevity.[4]

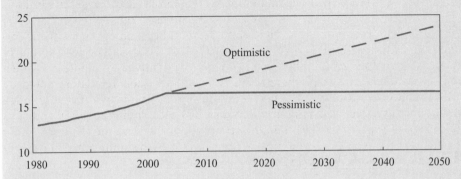

Exhibit 29.3 U.K. Male Cohort Life Expectancy at Age 65: Optimistic versus Pessimistic Projections
Sources: U.K. Government Actuary's Department; International Monetary Fund staff estimates.

One way to hedge longevity risk may be to transfer some of the exposure to investors via so-called longevity bonds or swaps.[5] However, it is difficult to find potential counterparties to such transactions who themselves are not already exposed to longevity risk (i.e., a potential one-sided market). Also, the need for long-dated longevity hedging instruments increases concerns about counterparty credit risks. Nevertheless, since January 2008 $2.6 billion of longevity swaps have been completed by pension funds in the United Kingdom.[6] Prior to the successful completion of these transactions, governments were frequently viewed as attractive counterparties, notwithstanding that most governments already have large exposures to longevity risk through their public pension and social security commitments. However, the unsuccessful attempt by the AAA-rated European Investment Bank (EIB) to launch a longevity bond in 2004–2005 illustrates how difficult it is to design such market-based longevity risk transfer instruments.[7]

---

[1]See Poterba (1997) for descriptions of the many variations on standard annuities, and Milevsky (2006) for the mathematics behind many of the concepts discussed here.

[2]The example assumes away survivor benefits, which would reduce the mortality credit. The one-year mortality credit is equal to $R * [M/(1 - M)]$, where R is the gross rate of return and M is the mortality rate. See Milevsky (2006) for more detail.

[3]See Watson Wyatt (2005) for a discussion of the drivers of the optimistic and pessimistic longevity projections.

[4]The life insurance business is occasionally viewed as providing some natural hedging opportunities (Cox and Lin 2005), but these are typically significantly less than some assume. Indeed, such hedging opportunities are typically quite limited due to

(*Continued*)

Box 4: Annuity Obligations and Longevity Risk
(Continued)

cohort mismatches—the age profile of a typical annuity pool cohort is much older (e.g., 55+ years) than that of a life insurance portfolio, which tends to reflect events earlier in an insured's life, such as marriage and having children (Brown and Orszag 2006).
[5]See Blake and Burrows (2001), Dowd et al. (2005), and Lin and Cox (2005).
[6]According to Aon Benfield (2009), legislative changes and new accounting rules are pushing U.K. pension funds to seek longevity risk mitigation solutions. Also, the legal and regulatory landscapes make longevity risk transfer more feasible.
[7]The failure of the EIB longevity bond has been attributed to several design flaws, including a somewhat narrowly defined underlying index (based on 65-year-old English and Welsh males) and (more importantly) its 25-year maturity, which left extreme longevity (i.e., above 90 years) uncovered (Blake et al. 2006).

PUBLIC POLICY CONSIDERATIONS

Through the use of various policy levers, governments influence the flow of risks in the financial system, and can encourage the development of new products and risk management tools, contributing to financial stability in the process. This occurred in the credit markets throughout the 1990s. Many observers believed previously that credit risk was inherently untransferable or untradable, which has proven not to be the case. Similarly, today many insurers and other market participants believe that certain of the risks highlighted in this chapter reflect one-sided risks or markets, and therefore may be appropriate only for traditional insurance risk management practices, such as portfolio diversification and pooling. However, governments may influence these markets and risk management practices. Some of the policy tools available to the authorities to encourage market innovation and alternative risk management activities have already been discussed (regulatory and supervisory frameworks, accounting standards, and data availability), and others include tax policy and compulsion. Moreover, as a practical matter, and in light of current and growing fiscal pressures on government finances, policy makers should explore means to attract more private capital to address these long-term risks and societal challenges.

Tax Policy

The structure of taxation can also significantly influence the development of risk management practices. First, governments need to consider whether existing tax systems may inadvertently penalize (and possibly prevent) the transfer of risk to other market participants.[32] For example, capital losses on derivative instruments and the costs of securitization should be taxed similarly for insurers to ensure neutrality of treatment between market risk transfer, reinsurance, and retaining risk on balance sheet.

In addition, tax incentives may be considered in some cases, even if temporarily, to encourage desired risk management practices. For instance, tax regimes for company pension funds should be designed to encourage prudent, possibly continuous funding policies, and to ideally incentivize companies to build reasonable funding cushions (e.g., two or three years of normal contributions).[33] With regard to the household sector, the clarity and stability of tax regimes are deemed essential to encourage the development of adequate long-term savings and investment products. More broadly, tax incentives may also be considered to facilitate the development of new markets, such as *macro swaps*, through which (for example) the pension fund and health-care industries could swap their complementary cash flows and exposure to longevity. Longevity increases lead to both greater liabilities for pension funds and higher revenues for health-care companies (from increased health-care spending by the elderly). The availability of an index reflecting the cumulative survival rate in a given population would provide the basis for both parties to trade their symmetric exposures, and to hedge against unexpected changes in longevity. Governments may encourage these transactions (for example) by introducing appropriate tax incentives for the health-care industry, perhaps conditioned on certain research or product development efforts targeting the needs of an aging population.

Compulsion

The need to pool diversified risks is an important feature of insurance, including annuities and health-care coverage. To help reduce adverse selection and bias, governments may require that a minimum degree of insurance be purchased by all persons. Such an option also helps to limit the potential costs that may ultimately be transferred to the public sector. With regard to longevity risk management, mandatory annuitization (similar to more specific risk measurement) may encourage the emergence of simpler annuity products, and potentially improve households' understanding and acceptance of such products. In the health-care sector, many Organization for Economic Cooperation and Development (OECD) countries have mandatory universal public or private health care, which may be a way for the government to overcome market limitations. For example, in 2006, the Netherlands introduced compulsory private health-care insurance, under which private insurers are required to accept any Dutch citizen for basic health-care coverage, regardless of the person's health condition or age.

CONCLUSION

Financial markets may play a greater role in the management of longer-term systemic risks. Governments should seek to encourage and positively influence market developments in these areas with the goal of completing incomplete markets. A clear and consistent regulatory framework can encourage innovation in risk management techniques. In some cases, governments may need to intervene directly in certain markets, perhaps temporarily, to provide some minimum and/or extreme insurance coverage, ideally to facilitate the development of private capacity.

The preceding discussion has highlighted how policy makers may influence financial market developments and market-based solutions to some of the challenges associated with managing longer-term systemic risks. It focused on how some of the policy levers available to governments may be utilized to progress or complement reform efforts. A central message is that governments need to approach these challenges as a risk manager, considering their explicit, implicit, and contingent obligations. In doing so, they are likely to benefit from greater market inputs and risk management instruments, including the ability to better measure and monitor such obligations (e.g., volatility measures).

To date, only a few governments have approached these financial challenges in this manner. Only in the past few years have longer-term projections been prepared and published by some ministries of finance and public auditors, addressing the issue of aging-related spending trends and longer-term fiscal sustainability. Similarly, few central governments publish balance sheets using accounting standards similar to those applied to private corporations, and the risks and magnitude of contingent liabilities in government accounts are rarely quantified. These emerging practices and trends should be encouraged.[34]

Furthermore, given the focus that rating agencies, in particular, are increasingly applying to sovereign borrowers' long-term fiscal issues, and the potential for rating downgrades if such risks are left unaddressed, greater action may soon be required.[35] Indeed, while the often shorter-term focus of politicians and the electorate may inhibit more immediate efforts to address these challenges, greater scrutiny from public auditors and legislators, financial media, international financial institutions, and investors will increase the emphasis on these systemic challenges and on the need for governments to pursue more comprehensive risk management strategies.

The issues related to these longer-term and other systemic risks, and their implications for financial markets, are relevant to all countries. Several governments and international institutions have acted to raise public awareness of the challenges related to these risks, and have begun to address some of the issues. However, these issues are not going to fade away. On the contrary, these tend to be cumulating risks, and with time may well exacerbate a number of related social, economic, and financial challenges. Moreover, governments, domestic businesses, and financial markets compete globally for investment capital. The potential economic and financial market impact of pension and health-care-related obligations, as well as food and energy security, may adversely influence the competitive positions, as well as the macroeconomic and financial stability of nations. These prospects should strongly encourage policy makers to build greater public support for more immediate policy initiatives designed to mitigate such adverse impacts. Given the multigenerational nature of the challenges and most of the likely reforms, it is important to move forward more ambitiously and more comprehensively to address these risks.

NOTES

1. These data do not include "life settlement" transactions, where a whole-life insurance policy is sold by the beneficiary or insured for an amount greater than its surrender value, but lower than the policy's face or insured value; see Stone and Zissu (2006).
2. For a typical CAT bond, issuance proceeds are invested in collateral to ensure that all interest, principal, and CAT-contingent payments can be made in a timely manner. The issuers of the four bonds in question opted to hold lower-quality collateral, coupled with a total return swap with Lehman Brothers, to protect against any collateral deterioration.

3. According to Goldman Sachs, at year-end 2009 there were about $24 billion life insurance transactions outstanding and almost $13 billion of CAT bonds and sidecars (see following). There had been almost $18 billion of CAT bonds and sidecars outstanding at year-end 2007.

4. Swiss Re has issued four parametric extreme mortality bonds (Vita Capital I, Vita Capital II, Vita Capital III, and Vita Capital IV) totaling $1,537 million, and Scottish Re followed with a similar $155 million issue (Tartan Capital), AXA with a $444 million transaction (Osiris Capital), and Munich Re with a $100 million transaction (Nathan Re).

5. The policies are reinsured through a captive special purpose reinsurance vehicle that does not face similarly high reserve requirements, and the transaction is structured so that the losses that exceed economic reserves are transferred to capital markets.

6. About $4 billion of embedded value bonds were issued in 2007 (the peak year) and about $7 billion prior to 2007. By comparison, according to the American Council of Life Insurers, U.S. life insurers collected $149 billion in premiums in 2006, and the amount of life insurance in force was $19 trillion.

7. Between 1997 and 2005, natural CAT bond issuance fluctuated between about $700 million (1997) and $2,000 million (2005), increasing to about $4,700 million in 2006 and $7,000 million in 2007 (GC Securities 2008). From 1997 to 2007, of the total $22 billion in CAT bonds issued, in terms of expected loss, $14 billion covered U.S.-based perils, $5 billion European-based perils, and $3 billion Japan-based perils (GC Securities 2008; Lane Financial 2008). In comparison, global insured natural CAT losses were about $23 billion in 2007, and ranged from $10 billion to $30 billion in 1990–2006 (indexed to 2007 U.S. dollars), except for 2006, which spiked to over $100 billion (Swiss Re 2008).

8. In fact, achieving high-end investment-grade (IG) credit ratings (e.g., AAA and AA) may be a key to CAT bond market growth. The bulk of the issuance has been non-IG, and rating agencies have been reluctant to break through the AA ceiling. In fact, S&P has set an explicit AA rating on natural CAT bond ratings, and Moody's seems to have set an Aa1 ceiling.

9. An ILW incorporates indemnity and index triggers, both of which must be realized for a claims payment to be made (see also Green 2006).

10. Sourced from various Aon Benfield (www.benfieldgroup.com) publications.

11. See Moody's Investors Service (2006b).

12. In 2006, Credit Suisse introduced a U.S. longevity index based on publicly available U.S. government mortality tables. The underlying U.S. mortality tables are updated annually with a three-year lag, which is typical of the timeliness of G-10 official mortality data. In 2007, J.P. Morgan introduced similar annually updated indices (LifeMetrics), which currently cover Germany, the Netherlands, the United States, England, and Wales. Also in 2007, Goldman Sachs introduced a mortality/longevity index (QxX) aimed at the U.S. insured population over the age of 65, directed primarily at the life settlement industry (see note 2). However, Goldman shut that operation down in late 2009. In 2008, the Deutsche Bourse introduced longevity indexes (Xpect), which cover Germany and the Netherlands with a monthly frequency.

13. See Case and Wachter (2005). Due to poor liquidity in the initial CME contracts, two paired exchange-traded funds were launched in 2009 that allowed investors to take a leveraged position on the extent to which the 10-City Composite Case-Shiller house price index would rise or fall over the next five years. However, greater trading activity now occurs in the brokered over-the-counter (OTC) market in contracts tied to Radar Logic's RPX indices for prices per square foot paid for residential real estate in 25 U.S. metropolitan areas. The United Kingdom has a reasonably liquid OTC market in futures and swaps on the national Halifax house price index.

14. See Milliman's web site (www.milliman.com/expertise/healthcare/publications/mmi/).

15. See also Swiss Re (2009) for a comprehensive discussion of the use of indices in transferring insurance risks to the capital markets.

16. See Groome et al. (2006) for a fuller discussion of the scale long-term costs and risks faced by governments with respect to aging-related and health-care costs and liabilities.

17. For example, the annual *Financial Report of the United States Government* is intended to show, among other things, the implications of the government's long-term financial commitments and obligations. However, the Comptroller General's statement on the 2005 report suggests that the financial reporting system used by the government does not clearly or transparently reveal all of its future liabilities; see U.S. GAO (2006) for details. To present a more accurate and complete picture of the central government's net worth and financial position, France adopted a revised and more comprehensive government accounting framework in 2001 (*Loi Organique Relative aux Lois de Finances*), adapted from standards used by private-sector companies. However, this effort remains a work in progress, insofar as such accounts currently include only the central government, and omit future/contingent liabilities of public pensions, which are broadly summarized in an annex. Similarly, the United Kingdom has developed a system of balance sheet accounts (Whole of Government Accounts) that follow U.K. GAAP standards, and are expected to be published for the 2010–2011 fiscal year.

18. See Mills (2008) for an overview of carbon trading and weather derivatives.

19. See also Group of Thirty (2006).

20. See the Swiss Federal Office of Private Insurance (2004) solvency test white paper.

21. U.K. FSA (2006).

22. See, for example, the speech by Mr. Ong Chong Tee, deputy managing director, Monetary Authority of Singapore, at the Singapore International Insurance Conference, May 17, 2006.

23. Industry and public officials have also noted that the fragmented U.S. insurance regulatory framework restricts the U.S. authorities' ability to assume a more influential role in international forums on these important issues (e.g., Davies 2006).

24. Swiss Re (2006).

25. See Fitch Ratings (2006), Moody's Investors Service (2006a), and Standard & Poor's (2006a).

26. See IMF (2005, Chapter III, Module 4).

27. Mutual insurers operate to maximize the benefits to their members, which may include providing coverage at lower cost than otherwise required by a market rate of return on capital.

28. Industry observers have noted that Solvency II may add pressure for further consolidation in the (European) insurance sector (see Standard & Poor's 2006c). See also comments by Walter Kielholz, of Swiss Re, in Ladbury (2006), and Swiss Re (2006).

29. Some health-care providers have realized the value of their in-house data/information, and have organized subsidiaries to collect, collate, and sell such data.

30. The development of liquid housing price index markets may also facilitate the growth of reverse mortgage products, allowing households to more easily realize an annuity-like income stream, and thus better hedge longevity risk.

31. See Fabozzi et al. (2010) for more detail on recent developments in European property derivatives markets.

32. In some instances, however, achieving neutrality in the taxation of a financial instrument may be effectively impossible for most taxpayers. For instance, the tax-favored position

of owner-occupied housing in most countries makes it difficult to treat house price derivatives in a similar manner.

33. Indeed, the 2006 Pension Protection Act in the United States, for example, raised the maximum tax-deductible contribution to approximately 150 percent (including other criteria) of the applicable funding target (against 100 percent previously).

34. The IMF's *Government Finance Statistics Manual* (2001) and the *Fiscal Transparency Manual* have sought to go further by also encouraging contingent liabilities to be included in government budget documents.

35. Standard & Poor's (2006b).

REFERENCES

Aon Benfield Securities. 2009. "Insurance-Linked Securities 2009: Adapting to an Evolving Market." December.

Blake, David, and William Burrows. 2001. "Survivor Bonds: Helping to Hedge Mortality Risk." *Journal of Risk and Insurance* 68:2, 339–348.

Blake, David, Andrew Cairns, and Kevin Dowd. 2006. "Living with Mortality: Longevity Bonds and Other Mortality-Linked Securities." Cass Business School Pensions Institute Discussion Paper, PI-0601, January.

Bodie, Zvi, and Robert C. Merton. 2002. "International Pension Swaps." *Pension Economics and Finance* 1:1, 77–83.

Brown, Jeffrey R., and Peter R. Orszag. 2006. "The political economy of government issued longevity bonds." Paper presented at the 2nd International Conference on Longevity Risk and Capital Market Solutions at the Cass Business School, April.

Case, Bradford, and Susan Wachter. 2005. "Residential real estate price indices as financial soundness indicators: Methodological issues." In *Real Estate Indicators and Financial Stability*. Proceedings of a joint BIS-IMF conference in Washington, DC, October 27–28, 2003. Bank for International Settlements.

Cox, Samuel H., and Yijia Lin. 2005. "Natural Hedging of Life and Annuity Mortality Risks." Georgia State University Center for Risk Management Insurance Research Working Paper 04–8, July.

Davies, Sir Howard. 2006. "A Word of Advice to Hank Paulson." *Financial Times*, July 5, 15.

Dowd, Kevin, David Blake, Andrew Cairns, and Peter Dawson. 2005. "Survivor Swaps." *Journal of Risk and Insurance* 73:1, 1–17.

Fabozzi, Frank J., Robert J. Shiller, and Radu S. Tunaru. 2010. "Property Derivatives for Managing European Real-Estate Risk." *European Financial Management* 16:1.

Fitch Ratings. 2006. "Exposure Draft: Insurance Capital Assessment Methodology and Model (Prism)—Executive Summary." Fitch Ratings Insurance Criteria Report, June.

GC Securities. 2008. "The Catastrophe Bond Market at Year-End 2007." GC Securities.

Green, Meg. 2006. "Hot CAT Contracts." *Best's Review*, April.

Groome, Todd, Nicolas Blancher, Parmeshwar Ramlogan, and Oksana Khadarina. 2006. "Population Ageing, the Structure of Financial Markets and Policy Implications." G-20 Workshop on Demography and Financial Markets, Sydney, Australia, July 23–25.

Group of Thirty. 2006. *Reinsurance and International Capital Markets*. Study Group Report. (Washington, DC, January).

IMF (International Monetary Fund). 2005. "Global Financial Stability Report." World Economic and Financial Surveys. Washington, DC, September.

IMF (International Monetary Fund). 2006. "Global Financial Stability Report." World Economic and Financial Surveys. Washington, DC, April.

Ladbury, Adrian. 2006. "Head for the Capital." *Insurance Day*, May, 24–25.

Lane Financial. 2008. "The 2008 Review of ILS Transactions." Lane Financial LLC, March 31.

Lin, Yijia, and Samuel H. Cox. 2005. "Securitization of Mortality Risks in Life Annuities." *Journal of Risk and Insurance* 72:2, 227–252.

Mahul, Olivier, and Jerry Skees. 2006. "Piloting Index-Based Livestock Insurance in Mongolia." World Bank Group *AccessFinance* Newsletter, March.

Milevsky, Moshe A. 2006. *The Calculus of Retirement Income: Financial Models for Pension Annuities and Life Insurance.* Cambridge, U.K.: Cambridge University Press.

Mills, Paul S. 2008. "The Greening of Markets." *Finance and Development*, International Monetary Fund, March, 32–36.

Moody's Investors Service. 2006a. "Company Built Internal Models Expected to Play Greater Part in Moody's Insurance Rating Process." Moody's Investors Service Global Credit Research Special Comment, June.

Moody's Investors Service. 2006b. "Reinsurance Side-Cars: Going Along for the Ride." Moody's Investors Service Global Credit Research Special Comment, April.

Poterba, James M. 1997. "The History of Annuities in the United States." National Bureau of Economic Research Working Paper 6001, April.

Standard & Poor's (S&P). 2006a. "Credit FAQ: An Advance Glimpse at the Upcoming Changes to the Insurer Capital Model." *RatingsDirect*, June.

Standard & Poor's (S&P). 2006b. "Global Graying: Aging Societies and Sovereign Ratings." *CreditWeek*, June 7, 55–66.

Standard & Poor's (S&P). 2006c. "Credit FAQ: The impact of Solvency II on the European insurance market." *RatingsDirect*, July.

Stone, Charles A., and Anne Zissu. 2006. "Securitization of Senior Life Settlements: Managing Extension Risk." *Journal of Derivatives* (Spring).

Swiss Federal Office of Private Insurance. 2004. White paper on the Swiss solvency test, no. 2, November.

Swiss Re. 2006. "Solvency II: An Integrated Risk Approach for European Insurers." *Sigma*, no. 4.

Swiss Re. 2008. "Natural Catastrophes and Man-Made Disasters in 2007." Swiss Re.

Swiss Re. 2009. "The Role of Indices in Transferring Insurance Risks to the Capital Markets." Swiss Re.

Syroka, Joanna. 2006. "Macro-Level Weather Risk Management for Ethiopia." International Task Force on Commodity Risk Management in Developing Countries, presentation given at annual meeting, Pretoria, South Africa, May.

UK FSA (Financial Services Authority). 2006. "Implementing the Reinsurance Directive." CP06/12, June.

U.S. GAO (Government Accountability Office). 2006. "Fiscal Year 2005 U.S. Government Financial Statements." Washington, DC, March.

Watson Wyatt. 2005. "The Uncertain Future of Longevity." Watson Wyatt/Cass Business School Public Lectures on Longevity, March.

World Bank. 2005. "Managing Agricultural Production Risk: Innovations in Developing Countries." World Bank Agriculture and Rural Development Department, Washington, DC.

ABOUT THE AUTHORS

Todd Groome, former advisor to the Monetary and Capital Markets Department for the International Monetary Fund (IMF), was appointed chairman of the Alternative Investment Management Association (AIMA), the global organization of the hedge fund industry, in January 2009. Mr. Groome has significant financial markets experience, developed over an extensive career in capital markets, in both the public and private sectors. Before the IMF, Mr. Groome served as managing director and head of the Financial Institutions Groups of Deutsche Bank and Credit Suisse in London, focusing primarily on debt capital markets and on capital and balance sheet management for banks and insurance companies. Prior to that, he worked with Merrill Lynch in London and New York as part of the Financial Institutions Corporate Finance Group working on mergers and acquisitions (M&A), advisory, and debt and equity financing for banks and insurers. Before moving to London in 1989, he worked as an attorney with Hogan & Hartson in Washington, DC, as part of the Financial Institutions Group. Mr. Groome holds an MBA from the London Business School, a JD from the University of Virginia School of Law, and a BA in Economics from Randolph-Macon College (where he was awarded the Wade C. Temple Scholarship for Economics, and graduated Phi Beta Kappa). He is also currently a visiting scholar at the Wharton Business School, University of Pennsylvania.

John Kiff has been a senior financial sector expert at the International Monetary Fund since 2005. Prior to that he worked at the Bank of Canada, where he was involved in various financial markets analytic and trading activities. Since 1999, John was heavily involved in several BIS working groups that focused on credit risk transfer markets, and he published a number of articles and papers around these projects. At the IMF, John is part of the team that produces the semiannual "Global Financial Stability Report," and he has continued to publish articles and papers on risk transfer markets. More recently, he has been focusing on mortgage securitization markets.

Paul Mills joined the U.K. Treasury in 1992, after having studied for a PhD in financial economics at Cambridge University. After periods in macroeconomic modeling and financial regulation, he specialized in government debt management, culminating in establishing the U.K. Debt Management Office in 1998. Paul remained at the DMO as head of policy and deputy CEO until returning to the Treasury in 2000 to lead policy sections managing the U.K. government's balance sheet (debt, cash, and currency reserves), then financial stability and regulation. He joined the International Monetary Fund in 2006 and has worked on global financial stability, the U.S. financial system, innovative risk transfer, climate change and financial markets, and Islamic finance. He now works in the IMF's London office focusing particularly on financial stability and regulatory policy.

PART VI

Appendices

APPENDIX A

IT Tools for Financial Asset Management and Engineering

LUCAS BERNARD
New York City College of Technology

INTRODUCTION

The study of finance concerns itself with both theoretical and practical issues. The relationship between the volatilities and correlations of individual securities, and the volatility of a portfolio consisting of those securities, is an example of a theoretical issue, whereas the speed with which a stop loss order can be executed once it has been triggered is an example of a practical issue. Theoretical issues and practical issues are, of course, not necessarily independent of one another, but they are typically addressed by different groups of people. The solution to theoretical problems typically leads to efforts to implement the theory and that, in itself, can pose a number of computational problems. These computational problems can often be addressed with the aid of appropriate information technology (IT) tools. In this appendix, we will consider the role these tools can play in addressing computational problems. In the process we will touch on modeling tools, mathematical/statistical tools, and data tools. Numerous books have been written on each of these types of tools and this short appendix cannot possibly do these tools justice. But we hope that the new student of financial engineering will get a sense of what is available when he or she encounters problems where these tools may have a use.

In general, we can distinguish among four classes of problems:

1. Problems that are hard to solve because we do not have enough time or computing power to solve them.
2. Problems that are hard to solve because we do not understand how to solve them.
3. Problems whose parameters are constantly changing, resulting in a need for constant updating.
4. Problems wherein having accurate and well-defined input data is key.

Importantly, these classes of problems are by no means mutually exclusive; there is much overlap.

We will consider an example of each type of problem and illustrate approaches and tools that have proven useful in addressing them. It will come as no surprise to the reader that the principal tool will be the computer. But, more broadly, it is the whole computational/information-system infrastructure that has developed over the past 20 years that is key. Specifically, this includes the personal computer, the local area network, the Internet, and the software used to manage these things.

Let us begin by considering a problem of the first type (i.e., a problem that we know how to solve, but we do not have the necessary time and/or computational resources). Imagine, for the sake of argument, that we have a large pool of subprime mortgages. Let us suppose that each of these mortgages has the same probability of going into default and subsequent foreclosure. Further, let us suppose, for simplicity, that the mortgages default independently of each other (i.e., that the cross default correlation is 0). Thus, given independence, the joint probability that, for example, any two of these mortgages, x_i and x_j, defaults is simply given as follows:

$$\Pr(x_i, x_j) = \Pr(x_i)\Pr(x_j)$$

Where $\Pr(x_i, x_j)$ denotes the joint probability of default and $\Pr(x_i)$ and $\Pr(x_j)$ denote the individual probabilities of default for x_i and x_j respectively. Because the probability of default is the same for each mortgage, let's denote this probability simply by p. So far, so good. Now let's add some meat to the problem. Suppose we have a very large pool consisting of 100,000 equal size mortgages and the probability of any one mortgage defaulting over the coming year is 0.05 (i.e., 5 percent). Now consider a mortgage-linked product whose payoff is based on the behavior of this pool. More specifically, suppose that it is a barrier option that will pay off if and only if the number of defaults over the next year, denoted by X, falls within a specified range whose lower bound is a and whose upper bound is b. That is, we are interested in the probability that X, the total number of defaults, will lie between a and b. That is, we seek to find $\Pr(a < X < b)$.

In this case, the problem is well understood by statisticians as having a binomial distribution, and the answer, therefore, is given as follows:

$$\Pr(a < X < b) = \sum_{i=a}^{b} \frac{n!}{i!(n-i)!} p^i (1-p)^{n-i}$$

Finally, let's suppose that $a = 5{,}100$ and $b = 10{,}100$. Now, the issue is this: If the number of mortgages in the pool was small, anyone with a scientific calculator could perform this operation. However, in our example, $n = 100{,}000$ and i may range from 5,100 to 10,100. Among the many computations that need to be made is this one (which is just part of the first term in the summation):

$$\binom{100000}{5100} = \frac{100000!}{5100!(100000 - 5100)!}$$

Plugging this into a TI-83 calculator would result in the following: ERR: OVER-FLOW. And this is only the first of 5,000 similar computations needed to find out the probability of having between 5,100 and 10,100 defaults.

The issue is not one of theory, but rather one of computing power. The TI-83 does not have the capability, but the more powerful TI-89 does. Nevertheless, there are still 4,999 similar computations to do. Even if each computation could be done in just 30 seconds, it would still take more than 40 hours to achieve a viable solution. A derivatives trader requires an answer in a fraction of a second! Thus, an understanding of theory alone is not helpful to the trader.

This particular problem has an easy solution, and we can use it to illustrate, first, how theory can inform on issues of computability and, second, how certain features of common software can be used to solve the problem even faster.

Statistical theory tells us that a binomially distributed random variable can be approximated by a normally distributed one, where $\mu = np$ and $\sigma = [np(1-p)]^{1/2}$. Thus, the computation above can be well approximated by:

$$\Pr(a < X < b) = \frac{1}{\sigma\sqrt{2\pi}} \int_a^b e^{-\frac{1}{2}\left(\frac{x-\mu}{\sigma}\right)^2} dx$$

Now, at first blush, this seems worse than before. However, the ubiquitous MS-Excel® is actually capable of solving this problem in one step.[1]

BASIC MS-EXCEL® TOOLS

MS-Excel has a huge amount of computational power built into it and we shall examine several of its features. But, first, let us finish the problem. In MS-Excel, one would enter the expression:

$$= \text{NORMDIST}(b, \mu, \sigma, \text{true}) - \text{NORMDIST}(a, \mu, \sigma, \text{true})$$

That is, provided we can assume normality, MS-Excel comes preprogrammed to solve complex integration problems for us. In this case, the solution is 7.34 percent. Thus, we conclude that there is a 7.34 percent probability that the option will pay off.

Other preprogrammed features that are particularly useful in financial modeling include arithmetic means, geometric means, standard deviations, variances, maximal/minimal element (of a set), binomial distributions, matrix computations, and correlations, as well as a complete Visual Basic programming environment. These represent only a tiny fraction of the tools available, and we will use some of them in the following examples. For the reader who has little to no experience with MS-Excel modeling, it is useful to know that the software provides an extensive "Help" reference with detailed instructions. If one does not know the name of a particular MS-Excel function, or is unsure of which function is appropriate, one can select "Function" from the "Insert" menu (alternatively, one can click the f_x icon toward the top of the worksheet area). This allows you to navigate to the appropriate function, and will tell you the function's arguments.

Suppose we wish to compute the average rate of return over a period of years given a list of the n individual yearly rates, r_i. In this case, the average rate is given by:

$$\bar{r} = \sqrt[n]{\prod_{i=1}^{n}(1 + r_i)} - 1$$

One can solve this in MS-Excel, by utilizing the function =**GEOMEAN()**. In a new column or row, simply add 1 to each annual rate. Then use the GEOMEAN function on this new series, and subtract 1 from the result to obtain the geometric mean rate.

If there is a specific function that you expect to employ frequently and MS-Excel does not include it as one of its built-in functions, you can simply create it. This is called a "user-defined function," and it is created using the Visual Basic Editor. We will demonstrate this with a simple example. Suppose we wish to define a function, which we will name "OurFunction," that squares a number and then adds 5 to it. In other words:

$$F(x) = x^2 + 5$$

We simply go to the "Tools" menu, navigate to "Macros," and open the "Visual Basic Editor." A screen opens where we insert a module as shown in Exhibit A.1.

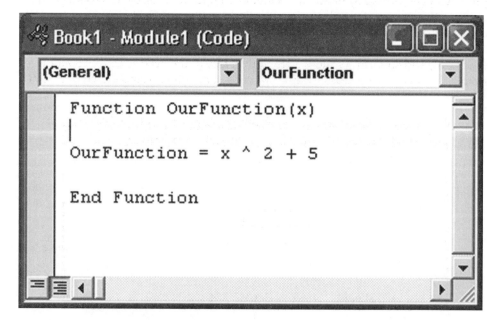

Exhibit A.1 Creating a User-Defined Function

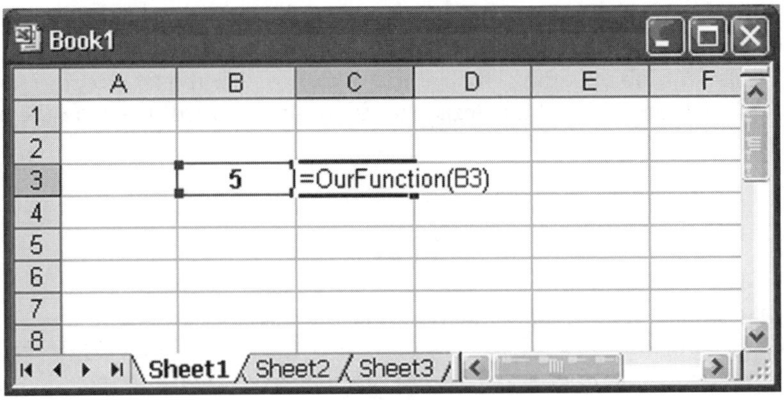

Exhibit A.2   Employing a User-Defined Function

Now, we close and return to MS-Excel. We have just constructed a simple function that we can use by going to any cell in our spreadsheet and entering it as shown in Exhibit A.2.

The result is shown in Exhibit A.3.

MATHEMATICA®, GAUSS™, MAPLE®, AND MATLAB®2

Computers have long been able to assist researchers, analysts, and engineers with numerical computation, such as the approximation of a definite integral, that were previously performed by hand. But symbolic computation, also known as algebraic computation, was not, until recently, similarly readily available. Thus, systems of equations had to be solved by hand, difficult integrals had to be looked up on tables, similarity methods had to be employed to obtain solutions to partial differential equations, and so forth. While we are not yet free of the need to think about these things, Mathematica, Gauss, Maple, MatLab, and other symbolic computation

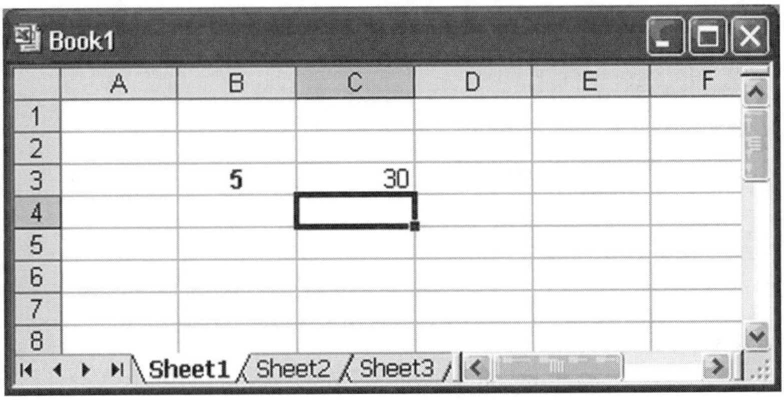

Exhibit A.3   Output Generated by the User-Defined Function

engines are now available and can be used to great effect. We will use Mathematica for purposes of illustration in this section.

First, let us recall the straightforward but complex integration from before—that is, computing the cumulative distribution function (*cdf*) of the normal distribution:

$$\Pr(X < b) = \frac{1}{\sigma\sqrt{2\pi}} \int_{-\infty}^{b} e^{-\frac{1}{2}\left(\frac{x-\mu}{\sigma}\right)^2} dx$$

In Mathematica, one enters the integral symbolically as shown:

$$\text{In}[16] := \frac{1}{\sigma\sqrt{2\pi}} \int_{-\infty}^{b} e^{-\frac{1}{2}\left(\frac{x-\mu}{\sigma}\right)^2} dx$$

$$\text{Out}[16] = \frac{1}{\sqrt{2\pi}\,\sigma} \text{If}\left[\text{Re}[\sigma^2] > 0, \sqrt{\frac{\pi}{2}}\left(\sqrt{\sigma^2} + \sigma\,\text{Erf}\left[\frac{b-\mu}{\sqrt{2\pi}\,\sigma}\right]\right),\right.$$

$$\left.\text{Integrate}\left[e^{-\frac{(x-\mu)^2}{2\sigma^2}}, (x, -\infty, b), \text{Assumptions} \to \text{Re}[\sigma^2] \leq 0\right]\right]$$

Mathematica does not know what we are doing and therefore warns us that the variance must be positive. However, it correctly computes the *cdf*, after canceling a few terms, as:

$$\Pr(X < b) = \frac{1}{2}\left(1 + \text{Erf}\left(\frac{b-\mu}{2\sigma^2}\right)\right)$$

where *Erf* is the Gaussian error function:

$$\text{Erf}(x) = \frac{2}{\sqrt{\pi}} \int_{0}^{x} e^{-t^2} dt$$

If one wishes to find the first few terms of the Taylor Series approximation for this function around the point $x = a$, in Mathematica one simply enters the problem in symbols as shown:

$$\text{In}[18] := \text{Series}\left[\frac{2}{\sqrt{\pi}} \int_{0}^{x} e^{-t^2} dt, \{x, a, 3\}\right]$$

$$\text{Out}[18] = \text{Erf}[a] + \frac{2e^{-a^2}(x-a)}{\sqrt{\pi}} - \frac{2(ae^{-a^2})(x-a)^2}{\sqrt{\pi}}$$

$$\times \frac{2(-1+2a^2)e^{-a^2}(x-a)^3}{3\sqrt{\pi}} + 0[x-a]^4$$

$$\text{In}[15] := \text{Series}\left[e^{-x(x-t)}\frac{x^\beta(a \times x)^{1-\beta}}{x!}, \{x, 1, 2\}\right]$$

$$\text{Out[15]} = a^{1-\beta}e^{-r+rt} + (a^{1-\beta}e^{-r+rt}(-1 + \text{EulerGamma}) + a^{1-\beta}e^{-r+rt}(1-\beta)$$

$$+ a^{1-\beta}(-e^{-r+rt}r + e^{-r+rt}\beta))(x-1)$$

$$+ \left(a^{1-\beta}e^{-r+rt}\left(1 - \text{EulerGamma} + \frac{\text{EulerGamma}^2}{2} - \frac{\pi^2}{12}\right)\right.$$

$$- \frac{1}{2}a^{1-\beta}e^{-r+rt}(1-\beta)\beta + a^{1-\beta}(1-\beta)(-e^{-r+rt}r + e^{-r+rt}\beta)$$

$$+ (-1 + \text{EulerGamma})(a^{1-\beta}e^{-r+rt}(1-\beta) + a^{1-\beta}(-e^{-r+rt}r + e^{-r+rt}\beta))$$

$$\left.+ a^{1-\beta}\left(\frac{1}{2}e^{-r+rt}r^2 - e^{-r+rt}r\beta + e^{-r+rt}\left(-\frac{\beta}{2} + \frac{\beta^2}{2}\right)\right)\right)(x-1)^2 + 0[x-1]^3$$

Here, Series[f, {x, x_0, n}] generates a power series expansion for f about the point x = x_0 to order $(x - x_0)^n$.

BLOOMBERG®[3], INFORMATION, AND THE API

So far we have seen that with the use of software we can solve problems of the first two types. That is, we can solve (1) problems that are difficult to solve due to time constraints or insufficient computing power, and (2) problems that are hard to solve because we do not understand how to solve them. We now turn to the third type of problem: those whose parameters need constant updating.

In finance, we are often confronted with data sets that are constantly changing. Quotes, for example, on liquid instruments can change by the millisecond. Even if one has constructed a model wherein the theory is sound and where issues of computability have been resolved, a lack of current data may still block our path to a solution.

Consider California in 1849. Gold was discovered at Sutter's Mill in 1848 and by 1849 the gold rush was on. Some prospectors, of course, became rich, but the majority did not. Most, in fact, did not find any gold. There is one thing, however, that almost every prospector did do: He bought a shovel. Thus, selling shovels was a less exciting but more reliable business to be in than prospecting. This is the principle that Michael Bloomberg understood in the 1970s. He realized that although most investors would not get rich in the (then) new computer era, almost all would demand up-to-date information. Thus, in the spirit of Reuters, Bloomberg founded his company to sell financial information terminals to Wall Street. To make a long story short, his net worth is now over $10 billion.

The Bloomberg terminal is the financial engineers' shovel. With this terminal he or she gains not only real-time trading data, but also analysis, news, and much more. However, it provides such a vast amount of information that one can be lost before one even begins. Being able to look up all this data is wonderful, but the real power of the Bloomberg system is only fully realized when the information-retrieval services it offers are married to modeling software that takes the data as input. In this section, we describe some of these features.

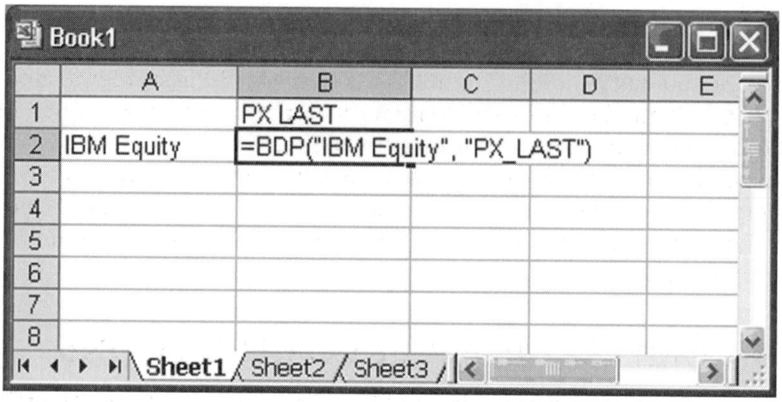

Exhibit A.4 Direct Code to Retrieve the Last Trade Price for IBM

When a Bloomberg account is opened, it is important that a feature called API be activated. API stands for Application Programming Interface. It is the bridge that allows a Bloomberg terminal to "talk" to MS-Excel.

Data requests may be specified either by selecting appropriate options from the Bloomberg menus or by entering direct codes. For example, a direct code might look like Exhibit A.4.

Alternatively, one could incorporate cell references in the code to achieve the same result. This is illustrated in Exhibit A.5 for the same example employed in Exhibit A.4.

Through the API, we can easily and quickly populate an entire table with real-time data. Much more complex information is also accessible. For example, the BDS (Bloomberg Data Set) command returns multicell descriptive data to your MS-Excel spreadsheet using the following syntax:

$$= BDS(security, field, opt\ arg\ 1, opt\ arg\ 2)$$

The "security" entry may be any valid identifier such as a ticker symbol or a ticker/exchange, CUSIP, or ISIN, followed by the relevant sector indicator

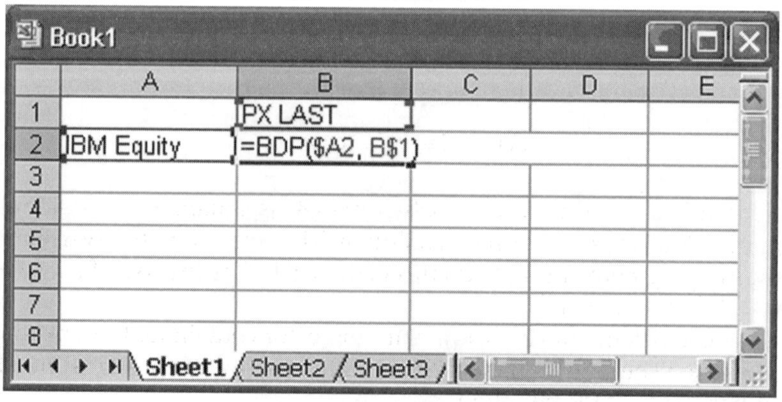

Exhibit A.5 Direct Code Incorporating Cell References

(e.g., Equity or Corp). The "field" indicates the type of information you want (e.g., last bid, etc.). Last, the optional arguments are for settings that may have particular relevance, but are not needed. Committee on Uniform Security Identification Procedures (CUSIP) numbers are used to identify North American securities. International Securities Identification Numbers (ISINs) are similar in function.

Almost any sort of information may be retrieved in this way. Thus, with a Bloomberg terminal, the only limits on data inputs are the limits of one's own imagination. Since the API software updates continuously, real-time model creation is straightforward.

MORE COMPLEX MS-EXCEL COMPUTATIONS

We have already discussed a number of MS-Excel's useful features. The following list expands on this a bit.

Use **Tools | Data Analysis | Descriptive Statistics** to compute the descriptive data.
Use **Tools | Data Analysis | Correlation Analysis** to compute the correlation matrix of an n-return series.
Use **Tools | Data Analysis | Histogram** to compute either an empirical distribution of data or the cumulative distribution of data.
Use **Tools | Data Analysis | Linear Regression** to perform regression.

MS-Excel can also do matrix computations. The following matrix functions are available:

Use **MMULT** to compute matrix products.
Important Note: In matrix operations, one must highlight the matrix and type *Ctrl-Shift-Enter* to validate.
Use **TRANSPOSE** to compute the transpose of a matrix.
Use **MINVERSE** to compute the inverse of a matrix.

As a first example of the manipulation of matrices, consider the problem of solving the following system of linear equations:

$$x_1 + x_2 + x_3 = 1$$

$$1.2x_1 + x_2 + 0.4x_3 = -0.5$$

$$0.4x_1 + 2x_2 + 1.1x_3 = 5$$

Note that if the matrix of the coefficients (A) is square and nonsingular, the system $AX = Y$ always has a unique solution. The solution to the system is found by premultiplying both sides of equation $AX = Y$ by the inverse of A: $AX = Y \Rightarrow A^{-1}AX = A^{-1}Y \Rightarrow X = A^{-1}Y$.

A is the coefficient matrix, X is a column vector containing the unknowns for which we seek a solution (x's), and Y is a column vector of constants (numbers at the right-hand side of the equations).

Thus, in MS-Excel, we have Exhibit A.6 and Exhibit A.7.

	A7	▼		fx	{=MINVERSE(A2:C4)}			
	A	B	C	D	E	F	G	H
1	Original Matrix				X Vector		Y Vector	
2	1	1	1		x₁		1	
3	1.2	1	0.4		x₂		−0.5	
4	0.4	2	1.1		x₃		5	
5								
6	Inverse Matrix				Y Vector		Solutions to X Vector	
7	0.26316	0.78947	−0.52632		1		−2.76316	
8	−1.01754	0.61404	0.70175		−0.5		2.18421	
9	1.75439	−1.40351	−0.17544		5		1.57895	
10								

Exhibit A.6 Original Matrix and Inverse Matrix with Solutions Showing Inverse Matrix Function

The solution is: $x_1 = -2.76316$, $x_2 = 2.18421$, $x_3 = 1.57895$.

Now, for a more complex application, we return to our example of a basket of risky mortgages. We are interested in building a model of credit default for the entire structure. Several steps along the way are of particular interest to us as they exemplify methods introduced earlier. Specifically, we use Robert Merton's definition of default, wherein default occurs when the size of the debt exceeds the value of the asset. In Merton's (1974) model, asset valuation may be expressed as follows:

$$V_t = V_0 e^{\left(r - \frac{\sigma_V^2}{2}\right)t + \sigma_V \sqrt{t} \times z}$$

Where V_t denotes the value of the asset, and V_0 denotes the value of the debt (i.e., debt principal), and z is a Weiner process, such that $z \sim N(\mu, \sigma)$.

	G7	▼		fx	{=MMULT(A7:C9,E7:E9)}			
	A	B	C	D	E	F	G	H
1	Original Matrix				X Vector		Y Vector	
2	1	1	1		x₁		1	
3	1.2	1	0.4		x₂		−0.5	
4	0.4	2	1.1		x₃		5	
5								
6	Inverse Matrix				Y Vector		Solutions to X Vector	
7	0.26316	0.78947	−0.52632		1		−2.76316	
8	−1.01754	0.61404	0.70175		−0.5		2.18421	
9	1.75439	−1.40351	−0.17544		5		1.57895	

Exhibit A.7 Original Matrix and Inverse Matrix with Solutions Showing Matrix Mutliplication

It can be shown that the probability of default, given the preceding definition of default, may be expressed as:

$$\Pr(\text{default}) = 1 - \frac{1}{\sigma\sqrt{2\pi}} \int_{-\infty}^{d} e^{-\frac{(x-\mu)^2}{2\sigma^2}} \, dx$$

$$d = \frac{\ln\left(\dfrac{V_t}{V_0}\right) + \left(r - \dfrac{\sigma_V^2}{2}\right) \times t}{\sigma_V \sqrt{t}}$$

The value and implied risk probability, at any moment, are found using the following MS-Excel expressions (employed in the spreadsheet depicted in Exhibit A.8):

= B20 * EXP((B21 − 0.5 * B22 ∧ 2) * B23 + B22 * (|11) * SQRT(B23))
= 1− NORMSDIST((LN(B19/B20) + (B21 − 0.5 * B22 ∧ 2) * B23)/B22 * SQRT(B23)))

Note that d is simply the upper limit of the integral shown, i.e., the cumulative normal distribution. For simplicity, we assume a simple mortgage-backed security (MBS) structure with only five reference assets (mortgages) and three tranches: equity, mezzanine, and senior, absorbing the bottom 10 percent, the second 10 percent, and the last 80 percent of the default risk, respectively. We relax our earlier assumption of no cross default correlation.

We assume that a default event has occurred when $V_t < V_0$. In this case, the loss to the special purpose vehicle (SPV) is given by $L_i = (1 - \delta_i)V_t$, where δ_i is the recovery rate for the ith asset, which is allocated to the lowest tranche first.

The problem is that we wish to incorporate contagion and/or hedging effects; so, we assume an initial correlation matrix:

$$P = \begin{bmatrix} 1 & 0 & 0 & 0 & 0 \\ \rho_{2,1} & 1 & 0 & 0 & 0 \\ \rho_{3,1} & \rho_{3,2} & 1 & 0 & 0 \\ \rho_{4,1} & \rho_{4,2} & \rho_{4,3} & 1 & 0 \\ \rho_{5,1} & \rho_{5,2} & \rho_{5,3} & \rho_{5,4} & 1 \end{bmatrix}$$

We now compute the Cholesky transformation, Π, which is defined as:

$$\pi_{i,j} = \frac{\rho_{i,j} - \sum_{k=1}^{j-1} \pi_{i,k}\pi_{j,k}}{\sqrt{1 - \sum_{k=1}^{j-1} \pi_{j,k}^2}}; 1 \leq j \leq i \leq n$$

A convenient property of the Cholesky transformation is that given a vector, $z = (z_i)$, of n random numbers drawn from a standard Gaussian distribution, then for $\rho_{i,j} = k$, the vector $c = P \times z$ is a vector of n random numbers that are correlated with $\rho_{i,j} = k$.

	A	B	C	D	E	F	G	H	I	J	K	P
1			Correlation	Matrix								
2	1.00							Correlation	0.600			
3	0.60	1.00						Risk-free Rate	0.040			
4	0.60	0.60	1.00					Default Rate	0.030			
5	0.60	0.60	0.60	1.00				Recovery Rate	0.400			
6	0.60	0.60	0.60	0.60	1.00			Coupon	0.065			
7								Volatility	0.200			
8								Time to Maturity	1.000			
9												
10		Cholesky		Reduction			V	Random	C		Sigma	
11	1.0000	0.0000	0.0000	0.0000	0.0000		1.7500	1	1.7500		0.75	
12	0.6000	0.8000	0.0000	0.0000	0.0000		1.7500	1	0.3500			
13	0.6000	1.2000	0.8000	0.0000	0.0000		1.7500	1	4.5500		Attachment	P
14	0.6000	1.2000	1.2000	0.8000	0.0000		1.7500	1	3.1500		Senior	5
15	0.6000	1.2000	1.2000	1.2000	0.8000		1.7500	1	3.1500		Mezzanine	1
16											Equity	1
17												
18	Asset	1	Default	Loss	Income	Implied Default Rate		Expected Loss Per	Tranche	%	$ --> Investors	
19	Asset Value	1447734.61	FALSE					Senior (Above 20%)	0.00	0.00%	0	
20	Principal Value	1000000.00		0.00	66000.00	0.02558806		Mezzanine (2nd 10%)	382792.44	76.56%	382792.4388	
21	Risk-Free Rate	0.04						Equity (1st 10%)	480394.72	96.08%	480394.7196	
22	Volatility	0.20										
23	Time to Maturity	1.00						SPV Profitability	733187.16			
24	Recovery Rate	0.40										
25	Coupon	0.07										

Exhibit A.8   Model of Default

```
MBS_run_1.xls - Module1 (Code)

(General)

Function Cholesky(Mat As Range)
Dim A, L() As Double, s As Double
A = Mat
n = Mat.Rows.Count
M = Mat.Columns.Count
If n <> M Then
    Cholesky = "?"
    Exit Function
End If

ReDim L(1 To n, 1 To n)
For j = 1 To n
    s = 0
    For k = 1 To j - 1
        s = s + L(j, k) ^ 2
    Next k
    L(j, j) = A(j, j) - s
    If L(j, j) <= 0 Then Exit For
    L(j, j) = Sqr(L(j, j))

    For i = j + 1 To n
        s = 0
        For k = 1 To j - 1
            s = s + L(i, k) * L(j, k)
        Next k
        L(i, j) = (A(i, j) - s) / L(j, j)
    Next i
Next j
Cholesky = L
End Function
```

Exhibit A.9 VB Code to Automate Cholesky Transformation

By substituting c for z in the preceding valuation equation, we can generate default events with known correlation. Further, by using Monte Carlo simulation, we can determine an appropriate pricing structure for each of the tranches.

Even with MS-Excel's predefined functions, this matrix would be tedious to compute. Therefore, we use the VB program shown in Exhibit A.9.

The result is shown in Exhibit A.10.

MONTE CARLO SIMULATION

We have seen how modern software can help us solve all four categories of problems that were described in the introduction to this appendix. But there are times

	A	B	C	D	E	
1			Correlation	Matrix		
2	1.00					
3	0.25	1.00				
4	0.25	0.25	1.00			
5	0.25	0.25	0.25	1.00		
6	0.25	0.25	0.25	0.25	1.00	
7						
8						
9						
10			Cholesky	Reduction		
11	1.0000	0.0000	0.0000	0.0000	0.0000	
12	0.2500	0.9682	0.0000	0.0000	0.0000	
13	0.2500	0.3227	0.9129	0.0000	0.0000	
14	0.2500	0.3227	0.4564	0.7906	0.0000	
15	0.2500	0.3227	0.4564	0.7906	0.0000	
16						
17						
18	Asset	1	Default	Loss	Income	Implie

Exhibit A.10 VB Generated Cholesky Reduction

when we need to solve a problem when very little is known about the structure of the problem and/or no analytical approach is available. In these situations, Monte Carlo simulation is often an applicable tool. The technique, which is extremely versatile, works by generating random observations on a variable of interest. With a sufficient number of observations, the average tends to converge to the true value of the variable. Importantly, Monte Carlo simulation is also often useful as an alternative approach when we do have an analytical model available. Consider a very simple application. Suppose that we want to know the value of "pi" (denoted π), which is defined as the ratio of the area of a circle to the square of the circle's radius:

$$\pi = \frac{\text{Area}}{\text{Radius}^2}$$

We can easily measure the radius, denoted below by r, but it is far more difficult to directly measure the area of the circle. So let's try to derive the area of the circle via Monte Carlo simulation using nothing more than the built-in functions of MS-Excel. We'll begin by drawing a square such that each side has a length of 1. Next, draw a quarter circle inside the box from the upper left corner to the lower right corner. This is depicted in Exhibit A.11.

The area of this quarter circle is exactly one-fourth of the area of a full circle. Now imagine that we randomly throw darts at the box in such a fashion that each dart lands in the box with equal probability of hitting any spot in the box. After throwing a sufficiently large number of darts, we can count the number of darts that land within the quarter circle (i.e., below the curve) in Exhibit A.11. Because the length of each side of the box is the same as the radius of the circle, it is clear that the box has an area of 1. The fraction of the total number of darts thrown that land below the curve (i.e., within the quarter circle), then gives us an approximation of the area of the quarter circle. Denote this fraction by g.

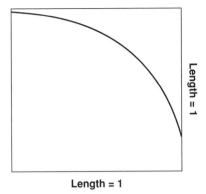

Exhibit A.11 A Quarter Circle

But how do we simulate the throwing of darts, such that there is equal likelihood of hitting any spot within the box? The answer is we employ the random number generator in MS-Excel, =RAND(). Each time this is run it will generate a value between 0 and 1 and every possible value is equally likely. If we run =RAND() twice, we can think of the two simulated values as x,y coordinates within the box.

Because we only drew a quarter circle for a circle having a radius of 1, the total area of the full circle having a radius of 1 is 4 × g. Thus, π is approximated by:

$$\pi \approx \frac{4 \times g}{r^2}$$

And since, in this case, the radius squared equals 1, the solution becomes:

$$\pi \approx 4 \times g$$

In addition to employing the random number generator to generate simulated dart throws, we also employ the counting and logical test features of MS-Excel in the application.

Consider the spreadsheet illustrated in Exhibit A.12. Column A shows the dart count, columns B and C show the x,y coordinates generated using =RAND(). Column D is the logical test: "TRUE" if the dart is within the quarter circle, and "FALSE" if the dart is outside the quarter circle.

	B101	▾	f_x =RAND()				
🗐 **MonteCarloPi.xls [Read-Only]**						▭◻☒	
	A	B	C	D	E	F	
100	99	0.298518916	0.432629481	TRUE	74	2.98989899	
101	100	0.642296557	0.435570858	TRUE	75	3	
102	101	0.706897018	0.659515207	TRUE	76	3.00990099	
◄ ◄ ► ►◄ \ **Sheet1** / Sheet2 / Sheet3 /							

Exhibit A.12 Monte Carlo Simulation of Dart Throws

| D101 | ▾ | f_x =(B101^2+C101^2<=1) | | | | |

MonteCarloPi.xls [Read-Only]

	A	B	C	D	E	F
100	99	0.298518916	0.432629481	TRUE	74	2.98989899
101	100	0.642296557	0.435570858	TRUE	75	3
102	101	0.706897018	0.659515207	TRUE	76	3.00990099

Sheet1 / Sheet2 / Sheet3 /

Exhibit A.13   The Use of the Logical Test Function

Consider dart number 100 (from column A). We can see that the logical test has determined that this dart fell within the quarter circle (as did darts numbered 99 and 101). The logical test function is depicted in Exhibit A.13.

Finally, note that column E provides a running count of the "TRUEs" and column F provides a running estimate of the value of π, by taking the running count of the number of TRUEs, divided by the total darts thrown, and then multiplying this quotient by 4. See Exhibit A.14 for the count function.

The final exhibit, (Exhibit A.15) shows a graph of the estimate of π plotted as a function of the number of darts simulated. It is easily shown that the larger

| E101 | ▾ | f_x =COUNTIF(D2:D101,TRUE) | | | | |

MonteCarloPi.xls [Read-Only]

	A	B	C	D	E	F
100	99	0.298518916	0.432629481	TRUE	74	2.98989899
101	100	0.642296557	0.435570858	TRUE	75	3
102	101	0.706897018	0.659515207	TRUE	76	3.00990099

Sheet1 / Sheet2 / Sheet3 /

Exhibit A.14   Running Count of the "Trues"

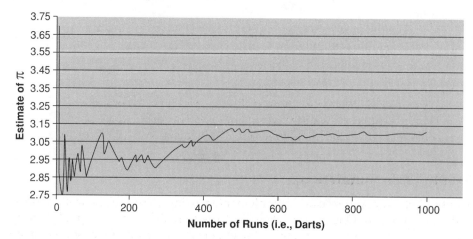

Exhibit A.15   Monte Carlo Simulation Convergence

the number of runs (i.e., simulated darts), the more accurate the estimation. This is typical of the convergence to the true value sought as the number of "runs" increases when employing Monte Carlo simulation.

CONCLUSION

We have seen that modern software allows the financial engineer to attend to multifaceted problems without having to learn complex programming, advanced mathematics, or even much about databases. That does not mean that one should not strive to learn these things, only that, for some purposes, it is not necessary to know them at the same depth that the highly quantitative segment of the financial engineering population does.

Because the length of this appendix does not permit a truly in depth discussion of any one of the techniques illustrated, a useful list of resources has been included below.

READER RESOURCES

Books on Financial Engineering Careers

Derman, Emmanuel. 2004. *My Life as a Quant: Reflections on Physics and Finance.* Hoboken, NJ: John Wiley & Sons.

Jui, Brett. 2007. *Starting Your Career as a Wall Street Quant.* Denver, CO: Outskirts Press.

Neftci, Salih N. 2004. *Principles of Financial Engineering.* New York: Academic Press.

Schachter, Barry, and Richard R. Lindsey, eds. 2007. *How I Became a Quant: Insights from 25 of Wall Street's Elite.* Hoboken, NJ: John Wiley & Sons.

Financial Modeling Using MS-Excel
Benninga, Simon. 2008. *Financial Modeling*, 3rd ed. Cambridge, MA: MIT Press.

Mathematica
Stinespring, John Robert. 2002. *Mathematica for Microeconomics.* New York: Academic Press.

Visual Basic
Bovey, Rob, Dennis Wallentin, Stephen Bullen, and John Green. 2009. *Professional Excel Development: The Definitive Guide to Developing Applications Using Microsoft Excel, VBA, and .NET*, 2nd ed. Ann Arbor, MI: Addison-Wesley Professional.

Monte Carlo Simulation

Monte Carlo simulation can be implemented using MS-Excel as well as other software packages. One such package is Crystal Ball®, which is published by the Oracle Corp. This software allows the engineer to take any spreadsheet and define his or her input and output variables so that the simulation can be performed.

Another popular software product (particularly in the health-care industry) is TreeAge Pro which is published by, and is a trademark of, TreeAge Software, Inc.

Bloomberg

Bloomberg data requires access to a Bloomberg terminal. Once one has access to the terminal, as well as a username and password, the BU command takes you to Bloomberg University, which contains an enormous amount of documentation, as well as access to staff to assist you around the clock.

Other Interesting Sources

www.contingencyanalysis.com/
www.defaultrisk.com/
http://fisher.osu.edu/fin/journal/jofsites.htm#otjnl
www.iafe.org/
www.isda.org/
www.securitization.net/
www.vinodkothari.com/

NOTES

1. Excel is a registered trademark of Microsoft Corporation.
2. Mathematica is a registed trademark of Wolfram Research, Inc.; Gauss is a trademark of Aptech Systems, Inc.; Maple is a registered trademark of Maplesoft, a division of Waterloo Maple Inc.; and MatLab is a registered trademark of The MathWorks, Inc.
3. Bloomberg is a registered trademark of Bloomberg, LP.

REFERENCES

Chacko, G., A. Sjöman, H. Motohashi, & V. Dessain, 2006. *Credit Derivatives: A Primer on Credit Risk, Modeling, and Instruments*, Upper Saddle River, New Jersey, Wharton School Publishing.
Merton, Robert C., 1974. "On the Pricing of Corporate Debt: The Risk Structure of Interest Rates," *Journal of Finance* 29: 449–70.

ABOUT THE AUTHOR

Lucas Bernard has been working in the financial and risk-management arenas, in their broadest interpretation, for many years. Possessing a varied background ranging from entrepreneurship and small business to academic research and consulting, Dr. Bernard is no stranger to the "real" economy, industry, and engineering. In addition to his PhD in Financial Economics (his doctoral dissertation concerned endogenous models of credit default), from The New School for Social Research (NSSR), he also holds masters degrees in *both* Mathematics, from The City University of New York (CUNY), and Computer Science, from NYU's Courant Institute of Mathematical Science (CIMS). His business background ranges from urban infrastructure planning and pharmaceutical consulting to franchising and even a "dot-com" start-up. He is also certified as a Financial Asset Manager & Engineer by the Swiss Finance Institute (SFI), a private foundation created by Switzerland's banking and finance community in cooperation with leading Swiss universities. An experienced teacher, Dr. Bernard has taught Statistics, Econometrics, and other financial topics at New York University (NYU), at the Polytechnic Institute of NYU (NYU-Poly), where he is a Research Fellow, and in the MBA program at Long Island University (LIU). His current and full-time affiliation is with The City University of New York, College of Technology (CUNY-CityTech), where he is an Assistant Professor in their Business Department. His personal web page is http://www.lucasbernard.com.

About the Companion Website

The companion website for this book can be accessed at www.wiley.com/go/bedermarshall (password: kolb). The site includes:

- A glossary of key terms from the book
- Data from a survey of financial engineering programs around the globe

MORE ABOUT THE SURVEY

One hundred thirty colleges and universities were asked to participate in the survey, which provides students looking for a Financial Engineering program with a centralized location where they can research programs that match their academic and career objectives. Of the original 130 schools worldwide that were asked to participate, 60 responded, including:

School	Location	Programs
American University	Washington, District of Columbia, USA	Master of Science in Finance; Master of Science in Real Estate
Bar-Ilan University	Ramat-Gan, Israel	MSc Financial Mathematics (without thesis; with thesis)
Baruch College, City University of New York	New York, NY, USA	MS in Financial Engineering
Bogazici University	Istanbul, Besiktas, Turkey	MS in Financial Engineering
Boston University School of Management	Boston, MA, USA	MS in Mathematical Finance; PhD in Mathematical Finance
Carnegie Mellon University	Pittsburgh, PA, USA	Master of Science in Computational Finance; MBA in Financial Engineering; PhD in Mathematical Finance
Case Western Reserve University	Cleveland, OH, USA	MSM-Finance; MSM-Finance/MBA dual degree; undergraduate early admissions—MSM-Finance

(*Continued*)

School	Location	Programs
Case Western Reserve University	Cleveland, OH, USA	MSM-Finance; MSM-Finance/MBA dual degree; undergraduate early admissions—MSM-Finance
Claremont Graduate University	Claremont, CA, USA	MS in Financial Engineering (MSFE)
Clark University	Worcester, MA, USA	Master of Science in Finance (MSF); MBA/MSF
Columbia University	New York, NY, USA	MS in Financial Engineering; MA in Mathematics of Finance
Cornell University	Ithaca, NY, USA	Master in Engineering with Financial Engineering concentration; PhD in Operations Research and Information Engineering with Financial Engineering focus
DePaul University	Chicago, IL, USA	MSc in Computational Finance
Dublin City University	Dublin, Co. Dublin, Ireland	MSc in Financial and Industrial Mathematics
Ecole Polytechnique Fédérale de Lausanne	Lausanne, Vaud, Switzerland	Master of Sciences in Financial Engineering
Florida State University	Tallahassee, FL, USA	Master's; PhD in Financial Mathematics
Fordham University	New York, NY, USA	MS in Quantitative Finance program; Advanced Certificate in Financial Computing jointly with Computer Science department
George Washington University	Washington, DC, USA	MSF Regular Program; MSF Intensive Program
Georgia Institute of Technology	Atlanta, GA, USA	Master of Science in Quantitative and Computational Finance
Georgia State University	Atlanta, GA, USA	MS in Mathematical Risk Management (MS MRM); Master of Actuarial Science (MAS); dual degree: MAS and MS MRM
Hong Kong University of Science and Technology	Hong Kong, China	MSc Investment Management; MSc Financial Analysis
Imperial College Business School	London, United Kingdom	MSc Risk Management and Financial Engineering
Kent State University	Kent, OH, USA	Master of Science in Financial Engineering
Lehigh University	Bethlehem, PA, USA	Master of Science in Analytical Finance
McMaster University	Hamilton, Ontario, Canada	Masters of Science (Mathematics)
Nanyang Technological University	Singapore	MSc (Financial Engineering)

School	Location	Programs
North Carolina State University	Raleigh, NC, USA	Master of Financial Mathematics; Bachelor of Applied Mathematics, concentration in Financial Mathematics
NYU-Polytechnic Institute	Brooklyn, NY, USA	Master of Science in Financial Engineering; Certificate program in Financial Engineering; Certificate program in Financial Technology Management; Certificate program in Risk Management
Oklahoma State University	Stillwater, OK, USA	Master of Science in Quantitative Financial Economics
Princeton University	Princeton, NJ, USA	MSE and PhD in Operations Research and Financial Engineering; Master in Finance; Undergraduate Certificate in Finance
Queens College, City University of New York	Queens, NY, USA	MS in Risk Management: Concentrations in Accounting, Finance, and Dynamic Financial Analysis Modeling
Rensselaer Polytechnic Institute	Troy, NY, USA	MS in Financial Engineering and Risk Analytics
Stanford University	Stanford, CA, USA	MS Financial Mathematics
Stevens Institute of Technology	Hoboken, NJ, USA	Master of Science in Financial Engineering; MS, Financial Engineering with Quantitative focus; MS, Financial Engineering with Systems & Management focus; MS, Financial Engineering with Software & Technology focus; PhD, Financial Engineering; MBA, Technology Management with Financial Engineering concentration
Technical University Vienna	Vienna, Austria	Programs in Financial and Actuarial Mathematics
University of Alabama	Tuscaloosa, AL, USA	Master of Science in Finance
University of Arizona	Tucson, AZ, USA	MS–Management, with concentration in Finance
University of Birmingham	Edgbaston, United Kingdom	MSc in Mathematical Finance
University of California at Berkeley	Berkeley, CA, USA	MS in Financial Engineering
University of California at Los Angeles (UCLA)	Los Angeles, CA, USA	Master of Financial Engineering
University of California at Santa Barbara	Santa Barbara, CA, USA	BS in Financial Mathematics and Statistics; PhD in Statistics and Applied Probability with emphasis in Financial Mathematics and Statistics
University of Connecticut	Storrs, CT, USA	Master of Science in Applied Financial Mathematics

(Continued)

School	Location	Programs
University of Dayton	Dayton, OH, USA	Master of Financial Mathematics
University of Florida	Gainesville, FL, USA	Master of Science in Finance
University of Illinois	Urbana, IL, USA	Master of Science in Financial Engineering
University of Limerick	Limerick, Ireland	MSc in Computational Finance
University of Minnesota	Minneapolis, MN, USA	Master of Financial Mathematics (MFM); Post-Baccalaureate Certifications in Fundamentals of Quantitative Finance (FQF)
University of Neuchatel	Neuchatel, Switzerland	MSc in Finance
University of Oxford	Oxford, Oxfordshire, UK	MSc in Mathematical and Computational Finance
University of Oxford	Oxford, Oxon, UK	Postgraduate Diploma in Mathematical Finance; MSc in Mathematical Finance
University of Southern California	Los Angeles, CA, USA	MS in Mathematical Finance
University of Technology, Sydney	Broadwasy, NSW, Australia	Master of Quantitative Finance
University of the Witwatersrand, Johannesburg	Johannesburg, Gauteng, South Africa	BSc Honours in Advanced Mathematics of Finance; MSc in Advanced Mathematics of Finance; PhD in Advanced Mathematics of Finance
University of Tulsa	Tulsa, OK, USA	MS in Finance; dual MBA/MSF; dual JD/MSF; dual MSF/MS in Applied Mathematics
University of Twente	Enschede, Overijsel, The Netherlands	Master in Applied Mathematics; Master in Industrial Engineering and Management
University of Waterloo	Waterloo, Ontario, Canada	Master of Quantitative Finance
University of Western Ontario	London, Ontario, Canada	MSc; PhD Applied Finance-Financial Mathematics
University of Wisconsin–Madison	Madison, WI, USA	Master of Science in Business
Washington University in St. Louis (Olin School of Business)	St. Louis, MO, USA	Master of Science in Finance
Worcester Polytechnic Institute	Worcester, MA, USA	MSc Financial Mathematics
York University	Toronto, Ontario, Canada	Graduate Diploma in Financial Engineering; Diploma in Financial Engineering; Certificate Program in Financial Engineering

Participating schools were asked to provide:

- Program contact and website.
- Description of awards/recognition of the program.
- What aspects of the program distinguish it from similar ones offered at other universities?
- Degrees offered (up to six).
- What are the core classes (fundamental and advanced)? (up to six)
- What are the available electives? (up to six)
- What course tracks are available? (up to six)
- What type of research is required? (up to six)
- Dean/department chair.
- Program email address.
- Students per faculty member.
- Professor/instructor (up to six).
- Admission statistics.
- Student makeup (percentages).
- Primary nationalities (country).
- Total number of countries represented.
- Work experience.
- Minimum time to complete the program.
- Employment statistics (percentages).
- Additional comments or suggestions.

The content supplied is at the discretion of the college or university and may not always be complete. Responses that did not meet the question criteria were not included in the results. Neither the editors nor their affiliated firms or universities make any representations regarding the accuracy of the submissions by the individual schools.

Schools that wish to be added should contact survey@sbccgroup.com to participate in updates and future surveys.

About the Editors

Tanya S. Beder is founder and chairman of SBCC Group Inc. (www.sbccgroup.com) where she heads the global strategy, risk, derivatives, and asset management practices. Clients include banks, broker dealers, family offices, pension funds, mutual funds, hedge funds, insurance companies and corporations from around the world. Previously Ms. Beder was CEO of Tribeca Global Management LLC, a $3 billion multi-strategy fund with offices in New York, London, and Singapore, and Managing Director of Caxton Associates LLC, a $10 billion asset management firm in New York. She is a member of the board of directors of American Century Investment Management Inc., serves on the National Board of Mathematics and their Applications, the Advisory Board of Columbia University's Financial Engineering Program, the Mathematical Finance Advisory Board of New York University's Courant Institute and is an appointed fellow of the International Center for Finance at Yale. For five years Ms. Beder was Chairman, and now serves on the Board, of the International Association of Financial Engineers where she co-chairs The Investor Risk Committee. *Euromoney* named Ms. Beder one of the top 50 women in finance around the world and *The Hedgefund Journal* named her one of the 50 leading women in hedge funds. Ms. Beder has appeared as an expert before Congressional hearings, as well as before the OECD, IOSCO, the World Bank, the IMF and other bodies around the world. She is a featured speaker at large international conferences and an invited commentator on CNBC, Bloomberg, Reuters, Fox Business News, and other media. Ms. Beder was an author of the Risk Standards for Institutional Investors and Institutional Investment Managers and has written numerous articles in the financial area that have been published by *The Journal of Portfolio Management, The Financial Analysts Journal, The Harvard Business Review, The Journal of Financial Engineering,* Probus Publishing, John Wiley & Sons, and Simon & Schuster. Ms. Beder holds an MBA in finance from Harvard University and a BA in mathematics and philosophy from Yale University.

Cara M. Marshall is a professor of finance at Queens College of the City University of New York. Cara holds a PhD in Financial Economics from Fordham University and an MBA with a focus on Quantitative Analysis from St. John's University. Her research interests focus on financial engineering, Monte Carlo Simulation modeling, risk management, and derivatives, as well as behavioral and experimental methods in finance. Cara's doctoral dissertation examined the efficiency of the pricing of volatility on U.S. options exchanges. Prior to academia, Cara worked in Internet engineering, developing websites, and a platform for online course delivery. She has also worked as a marketing manager for a conference and training company. Over the years, Cara has consulted to several leading commercial and investment banks where she trained new hires in the use of financial analytics. In this capacity, she taught financial modeling to bank employees in New York, London, and Singapore. Cara has also performed analysis for hedge funds and for firms in other industries. She has published papers in several scholarly journals and contributed a number of chapters to books published by John Wiley & Sons.

Index